Dance Writings

UNIVERSITY PRESS OF FLORIDA

Florida A&M University, Tallahassee
Florida Atlantic University, Boca Raton
Florida Gulf Coast University, Ft. Myers
Florida International University, Miami
Florida State University, Tallahassee
University of Central Florida, Orlando
University of Florida, Gainesville
University of North Florida, Jacksonville
University of South Florida, Tampa
University of West Florida, Pensacola

Dance Writings

EDWIN DENBY

EDITED BY

Robert Cornfield and William MacKay

University Press of Florida
Gainesville/Tallahassee/Tampa/Boca Raton
Pensacola/Orlando/Miami/Jacksonville/Ft. Myers

First published 1986 by Alfred A. Knopf, Inc.
Printed in the United States of America on acid-free paper

Grateful acknowledgment is made to the following for permission to reprint previously published material:
Dance Magazine: "Pilgrimage to the Altar of Terpsichore," by Edwin Denby. Reprinted courtesy of *Dance Magazine*, June 1966.
Copyright renewed 1986 *Dance Magazine*.
"Edwin Denby on Balanchine, from an interview by Richard Philp." Reprinted courtesy of *Dance Magazine*, July 1983. Copyright 1983 Richard Philp.
Simon & Schuster, Inc. "Criticism, Dance" from *The Dance Encyclopedia*, by Anatole Chujoy and P. W. Manchester. Copyright 1967 by Anatole Chujoy and P. W. Manchester. Reprinted courtesy of Simon & Schuster, Inc.

12 11 10 09 08 07 6 5 4 3 2 1

A record of cataloging-in-publication data is available from the Library of Congress.
ISBN 978-0-8130-3057-9

The University Press of Florida is the scholarly publishing agency for the State University System of Florida, comprising Florida A&M University, Florida Atlantic University, Florida Gulf Coast University, Florida International University, Florida State University, University of Central Florida, University of Florida, University of North Florida, University of South Florida,and University of West Florida.

University Press of Florida
15 Northwest 15th Street
Gainesville, FL 32611-2079
http://www.upf.com

Contents

From *Modern Music*

From the *New York Herald Tribune*

Reviews and Appreciations

Balanchine and the New York City Ballet

Essays

EDWIN DENBY

Dance Writings

Introduction

In preparing this book, William MacKay and I reviewed the first journal and newspaper appearances of Edwin Denby's articles and reviews and compared these with the texts published in the two previous collections, *Looking at the Dance* (1949) and *Dancers, Buildings and People in the Streets* (1965). Where they differed, we selected what we considered the better version, and there are cases where we have recovered cut passages and rejoined them to sections that had been revised for their book appearance. Whenever possible, we have compared published versions with manuscripts and typescripts in the Denby archives. Many of the pieces in the first and second sections of this book have not been published in book form before. They replace in more generous sum pieces that we have left out, because they were either repetitious or less consequential than might have seemed years ago.

The first collection, *Looking at the Dance*, was imaginatively edited and arranged by the critic B. H. Haggin. Sections were devised called "Dancers in Performance," "Events of Earlier Seasons," "Modern Dancers," etc. Here we have opted for a simpler device. The first section includes in chronological order Denby's articles for *Modern Music*; the second, his reviews for the *Herald Tribune*. In this way they offer an unintended yet curious history of dance in New York from the mid-thirties through the mid-forties. Glimpsed among the chronicles of the major dance companies are views of some vanished occasions that provide period nostalgia as well as information: reports on nightclub floor-shows and dance in concert (at the YMHA, at the Little Theater on Forty-third Street, at Hunter College, in Carnegie Hall studios, at the Henry Street Settlement, in union halls and high school auditoriums), ice shows, Harlem revues, ethnic recitals. An advantage in this ordering is the demonstration in sequence of Denby's exploration in critical writing: his extension and refinement of his dance theory and of his ways of reviewing.

At the urging of Aaron Copland, Minna Lederman, in 1936, invited Denby to contribute articles on dance to the bimonthly *Modern Music*, a journal for the composer and serious musician, and in his contributions Denby pays particular attention to that audience. In 1942, another distinguished composer, Virgil Thomson, who was then music critic for the *New York Herald Tribune*, suggested to his editors that Denby would be an able substitute when dance critic Walter Terry and his replacement,

Robert Lawrence, were both drafted. Denby's stint concluded with Terry's return to civilian life.

At *Modern Music* Denby had a relatively relaxed deadline and as much space as he needed; but more important, he had a meticulous and demanding editor, and in later years he readily credited Minna Lederman for his training as a critic. At the *Tribune*, he contended, and rather well, with the strictures of daily reviewing. Though he "hated" being forced to write immediately after a performance, the result was of a remarkably high critical order, and his most-quoted remarks come from these reviews—"Miss Toumanova with her large, handsome, and deadly face," or this evocation of *Concerto Barocco*: ". . . at the culminating phrase, from her greatest height he very slowly lowers her. You watch her body slowly descend, her foot and leg pointing stiffly downward, till her toe reaches the floor and she rests her full weight at last on this single sharp point and pauses. It has the effect at that moment of a deliberate and powerful plunge into a wound. . . ."

After the *Herald Tribune* post, there were passes at regular reviewing as a contributor to *Dance Magazine* and for Richard Buckle's British journal *Ballet*. But without the constant pressure of deadlines and an editor's nagging, there was less reason to overcome his writer's resistance to getting the job done. What did overcome all obstacles was an urgent need to write about George Balanchine's latest work. His post-*Tribune* writing on Balanchine and the early years of the New York City Ballet make up the fourth section. Other reviews from 1945 on make up the third, and the fifth contains essays and lectures on general dance topics.

During the last years of Denby's life, admirers regretted he hadn't written more—that he had not found after the *Tribune* a steady forum that compelled him to produce. But his most productive period as a dance writer spanned over twenty-five years, and there is in his work variety, volume and consistency in thought. He was an active though infrequently published poet, and *Edwin Denby: The Complete Poems* shows how steady a writer he was.

There was a part of him that had dreaded presumption; he distrusted assertive behavior, and this caused him to think of himself as a poet who wrote dance criticism. He brought to criticism the finicky care for precise emotional tracing that is his poetical manner. Because this style highlights clarity and concision, he makes the complex questions of dance seem to be simple ones. (The fault in some of his imitators is that they emulate his laconic phrasing and imagery without finding the base of complex experience from which these arise.) His voice and method have proved to be a telling influence on American dance criticism. There are other ways of doing the job, but he achieved what he set out to do: to find an American voice that spoke convincingly of the power of dance.

He had practical experience and dance schooling. In the late twenties and early thirties he had performed modern dance in Germany and Austria, and soon after his return to the United States he had choreographed, though not with success, Kurt Weill's Broadway musical *Knickerbocker Holiday*. Dance technique was of great importance to him, and many of his articles are filled with teacherly correction. But he worried more about the impetus of dance, what it was that held a piece together. In literary terms, these were aspects of structure, theme, style. In dance terms, Denby was concerned with rhythm: the overall rhythm of the work and the rhythm of a phrase. A dancer's rhythmic attack creates his distinction. Throughout his writing career, Denby develops this theme, and the concern provides a constant critical focus.

Personally Denby was admired for his courtly manners, and he worried always that he had not behaved with sufficient concern and kindness. For him decent behavior was a moral virtue, and his attraction to dance included the notion that it was not only a social activity but a moral one. And it was a joyous one at that, for it affirmed the beauty of the human spirit. In the following pages you will see how often George Balanchine's ballets are celebrated for their perfect manners, happy spirit, aptness for the human body, revelation of a dancer's special distinction—in short, for their classical virtues. Balanchine's ballets, Denby claims, revere the human possibility, and in this way they are without selfish or self-centered concern. They seem objective because their impulse is outward, toward the other. Denby easily returns to the words "pleasant," "pleasure," "modest," "gentle"; for him these are dynamic qualities. Arlene Croce calls him the kindest man she ever met.

His severity came when what he loved was abused. In his introduction to *Dancers, Buildings and People in the Streets*, Frank O'Hara relates how sharply Denby dealt with a first-nighter who told Denby that Balanchine's *Don Quixote* moved her right out of the theater. "That's where you belong, then," he assured her. After the premiere of a new work of hers, a famous choreographer called to him, "Oh, Edwin, if only you were still reviewing!" He waved off the remark, stammered something congratulatory, and let her move on. When she was gone, he turned to me, furious: "Horrible, disagreeable person. All she wants is more praise."

All this is in his criticism: generosity to performers, forbearance with the sincere but misguided, censure of the overreaching and pompous. When he chastises, he tries to turn it into a joke. Of a dancer whose name you will find in the text he says: "Of her present style I can find nothing good to say. She hams with a heartlessness that is frightening. She ogles, flounces, capers, and cuddles, jumps, turns, and stands, slapping down each effect like a virago operating a cash register. She seems to want the title of 'Miss Ironpants.' I hope so intelligent a dancer as she is will quickly get over this phase, or else team up with the Three Stooges, where her present manner properly belongs."

He complained once of a young critic that her reviews were made up of a ballet master's corrections, fit only for the studio; but he himself was the teacher too, and the freshness of the pieces in *Modern Music* and the *Herald Tribune* comes from his telling us what he had so recently decided on. Though he knew the dance writing of the past, and respected it, he had come to dance with no formulas, no prejudices. He learned from what he saw, and this kept him alert throughout his life. His appreciative curiosity was rewarded by the extraordinary devotion of so many young performers and poets. I think Denby was happiest with young people; he liked giving instruction and affirmation.

In his first article for *Modern Music* (not included here), on librettos, he names Gertrude Stein as America's best poet. What he esteemed in Stein was the precision, the quick, barely visible metaphors, the simple formulations that spoke for inchoate feeling, and especially the warmheartedness. It is what we find in his critical writing, too. With Lincoln Kirstein he might have been among the very few serious American writers of the thirties and forties to have some professional care for dance, but his style joins him with artists of that period. He is a New York writer (though he spent much of his childhood in China and spent the twenties and early thirties in Europe), and the city landscape and the city's crowds and complex social arrangements are background and image for talking about dance. This Americanness made him a guiding figure for the New York poets Frank O'Hara, Anne Waldman, James Schuyler, John Ashbery, and Ron Padgett. In the early years of his critical writing, he included among his close friends Elaine and Willem de Kooning, Aaron Copland, the photographer and filmmaker Rudolph Burckhardt, and Virgil Thomson, whose directness, authority, and tough good sense he applauds often.

Denby's critical duty was to delineate the way dance spoke to the soul, how its blunt imagery could terrify, where and by what means it dazzled the senses. He had the advantage of writing in defense of an art at a time when it needed explication and when it needed a gallant knight. American modern-dance enthusiasts contrasted their enterprise's earnestness, social responsiveness, emotional and psychological rigor with the decadence of European ballet. In answer, Lincoln Kirstein, another quintessential American poet and ballet proselytizer, shot back by decrying modern dance's lack of discipline, vocabulary, and technique, its emotional unruliness, and artistic vacuity. Denby assumes a conciliatory stance and encourages both worlds, taking each one's proclaimed virtues and applying them to the other: he places Graham within a theatrical and literary tradition and he shows Balanchine's classicism to be revisionary and his sophistication a revolutionary stance.

By the late thirties ballet was not an unfamiliar form to the New York public, but with the formation of Ballet Theatre and the regular seasons of the Ballet Russe de Monte Carlo, dance was dealt with in print more frequently and of necessity more seriously. The audience asks questions, and how full of instruction and information Denby is: he tells how a ballet is or should be structured, when it is absurd and when it is proper, who the better choreographers are; he firmly corrects the reputations of Fokine, Massine, and Balanchine; he tells what the toe shoe does, and what companies are to be applauded; he provides direction to ballerinas—and explains their function: "In classic ballet the queen ballerina of a company is its central dynamo; she sets the style, she exemplifies it at its most completely expressive. It is through watching her that the audience understands the style of a piece, and the style creates the poetic illusion in which the drama becomes real. She projects not only her own role but the entire world of fancy in which that role becomes dramatic, in which everybody and everything on stage can play a part."

There is no mere assumption of the importance of all this; he insists on how crucial the performance and appreciation of dance is, for at the heart of the matter is poetic possibility, and what is at stake is the quality of existence. Therefore, those who produce dance have a heavy responsibility. "The history of management teaches that only poetry confers prestige on entertainment, and that without prestige ballet can't get private citizens to pay its deficit. Another fact is that a company loses its self-respect without serious new works, without a sense of fresh poetry in the routine; and the management is responsible for the development of its dancers."

The lesson applies just as forcefully today.

Enthusiasm for dance includes choosing favorites, and Denby is passionate about his. His exemplary artists are the ballerinas Alicia Markova and Alexandra Danilova and the choreographers Martha Graham and George Balanchine. When he writes of them the words brighten, and he outlines the perfect forms of the art by their achievements.

Markova is the genius of phrasing, that signal aspect of the dancer's musical sense by which she plays with the relationship of the steps to the music and thus creates tension, surprise, and drama. Of her performance in Antony Tudor's *Romeo and Juliet* he writes, "Markova's rhythm is not only due to her remarkable freedom in attacking her steps a hair's breath before or after the beat, a freedom in which she shows a perfect musical instinct. I think one gets closer to it by noticing her phrasing. . . . In musical terms there is a rubato within the phrase, corresponding to the way the balance of the body is first strained, then is restored. . . . Now I see that Markova can sense and can show the dance rhythm that underlies [Tudor's] visual phrases. She finds their point of rest. She is easily equal to his dramatic meaning and passion, but she also gives his drama the buoyancy of dancing. As I watch her, Markova—like Duse in Ibsen—seems to be speaking poetry to the company's earnest prose."

Technically brilliant always, Danilova is also the paragon of responsible performing. He is ravished by her ready ability to gauge the needs of whatever she dances, to dance exactly within the frame of the dance, to show the work's spirit and point precisely—and to improve on it when necessary. She places herself vibrantly at the service of the work, and this vibrant commitment becomes stage vitality. In both these great dancers he sees seamless, utter concentration and selflessness before their craft.

When he first writes about Martha Graham, it is with caution: "She seems to watch over her integrity with too jealous an eye." In general he is suspicious of the insistence on individuality and self-dramatization in American modern dance. (Perhaps he was happier with later modern dancers and with the postmoderns because they are less "personalized.") Graham quickly breaks down his resistance, and, as he might say, it is a happy discovery to see her ample intellectual stature, her supreme dramatic gift, her beautiful seriousness. Of her Brontë work, *Deaths and Entrances*, he writes: "Our forebears when they saw these tragedies started with horror and wept. They sensed their secret obscenity. Miss Graham brings back the true Romantic impact and effect: it is as immediate now as then, and this is an achievement of genius."

George Balanchine vitalizes the critic as he vitalized classical ballet in America. Dante was finally Denby's onlie poet, and finally Balanchine is Denby's onlie choreographer. Among critics of these years, Denby was Balanchine's most constant, perceptive, and eloquent apologist. He perceived in Balanchine a beneficent generosity that complemented his artistic pre-eminence.

"Balanchine has an extraordinary gift for bringing performers to life on their own personal terms, so that the unconscious grace that is in each one of them can shine out in the work they do, giving it the momentary and mortal expression of beauty. The plan of a choreography is a great pleasure. But it is the brilliancy of young dancers entirely in the present, the unique liveliness of each dancer caught entirely in the present instant that at once, we all know it, will be past and irretrievable forever—it is this clear sharp sense of our own natural way of living that makes a moment of ballet speak to the complete consciousness, that makes choreography look beautiful. As Balanchine's has again and again."

This aspirational resemblance between Denby and Balanchine allows Denby to find and name the poetic core of the choreographer's *Agon*, *Ballet Imperial*, *Opus 34*, and *The Nutcracker* in his celebrated essays on these works. In memory, he retains not only the steps but their vitality and suggestion: the reading of *Agon*, for instance, is about the voyage of exhilaration and wonder it takes the audience on.

For his reader, Denby wants to be an informative but not overbearing companion, and the delight in these pieces comes from their direct, conspiratorial appeal. There is no autobiography here, except for the noting of his companions: the poet, the bright woman friend, the composer of genius, the child who is a wonder of attention and quotes. And there is no gossip or politics either—though once he anxiously reports the rumor that Markova had fainted after a performance and scolds her employers for not taking proper care of her.

His mission is to make known the unique emotional power of dance. Ballet is a towering art, not fragile or secondary. He reiterates the splendor of the endeavor, and because dance by its nature is about impermanence, it is an emblem of life's poignant glory.

It is how he valued dance, as it is valued in Greek myth, that altered the way we talk and think about dance. He makes grateful obeisance to its makers and performers. This generous vision was also the gift he gave to his friends. By his attention and care he ennobled them; he made them wiser, funnier, more gifted. For the Elysian atmosphere he created (exactly like the one in Balanchine's *Chaconne*), they wanted to be with him all the time, and that is why his readers return to him again and again.

—R. C.

Edwin Denby, 1903–1983

Biographies irritated Edwin. "They are too simple and too complicated," he once told me. "People want to tell stories," and lives were not always completely stories. This distrust, combined with a courtly modesty, made him a difficult subject. When editor Ron Padgett began gathering details about Edwin's life for the 1975 *Collected Poems*, he agreed (more than a little reluctantly) to help. Hours of interviews followed, Ron and Rudy Burckhardt painfully coaxing answers from Edwin between disclaimers and silence. But by the time the book appeared, Edwin's relentless scalpel had reduced the biography to three authorized sentences:

"Edwin Denby was born in Tientsin, China, in 1903. He received his early education in Europe, to which he returned after several years at Harvard. Since the early 1930s he has lived mostly in New York."

Edwin Orr Denby was, indeed, born in Tientsin, China, on February 4, 1903.

On the northeast coast, sixty miles from Peking, Tientsin was at the time a city of seven hundred thousand Chinese dominated by a few thousand Europeans and Americans. It offered its foreigners lush Victoria Park, ambitious Western architecture, golf courses, cricket clubs, concert halls, and several English-language newspapers. Its opera house featured Verdi, Elgar, and Gilbert & Sullivan. Decades later, Edwin still delighted in his mother's recollections of a Tientsin production of *The Mikado*: "So many Chinese playing so many Japanese! Imagine all those extras!"

Much of the foreign enclave considered the Chinese little more than walk-ons anyway. Life in China was simple, Edwin told me. Americans pretended they were in Europe, and the Chinese made believe they were invisible. Edwin's version of the 1900 Boxer Rebellion, which snapped this charade, was wryly Jamesian. "To many of my parents' friends it was a great crisis," he said. "They were never again able to trust their servants."

Few were better positioned than the Denbys to enjoy the fruits of such unapologetic imperialism. Edwin's grandfather, Charles Denby, Sr., arrived in Peking in 1885 as President Cleveland's appointee as minister to China. He served in that post an almost unparalleled thirteen years. A vigorous advocate of the Open Door policy, he was so respected that

China rejected several possible replacements and Japan entrusted him with its interests in China during the 1895 hostilities.

In many ways, Charles Denby, Sr. (who died when grandson Edwin was one), was less remarkable than his namesake son. Charles Denby, Jr., only twenty-three, accompanied his father to China as second secretary of legation. (Actually, the Denby family contribution to world diplomacy was almost washed overboard the S.S. *Rio de Janeiro* by a typhoon in mid-Pacific.) Not content to be a nepotist, the younger Denby tutored himself until he became "one of the best American scholars of his day in the Chinese language, literature, history and philosophy. . . . In the Chinese official and written language he attained unusual proficiency, and many important negotiations between the legation and the Chinese government were conducted by him entirely in that tongue." Indeed, as first secretary of legation, Charles Denby, Jr., was the chief draftsman of the treaty ending the Chinese-Japanese War.

By the time of the treaty signing, Edwin's father was already a married man. The match seemed made in heaven—or, more precisely, in Evansville, Indiana. Martha Dalzell Orr had been born and raised in that small town only a few blocks from the Denbys. But it took an around-the-world trip with her family and outgoing Secretary of State John W. Foster (also from Evansville) to pair her with Charles Denby, Jr. They met in Peking in 1894 and exchanged vows in their hometown the following year.

Martha Orr Denby was, by every account, a fearless, intelligent woman. A college graduate, she had waded through crowds of beggars to see the burning ghats on the Ganges, wandered teeming Beirut streets, visited a wolf-child in India, celebrated Thanksgiving on the Nile. During the Boxer siege of Tientsin, she hid with her infant son James in basements, while above, the bad situation worsened, people eating household pets and planning "preventive" group suicide.

To Edwin, his articulate, opinionated mother was one of the main arbiters of his life. He never stopped trying to please her, and felt he never quite had. She was certain, he told me, that there was one fine writer in the family but hadn't decided which of his two brothers it was. Even Edwin's choice of genre disturbed her. "She could imagine people dancing, and even people going to watch them dancing; but to imagine people writing about people dancing seemed more than she could bear."

The Denbys left Asia for the last time when Edwin was seven. Consequently, he had few Chinese memories and doubted the authenticity of most of them. His best recollections, he liked to say, were of the Boxer Rebellion, which occurred several years before his birth. From Shanghai,

Edwin remembered a fallen pagoda, Chinese peasants scurrying around "as they would be encouraged to do," and vases in a large, high-ceilinged room, "but perhaps this is another room, later." And he remembered, too, one kindergarten image of simple animal choreography: "There was a pony and a two-wheeled wicker cart which took me and my two older brothers to school. . . . When you got to school you could throw the reins back into the cart and the pony would go home."

The Denbys globe-trotted, following father Charles from one State Department appointment to another: Tientsin, Washington, Shanghai, Vienna. Precocious and frail, Edwin was educated on three continents, usually in schools, sometimes by tutors. Already class recitations gave less satisfaction than his voracious outside reading. The martial spirit of German and Austrian education was perhaps partly responsible. Decades later, Edwin slyly confessed that his recollections of German schools had become hopelessly conflated with images from war movies. Whatever the cause, his mastery of languages, literature, and classical history was far beyond his years.

If Edwin had too few Chinese memories, he probably had too many diplomatic ones. Charles Denby, Sr., reminisced sentimentally about "the endless round of balls, picnics, and private theatricals" he encountered in the foreign service. His grandson recalled instead painful "dress-ups," being dragged to tedious receptions to be shown off to his elders: "reciting, speaking languages, that sort of thing."

One outing, though, left an indelible, joyful imprint on a seven-year-old Denby: a Christmas performance of *Die Puppenfee* at the Vienna Opera House gave Edwin his first vision of ballet. Seventy years later he still remembered with pleasure Tony Birkmeyer's leaps and entrechats. When, a year after his opera house excursion, his mother asked him a predictable maternal question, Edwin said yes, he knew. He wanted to be a dancer. Or pope.

European education may have been all stiff collars and repetition, and diplomatic rounds an adolescent torture, but life in Austria was heaven. (Charles Denby served as consul general at Vienna from 1909 to 1915.) Everything about the country delighted Edwin: the palaces, the parks, the people. Even Viennese bonbons seemed unequaled. When the Great War struck, the Denbys were vacationing at one of the grand hotels on the Lido. The announcement emptied the resort overnight. The Denbys stayed another year before leaving Austria, "the enemy country we had all liked so much."

After attending school in Detroit and being tutored in Washington, Edwin entered Hotchkiss, the prestigious Connecticut preparatory school. He was thirteen. Returning to the United States had not been easy. "I have been scared of America all my life," he wrote to a friend decades later. Hotchkiss could scarcely have been more American; indeed, a 1917 *Lit* editorial claimed no school was. Another Chinese-born Hotchkiss boy, Henry R. Luce, '16, had been stigmatized as "Chink" while there, and Edwin was no better versed than he in teenage slang and folkways. In his senior year, his classmates voted him "The Biggest Grind."

But Hotchkiss was no disaster for Edwin. He had a few close friends, two of whom became his Harvard roommates. Academically, he excelled. He graduated with honors, won the senior Greek and English prizes, and shared in Hotchkiss's victory in the Phi Beta Kappa interscholastic competition. His scores in the college entrance examinations were unsurpassed in the country.

More important, he was writing. He served on the editorial board of *The Literary Monthly* and contributed poetry and fiction to the magazine. The poems are delicate if rhetorical inventions, most of them sonnets influenced by Milton and Wordsworth. (Edwin's only non-sonnet was named the 1919 class poem.) The stories are allegories of concealed loyalties and unrecognized gifts, set in countries as remote as those he had known as a child.

At sixteen, Edwin became a Harvard freshman. His record of academic achievement continued, but underneath, something was bubbling. "Nothing made sense," he told me. Finally, in December 1920, midway through his sophomore year, he abandoned college and left the country, secretly catching the steamer *Adriatic* to England with his friend Frank Safford. Somewhat implausibly, the two planned to work and study abroad. Anxious parents, however, cut this planned escape to a two-week escapade; Denby and Safford booked on the *Adriatic*'s return passage.

A faculty friend arranged a job for Edwin as a farmhand in New Hampshire. He stayed five months, milking cows and collecting eggs. "I didn't write anything while on the farm," he told an interviewer, "because I was completely idiotic. I was quite astonished." Finally, chastened, "in my dazed state," he went home to his parents. When he told his mother he was suffering from a nervous breakdown, she assured Edwin he was too young for such a malady. He returned to Harvard.

The honor student who had withdrawn a year before was replaced by someone older and more diffuse. "Today we didn't get drunk," he confided proudly to his diary. "I got up late, too late for my classes." When he did go to lectures, he sometimes listened little, "drawing pictures instead, and looking at some finely curved elm branches." He lounged in his room reading Shelley and Shakespeare, or simply wandered, "shallow-heartedly enjoying the adventure of the moment," distracted by a stream of melting snow, a statue of Buddha, an attractive man. He was confused by these yearnings, and then confused by his own confusion. Most of all, he longed for Europe and escape.

Europe was far away, but, for a while, escape seemed closer. Safford and his new wife moved to New York, and Frank asked Edwin to share an apartment with them near what is now Sheridan Square. The choice between Greenwich Village and a junior year at Harvard was decided with no apparent difficulty, and Edwin was soon hunting work to pay his part of the twenty-dollar-a-month rent. Finally, he landed a job installing phones for New York Telephone. Whatever the facts might have been, Edwin liked to say he never unraveled the mysteries of colored wires and that only the generosity of his foreman kept him from being fired.

The happy but unproductive year in New York ended when the Saffords packed for Austria, where Frank was to study medicine. Once again, after false starts, side trips, and evasions, Edwin was at crossroads. Two more years of Harvard seemed unsurmountable. This time he resisted parental pressure to return by promising to enroll in courses at the University of Vienna. The half-trick worked: the Denbys agreed to finance his stay in Austria. Except for a reunion with the Saffords, Edwin had no fixed intention. "I wanted to write; and of course, there was no plan at all." When he left America, it was 1923. When he returned, it would be 1935.

"Europe meant so much," Edwin told me. "After all, I grew up there"—adding a twist of silence—"twice." At Harvard, he had been "thrilled" by Safford's suggestion that he continue his education in Vienna. In Austria, harsher realities quickly intervened. Friendship with the Saffords became difficult; Frank was preoccupied with learning medicine (and German), and Edwin's relations with Mrs. Safford, always complicated, became strained. The mail brought unwelcome questions and bad news. From Washington, his mother wondered about his future and passed along grim clippings about beloved "Uncle Edwin" Denby faltering under the pressure of the Teapot Dome scandal, finally resigning as secretary of the Navy. Edwin's depression poisoned his writing; a long autobiographical poem meandered nowhere. He spent a winter contemplating suicide. "It was one of my preoccupations."

Someone hinted Freud might help. A "crestfallen" Edwin climbed the ten steps of 19 Berggasse expecting to see the father of psychoanalysis. Instead, Freud's maid (or daughter Anna; Edwin could never decide) said the doctor was too ill to see new patients and directed him to Dr. Paul Federn, one of the Master's earliest acolytes. What Edwin thought a particular act of mercy was actually house policy; as an old loyalist, Federn received Freud's referrals.

Edwin entered analysis. "I worked with Dr. Federn for a number of years. It helped a great deal. . . . I forgot it very fast when it was over." Others, including Freud, believed Federn too optimistic, too romantic, too involved, too vague a Freudian, but Edwin's gratitude lasted a lifetime. "He saved my life," Edwin insisted. He wavered between thinking it was the analysis itself, the distraction it offered, or simply the friendship that salvaged him, but Federn remained an intimate, "someone to tell," long after Edwin had broken off the analysis as "too painful."

At Harvard, he had confessed in his diary his resolve to "have a fine body." When the Boston Symphony was playing Wagner, the teenaged Edwin liked to sneak into a passageway outside the balcony and dance—"just whatever came to me." (He stopped when he saw others doing the same and "they looked so absolutely foolish; I felt embarrassed.") Now, at the encouragement of Federn and some friends, he edged toward this odd form of expression. Returning on a train to Vienna, in an act of misplaced gallantry he blundered into meeting a French girl. (In renderings of this past, Edwin often assumed the persona of Chaplin's Little Tramp.) The girl was a student at the Hellerau-Laxenburg School, located in a castle outside Vienna. She offered a prospectus. Edwin was amused and intrigued by the dance school's promise to teach pupils "the experience of time and space, and the relations of time and space."

He remembered the place from his childhood, scolding himself for thinking the mock Gothic castle real and for being frightened by the swans. Gathering his courage, he went to the school for a morning tour. Christine Baer-Frissell, the director, sensed the timid interest of her countryman and nursed it along. She invited him back, first for an afternoon, then a week, then a month. He stayed three years and graduated.

One Vaslav Nijinsky had visited Hellerau also, though in its Dresden incarnation, and only long enough to get help mastering the difficult rhythms of Stravinsky's *Sacre du printemps*. Marie Rambert, Hanya Holm, and Yvonne Georgi were more formal students, and Mary Wigman, after searching "for a mystic answer to a wordless riddle," became a dancer there. The creation of Emile Jaques-Dalcroze, Hellerau by Edwin's time had far outgrown the simple "eurhythmic" exercises Dalcroze first devised for his music students. It had become a center for *Ausdruckstanz*, a school teeming with influences: Duncan, Laban, Wigman, and, not least, teachers Rosalia Chladek and Valeria Kratina.

Edwin studied not dance but *Körperbildung* (literally, "physical development," but more akin to gymnastics). The acclaimed Tanzgruppe Hellerau was, as he noted, an all-girl ensemble. Besides, he was convinced that he was "the most ungifted person for dance that anybody had ever seen." Nevertheless, he took several dance classes and participated in a scene he characterized as both carefree and overserious. He attended German Dance Congresses, went to performances ("If Wigman was bad, we were depressed for a week"), and "solved" the usual aesthetic questions over innumerable cups of coffee ("Oh, it was very polemical"). Such heady memories were pleasantly interlaced with images of midnight swims and outdoor acrobatics, walks in the Vienna Woods, and classroom impersonations of the famous. (Half a century later, Edwin still charmed friends with his gentle mimicking of Harald Kreutzberg and Isadora Duncan.)

An advertisement handed him his dance debut. The aging, notorious Adorée Villany wanted extras for a performance, and, needing money, Edwin signed up. He recalled an evening of wearing "silly costumes, doing Egyptian things" while Villany romped behind a screen. He was unclear as to whether she was naked or merely seemed so, but her history shows Villany had no fear of "artistic nudity." Indeed, she had been performing dances in various degrees of "historically accurate" undress since 1905, and had suffered in predictable legal ways. (Once she insisted she could be judged only by Rodin, not by a magistrate.) To Edwin, the author of *Tanz-Reform und Pseudo-Moral* was a sincere woman caught in a temporal warp, "ahead of her time, behind Isadora's." After the concert, Villany thanked Edwin, then offered him a book of manifestos and reviews fleshed out with photos, and an overnight invitation. Bewildered, Edwin accepted the book.

He was toying with literature in other ways. From Shakespeare & Company he ordered copies of *Ulysses* and Gertrude Stein, and he followed *transition* through years of experimentation, even submitting a manuscript, which "they were kind enough to ignore." Other attempts at publication were more successful. *The Drama* accepted a 1925 piece on theatrical production, and a year later, Harriet Monroe's *Poetry* printed two Denby poems. He fiddled with translation and began at least one novel, a queer story about a young dancer immobilized and illuminated by a mirror.

In 1927, he visited the Soviet Union for six weeks. A Constructivist theater exhibit in Vienna had rekindled his Harvard interest in Russia, and two family weddings in America made the trip possible: within eight days of each other, his two brothers married, exchanging places as best man. President Coolidge, cabinet members, and senators attended. Edwin, pleading busyness, remained in Austria, odd man out. A brother's generosity allowed him to use for his own purposes family "traveling money," diverting it, in effect, from Washington to the Kremlin. His trip financed, Edwin railroaded through dimly lit Warsaw and then on to Moscow, "the cubical city."

A piece of paper paved the way. A typed memo admonished the management of Soviet theaters to assist "the American art historian E. Demby [*sic*], who has come to Moscow specifically to study theater production in the USSR." The directive, which doubled as a pass, was signed by Anatoly Lunacharsky, People's Commissar of Education. Lunacharsky was no mere bureaucrat. He had convinced Lenin that the Bolshoi Ballet was not sufficiently unrevolutionary to scrap and had lured Isadora Duncan to Russia with telegrammed promises (some of them kept). At times he had stayed above Bolshevik strife by peppering his department with the wives of bigwigs. But Edwin seemed less impressed by Lunacharsky's credentials than by his economy. The commissar had extracted the paper from his typewriter, creased it, recreased it, then tore it neatly in two with his fingers. A diplomat's son could not fail to recognize such behavior as revolutionary.

More important revolutions were taking place on stage. Edwin witnessed as many as possible, attending lectures, classes in "biomechanics," Meyerhold productions, Yiddish theater, Prokofiev concerts, even the circus and a choral reading of John Reed's prose. He returned from the Bolshoi with few kind words about Ekaterina Geltzer's Esmeralda ("hollow and dull") but greeted the appearance of a live goat on stage with exclamation points. Already the writer in him was elbowing out the performer. A choreographic olympiad elicited uncommon invective: "formless, inventionless, hideously costumed, unmusical." *Joseph the Beautiful*, by Balanchine favorite Kasyan Goleizovsky, he found "never uninteresting, but a show, not an experience. . . . One pose succeeds another," he complained in his journal. "Bodies are used as materials for complicated line composition, almost no flowing of movement."

Back in Vienna, Edwin approached graduation day at Hellerau with some confidence, his independence buoyed by his sense that all Austrians believed young people to be crazy anyway. Hellerau had taught him ease with his self, familiarity with others. "It was not just an interlude," he corrected me once. "Interludes never are." He came home from the 1928 German Dance Congress to his typewriter, piecing together an essay, half tribute to his school, half question mark about the future of dance. Sandwiched between a Djuna Barnes piece and photos by Man Ray, this curious amalgam of experience and worry appeared in the January 1929 *Theatre Guild Magazine*, the first published article on dance by Edwin Denby.

A month later, he compounded his entry into the writing world with a paper, sanctified by Dr. Freud himself, in *Zeitschrift für psychoanalytische Pädagogik*, ominously titled "On the Soul's Reactions to Gymnastics." Federn (who numbered Rainer Maria Rilke and Hermann Broch among his clients) shepherded the project to completion and sponsored its publication. In a way, the article served as Edwin's swan song to both psychoanalysis and Hellerau. Now matriculated, tempted by careers in writing and therapy, he turned instead to dancing.

In Essen, he auditioned for Kurt Jooss, was accepted into the fledgling company, then quit the first week, a victim of his own nervousness. (Jooss was still years away from the international renown of *The Green Table*.) Edwin's next job choice was more fortunate. The Hessisches Landestheater in Darmstadt needed a dancer for its chorus. Edwin wanted to direct or act, but the enthusiasm of his interviewers and a late-night guided tour of the city convinced him to accept a tiny job "in this small German company in a small German town."

Darmstadt was no refuge for backwoods Barrymores. The city of a hundred thousand boasted two theater houses and a ten-month season. By the time Edwin signed on, the theater was (in Virgil Thomson's words) "quite famous for its modernistic productions." Brecht's *Mann ist Mann* had its premiere there, and the management under Carl Ebert offered operas by Falla and Hindemith, ballets by Milhaud and Satie. Arthur Maria Rabenalt, "young and gifted," directed *Musiktheater*, and a young Rudolf Bing assisted Ebert. Wilhelm Reinking (always considered by Edwin a genius without a reputation) designed sets that were alternately awesome and intimate.

Cläre Eckstein was the *Ballettmeisterin*. A former Wigman student, she could choreograph social satires as adeptly as brisk lyrical duets. Hindemith was so smitten by the dances she created for his opera *Neues vom Tage* that he offered to compose a piece for her. (Circumstances, including Hitler, interceded.) Edwin remembered Eckstein as relentlessly inventive, incorporating mistakes into performances, improvising and refining constantly. "She did things that no other choreographer was doing . . . from a theater point of view." A recent German memoir agrees, insisting that her rhythmic pantomime earns her a place as "a forerunner of the generation of Pina Bausch."

Edwin believed that he was among the mistakes Eckstein incorporated onstage. She discovered his potential as a comic dancer, quickly featuring him as her partner. "I didn't want to be funny; I was," he pleaded, but newspaper accounts of ovations lasting several minutes belie this as mere self-effacement. Probably Eckstein, a "ravishing" performer herself, recognized that Edwin's Buster Keaton features, elegantly understated gestures, and acrobatic gifts were a snapping match to her graceful, more outgoing exuberance. Whatever the case, reviews and photographs attest the rapport and virtuosity of the pair in *Soirée*, *Die Hochzeit in Cremona*, and *Die Regimentstochter*.

To Edwin and many others, Darmstadt in the twenties was idyllic; "*mein Frühling*," one account calls it. He spent "days and days" in the outdoor *Kaffee* in the square near the theater. And because writing was an important part of café life ("a reason for being there"), he wrote, mostly in German: stories, plays, a radio talk on Georg Trakl. Such industrious scribbling had its reward. Ebert and Rabenalt commissioned Edwin to modernize (or "jazz up," as the Paris *Herald Tribune* suggested) *Die schöne Galatea* by Franz von Suppé. If this nineteenth-century classic needed revitalizing, Edwin seemed the man equipped to do it. After the operetta opened to a crowded house in June 1929, reviewers lauded the "scintillating dialogue and delightfully naughty lyrics, adroitly fitted" to Suppé's melodies. (Lest readers draw improper conclusions about Denby's "perfect German," one reassured them that Edwin's "Americanism is of Mayflower vintage.") Praise reverberated sufficiently to justify publication of *Die neue Galatea*. Edwin's first book, now virtually unobtainable, bears the imprint of B. Schotts Söhne, Mainz.

His next project formed an important friendship and caused a counterrevolution. Now an assistant régisseur at the Landestheater, Edwin wrote to Virgil Thomson, proposing to give the still-unproduced *Four Saints in Three Acts* an airing in Darmstadt. "Almost bilingual," he promised his own help in "verifying a translation." The ensuing correspondence unfolded a comedy of errors and postponements, Gertrude Stein refusing at one point to finance Thomson's trip to Darmstadt because "the libretto had already been accepted" (presumably by Edwin, a stranger to her). Meanwhile, the enemies of experiment festered. Officials merely miffed at retouching Suppé thrashed at the thought of the words of Stein being sung from a German stage. Music director Karl Böhm was especially appalled. Lines were drawn and hardened. Within a year, Ebert and Bing were gone, replaced by less progressive managers. Instead of culminating in a decisive world premiere, Edwin's brainchild helped truncate what

Thomson called "Darmstadt's bright history in producing left-wing or far-out opera and ballets."

After the opera explosion, Edwin stayed on only to the end of the season. He and Eckstein performed in Darmstadt for the last time in June 1930, unveiling three pantomimes, then hopped to Munich the same month for the German Dance Congress. There, *Soirée* earned them plaudits, and, on the final day, a showcase of *"Junge Tänzer"* featured a Denby solo, *Ein höherer Beamte*. Edwin reminisced not at all about his performance, and very little about the "odd, very odd" *Totenmal* Mary Wigman premiered the same day, but he loved to tell of the moment during a group discussion when Wigman rose to speak: her standing cut the room with silence, and all around, in odd contortions, a hundred dancers froze "like statues, or mimes." ("Whose speaking could be so important now?" he liked to ask. "I know of only two.")

Denby and Eckstein continued their triumphs in Berlin—first at the Theater am Schiffbauerdamm, next at the Berliner, then the Volksbühne, then wherever they played. Several audiences forced mid-performance encores for the pair, and reviewers were appreciative, although one did complain that the dances were always "*Groteske, Parodie und Ironie*." In May 1932, the troupe followed the Loie Fuller Dancers into the Wintergarten. Later, they played the Berlin cabaret Katakombe and the Bonbonnière in Munich.

But the clock was ticking; the Reichstag was burning. Edwin, who believed the Germans "the most civilized people, the brightest," was astonished they would elect as chancellor a man whose radio speeches were such a joke. He was dismayed that his communist friends took a street-gang glee in their night battles with the S.S. Nevertheless, he badgered a Soviet embassy official into granting a return visa to one young Red he thought in immediate danger, and once "chaperoned" an activist "between arrests" across the border, always afterward remembering the Bavarian Nazis on the train glaring at his friend's prison haircut.

Edwin himself had reason to worry. His associations were suspect: "I knew a lot of *Threepenny Opera* types," he once told me, characteristically neglecting to mention he already knew *Die Dreigroschenoper* authors Brecht and Weill as well. Besides, what could be worse than an "*amerikanische Grotesktanzer*" ("son of a war minister," to boot) satirizing German middle-class pretensions? One popular role cast him as a physical-culture fanatic, absurdly garbed, overstuffed as a George Grosz creation or a Goebbels. Edwin never developed political interests; he merely perfected fears. He watched quietly as bookings were canceled, theatrical agents began to disappear; "all our contracts were voided." His explanation was cryptic: "Suddenly, jugglers became very popular." (Files of *Der Tanz* uphold him, pictures of acrobats and animal acts gradually outnumbering those of performers less *völkisch.*) Finally, in 1933, one communication panicked him completely. He fled the country.

In Paris that June, he saw choreography that transformed his life. Eleven years earlier, he had seen Isadora at Carnegie Hall and had been struck by her dancing—"very slow and very simple, absorbing and very grand." But he had witnessed nothing since comparable to "those flashes." The Diaghilev Ballets Russes, seen in Vienna, had thrilled him, "but the complications and delicacies I didn't understand at all." (When I asked Edwin if, like the Kirsteins, the Denbys had discussed attending Nijinsky's "scandalous" American performances, he responded with mock horror: "Oh, no, of course not. My mother was a diplomat's wife; she knew quite well what she must not know.") In 1930, he watched Lifar and the ill-starred Spessivtseva in George Balanchine's *Prodigal Son*. It washed over him. Three years later, perhaps lured by Balanchine's remaking of the Brecht-Weill *Die sieben Todsünden*, Edwin attended programs of Les Ballets 1933. One performance of Balanchine's *Mozartiana* left him speechless, helpless, a victim of pleasant lightning: "It wouldn't stay out of my mind."

He moved from Paris to Majorca, rejoining his parents there and enjoying their subsidy. As "an excuse to stay in my room," he began composing a gothic adventure novel he called *Scream in a Cave*. Three times in as many years he rewrote the cliffhanger as "an exercise, to teach myself." (The experiment worked, but the novel nearly died, tanning thirty-five years until published as *Mrs. W's Last Sandwich* in 1972.) When not occupied with revisions, he wandered around the island on foot, with only a dog as companion, deciphering architecture and exploring Moorish ruins. In May 1934, he stepped a little closer to his future, launching his career as a newspaper dance critic with a review of Miss Hutter and her pupils for the *Majorca News & Spanish Times*. Drawing particular Denby praise were "dainty Stella and watchful Irene."

His career as a performer was not quite finished. He joined Mariette von Meyenburg's company, providing "*collaboration artistique*" and dancing several parts in her *Mercure*. He appeared also in another Meyenburg piece set to Satie, *Parade*, which he had performed earlier in an Eckstein version. Between tours of France and Switzerland, Edwin taught gymnastics at Meyenburg's school in Basel.

Needing a new passport picture, Edwin took a dance friend's advice about a photographer and tracked down an unfamiliar Swiss address. On the other end of the experience was Rudy Burckhardt: "There was a knock on the door and Edwin walked in." The visit lasted almost fifty years. Rudy moved and re-moved, married and remarried, fathered two sons, but to the last day of Edwin's life remained his essential friend, his confidant and confessor.

When the door opened, Burckhardt was a twenty-year-old medical-school dropout. He was from a "good" Swiss family: "We descended from Jacob Burckhardt, the historian," he told me, stressing the verb. To Rudy, Edwin was "cosmopolitan, dashing, big world." Indeed, who could remain immune to a man who had smoked opium with Cocteau, exchanged pleasantries with Meyerhold, met Diaghilev, talked with Freud about self-analysis ("impossible for non-Freuds"), and been bored by the conversation of James Joyce? "He knew famous people I had never even heard of," Rudy confessed. But none of Edwin's other acquaintances had the gift his "little Swiss friend" had for witty, self-deprecating insight, or his refreshing vision. Once, talking about him, Edwin used the phrase "he carries his own eyes."

Edwin was poor, surviving on teacher's fees and a small allowance from his family. To save money, he lived at the Meyenburg studio; Rudy remembers him bleary-eyed, shuffling across a morning dance class, toothbrush in hand. Days he spent in various cafés, still shedding drafts of his novel. Nights, he and Rudy went to "working-class bars on the wrong side of the Rhine." When Burckhardt's parents sent some money, the pair scooted to Paris for a few weeks. There, large "brand-new Picassos" occupied them more than the Louvre, and they "played bohemian" in a nightspot favored by criminals and circus people.

One Carnaval in Basel later, it was time to go. Edwin left first, returning by boat to the States, while Rudy lingered awhile, awaiting his inheritance. In April 1935, he joined Edwin in New York. One cannot imagine a more unemployable pair: one a prodigal photographer who spoke only "*ein bisschen* English"; the other a broken-down dancer and would-be writer.

The apartment on West Twenty-first Street was bad. Unheated, the fourth-story walk-up had electrical problems and only cold water. The hallways were dark, and thick with the smell of cats; the streets, loud around the clock with truck deliveries and taxis. But the eighteen-dollar-a-month rent was affordable, and Rudy saw the loft's possibilities. They took it.

New York was a great pleasure. "We were happy," Edwin remembered, "to be in a city the beauty of which was unknown, uncozy, and not small-scale." Quickly, they found friends. Or, according to Rudy, rediscovered them: "Edwin knew everybody in Europe, and then everybody came over here," as if, in some twisted way, Hitler was responsible for their social success. In fact, many friends were émigrés or, like Aaron Copland, Virgil Thomson, and Paul Bowles, repatriated Americans Edwin had known in Europe. He and Rudy watched dawns at Madison Square and slept until four or five in the afternoon.

Edwin could approach interviewers with unswerving purpose. "Three things happened to me in the thirties," he lectured one. The first was that "Rudy Burckhardt, whom I'd met in Basel, came to New York." (Not "I returned to New York"; to Edwin, autobiography was an occasion for gathering bouquets.) "The second . . . was meeting Minna Lederman." On a photograph, Edwin articulated his debt more clearly: "To Minna," the inscription began, "who made me a dance critic."

From a narrow extra room in her parents' apartment, Minna Lederman edited *Modern Music* for the League of Composers. Though finances were a constant problem and interference from the League board an intermittent danger, Minna animated the magazine with her vigorous intelligence. At a penny a word, she recruited as writers legions of the famous and soon to be: Berg, Bartók, Schoenberg; Cage, Shostakovich, Prokofiev; Carter, Kirstein, Varèse; Bernstein, Blitzstein; Piston, Cowell, Ives. Not even André Breton could resist her call, though his "Silence Is Golden" article savaged all music.

Accepting Thomson's pointer, Edwin submitted to *Modern Music* a lengthy manuscript he had been dawdling over. Some negotations later, it surfaced in the March–April 1936 issue as "A Good Libretto," several ellipses apparently registering the distance between authorial intention and editorial restraint. Three contributions followed before "Aaron and Virgil suggested to Minna that I write a dance column for the magazine, and so I did." (Copland and Thomson, as well as Denby friends Bowles and Roger Sessions, were already *Modern Music* regulars.) Edwin rationalized the job as a source of free tickets; besides, he thought, subscribers to a music magazine would not demand much from a dance critic.

But he had at least one auditor. Minna was not just the "first-class editor" Thomson knew firsthand; she was "that impeccable trainer." Edwin said, "I was a writer; I never *supposed* readers." Others offered vague praise or wondered why you hadn't written the article they wanted to; Minna edited, interrogating every phrase, plucking out poetic gauze with blue pencil or question. "At first," Edwin joked, "it seemed very impolite: she insisted on understanding." Their marathon sessions could be painful. Sometimes, when proposed excisions cut too deep, they took to the phone. But Minna's gentleness matched her persistence, and she shared Edwin's concern with blending sound with sense. "Gradually, I learned," he said. "Consonants are part of it, and vowels are part of it, ways of saying what you finally wanted said, not obtrusively, but with some general meaning." Or, another time, more simply: "Minna made me intelligible."

The third, and apparently final, thing that happened to Edwin during the decade required meteorological and feline assistance. "I met Willem de Kooning on the fire escape, because a black kitten lost in the rain cried at my fire door, and after the rain it turned out to be his kitten." Thirty-two, successful as a stowaway from his native Rotterdam, de Kooning lived one building over, one floor down. Already his interminably active phonograph had marked him as a man to know, Edwin admiring his pastiche of flamenco music and Mozart. Soon the two were habitually sharing midnight coffees with Rudy at Stewart's, a Twenty-third Street haunt, sometimes bringing along friends, including Kurt Weill and Lotte Lenya, Fairfield Porter, and de Kooning's painter friend Arshile Gorky (Edwin described the pair as "brothers with a secret"). Eventually, this little nest of misfits almost supplanted another Stewart's crowd, several tables of deaf-mutes. Edwin remembered them wheezing laughter, gaily bantering with their hands, "the happiest people I have ever seen." He harbored no doubts about which group the waitresses thought more crazy.

For a while, Edwin relinquished the Twenty-first Street loft to Rudy and his new girlfriend while he lived a block away in a space vacated by de Kooning. His friend had so transformed the apartment with the wizardry of his carpentry and color schemes that Edwin never forgot the interlocking perspectives it unfolded. Another time, he shared the original loft with Paul Bowles, while the latter composed music for Charles Henri Ford's *Denmark Vesey*. Friendship did not prevent Virgil Thomson from dismissing this story of slave revolt as "another negroid opera," a view perhaps bolstered by the curious nature of some Bowles-Denby "research." The two gathered atmosphere almost nightly at the Apollo, the Cotton Club, and several other Harlem hot spots. They also found time to attend Father Divine sermons, attracted less by His message than by the ample free breakfast it accompanied. That a deity would feed His flock so sumptuously seemed to Edwin an important extenuating circumstance.

Once, not long after de Kooning had renounced all womankind to his friends as obstacles to art, a new face appeared at Stewart's. The visage, "with eyes so attractive," belonged to Elaine Fried, only a year out of high school but soon to be de Kooning's bride. She and Edwin quickly entwined as friends and ballet companions, he admiring the way her sense of telling visual detail imposed no grid on the dance. They all met at the cafeteria, the automat, and each other's lofts. Already, he was no stranger. "The paintings Bill was working on when I first met him were all of men, and they all had round eyes," Elaine remembers. "These were always Edwin's eyes." Sometimes, when he came for a sitting or simply to visit, he would show them poems he had just completed.

Horse Eats Hat called for writing more madcap. Orson Welles and John Houseman commissioned Edwin to "freely adapt" Eugène Labiche's *Un Chapeau de paille d'Italie* for their 1936 WPA Federal Theatre production. Freely adapt he did. "Aided, driven, and abetted" by director Welles, Edwin exploded the farce into a dizzying series of chases, his "demented piece of surrealism" leaving the 1851 plot as mangled as the straw hat of the title. (By comparison, W. S. Gilbert's version seems a chaste English garden party.) When the play opened on September 26 at the Maxine Elliott Theatre, many were delighted, everyone was confused. The *Times* critic at least intuited influence: "It was as though Gertrude Stein had dreamed a dream after a late supper of pickles and ice cream, the ensuing revelations being crisply acted by giants and midgets, caricatures, lunatics, and a prop nag." (The back half of the horse was played by Edwin himself, a fact uncharitably evoked by a few reviewers.) Everett Dirksen, just beginning a long career as Congress' "Wizard of Ooze," sourpussed that the play was "salacious tripe"; and the WPA dispatched a guardian from Washington to search the text for possible double-entendres. Even rewrites were censored. Edwin was overworked and jubilant.

After lending a translating hand with Erika Mann's *Pepper Mill* revue, he turned to other projects. Aaron Copland wanted an opera. Edwin's first inspiration was a costume maker's nightmare: "Every time I closed my eyes I would see penguins, an entire stage crowded with penguins." Fortunately, these fat black-and-white flappers gradually gave way to contemporary American teens, and *The Second Hurricane* was born. It told a gentle tale of adolescents marooned in storm country slowly kindling a social sense against the regathering winds. With the project nearing feasibility, Edwin convinced Copland to name Orson Welles director. Edwin knew the twenty-one-year-old Welles as "the most talented person in town." He also knew him as impossible. Remembering Welles's manic *Horse Eats Hat* revisions and autocratic directing ways, Edwin decided to put a continent between himself and the production. He and Rudy left for Haiti two months before the premiere.

Before their getaway, Rudy screened his first film, *145 West 21*, at a fund-raiser for the opera. The one-reeler paired Edwin and Paula Miller, Lee Strasberg's first wife, as newlyweds. Sound accompaniment was provided by Paul Bowles, who "played piano, sang, whistled, clicked my tongue and made percussive noises." Lyricist John Latouche played a less audible role, and a burlesque crowd in the movie featured the unconvincing leer of Virgil Thomson. (Rudy was a little irked that Miss Miller refused to bare her breasts in the sequence.) Copland himself impersonated a spackle-splattered roofer turned house thief. Edwin believed that Aaron "enjoyed acting as only a composer could." The film premiered at its title, the Denby-Burckhardt loft, to an audience including Carl Van Vechten, Sandy Calder, Lincoln Kirstein, Joseph Cornell, Jane Auer (Bowles), and the usual refugees from Stewart's.

Through conductor Lehman Engel, the Henry Street Settlement offered rehearsal and performance space for the opera. Its proletarian underpinnings sometimes gave the Lower East Side center a resolute pink tinge. Only a few years previously, Ethel Greenglass (Rosenberg) had taken modern-dance classes there. When *The Second Hurricane* opened on April 21, 1937, the Settlement Playhouse seemed a proper place for its modest sets and vaguely Pop Front themes. Edwin was bashfully proud of the opera. Once, incognito, he attended a high school production in Akron and left radiant, relieved that the football player–cheerleader cast had not bruised the tender repetitions of his lyrics.

Even with the opera safely over, Edwin loitered in Haiti and Mexico, applying varnish to his much-traveled novel. Finally, he returned stateside in time for his father's funeral: Charles Denby, Jr., died on February 14, 1938. He and his youngest son had never been close; he had greeted his offspring's dancing with inquiries about his appetite for foolishness. But in larger ways, Edwin was a beneficiary of his father's intelligence, high expectations, and mastery of a more courtly world. Others had benefited, too: Ballet Russe de Monte Carlo impresario Sergei Denham renamed himself in honor of the senior Denby's help with his immigration case.

Once settled back into New York routines and *Modern Music* deadlines, Edwin tried some choreography, staging dances for the Boston premiere of *Knickerbocker Holiday* before abandoning Broadway as too much fuss. Parties, given or gone to, were another distraction. Edwin remembered particularly the festivities of the Askews—sometimes, with guests like Dali, Tchelitchev, and Lifar, more performance than party. Kirk and Constance Askew were, in fact, the most important hosts in American dance history, the loan of their London kitchen enabling Lincoln Kirstein to woo George Balanchine across the Atlantic. Being a critic made parties "prickly," Edwin said, forcing one not to say certain things and not to hear others. But such constraints hardly throttled Thomson. Virgil would hold forth in a corner, delivering his most opinionated opinions until the get-together came to him. Edwin envied his friend's ability to think and speak anywhere, and always contrasted his own writing difficulties with Thomson's supposed ease.

In 1940, Edwin trekked West, first to Hollywood to visit his friend Copland, and then to Texas to research the "adult opera" the two had contemplated. While in the Southwest, he attended a Zuni ritual dance. (At this point in the story, Edwin would always pause significantly before "And it was the worst thing I ever saw.") Somewhere between the City of the Stars and Carlsbad, New Mexico, he concluded that civilization was no longer tenable. With typical whimsy, the dance critic decided to become a cowboy. The ranch owner who interviewed him was understandably skeptical; Edwin parried with half-stated truths and enthusiasm. Finally, suspicious of his smooth fingers, the rancher asked if Edwin had any experience with horses. "Of course," came the quick response; he had done show-riding while still a boy. The rodeo's loss was literature's gain.

New York projects piled up. With Rita Matthias, Edwin translated Ferdinand Bruckner's *The Criminals*, which opened at the New School auditorium two weeks after Pearl Harbor. In Bruckner's timely remake of the 1928 play, which Edwin had seen at Darmstadt, Nazis replace homosexuals as the main villains. Meanwhile, Edwin's theatrical career was buckling under the weight of manuscripts going nowhere. "I had never known anyone with such a passion for writing librettos," Minna recalled, but "no large opportunity seemed to come his way." Copland and Denby had multiple thoughts about the opera-western *Sonntag Gang* Edwin completed in 1940; *Miltie Is a Hackie* and a ballet libretto, both finished the following year, also remained unproduced.

After the disappearance behind Japanese lines of a beloved cousin who shared his name, Edwin tried to enlist. "He would have made a terrible soldier, even worse than me," was Rudy's verdict. A Selective Service official apparently agreed, and refused the thirty-nine-year-old volunteer. (Rudy himself was drafted.) Meanwhile, the Army was inadvertently shaping Edwin's future, first calling up *Herald Tribune* dance critic Walter Terry and then mobilizing his replacement, Robert Lawrence. Needing to fill the chair with someone brilliant, experienced, and draft-proof, music editor Thomson turned to friend Edwin, "knowing I was poor." The pay was fifteen dollars a week. The June 25, 1943, *Tribune* carried an article by its new "official reviewer."

Edwin had written twenty-eight articles in his seven years at *Modern Music*. At the *Herald Tribune*, he was expected to produce three or four reviews a week and a longer article every Sunday. Instead of bimonthly musters, he faced deadlines two hours after he left his theater seat. Witnesses to his frantic *Modern Music* "all-nighters" wondered how Edwin would survive the job.

One answer, predictably, was Minna. She phoned each week with patient criticism and quick praise, and listened to shards of his Sunday column, each of which cost Edwin several weeks of worry. But Edwin himself was strangely changed, suddenly capable of "composing" an article as he walked the few blocks from the City Center to the *Trib* building. (Once, when he wandered off a curb unawares, he was pleased that the cab that lightly bumped him had not jostled his lead.) In the large common office of the newspaper, Edwin would find an unused typewriter and sit down, jotting occasionally on a pad as he pecked out his final copy. "At quarter to twelve I would take the article upstairs." His piece set and proofread, he would often save a subway nickel and walk downtown, trying to reconstruct what he had written.

If this sounds simple, it was only deceptively so. "He found his new work very taxing, just barely possible," Minna wrote. Articles badly done were irretrievable; some mornings after (afternoons, actually) found Edwin over coffee and paper, biting his lips in self-derision. "Every week or two, I'd want to resign." One night a head cold left him blank at the typewriter. Other times, the imprecision of program notes forced him to improvise. Saturday he was obliged to apologize for Friday's description of Nora Kaye as "Miss Markova." Sometimes, problems were ethical: he fretted over panning ballet companies already hurting at the gate, and one phone call from a dancer devastated by his critique made him reconsider writing about beginners. Another time, his fears were more personal: a marine promised to thrash him because a review of Sonja Henie was not sufficiently starstruck. Overnight, skating took on a new importance.

When the war ended in 1945, Edwin was as exhausted as General Eisenhower. He submitted his final *Tribune* article in November, welcomed Walter Terry back to his civilian job, and fled to Mexico for a rest. A year passed before he again took up his dance pen, and even when he resumed, he wrote little: four articles in 1946, one in 1947. The following year, his first book of poetry, *In Public, In Private*, appeared in two postponed, subsidized, misprinted editions, each with its own de Kooning frontispiece.

More important, under B. H. Haggin's firm editorial hand, *Looking at the Dance* was approaching publication. In 1945, Edwin had provided a brief text for Alexey Brodovitch's photographic *Ballet*, and a year later,

Dance Index had devoted an issue to Denby criticism with an introduction by Elaine de Kooning and Walker Evans photographs. But an entire volume of dance reviews seemed risky; too ephemeral, commercially unfeasible. Allen Tate warned one publisher against this pressing of gossamer, and the collection, announced for Holt, was issued instead by Pellegrini and Cudahy. The book's greatest enemy, though, was Edwin himself. Surviving typescripts and tearsheets plot a widespread battle between Denby's "omit" and Haggin's "restore." Published almost against its author's will, *Looking at the Dance* became the most acclaimed terpsichorean book in this country's history.

Edwin read the reviews in Europe. In 1948, he arrived in Paris, toting a Guggenheim and stomach ulcers. He treated both with worry. His fellowship project, a book about comparative dance styles, crumbled into a few essays; as always, Edwin preferred ballet to writing about it. His medical condition he ignored more dangerously, finally collapsing under the kniving throbs. Mending took years. There exists a 1955 photograph taken by Jerome Robbins of a bow-tied Edwin squatting by a pillar in Venice, his eyes squinting against the sun, his face the very picture of pain.

Before his breakdown, Edwin had sidetracked to Fez with friends Jane and Paul Bowles, making a combination of people and place Tennessee Williams found "deliciously mysterious, very Kafka!" With the Bowleses, Edwin stayed three months, sampling hashish and the conversation of camel boys. At the airport in Tangiers, he saw a Moroccan princess, almost invisible beneath silk, communicate a message, and her royalty, with just fingertips; and he remembered with proper glee the care one North African herdsman took orchestrating the bells of his goats.

In Europe, he surprised himself with leisurely articles for the English periodical *Ballet*. Editor Richard Buckle judged Edwin's contributions "the ultimate justification for the magazine's existence." From bases in Italy, he would make "sallies" to Copenhagen, Paris, or London for concerts. In 1951, he took breaks from writing chores to share this familiar continent with the Burckhardts: Rudy, wife Edith, and Jacob (the son, not the historian). They toured Greece, the Italian mainland, and Sicily, and lived half a year on Ischia, off the coast of Naples. Early the following year, Edwin ended his happy quadrennial exile, docking in Manhattan aboard the *Queen Elizabeth*.

"I hadn't expected so intense a pleasure, looking at New York again, in the high white February sunlight." Much of his pleasure centered on "New York City's Ballet," Kirstein's company in its new incarnation. Edwin responded to its flowering with articles more frequent than any since his *Herald Tribune* days. New friends appeared, too: "Met these four boys Frank O'Hara, John Ashbery, Kenneth Koch, and Jimmy Schuyler (who I had met first abroad) at the Cedar Bar in '52 or '53." Gravitation worked other wonders. Alex Katz entered Edwin's life not as a painter but as a dancer, demonstrating new fandangos on the floor of the old Palladium. (Edwin returned the favor, introducing set designer Katz to collaborator-to-be Paul Taylor.) Franz Kline and Red Grooms and Larry Rivers slid into Denby orbits, and at parties, this frail, white-haired figure mingled with Lenny Bernstein, W. H. Auden, and "that fellow named Kerouac."

To European friends, he dispatched transatlantic kisses, filling rooms of "the exquisite Miss Toklas" with the fragrance of lilies delivered by flower-boy Virgil Thomson, and offering "laughing Olga," Duse biographer Olga Signorelli, his only book dedication (to his 1956 *Mediterranean Cities* poems). Summers he lolled in Provincetown, inhabiting a shack among the shifting dunes. There, "to teach myself to see distance in the air," he tried his amateur's hand at painting. Artist Mimi Gross describes a recurring double apparition: Edwin perched on sand with special friend Peg Watson, whose looks and grace made her seem "a feminine Edwin."

By the late fifties, he was writing almost no prose. O'Hara roused him into finishing "Three Sides of *Agon*" for a 1959 *Evergreen Review*. The choreographer in question passed along his copy, Balanchine believing it worth Stravinsky's attention. (Edwin had helped Mr. B shape his *Dance Encyclopedia* articles, and a few other pieces by Balanchine and de Kooning bear the imprint of Denby rhythms.) Robert Cornfield, a young friend introduced to Edwin by painter John Button, proved a double boon. He matched favorite dinner companions Edwin and Arlene Croce, and lullabied Denby's self-doubts while editing his *Dancers, Buildings and People in the Streets*. The essay collection was published in 1965, its author grateful that Jacqueline Maskey, who gathered the articles, "had made it possible, and Bob had made it necessary."

The following August the accidental death of O'Hara pierced Edwin. "Frank O'Hara was a catalyst for me, although I was much older. But, then, he was everybody's catalyst." Edwin spoke at his funeral, calling Frank "our greatest living poet." Two years later, writing to another friend, he suddenly interjected, "I miss Frank very much," and left the letter there, hanging in the air. Only five years before he himself was gone, he walked me slowly twice around his block, trying to convey the importance of this man, his gifts, the vacancy: "Some people never recovered; in ways, I never did."

Grief could not stagnate Edwin. Ted Berrigan, a jovial bear of a poet, had introduced him to downtown readers with a 1963 issue of *C*, and, gradually, "Frank's children," the writers around St. Mark's Poetry Project, gathered him in, adopted him. Edwin finally permitted friends Ron Padgett, Anne Waldman, and Joan Simon to publish poems he could not bring himself to read: the 1975 Full Court Press *Collected Poems* appeared unseen by its author. Small presses and mimeo magazines left him unembarrassed. The critic's critic, the man who evaded a writing project with Bertolt Brecht, could not resist appeals from the editors of *Mag City* and *Salome*. "I've always been underground," he assured me, and delivered a little lecture on The Importance of Being an Outsider Everywhere.

Surely, some prescience guarded him, allowed him to anticipate successive "next waves." The Judson Church series, David Gordon, Douglas Dunn, Kenneth King, William Dunas, Lucinda Childs, Twyla Tharp, Robert Wilson, Karole Armitage: all paraded by and were recognized, just as Duncan and Schlemmer and Balanchine and Cunningham had been. One pleasure did not blunt another: openings on Avenue B were greeted with the same attention as those at Lincoln Center. Jennifer Dunning believed that the old man she saw one night rising above bleak punk cacophonies watched dance "with a curious yet sustaining private morality."

He was, as he told one questioner, "not quite retired." His image flickered through a dozen films, by Yoshiko Chuma, Red Grooms, and two generations of Burckhardts. He lent advice and an author's applause to Bob Holman's retrieval of *Four Plays* written for an old Warhol project. As a live performer, he accepted emergency calls. When winter colds sent shivers through a children's Christmas pageant, Edwin took to the boards in long johns borrowed from Paul Taylor and a wreath of backyard leaves and as a stand-in Jolly Green Giant danced a dance that artist Helen De Mott will never forget. Others remember him onstage in Robert Wilson performances, intoning passages from Nijinsky's autobiography or whispering his own poetry in a corner.

"Well, then, you were the last person to see me alive." I had just told absentminded Edwin that it was I who had accompanied him to *Einstein on the Beach* when it opened at the Metropolitan Opera in November 1976. A few days after *Einstein*, he suffered attacks that shattered his health and nearly broke his spirit. Eyes, heart, stomach, feet; nothing ever again seemed exempt from pain or surgeons. Edwin wanted to die. He poked at the meals his doctors allowed him and tore up overdue notices for his pacemaker batteries. Then Rudy called in the cavalry: old friend Katie

Schneeman, disguised as a hired cook, conspired daily to keep Edwin fed and busy and well. For six years, it worked.

While his eyes were healing from an operation, Edwin encouraged visitors to read to him, the texts usually chosen from Ashbery books or Croce's *New Yorker* articles or the *Times* shredded down to its dance reviews. "Please, that sentence again," he would say half a dozen times an evening; lids shut, savoring each phrase like a cat licking a peach. During one recovery, dancer Kenneth King played morning nurse, administering eyedrops every a.m. "Kenneth's talk is stimulating, his coffee is overstimulating," was Edwin's light complaint.

When Dana Reitz, another Denby favorite, appeared at the performance space at The Kitchen, Edwin insisted I go. Finishing errands, I arrived hopelessly late to the final concert. My reservation lost, I was reduced to peering up from the street, catching scattered glimpses of Dana's solo through a second-story window. Finally, frustrated and disappointed, I left. Two nights later at Edwin's, I could not wait for the question. Guiltily, I told him what had happened. "Yes," he beamed, "*but what did you see?*"

"We were all so bright around Edwin," poet Alice Notley told me. Jerome Robbins thought that walks with him had a Mary Poppins quality: "It looked like the everyday world to me until I saw things with Edwin around. Then it all changed." Jacob Burckhardt noticed that just when he had convinced you he was actually senile, someone would mention *Liebeslieder* or Jane Freilicher's show or the way clouds drift at different speeds, and Edwin would be off again, perceiving. "The guy never stopped," Alex Katz decided.

But he was tired. In 1965, Frank O'Hara had written of him, "He sees and hears more clearly than anyone else I have ever known"; and now no one was more acutely aware of these things fading than Edwin himself. Balanchine's death in April 1983 left Edwin standing on the wrong side of an epoch. When, after the news, he met Edward Villella on the street, the two wept together. "How far he has taken us," he scribbled in a sympathy note to Lincoln Kirstein. Himself now "a white old man, approved," he did not want to go much farther.

Every year, it was the same. I would take off a summer day to get Edwin to the airport for his vacation in "lucid Maine." But no matter how early I arrived, there was never enough time. Eyeglasses were always missing, suitcases always needed to be frantically ransacked or methodically repacked; even checklists disappeared. Edwin was "as nervous as a cat on moving day." His phrase was apt, much of his departure anxiety centering on his beloved furry things. (One friend hinted that these mornings might be calmer if Edwin himself took the pet tranquilizer.) Finally, with his notebooks, his raincoat, his Beckett, his visor, his Ashbery, pockets full of tiny bilingual Dantes, his second-favorite sneakers, he would climb down the buckling staircase. The closing of the cab door would remind him of something else.

This Wednesday was different. When I entered, Edwin was gazing out the window. He was oddly calm, wanted only to converse; there was no urgency about luggage or arrival time. For an hour, in the apartment where he had lived almost half a century, we quietly talked, sitting at the table "Bill made me." His banter that day was as placid and uncluttered as his loft, with its white, layered extremities. After Katie arrived, he read a letter (a thank-you card from Effie Mihopolous, his last interviewer), wrote a note (to Alice Notley, widowed suddenly that July week by Ted Berrigan), and autographed one book (inscribed to Tazewell Thompson, who in 1985 would revive *The Second Hurricane*). Then we gathered his things, and, with a banana and a *Paradiso* stuffed in his suit-jacket pockets, Edwin descended the steps.

"I think now he must have been saying goodbye to us all spring," Marcia Siegel wrote. Surely, all that final week he had been tucking in friendships: dinner one night with Minna, Merce, and John; supper the next with much-loved Jacob. The day he died, he spoke by phone with Frank Safford, "since freshman spring intimate."

One of my first memories of him was of his crossing and recrossing a broken floorboard at St. Mark's Church, mastering its creak, practicing even more unobtrusive exits.

On Tuesday, July 12, 1983, Edwin Orr Denby died "by his own hand" in Searsmont, Maine. Critic, self-critic to the last, he left two notes, took his overdose, then sat down to watch his own dying. When Rudy found him the next morning, he was in the chair, by the table, head resting on his folded arms. —W. M.

From "Modern Music"

NIJINSKA'S "NOCES"

Noces in the choreography of Nijinska (revived this spring by the Monte Carlo Ballet) is, I'm sure, one of the finest things one can see anywhere. And if I could think of higher praise I would write it.

Noces is noble, it is fierce, it is simple, it is fresh, it is thrilling. It is full of interest. It is perhaps an indication of the heroic age of Nijinsky. There is a realness in the relation of dance and music like a dual force, separate but inseparable. The movements, odd as they are and oddly as they come, often in counteraccent, are always in what theoreticians call "motor logic": that is, they are in a sequence you get the hang of, to your own surprise, and that has a quality of directness when performed. Amazingly few movement motives are used, and only the clearest groupings and paths, making the rhythmic subtlety obvious by contrast. That all these movement motives should be accentuating the direction into the floor leads to such interesting results as that ballet dancers, more familiar with the opposite direction, do these movements with a curious freshness; that the leaps seem higher; that the "pointes" get a special significance and hardness (almost a form of tapping), a hardness which all the performers, by the way, had not understood; and, as a further example, this general downward direction gives the heaped bodies a sense beyond decoration and gives the conventional pyramid at the end the effect of a heroic extreme, of a real difficulty. This sense of the realness of what is being done is underlined by the constant use of people at rest contrasted with people dancing—in the last part, people actually at rest on chairs. How often in other ballets have people stood about while others danced without adding by their contrast, because the contrast was not being used. And the stillness of the whole company at the end after all their frenzy is a climax of genius. During the whole last scene, the climax is a sort of steady inevitable expansion, a motion from the particular to the abstract.

Of the dancers themselves I would like to say that, though they seemed handicapped by insufficient rehearsal, they danced, especially at the last performance in New York, with a fine fervor. In fact the group of the Ballet Russe deserves every praise; the way they are overworked by the management is inhuman, because it is destructive of talent; and that they can still offer so much is a miracle.

Of the music of *Noces* I need not speak; it is as fine as the choreography.

The scenery and costumes I find satisfactory, though I should like to see the four pianos on the stage, and the bed through the door of the house. The production is fifteen years old, and scenery and costumes belong more completely than choreography or music to that "abstract" fashion, the didactic heroics of the early twenties (those were Mary Wigman's best days, too).

Of another addition to the repertory, a new version of *Jardin Public* (choreography Massine, music Dukelsky), I personally feel the less said the better. What I saw was an unpleasant confusion. In the mess of movements the Poet's bit of classic clarity did not help. Massine had found a few ingenious gestures for the Workers and odd ways of posturing for himself, rather reminiscent of Kreutzberg. But I saw no interest, or strength, or even intention of anything. Coming from our first ballet company, I found it thoroughly distasteful. MAY–JUNE 1936

NIJINSKY'S "FAUN"; MASSINE'S "SYMPHONIE FANTASTIQUE"; AMERICAN BALLET CARAVAN

During the last six weeks New York has been a pleasant place for a person who likes ballet. I have seen one absolutely first-class piece, Nijinsky's *Faun*; Bérard's sets for the *Symphonie Fantastique*, the second and third of which are as good as the best ever made—probably the best we'll see all winter; and then a new dance group that is full of freshness and interest, the American Ballet Caravan. I have also seen other things I liked more or less, or not at all, and I have not by any means seen everything that has been done.

The revivals of the de Basil Ballet Russe are as carefully rehearsed and as freshly executed as its novelties. Last year's *Noces* and this year's *Faun* are things to be very grateful for. The *Faun* is an astonishing work. After twenty-three years it is as direct and moving as though it had been invented yesterday. It gathers momentum from the first gesture to the last like an ideal short story. From this point of view of a story, the way the veil is introduced and re-emphasized by the Nymph is a marvel of rightness. From the point of view of visual rhythm, the repetition of the Nymph's gesture of dismay is the perfection of timing. It is, of course, because so few gesture motives are used that one can recognize each so plainly, but there is no feeling of poverty in this simplification. The rhythmic pattern in relation to the stage and to the music is so subtly graded that instead of monotony we get a steady increase in suspense, an increase in the eyes' perceptiveness, and a feeling of heroic style at the climax.

It is true that most of the gestures used have prototypes in Greek reliefs and vase paintings, but, in addition to that intellectual association with adolescence, the fact is that when the body imitates these poses, the kind of tension resulting expresses exactly the emotion Nijinsky wants to express. Both their actual tension and their apparent remoteness, both their plastic clarity and their emphasis by negation on the center of the body (it is always strained between the feet in profile and the shoulders en face)—all these qualities lead up to the complete realization of the Faun's last gesture. The poignancy of this moment lies partly in the complete change in the direction of tension, in the satisfying relief that results; and the substitution of a new tension (the incredible backbend) gives the work its balance. But besides, the eye has been educated to see the plastic beauty of this last pose, and the rhythmic sense to appreciate its noble deliberateness. That it is so intensely human a gesture, coming after a long preparation of understatement, gives it, in its cumulative assurance, the force of an illumination. This force of direct human statement, this faith in all of us, is the astonishing thing about the *Faun*. It is as rare in dancing as in the other arts. These last moments of the *Faun* do not need any critical defense. But they have been so talked about that I am trying to point out for intellectuals that they are not a sensational tag, but that the whole piece builds up to them, and reaches in them an extraordinary beauty.

The de Basil company danced the *Faun* beautifully. Lichine in the title role excelled. It is a part that demands exceptional imagination as well as great plastic sense. And Lichine had besides these a fine simplicity.

His own ballet *Pavillon* (music by Borodin) was pleasant but left no definite impression as a piece. Its lightness was often commonplace, and its inventions often plastically ineffective. I hope he will show us a new ballet next year in which his admirable sense of dance will find a more definite form.

The other novelty, Massine's *Symphonie Fantastique* (music and book by Berlioz) was at the opposite extreme from *Pavillon* in point of definiteness and effect. Massine is without doubt the master choreographer of today. He has the most astonishing inventiveness and the most painstaking constructivity. He is an encyclopedia of ballet, character, specialty, period, and even of formulas from modern German dancing. In the *Fantastique,* for instance, his Musician runs the whole gamut of late romantic gesture, and the prison scene is glorified Jooss. Besides this gift of detail he has a passion for visual discipline, a very good sense of dramatic variety and climax, and one watches the whole *Fantastique*—except perhaps for the last finale—with a breathless attention. The prison scene in particular moves as fast as a movie thriller. In the *Fantastique* Massine uses even more successfully than in *Présages* or *Choreartium* the device of a number of simultaneous entrées, giving an effect like a number of voices in music; and his gift for following the details as well as the main line of a score is remarkable.

But notwithstanding these many great attainments, I personally do not enjoy his work. For me, the activity of his ballets is an abstract nervousness that has no point of reference in a human feeling. The physical tension remains constant; it has no dramatic subsequence. The gesture motives are ingenious, but they allow no projection of any imaginative reality; they allow only the taut projection of a gesture in the void. His characters are intellectual references to types; they do not take on a mysterious full life of their own. And I imagine that it is this lack of humanity in his work that has limited such dancers as Toumanova and Jasinski, though he has developed a fine visibility in Zoritch.

For me the great treat of the *Fantastique* is the extraordinary sets of Bérard. Their proportion, both in themselves and to the dancers in the course of the scenes, their space, repose, and coloring are miraculous. Much of the lighting was fine too, among other things the dark opening of the ballroom scene, which disappeared in a later performance.

The American Ballet Caravan, composed of members of the American Ballet, presented, the evening I saw them, *Promenade* (Dollar-Ravel), *The Soldier and the Gypsy* (Coudy–de Falla), and *Encounter* (Christensen-Mozart). The Mozart was the best, with the right quality of definiteness and play, of stage magic and tender friendliness. The Spanish number had an interesting and appropriate attempt to combine dancing with parlando movement, so to speak; and the Ravel had a sense of style and several happy inventions. The costumes were interesting, those for the Ravel remarkable. But it is a shame they chose to dance against that old eyesore, black curtains. The company is well trained and unspoiled. They are pleasantly un-Russian. There is an American freshness and an American modesty that is charming. There may be as yet the usual faults of beginners—lyricism, too timid a dramatic attack, too little concentration choreographically, and occasionally by some dancers more projection than the moment warrants. But the important thing is that young talents get a chance and that the enterprise as a whole is lively and real and part of us. I regret that I missed the second program, which contained a ballet by a young American composer, Elliott Carter, *Pocahontas* (Christensen), and *Harlequin for President* (Loring-Scarlatti).

The novelty by the Jooss Ballet, *The Prodigal Son* (music by Cohen), was not a success, but I do not think it necessary to analyze it, as it may well be thoroughly revised. The Jooss Ballet, accurate as they are, could learn a good deal in theater effectiveness and in invention from Massine.

From the standpoint of new music the season has not been very rich. *Concurrence* by Auric is nice but not new. Tansman's new version of his *Sonatine Transatlantique* for Jooss is excellent music and good for dancing. I didn't like Cohen's *Prodigal*. The best new ballet music I heard was Paul Bowles's score for *Horse Eats Hat*. This whole production is much the most interesting thing in the season's spoken theatre from the standpoint of movement. NOVEMBER–DECEMBER 1936

GRAHAM'S "CHRONICLE"; UDAY SHANKAR

In December Miss Graham presented a new heroic dance suite for herself and her group called *Chronicle*. It deals with division, grief, and final adjustment. I wish I had seen it again to clarify my own impression and to be able to point specifically to its more or less successful elements. As it is, I can only speak of it in general terms, and confusedly.

Seeing Miss Graham with her group and in solo recital, I was impressed by her courage and integrity. She believes in the biggest possible gesture; so she has trained herself to execute these extraordinary movements as accurately as a ballerina would her own most difficult feats. She believes in unexpectedness of composition, and she succeeds in keeping up an unremitting intellectual tension. There is no slack anywhere, physically or intellectually. She has, besides, an emotional steadiness in projection that binds together her constantly explosive detail, a determination which controls what might otherwise seem unrelated and fragmentary.

These are certainly rare qualities. I think anyone who likes dancing will admire her. But it seems to me her courage could go even further. She seems to watch over her integrity with too jealous an eye. She allows her dance to unfold only on a dictatorially determined level. But a dance unfolds of its own accord on a great many contradictory levels. And I miss the humanity of these contradictions.

To speak more in terms of dance, it seems as though Miss Graham were too neat. Her group is excellently trained. They do each motive given them with accuracy and decision. But from time to time, accidentally it seems, Miss Graham herself has a softening of contour between moments of emphasis where her natural subtlety of body substitutes shading, continuity, and breath for the geometry of constant tension; and it is at these very moments, which seem unintentional, that Miss Graham gets her audience most, gets them to feel something of the drama she is trying to tell about. I have the impression that Miss Graham would like to keep a dance constantly at the tension of a picture. She seems to be, especially in her solo dances, clinging to visual definition. Even her so-called angularity springs partly from a fear that the eye will be confused unless every muscle is given a definite job. The eye would be confused. But our bodily sense would not. Our bodily sense needs the rebound from a gesture, the variation of hard and soft muscle, of exact and general. As I said, Miss Graham herself has an instinct in this direction; but she seems to hesitate to rely on it in composition. I think it is this lack of confidence that she can communicate her tension directly to the body of anyone in the audience that makes her dances so "difficult." Isadora did not have this lack of confidence, and so her dances—though perhaps pictorially undistinguished—were always compelling, and gave the effect of beauty. But I don't want to go off on too theoretical a discussion, though Miss Graham is a controversial figure and important to us.

For musicians Miss Graham's programs are especially interesting because a number of modern American composers write for her, setting her dances to music after the dance has been composed. In general they seem anxious to stick literally to the rhythmic detail of her dance, the way many dancers—inversely—might try to stick to the rhythmic detail of music. It isn't a good method. Especially because Miss Graham's motives are so obvious, they need no reiteration in music, and they are structural body rhythms rather than ornamental gestures. For the musicians the result of following her is that instead of making their piece a whole, they divide it up into a series of brief phrases, each stopping on an accent. It seems to me that the rhythmic structure of dance and that of music are parallel but not interchangeable. Time in music is much more nearly a mathematical unit than in dance—in the dance-pulse stress and recovery (the down- and upbeat of the measure) are often not of equal time length as in music, and stress in music is more regularly recurrent. A good dance goes along with a piece of music with plenty of points of contact but many of duality. A dance needs a certain rhythmic independence—similar in a sense to the rhythmic elasticity the voice is given in our popular songs. But to give this freedom to the dance the music must have a life of its own as music; and the more unassuming this life is, the more definite it should be. In any case it is no fun seeing a dancer dance smack on his *Gebrauchsmusik*, and he looks as dramatic doing it as a man riding an electric camel.

One very good kind of dance music is that of Uday Shankar. I do not mean to criticize it as music, much less as Hindu music. But to a lay ear it sounds pleasant, it sounds as though it made sense without being emphatic, it repeats itself without insistence. The Oriental music I have heard always has this independent friendliness toward the dancers. It may have something to do with the fact that the music is made in sight of the audience, and that the musician exists not only as an instrument but also as a person. To me it is theatrically much pleasanter to see the people who make the music for dancing. It puts the dancer into a human perspective; it takes the bombast out of his stylization, and instead shows its real reference to the more usual look of a body. Human beings don't look any better for being alone; on the contrary, their beauty is a relative thing, and even their solitude is more lonely when it is imaginary.

Uday Shankar is a fine dancer. What struck me most about him was that though he is a star, though he projects as vigorously as any Broadwayite, he still gives a sense of personal modesty. Many gifted dancers seem to say on the stage, "I am the dance." He says, "Hindu dancing is a beautiful thing and I like to do it as well as I can." We see him and admire him. His exact control of every gradation of dancing—fluidity or accent, lyricism or characterization, space movement or stationary gesture, virtuoso precision or vigorous generality—is marvelous. His intention is always clear and his surprises never offend. Within the limits of what may seem to us supercivilized and adolescent suavity, without either our classic footwork or our modern backwork, he finds it easy to run the whole gamut of dancing. Another style of dancing might have a different range, so to speak, but none can have a more complete expressiveness. Although he shows us all this in his own person as a dancer, we do not feel that he is showing us himself; he is showing us something that is beautiful quite apart from his own connection with it. He is a friend of ours who thinks we will enjoy too what he would enjoy so much if he were a spectator. As a result, he is glad to show us his company—the coquetry and wit of Simkie, the juvenile eagerness and delight in his own gifts of Madhavan. He shows us even the least expert of his dancers as they are—not subtle, of course, but agreeable. All these shades of dance personality are allowed to flower according to their nature, and add up to the sense of harmonious and natural completeness. I believe that this use in a troupe of whatever gifts are present—like the sense in a star that he is not the only person, that he is in fact only a detail in the whole of dancing—is the only thing that makes the theater real. Considerations of accuracy, of form for the group, of personal projection or style for the star are not secondary, they are an integral part of the artist's life. But they belong at home in the routine of preparation; they are his private life. In the studio the artist is more important than the whole world put together. On the stage he is one human being no bigger than any other single human being, even one in the audience. The big thing, the effect, is then at an equal distance from them both.

JANUARY–FEBRUARY 1937

BALANCHINE'S AMERICAN BALLET

Classic Ballet, the new work at the Metropolitan by Dollar and Balanchine (to the Piano Concerto in F Minor of Chopin), is excellent. It is swift, pleasant, interesting, and very well danced. And its moving quality (which a first night is bound to flatten out) will increase the more often it is repeated.

Beyond this, it shows that the American Ballet has grown up to be the first-class institution it was meant to be. George Balanchine has done more than anyone could have expected in so short a time. The company is at home on the huge stage. They are becoming brilliant in virtuoso passages. Without losing their freshness, they emerge as individually interesting—by which I mean that last, most exciting, and most dangerous phase in a dancer's development when he not only can do brilliantly what he is supposed to, but adds to that an illumination from individual feeling.

I admire Balanchine extremely for the way he fosters this personal quality in his dancers. It is real theater personality, in distinction to the fictitious kind common on Broadway, which consists of projecting yourself with a fanatic intensity regardless of anything else on the stage. There are moments when this is fine, and occasions besides when a performer has to do it to save a show, the way the boy stuck his arm in the dyke. But too many soloists appear only in this catastrophic role. And they never get or give the variations of intensity that make a whole piece, and the soloist, too, theatrically satisfying. It is worth pointing out that the projection Balanchine encourages is the satisfactory kind, and that he is beginning to get it.

Dollar's choreography shows an honest and well grounded talent. In style it reminds me of Balanchine's *Nocturne*, but Dollar's application is so intelligent, it speaks well for his integrity. Balanchine seems to have two styles. One, like his *Mozartiana*, is brilliantly complex, full of surprising realizations and poignant interchanges and a subtle, very personal fragrance. The other (to which belonged *Nocturne*, *The Bat*, and the "Abstract Ballet" in *On Your Toes*) looks like the opposite of the first. It minimizes detail for the soloist or the ensemble, and avoids technical feats. Instead it builds on unmistakable clarity of groupings and of directions; on rapid oppositions of mass, between single figures and a group; and above all on an amazing swiftness of locomotion. (The entrees are brief and, by simplifying the leaps, cover an astonishing amount of space.)

This style may have been due originally to the lack of training with which the American Ballet started. At any rate, Dollar now uses it very well. He has been able to add to it interesting feats, where they were worth doing. But he has not forgotten its essentials: mass, direction, clarity, and above all swiftness, a fine swiftness even in more complex passages that gives physical exhilaration to the whole. In addition, Balanchine has contributed a middle section which is more elaborate both in detail and in feeling, and which fits in astonishingly with the more abstract speed of the rest, heightening it with its greater warmth.

I think there is another reason besides Dollar's integrity as a dancer that makes this collaboration between teacher and pupil come off so agreeably. It is that Balanchine, no matter how odd some of his choreography may appear, has always composed in a way that is natural for a dancer to dance. He has no interest in effects which are not danced, which are merely seen. His poses are not arbitrary, they are the point at which a certain kind of gesture in a definite direction is arrested by a complementary tension. The method of movement may be classic ballet, and the source of material, intellectually speaking, the practice room, but the practice room is as much a part of life as the factory or the jungle, intellectually speaking. It is because all his movement has this living quality that it can have a continuation in someone else's, or combine with any other kind of living movement, I imagine, without anything being lost. It is also for this reason (that Balanchine's movement is natural to the body) that the technical training of the American Ballet has been so happy. Its members are now both exceptionally well grounded in the essentials of dancing and proficient in the technique of the ballet. Personally I am not a "balletomane." But dancing that makes sense is so rare it is worth being serious about. MARCH–APRIL 1937

BALANCHINE'S "APOLLON"; AMERICAN BALLET CARAVAN

Now that the Metropolitan does have a ballet masterpiece in its repertory—one as good as the very best of the Monte Carlo—there's a conspiracy of silence about it. It's true people ignored this ballet last year, too, when it came out, but I think they'd better go again, because they are likely to enjoy it very much. It's the Stravinsky-Balanchine *Apollon* I mean, which the Metropolitan is repeating this year, and which it does very well, even to playing the music beautifully.

It is a ballet worth seeing several times because it is as full of touching detail as a Walt Disney, and you see new things each time. Did you see the way Balanchine shows you how strangely tall a dancer is? She enters crouching and doesn't rise till she is well past the terrifically high wings; then she stands up erect, and just standing still and tall becomes a wonderful thing. Did you see how touching it can be to hold a ballerina's extended foot? The three Muses kneel on one knee and each stretches her other foot up, till Apollo comes and gathers the three of them in his supporting hand. Did you notice how he teaches them, turning, holding them by moments to bring each as far as the furthest possible and most surprising beauty? And it isn't for his sake or hers, to show off or be attractive, but only for the sake of that extreme human possibility of balance, with a faith in it as impersonal and touching as a mathematician's faith in an extreme of human reasoning. And did you notice the countermovement, the keenness of suspense, within the clear onward line of Terpsichore's variation (what the moderns call the spatial multiplicity of stresses)? The intention of it—the sense of this dance—is specified by a couplet quoted in the program, a couplet by Boileau which contrives to associate the violence of cutting, hanging, and pointing with an opposite of rest and law, and makes perfect sense, too:

> Que toujours dans vos vers le sens coupant les mots,
> Suspende l'hemistiche et marque le repos.

Aren't you curious to see how incredibly beautiful this couplet is when danced? Or did you notice how at the end of a dance Balanchine will—instead of underlining it with a pose directly derived from it—introduce a strange and yet simple surprise (an unexpected entrance, a resolution of the grouping into two plain rows), with the result that instead of saying "See what I did" it seems as though the dancers said "There are many more wonders, too." And did you notice how much meaning—not literary meaning but plastic meaning—he gets out of any two or more dancers who do anything together? It's as though they were extraordinarily sensitive to each other's presence, each to the momentary physical strain of the other, and ready with an answering continuation, so that they stay in each other's world, so to speak, like people who can understand each other, who can belong together. And he combines this intimacy with an astonishing subtlety on the part of each individually. The effect of the whole is like that of a play, a kind of play that exists in terms of dancing; anyway, go and see if you don't think it's a wonderful ballet. The subject is the same as that of the music, which as you know is "the reality of art at every moment."

The dancers at the Metropolitan do these extremely difficult dances very well. Lew Christensen (from the Caravan) has, it is true, a personal style that is easy rather than subtle; but, besides being an excellent dancer, he is never a fake and at all times pleasant. The girls have a little more of the Balanchine tautness and they too are excellent dancers and appealing. The costumes are good.

The intelligentsia turned out in full for the All-American Evening of Kirstein's American Ballet Caravan; they approved the whole thing vociferously, and they were quite right. There was a happy community feeling about the occasion, a sort of church-social delight, that would have surprised the out-of-towners who feel New York is just a big cold selfish place, where nobody has any interest in anybody else. The ballets—*Show Piece* by McBride and Hawkins, *Yankee Clipper* by Bowles and Loring, and *Filling Station* by Thomson and Christensen—taken together show that an American kind of ballet is growing up, different from the nervous Franco-Russian style. From Balanchine it has learned plasticity, and openness, and I imagine his teaching has fostered sincerity in these dancers as in others he has taught. But our own ballet has an easier, simpler character, a kind of American straightforwardness, that is thoroughly agreeable. None of these ballets is imitative or artificial, and there is nothing pretentious about them. Hawkins shows us a good-humored inventiveness, Loring a warmth of characterization, and Christensen a clear logic of movement that are each a personal and also specifically American version of ballet. I think this is the highest kind of praise, because it shows the ballet has taken root and is from now on a part of our life. And the dancers themselves have an unspoiled, American, rather athletic quality of movement that is pleasant. As a group they are first-rate in their legs and feet and in the profile of the arms. I think they still lack an incisive stopping, and the expressiveness across the shoulders that will shed light through the correctness of movement; but their improvement in the last two years has been so phenomenal that these reservations aren't serious. At present the boys steal the show, especially Christensen, with his great ease, and Loring, with his human quality, but they don't try to steal it; and Albia Cavan and Marie-Jeanne show they intend to catch up with them. But one of the very good things about the Caravan is its homogeneity as a group. And I congratulate them all wholeheartedly, just as the audience did.

Of Balanchine's ballet in the *Goldwyn Follies* I would like to say that it is worth seeing if you can stand the boredom of the film as a whole (but don't leave before the mermaid number of the Ritz Brothers). It is worth seeing because the dancing is good, and one can see it; and because there's something moving left about the piece as a whole. But it is particularly interesting because you see a number of dance phrases that were composed into the camera field—an effective and necessary innovation anyone could have learned from Disney, but which nobody tried till now. It is the only way dancing can make sense in the movies.

MARCH–APRIL 1938

THE WORLD'S FAIR

I like what the World's Fair looks like now, and I think it will be still better when it's finished. It isn't art, but it's something pleasant. It's like "folk" art when it's neither foreign nor historical—that is, when it's something you don't think about, like postcards or skyscrapers or radio sketches. It hasn't any rational style of architecture; neither shapes nor colors nor sizes mean what they ought to, rationally. I guess they never do in folk art, just as they don't in swing. The Fair is in gas station style, and gas stations are one of our liveliest and folkiest Americanisms. It's functionalism as she is spoke. It makes no sense and leaves no headaches. There is nothing to be critical about, so when you stop enjoying yourself you don't have a moral obligation to hang around and gripe.

I hope the Fair gives us some spectacles in the same vein—as big and as cheerful. The Preview Motorcade and Festival wasn't up to that because it was timid and endless. Certainly the circus had done much better just before. I don't mean to say we shouldn't have artists. But we should have artists who for the moment aren't doing art—even commercial art—but are doing a fantastic stunt for everybody's amusement, like Chaplin acting in a charade at a party. We ought to have pageants, but not "The Battle of Roses" or "Peter Minuit and the Indian Braves"; we ought to have something to astonish you so much you haven't time to look at your program. I suggest some thirty-minute pageants—say, *A Martian Tragedy* by Orson Welles, or *The Subconscious of Tomorrow* by David Sortor. I'd like to see—under the pretext that it's art—Monteverdi's *Combattimento* with two-story armor and sixteen-foot swords, and a string quartet and voice amplified mile-wide from the top of the Trylon. But we need bigger marvels—Sandy Calder doing skywriting in colors, Aaron Copland improvising a cannon concert during a thunderstorm, Virgil Thomson lecturing on Wagner from a parachute, his voice all over the fairgrounds. It's true the pleasantest things at a fair are those that happen by accident, as in the Plymouth Rock pageant, when the Pilgrims couldn't land because the Rock floated out to sea, and the Indians had to wade in after it, and their color came off, and by that time the rock was so wet the Pilgrims slipped off. But if a thing is done in the right spirit happy accidents are bound to come, especially to artists. I hope none of this sounds supercilious or ironic, because I don't mean it that way. I like the bigness and the naturalness that the Fair suggests. It makes you want some popular wonders. We're all ready for a good time, and being crazy is what we like a lot just now. Let's go crazy in a big way. Let's be ourselves. The start is in the right direction.

But—to be practical—the open-air stage at the Fair is no good. A human figure can't look interesting from a distance without something to scale it by, something fixed by which you can judge its movement. Indoors the proscenium gives such a scale, and out of doors the field on which the figure moves, if seen from above—seen, for instance, from balconies or steep tiers. An open-air theater has some special possibilities (the supertheatrical distances between figures, the length of entrances and exits), and these have to be conveniently arranged by the builder. And you can't have much fun without machinery. There are plenty of people who know all about these things and who could give practical advice.

For serious dancing the open air is not a good place anyway. People are apt to look silly expressing their bits of individuality where the eye of the audience is not artificially concentrated. The effect is like that of a lady at a grand piano singing Schubert in Times Square. Outdoor dancing is most effective when the audience accepts the style it is in without effort—dancing like that at the Savoy, or even tap dancing if the performer (like Paul Draper, whom I saw at Loew's State) has the rare gift of a friendly intimacy with the audience.

Paul Draper has of course an even rarer gift than that—the one of communicating the emotion of dancing, of a leap, of a port de bras; not that he does these things technically better than other dancers, not that you admire feats when you see them, but that you feel the pleasure that lies in doing them, the rare pleasure of dancing.

I suppose people who like dancing go to the Savoy frequently on Tuesdays for the "400 Club" competition. It is always a pleasure. The Cuban Negroes (Nanaga) on Friday at the Café Latino are completely different and very good, too. Their rhumba is as fierce as the one I saw at the Tres Hermanos in Las Fritas (near Havana). I particularly like the way they do some steps and then stop dancing a moment and then start in again. This is also a matter of giving a scale, so to speak, a trick that modern dancers and even the ballet too often overlook. And—though this is a different world—during the voodoo dance the dancer was for a few moments really on the verge of becoming possessed.

MAY–JUNE 1938

MASSINE AND THE NEW MONTE CARLO

The oddly written publicity for the new Monte Carlo states: "The arrival each year of the Ballet Russe de Monte Carlo automatically mobilizes the ballet fans of the nation, and the resulting enjoyment is prodigious." This sounds as though we were to derive prodigious enjoyment from being automatically mobilized—almost as though we were to plunk down our shekels, raise our right arms, and shout "Heil Hurok." Of course, the sentence quoted and others like it are ridiculous. It was a great pleasure to see the new Monte Carlo; it was a pleasure too that it was such a success. But it isn't yet all it set out to be; it hasn't kept as many of its campaign promises as it could have.

This new Monte Carlo is subsidized by our own money, so it isn't a gift horse; we have a right to look it over, and there are several front teeth missing. One of them is music by our own composers, whom we have a hard enough time hearing anyway. Thanks to the WPA and more to the Ballet Caravan, anyone interested in ballet music already knows that you can get it as satisfactorily here as abroad. We want it not for the pleasure of saying it's ours but because we are curious to hear it, and an American enterprise seems a natural place, especially an enterprise which promisingly entitles itself "Universal Art, Inc."

So much for propaganda; now to the pleasure of praising. Massine deserves the greatest praise for the company he has chosen. The freshness of the corps de ballet is wonderful. Especially the girls, as Wilis, as swans, as sylphides, as Parisiennes, as Transylvanians, are a constant pleasure. The soloists are excellent, with a clarity of profile and a physical zest that are first-rate; and the boys even outdo the girls. I particularly enjoyed the intelligence of Platoff and the limpidity of Guérard; and I remember half a dozen others in great moments. These soloists have not reached the completeness of personal projection that would transform them into stars, but they are all wonderfully free from faking either technique or personality; and with what wholeheartedness they all dance. In fact, I think the very best thing about the new Monte Carlo is this real sense of dancing it gives you all the time.

I saw two stars in the New York season—Danilova and Lifar—and for complete satisfaction two stars are not enough, especially as before the season was half over Lifar had left. (I missed Markova.) Danilova is not only a prodigious technician, but the way she points up a technical feat with a personal wit and distinction makes her the equal of any great actress. Her pointes, her ballonnés, and above all the poses in which she rests on her partner's shoulders are among the joys that genius gives us. Lifar is neither such an impeccable technician nor such a wit. He is frequently brilliant, but he can sometimes be awkward, and even dull. I seem to forget these lapses and only remember that more than any other dancer, he touches me. Look at his Faun standing next to the Nymph, look at his attempted flight in *Icare.* It is dancing, but something else is there too, a kind of naturalness in the part that goes beyond the gestures required, as though the character were as much alive as anybody living. As though on the stage, he seems to believe in the life that is going on outside of the theater in the present. He seems to believe that his part makes sense anywhere, that his part (in the words of Cummings) is competing with elephants and skyscrapers and the individuals watching him. They all seem real at the same time, part of the same imagination, as they are really. There is something unprofessional about carrying reality around with you in public that goes straight to my heart. This is the kind of criticism it is hard to prove the justice of; I wish we could see Lifar more often so I could try. To me his ballet *Icare* seemed a strange real story sincerely told. It wasn't always successful (the percussion is quite bad), but it was far more warm and human than the agreeable cuteness of Fokine's new pieces, or the brilliantly calculated blatancy of Massine's. Massine is certainly brilliant, whether he appears as a performer or a director. He knows how to keep things going, how to make them look like a lot, how to get a big hand. He can get away with murder. If one took him seriously, he would be guilty of murdering the Beethoven Seventh, the Scarlatti, and even tender little Offenbach (though there wasn't much of Offenbach left in that new orchestration). There is of course no reason for taking Massine seriously; he doesn't mean to be, he doesn't mean to murder. Like a cigarette company, he is using famous names to advertise his wares. But I cannot help resenting it, because they are names of living things I have loved. It is hardest to bear in the case of his *Seventh,* where the orchestra is constantly reminding me of the Beethoven original.

Trying, however, to put aside this private resentment, I still am disappointed. Well, I'll exaggerate, and be clearer. I could see a kaleidoscopic succession of clever arrangements, but there was no thrill in the order in which they came. There was no sequence in the movement that awakened some kind of special feeling, some kind of urgency. It all occupied the eye as long as it lasted, and left no reality, no secret emotion behind. I missed the sense of growth and interplay, of shifting kinds of tensions, the feeling of drama, almost, that makes the best choreography mean much more than a string of effects. As a pictorial arranger Massine is inexhaustible. But dancing is less pictorial than plastic, and pictures in dancing leave a void in the imagination. They arrest the drama of dancing which the imagination craves to continue, stimulated by all the kinetic senses of the body that demand a new movement to answer the one just past. Until a kind of secret satisfaction and a kind of secret weariness coincide.

This dramatic progression of different qualities of movement is what means so little in these ballets. Take the *Seventh*. Every gesture is visually clear, but every gesture is at the same pitch, hit equally hard. The picture changes, but the tension remains the same. It's all very agitated. There are sometimes more, sometimes fewer people on the stage; they get on top of each other, lie down, run around, jump, crouch, whirl, pose, wave, or huddle, and they never give any sense of getting closer together or farther apart, of getting lighter or heavier, more open or more shut in, more soft or more hard. It is showmanship with a vengeance, it is a drill of automatons. Notice Massine's use of ballet technique. The extended silhouette is used as though it were a constant, like a military position, with none of the thousand subtleties of direction and intensity with which Balanchine gives it so much variety and purpose. And consequently with Massine it breaks in the middle, in the small of the back, instead of growing out from there by reaching up and down in a thousand human ways.

Because Massine's tension is static he can never make us feel the curious unfolding that is like tenderness. Like a Hollywood director, he gives us no sense of human growth (there isn't time), he keeps everything at a constant level of finish; everything is over as soon as it starts. He has no equivalent for mystery except to bring down the lights. So the *Seventh*, though danced with fervor and transfigured by the most wonderful sets and costumes in the world, leaves a sense of cheapness; and if you remember the mystery of Beethoven dynamics, it is unpleasant. *Gaîté Parisienne* seems just another empty revue number, where sex is a convention and not an emotion. Smarter, of course, than Broadway, and marvelously danced. And *St. Francis* seems a slinky posturing, a Sakharoff-Kreutzberg parody of illuminated Books of Hours and Minnelieder, with a grand finale of anthroposophic chorus girls.

No one but Massine could have got any theatrical effect out of this hodgepodge of minor pictorial devices, no one but he could have held the stage with a solo only half executed—but everyone acknowledges his stupendous gift of showmanship, and eminence, for that matter. We should miss a great deal if we were not to have a new Massine ballet; but we miss more by not having a new Balanchine ballet, or at least an old one like *Apollon*, a work of genius that reminds us of the sort of thing the greatest choreography is. The Monte Carlo has plenty of effective pieces; it should also have a great one.

All this schoolmastering leaves me only room enough to say that the purest pleasure I had was from the old *Coppélia*, which spread a kind of gentle radiance. NOVEMBER–DECEMBER 1938

ARGENTINITA; SOME MUSICALS; GRAHAM'S "AMERICAN DOCUMENT"

I think Argentinita is a wonderful dancer, because she gives you a pleasure like that of being in good company. She is a lady who makes you feel at home in her house. Most people must find her very natural; she doesn't try to impress you or grip you or any of those things. She treats you as an equal, and you leave the theater feeling as though you'd spent the evening with a friend. I say Argentinita, but it's her company too, all five, who are like that. It is a subtle entertainment, warm, witty, expert, and unpretentious.

As a dancer she is certainly wonderful. The structure of her numbers and the flow of them, the exactness of the rhythms and the clearness of the gestures. Even when she hardly moves, there is in the air that extra sense of well-being all over that is dancing. And especially her waist; if you haven't noticed how beautiful the middle of a dancer is, you can learn from her.

It's the bearing of any Spanish gypsy dancer that makes me feel so good, the lift of the waist, the expressive stretch from the pit of the stomach to the small of the back. It's the bearing of a bullfighter too, when he makes his passes. It lifts the hips and lightens the feet, it settles the shoulder, eases the arm, and frees the head. And it seems to heighten the dancer's visibility. Perhaps expression in dancing, the sense of an impulse, comes from the diaphragm, as Isadora said. A flamenco dancer always seems to have more expressiveness than he needs for a gesture, a kind of reserve of it that gives him an independent distinction—or dignity, as I have heard Spaniards say, who are very sensitive to this quality. Perhaps, looking at it technically, it is the strictness of this fundamental position that gives coherence and point to everything within the flamenco range; that gives the dancer the freedom to shift from serious to funny; that keeps the male dancer from getting all wet with stagey glamour. You see, these are all problems that the modern dancer is puzzled by. Another thing that a gypsy dancer can do is go into or come out of a dance without embarrassment. She walks up to the guitarist and stands there clapping her hands a few times and then starts, or she stops dancing and sings a little, or she stops and lets someone else dance while she merely stands around or walks. This change between heightened movement and ordinary movement is a wonderful contrast on the stage; it puts the performer on an equal footing with the audience, it makes him a casual human being and his big moment all the more interesting. We have it in tap dancing, and the ballet can have it; and I wish our theater could have more of it. For the gypsy of course it is no problem at all, except one of personal "dignity."

To get back to Argentinita in particular. Her program arranges all sorts of Spanish and Spanish-American dances that are not flamenco, but which, thanks to her good taste, her excellent company, and I imagine the flamenco discipline, are very agreeable. Pilar Lopez and Antonio Triana, her partners, are fine dancers (he especially in gypsy numbers), the two musicians are a pleasure, and it's a particular pleasure to hear the little, accurate singing voices. Neither Argentinita nor her company showed the ferocity of some flamenco, the sudden stops, the incredible pressed timbre in singing or the savage coloring in costume. But I liked what I saw, integrity of refinement and a sovereign grace. And I liked, too, to feel again the personal independence a Spaniard cherishes, the sense of human dignity he has. He can never accept the fascist requirement to grovel. And he doesn't enjoy seeing other people grovel, either.

I made a round of the musical shows in town to look at the dancing but I didn't see anything very special. In *The Boys from Syracuse* there is a good threesome by Balanchine combining acrobatics and tap with a bit of ballet expression; I really liked the end, where the two couples walk off quietly into the dark; it was the one time I saw something with sexual feeling in a musical. In *Sing Out the News* there is a funny dance by Joey Faye as a little socialist that is extraordinarily mysterious. But the only show for me is *Hellzapoppin* (cheerfully imbecile), which also has the most cheerful dancing: Barto and Mann, Hal Sherman, and Adams. I saw the world's best striptease at the Apollo one Saturday midnight, done by Willie Bryant, who went only as far as his suspenders. And I hope everybody has seen the wonderful "Giants" dance in the movie *Dark Rapture*.

Martha Graham's *American Document* is a major work, as everybody knows, with a moral to which everyone subscribes, stated by a narrator. It wants "to capture the feeling of America." I see Miss Graham's sincerity, her fine technique, her intensity. But I am troubled by the monotony of equal thrusts, the unrelaxed determination. There is something too constantly solemn, too unhumorous, too stiff about it; something sectarian. Even the "Walk Around" looks like an effort to me. Well, in detail there are many interesting things, and Martha and Erick did very well. But I missed the point of it.

JANUARY–FEBRUARY 1939

MODERN DANCERS AND HUMAN BEINGS

When I saw Agnes de Mille's dancers standing in profile making an arm gesture, it looked so natural that it looked just like Margie, Amy, and Sue lifting their arms. It looked concrete, as though there were nothing else to it but what you saw; as in a morris dance, they were doing what they were doing and they were whoever they were. They looked human. It may sound harmless enough, but it was a pleasant surprise. And then it occurred to me that one of the things that has made me uncomfortable at recitals of modern-dance groups is the way the dancers seem to disappear as human beings and only function as instruments. When you see six of them on the stage, all you can do is count six, you can't tell six what. They don't seem to be girls combining with other girls, they don't seem to have any human relation to one another. They seem artificially depersonalized, and their bodies operated from offstage. I smell a Führer somewhere, and I get uncomfortable. I wish our dance groups would look as if they were free agents. I wish they would look as if they liked being together, at least as much as folk dancers do, or lindy-hoppers.

Well, another thing that makes me uncomfortable with modern groups is that they don't even look as if they enjoyed dancing. We all know that expression of sobriety they wear not only on their face but on their body, too. It covers a group of them like an unattractive army blanket. From their programs, from their choreographies, they mean to express all sorts of things; but they don't show them. They seem to be thinking of the next movement as though they were afraid they'd forget it, instead of enjoying the one they are doing while they are doing it. When I think of the natural kind of dancing, or folk dancing, I notice it doesn't express anything but the pleasure of being in a dance. The ballet (and vaudeville dancing too) teaches in school to express, to project the natural pleasure in just movement. But the modern schools pay little attention to projection even of this simple pleasure. I think that is a serious weakness as far as appearing on the stage goes. When a dancer learns to show his delight, the audience begins to "understand" him. You cannot understand without liking, and how can the audience like unless the dancer shares his liking with them. But our dance groups set themselves problems in expression far beyond this simple one. They skip it and jump in at the second story. They don't care about your liking; they want you not only to understand but to believe. They want their movement to awaken your imagination, so that it will join the movement you see to others you consciously or unconsciously remember. This would be really sensational dancing.

Real sensationalism is wonderful, but besides emotional control it requires physical ease. Really sensational dancing will pass through violent shifts of balance without breaking down the body's assurance. The balance is real; you can see it shift back and forth and all the while the body continues moving as a whole. This is what our modern groups expect of themselves and often pretend to be doing; but actually a violent step or gesture upsets the relation of one movement to the next, breaking the dance, forcing it to start up in the middle. Natural dancing avoids this difficulty, limits steps and gestures to amusement, so that the body moves consistently as a whole. But our groups, afraid of being too simple, would rather fake sensationalism even if they leave us with a not quite pleasant feeling afterwards.

I am not trying to "invalidate" the modern-dance groups; on the contrary, I would like to clear the confused prejudice against them, by pinning down the unfavorable impression they make to specific aspects. We all know they have made discoveries from which the dance world is benefiting. Perhaps the modern-dance group should establish its own technical and emotional academy; but that would mean abandoning the semi-professional status which is one of its virtues. Anyway, it is interesting that there may be now a tendency toward a new method, toward a more natural and "concrete" style. Besides finding it in Agnes de Mille's group, I thought I saw it too in Anna Sokolow's *Opening Dance* and—though in a more proper form—in Hanya Holm's *Dance Sonata*. These pieces are easier to do, more danced, less sensationalistic. They haven't much propaganda, but in point of propaganda I think our groups will find a warmer audience, and their themes will come across with more meaning, when they give more meaning on the stage to what they themselves are: natural young people who enjoy dancing, recognizable grade-A proletariats.

MARCH–APRIL 1939

ASHTON'S "DEVIL'S HOLIDAY" AND MORE MONTE CARLO

The Monte Carlo, which I am always happy to see, began the season with a new ballet Diaghilev would have been proud of: *Devil's Holiday*. And Massine, who has been the Diaghilev for this production, deserves equal praise. I have seen it three times and I like it better each time. Everything about it is full of zest, sincerity, freshness, and charm. Tommasini, as Mr. Martin so well said, seems to have had the time of his life writing the music on Paganini themes, and the variations in the first half of the last scene struck me as particularly beautiful. Berman, from whom we had wonderful drops for *Icare* last season, has given us five more which are as brilliant as any baroque Burnacini, but full of a contemporary intimate and personal sentiment, and also scenically discreet; and his costumes are the most wonderful imaginable—just look at the two Servants of the Devil, at the Devil's horrible disguise, or at the farandole in the last scene, like a fashion show in heaven. (Judging from the published sketches, the drops were not as well executed as they should have been—especially the landscape—nor all the costumes; but even so they were wonderful.)

And I am delighted too with the new choreographer, Frederick Ashton, the young Englishman who several years ago did the dances for *Four Saints*. His style is original, and originality usually looks awkward at first, or unnecessarily complicated, or arbitrary, or something. His at first looks jerky, and you miss the large simple phrases you have come to like in

Fokine, or the expert mass climaxes of Massine, or the incredible long moments of extension and tenderness of Balanchine, like speech in the silence of the night. But you can praise all that and still praise Ashton too. If he derives from anyone it is, I think, Nijinska, with her hasty, almost shy elegance, her hobbled toe steps. He derives too, it seems to me, from the kind of awkward and inspired dancing that young people do when they come back from their first thrilling ballet evening and dance the whole ballet they have seen in their own room in a kind of trance. The steps do not look like school steps (though they are as a matter of fact correct); they are like discoveries, like something you do not know you can do, with the deceptive air of being incorrect and accidental that romantic poetry has. But how expressive, how true to human feeling the dances are. The perverse solemnity of the betrothal guests, the noble and pathetic stiffness of the betrayed betrothed, the curious frenzy of cruelty after the scandal; these are real emotions. The lovers' dream dance is restlessly hurried, like a dream in which you know you are only dreaming; and what a final and brief conclusion it has into a deeper sleep. Like a Sitwell poem, the hunting number is fussy and witty to heighten the lonely and frantic despair of the lost lover, interrupted by a diabolically hysterical substitute love. And the last scene is a whirl of inventions, of young eagerness that can hardly stop for the tenderness it dreams of, and that is tender without knowing it. A choreographer who can call up so many sincere emotions, who keeps a steady line of increasing interest (and animation) throughout a long ballet and does not fall into conventional tags at important moments, is a real rarity who is worth being enthusiastic about, and, what is more, worth paying for a ticket to see. Personally, the only part I do not care for is the fox's dance, which, however, gets a laugh and a hand.

Devil's Holiday is probably difficult to dance and it is danced very well by everyone. The type of expression is not mimetic but like that in classic ballet, in which the entire personality illuminates a role that the dancer has to conceive without the aid of detail. Danilova is particularly fine, of course; Krassovska is brilliant; and Franklin is magnificent. Platoff, of whom I think very highly as a dancer, was good but not as good as he generally is. All the dancers in the divertissement of the last scene were splendid.

As to the other novelties: *Igrouchki* (Fokine) is a doll skit in the Chauve-Souris style, which looks a little silly blown up to the proportions of an opera stage. *Capriccio Espagnol* has the benefit of Argentinita's exhaustless repertoire of regional steps, and of Massine's equally exhaustless repertoire of effective theater. Most of it is pleasant to watch and the end is one of those bang-up finales that are indispensable to ring the curtain down if you have a lethargic audience. Massine has a solo, and in it he makes the other men look like little boys. The showmanship, the bite of his stage presence is superlative; look at the slow curling of his hands as his dance begins. It is inaccurate to call such a dance as his Spanish in the specific sense (see the difference in stance, in the relation of the partners, in the casual interruption of dancing) and foolish to compare him with a real gypsy, who would probably have no gift for dominating a crowded stage and would hardly be visible at that moment to an ordinary audience. (Eglevsky, the new star, is very agreeable in this ballet; he has the world's finest plié, which delighted me in *Swan Lake*; his *Spectre de la Rose* was more brilliant than Guérard's but less distinguished. Theilade was fine in the *Spectre*, too.)

The other major novelty so far, the Massine-Matisse-Shostakovich *Rouge et Noir*, was a disappointment to me. The set and underwear costumes, effective for a while, became rather professorially meager long before the piece is over (and rather unpleasantly indecent). The music sounds like a young man confusing himself with Brahms while in the next room somebody is cooking cabbage soup. (Such emotions were more charming with Mahler.) The choreography I am at a loss to describe because it does not seem to relate itself to anything I feel. I will gladly accept it as my fault that it all seems to me to happen in a vacuum. I can see ingenious arrangements and good technique, a touching opening in the third scene, and an odd feeling of a conventional anecdote at the very end. When I like something I am sure I am right; when I don't, I'm not. I should like to read a sympathetic criticism of this ballet to help me get interested.

Bacchanale (Dali's Venusberg ballet), notwithstanding a fine easel painting for a backdrop, turned out to be a kind of charade. There was a moment during the first entrance of the Sacher-Masochs (Platoff and Lauret, who were excellent) when it began to come to life and be at least a little horrid. It is a shame it didn't jell, because the idea was all right. Anyway, the audience had a few laughs and didn't mind.

Ghost Town won an ovation. Rodgers's music is Rodgers at his own best; it is catchy and unpretentious and keeps going, and I enjoyed the clarity of it. It also sounded repetitious and orchestrally sour and melodically saccharine, but that is not the point; it does say something of its own. The set and costumes (du Bois) too are musical comedy, and yet they have a callow freshness that isn't fake. The Picasso, the Derain, the Berman or Bérard decorations all have space under wonderful control; and their colors even during dancing stay in place, so to speak, and don't mess up the stage. There is nothing of that in this du Bois, which is obviously awkward and keeps going all the time all over the place, without rest or coherence; but it's not an imitation any more than the Rodgers is. You can call it vulgar, but in its own way it is sincere.

The choreography, which is Platoff's first work, strikes me as much more interesting than either the music or the décor, although it is even less orderly. It too keeps going all over the place, messes up dances by realistic gestures, by awkward spacing and operatic arm waving. But there is an exuberant energy in it. There are also, even at a first view, bold details, such as the double action of the two rival groups of prospectors, which are remarkable and very promising for the future; the second Mormon entrance and Ralston's dance of jubilation looked especially good too. But I think better than any detail was a something direct in the whole attack. It was not an imported atmosphere. For the first time the Broadway audience felt at home at the Ballet Russe; and before anybody knew it, the Metropolitan itself turned out to be only two blocks from good old Times Square. It was a historic event.

The whole company danced *Ghost Town* with enthusiasm. In general the whole company has been better than ever all through the run, and everybody, including the management, deserves warm praise. I would also like to say that the revivals this year have been particularly good: *Boutique Fantasque,* for instance, is a delightful Massine that looks as fresh as ever. I hope Massine can revive his *Pulcinella* for next year.

And Danilova is very, very wonderful.

The Bali ballet (so called) was very interesting. It is not "touristy" at all. It is the Malay version of our own casino show, without jokes. As we garble our own classic style for such purposes, so they do theirs, and only variety numbers can retain their dignity; and musically Malay jazz hits an all-time low. Evidently the tired businessman of Singapore likes the same emptiness of feeling as the tired businessman of Manhattan. If you are shocked by Devi Dja doing a temptation of Buddha in the style of the "Scandals," look at the enormously successful Easter stage show with the Rockettes in cross formation on Sixth Avenue. It goes to prove that the East and West have been meeting for quite a while behind Kipling's and Spengler's backs, and that art is made for the few who like it anywhere in the world. OCTOBER–NOVEMBER 1939

A NOTE TO COMPOSERS

A composer unfamiliar with the theater who is interested in writing ballets should certainly see the big companies as often as possible and watch what happens. I think he should start by watching *Sylphides* or *Carnaval* (now in the Monte Carlo repertory), because both are obvious and successful; the relation of dance steps to music in both ballets is blunt but bold. If he watches the dancers and listens to the music at the same time, he will see how the visual rhythm frequently goes against the acoustic one. He can see how the choreographer runs over the end of a phrase, distributes effects and accents sometimes with, sometimes against the pattern of the music. Look at the group accents in the final measures of most of the *Sylphides* numbers; or at the way in the Schumann the same motive is danced with different steps, or the rhetoric of a piece is broken into by different entrances.

If he looks more closely he will see how a dance phrase rests on several accents or climaxes of movement which other movements have led up to or from which they will follow, as unaccented syllables in speech surround an accented one. He will see that the dance accents frequently do not reproduce the accents of a musical phrase, and that even when they correspond, their time length is rarely identical with musical time units. (A leap, for instance, that fills two counts may end a shade before, and the next movement begin a shade after, the third count.) The variations of energy in dancing around which a dance phrase is built are what make the dance interesting and alive; and they correspond to a muscular sense, not to an auditory one. I think it is the fact that in ballet technique these instants of emphasis are not expected to be identical with the metrical values, but increase or decrease in time values of their own. (The beat and offbeat as the dancer executes them are differently long.)

Many musicians are bothered by noticing that dancers "can't keep time." I often notice how dancers who are keeping time become dull and unrhythmic. Keeping time at all costs destroys the instinctive variability of emphasis; it destroys the sense of breathing in dancing, the buoyancy and the rhythmic shape of a dance phrase. To be sure, an exaggerated rubato, on the other hand, looks loose; and it destroys the spring and force and cumulative sweep of the beat. In performances of music, musicians understand very well this problem of adjustment; dancing presents another form of it, made more complicated by the fact that the edge in accentuating a bodily gesture (which underlines its correspondence with the musical beat) is a device that rapidly becomes monotonous to the eye and that tends to dehumanize the look of a dancer onstage. A dancer onstage is not a musical instrument; she is—or he is—a character, a person. The excitement of watching ballet is that two very different things—dancing and music—fit together, not mechanically but in spirit. The audience feels the pleasure of a happy marriage at least for the fifteen minutes the piece lasts.

Ballet music is conceived as music that is marriageable—its inherent animation will not be destroyed by the physical presence of dancing, or even by the unavoidable racket that dancing makes onstage, and its continuity will not collapse under the rugged conditions of theater presentation. The more delicately hermetic the composition, the more necessary it becomes to listen with absorption and the more necessary it becomes to play it in just one way. For dancing, however, the conductor has to see to it that dancers hear their cues and can meet the tempo—and even (as in opera) temperamental variations of tempo are inevitable with good dancers. So a composer is safer if he does not count on orchestral subtlety of emphasis in theater execution, which the poor quality of ballet orchestras, the lack of rehearsal time, the physical necessities of dancing, and the plan of the choreographer are each likely to endanger.

No one who watches a good ballet with attention can hear the score as distinctly as he would in concert. Once the curtain is up the music functions in the show as a spiritual atmosphere for the stage action; as giving the general emotional energy of the piece, its honesty, cheerfulness, steadiness, or amplitude; with occasional bursts of danciness, of lyricism, of wit or rhetoric, and an effective conclusion, which are more consciously heard. A composer cannot count on finding a choreographer as exceptionally musical as Balanchine. But he should count on finding a choreographer, a dance company, and an audience who respond to the inherent character of his musical communication. He can count on an audience that appreciates perfectly well the largeness of imagination—if not the technical detail—of ballet scores like Tchaikovsky's or Stravinsky's, and responds to their imaginative scope with an eagerness rare in concert audiences.

OCTOBER–NOVEMBER 1939

BALANCHINE AND STRAVINSKY: "POKER GAME" AND "BAISER"; THE MONTE CARLO SEASON

Balanchine's *Poker Game* (set to Stravinsky's *Jeu de Cartes*), revived this fall at the Monte Carlo, is a ballet in a minor genre but it is as good ballet as one can possibly have. And it creeps into your heart as unpretentiously as a kitten. To be sure, its range is limited. It is no more than a new twist to the animated doll subject, which by nature is witty, ironical, appealing, and playful, and rather likes to stay within the bounds of pleasant manners. Ballet certainly can have a wider range if it chooses; and *Petrouchka,* even though it starts with the doll idea, does choose. *Poker Game* doesn't, and yet it succeeds in becoming a "minor masterpiece." I think when you see it you will notice yourself how easy it is to look at, how agreeably it shifts from group to ensemble or solo, with an unexpectedness that is never disconcerting; how lively the relation is between still figures and moving ones; how distinct the action remains; how clear the center of attention, or the division of interest, so your eye does not take to wandering on its own and confuse the rhythm intended.

But besides being easy to look at, what you see is amusing. The steps emphasize a kind of staccato and a lateralness that may remind you of playing-card figures; many of the steps you recognize as derived from musical comedy. But the variety, the elasticity of dance impetus, the intelligent grace are qualities you never get in musical comedy routines. Nor does the musical comedy routine allow everyone onstage to project intelligent and personal good spirits. *Poker Game*, by allowing the dancers just this, makes you feel as if you were for a while in the best of company, with everybody natural and everybody interesting.

It is Balanchine's merit that all this is so. He keeps the dance placed in relation to the actual stage frame, which gives it a common-sense point of reference. He has the sense of timing, the sense of distances, which make the movement distinct. He has the wit which makes it amusing and the invention both plastic and rhythmic to keep it going in a lively way. He has the good sense to keep the numbers to their obvious subject: you see the Durante-like Joker egging on the silly Queens against the Aces, you distinguish between Jacks and Kings, you can tell who is winning or losing, and he does not make either too serious for the other. The subject in other words remains real and aboveboard; and the emotion it leads to, whether witty or sentimental, kept in relation to this subject, does not take on a faked or a private urgency.

But Balanchine has a profounder choreographic gift. His steps, no matter where derived, are steps that a ballet dancer specifically can do and do best, steps a ballet dancer can be brilliant in. His rhythms, however complex, are grateful to ballet dancers. He seems never to violate the real nature of a dancer's body, the part-native, part-trained relation of trunk and arms and head and feet; so that no matter how odd the movement required, the dancer still remains himself and does not congeal to an impersonal instrument. And so the choreography does not violate the dancer's best gift, which is his natural human warmth. It is a fact that Balanchine has been able to make the same dancers seem real and true in his ballets who have seemed conventional or stupid in others. All these qualities, being the best qualities of choreography there are, make a good Balanchine ballet as good ballet as you can get. It is true his style is very complex, and some people don't like complex dancing. There is also a joyous irony in his tenderest pathos, and irony in sentiment seems subversive to good people who like to think that sentiment is something comfortable, secure. But this issue does not arise in *Poker Game*.

I found the entertaining music of *Poker Game* wonderful to listen to and, thanks to the play of counterrhythm and counterdynamics on the stage, easy to follow. (The light orchestration, obvious accents, and sharp eighth notes seemed helpful for dancing, making counting easier.)

I cannot resist adding by way of footnote that I urge you to see and see again the Balanchine-Stravinsky *Baiser de la Fée*, now also in the Monte Carlo repertory. Unlike *Poker Game* it is ballet at its grandest. It has a range of expression that includes the brutality of the peasant dances, the frightening large mime gestures of the fortune-telling scene, the ominous speed-up of the wedding party, the hobbled tenderness of the bridal duet, the clap-of-thunder entrance of the veiled Fairy, the repulsive dissolution of the last scene—all of it fascinating and beautiful. Its images of destiny, its tragic illuminations, are as convincing as any I know in literature; but the lightness, the grace with which these dramatic scenes develop is peculiarly Balanchinian. *Baiser de la Fée* is poetic theater at its truest.

Balanchine's third piece for the Monte Carlo, a revival of *Serenade*, I was not invited to by the organization's publicity department; well, I remember liking it some years ago at the Stadium.

The other revival of the Ballet Russe, Petipa's [*sic*] classic *Nutcracker*, has a charming and straightforward first scene, which is also a good example of ballet "recitative." In this scene Miss Lauret was very fine indeed, and Miss Etheridge also. The second scene is a virtuoso adagio and variation, in a noble and extensive style, beautifully composed; the dancers did it full justice technically but were unable to give the real presence of nobility. The third scene seemed pretty dull. I do not care for the décor of any of it. Which leaves the two actual novelties: Massine's *Vienna—1814* and *The New Yorker. Vienna* is unfortunate in every way (Massine-Weber-Chaney). *The New Yorker* I thought entertaining, with many excellent caricatures (Danilova, Semenoff, Yazvinsky, Chamié, Lauret). It's nothing you remember as ballet. Nor has Gershwin's nice Bronx nostalgia (in a corny orchestration) anything to do with what goes on.

Looking back on this season and the repertory as a whole, I thought the dancers seemed better than ever in technique and verve. But I am disappointed that Danilova and Massine are still the only artists who seem to have got over the limitation and the prejudice of being invariably juvenile. Maybe I do Rostova, Lauret, and Krassovska an injustice; and Markova—whose second act in *Giselle* was so miraculous last year—showed real warmth this time as Queen of Hearts. But I believe that she and Franklin and Eglevsky are greater dancers than they have dared to prove in their repertory this season. I missed in general the performer's passionate and uninhibited belief in his part, which can give to a dancer the most luminous theater presence in the world.

And in another way, too, the season discourages me. It looks as if the Monte Carlo were reviving not the Diaghilev tradition of intelligent dancing but the Petersburg tradition of attractive performers. The last score one could be eager to hear was *St. Francis*, which was also the last time Massine took a chance with novel choreography; and that happened long before the war. *Devil's Holiday*, also prewar, is still the last interesting décor or choreography to be shown, excluding the Dali backdrop, which a year ago looked lonely enough in the foolishness in front of it. That isn't much of a record for so pretentious an institution.

The American contributions, so condescendingly promised, have been pathetically stupid, and seem to have been chosen with a kind of inverted snobbishness—commercial art for commercial art's sake. Commercial art is, as Cocteau said of New York's Jewish and Negro populations, the rich manure of our intellectual life; but to dump that manure on the stage in full view is not the proper function of Universal Art, Inc. Broadway does it more naturally. Our local artists may not have the easy sweep of the great Paris period, but at least they are in the real art business, and they are the people to go to if you do want American art—they have all there is, and there isn't any more. This season the only local contribution that can be mentioned among educated people is Irene Sharaff's—the pretty costumes for *Poker Game*; and they were bought up from a previous show.

Nothing risked, nothing gained. Still, at this date, it's hardly such a risk. Thomson, Copland, and Bowles have all been on Broadway. As for painters, there is Stuart Davis, who is a ballet natural; Cristofanetti, with his exquisite taste; last year there was a show of ballet sets by New Yorkers at Valentine's, and the sketch of Rudolph Burckhardt, for instance, was far better ballet than anything the company commissioned this year; I have also seen two good ones by Lorna McIvor. But the organization of the Monte Carlo, it appears, pays for the pretense of intelligence, not for its reality. It is unjust, I think, to blame Massine. But it begins to make a stuffy atmosphere that I have no great pleasure smelling. NOVEMBER–DECEMBER 1940

LIFAR AS WRITER

If you feel ballet is a real thing, as I do, you will find the first part of Serge Lifar's new book *Serge Diaghilev* excellent, and the second part wonderful. The first is an account of what was said and done and thought by and around Diaghilev from his childhood till the end; the second is what Lifar saw happening from the time he joined the company (1923) till his friend's death. It is all clear and concise; and it is brilliantly translated.

In the first part what interests me more than the history is Lifar as a dance critic. He is the best dance critic living. It isn't that I subscribe to his decisions. To be sure, it's fun when he demolishes a stage rival with a few appreciative words; but I often violently disagree. No, it's not Lifar's opinions I stand up for; it's his attack. Because, first, he has the professional experience which turns dancing from a thing you buy ready-made into a thing you make yourself. And second, he sees dancing with the eyes of intelligence, as an ordinary person sometimes sees a friend or sees the weather; sees and believes at the same time. "The eyes of a poet," people say who know what poetry is about. If criticism makes any sense at all, which I often doubt, the sense it makes is that it suggests to others this way of seeing. And opinions are no more than one of the ways of doing it.

But I recommend you try the second part of the book first, the autobiographical part. It reads like a house afire, like a Russian novel. Hotel furniture is smashed all over Europe; broken ankles lead to triumphant premieres; apathy turns to illumination, too deep a love takes the form of estrangement, and passion rises dialectically by its reversal. It all sounds very improper in our flat country. A decent American finds it too personal, too portentous, too eloquent; even possibly too aptly fitting a classic pattern. But you will notice there is no snobbishness or vanity or cynicism. It is a foreign way of telling a story, but the real surge of dancing is in it, as it is in Isadora's *My Life* and Nijinsky's *Diary*. As from those two books, you will get from Lifar's the sense of what a living dancer is. Not directly as you would out of a poet's novel, but indirectly as you would out of a long letter. It is as real and as strange as what a living businessman is.

NOVEMBER–DECEMBER 1940

THE ORIGINAL BALLET RUSSE

The Original Ballet Russe is not just another version of the Monte Carlo; it has a quality of its own, and a particularly pleasant atmosphere. It hasn't of course so much prestige, but it seems to have more dance to it, more buoyancy. I think this is due especially to Lichine. He used to be a handsome star with, to my taste, rather too glamorous a manner. He is now a comedian of genius and a choreographer of the first class. The directness he himself has seems to have cleared the air for the whole company. Their dancing is not weighed down with mannerisms.

Lichine's *Graduation Ball* is in its type just an operetta to Strauss music, the stock item every company offers. But Lichine's piece, without visible effort to be special, turns out to be a pleasant surprise. You may think you are looking at the same old thing, but you don't feel as if you were. The very first waltz strikes you right away as a little human scene. And the show-off "Perpetuum Mobile," which is a feat of new steps and trick technique, doesn't impress you, it delights you as spontaneously as the best lindy-hop does. *Graduation Ball* has its weak spots too, but they do not seem important because you feel the piece directly as a whole; you feel its wholehearted impulse before you judge its detail.

Though *Graduation Ball* is ballet comedy, the conventional marionette gestures that belong to the type have almost disappeared. In modern ballets they have not often been amusing; they have not often been jokes of character, but only professional jokes of dance style. Dancers think them terribly funny, but no one else does. Lichine's numbers, instead of being made up out of smug references to what is supposed to be funny, are the actions of real dance characters in a plausible situation; they are real dancers with all the exuberance of dancing. Such direct humor puts *Graduation Ball* in the best class of comedy, which Massine's recent comedies, for all their wit, do not reach.

Character dancing is not like lyric dancing. Lyric dancing is concerned with the secret reality of proportions in space; to character dancing space is more practical, it's a question of having room enough. The lyric effect is lovely. But its method (under the absurd name of modern and abstract) has become so canonized in the last two decades that it is now the only respectable way to do choreography whether one has the gift for it or not. Lichine's gift is too concrete to get very far among secrets; and it is a pleasure to see him drop what he could continue only as a respectable convention. You can forgive him his plain floor patterns, his unrefined spacing, his lack of subtlety for the sake of the true gift he gives free play to instead. Lichine is not "translating ideas into terms of dance"; he is dancing in the first place. His mistakes are not correctible according to another choreographer's style; the impulse is too original, an originality so spontaneous you get the happy feeling he can go on inventing forever, that he draws not on his taste but on a world he was born with, a whole world new to us.

Graduation Ball, though by nature a minor piece, struck me as proving Lichine's gifts most conclusively. Of his other pieces, *Protée* seemed like a grave finagling of nothing much. *Francesca da Rimini* was empty in its elaborate love scenes, but it had a few fine group moments, which suggested that life in a thirteenth-century castle was actually brutal, crowded, and public. Lichine's version of *The Prodigal Son* was more convincing as a busy night on the waterfront than as a parable. The action parts were lively, striking dances; but the lyric parts, the scenes of warning, of remorse, of reconciliation, were mostly dumb show and not interesting at all. In our hearts, as in the parable, forgiveness is more wonderful than sin and lends sin its wonderful horror. Lichine doesn't manage to say this, and it isn't the kind of emotion he can express. Instead he shows us concrete human actions, a concrete story in dancing. But what makes him a choreographer of real importance is his exuberance of physical rhythm, his exuberant impulse to dance.

The other major premiere by the Original was Fokine's new ballet *Paganini* to Paganini music. Fokine is of course a genius and his ballet is about a genius and it was highly praised. I myself found no pleasure in it, so I cannot speak of it fairly. Perhaps it was an error to make the central figure of a ballet a role without dancing, because you keep wanting to see it dance and get at the heart of the matter. But I will say in favor of *Paganini* that you cannot help watching it with attention, and that it made me definitely uncomfortable; that is certainly a mark of personality. Another novelty was *The Eternal Struggle*, staged by Schwezoff, an intelligent dancer in the company itself. It is something of a tour de force in keeping allegorical figures properly busy to the music [Schumann's *Etudes Symphoniques*], but more ingenious than interesting. And still another novelty, *Quest* (Verchinina-Bach-Cristofanetti), is coming.

The repertory of the Original is enormous. The older masters are represented by a fine *Aurora's Wedding* and *Swan Lake*. Among the familiar Fokine classics there is a wonderfully fresh revision of *Carnaval*, and the Stravinsky *Firebird*, which, apart from the Bird's long solo, isn't very interesting. Massine is represented by the earlier symphonic ballets, some travesties left over from the twenties, *Union Pacific*, and the Bizet-Miró *Children's Games*, full of witty invention and very pretty to look at. There is also an unsatisfactory Lifar number and a confused *Faun*. And last comes Balanchine's *Cotillon* (Chabrier-Bérard), the classic in dancing of the later School of Paris and to me the glory of the Original's repertory. This piece profoundly affected the imagination of the young people of my generation. It expressed in a curiously fugitive and juvenile movement the intimacy, the desolation, the heart's tenderness and savagery, which gave a brilliant unevenness to our beautifully mannered charm. The thirties had not only a kind of Biedermeier parochialism, they had also insight into the eternity of a moment of grace. We are all out of them now, and it is strange to see now that what we then believed is still as true and absorbing in itself as any subsequent discovery.

I have already praised the dancers of the Original as a whole. First of the stars is Riabouchinska, the wonderfully overrapid dancer who can transform herself completely in comedy—everybody loves her; Toumanova, a marvel of the sternest technique, an actress who more than anyone can create a tragic isolation on the stage; Baronova, lovely, now uncertainly feeling her way toward a warmer, more womanly style. Among the men is a dancer for whom I feel a particular affection, Jasinski, the most modest and most poetic of the stars. The flexibility of his upper spine, his déboîté, shows you how elastic ballet dancing can be, against the military rigidity many people think the back of a male classicist should be confined to; and his arms are correct enough, and free. He shows you that the batterie of the feet can be a game instead of a test, and that at some brief moments you can hold your shoulders too high and still be right. I wish I could see him in the *Spectre*, the touchstone of unaffected lyricism. Among the other dancers: Leskova, as true a comedian as Riabouchinska; Osato, Denisova, Moulin, the frank Petroff, Lazowski, Runanin, Orloff (in *Good-Humored Ladies*), and the rest. I am glad we have them all, and glad of the atmosphere of healthy development the company has. Incidentally, its musical taste (especially clear in the novel Strauss selections for *Graduation Ball*) is very good indeed.

JANUARY–FEBRUARY 1941

GRAHAM'S "EL PENITENTE" AND "LETTER TO THE WORLD"; BALANCHINE'S "BALUSTRADE"

Martha Graham has now presented to New York her two dance works *El Penitente* and *Letter to the World*, which are full of interest and full of poetry. *El Penitente* looks like a mystery play. A young woman and two young men come on the stage carrying a bright banner. Their manner is collected and cheerful. You watch them act out a play which tells that though man's duty to Christ is hard, his pain is relieved by a Divine Grace visiting him in turn as a virgin, a seductress, and a mother. Sometimes they use their banner as a little curtain from which emerge supernatural apparitions; once, they strip off the cloth, and the frame suddenly is a cross. When the play is over, the three performers add a little dance of jubilation in their character as farmers. The style of gesture reminds you of New Mexican primitives—the votive pictures and *bultos*. It suggests—as they do—a double emotion of unlimited space all around and of solid weight at the center, there where you are. There is an apparent naiveté of timing and placing which is charming in detail and carried through with distinction. All this might be true either of a real Catholic piece or of an exquisite tour de force. But the dance seemed to have a poignancy other than Catholic and a reality beyond that of charm. The gestures are not made so much for their symbolic meaning as for their shape and rhythm as dancing; the dancing does not exploit its own limpidity, invention, and restraint but moves you by its dynamics as a whole, a personal meaning which makes the form real, which makes the religious style real too, but in an oblique way. Partly because the scenes between the man and the woman are placed downstage, partly because they are the most expressive, partly because it is Miss Graham who dances in them, it was not the relation of man to the Divine but the relation of a man and a woman that seemed the true subject. On me the effect was that of a tender and subtle love poem, a real love held nearly in suspense by a remote terror. It was as though Miss Graham had used the Spanish-Indian farmers' expression of religious faith as a metaphor for her own faith in the strangeness love can have. It is a sincere and touching and very attractive work, whether you choose to describe it in these terms or find better ones.

Letter to the World is a longer, richer, and more uneven piece. Much of it is not clear to me after seeing it once. But it contains such astonishing passages that one is quite willing to forgive the awkward parts it also has, and remember it as a masterpiece. *Letter to the World* is about Emily Dickinson. There is a legend that Emily Dickinson fell in love with a married minister, whom she saw once or twice and might have run away with. On the stage you see the garden door to a New England house and a garden bench. You see a woman move about as though she were dancing to the rustling in the trees and with the odd swirl of the breeze. She appears and disappears mysteriously, suddenly or delayed, like a leaf, or a mouse, or a word. Other figures, too, appear, sometimes one, sometimes several. You see a tall and dominating woman in black, you see a crowd of stiff boys and girls, you see a solemn and violent man, and a boy who is ironic to the heroine and exuberant alone. The heroine herself appears at one point in a funny dress with trousers under it, and plays games with herself like a schoolgirl, even upsetting the bench and doing happy stunts on it. Much later, the man pays little attention to her, and in the end, according to the program, "out of the tragedy of her loss will be born the poet."

The passages for the other characters, except the "Death" dance for Jane Dudley and the "March" leaping dance for Merce Cunningham, did not seem very interesting; but many of those for Miss Graham are extraordinary for their devious grace, their unpredictable and fascinating current. Often they have a round buoyancy like that of waltzing, with poignant gradations of greater and less airiness. Her funny dance, "The Little Tippler," is a sort of polka of impish pranks, like Thoreau's squirrel—"all of his motions, even in the depths of the forest, imply spectators as much as those of a dancing girl." And altogether wonderful is her sitting on the bench toward the end, half turned from the audience and reflective in a pure, Victorian attitude, with a passionate heroism of repose that has all the amplitude of Isadora Duncan. The continuity of a lyric line, the contrast of dynamics (the sense that a gesture is not always a thrust but often a caress)—both of these are a new development in Miss Graham's way of composing, as is also the use of different kinds of projection (the sense that she dances at times more publicly for the audience, at times more privately for herself). From many points of view *Letter to the World*, no matter how uneven it appears at first sight, is a moving and noble work one cannot praise too highly.

Miss Graham's technique is as always impeccable. And she has three fine dancers with her, Jane Dudley, Erick Hawkins, and Merce Cunningham, who by having dance characters of their own throw her personal quality into relief. Cunningham, the least finished dancer of the three, delighted me by his humor, his buoyancy, and his wholeness of movement, a singleness of impulse like that which makes Negro dancers so graceful. The empty lightness of his upheld arms when he leaps I have never seen elsewhere. I did not think the music for *El Penitente* (Horst) had much character of its own; but I liked that of *Letter to the World* (Hunter Johnson), which, though modest and gentlemanly, contributes another personality to the piece.

Balanchine's *Balustrade*, with a Stravinsky score and a Tchelitchev décor, was a ballet in the Diaghilev tradition, a collaboration of first-class artists where one can expect to feel movement, look, and listen with the same degree of sensibility. In such collaborations you can see the poetic quality of dancing better, because all the different aspects of the spectacle have been made by people who believe in its poetry. When there is only one artist working on a show at a time, there is mostly something pathetic and provincial about the theater; one feels too sorry for him to pay undivided attention. At any rate it is a fact that such collaborations created the Diaghilev tradition: the tradition that dancing can be as poetic (or, if you prefer, as serious) as any other art; the tradition that painters and musicians should not give up their character when they work for dancers; the tradition that a dance evening is a natural pleasure for a civilized person.

Balustrade is danced to Stravinsky's Violin Concerto, music that seems to me easy to go along with from the rhythmic side. The choreography too is easy to go along with from the rhythmic side, as it is full of references to our usual show dancing, the kind you see anywhere from a burlesque to a Hollywood production number. I noticed two elements, or "motifs": the upstretch on the downbeat, and one knee slipping across the other in a little gesture of conventional shame. The first, syncopated element Balanchine enlarges into the liveliest and lightest ensemble dances; the second element, one of gesture, he elaborates into a long acrobatic trio in which all sorts of "slippings across" are tried—of legs, of bodies, of arms—and this trio ends by a separation, the girl looking reproachful, the boys hanging their heads in shame. How strangely such a concrete moment tops the abstract acrobatics before it—a discontinuity in one's way of seeing that is bridged by the clearness of placing and the sureness of timing.

Balustrade is complex (or "contradictory") in this way as the eye adds up its successive phases. Its novelty is that it is not complex at each moment in the manner we are accustomed to. The individual dance role has almost no countermovement, no angular breaking of the dance impulse or direction. The impulse is allowed to flow out, so to speak, through the arms and legs, which delineate the dance figure lightly, as it were in passing—as they do in our show dancing. This is all something else than the "European" style of the thirties. There is in this new "undissonant," "undeformed," or "one at a time" way of dancing a kind of parallel relation to Miss Graham's new modern-school manner in *Letter to the World.* Once more, dancing, like any living art, has moved ahead of what we had come to think of as the modern style, and this time without even any manifestos to warn us.

I must add that in *Balustrade* the costumes are elegant but annoying. Though they have imagination and a sort of super-Hollywood pruriency, the materials are such that after the first minute or so they look like a wilted bunch of rags cutting the line of the body at the knee, obscuring the differentiation of steps, and messing up the dance. And the trio costumes look too publicly sexy; they take away from this erotic dance its mysterious juvenile modesty. Still, it was right of the management to take a first-rate painter for a work of this kind; an artist's mistake is infuriating, but not vulgar.

MARCH–APRIL 1941

HANYA HOLM; AT THE CIRCUS

Miss Hanya Holm and her group have presented us with a serious surrealist alchemistic fantasy. First a prologue: dancers in androgynous red tights and beautiful long blond wigs did some calisthenic weaving and leaping. Then the main part: several dancers appeared in elaborate costumes, a nest of light bulbs on the head, for instance. The audience recognized these as "surrealist" and tittered. But after the dancers came on, all they did was wiggle a bit, stand around, walk off, come back on, and do it all over. They looked afraid of messing up their pretty, fancy dresses. It was timid and dull; and it could have been dismissed as a minor mistake if the program had not implied that this was official surrealism. Official surrealism, which kept clear a few years ago of Dali's decorous and cute Monte Carlo ballet, has its own terrific eighteen years of history, its cruel Peeping Tom thrills—the thrills of a Peeping Tom who gets to see only the empty part of the horrifying bedroom. I looked up an old Dali ballet libretto, from the pre-*House Beautiful* period of surrealism, published in Georges Hugnet's official *Petite Anthologie du Surréalisme* (1934). At a quiet moment, for instance, a dancer, who has unbandaged his arm, sops a piece of bread a lady has sat on in a glass of tepid milk, and then—his face expressing a sweet and infinite nostalgia—he presses the wet bread under his armpit. At the end, while a chorus of legless cripples dressed as Japanese are yelling the tango "Renaciamento" (among other things), a woman with opulent breasts and metal shoes is savagely treading a heap of bread, as though seized with a delirium of the feet incident to wine pressing; then a lot of motorcycles tied to ropes come roaring through the backdrop, and several electric fans and sewing machines fall from the top boxes and are crushed on the stage. The curtain falls slowly.

Miss Holm had another new number, in her familiar agreeably fluid style in which the body is kept well in balance and the movement correctly produced from the small of the back. Some people find this agreeably lyric, and others agreeably innocuous. I think it is all right, but it seems rather more proper than anything I know outside the theater. Miss Holm herself is obviously an excellent dancer, and I would like to see her in a solo.

I went to the circus expecting to be shocked by the Bel Geddes "streamlining," and found he had done more of a pants-pressing, hat-blocking job; the circus is still the mess we all like it to be. For the dance lover there is a graceful lady elephant who dances the conga with delight; an incredibly beautiful dancing horse called Belmonte; and a happy pack of leaping dogs who play volleyball with a balloon. There is one completely aesthetic human act of two Japanese who walk up a tightrope to the gallery and slide down again backward, standing; why it seems so beautiful I don't know. I also liked a camel that went around disguised as a goose.

Some Colorado high school boys and girls called the Cheyenne Mountain Dancers were to appear up in the Rainbow Room one night at one o'clock. But the dancers I found were Indo-Chinese, doing what seemed a Portuguese rhumba. The headwaiter told me there had been a last-minute change of schedule, and the cowboys had left. I asked how they were and he said, "Very colorful and neat."

The machine-gun dance in the second scene of *Native Son* gives me a chance to state that, among other things, Orson Welles is the greatest dance director in our theater. And also that he is the only producer who gives us scenery which is a delight to look at; the only scenery that sets the size of an actor in a dramatic proportion to the frame of the set. I imagine it is the proportion of the actor to the set (as it is in dancing), and not the real detail on the stage, which makes scenery feel real. You can't help but see him in a real relation to the set, instead of as a man wandering about a decorated stage. MAY–JUNE 1941

KURT JOOSS; THE MONTE CARLO BALLET

The season opened with the Jooss Ballet, presenting eight or nine pieces by Jooss and one brand-new one by Agnes de Mille. First, Miss de Mille's *Drums Sound in Hackensack*. It is about New Amsterdam, the fur trade, how the cheated Indians found a Dutch girl in the jungles of Jersey, and what happened then. To show us New Amsterdam, Miss de Mille begins with a folk dance, adds a Puritan hop and a de Mille wiggle, and we all get the joke and smile easily. When she comes to the serious parts, terrors of the forest and Indian savagery, she invents some gestures as simple as those an earnest child would hit on. Again everybody gets the point and is perfectly satisfied to go on watching until something else happens. So the piece comes out a hit. The stage Indians, either woodenly noble or tomtomish, I liked especially. I like Miss de Mille's work in general. Though her heroines are inveterate wigglers, she has a real sense of how the body dances, she composes properly, and she has a gift of rhythm completely congenial to Americans.

Jooss's works, however, one looks at very seriously. They are on the plane of "masterworks." Jooss has a great reputation, too, as a leader in serious theater dancing and as a systematizer of modern technique. Just the same, watching the stage, what I saw was one dud after another. There is one exception—the famous first scene of his *Green Table*. This is brilliant and curiously different from all the rest: different in rhythm, style, humor, and theatrical punch.

The Jooss dancers are engaging, accurate, lively, and devoted executants, without mannerisms or bad manners, dancers by nature. They were fine for Miss de Mille. But when they dance the Jooss choreography, what do you see them do on the stage? Well, the best thing you see is a controlled, clear, wide movement in the arms. (And they can stop an arm gesture more neatly than most good dancers.) Their hands and necks are plain and good. The breastbone is held high and the chest is open. This upper third of the body is excellent. But below it, the belly is dull, the buttocks heavy, the small of the back sags in. Where is the shining tautness across the groin, a glory of Western dancing? These people might as well be sitting down, as far as the expressiveness of their middle goes. And below, the leg gestures are forced and heavy. The leaps are high and strong, but they have only bounce, they don't soar (except one boy in *Old Vienna*); they don't hang in the air, either. (The low wide leaps are the interesting ones but get monotonous.) The feet in the air look thick. On the other hand these dancers land better from a leap than most ballet dancers. Does this add up to a satisfactory new norm of technique? It does not. Neither does it exhaust the possibilities of the modern school. Because the Jooss norm of the outward chest and inward middle is fixed, and modern technique demands that any portion can vary at will from outward to inward. It's a terrific demand, but it's the essence of widening the expressive range beyond that of classic ballet.

Or take the Jooss stylization of rhythm. I see an emphatic pound (this is, a gesture stopped and held). Then comes an unaccented moment (no gesture, change of position). Then comes another equally emphatic pound (a new gesture, stopped and held). This keeps up all evening. In the pit the music pounds down on the beat at the same moment the dancer pounds out his gesture. The effect is very dispiriting.

What happens is that there is a systematic alternation between emphatic and unemphatic movement, like that between beat and nonbeat in a bar. There is also an unusual continuousness about the time quality of the movement. Many people are dissatisfied with a kind of hoppitiness in classic ballet. They point out that there is a fraction of a second between steps, between arm positions, that goes dead in the way a harpsichord goes dead, but not an orchestra, or even a piano. Jooss has stretched a movement to fill the time space completely; he uses a pedal. It was Dalcroze who thirty years ago made us most conscious of this possibility in moving.

When a dancer makes his gesture coincide as closely as possible with the time length and time emphasis of musical rhythm, he is apt to be as pleased as a hen is who has laid an egg. He tells everybody "Look how musical I am," and everybody cackles back "Isn't he just the most musical thing!" Rationally it seems odd to confuse the metrics of music with musicality. And also to assume that the metrics of dancing are identical with those of music. It strikes me that there is in fact an inherent disparity. The proportioning of time, as well as the proportioning of emphasis, between the stress and the follow-through of a single metric unit is much more regular in music than it is in movement. Apart from theory, in practice this kind of measured gesture draws attention to itself and away from the body as a whole. In practice, too, the dancer loses a certain surprise of attack, which is one of his characteristic rhythmic possibilities.

Well, in point of musicality, listen to the music Jooss uses. True, the dancers obey the metrics of music, but the music in its rhythmic development obeys beat by beat the rhythmic detail of the dance. The piece makes no musical sense. It is merely a cue sheet for the dancers. It sounds as if it kept up a continuous gabble about the mechanics of the steps. It's like a spoken commentary in a documentary film that names every object we see while we're looking at it. Music that can't make any decision on its own is functioning on a bare subsistence level, and it is apt to be as glum as that. Poor Frederic Cohen's voluble cue-sheets for Jooss are utterly depressing; they reminded me most of cafeteria soup gone sour. I don't think much of the musicality of a director who makes me listen to such poverty. If this is collaboration, it must be the Berlin-Vichy kind. I detest a dancer who is satisfied with it.

I don't go to the theater to see a servant problem solved. Jooss of course isn't the only choreographer who has music in to do the dirty work and keeps all the dignity for himself. Modern dancers have made the same error often enough in the past. They commission a new composer, but when the piece is played it has (like a poet's advertising copy) no character, it only has manner. For a while it was fun enough to listen to a new manner, and affix at least an ideological, a historical meaning. But the historical significance of style is a parlor game that gets tiresome. I wish all kinds of dancers would let us hear pieces of music old and new, and do, while they are played, whatever they like to. I wish they would put themselves on the spot in the presence of serious music. When the dancer acts serious and the music is trivial, he can't escape seeming petty and provincial. Anyway, in the theater I want the dancer to dance, the orchestra to make music, and the décor to be a stage picture. If these three don't come out in accord, I am angry but still interested. If only one of them is allowed to speak up, the production isn't big time.

But the issue of dance music has led me away from the subject of Jooss. Besides technique, rhythm, and the use of music, there are many other aspects to choreography. In the Jooss ballets I did not see any I cared for. He has systematized grouping so that diagonals, cubes, and spheres cut across each other by the dozen. But they look stupid because they have no relation to the size of the human figure on the stage. He has systematized the representational aspect of movement, with the result that every gesture can be translated so exactly into words, the dance might as well be a series of signals for deaf mutes. You imagine it would have the same meaning if performed by nondancers. The dancers add neatness, but they don't by dancing create the meaning, a meaning which undanced would not exist. Looking at it another way, all the gesture is on the same level of signification. The wonderful shift possible from pantomime to lyric (like a new dimension of spirit), or the shift as in Spanish dancing from standing around to taking the stage—all this, with all the rest in dancing that is tender and variable and real only the moment it happens, has been systematized away.

A systematization of modern dancing, like the literary adoption of the heroic couplet, makes a great deal of sense to dancers floundering between the arrogant academicism of the ballet on the one hand and the uncompromising private language of some studio dancers on the other. I remember fourteen years ago in Germany the attempt to establish a new academy, a new order, seemed of the greatest importance, and we all watched Jooss's gradual discoveries (for he was the leader of the movement) with delight. The results shown here this fall are well worth acrimonious theoretical dispute. But what I actually looked at on the stage was a stodgy, self-satisfied, and petty solemnity, pretending to be serious and, worse, significantly ethical.

. . .

With the opening of the new season, the Fleischmann Monte Carlo Ballet also returned—world premieres, stars, rich refugees, and all. Dali's *Labyrinth* is the pudding's plum. It is the height of fashionableness and of bad manners. Dali hogs the show so completely he won't let you see Massine's part of it, or hear Schubert (whose Seventh Symphony is played throughout). He focuses your eye at a spot so high on the drop that every time you pull it down to look at the dancers below you feel acutely uncomfortable. Besides dwarfing the dancers he dresses them in incredibly bad taste, as if in the rented rags of a burlesque chorus. The colors and materials coalesce like a stew. He jams the dance between a drop hung too far forward and a litter of props, and finally distracts the audience by some idiotic revue tricks, doves, dolphins, and roosters, which are all that emerge recognizable from the hectic mess. The dance looks like the milling Times Square subway platform on New Year's Eve. And the music is an irritating noise that keeps on and on. There is no doubt that this is what Dali wanted. The drops, four of them, which alone survive the general rape, are grandiosely frantic and frozen. The effect of it all is absolutely real, as acute as discomfort. And its complete disregard for the audience's comfort is what makes it so terrifically fashionable. The first time I saw it, it put me in an excellent humor. There was nothing secondhand, nothing pedantic about it. It was a real world premiere, something made this minute and made for all the world to look at. At the second performance of course there wasn't any novelty left and I was bored. That no doubt condemns the piece as art, but not as a production. I think the Monte Carlo owes us such manifestations among other things; this is the first time it has given us a real one, and I feel very pleased about it.

Oh yes, the subject of *Labyrinth* is the return of art to the classic tradition. If you think art can leave I suppose you think it can return. That's all nonsense to me, so I wasn't bothered by Dali's little blasphemies either.

A different kind of discomfort was that of the Massine-Weinberger *Saratoga.* The music is as ingratiating as a restaurant waiter. The dance is inept and half unfinished. Franklin to be sure danced brilliantly whenever he could. But still *Saratoga* marks an epoch in our ballet. Way at the back of the stage hangs a drop neighbored by a little kiosk, done by a new designer, Oliver Smith. It is the first time I have seen anything on our own stage that has color, size, and air quality all completely personal and right. And then you see that the rest of the set helps, too. You see it doesn't fade as time passes, but grows brighter. (And to put white in the sky is quite an achievement.) It is as poetic and as real as anything the Parisians used to make. For this discovery Massine—who up to now has been as unlucky as Broadway in his local designers—deserves cordial thanks. Alvin Colt's costumes—well, never mind.

On the other hand, the ultimate, inexcusable worst in local stage design was the third premiere, *The Magic Swan*, an act [Act Three] resurrected out of *Swan Lake* (Petipa-Tchaikovsky). There seemed to be some unhappy misunderstanding in this production about what constitutes classic dancing. Such fine dancers as Mladova, Rostova, in fact a whole string of soloists of both sexes, appeared as smooth and languid as ballroom performers. And then, exactly on this subject, *Magic Swan* brought a magnificent revelation: Toumanova in her pas de deux and finale with Eglevsky. Her classicism doesn't express any emotion; it is passionately just itself. Her incredibly swift tiny battements on the ankle are somehow magnified so that the moment fills the whole opera house. There is no being nice to the audience; there is no letting go of them either. When she dances it is a matter of life and death. Dancing can be other things than this, but I don't see how it can be any greater. . . . Toumanova has gained since last spring, in contact with her partner, a kind of emotion deeper than playacting, until now Danilova's undisputed territory. Eglevsky too has gained; he seems drawing ahead of the other men in emotional power. His solos were admirable, of course; better still were his duets; and I was impressed especially by his final pantomime gesture of despair. I feel Toumanova is still a bit solemn in serious classic pantomime, but that is a minor reservation. Both of them are wonderful too in *Baiser de la Fée*. And in *Coppélia*, in which she and Franklin are radiantly brilliant, she reveals a gift for comedy as true as the great Danilova's; here ballet pantomime and dance style are both wonderfully personalized by her own happy intelligence.

The other dancers are all as good as ever, though they seem overworked, too. One doesn't notice it in technique so much as in the personal warmth they don't always project. But of course the fact is that the company is too small to carry off the heavy repertoire it has in the finest style.

Just as the orchestra is too small to sound as good as it might. For this season's repertoire, however, I am full of admiration. Though some of the pieces are duds, the list covers the complete range of style and subject and novelty, and each piece has some aspect of interest. For Petersburg classics you can see *Magic Swan*, *Swan Lake*, *Nutcracker*, *Coppélia*. For early Diaghilev there is *Sylphides*, *Prince Igor*, *Schéhérazade*, *Petrouchka*, the *Spectre*, and the *Faun*. For the postwar period there is the *Toyshop* and *Tricorne*—two of Massine's masterpieces—and his renovated *Bogatyri*.

For his symphonic style there is his Beethoven and his Shostakovich. For his musical comedy side there is the *Danube*, *Gaîté*, *Capriccio Espagnol*, and *Vienna—1814*. For Balanchine choreography there is the *Baiser*, *Poker Game*, and *Serenade*, all three fascinating to watch. For English choreography there is Ashton's *Devil's Holiday*, which is still my favorite among the English works shown here. There are two Dalis, *Bacchanale* and *Labyrinth*. And for the American angle there are Massine's *New Yorker* and *Saratoga*—that is still the weakest side of the collection, but let's hope we get a more enterprising piece in the spring. Apart from "American" it adds up to the best all-round ballet repertoire we were ever offered.

I am shocked to find that the last scene of the *Baiser de la Fée* has been mutilated. The slow rope climbing in its finale used to open up, both in style and emotion, an obscure and terrifying further perspective, which set the proportion of everything that had gone before just as the music here does. This year the rope ladder has been cut and there is some creeping around on a ramp, which can't look other than stupid and is completely ineffective. The substitution is an act of vandalism. Whoever is responsible for it should be watched; he is dangerous.

NOVEMBER–DECEMBER 1941

BALLET THEATRE; GRAHAM'S "PUNCH AND THE JUDY"

The reorganized Ballet Theatre presented a season that was timid and on the musty side. Only one new feature was a real pleasure: the presence of Alicia Markova, the great English dancer. The management had commissioned no new American choreography, or score, or set. It did not even offer a new piece by its own Antony Tudor, one of the most interesting choreographers in America, and even abandoned the best of his previously presented works, *Dark Elegies*. This season's novelties were Dolin's version of *Aurora's Wedding*, called *Princess Aurora*; a revival of Nijinska's *Beloved*; a piece called *Slavonika*, which was nothing; and a *Bluebeard*, which at least was a new work by Fokine.

To take them in detail: *Princess Aurora* (a Dolin arrangement of bits from the Petipa-Tchaikovsky *Sleeping Beauty*) was supposed to revive the Bakst décor. Some of the costumes were magnificently executed, others had an unconvincing lushness more like the old Follies than like Bakst, and the backdrop looked very sad indeed. In the dance, the Gibson-Conrad Bluebird was extremely attractive and, surrounded as it was by dull dancing, it brought down the house.

Beloved (1928) has a very beautiful and interesting score, a Milhaud free-rendering of some Schubert and Liszt, and it has choreography in Nijinska's "amateurish" or "*primitif*" ballet style, which I found oddly poetic in the whole effect of it. And Markova's dancing of a Romantic Muse ("half in love with easeful death") is terrific. *Slavonika* was one of those washouts that are natural in any theater routine, and harmless. And it did have costumes by a talented local designer, Alvin Colt. Unluckily they were in a dressed-doll style that is fine for revue but too cute for ballet, and the lace-trimmed stage looked like a Christmas window at McCutcheon's, gigantically blown up.

Bluebeard, the Fokine-Offenbach farce, was something of a hit. The choreography tells a very complicated story with admirable clarity, and it is full of effective gags, a little in the manner of a college show. In this collegiate style Dolin dances charmingly, and everybody around is pretty busy. I was sorry, however, that the Offenbach love lyrics which contrast with the action had been cut down to short bits, and that the dances set to them were conventionally nice instead of really poetic. The result was more like the mechanical balance of Sullivan than the delicate equilibrium of Offenbach. It seems to me that Offenbach's humor, like Mozart's, is poised on the suggestion that false love and true love are not as different as one might wish; they are both of them really tender. The joke isn't that romantic love is just a fake, and therefore ridiculous; the joke is that romantic love is real and real love is full of incongruity. I am sorry that neither Massine's *Gaîté* nor Fokine's *Bluebeard* conveys the fragrance of this tender irony that makes Offenbach a real friend. For in neither ballet is anybody ever really in love, neither with the right nor the wrong person. The music is better in *Bluebeard*, however, than in *Gaîté*, because the original orchestration (which is perfect) has been less tampered with. The décor of *Bluebeard*, by Vertès, the fashionable magazine artist, is fussy and boring. There is no color and no shape which stays alive longer than a couple of minutes. There is no sense of air or space. A few of the costumes are pretty. Mr. Vertès is fine in his own profession. But to do a ballet set a man must make a decoration one can look at for at least fifteen minutes steady and still be interested in; it is obvious that this is just what a serious painter spends his time trying to accomplish. It is among serious painters that ballet designers should be looked for. This is a responsibility of a first-class management.

Markova has appeared here before, but the more you see her the higher you value her. Seen merely as a virtuoso she is extraordinary; the adagio movements "bloom in space," the allegros "scintillate evenly," the leaps soar and subside, when lifted she looks fluid—well, in every department of classic technique she is flawless. And she has all those peculiarities of physical structure that ballet enthusiasts gloat about—like the overlong arms, the lateral overmobility in the hip joint, the outward set of the shin, and of course the fabulously high arch—all of which add to the poignancy of the gesture because you seem to be seeing what it is impossible to do. Musically too she is a virtuoso, even to dancing an imperceptible fraction ahead of or behind the beat, for the special attack or pathos it gives to dancing. And she holds your eye on her. Not that she is sexy; she is very proper, but you watch her as intently as if you were perturbed.

Markova has power too as an actress. She alters her style to characterize her part, even to giving her virtuosity no special play. A few details of characterization, such as Giselle's mad dance, I do not agree with; but it is a disagreement of taste, not of principle. For she builds and holds a scene as steadily as an actor like Evans. And there is something more to it than the proper control. She does not make the part a vehicle for her own glamour. She takes it disinterestedly. And what you see is not Markova as Giselle, but Giselle in the figure of Markova. In this unselfconsciousness, so to speak, her dancing becomes serious and sincere poetry. When you watch her, the whole body shows that unpredictable burning edge of movement that the living images of real life have, which continue so mysteriously to live inside our hearts, and out of whose inexhaustible light art is made. It is an equivalent of the absorbing "living line" in poetry and drawing. Out of hundreds of good dancers of all nationalities, there have been perhaps a dozen in whose dancing I have seen it continue as the characteristic of the whole body for minutes at a time.

The other star ballerina, also new to the Ballet Theatre, is the sumptuous Baronova, who used to be a very fine dancer indeed. Of her present style I can find nothing good to say. She hams with a heartlessness that is frightening. She ogles, flounces, capers, and cuddles, jumps, turns, and stands, slapping down each effect like a virago operating a cash register. She seems to want the title of "Miss Ironpants." I hope so intelligent a dancer as she is will quickly get over this phase, or else team up with the Three Stooges, where her present manner properly belongs.

Martha Graham's *Punch and the Judy* is a comedy taking place in a white-collar apartment; the reiterated "squabble and scuffle," as the program says, between a husband and wife. Most of the audience thought it was very funny, the indicated kicks and slaps, the parodies of tragic gesture, the general air of middle-class self-importance and nervous activity. It happens that continuous stylized pantomime doesn't make me laugh much; so I was following the action. It seemed to me that the protagonists were quite untroubled by their quarrels, untroubled by sex, too, and not much interested in their child. Their infidelities didn't seem to interest them especially; neither did jealousy. And the wife had nice dreams. So I gathered that they were a good-natured conventional young couple who didn't notice much. Then what is the piece about? Maybe, as in Noël Coward, the theme is the unfeeling couple's incidental charm and liveliness. Occasionally the husband reminded me of the charming Dagwood in the comics. But that didn't offer a clue to the theme. I was confused by the multiplicity of detail in gesture and rhythm, and the brusque shifts of spacing, the clutter, the unsympathetic staging and costuming, and the clumsy spoken words. I could find no appreciable point of repose from which to see the figure of the movement. I was rather appalled by the stubborn parody in all the expression. Maybe the real theme is something sinister, even malevolent. Or maybe, as so often happens to me at a new Graham piece, I will get a very different impression when I see it again.

It was clear, however, that Martha Graham and Erick Hawkins in the title parts danced with an admirable fluency, a complete control of the timing, the attack, the extent, and the transformation of a gesture, keeping it perfectly placed in style, in character, in quality. They made other modern dancers look wooden and awkward, as you watched. And the music, by Robert McBride, I liked very much indeed. It is in his quite personal style, completely unromantic (or "unexpressive"), but not uninteresting, and very agreeable to listen to. It does without seasoning as well as an apple.

Letter to the World, last year's piece about Emily Dickinson, I again found very beautiful; and Miss Graham danced it magnificently. Beautiful too was Merce Cunningham's dancing in this; he is in his own way as noble and as touching a dancer as I know, one of the finest dancers in America.

Ruth St. Denis appeared, doing dances that went back to 1905. It is extremely interesting to see how decorative these famous dances are, how boldly and happily unauthentic, and how charmingly ladylike in their tone. As theater there is no foolishness, no fake in them whatever. The power of these dances is not in their composition but in the extraordinary projection Miss St. Denis gives them, the flood of unspecific good intentions and the personal charm by which she makes the whole house feel comfortable and friendly. She would have no trouble at all winning the Broadway audience all over again.

JANUARY–FEBRUARY 1942

CARMEN AMAYA; ISADORA RECONSIDERED; DANCE PHOTOGRAPHS; "PUNCH AND THE JUDY" REVISITED

On the Carmen Amaya question, it was her comic "Hay que tu" number that convinced me she is an extraordinary dancer. A gypsy girl sings to her lover, "You can't make me jealous; you go on pretending to make love to others, but you always come back to me and say, 'There's only you, beautiful, there's only you.' " Amaya was wearing the typical flamenco dress, with its many flounces and a long train, but she looked like a girl of thirteen, angular as a boy, in her first evening gown. She fought her train into place like a wild-animal trainer. Her voice was hoarse and small, her gesture abrupt and awkward. All this with the defiance of the song made the dance comic. But the figure of the tough slum girl Amaya suggested was as real to you as the stranger sitting next to you in the audience. You felt its private individual life, its life before and after the glimpse of it you were catching. And there was nothing pathetic, no appeal for help in it. So you grinned and laughed, as much at home as with Villon, "*en ce bourdeau où tenons notre estat*"; and the fierce adolescence on the stage looked as wonderful as tragedy does.

Realness in comedy is very rare among dancers; and the cruelly comic is of course one of the special gifts of Spain. Now that I've seen Amaya do it, I have the greatest admiration for her. Before, I had been rather disappointed. Compared to the other Spanish stars in town, I had not found in her dancing the limpidity, the exquisite flow and nuance of Argentinita, nor the diamond glitter, the superb force of Martinez, the greatest of the Spanish dancers here; Fernandez, the Mexican, had seemed more plastic. And Rosario and Antonio—somewhat like Amaya in fiery temperament, in exuberant blurring of detail, in speed and theatricality—have the advantage of being a couple of kids happily matched, a relation which makes the dance look open and natural.

True, even in disappointing numbers Amaya has first-rate personal qualities. She has sometimes for instance a wonderful kind of rippling of her body in movement, more like a young cat's than a girl's; she has an extraordinary cutting quality in her gesture, too, as if she meant: here only, and never elsewhere. She has a thrilling speed and attack. But these impressions of real moments were confused by others when she seemed to be faking: forcing her "temperament," or driving her dance into the floor, like a pianist who pounds too hard. Or she would lose control of the continuity of her dance, put all her fire into half a minute of it and not know what to do with the remaining two minutes, so they went flat. Sometimes she seemed determined to cow her audience, and I had the feeling I was watching not a dancer but an ambitious person. On the other hand, that in the course of her first recital she could adjust herself to the glum expanse of Carnegie Hall and finally take charge was a proof of her personal stage power. But Amaya's unevenness does not bother me anymore. Instead, I now understand why all the other flamenco dancers respect and admire her. And the other evening at Broadway and Forty-sixth, when I looked up at those Wilson's Whiskey shadow-movies and recognized Amaya doing a turn up there, I was as pleased as if I'd unexpectedly caught sight of a friend.

The recital of Maria Theresa (one of the original Duncan dancers), who danced several of Isadora's Chopin pieces, was interesting because it brought up again some of the technical procedures of Isadora: the large plain phrases in which a single gesture is carried about the stage; the large, clear contrast between up and down, forward and back; and the way the body seems to yield to the music and still is not passively "carried" by it, but carries itself even while it yields. It seems to me the effect of these dances, technically speaking, comes from the kind of support the gesture has, rather than from the interest of each new gesture. The gesture in itself, in the softness with which it begins, in the shape it takes and its accentual rhythm, is monotonous enough; but the support it has is a kind of invention. The support seems continuously improvised and always active, always a little stronger than the gesture in energy and just ahead of it in time. Such an accurate proportioning of energy, as it decreases from a central impulse in the torso through the joints to the extremities, gives the limbs an especial lightness; the hands, head, and feet an attractive, as if careless, bearing. It also gives the observer's eye a definite center from which to appreciate the body movement as a whole, and a feeling of following the dance continuously. It requires a technique on the dancer's part, and no easy one. Just remember how even good dancers confuse your attention by jerking your eye from one detail to another; how often even good dancers give you the sense that their impulse to move operates by fits and starts; how often they seem to be dancing now and then during their number and the rest of the time merely executing according to plan. It struck me that in the Duncan method the dynamics of movement (the flow and current of the impulse) becomes intentionally the most carefully controlled and the most expressive aspect of dancing. In ballet this aspect is not systematically taught; it is left individual and instinctive. The modern-school method, from Mary Wigman on, has tried to analyze dynamic control; but it replaced the Duncan gesture with an infinitely more varied kind, and in consequence the problem of making the dance coherent became far more difficult to resolve, technically. I am speaking here of technique in its gymnastic aspect; the Duncan coherence, which derives from the coherence of the music you hear as you watch, and the "modern" coherence, derived from the nondance ideas you are invited to recall while watching—these I am not now considering.

I am less convinced than I was ten years ago that classroom instruction in dynamics is much use to the dancer. A panacea against absurdity, as many hoped it would be, it certainly has not proved; and even with Duncan dancers, her own method did not turn out to be foolproof. But I think Isadora's technical approach to dancing (I mean distinct from her unique greatness as a dancer) is an interesting subject to clarify. It seems to me nonsense to imagine that she could have had so sweeping a success with highly perceptive audiences, could have created so disinterested an enthusiasm by numbers that she performed over and over, without (as many affirm) having a technique. The photographs seem to me not to show very much, but in several one notices a neck and shoulder line that is strikingly plastic, strikingly aware of three-dimensional expression. On her last American tour I watched a program from up in the Carnegie Hall gallery, from where she looked, all alone on the stage and facing the full blare of a Wagnerian orchestra, very small indeed. But the slow parts of her Venusberg dance and her Siegfried Funeral March remain in memory two of the very greatest effects I have seen; I can still feel their grandeur and their force.

Incidentally, when you observe the early Chopin numbers of Isadora's which Maria Theresa now has revived, you get to thinking that Fokine's *Sylphides* (also to Chopin) is hardly at all characteristic of the dancing of Taglioni and Grisi, as often supposed, but instead is full of Duncanisms. I mean in the "sensitiveness" of its extended phrases; in the stress it gives to contrasts in space—downward, upward, forward, backward; in the yielding quality of many arm gestures and back bends. These last look correct as ports de bras and renversés, but the timing is unclassical. And maybe too the rose-petal hands, the loosely drooping fingers that Fokine or Nijinsky invented for the *Spectre*, were suggested by a gesture of Isadora's. It is of course equally true that the relaxedness of her manner superimposed on the solid leg and hip rigor of ballet created a very different effect from hers: an effect of inherent contradiction, a poignant sense of perversity that has gone to the heart of most civilized people during the last thirty years.

At the Modern Museum there was a show of dance photographs by Gjon Mili, many taken by his new stroboscopic and multiflash process, which records successive phases of a movement at intervals of fractions of a second on a single plate. All of his pictures are intelligent documentation, and phototechnically they are very handsome indeed; and often they have a kind of friendly drollery in stopping the dancer dead just when he was making so very earnest an effort to rush ahead. Well, as I was looking at them and thinking of the many dance photographs I have seen, I wondered why most of them depress me so. Of course I like to look at dance pictures of myself as much as any ex-dancer does. But other people's—documentation aside—generally look pretty foolish to me; the dancers in them look so busy getting nowhere. A shot can show you only one gesture, which is like hearing only one note of a piece of music, or one word of a poem. The more painstaking the photograph, the more pointless the effect. You don't see the change in the movement, so you don't see the rhythm, which makes dancing. The picture represents a dancer, but it doesn't give the emotion that dancing gives as you watch it. A dancer onstage doesn't look strained, and she isn't a dry amoeba-shaped blob, a configuration of swirls of cloth and rigid muscles and swollen veins fixed forever in a small square of nothing, like a specimen on a slide. The dancer isolated in the camera field seems to be hanging in a void, in a nowhere.

Dance pictures get livelier the more sure you are of just where it happened, and the more air there is all around. My favorite photographs of violent motion are the strange series Rudolph Burckhardt took of Orson Welles rehearsing *Horse Eats Hat* among half-built scenery on the stage of the Maxine Elliot. In these pictures the place and purpose of the movement are clear. And so the monstrousness of arrested motion on the photograph and the subhuman shapes makes sense. But the movement in this case isn't the special kind that is made by dancers.

Among ballet photographs I should like to mention some thirty-year-old ones I very much like to look at. Curiously enough, many of them were not even taken in action, or by the same photographer. They are the photographs of Nijinsky. In nearly all his pictures one feels, besides the documentary interest, an immediate sense of movement, of the impulse to dance. Is it because they so clearly give the sense of expressive energy radiating from the pit of the stomach up out at the top of the chest and the base of the neck, and radiating down through the small of the back and out along the legs? This might be one explanation. But one can also note that the photographers did not so much try for an elegant or a novel two-dimensional outline in the dancer's pose as for a three-dimensional and plastic interest. Since the interest of the pose is a three-dimensional one, you notice the air all around it; and since the ornamental outline of the limbs isn't the main thing in the picture, you see the weight of the body better, and the movement indicated looks more like a voluntary action and less like a freakish explosion. Nijinsky's own personal dance intelligence illuminates his poses, and because in them you see his easy control of action-in-repose expression, you have confidence too in his control of expression in the livelier parts of the dance that are not photographed. He looks to me as if his body remembered the whole dance, all the phases of it, as he holds the one pose in the picture; he seems to be thinking, I've just done that, and then I do that, and then comes that; so the body looks like a face lighting up at a single name that evokes a whole crowd of remembered friends. As you look at him you see the pose breathe and move and start to glow. Quite apart from the style of movement they represent, some of his pictures should be in the hotel room of every dancer, to remind him of the real radiance of movement, to cheer him up when he wonders what it's all about anyway. And dance lovers need such reminders and such cheering up from time to time, too.

At the first view I was puzzled by the emotional effect of *Punch and the Judy*—what the piece really means. So I am coming back to it again, now

I have seen it a second time: I leave you to judge, by comparing your own impressions with mine, whether I get it this time either.

The program says it is a domestic comedy. The dance opens with some silly words and foolish ornamental overlarge gestures by three unsympathetic ladies, billed as the Three Fates. Then you see a young wife waking up with a headache. Her husband on the other hand wakes up at the top of his form. You get the situation, the joke of the ensuing friendly roughhouse. You think it's a comedy. You see too that the characters move in marionette style: they are Punch and the Judy. But you notice that their movement has not merely a puppet style (familiar in dancing, and rather a bore); it also seems real human movement, with a motor force not outside but within the torso. You admire the subtle adjustment of the two opposite styles. You admire how clearly you can follow the "meaning" of the separate gestures, as in a pantomime, and how at the same time these gestures in cut, contrast, and rhythm form a dance sequence. Nor do the gestures repeat themselves, or mark time, or utilize clichés; they are packed with inventive detail. And a kind of brutal plainness in the stage spacing is very deftly suggested.

As the story continues, you notice that the other characters are less real than the protagonists; they are straight puppets. Their dances amuse you as gags, but they don't have any inner drive of their own. Even the Three Fates, though they dance witty parodies of decorative movement, don't become a dynamic factor. The Power of Dreams, which appears as Pegasus, has a mysterious airiness in dancing, but the influence remains remote and brief and plays an ornamental and not a dramatic part. The two central characters are left with only unreal puppet foils. They themselves, part puppet, part human, never can act toward the others humanly. I had hoped till the end that at least in conflict with each other they would break through their own stylization, become completely human, and that then the emotion would open up, become a real conflict with a real resolution. It did not happen. Their relation to one another is unchanged after they have gone through all their puppet antics. And the futility of the action is expressed in the last spoken words: "Shall we begin again?"

It is then that you realize the action you watched was not as aboveboard as you at first imagined. Was there a kind of slyness, the way you were lured on to a pointless result? No, you were warned by the unpleasant opening. But now the jokes have a bitter taste, when you find they were not real people who made them. It has been a puppet story; not a drama but a monologue. The gags were the author's wisecracks at life, and she didn't give life a chance to answer back. You expected to see the humor of man and wife living together, but what you have seen is the folly of it, the pointless folly. The folly might have found a point if it had had the contrast of sentiment, or if it had had the added force of fury to drive it into the vastness of the unconscious, where folly is at home. But the point this work gives folly is a different one; it is the very care of its workmanship and execution. It is a high-class folly.

And so I found the piece easy to watch and hard to take. I found it not pleasant or open, but in its peculiar prejudice serious and interesting.

MARCH–APRIL 1942

FOKINE'S "RUSSIAN SOLDIER"; TUDOR'S "PILLAR OF FIRE"; BALANCHINE'S ELEPHANT BALLET

In *Russian Soldier* (Fokine-Prokofiev-Doboujinsky) at the Ballet Theatre you sat and watched a Russian soldier dying on a battlefield as a pretext for a dancing Radio City spectacle in brightly harmonizing colors. "How perfectly lovely," the suburban lady next to me exclaimed when he was dead. She was seduced probably by the coy folksiness of the show—eternal Russia, tea-room style. As for me, before the war the piece might have slipped by as vulgar and adroit. Presented now, with a title so full of immediate association, it is obscene. The balletomanes, less irritable than I, expressed their opinion by reviving Samuel Barlow's classic pun, "Standing in tears amid the alien corn," and adding another, "I was bortscht to death." About the score (the suite *Lieutenant Kije*), it went on indefinitely with no modesty whatever, a smart workout for all the old gags about the good earth. Fokine says he fell for it. Prokofiev says it's travesty music. It certainly is heartless.

I grant that my disgust with *Russian Soldier* is more a matter of general viewpoint than of dance viewpoint. And I still take something of the same mixed point of view when I object violently to the coyness of the piece, apart from its subject. I object to it in itself but even more because I find coyness has been the keynote of the Ballet Theatre. Its management has consistently specialized in the large-scale cute. In light pieces it tries for a knowing giggle. In versions of serious classics about tragic love it injects cute "period" effects. Until this spring the Ballet Theatre has never been able to put on a serious and poetic work on its own initiative under any circumstances. As novelties it has given us over and over again some sycophantically simpering piece, the very kind of ballet our fathers and mothers drove off the stage in the great dance wars of thirty years ago. The history of management teaches that only poetry confers prestige on entertainment, and that without prestige ballet can't get private citizens to pay its deficit. Another fact is that a company loses its self-respect without serious new works, without a sense of fresh poetry in the routine; and the management is responsible for the development of its dancers. Certainly the Ballet Theatre has plenty of talent in its company, besides having a kind of touchstone in Markova, who is one of the most poetic dancers of our time.

Ballet Theatre celebrated its first season at the Metropolitan by putting on the first large, completely serious and poetic work it has ever created on its own initiative. Tudor's *Pillar of Fire* (Schoenberg-Mielziner) is the one really good ballet that has been launched in New York since the de Basil company's *Balustrade*.

The audience watched *Pillar of Fire* almost breathlessly. For me, I see the dancers continuously transforming and contrasting their dance, as if no possibility open to them were to be left out. And the moving effect of the piece is that all this real complexity and power seem barely able to cope with the shadowy, immense space of the stage above them that becomes, as you watch, vast and real as the doom of fate. It seems to shut down from all sides on the dancers. Tudor is a master in what the painters call negative space. It gives the movement a peculiar privacy, as if it took place in an immense silence.

In point of dance style, *Pillar of Fire* is a work of originality and precision. The devices used are dramatic ones: brief phrases urgently interrupted—they re-emerge and amplify; gesture that tends in or braces itself against a direction, an imperative direction in which the dance is driving, urgently into an imminent future. It is the thrill of needing, not the delight of having. And the need is so intense, so unrelieved, it is unbelievable in any but a private faith.

Or looking at the style statically as a complex of devices, you see it employs three separate techniques of body carriage, of body tension. The ballet technique—firm, with gesture flowing controlled, with taut leaps and high lifts; a kind of modern-school technique—flexible, with impulsive gesture explosive as jitterbugging, loose low leaps, low lifts; and, third, a technique of the body as in everyday life, modest, unstraining, as if at ease. Absorbing are the variations of these three seen simultaneously in adjustments of speed to delayed movement, of diving into space to holding back, of tautness to being relaxed.

But there is another aspect of the choreography that gives me a more convincing intimate pleasure. This is that the technical devices don't have the effect of tricks; the effect of them isn't that of professional symbols of style or pattern or meaning. While you watch the dance, the eye sees everything plain. If Tudor uses a grand jeté, with high carriage and legs spread taut in the air, the carriage, the taut legs don't tickle you as a gadget would; they are a direct act. And if two dancers are close together, the knees, the hands, the shoulders, what they do to each other, how they mix—this is what holds your attention, the actual moves made. You don't have to make allowances as if anatomical facts were to be glossed over, as if you were for the sake of ulterior generalization to ignore one left arm, or the place where you know an organ is. In other words, at every moment you see the dancer as a person, as a man or a woman dancing, not as an unhappily defective instrument of a choreographer's flights of fancy. This is honesty in dancing. It makes not theoretical perfection the paramount issue, but the merely intensified expressivity of a dancer's movements over our common movement. In sequence all of it—the dance—has an emotional effect. And this effect is real and poetic thanks to the continuous certainty of the physical impression all along. Here is an example. It happens to one side of stage front, as if painfully placed. The frantic heroine leaps and the passionate young man she wants but does not love catches her in a split in midair firmly between the legs with both hands, catches her close to him at the level of his waist; for an instant she hangs against him, rigid as in mid-leap and caught. This is a technical device, a concrete act, and an image all at once. The audience watches spellbound, shocked and moved at the same time. Such a moment would be merely vulgar in the unpoetic theater.

The dancing of *Pillar of Fire* is perfect. Of course the dancers of the Ballet Theatre are very good indeed, but they don't always look as good as that. Tudor, like Balanchine, is one of those rare choreographers who make dancers look technically superb and accurately expressive. I have never seen Miss Kaye, Miss Chase, and particularly Miss Lyon look quite so wonderfully interesting. Laing is always remarkable.

As for Tudor's musicality, like Balanchine's again, it is a marvel worth seeing. The seams of the music are never patched over by the dancing. At climaxes Tudor may use arrested movement, at other times he holds back or hurries the steps ahead; but music and dance seem to have equivalent phrasings that don't get in each other's way, and don't double for one another either. The score (it is *Verklärte Nacht*) comes out limpid and clear. Incidentally, the orchestra sounded very good too.

I do just the same have a reservation about the ending of *Pillar of Fire*. Here the dance becomes so subdued it turns static, and the effect is indistinct. The heroine seems still sad and strained. It is rather a sense of exhaustion and retrospection (as it is in the music, too) than a sense of fulfillment; though the latter would be expected from the story's happy ending and the (rather overwarm) Threshold-of-the-Future lighting effect that ends the piece. I was bothered by this discrepancy, and then retrospectively fell to wondering if the real subject of the piece isn't "Nevermore" despite the story. But though I was confused, the happy end does not really carry, anyway. The long tortured and humiliated parts stay with you, not comforting, but very moving in their pathos.

As a footnote, the weight of the materials of the costumes, and the cut, especially of the little girl's dresses, were miraculous.

It was the circus that this spring played the trump card of ballet, beating the Opera House Gang at their own game by putting on a Balanchine-Stravinsky novelty. It was also the world's first elephant ballet, and it was a fine number. The elephants do all their charming old tricks and one new one—the classic adagio pirouette supported by the partner. The elephants are lively and feminine, and the many pretty girls with garlands are very exact and very pleasant. Balanchine as usual has deployed counterrhythm, asymmetry, and adagio invention. And there is none of that drill-sergeant emphasis on uniformity that destroys the real flavor of dances by animals or athletes. The Stravinsky polka is a bit jumpy, but he's an old friend, we're glad to meet up with him, and even if we can't quite make out what he's saying in the general din, I'm willing to give him the benefit of the doubt. "There goes Igor," as *The New Yorker* reports the band saying.

There was a Chinese wirewalking number with a completely beautiful flower-table that made me think how sumptuous the circus would look if the whole décor could be designed and executed by Chinese. The Bel Geddes color is all aniline, and it's like playing in one key very loud for three hours.

MAY–JUNE 1942

DE MILLE'S "RODEO"; NIJINSKA'S "CHOPIN CONCERTO"; MASSINE'S "ALEKO"

The ballet season (Ballet Theatre and Monte Carlo Ballet sharing a month at the Met) has not been very startling, but it has been unusually pleasant. Both companies danced almost constantly at dance pitch, which had never happened before. The audience was less jittery and more cordial. People didn't seem to come to ballet because they "must" see it, they just naturally were there; and the house wasn't any too big for them. A few older people may have wished for a little more nervous stylishness in the air. But I had the impression that the elegance we are headed for is a less quivering, a less immodest and more amiable one.

The success story of the season was the Monte Carlo's all-American *Rodeo*. I never heard so friendly an enthusiasm as on the opening night. The noise didn't have the harsh fierce sound of a demonstration, either artistic or regional. It sounded like a sincere pleasure, easy and full and sort of homey.

The effect of the ballet, as a friend of mine said, is like that of a pleasant comic strip. You watch a little coy and tear-jerky cowgirl-gets-her-cowboy story, and you don't get upset about it. What you are really recognizing is what people in general do together out West. Somehow the flavor of American domestic manners is especially clear in that peculiar desert landscape; and that is its fascination. The dance, the music, the décor (Agnes de Mille–Copland–Smith and Love) each are drawn to that same local fact with affection; and so they have a mysterious unity of a touching kind. They also have the unity of being each one of superior workmanship. It is a modesty of the work that their relationship otherwise looks quite casual.

Choreographically, too, *Rodeo* looks like something improvised. Its truest and luckiest overtones come from style mixtures. For instance, the long first and third scenes to full orchestra are made up of stylized pantomime, plot, gags, and stylized folk-dance effects. But the brief second scene has none of that. It's a fast cowboy dance or running-set—a real one—danced just to handclapping and some calling. By themselves the other two stylized scenes would turn cute and corny. But thanks to the little interlude, you feel like continuing through the others, the long silence and the cheerful loneliness of the real place. It's a fine effect; and it also escapes the sourpuss these-are-my-roots claptrap.

The dances proper, which take up most of the time, are full of quick invention, lively and very attractive; the best we've had on the prairie subject and the best Miss de Mille has done. The ballet was danced very handsomely, with an accurate sense of what American movement (and the pokerfaced expression it has) is like. It was no trouble at all to the Ballet Russe. What I particularly liked about Miss de Mille in the lead was how—by imaginative projection—she gave a completely clear sense of the West as a place she had lived in, quite independently of anything she did. It gave her performance the extra dimension of style; and the audience took to her completely. The drawing and sense of space in the drops by Oliver Smith are remarkably fine, too.

Well, there was a dispute whether the ballet imitated *Billy the Kid*. It didn't. What in *Billy* is local color in *Rodeo* is the main subject. (*Billy* was revived by the Ballet Theatre afterwards. The score sounded fine but was played slowly and roughly. Gibson, as Billy, is of course a better dancer than Loring; on the other hand he hasn't Loring's command of the dramatic pause. The spacing of the figures as well as the flavor of the movement has not the old clear focus, and the Sheriff has lost his mysterious quiet. Not enough rehearsal.)

The season brought one novelty that is in the big-time tradition and with a fresh approach—in all respects a work of highest quality: Nijinska's *Chopin Concerto*, also presented by the Monte Carlo. It is danced to the E-minor Piano Concerto, in a self-effacing, attractive décor by Ignatieff. It is a kind of *Sylphides* thirty years after—just dancing, without a story, in the academic classic style. (But it doesn't feel at all like *Sylphides*, and the style as a matter of fact is much more correct than Fokine's.) Two independent girl soloists are contrasted in movement with several close groups of dancers, either girls or boys. There is no psychology, no nostalgia; there is only limpid and constantly interesting change. There is a real subject, the weight and the lightness of the body seen in motion. The dance does not go to either extreme of violence or pathos, but it makes the difference clear and also very moving. And from a slow, awkward beginning it takes flight toward the end in several more and more extended solo variations, a continuous flutter of little steps and low rapid leaps, astonishingly unforced in conception and fantastically brilliant in execution. (No wonder—Danilova and Krassovska were the dancers.) The work is big-time because it is ample and consistent and doesn't leave any emotional loose ends around. To me it also seemed a clear example of the new reticently ingratiating and unstrained and gently corny fashion.

Nijinska's other new ballet, *The Snow Maiden*, also done by the Monte Carlo, I liked very much too. It is set to an arrangement of Glazounov's *Seasons*. It has a Russian folk-tale plot about a daughter of Frost and Spring, a maiden who is cool until a shepherd wins her love at a village festival; she loves, melts, and dies in his arms. Spring has come. The ballet, especially in its Aronson setting, gets pretty close to greeting-card art, but by some gift of vivacity and unpretentiousness its sentiment turns out to be fresh and light like the pleasure of walking alone to the wood lot on a day in early spring. The simplified Russian folk dances come off very happily too, and Danilova, as the Spring, is poetic just being carried around the stage—what delicacy of stage presence!

These were the three novelties of the Ballet Russe de Monte Carlo. Ballet Theatre also had three: *Aleko* (Massine-Tchaikovsky-Chagall), *Don Domingo* (Massine-Revueltas-Castillanos), and *Romantic Age* (Dolin-Bellini-Merida). They weren't so novel. *Romantic Age* is a decorative little parody of conventional ballet, too harmless to be as elegant as it might. Its Bellini music doesn't suit the purpose; it is much too interesting nowadays. The happy feature of *Romantic Age* is the special wit of Markova in the lead. First she pretends—exquisitely—that she can't dance; later she goes that one better and pretends she can. Her parody of Victorian ballet, the self-satisfied slow-motion floating in adagio, the prim placement of the extremities in allegro, is the sweetest joke in the world. Markova, too, this time showing her peppery little feet, is the only pleasure on the stage in *Don Domingo*—a welter of complicated plot, seven or eight badly imitated Mexican folk dances, a second-rate nightclub plastique number in a spotlight, agitated groups that don't know where they belong, and heaps of décor in the official Mexican-art style with too much indigestible color. The Revueltas music is of course something to be grateful for.

The one big-time novelty of the Ballet Theatre is Massine's *Aleko*. It has the only Paris School décor of the season, by Chagall, and besides giving the satisfaction and having the fine presence of a great painter's work, it is also beautifully executed. The ballet is Massine's finest since *Fantastic Symphony*. It has lots of his expert stylization of local color (in this case, Russian gypsies and peasants), lots of his stylized dance-pantomime, lots of his ballet counterpoint (different dancers doing different things at the same time). It has as prize plum a long last scene with the breathless melodramatic thriller rush that Massine does better than anyone else. And it even has an admiring bow or two in the direction of Tudor choreography. For me, however, it has also plenty of the qualities I dislike in Massine's work—an agitation that seems senseless, a piling up of scraps of movement and bits of character like so much junk from Woolworth's, patterns but no room for them, accent and meter but no rhythm and flower of phrase. The duets are bizarre without intimacy; the man has to jerk from one position to another by turning his back awkwardly on his partner. For me *Aleko* has a real subject only in its décor; the dance is just a hectic show, and whenever it slows down it goes flat. Well, the public at any rate loves the hubbub of it, and it loves the junk. Anyone can very well love all the dancers of it; they work as hard as possible, and everyone dances his or her best.

It seemed to me that the audience this season wasn't taking sides on the question of choreography and décor, it was so eager to enjoy all the dancing. Each of the companies had its familiar and wonderful star, Danilova for Monte Carlo, Markova for Ballet Theatre. This year Markova added to her glory by doing each of her many parts in a different ballet style—each accurate and complete. As a Markova enthusiast I was especially delighted with her *Aurora's Wedding* role, which she chose to do in the *grande courtisane* manner. It was the last trick one would have expected of her, and of course she was right. It made that sermonlike Rose Adagio for once deliciously breathless. In the Monte Carlo company, Slavenska appeared with a new friendly Viennese manner, and for the first time in years she was admirable in a classic piece. Youskevitch, as her partner, had got over the little foolish stiffness between the shoulder blades that used to look so boyish; and his knees give now as sumptuously as Eglevsky's when he lands. He is very fine.

But it is Gibson, of the Ballet Theatre, who wins the hearts this year, because you watch what looks like a great star just emerging. What's new for a lyric star too is that he hasn't the 1930 Russian mannerism of a certain greasy sexiness. So far he is at his best only in *Aurora's Wedding* and in *Naughty Lisette* (*La Fille Mal Gardée*). But his *Spectre of the Rose* is more promising than any recent one has been. He has the gift for the poetry of leaping, and the basic trick of stopping in midair; now he is teaching himself to continue dancing on the ground, too. Best of all, he begins to show personal imagination and personal dance rhythm. He and Miss Conrad and Miss Lyon seem to be the only ones who are learning this fundamental of style from the great example of Markova, as in the other company Krassovska has learned her freer rhythm from Danilova's example.

It is quite right for the management of Ballet Theatre to be developing its better dancers by rotating the solo roles. I hope it can also do something to give the ensemble more real style. (The Monte Carlo still is the better company in that respect.) A sense of style in the ensemble is what really brings a ballet to life. Style is the expression of the secret meaning of the piece as far as it relates to the individual dancer; in that way it is the dancer's deportment. In another way, style is a question of giving a phrase of dancing an edge or vivacity by timing the point of emphasis, as in reciting poetry. Virgil Thomson, who saw a performance of *Swan Lake* in which Markova was magnificent, told me that in the old days with the magnificent Doubrovska in the part he had not had so sharp a sense of a distinction between star and chorus; in style they were related to her style, they were all enchanted swans. The ensemble of the Ballet Theatre are accurate technically, they are lively and pleasant and good-looking. But nobody has yet taught them classical deportment, which is delicate and grand and personal; it also allows the girls a special femininity which would be interesting. NOVEMBER–DECEMBER 1942

BALANCHINE AND TCHAIKOVSKY: "BALLET IMPERIAL"; CARMEN AMAYA; DORIS HUMPHREY

Ballet Imperial (Balanchine-Tchaikovsky-Doboujinsky; danced by and created in 1941 for Kirstein's American Ballet) was the single full-length ballet offered at the New Opera and it is the most brilliant ballet of the season. In intention it is a homage to the Petersburg ballet style, the peculiarly sincere grand manner which the Imperial Ballet School and Petipa evolved. We know the style here from the choreography of *Swan Lake*, *Aurora's Wedding*, and *Nutcracker*, even of *Coppélia*, though all of them have been patched out; we know it from glimpses of grandeur in the dancing of the Russian-trained ballerinas; from photographs, especially of the young Pavlova and the young Nijinsky; and from the legend that persists and which is distinct from the Diaghilev legend. Balanchine of course knows it thoroughly from having been trained in the actual school. But even with little knowledge, homage to this manner is natural for a dance lover. The Petersburg style was the one that vigorously continued our whole tradition of serious dancing during the increasing barbarism of 1850–1900. It was also the solid foundation for the extraordinary glory of ballet in the Diaghilev era, a glory which still pays the expenses of our ballet companies. And there is another attraction toward it, more compelling and more personal: it is the force of the mysteriously poignant images of the style—an expressive force which keeps returning them to the mind. And they so return, even after the context of them is gone and their outline altered, marked among other images by their singularity of expression.

Such images spontaneously arising are *Ballet Imperial*'s theme. It does not reproduce the period as a decorator would. You don't find the fairy-tale plot, the swans, the dance variations strung on a story. Instead there is a backdrop that makes you think of the concrete St. Petersburg, and in front of that a brand-new ballet with lots of novel steps. Actually you see a stage full of dancers who, say, arbitrarily disappear, who reappear in peculiarly rigid formations that instantly dissolve, or else stop and stand immobile. You see the vivacity of the star set over sharply against the grand pose of the ensemble, or else the solo dancer lost and still while the full company hastens happily. You watch the solo partners discover each other, two individuals in the noncommittal cheerful society of the company; you follow their touching individual response. And afterward you see them alter their natures from having been tender personages to being star performers, an inexplicable duplicity that leads to no heartbreak but culminates instead in the general dazzle of a virtuoso finale for everybody all over the stage at once. So described, *Ballet Imperial* might be a typical Petersburg ballet. But the fact is that each of these typical effects is arrived at by so novel a technical procedure that it comes as a surprise. We feel the effect first, we recognize the feeling, and from that we remember the old effect. One might say the new effect is as fresh as that of the Petersburg ballet was in its own time. Or that the past and the present seem to happen at the same time, as they do in the drama of personal memory.

As dancing, *Ballet Imperial* is full of freshness. In point of form, it is an abstract ballet interpreting Tchaikovsky's Second Piano Concerto. Interpretive dance reveals one of the structural aspects of a piece of music—Fokine is apt to show how the periods sit, Massine goes for the tangle of musical motives. Balanchine draws our attention to the expressive flow under the syntax, and we have a vivid sense of the free musical animation. I was delighted in *Ballet Imperial* how the concerto, a showpiece I had thought forced, came to life and sounded fresh and direct. The dance focuses the interest like a good musician's playing: certain moments get an imperceptible emphasis, a long passage is taken in at a swoop, another is subdivided; and thanks to a happy interpretation the piece comes out as good as new.

In dance steps and dance figures Balanchine has always been inventive. But most people think of his choreography as full of specifically poignant detail—quick thrusts backward and sideways, odd pauses, hobbled leaps, extraordinary group poses, indecently upside-down lifts. Most of us recall how his dancers have looked torn in three directions at once, and so were we, and it was wonderful. *Ballet Imperial* has a certain oddness, but it isn't in that earlier manner in the least. It does have a slow middle section, a very beautiful one (it's in a free style of ballet movement derived from classic pantomime), which has for sentiment the pathos of a love story. A boy and girl find each other, they misunderstand, become reconciled, and lose one another. The tone is intimate. But there is not one indecent image or lift. The gestures are easy, the figures simple. And at the end the movement is brushed away, and the solitary "frustrated" emotion left in the air is very simply succeeded by a general comradely liveliness of tone in the next section, a long finale which like the long opening section has no pathos at all.

And in the slow pantomime part as well as in the rapid other two parts one comes to notice how the detail of gesture does not run counter to the main line of movement. It is not an accent, it does not draw attention to itself. The arms are easy, the dance is lighter, faster, more positive, presents itself more openly. The dance figures throughout are readily grasped. Balanchine maintains interest by an extraordinary flickering rapidity of dance steps and quick shift of dance figures. I found the speed, perhaps because it is still unfamiliar, at times confusing; but the positive style was unexpected and it had a pleasantly fresh aroma. And the brief solos in the last section reminded me of the bold large manner Petipa seems to have had, where the dance stands out so plain you see it right off with delight and you don't stop to think of the choreographer.

I was sorry the ensemble performing *Ballet Imperial* had the weakness that young dancers always show—an insufficient power of projection. It is hard to feel them if you watch from the back of the house. Looking at this question in another way, in inexperienced dancers the movement never quite comes to rest, so that the dynamic scale is a bit blurred, and the movement does not lift to its flower, shine, and subside completely, leaving a completed image in the mind. This is rhythm in dancing (as distinct from musical rhythm) and it is what gives to dancing the air of style. It is a quality of expression independent of choreographic or virtuoso effects (or of characterization) and much more communicative than they are. To have it a dancer must be unusually sturdy and self-possessed. But as *Ballet Imperial* progresses, the dancers do give you a sense of dance style. You begin to feel it in the air. You see it as vivacity and then you recognize that the freshness of movement comes from their personal animation. And you realize in the end how badly you missed, in the celebrated ensembles at the Met this fall, an air of intelligence that the sense of style gives to dancing. I remember too that dancers Balanchine rehearses, whether stars or students, always tend to show their natural dance intelligence. They have an indefinable grace in dancing that seems to come naturally to them, that seems extemporaneous. They look not so much like professionals but like boys and girls who are dancing.

Balanchine has an extraordinary gift for bringing performers to life on their own personal terms, so that the unconscious grace that is in each one of them can shine out in the work they do, giving it the momentary and mortal expression of beauty. The plan of a choreography is a great pleasure. But it is the brilliancy of young dancers entirely in the present, the unique liveliness of each dancer caught entirely in the present instant that at once, we all know it, will be past and irretrievable forever—it is this clear sharp sense of our own natural way of living that makes a moment of ballet speak to the complete consciousness that makes choreography look beautiful. As Balanchine's has again and again.

Several straight flamenco numbers ended Carmen Amaya's Carnegie Hall program. They were each one much too short to have their full effect, but in them everybody can see that she is a great and a very individual dancer. That, however, isn't the curious part of the story. Four-fifths of the evening was reserved for Spanish dancing, recital style, a form made illustrious by the great Argentina, and of which Argentinita is now the star (at least here). Amaya, as a flamenco dancer in process of becoming a recitalist, has naturally chosen the best model she could find, and she has worked hard—the improvement in detail over last year is obvious. But actually, in the kind of number Argentinita turns into a marvel of polish, Amaya right after some real stroke of genius next looks as if she had lost the thread of her story, she looks plain or out of place. Well, she carries off the number by the force of her presence on the stage, and it is wonderful how silly she invariably makes the Granados or Albéniz music sound by the edge of her attack; but the whole thing is off balance.

Off balance, but highly interesting. Because Amaya is a completely honest character, and what you watch is the struggle between two opposite dance natures—Argentinita's, which she wants to reproduce, and her own, which she can't destroy. Argentinita's nature is that of a sensible artist; she completely understands the logical line of a recital dance, she dances a piece through from A to Z without a false stress or a gap. Similarly she is a purist of movement and her transitions from one gesture to the next are a technical delight. She is also a witty and charming lady, who takes the audience into her confidence in a vivacious and cultivated way. (Some lovers of Spanish dancing even find Argentinita too polite to be thrilling.) Amaya on the other hand has none of these qualities. Form for her is not logical, it is a successive burst of inventions; the rhythmic shock is wherever you don't expect it; gesture is expression and attack, it's a gamble and there is no sense in saving and budgeting; and she has no patience with illuminating and delightful anecdotes on Spanish life, she wants to say straight out what she knows is so.

I admire in Amaya the effort of a great natural dance intelligence to master a form so foreign to it; it strikes me as a noble struggle. The first indication of a new form of her own seems to me the very original though not yet completely successful dance she has enthusiastically called a "supercreation," which though it is a recital number is a wild piece Argentinita wouldn't dream of performing. In Amaya's more imitative dances it is the flashes of genius that break up the form which I am happiest over.

Technically speaking Amaya's dancing was more controlled and more various than last year. She has also checked her former mannerisms: she doesn't repeat her lightning turns again and again, she doesn't shake down her hair every time, or dance male parts too frequently. Her magnificent rapidity, her power, her fine originality in handling the sex character of Spanish dancing are all singular virtues; and again and again she can dance as if nothing else existed in the world but dancing and death.

Angna Enters, who is of course a realistic mime and not specifically a dancer, appeared in new and old impersonations. The clarity and unobtrusiveness of her action, the elegance of her accessories, her pointed sense of "genre," and a certain rhythmic instinct in forming a scene—all this is expert and high class. So is the extremely intelligent piano tinkling offstage. The evening is a specialty of understatement and inference. But the emotion is not always distinct and it is mostly small. For me, grateful though I am for so much good taste and so little pretentiousness, I find an entire evening of it gives me an impression of timidity. Of course I know that for a century or more a notable characteristic of the American school in art and in taste has been timidity of expression. But now and then it seems to me an absurd standard for grown-up people.

At her studio theater Doris Humphrey presented an all-Bach program. It contained her well-known large composition to the Passacaglia and Fugue in C Minor; a new, very long solo by José Limón to the Chaconne for solo violin (it had interesting references to fencing style and was an honorable failure); and the program also contained two new pieces for small groups by Miss Humphrey, one set to four chorale preludes, the other to the Partita in C Major played on the harpsichord. These new dances, which are often gentle, pleased her faithful audience, but less than the old ones do. I thought them interesting as a further example of the general tendency of the "modern dance" choreographers to compose in a more continuously fluent manner. Five years ago they were chiefly concerned with the emphatic aspect of movement: they socked the active phases of gesture, stamp, jerk, thrust, or stop, they gave slow motion a knife edge or contracted with paroxysmal violence. A dance seemed like a series of outcries. The moderns had always cultivated continuity in their intellectual concepts of dancing, but they did not build their dances out of a continuity of expression. Now they are interested in the value of the unemphatic phrases as well, in the continuous support on which the continuous dance line rests (as in singing or piano playing). I think they are interested in the confidence the continuous line can express, and in the melody of a continuous movement.

Modern dancing is not dead, of course not. It has an appreciative public. Its intentions are extremely intelligent. Its execution varies from the studentlike to being fresh and real. But it sets itself the highest standards. Musically it has brought us this season several pieces by Cage, a novel music of freshness and delicacy; and *Modern Music* reported in the last issue two new ballets by Harris for Hanya Holm. Even when modern dancing is conventional, we who watch are happy over the disinterested love of serious dancing that motivates it. Any child knows by now that there is no money in it, and little enough glory. But young people do it just the same, with the obstinate generosity that keeps turning up in our species.

JANUARY–FEBRUARY 1943

MARKOVA'S DANCE RHYTHM; TUDOR'S "ROMEO AND JULIET"

The great event of any Ballet Theatre season is the dancing of Markova. And this season she danced even more wonderfully than before. She appeared night after night, and even in two ballets on the same program. Once the papers said she had fainted after the performance. There is only one of her. I very much hope she is gratefully taken care of and prevented from injurious overwork.

When she dances, everybody seems to understand as if by sympathy everything she does. And yet her modesty is the very opposite of the Broadway and Hollywood emphasis we are used to. A Russian girl I know who works in a defense plant brought along her whole swing shift one Sunday into standing room. They had never seen ballet, and they unanimously fell in love with Markova. Markova has the authority of a star, but her glamour comes from what the English so well call a genuine spiritual refinement.

Watching her critically in Petipa's [*sic*] *Swan Lake*, in Fokine's *Sylphides*, in Massine's *Aleko*, or in Tudor's novelty, *Romeo and Juliet*, I am constantly astonished how she makes each of these very different styles completely intelligible in its own terms. None looks old-fashioned or newfangled. Each makes straight sense. Her new Juliet for instance is extraordinary. One doesn't think of it as Markova in a Tudor part; you see only Juliet. She is like no girl one has ever seen before, and she is completely real. One doesn't take one's eyes off her, and one doesn't forget a single move. It doesn't occur to you that she is dancing for an audience, she is so quiet. Juliet doesn't try to move you. She appears, she lives her life, and dies.

One of the qualities that strikes me more and more in Markova's dancing is her dance rhythm. Anybody who has been to the Savoy Ballroom knows what rhythm in dancing is. But once you get away from there and start watching the art of stage dancing, you find rhythm very rarely. You find many beautiful things—exact control, intelligence, energy, variety, expression—but they aren't quite the same thing as rhythm. Of course rhythm in art dancing is not so simple as in the Savoy "folk" form. But you recognize it wherever you find it. And as anybody can hear that Landowska has rhythm, so anybody can see that Markova has it.

Markova's rhythm is not only due to her remarkable freedom in attacking her steps a hair's breadth before or after the beat, a freedom in which she shows a perfect musical instinct. I think one gets closer to it by noticing her phrasing. And what we speak of as Negro rhythm is perfection of phrasing in a very short dance phrase. What strikes me equally about their two-beat phrases and her very long ones is how clearly each separate phrase is completed. It is perfectly clear when the phrase rises, and when it has spent itself. I feel the impulse has been completed, because I have seen the movement change in speed, and in weight. (In the lindy the thrust is hard and quick, but the finish—or recovery—of the step is light and seems even retarded; in Markova's incomparable *Sylphides* phrases she prepares during five or six steps with a gentle, uniform downward martellato for one slow, expressive, and protracted upward movement in her arms.) In musical terms there is a rubato within the phrase, corresponding to the way the balance of the body is first strained, then is restored.

Markova's way of dancing adds a peculiar quality to a ballet by Tudor. Other dancers can make his dramatic intentions clear. They show that each of his gestures carries a meaning: a nuance of emotion, of character, of social standing. They show his precision of timing and placing, so that one appreciates his extraordinary genius for visual rhythms on the stage. They are personally self-effacing, and give a thrilling intensity to the drama he intended. But Tudor's style includes many hampered movements, slow-motion effects, sudden spurts of allegro arrested incomplete, arm tensions straining into space, pelvic displacements, and shifts of carriage. They are fascinating effects. On the other hand I notice that in execution the movement looks forced. The dancers have trouble with their balance, they are apt to look laborious and lose their spring. Perhaps Tudor meant the dance to look off balance, but it also looks airless. Now I see that Markova can sense and can show the dance rhythm that underlies his visual phrases. She finds their point of rest. She is easily equal to his dramatic meaning and passion, but she also gives his drama the buoyancy of dancing. As I watch her, Markova—like Duse in Ibsen—seems to be speaking poetry to the company's earnest prose.

Tudor's *Romeo and Juliet* was the world premiere that Ballet Theatre presented in its spring season at the Met. It was a great success and fully deserved it. It has a few unconvincing moments, but it has a great many original and very fine ones. (One of the most delicate effects is the special use of toe steps in the part of Juliet; they take on a quality different from any pointes I ever saw.) As a whole, I found the piece fascinating.

The plot of *Romeo* is that of Shakespeare's play. Tudor follows the action almost faithfully, but the individual thing about it is that the poetic message is not the same. The ballet's conception of mutual love is far less impetuous, far less straightforward, far less dazzlingly radiant. The difference is clearest in the character of Romeo, who in the ballet is never quite frank; he is like an object of love rather than a lover. But he is a perfectly real young man. And Hugh Laing—always a dancer full of real character—dances him as one. Tudor's piece strikes me as a personal version of the story, a reverie on the subject, with muted and oppressed images. Shakespeare's openness is its foil. And it is precisely the private deformation Tudor has made which gives to the ballet its core of poetic reality, its odd spell.

That Tudor had no intention of copying Shakespeare is clear enough in his choice of Delius for the music. The various pieces that together form the score have not the theatrical incisiveness of ballet music. But they are used as background music, as soundtrack; as such they are of high quality.

But I think the big event and most telling effect of the *Romeo* production is the extraordinary décor the painter Eugene Berman has given it. I have never shared the complacency with which we New Yorkers accept window-dressing (be it functional or "camp") as ballet décor. I think ballet sharpens the eyes and opens the heart, and under these circumstances a vulgar set is carrying our cult of lowbrow manners too far. I am shocked to see *Giselle* danced in front of a powder-room wallpaper, or to see the swans in *Swan Lake* troop out in so many little homemade Dutch outfits, just as if they had rolled up their sleeves for a bout of spring cleaning.

Berman's Italian Renaissance décor is a serious work of art, like Picasso's *Tricorne* or Bérard's *Cotillon*, like the works of the baroque designers. And I imagine later theater lovers who look at the record of it will marvel at the refinement of sensibility it presupposes in the audience. As a picture it is shut in and still it lifts and spreads, it comes forward, and it keeps its secret. As a stage design it has inventiveness and immense learning, everything has been made with tenderness and is useful. The blended perspectives, the contrasted weights of the materials, the originality of the colors, the animation of the proportions, the energy of the drops, all these show us the many kinds of visual pleasure the stage has to offer. And in *Romeo*, for once, the scene painting and the execution of costumes are superlative.

Ballet Theatre brought one other novelty to New York, *Helen of Troy* (Lichine-Offenbach-Vertès). It is a musical-comedy number—not as ponderous as a real musical comedy, not as bright as a real ballet. It has its good moments, but an awkward lack of fancy keeps cropping up too.

It's a great pity for the score, and a pity for Lichine, who is a good choreographer. Jerome Robbins as Mercury runs away with the show. He's real Third Avenue (as I heard a young lady giggle to her girlfriend) and everybody enjoys it.

Otherwise Ballet Theatre rounded out its repertoire by handsome reproductions of Massine's *Tricorne*, *Boutique Fantasque*, and *Capriccio Espagnol*. It also revived Balanchine's beautiful *Apollo* (to Stravinsky's *Apollon Musagète*), which received a fine ovation from the audience. The ballet itself I reviewed in this column five years ago, explaining and defending the choreography; now it turns out to be perfectly clear anyway. Everybody smiles at the little jokes, everybody appreciates the intimacy of tone and the wide-openness of line. I wondered, though, if the dancing of the Muses wasn't too slick; they used to look a bit more timid, more virginal. André Eglevsky as Apollo was excellent—he always was an exceptional dancer and this year he is better than ever.

Besides Ballet Theatre, the spring has brought a good deal of other dancing, and the summer promises more. Argentinita presented a new *Café de Chinitas*, a quadro flamenco number which García Lorca had long ago arranged with her. The first version shown at the Serenades was able enough; a second version, with a Dali décor, was performed at the Met with her Ravel *Bolero* and dances from *Carmen*, too late for comment here.

At the very active Humphrey-Weidman studio there were a number of new programs, including several guest stars. Here and elsewhere there have been numerous regional or historical American and Latin American numbers, new or revived. Among the new ones was Doris Humphrey's version of the *Salón México*. What is best about them all is a sort of casual homey charm. And I warmly recommend Weidman's revived *Impressions of Famous Dancers*. They are parodies of Doris Humphrey, Anna Duncan, Wigman, Ted Shawn, and Amaya. They are highly intelligent, infamous clowning and, especially if you know the models, terribly funny.

I apologize for not having previously mentioned this year, as I should have, the appearance of a new modern dancer of great promise, Valerie Bettis. As a generous rival said of her in admiration, "But she moves." Bettis too has dance rhythm. Her vitality on the stage, her technical facility are astonishing, and her compositions unusual. The other young modern dancer I find extremely interesting to watch is Merce Cunningham, of Martha Graham's company. His dance rhythm too is like a natural gift one watches with immediate pleasure.

A number of people have asked me the reason for the present wave of balletomania that is sweeping from coast to coast, and that packed the Metropolitan for the longest ballet season in our history. My personal opinion is that ballet—when it is well danced—is the least provoking of our theatrical forms. Nobody on the stage says a word all evening. Nobody bothers much about sexiness or self-importance. The performers are bright, tender, agile, well mannered, they are serious and perfectly civilized. It is good for one's morale, because it appeals to the higher instincts. You feel sociable and friendly and at the same time wide awake. I think that's why so many people are delighted. Civilization is really a great pleasure.

MAY–JUNE 1943

From the "New York Herald Tribune"

"THE NUTCRACKER"; MASSINE'S "THREE-CORNERED HAT"

The Monte Carlo Ballet Russe, continuing its season at the Metropolitan, last night danced *The Nutcracker*, *Three-Cornered Hat*, and *Prince Igor*, three familiar pieces, the youngest of which was older than most of the soldiers and sailors in the audience. Everybody knows, though, that these three old friends still have plenty of life in them. And the company can be excused for marking time a bit, preparatory to the world premiere of *Rodeo* tomorrow.

The Nutcracker was—but for the two leads—a repetition of the performance the day before. Last night the star parts were taken by the great Danilova and André Eglevsky. Miss Danilova did not seem at first to be at the top of her form, but both she and the audience warmed up progressively, and the second act found her as delicately natural in the grand style as she alone can be. Eglevsky, too, has a simplicity of manner and a certain imaginative warmth that marks him as a quite exceptional classic star. Technically he was, of course, magnificent.

Three-Cornered Hat remains one of Massine's masterpieces as a choreographer and one of his best parade numbers as a dancer. He still dances all of it, and especially the farruca, to great effect, though he dominates the stage more by his matchless stage presence than by technical virtuosity. He almost alone of ballet dancers seemed formerly to have something of the edge of the great Spanish dancers, something of their brilliant attack and unpredictable rhythm. Spanish dancing at its best is "hot" in the jazz sense. But it can be argued that ballet Spanish needn't be "hot," since its own non-Spanish rhythm is its inherent characteristic.

Miss Krassovska, who has been exceptionally brilliant this season, took the part of the Miller's Wife, and did it well, though to my taste it wasn't quite dry enough. James Starbuck's Governor was a ridiculous desiccated insect, and a very good version of the part. The Picasso set and costumes are as fresh and as positive as the day they were created; he is still the greatest stage designer of them all. OCTOBER 15, 1942

DOLIN'S "ROMANTIC AGE"

Dolin's ballet *Romantic Age*, the world premiere of which the Ballet Theatre presented last night at the Metropolitan Opera House, is cute as candy. And before it is over, it turns out to be a pretty big lump of confectionery to swallow. But the dancing of Alicia Markova in the lead is quite another thing. Wit and good nature, incredibly perfect technique and a fantastic grace quite of her own turned her part in the piece into one of those little jewels for ballet lovers.

Essentially *Romantic Age* is an expanded and beribboned sequel to Dolin's *Pas de Quatre*. It is another but much more elaborate Victorian pastiche—parody of ballet at its dullest. The story is of a Nymph, who alone among her sister nymphs is awkward. She can't dance ballet. Amor shoots her with his golden arrow and she becomes the best dancer of them all. A handsome Faun seems to please her for a while, but really a polite Youth turns out to be the better partner. The Faun's anger is appeased and that leads to a grand finale.

The various dances themselves are in Dolin's usual choreographic style, grateful for the dancer, in good taste, perfectly clear, and not very interesting. Dolin himself danced the Youth, and exhibited as always perfect manners and clean style. Everybody on the stage did well and the audience was willing, but without Markova the whole thing wouldn't have come through as a joke. When this most exquisite of technicians pretends she can't dance, she is a miracle of grace and a perfect showman.

The Bellini music deserves a better fate than to be used for a decorative parody; it has a real passion. The score was arranged by Antal Dorati.

OCTOBER 24, 1942

TUDOR'S "DARK ELEGIES"; "SWAN LAKE"

Last night's program of the Ballet Theatre at the Metropolitan Opera House had three interesting novelties: André Eglevsky as Alicia Markova's partner in *Swan Lake*; Robert Lawrence, the dance critic of the *Herald Tribune*, as orchestra conductor of the same piece; and, third, the only performance in two seasons of Tudor's ballet *Dark Elegies*.

Dark Elegies, danced to Mahler's *Kindertotenlieder,* is a work in which pauses, a naive solemnity, and the simplest of dance figures give a clear effect of pathos. The dance style is that of Northeast European folk dances; the style of expression is like the odd stiffness of English morris dancers. The relation of dance rhythm to the music, the timing of the accents, the spacing of the figures—these are, as always with Tudor, of an impeccable elegance and clarity.

It is true that the willful spareness of the movement—as if it were dragged out of the dancers—stands in contrast to the florid emotionalism of the music. And both dance and orchestra are far from the sweet domestic note that the words of the songs have. But none of this lessens the effect of the piece on the stage. It was another well-deserved triumph for Tudor. I thought the dancing of Miriam Golden and Hugh Laing especially fine, but the entire company danced, as this piece can only be danced, with oneness of feeling.

Swan Lake, opening the program, was a completely magnificent performance of one of the most poetic of stage works. This ballet makes little enough sense when done as a production number. It makes the best of sense if the three central figures can convey that the Swan Queen is really enchanted, the Prince really in love with her, and his Friend really his friend. Then the ballet turns out to be a tender and true poem about love where love is impossible; about the beautifully glittering ambiguity that is at the core of Victorian romanticism.

Last night's performance was perfect from this poetic aspect, as well of course as from the technical one. Markova's phrasing of a dance is a joy of intelligence. As an actress, she was by turns delicate as a pet bird, scintillating, trustful, and a girl imprisoned in a spell. Eglevsky was tender and modest and manly. His gesture of despair to his Friend in the pause in the midst of the central love duet was noble and true. In fact the brief pantomimic scenes last night between the Prince and the Swan Queen were of an extraordinary limpidity. The music to these moments was also exceptionally clear and it turns out to be very interesting.

OCTOBER 30, 1942

ARGENTINITA

The great Spanish dancer Argentinita and her company gave their only recital of the season last night at Carnegie Hall in a program that included new and old numbers.

Argentinita has not the dramatic intensity, the force, of Amaya, Martinez, or Rosario and Antonio. But she has other qualities of the first rank that have made her in the last five years the most popular of our Spanish stars. Her dances present either a little situation or one of the Spanish dance styles with extraordinary clarity.

She dances not as a gypsy but as a lady, and within this range her mastery of nuance, the accuracy with which she makes her point, is unparalleled. She is charming to her audience. The lightest of ironies colors her suggestion of passion, of speed, of grace. It enlivens her phenomenal knowledge of Spanish regional dances. And it keeps the performance within the bounds of what may be done with good taste in public.

Her technique—the purity of arm gesture, the lift of the waist that barely moves but is always alive—is admirable. But incomparable is the virtuosity of the feet. They perform miracles of shading in the sound of heel taps and sole taps. They also make the most charming and expressive little gestures of the ankle. The feet seemed last night more subtle and distinct than I had noticed before.

In Argentinita's company her sister, Pilar Lopez, is equally well known; she is more of a soubrette in type, with a more robust humor. She did an excellent alegrías of her own. The new men partners, Greco and Vargas, were young, handsome, and quick; but both seemed inexperienced, and Greco not serious enough.

Alejandro Vilalta, the featured pianist, played without Spanish dignity or precision of rhythm. The guitarist was Montoya.

MARCH 22, 1943

CHARLES WEIDMAN

Charles Weidman with Florence Lessing and Peter Hamilton introduced a new program last night at the Humphrey-Weidman Studio, which I am happy to tell you is going to be repeated on subsequent Fridays.

The program begins with five little parodies of various dance styles—parlor numbers that are neat and bright. It is like being at a family party, and everybody laughs at Uncle Charles, who is so quick with his hands and makes faces so slyly. But the evening ends with Weidman's celebrated *Impressions of Famous Dancers.* They are masterpieces of high clowning, and fantastically funny. They deal—and deal very penetratingly—with Doris Humphrey, Anna Duncan, Mary Wigman, Ted Shawn, and Amaya. They should be filmed for the Dance Archives of the Modern Museum, to show later dance lovers what these famous dancers were not quite like. I shall certainly go again, if only to see the superb Wigman piece, as ruthless a travesty as was ever invented. Miss Humphrey herself introduced the *Impressions* in a charming speech.

There were two new trios on the first part of the program, one a sultry tango (*La Comparsa*), the other an especially attractive scene in a ballet school (*The Dancing Master*). The latter, done to Alec Templeton's *Mr. Bach Goes to Town,* shows two local ballet pupils very properly practicing, but now and then they slip without noticing into a hot jive. Florence Lessing and Peter Hamilton were both of them fresh and spirited in all the numbers; they are very pleasant, straightforward, well-trained dancers.

And Charles Weidman is certainly a magnificent clown.

APRIL 3, 1943

"ALEKO"; KAREN CONRAD

There were three novelties in last night's program of the Ballet Theatre at the Metropolitan. Karen Conrad appeared as the Swan Queen in *Swan Lake*; Massine took the title part in *Aleko*; and Robert Lawrence, dance critic of the *New York Herald Tribune*, was guest conductor for both of these ballets. These novelties were each of interest.

The title part of *Aleko* is difficult because the character, who stands in opposition to the entire company, is at the center of the action only at the beginning and at the very end. At other times when he appears, he seems to express a sort of self-pity that is not especially communicative, and his gesture is "inward." Other stars do not hold the attention in these portions. Massine, however, dominated the stage with ease. He also gave the story a lively beginning by showing convincingly how pleased a city youth would be to be accepted by gypsies as one of their alien world.

Though Massine avoided a few technical feats Dolin adds to the role, his superior understanding of the story, and of its specifically Russian aspects, made the ballet itself clear. This reviewer is not happy over much of the abrupt, overloaded choreography, but last night's performance was excellent. Markova was better than ever as Zemphira—as arbitrary and temperamental as a gypsy princess. And Laing, as the Young Gypsy, was fine. The company did extremely well.

Miss Conrad is technically the finest classic dancer of the younger generation in this company. Her Swan Queen was executed brilliantly and with ease. But last night she missed the poetry of the part, which lies in the character of an enchanted bird. Unless there are enchanted birds, the whole ballet makes no sense. Miss Conrad looked lovely but too normal. And she lacked, too, the perfection of completing one gesture before the next one is begun, a perfection that gives a sense of endless moonlight to Markova's rendering. But the comparison is unfair to a young dancer.

APRIL 6, 1943

LORING'S "BILLY THE KID"

The Saturday-afternoon bill of the Ballet Theatre contained besides *Petrouchka* and *Princess Aurora* the season's first performance of *Billy the Kid*, the Aaron Copland ballet with choreography by Eugene Loring, revived by Michael Kidd. The matinee audience was, as usual, full of children, and the house was a very pleasant place to be in.

The children got an excellent performance of *Petrouchka*. Massine, who took the title part, is by far the most intelligible Petrouchka we have. He throws himself in despair through the paper wall. When he reappears on the roof he is eerily derisive; and his final collapse is scary. Reed's Blackamoor is comic in a way children really enjoy.

The performance of *Billy the Kid*, on the other hand, was not up to Ballet Theatre standard. The exactness of gesture and the spacing of figures have become blurred in many places, notably in the long Street Scene. Here everybody seemed restless and the sense of Western quietness was lost. Effective was the duet between Billy and his sweetheart, a scene beautifully danced by Kidd and Annabelle Lyon. Kidd, as Billy, has verve and a sinister elasticity; he is a fine dancer. But he missed this time the extraordinary dramatic pauses that made the part fascinating in Loring's own version of it.

But it was the orchestra in *Billy* that gave a really inferior performance. Not only that it played without animation or interest; it also played wrong, even in spots that present no difficulty. The brasses at the end sounded just like Donald Duck. One could hardly have guessed that the score is completely elegant and moving; that it is deservedly our first ballet "classic"; and that it can be a theatrical wow.

APRIL 11, 1943

TUDOR'S "ROMEO AND JULIET" REVISITED

The ending of the new Tudor-Delius-Berman *Romeo and Juliet*, omitted at the first performance, was given Saturday night at the Metropolitan Opera House. It completed the story and added two more extraordinary scenic effects to a ballet which for scenic beauty is unparalleled in our time.

At a second view, the quality of the ballet itself is clearer. It is made up of exquisite pantomime fragments ranging in style from quattrocento poses to a reference to judo. It is full of nuances in timing and placing, like an Eisenstein film. And it does not sweep through the story. It is, so to speak, a meditation on the play. But it is strangely moving. Its strength is that of an intensely and consistently poetic attitude. And so *Romeo and Juliet* turns out to be big news for dance lovers, because this attitude is the real point in dancing and it is not often shown.

In all this, of course, the marvelous Markova excels. And technically, no matter how odd the timing of her interrupted phrases may be, she gives them a rhythmic clarity and coherence which turns everything into dancing. But above all it is Juliet who dances.

The poetic realism of *Romeo and Juliet* is everywhere heightened by Berman's scenery and costumes. One can admire their elegance—the hats are better than John-Frederics'. Or their architectural learning, or their sense of the human figure. But it is their sincere homage to the glory of the Italian Renaissance, like a meditation on the beauty of the human spirit, that makes them look like living poetry.

APRIL 12, 1943

DANILOVA: PLEASURE IN THE GRAND STYLE

Among ballet stars Danilova has a special gift. At the height of a classical variation, while she is observing all the restrictions of the grand style, she seems suddenly to be happy to be dancing, with a pleasure like a little girl's. It gives her a sort of natural grace that is unique.

Last night, appearing in *Nutcracker*, which the Monte Carlo Ballet presented at the Broadway Theater, she showed this wonderful quality once more. Her assurance was remarkable, too. She was ably assisted by Youskevitch, who was himself dazzling in his variation in the final scene.

The production of *Nutcracker* was, however, hardly worthy either of the sweetly fanciful and famous score or of the touching flavor the ballet as a whole can have. The first scene especially was rudely done. Some years ago, in the de Basil company's production, this scene particularly had much more of the real E. T. A. Hoffmann domestic charm that is the point of it. But it is a great pleasure to see the piece again; it remains one of the great classics of dancing.

MAY 22, 1943

BALLET AT LEWISOHN: "LES SYLPHIDES" AND "PETROUCHKA"

Despite heat and curtailed bus service, nine thousand people found their way to the Lewisohn Stadium last night for the opening of a four-day summer season of Ballet Theatre. It is a very pleasant way to spend an evening, though not an ideal place to see ballet. For a dance lover, however, it is better to see Markova, Massine, and the Ballet Theatre company at a disadvantage than not at all.

The program began with *Sylphides* with so much light in the real sky that the artificial moonlight on the stage didn't have a chance. It was like watching a dress rehearsal. But by the time the snow was falling in *Petrouchka*, night had come; the dancers had gathered momentum and gave this piece an exceptionally fine last scene. They competed successfully with the night planes overhead. Ballet Theatre was back in form.

After thirty years Fokine's *Petrouchka* is still a fine, straightforward work. Fokine is not a subtle choreographer, but he goes straight to the heart of the story he is telling; that is what keeps his pieces alive. *Petrouchka* is helped immeasurably, to be sure, by the Stravinsky score, which is fresh as ever in all its subtlety. And last night the score sounded especially good.

The ballet itself stands or falls as a story according to the way the title part is danced. Massine last night, as usual, controlled the stage whenever he chose by the distinctness with which he can project the part. Miss Chase as the Ballerina, Eglevsky as the Moor, and Semenoff as the Charlatan were all in their best form. And the nursemaids, the gypsies, the coachmen, and especially the two grooms (Orloff and Bland) were full of zest. It was a pleasure to watch the dance scene catch fire; one forgot the heat and forgot that the dancers were, poor things, all of them in winter clothes.

In *Sylphides*, the first number on the program, Miss Markova, as well as Miss Hightower and Miss Svetlova, began extremely well; but there seemed to be a little trouble for the soloists toward the middle, and Mr. Dolin, in the only male part, didn't find the smoothness of line necessary for this piece.

Sylphides is a strange and charming mixture of academic ballet style in movement with interpretive dancing in spirit.

Soviet critics affirm that Ivanov, the choreographer who collaborated with Petipa on *Swan Lake*, was the first to interpret music in ballet dancing. *Sylphides*, however, seems to be more influenced by Isadora Duncan. She was the first to run, hesitate, turn, and yield to Chopin music. This effect Fokine has suggested, combining it, however, with ballet dancing to form a style of his own.

Seen as an interpretation of Chopin, *Sylphides* is a little rude, compared with the interpretive ballets of our day. The musical periods are broken apart; the harmonic progress of the music is carelessly ignored quite often. But *Sylphides*, too, has a boldness in its long lines, and a charm in its combination of stiffness with soft bends that still holds the attention.

JUNE 25, 1943

"SWAN LAKE" AND "ALEKO" AT THE STADIUM

Ballet Theatre, continuing its brief season at the Lewisohn Stadium, worked hard and with the best intentions. Whether it was the heat, or the lack of contact between company and audience that open-air productions suffer from, the performance didn't jell. It looked like ballet, all right, and good ballet, but it didn't feel like it. There was no concentrated and sustained emotion.

It was nobody's fault. The audience was attentive and it was even larger than the night before. The dancers danced handsomely and with all the verve in the world. The program was first-rate. The conductor tore himself to bits, trying to put over a show. The orchestra was an excellent one. And the music was Tchaikovsky. One can truthfully say that everybody concerned did his or her best.

First on the program was *Swan Lake*, with Miss Kaye dancing the Swan Queen for the first time. Miss Kaye is justly admired in the very difficult part of the heroine in *Pillar of Fire*. Last night as Odette, queen of the swans, she was excellent in the largeness of her movements, in the extensions of arms and legs. The shoulders seemed a trifle too high and square, however, to give the best line. I thought it was the raised-shoulder position that kept her from having the full poise that the part of a queen in classic ballet requires. From where I sat it was impossible to see the feet, and the nervous detail of one foot beating against the ankle of the other that is so expressive in this particular part was lost to me.

But I did not find that Miss Kaye projected the sense of being enchanted, the sense that there is an infinity of time for her to do whatever she does, since she is under the spell of fate. It would be unfair to judge her by this first try at so complex a part. Only last winter Miss Conrad failed at her first try as Odette, but showed very remarkable qualities at her second performance.

The company danced the ballet well, and Mr. Eglevsky as Prince Siegfried was a model of simplicity, elegance, and sincerity.

Aleko, second on the bill, brought Miss Markova in the part of Zemphira, and she was as scintillating, impetuous, and exact as she had been in the winter. Massine danced Aleko with a handsome directness, and Laing as the Young Gypsy was excellent, as he has been from the first. The company rushed, flung their arms about, stopped dead, and were off again, as the choreography requires. The four gypsy men were particularly spirited. Their quartet succeeds in covering a number of less interesting moments in the action.

But the orchestra had some little trouble in this piece; no doubt the mistake in bringing on the last backdrop one scene too early was confusing to everyone. However, the dancers kept the show going, and in the end everybody came out together.

It was hard on Robert Lawrence, former dance critic of the *Herald Tribune* and guest conductor for these two ballets, to have so jinxed an evening for his farewell appearance before joining the Army. He evidently was trying his darnedest to make this last evening a memorable one. Theater life is full of pitfalls. Better luck next time, and good luck to him until then.

JUNE 26, 1943

BALLET THEATRE AND THE MONTE CARLO

The rivalry between our two major ballet companies is a stimulus to anyone's interest in them and to enterprise by their managements. At the moment, the Monte Carlo is the smaller company, with a publicity not quite so effective; one is perhaps inclined to judge it more leniently, from a natural sympathy with the underdog, and with the ulterior motive of saving Ballet Theatre from the disaster of becoming a stodgy monopoly.

The two companies, however, do make a slightly different general impression, with something to be said for each. Ballet Theatre—admirable even in its standard of performance—seems to pursue its goal of solid success with a grand air of complacency. The Monte Carlo is likely to look scatterbrained, temperamental, and quite good or quite bad. The Monte Carlo doesn't always have its costumes in order, but it shows now and then the keener sense of style in its dancing. Style is a quality different from accuracy, energy, or stage charm; it is a vivacious quality like dance rhythm. I regret that the sense of style is not cultivated more carefully in both ensembles, but the dancers in both companies are pleasant, gifted, and hardworking. In fact, considering how overworked and underpaid they all are, they are all amazingly good. The public is clearly grateful to them. It loves them, and so do I.

This is an overall impression of the ensemble as units. If one thinks of the individual members, there are incomparable dancers in each of the two companies. It would be foolish for a dance lover to miss seeing either Miss Danilova at the Monte Carlo or Miss Markova at Ballet Theatre. And Massine is at Ballet Theatre too. Ballet Theatre, as the larger ensemble, has a few more dancers of exceptional talent, but one sees passages of beautiful dancing on any evening at either company. Though there are some points one cannot be satisfied with, there is a great deal a ballet lover from any country will at once enjoy.

In point of repertory both companies try to keep a proper balance between the three periods: nineteenth century, Diaghilev, and contemporary. Unfortunately, despite the genius of Miss Markova, the Ballet Theatre company has not yet quite grasped the sincerity of nineteenth-century romanticism; it still shows an inclination to toy cutely with the "period" aspect of these masterpieces. On the other hand Ballet Theatre presents a much more comprehensive contemporary repertory, including at least one piece by almost all the choreographers around, and it has the monopoly of Tudor ballets. That is a real distinction. This last year, however, in point of novelties of merit the Monte Carlo came out ahead of Ballet Theatre, with three of them (*Chopin Concerto*, *Snow Maiden*, and *Rodeo*) to Ballet Theatre's two (*Aleko* and *Romeo and Juliet*).

Why both companies have passed up the chance of a Balanchine novelty—and especially the obvious plum of the season, a Balanchine version of Stravinsky's new *Danses Concertantes*—is a mystery. Ballet management in no other country would ignore a prestige attraction so easy to put on, so sure of being violently discussed—not to mention that the piece might well turn out to be an artistic event.

Nor has it occurred to either company to bring over an English or a Soviet choreographer to rehearse here a ballet already set over there, and so give us an interesting glimpse, at least, of what is being done in other centers of dance activity. It would be a stimulating experience as much for the companies as for the public. JUNE 27, 1943

MASSINE'S "CAPRICCIO ESPAGNOL"; DE MILLE'S "THREE VIRGINS"; "GISELLE"

Saturday night's performance of Ballet Theatre at the Lewisohn Stadium was a full success. The first two ballets (*Capriccio Espagnol* and *Three Virgins and a Devil*) have the boisterous qualities that register most easily in the open air. *Giselle*, the third ballet, is anything but boisterous. But the passionate precision of Miss Markova in the lead made its subtle values intelligible a block away. It was a startling experience to see so delicate, so intimate a piece appeal without effort to an audience of ten thousand. It was a triumph for Miss Markova as a theater artist.

Capriccio Espagnol in Massine and Argentinita's choreography is a lively arrangement of Spanish regional and Spanish gypsy dances. It does not try for the special strictness of real Spanish dancing. The steps are authentic, but the rush and swirl of movement is Massine's. Massine has the secret of the surefire number for a large ballet company, and *Capriccio* is a happy example. Massine himself appeared in the part of the Gypsy, a role he does more sharply than anyone else. Miss Kaye was his gypsy partner; her lightning turns, her hip shakes, her wrist movements in the air were vividly temperamental.

Three Virgins, Miss de Mille's little satire on virginal vanity, makes all of its jokes very clearly. The dances slip from old country dance forms into burlesque bumps and bits of lindy steps (Flying Charleston, Susy-Q, and Pecking). The meaning of the pantomime is unmistakable. The five dancers were all excellent; and particularly Miss Karnilova, in the longest part, proved herself a masterly dance comedian.

These two ballets are meant as light entertainment. But *Giselle*, which followed them, is a tragedy. It is a hundred-year-old classic in which the great dancer Carlotta Grisi conquered Paris in 1841. The theme was inspired by two romantic poets; the plot was fixed by a successful librettist; and the choreography, credited to Coralli, is probably largely due to one of the greatest of choreographers and classic dancers, Grisi's husband, Perrot. The ballet is still danced in Paris, London, and Leningrad. And all the great ballerinas of the past have appeared in it.

Though so brilliant a history may add to the prestige of a ballet, all this seems remote from Amsterdam Avenue, 1943. But it is not prestige, it is its quality that keeps *Giselle* alive. The story of the ballet has poetic reality. The dances are in a large, open style. They are not intended primarily as exhibitions of virtuosity; they are meant to tell a tragic story and create a mood. And the score of *Giselle*, by Adam, is direct and animated; the more closely one listens, the more one notices how carefully made it is. But above all *Giselle* gives a great ballerina a superb chance to captivate, to dazzle, and to touch the heart. *Giselle* is the Lady of the Camellias, the Violetta, of the dance.

Miss Markova succeeded in the role on Saturday as completely as she already had at the Metropolitan. She captivated, dazzled, and touched. In the mimed passages—for instance, the conventional gesture of madness, staring at the audience with hands pressed to frame the face—she is somehow thrillingly sincere. In the dance passages of the first act, she is gay and light with a sort of chaste abandon; in those of the second, she is partly unearthly, like a specter, partly gracious, like a tender memory. It is as hard to color correct academic dancing with emotion as it is to give emotional color to correct bel canto. Miss Markova makes it seem the most natural thing in the world.

One reason she succeeds is that one sees every detail of the movement so distinctly. The movement of other dancers is apt to look fuzzy or two-dimensional in comparison to hers, which looks three-dimensional. Only the greatest dancers have this so-to-speak stereoscopic distinctness. Markova also has a complete command of the impetus of dance movement. She hits the climax of a phrase—say, a pose on one toe, or a leap—without a trace of effort or excess drive. The leap, the pose, seems to sustain itself in the air of its own accord.

She does not strain either in movement or in theater projection. She is so straight upright, so secure, that she does not have to thrust her personality on the audience for an effect; the audience is happy to come to her. This makes her dance seem personal, intimate, even in the open air.

JUNE 28, 1943

TUDOR'S "GALA PERFORMANCE"

Ballet Theatre closed its four-day run at the Lewisohn Stadium last night with an attendance over eleven thousand. The numbers on the program showed ballet fashions over a fifty-year span. The grand exhibition style of St. Petersburg was rather poorly represented by *Princess Aurora*; the story ballet of before the First War by *Petrouchka* and *Spectre de la Rose*; and a contemporary satire by Tudor's *Gala Performance.*

Last night it was *Gala Performance* that was the liveliest to watch. Its first scene is an engaging picture of ballet dancers onstage before the curtain goes up. Though the dancers represent their predecessors of fifty years ago or more, the characters of dancers are still rather similar. This scene incidentally is notable for the distinction of its fluid composition.

The second scene makes an acid comment on the futility of ballet virtuosity, and for it Tudor invents a ballet style never seen elsewhere, but quite recognizable. The dancers preen, strain, and disarticulate themselves without a let-up. They seem delighted with themselves, but actually succeed in looking like some absurd race of insects.

All the performers danced the piece with contagious good humor. They were excellent in dance technique and theater technique. Particularly fine were Miss Kaye and Miss Golden. JUNE 28, 1943

ON COMMISSIONING NEW BALLET SCORES

One of the normal activities of a ballet company is the commissioning of new scores. It was Diaghilev who established this function of ballet, and the fact that he commissioned the score of *Petrouchka* is to many people his enduring monument. The general good will Diaghilev won for ballet by his musical policy is still of use to the present companies. For the musical public his continuous production of new scores proved that ballet is a normal part of the intellectual life of its time and place.

Over here, the smaller American ballet companies, the late Caravan especially, have done extremely well in commissioning new music by local composers. But the big companies, Ballet Theatre and Monte Carlo, have been far too remiss in this matter. In the case of Ballet Theatre, the only independent musical contribution I can recall is Brant's uninteresting score for *The Great American Goof* several seasons back. The Monte Carlo can be praised at least for last winter's one new American score, Aaron Copland's *Rodeo*. But I have not heard of any further commissions for next season.

There is no lack of local ballet composers who have already written successful ballets. All three of Copland's scores have been successful in the theater. Marc Blitzstein, Paul Bowles, Theodore Chanler, Carlos Chávez, Camargo Guarnieri, Walter Piston, Virgil Thomson are all reasonable choices for ballet commissions. And there are others. Not to mention that Milhaud is here now, too.

Such a lack of interest by the big companies in living musicians of some originality is very sad. They seem to have no curiosity about the intellectual life around them. It is perfectly proper for a ballet company to choose old music of contemporary interest for some new ballets. But there is something fossilized about a company that cannot go out and buy itself a brand-new score or two every spring.

It is hardly a question of funds. Both companies find funds for handsome new productions set to existing scores. The six hundred dollars or so a commission costs (plus about three hundred for copying parts) is not a prohibitive extra charge. Nor does the public refuse to listen to new music. *Rodeo*, for example, was a phenomenal success all over the country; the Copland score evidently didn't discourage anyone from coming. And to go a little beyond the strict subject of new music, it struck me that during this last winter here in New York the general enthusiasm for anything approaching ballet "experiment" has been astonishing. The more novelty a ballet had in any respect, the more eagerly the public seemed to welcome its appearance. It was true of *Rodeo*, of *Apollo*, of *Romeo*, and even of *The Wanderer*.

This is one side of the argument: the public expects new scores, the composers available are adequate, and the financial risk appears to be slight. But even if the risk were greater, there is a necessity for ballet companies to experiment. They don't owe it to us, they owe it to themselves. The spirit of a company, the vitality of the dancers, begins to sag without an occasional contact with what is liveliest and boldest in the artistic activity around. Not that dancers understand intellectual values more sharply than other people. But they seem to require for their best efforts an occasional atmosphere of intense outside interest in the work they are producing. The reckless expenditure of spiritual energy by everyone concerned in it that goes with the making of a completely new, a so-to-speak disinterested work, revives them. It is so much fresh air in the ballet studio. And unless a management now and then considers this susceptibility on the part of its dancers, it will find itself with a dispirited, demoralized company on its hands, the public will lose interest, and our present active and healthy balletomania will pine away for lack of loving care.

JULY 4, 1943

TUDOR AND PANTOMIME

Many people who are disappointed to find little meaning in ballet dancing are struck by how much meaning the ballet figures in Tudor's *Pillar of Fire* and *Lilac Garden* convey to them. In *Lilac Garden*, for example, an about-to-be-abandoned mistress sees her lover standing alone, facing her at a distance. Desperately she rushes at top speed across the stage; she seems to leap straight onto his shoulder. He holds her tightly by the waist; she crouches there above his head, tensely arching her neck. He does not look up. The action is as sudden as the leap of a desperate cat on moving day. But the pose also brings up the sudden sense of a private physical intimacy. It has that meaning.

Again, in *Pillar of Fire*, a chaste and frenzied young woman sees a vigorous young man. He looks at her suggestively. She leaps at him though the air in grand jeté. He catches her in mid-leap in a split and she hangs against his chest as if her leap continued forever, her legs completely rigid, her body completely still. How is it one notices the momentary pose so distinctly?

It is partly because the stopped leap has a startling effect—like a fast tennis ball that goes dead. And the shock of the stop is heightened by the contrast to an onward full surge of the music. The timing, the placing of the pose, its contrast to the direction, the speed, the stopping and starting of the dance figures that went before—in brief, all the resources of what the cinema calls visual rhythm—have been used to direct the eye to this special instance of bodily contact. The attention is focused on the parts of the body, their relation to one another, the physical force involved in the leap and the lift, almost as if by a motion-picture close-up. And the moment so distinctly presented registers all the more, because it registers as a climax in the story, as a pantomime of a psychological shock.

One "reads" the climactic moments in these ballets in a pantomime sense because from the outset Tudor has emphasized the pantomime aspect of the dance. He begins with easily recognizable movements, gestures of greeting, of pushing back a strand of hair, of fiddling with clothes, of averting the glance, of walking or standing not as in a ballet but as in daily life. One's attention is caught by these gestures because they at once specify the characters of a story, the situation, the psychological tension. They are expertly stylized to fit the music and to form sequences of motion that please the eye. They combine smoothly with dance steps, and we unconsciously expect from the more complex dance figures that follow the same sort of narrative meaning, the pantomime exposition of story we have begun to look for. The two dance figures described above show how completely Tudor succeeds as a storyteller, using ballet images.

In fact, in these two ballets Tudor gives to the whole classic ballet system of movement a pantomime bias. He uses ballet technique to portray a particular attitude, an upper-class code of behavior. In *Lilac Garden* he purposely exaggerates the constraint of ballet carriage; the dancers dance rigidly, hastily, with dead arms—as beginners might. But the ballet constraint they show portrays the mental constraint of the characters in the story, who rigidly follow an upper-class convention of behavior. Artificial upper-class constraint is the theme and the pathos of *Lilac Garden*.

In *Pillar of Fire* Tudor goes further. He shows two different ballet styles: an improperly strained one that characterizes the anguished heroine, and a smooth, proper style for the nice untroubled neighboring boys and girls. In addition, both kinds of ballet are set against the nonballet dancing of the exciting lowlife crowd—they dance and whirl in a sort of wild rhumba style, swivel-hipped, explosive, and frenzied; while the calm hero, in contrast to everyone, comes on not as any kind of dancer, but walking across the stage as modestly as a Fuller Brush man. Tudor fuses these heterogeneous elements brilliantly, but the dance device I wish to call attention to is the use of ballet technique to describe a special kind of person, to represent a special habit of mind.

Tudor's meaning is admirably clear and his dramatic effects are intense. It is interesting, on the other hand, that the traditional ballet (whether of 1890 or 1940) tries for a radically different kind of meaning than that of pantomime description; it appeals to a different manner of seeing dancing and requires a different technical approach in the dancer.

JULY 11, 1943

ON MEANING IN DANCE

Any serious dance work has an element of pantomime and an element of straight dance, with one or the other predominant. When you think about it, it is curious in how different a way the two elements appeal to the intelligence, how differently they communicate a meaning.

Tudor's *Pillar of Fire* is a brilliant example of contemporary pantomime ballet. It is as absorbing to us as Fokine's *Schéhérazade* was to our parents in its 1910 version thirty years ago. The difference between the two is striking: *Schéhérazade* was bright and luscious, *Pillar of Fire* is gloomy and hot; Fokine hacked at his subject with a cleaver, Tudor dissects his with a scalpel. But—apart from the big orgy they each work up to—the two ballets both hold the attention by a continuous, clear story. Both belong to the tradition of the stylized drama, and not (as *Coppélia* and *Ballet Imperial* do) to the tradition of the dance entertainment. The pantomime ballet focuses the attention on stylized movement; the dance ballet, on a suite of dances.

What is a "stylized movement"? It is a movement that looks a little like dancing but more like nondancing. It is a movement derived from what people do when they are not dancing. It is a gesture from life deformed to suit music (music heard or imagined). The pleasure of watching it lies in guessing the action it was derived from, in guessing what it originally looked like, and then in savoring the "good taste" of the deformation.

Stylized movement has always been a perfectly legitimate pleasure in the theater. Sometimes it's merely a little quiz game thrown in for variety. In general, though, a stylized passage adds a pretty color to any dance. And stylization is one of the best recipes for a comic effect.

But in the pantomime ballet stylized movement is the main aspect of expression. It is what one looks at particularly, because it keeps making a serious dramatic point. Gesture by gesture, as if idea by idea, the drama is built up. The audience watches for each allusion in turn; it follows point by point. The interest becomes like that of a detective story. The audience peers eagerly, delighted to have caught on, anxious not to miss a clue. It solves harder and harder riddles. The storytelling gathers momentum; as in driving a car, it's the speed that is thrilling, not the incidental scenery. One is, so to speak, hypnotized by the future destination. One merely wants to know what happened, as in watching a motion picture.

On the other hand, a dance ballet (*Coppélia*, for example) has a very different kind of appeal. True, it also has a story and it has pantomime portions. But you don't take them seriously. The parts that show you the heart of the subject, that are the most expressive, are in the form of dance numbers, of dance suites. They are like arias in an opera. In a dance ballet the story is not a pressing one, and it can be delayed awhile for a lyric comment on the momentary situation. The audience has come to enjoy the dancing; it is in no hurry to get the heroine married or murdered and to be sent out of the theater again.

In a dance ballet there is a difference in the way the audience watches the movement. It does not identify the gestures with reference to real life; it does not search in each pose for a distinct descriptive allusion. It watches the movements in sequence as a dance. There is a sort of suspension in judgment, a wait and a wonder till the dance is completed, till the dancer has come to rest. When the dance is over one understands it as a whole; one understands the quality of the dancer's activity, the quality of her rest, and in the play between the two lies the meaning of the dance aria, the comment it has made on the theme of the ballet. One has understood the dance as one does a melody—as a continuity that began and ended. It is a nonverbal meaning, like the meaning of music.

The dancer in pantomime emphasizes what each of the gestures looks like, he appeals pictorially to intellectual concepts. The dancer in a dance number emphasizes the kinetic transformation, his dance is a continuity which moves away from one equilibrium and returns to another. Repose is as important to the meaning of a dance ballet as activity. But in pantomime a stop must be made to look active and pressing, it must keep the urgency of the history. This difference leads the dancer to a different emphasis in technique.

JULY 18, 1943

BALLET TECHNIQUE

When they watch a ballet in the theater some people can take ballet technique for granted as easily as school kids take the technique of basketball for granted while they watch a lively game in a gym. These ballet lovers see the dance impulses perfectly clearly.

Other people, however, are bothered by the technique. They watch the gestures without feeling the continuity of the dance; the technique seems to keep getting in the way of it. Ballet looks to them chiefly like a mannerism in holding the arms and legs, and in keeping the back stiff as a ramrod. They can see it must be difficult to move about in that way, but why try in the first place? Annoyed at the enthusiasm of their neighbors in the theater, they come to the conclusion that ballet technique is a snobbish fad, the perverse invention of some dead and forgotten foreign aesthetic dictator who insisted on making dancing as unnatural as possible.

But ballet technique isn't as unreasonable as that. Just as a dazzling technique in pitching, for instance, is an intelligent refinement of throwing a ball for fun (which everybody does somehow), so ballet technique is a refinement of social dancing and folk dancing, a simple enough thing that everybody has tried doing for fun in his own neighborhood. You know the main technical problem of dancing the first time you try; it's to move boldly without falling flat on the dance floor. You have to get the knack of shifting your weight in a peculiar way. Next you try to keep in rhythm, and then you try to give the conventional steps that extra personal dash which makes the dance come off. It's a question, of course, of doing all this jointly with others, sometimes in groups, sometimes in couples—when a little sex pantomime may be added, by common consent all over the world. And incidental acrobatic feats are welcome if they don't break up the dancers' happy sense of a collective rhythm.

Exhibition dance technique is a way of doing the same things for the pleasure of the neighbors who gather to watch. You see the simple elements of common dance technique refined and specialized, with a particular emphasis placed on one element or another. In recent generations we have seen our own normal folk and social dances evolve into professional tap dancing, into exhibition ballroom, and most recently into exhibition lindy.

Like these recent dance techniques, ballet, too, is the result of practical experiments by a number of exhibition dancers—a long line of professionals which in the case of ballet began in the seventeenth century and has not yet ended. The ballet dancers seem to have taken as their point of emphasis not the small specialty tricks but the first great problem everybody has in dancing—the trouble of keeping in balance. The problem might be described as that of a variable force (the dance impulses) applied to a constant weight (the body). The ballet technicians wanted to find as many ways as possible of changing the impetus of the movement without losing control of the momentum of the body. When a dancer is not sure of his momentum he is like a driver who has no rhythm in driving, who jolts you, who either spurts or dawdles and makes you nervous. Watching a dancer whose momentum is under control, you appreciate the change in impetus as an expression. You follow the dance with pleasure, because the dancer has your confidence.

The foot, leg, arm, and trunk positions of ballet, the way it distributes the energy in the body (holding back most of it in the waist and diminishing it from there as from a center)—this is a method of keeping the urgency of the movement in relation to a center of gravity in the body. The peculiar look of ballet movement is not the perverse invention of some dead aesthetic dictator. It is a reasonable method which is still being elaborated by experiment. On the basis of a common technical experience—that of equilibrium in motion—this method tries to make the changes of impulse in movement as distinctly intelligible as possible. There have always been great dancers who danced in other techniques than that of ballet. But there have always been great dancers, too, who found in ballet technique an extraordinary range of clear expression.

JULY 25, 1943

THE DANCE IN FILM

Pavlova enthusiasts will go on a pilgrimage to the Modern Museum this week to see the film of Pavlova dancing, which is being shown there in a program called "The Dance in Film (1909–36)." The Pavlova reel is a record of portions of six dances; it was made privately by Douglas Fairbanks in Hollywood in 1927, and it is probably the best film of Pavlova that exists. It will touch those who can remember her glamour on the stage. But without the help of memory it does not re-create the legendary

Pavlova effect. I think you can get a better suggestion of the effect the great dancer produced from some of the still photographs of her, especially the early ones (taken around 1910) from St. Petersburg.

Dance students, however, will be grateful that the film exists and is accessible. In itself it is plain and straight. It records several aspects of Pavlova's technique in motion, and to the student this is of great interest. He sees how firm her attack was for all the delicacy of her manner; he sees her clear control of speed, her ability to pause, her wide, simple arm gestures, her extremely rapid pas de bourrée—which the camera can't keep up with. And the student notes that she was not as strong or correct in the thighs and knees as in the ankles and feet and that she could overdo facial miming—details which her contemporaries criticized and which evidently did not detract from her effect on the stage.

The other items on the Modern Museum program are of varying interest. Incredibly absurd is a film from 1913 showing the celebrated Moscow ballerina Geltzer doing a fake Fokine Greek-tunic number. She is supported by a stout, mustachioed premier danseur, who observes her in ecstasies of rapture; what is disconcerting is that he looks like a respectable middle-aged bartender gone mad and doing ballet with a diaper over his tights. Another film shows Rudolph Valentino in a "passionate" Argentine tango, dancing it with an innocent sultriness that is very winning. There is also a Charleston by Joan Crawford, an Astaire trick dance with chorus, and the famous Disney *Skeleton Dance.*

Dance expression and dance recording are two separate functions in the cinema that rarely coincide. The motion picture is the only means of accurately recording dancing, but dance lovers are aware of how rarely it projects anything like the dance quality one knows from the theater. When we watch dancing anywhere, the more distinctly we can see the plastic quality—the three-dimensional quality—of the movement, the more clearly we feel the point of the dance. But the camera gives a poor illusion of volume; it makes a distortion of foreshortening and perspective, and it is plastic only at short range. A further trouble is the camera's narrow angle of vision. A dance on the stage becomes clearer by the relation of the movement to the architectural space around it—that is, to the permanent stage space and permanent stage frame in which the dance moves back and forth and right and left. Theater choreography is movement suited to a whole, fixed area. But the film cannot show the whole stage and also show the dancer large enough so we can see just what she is doing. When the camera moves up to her the stage frame is lost; when the camera follows her she seems to be flailing about without making any appreciable headway—she bobs around against a swirling, fantastically liquid background. Altogether, when a stage dance has been photographed from various distances and angles and the film assembled, the effect of the dance is about like the effect of playing a symphony for the radio but shifting the microphone arbitrarily from one instrument to another all the time. Listening at home, you can hear the noise all right, but the symphony doesn't make any sense that way.

When you watch the film version of a ballet intended for the stage, why should good dancers so often look unnatural in a way they don't in the theater? Well, for one thing, you watch a dancer on the cinema screen as you would if she were dancing for you in a living room. You see her close by, at a distance ranging from two to twenty feet. In the theater she makes her big effects across a distance of a hundred or three hundred feet. What looks expressive away on the stage looks absurdly overemphatic near at hand. The hard thrust with which a stage dancer attacks a movement, the spread-wide openness of gesture which is eloquent in the theater, the violent speed at which a dancer can cover a large stage space—these phases of dancing are effective only at a distance. They are proportioned to a large space and not to a small one; so is the physical effort involved in doing them, which looks unreasonable and unattractive at close quarters. (Even in the theater many people are disappointed when they watch a great dancer from the first row; they are embarrassed to see her work so hard.) In short, the present manner of filming a dancer close by puts her into an intimate relation to the audience; she is therefore restricted to intimate effects and cannot use the full dynamic range of serious theater dancing. She is most successful when she looks not like a dancer at work, but like a nondancer who incidentally does some winsome steps and when in expression she restricts herself to understatement.

A dance style like Astaire's, which makes a fine art of understatement, is for this reason the immediately effective style in a film. It looks natural a few feet away. It does so not merely for the psychological reason that tap dancing is what we think of as a natural way of dancing in this country, but much more because tap dancing lends itself technically to an exquisite salon style. The dynamic range is narrow but sharply differentiated; the dramatic miming is barely indicated but perfectly intelligible; the presentation is intimately charming; and the dance itself rarely needs much room. A complete dance phrase can generally be photographed close by in a single camera field, and the continuity to the following phrase is generally so casual that a shift in the camera between phrases does not interrupt very much. These are the technical advantages which allow Astaire—who is certainly a great dancer—to give a more complete sense of dance expression on the screen than good dancers in other styles can. But there are indications that dance expression of a less miniature sort may also be possible in films. In Chaplin's early pictures there were often dance numbers that were not salon pieces—such as his own acts on roller skates, as a boxing referee, as a drunk, or "choral movements" like those of the crowds in *The Cop*. The film technique of the day was not so obsessed with intimate nearness, and Chaplin often performed a full dance sequence in a single camera field, giving the complete continuity.

In the present film technique Disney's animals have been more successful than human dancers in giving a wide range of dance expression to movement; and Disney often composed the dance to fit the field, as a choreographer does for the stage. Balanchine (in *The Goldwyn Follies*) tried composing serious ballet dancing to fit the successive camera fields (and camera angles). And this procedure is the sensible approach to making dancing in the cinema more than a mere recording or more than an amiable incident; it is an approach that might make film dancing as variously expressive on the screen as theater dancing has become on the stage.

AUGUST 1 AND 8, 1943

BALANCHINE AND DE MILLE ON BROADWAY

Balanchine's dances for *The Merry Widow* are strikingly effective and they are also completely unlike the conventional musical comedy dancing. In the embassy scene, a houseman and a maid start a witty polka quite casually and they end it with no bid for applause. The Broadway style would have brought on the ballet ensemble at this point and built the number to a smash finish; it would, of course, have spoiled the light touch the incident now has. In the second act, too, the "Marsovian folk dance" could have finished with stamps, snappy turns, and tosses of the head; the brassiness of such a number would have won applause but it would have killed the sentiment of the scene and of the "Vilia" song that follows. Broadway tries for overemphasis, and Balanchine has avoided it. He has made the dance modest and unpretentious. Even the big ballet number doesn't try to impress you, doesn't try for a hand. It has no special acrobatics; the figures are extremely simple; its variety is in speed and attack. But the cumulative crepuscular swirl of it, danced in strange lighting effects, creates a real and a mysterious fascination.

Broadway dance routines all tend to look like a metronomic drill. But none of the *Merry Widow* dances do. They are not built for the stylized precision that the Rockettes excel at. The *Merry Widow* routines are easy for ballet dancers, so easy the dancers can do them with freedom. And so these dances get a spontaneity of movement that comes as a shock in the theater. In fact, in the can-can number at Maxim's the spontaneity of the girls gives the can-can a Parisian sting no stage can-can has had for many a year. The casualness of it is highly provocative and personal. Now casualness and spontaneity in dancing are hardly ever found together in Broadway ensembles, at least outside of colored shows. It is a shame that so happy a combination should be so rare.

To be sure, such an illusion of ease, such simplicity in refinement, is only possible with very finished dancers. Those in *The Merry Widow* are excellent. The soloists have all been soloists in the Monte Carlo company. Balletgoers already know the intelligent comedy of Miss Roudenko and Mr. Starbuck, the striking loveliness of Miss Mladova, and the Aubrey Beardsley poise of Mr. Volkoff. Altogether the effect of the little ballet is one of greater elegance than I have ever seen in musical comedy dancing anywhere.

It is interesting that the other great popular dance success on Broadway—Miss de Mille's ballet for *Oklahoma!*—is also completely unlike the usual show dancing. Miss de Mille's dances, too, emerge unpretentiously from the action of the play, they heighten the sentiment of it, they have a sincere point to make. *Oklahoma!* is about our modest Western way of life, the emotion and the myth of it. It is a subject we all cherish and believe in, like an image of home. When the audience recognizes the local flavor of Miss de Mille's dances, it is not just a cheery matter of some folk-dance steps. It is a way of moving that looks plain and open, and Miss de Mille seems to come closer to the secret of our common movement than other native dancers have. What is effective about the *Oklahoma!* dances is the overall sense of being in this country. In the detail of it, the most touching part to this reviewer is the brief adagio duet at the beginning of the dream ballet, where the heroine is held high by the hero and is poised outstretched on his shoulders, as if she were in a dream of flying with him through the air.

The excellent dancers in *Oklahoma!* have been praised before in this column by Mr. Lawrence; they also are former Russian Ballet soloists—with the exception of Erick Hawkins (who at the moment takes the part of Mr. Kostenko), who is usually Martha Graham's partner. It goes to show that if a dance is to be expressive, it requires dancers who have learned not only technique but also serious dramatic expression.

AUGUST 15, 1943

CONCERT DANCERS IN NIGHTCLUBS

Charles Weidman, Florence Lessing, and Peter Hamilton, appearing as the featured trio at the Versailles, do unserious dancing, and do it intelligently. They dance with a rush, but a rush that is accurately modulated. The movement has an air of elegance that comes from serious training. The arrangements (choreography is too solemn a word) are clear and proper, the performers look like intelligent people dancing, and the jokes they make are mild and come naturally. For instance, their Hindu number (Singhalese, to be exact) is so lively it slips into a jitterbug step and out again without losing its Oriental deadpan expression. Mr. Weidman paces about beating intently on two finger drums tied to his belt, like a frenzied Fifth Avenue bus conductor. Peter Hamilton leaps high, and Miss Lessing smirks complacently—Hindu style—through this New York hullabaloo. The number makes no pretensions, but it has the grace of freshness (and that in a genre—the travesty Hindu—that has become the standard bore of nightclub programs). Altogether, the nightclub work of these three serious dancers has the charm of personal good manners, a quality one is particularly grateful for in a café atmosphere.

Another concert dancer, a discovery of last season, Miss Pearl Primus, is appearing at Café Society Downtown. She does serious dances, including some Josh White "blues" accompanied by Josh White in person; but her serious style is not inappropriate to this slightly earnest club. She is an unusual dancer and deserves her quick celebrity. All her movement has a native Negro quality—an unction and a spring—that is a great pleasure to watch. In schooling she is a straight "modern"; but the personal simplicity of her dances and her clear sense of drama and climax make her numbers easy for any audience to follow. For her best effect she needs a good deal more room than she has on the floor of Café Society, but at least she couldn't find a more attentive nightclub public.

A complete disappointment to this department are the Horton Dancers, a modern group from Los Angeles, three couples of which dance at the Folies Bergères. From the numbers they show, it is impossible to guess what their reputation is based on. The floor show has, however, an interesting Chinese contortionist (or control dancer), Miss Lowe. She does her dreadful feats not only with charm, but also with a certain intellectual distinction. She phrases her numbers coherently, like a dancer, beginning each new sequence with a clear-cut dynamic impulse, which she sustains through her contortions till she lets it subside at the close of the phrase.

Rosario and Antonio, the Spanish gypsy team who are in *Sons o' Fun*, are now appearing in the Havana-Madrid too. They are young, attractive, full of magnificent fire, the darlings of the audience. Together, as a flamenco pair, they are unapproached in this country. The program I saw was not straight flamenco, however. It consisted of concert versions of gypsy and Andalusian dances (one of them adapted from Massine's duet in *Capriccio Espagnol*). Antonio's tough gypsy flamboyance has a roughness of finish that is not in proper concert style. On the other hand, these two young people throw themselves into any step they do with a sincere and passionate abandon that is extraordinary, that looks like the actual lifeblood of dancing.

At the Havana-Madrid you also see some expert, elaborately shuffled rhumbas done by the customers, in particular by a sailor the night I was there. And the little showgirls have a gaily irreverent way of doing their foolish little drills—in contrast to the pious Ziegfeldian ritualism that is de rigueur for the longer girls who decorate the establishments with higher ceilings.

AUGUST 29, 1943

ICE-CAPADES FOR WAR BONDS

The 1944 Ice-Capades, which celebrated its world premiere last night at Madison Square Garden, is, like its predecessors, a charming, well-paced, $200,000 Hollywood-style extravaganza that can pride itself on its good manners. The Garden was packed and the audience was perfectly happy.

The new Ice-Capades was a smash hit in another way, too: its world premiere was also a war bond rally, and the evening topped the goal of $5,000,000, bringing in $6,025,994.

Chester Hale, who staged the production and the dances, has again succeeded in bringing variety of all kinds into the show. It opens and closes with military numbers, the first of these being dedicated to the Marines. Sergeant Frank French had the lucky task of drilling the highly personable chorus of the Ice-Ca"pets" in close-order work and manual of arms. It looks a little different when they do it from what it would be otherwise—what with spangles, smiles, and skates—and makes a very fetching introduction to the evening.

Then came in quick succession a comic number, a jitterbug trio, and an adagio team. Miss Bohland in the adagio number had a firm finish in her poses that was fine. Marilyn Quinn, in the "Junior Miss" number following, has a fiery temperament and makes leaps of extraordinary swiftness. All of a sudden the ice is full of cowgirls on horseback—the lively Ice-Ca"pets" again—in a "Ro-Day-O Daze." One of them got a special hand when her mount fell (unintentionally) on the ice; she picked it up and, like a good horsewoman, patted it on its wooden neck.

Into the rodeo comes a "Laria-trix" named Trixie, a very pretty girl who—believe it or not—can do a number of the great Rastelli's feats and do them on skates. Let us hope nobody is going to learn to skate a tightrope. Trixie deserved the big hand she got.

This and more leads into the big first-act finale, a Tahitian-Hawaiian fantasy where the featured stars of the show appear, Donna Atwood and Jamie Lawrence. Donna has a youthful suavity, a sort of easy, sweet way of doing everything she does that is most attractive. Then comes a moment when the lights go dim and the audience all says "Ah!" It is a lovely moment, but I won't spoil it by telling you what happens.

There was, of course, plenty of breathtaking skating, especially by Robert Dench and Rosemarie Stewart, and by Jamie Lawrence in his handsome bombshell solo. But the characteristic of these Ice-Capades is that Hale has put the accent more on grace and natural bearing than on straight virtuosity. He has made it a friendly and altogether pleasant show. And the costumes, music, and lighting are all first-rate, as you would expect.

SEPTEMBER 15, 1943

KATHERINE DUNHAM

Katherine Dunham's tropical dance revue is a box-office hit; its run has been extended to six weeks, and that establishes it already as a unique success for an entire evening of dance entertainment. In addition Miss Dunham expects to add new numbers during the run, including one to a piece by Aaron Copland, written expressly for her; and a second edition is promised for the spring with musical additions by Duke Ellington and Ernesto Lecuona. But here I want to talk about the present show as though it were a dance recital, which, of course, strictly speaking, it isn't. Considering the evening as a recital, or as a revue, the central interest remains the same: Miss Dunham herself in her prize numbers—*Bahiana*, *Shore Excursion*, and *Barrelhouse*—which give us her impressions of three "hot" styles, the languid Brazilian, the tough, fast Cuban, and the strident Jungletown. She has observed these fashions of tropical entertainment intelligently, she knows what they are each after. Better still, she knows there is nothing arch about a hot style, that its expression is serious and sometimes even angry.

In composing these three numbers she tries to re-create an atmosphere, she does not try for choreographic or virtuoso values, or for abandon. Her dancing is representational; she acts her dance, so to speak. One admires her projection, her stage presence. She does not force herself on your attention, she allows herself to be seen. Her gestures are provocative and yet discreet and she can even keep a private modesty of her own. As a dance entertainer, she is a serious artist.

But she is also on view as choreographer of the evening. The Brazilian, plantation, and jazz numbers for her group are in the main lively and easy; and her company, which is strikingly spirited, handsome, and graceful, is very pretty to watch in them. She has, happily, avoided giving them arm and leg tensions which would be out of key with their pelvic litheness, but she has found a good deal of variety in her dance-hall material and she has made sequences which flow naturally. She has not been as fortunate in her own part in these groups; her passages are often too fast and too scattered for her to shine in them, and in duets she does not make the man's part strong enough for her to play up to. In general, however, the group numbers are effective when they are a playful representation of some actual dance. But when the subject is the abstract idea of a dance, and the gesture becomes stylized and strict, the piece is likely to wander off into pleasant decorative effects.

Miss Dunham's instinct for the decorative values of abstract dancing is good. Her handling of the dramatic values of abstract form is uncertain. This uncertainty shows most clearly in her most serious numbers, the stylized rituals of fertility, male puberty, and death, which fall very short of their dramatic intention. Their failure is also complicated by a confusion of technical procedures. The movement is based on African dance elements but the choreographic plan is that of the American modern school. The latter (like any Western art dancing) gets major effects from many kinds of displacement within the stage area, and out of sharply varied gesture. In African dancing, on the contrary, displacement values are of minor importance, individual variations are permissible, and gesture gets its value by plain reiteration. To reconcile two such different expressive methods is a big problem. It is a problem that faces all those racially conscious artists who insist on reconstructing a style whose creative impulse is foreign to their daily life.

Not that ritual emotion is in itself a theme foreign to a civilized person. The force of primitive ritual was successfully expressed in terms of ballet dancing, for instance, by Nijinska's *Noces*. But Miss Dunham does not set out to make the complete abstract contrasts between lightness and heaviness, between rest and motion, between movement closed in and movement wide open by which she could give dramatic meaning to nonrepresentational dancing. For in any technique of art the transport of faith can be represented by the distinctness of contrasts and their surprising reconciliation, as indeed ritual forces are represented in West African sculpture, which is the prime example in human art of the abstract intensity of volume contrasts. SEPTEMBER 26, 1943

ABOUT TOE DANCING

To a number of people ballet means toe dancing, that is what they come to see, and they suspect that a dancer only gets down off her "pointes" to give her poor feet a rest. But toe steps are not what ballet is about. They are just one of the devices of choreography, as the sharp hoots of a soprano are one of the devices of opera. Toe steps were invented, the historians say, "toward 1826" or "toward 1830." And the historians also explain that ballet during the century and more before the introduction of toe steps was quite as interesting to its audience as performances at the Metropolitan are nowadays to us. It was fully two hundred years ago that the audience enjoyed the difference between Mlle Camargo, that light, joyous, brilliant creature, and Mlle Sallé, the lovely, expressive, dramatic dancer. In 1740, too, the public was applauding with enthusiasm the plastic harmony of M. Dupré, "who danced more distinctly [*qui se dessinait mieux*] than anyone in the world." There was evidently plenty to watch before there were any toe steps. Still without toe steps choreography became so expressive that first Garrick and later Stendhal compared dance scenes they saw to scenes of Shakespeare. And long before toe steps Noverre's *Letters on Dancing* discussed the aesthetics of ballet so clearly that ever since ballet has been judged by the general standards of art, or has not been judged at all. You can see that toe steps are not the secret of ballet.

I do not mean that the feature of toe dancing is foreign to ballet—quite the contrary. As a matter of fact the principles of ballet technique—its gymnastic as well as its plastic principles—were accurately defined shortly before toe steps were invented, and their addition did not require any revision of the fundamental exercises or postures. Toe steps are an application of an older ballet device, the rigid stretch of knee, ankle, and instep to form a single straight line. During the eighteenth century this special expression of the leg was emphasized more and more, though used only when the leg was in the air. Finally a girl discovered she could put her whole weight on two legs and feet so stretched (as in an 1821 ballet print), and even support it on one; that became our modern toe step.

Perhaps toe technique was due to the exceptionally severe exercises to which the dancer Paul Taglioni subjected his brilliant daughter, Marie; certainly it was her expressive genius that made the trick a phenomenal one. But she was a great dancer before she did toe steps, and she had at least six and perhaps ten years of success behind her when the new fashion began. The uncertainty of history over the exact date suggests that these initial toe steps were far less precise than ours. In any case, in the 1830s other dancers besides Marie Taglioni learned them, though, done as they then were in a soft slipper darned across the toe every evening, they were often uncertain and dangerous. Now of course any student learns them painlessly and with no heartbreak at all.

But to do them expressively, as Taglioni, Grisi, and Elssler did, is still not common. Gautier, the poet-critic of a hundred years ago, described expressive "pointes" as "steel arrows plunging elastically against a marble floor." Unfortunately we have all seen dispirited performances of *Sylphides* where they have been merely a bumpy hobbling. Toe steps inherently have a secret that is not easy for either the dancer or the public: it is the extraordinary tautness of the completely straight leg-and-foot line which seems to alter the usual proportions of the body, not only the proportion of trunk and leg but also the relation of hard and soft. Dancing on and off the toes may be described in this sense as an expressive play of changing proportions.

But "pointes" have a psychological aspect, too. There is a sense of discomfort, even of cruelty in watching them, a value that often shocks sensitive persons when they fail to find in the emotion of the dance a vividness that would make this savage detail interesting. Well, from a psychological point of view, toe steps have here and there a curious link to the theme of a ballet. In *Giselle* they seem consistent with the shocking fascination of death that is the core of the drama; in *Swan Lake* they are a part of the cruel remoteness of the beloved; in *Noces* they hammer out a savage intoxication. Elsewhere, in scenes of intelligent irony, they can look petulant or particular, absurd or fashionable.

But it would be a complete mistake to tag toe steps in general with a "literary" meaning. Their justification is the shift in the dance, the contrast between taut and pliant motion, between unexpected and expected repose, between a poignantly prolonged line and a normal one. Toe steps also increase the speed and change the rhythm of some figures. On paper these formal aspects sound less dramatic than psychological ones; but they are what one actually sees on the stage, and out of them, seeing them distinctly, the better part of the dance emotion is made.

OCTOBER 3, 1943

HOW TO JUDGE A DANCER

When you watch ballet dancers dancing you are observing a young woman or a young man in fancy dress, and you like it if they look attractive, if they are well built and have what seems to be an open face. You notice the youthful spring in starting, the grace of carriage, the strength in stopping. You like it if they know what to do and where to go, if they can throw in a surprising trick or two, if they seem to be enjoying their part and are pleasantly sociable as performers. All this is proper juvenile charm, and it often gives a very sharp pleasure in watching dancers.

But you are ready too for other qualities besides charm. The audience soon notices if the dancer has unusual control over her movements, if what she is doing is unusually clear to the eye, if there are differences of emphasis and differences of urgency in her motion. Within single slow movements or within a sequence you enjoy seeing the continuity of an impulse and the culmination of a phrase. Now you are not only watching a charming dancer, she is also showing you a dance.

When she shows you a dance, she is showing how the steps are related, that they are coherent and make some sense. You can see that they make some sense in relation to the music or in relation to the story; and now and then the dancer shows you they make sense also as dance phrases purely and simply. You may notice that a dance phrase holds together by its rhythm in time (a rhythm related to that of music), as a sequence of long and short motions set off by a few accents. Again in other passages you may be most interested by the arrangements in space, motions that make up a rhythm of large and small, up and down, right and left, backward and forward. You watch dance figures that combine several directions, done by single dancers or by groups, in place or while covering distance. Such dance phrases are plastically interesting. But at still other moments you notice especially the changes in the dancer's energy, the dynamics of a sequence, which contrasts motion as taut or easy, active or passive, pressing or delaying, beginning or ending. Dynamics, space, and time—the dancer may call one or another to your attention, but actually she keeps these three strands of interest going all the time, for they are all simultaneously present in even the simplest dancing. But a dancer who can make the various factors clear at the proper passage so as to keep you interested in the progress of the dance is especially attractive because she is dancing intelligently. She makes even a complicated choreography distinct to see.

Intelligent dancing—which might as well be called correct dancing—has a certain dryness that appeals more to an experienced dance lover than to an inexperienced one. In any case, everyone in the audience becomes more attentive when he recognizes a personal impetus in an intelligent dancer's movement, when she has a way of looking not merely like a good dancer, but also different from others and like her own self.

Her motions look spontaneous, as if they suited her particular body, her personal impulses, as if they were being invented that very moment. This is originality in dancing—and quite different from originality in choreography. The original dancer vivifies the dance—plain or complicated, novel or otherwise—that the choreographer has set. She shows a gift like that of an actor who speaks his lines as if they were being uttered for the first time that very moment, though they have been in print a hundred years or though he has spoken them a hundred nights running.

Such vitality in dancing is not the same thing as that punch in projection sometimes called a "dynamic stage personality." A lively dancer does not push herself on the audience, except, of course, during curtain calls. Projection in serious dancing is a mild and steady force; the dancer who goes out to the audience with a bang cuts herself off from the rest of the stage action. Galvanic projection is a trick appropriate to revue, where there is no drama to interrupt. But in serious dancing the audience must be kept constantly aware of the complete action within the stage area, because the changes—and, therefore, the drama—of dancing are appreciated clearly in relation to that fixed three-dimensional frame. So the best dancers are careful to remain within what one may call the dance illusion, as an actor remains within the illusion of a dramatic action—when you cannot help imagining he is a young man speaking privately to a girl in a garden, though you see perfectly well he is middle-aged, that he is talking blank verse for you to hear and standing on a wooden floor.

And just as you become really absorbed at a play when Romeo is not only distinct and spontaneous but also makes you recognize the emotion of love, which has nothing to do with the actor personally or with acting in itself or with words in themselves, so the dancer becomes absorbing to watch when she makes you aware of emotions that are not make-believe at all. Some of my friends doubt that it is possible to give so much expressive power to dancing, though they grant it is possible to performers of music or of plays. To recognize poetic suggestion through dancing one has to be susceptible to poetic values and susceptible to dance values as well. But I find that a number of people are and that several dancers—for example, Miss Danilova and Miss Markova—are quite often able to give them the sense of an amplitude in meaning which is the token of emotion in art. I myself go to dancing looking for this pleasure, which is the pleasure of the grand style, and find a moment or two of satisfaction in the work of a dozen dancers or more. In these remarkable flights the choreographer may be admired even more than the dancer, but here I am describing the merits of dancing only.

What I have said applies to any dance technique, and now that the ballet season is opening, it is a simple matter for anyone to go to the Metropolitan and check for himself the accuracy of it or the mistakes.

OCTOBER 10, 1943

MASSINE'S "MADEMOISELLE ANGOT"

Ballet Theatre opened its four-week season at the Metropolitan Opera House last night to a packed and very friendly house. It presented three old pieces and a world premiere, Massine's *Mademoiselle Angot.* The last-named isn't much of a piece, but the audience took it in its stride, delighted to have ballet back in New York, and looking forward hopefully to the next world premiere on Wednesday.

The program opened with *Capriccio Espagnol*, with the standees packed together as in a rush-hour subway, and the orchestra-seat patrons mostly coming late. The ballet itself was remarkable for two reasons. First, the difficulty the orchestra had playing this easy piece, a difficulty that placed the dancers at a considerable disadvantage. The second point of interest was the dancing of Alicia Alonso and Jerome Robbins in the gypsy parts, usually done by Nora Kaye and Massine. Both the young dancers were precise and spirited, Robbins in particular. They were much applauded.

The fine performance of the evening was the dancing of the second ballet, Tudor's well-known *Lilac Garden.* It is a psychological story ballet, and tells how on the eve of marriage a man and a woman meet their previous lovers for a last time at a formal garden party, where the guests observe them. The drama is in their reluctant acceptance of the coming separation and in their consciousness of being observed.

The piece was danced with an unusual smoothness and reticence. The orchestra and in particular the unnamed solo violinist were excellent. Miss Karnilova, taking one of the major parts for the first time, seemed in contrast to the others a little angular, but the piece as a whole was very moving and showed Ballet Theatre at its best.

Then came the novelty, *Mademoiselle Angot.* As dancing it is a constant jumping about, fluttering of dresses and arms and legs that has no cumulative effect. The plot is adapted from Lecocq's famous operetta *La Fille de Madame Angot*, but it has kept neither the amusing social contrasts of the original story nor the characterization of the heroine as consciously and deceptively demure.

The plot of Massine's ballet disappears in fact under a load of separate dance numbers that have neither logical connection nor dramatic destination, nor even any very clear form as dance.

What remains is the appearance of the four leading dancers in the ballet, Massine himself, the Misses Kaye and Hightower, and André Eglevsky. As balletgoers know, they are all four dancers of the highest quality, but they have a hard time being interesting in the superactivity they are supposed to execute. Miss Kaye comes off best, dancing the role of the soubrette with a sharpness of outline in her high speed that has distinction. Massine resorts to heavy "funny" actions, Miss Hightower is unhappy every time she is lifted, and Eglevsky dances his prestos correctly but with little glamour.

Simon Semenoff has the best part, as a fat comic. His minuet with Miss Hightower in the second scene is the one really funny moment in what should have been a comedy.

The décor by Doboujinsky is attractive, old-fashioned, and the work of a perfectly good painter. It is very good in the beginning of the third scene, where the colors of the costumes and those of the backdrop make a handsome contrast.

Lecocq's music would probably sound better if it had been left in its original light orchestration. Mr. Mohaupt has done the usual thickening required by Hollywood and radio standards, but it takes the animation right out of the notes, as much as if they had grown middle-aged and corpulent.

OCTOBER 11, 1943

TUDOR'S "PILLAR OF FIRE"; DOLIN'S "PAS DE QUATRE"

Ballet Theatre at last night's performance at the Metropolitan Opera House featured two contemporary ballets (made in America) which are both of real interest though they are very different indeed in their manner.

Pillar of Fire, Tudor's much-admired psychological study of sexual repression in a young woman of the middle classes, was the first. Dolin's *Pas de Quatre*, with Markova in one of her comic roles, was the other.

In *Pillar of Fire*, Tudor combines ballet technique—its high carriage, taut legs, toe steps, and wide-open arm movements—with nonballet dancing—swivel hips, leaps with bent legs and knees not turned out, arms thrust out violently. He combines both of these with naturalistic gestures—bowing, lifting a chin in disdain, passing the hand across the forehead, or ordinary walking.

These different styles are so sharply defined for the eye of the audience by their timing in the phrase where they appear that one cannot help feeling the differences of physical tension which shape them. And one instinctively translates these shifting and contrasting tensions into psychological meanings. Their succession forms a psychological narrative that is clear, intense, and highly dramatic.

Pillar of Fire was given a very fine performance by the Ballet Theatre company. Miss Kaye and Mr. Laing in the leading parts had in the first scene especially a spontaneity, an abandon in their dancing that I had never seen before. Miss Reed, taking Annabelle Lyon's part of the Youngest Sister, was excellent; in her characterization the role is less ingenuous, but it is convincing. Miss Chase was perfect; this is indeed her best role in the repertory. Mr. Tudor was excellent, as usual.

Pas de Quatre, on the other hand, is a joke on Victorian ballet. Four great historic dancers of the 1840s dance a foursome, each has a tiny solo, all exhibit their proficiency and their graciousness. Miss Hightower impersonates a majestic Grahn, Miss Alonso a lively and spirited Grisi, Miss Reed is a simple and fresh Cerrito.

But it is Miss Markova in the part of the greatest of the four, Marie Taglioni, the Sylph, who brings this little academic joke to life. She not only dances the steps with incredible "correctness," and with the lightness that the greatest dancers alone achieve, she accentuates the "dying grace" of her slow phrases, the sharpness of her attack in a presto, the angle of the head on the neck or of the spine on the hips, just far enough so that the "style" becomes ridiculous without losing its perfection. It is a masterpiece of dance wit, a joke that has only the gentlest sting.

OCTOBER 13, 1943

LICHINE'S "FAIR AT SOROCHINSK"

Fair at Sorochinsk, a ballet on a Ukrainian folk theme by David Lichine, was given its world premiere last night by Ballet Theatre at the Metropolitan Opera House, and it was an event worthy of a great ballet company. Again and again in the course of the ballet there are choreographic inventions that reveal an originality of the first class. Lichine's gift as a choreographer is vigorous, and it is different in quality from any other choreographer's in the country.

The plot of *Fair at Sorochinsk* is not that of the Mussorgsky opera, though some of the characters are the same, since the ballet too is based on Gogol's stories about his own birthplace. In the ballet, a witch who is intimate with Red Coat, the Devil of the Ukraine, tries to thwart the true love of her beautiful stepdaughter and a handsome village boy. The Devil and the witch succeed in luring the boy and girl as well as many other villagers to a witches' sabbath; but the innocence of the lovers preserves them at least from harm.

The ballet opens with a half-pantomime, half-dance scene at the witches' inn, then moves to a scene at the fair, where after some Russian-fair pantomime there are two big folk-dance scenes; then comes the "Night on Bald Mountain" scene, with dances of witches and bedeviled villagers; and last is a quiet ending with almost no movement at all.

The general dance style of the piece is in Ukrainian or Cossack folk steps, heightened and varied for the stage. The group figures, however, the massing or thinning out of movement, the dead pauses and sudden rushes are where the choreographer's instinct for dance form shows itself brilliantly. These folk dances are not hackneyed ballet reproductions; they have an impact and a decision in their contrasts that is altogether Lichine's. It is the same instinct for vigorous dance dynamics that Lichine has shown in his own dancing.

There are also original details in the dancing. Dolin's Cossack toe steps and toe pirouettes (Dolin takes the part of the Devil and dances it with the greatest brilliance) are a happy invention and suit the part perfectly. Lichine has always shown a gift for direct characterization in dancing, and all his characters are defined not by mugging, but by dancing.

The performance by the entire company was brilliant. André Eglevsky was remarkable, Miss Banks and Miss Chase excellent.

The evening began with *Princess Aurora*, the dance suite drawn from the 1890 *Sleeping Beauty* of Petipa, to the exquisite Tchaikovsky score. Miss Markova in the title part gave a magnificent performance. She has added to her rendering those subtle back bends of the neck that intensify the plastic line of the body and that the great Russian ballerinas seem to have discovered. They give warmth to the severity of the pure classic line, and Markova does them to perfection.

OCTOBER 15, 1943

A CORRECTION

In yesterday's review of Ballet Theatre this reviewer praised particularly the execution of the part of the Princess in *Princess Aurora*, and he named Miss Markova as the dancer of it. It was, however, Miss Nora Kaye who took the part, and to whom the praise belongs; and the reviewer apologizes to the two dancers and to his readers for his mistake. Miss Kaye's performance was a notable one indeed, and in the purest classic grand manner.

OCTOBER 16, 1943

BACK TO THE "FAIR"

During the intermission of Ballet Theatre's matinee yesterday, the five golden tiers of the Metropolitan buzzed with children's conversations, and a little girl in the aisle downstairs, after gazing into the orchestra pit, couldn't quite keep her feet from trying a dance step.

The program began with Prokofiev's *Peter and the Wolf*, staged some years ago by Bolm. This reviewer finds that the steps that characterize the animals and people of the story are too often coy and conventional where one expects them to be fresh and true; to be sure, Disney has set an extremely high standard for dancing animal impersonations. I also miss in this ballet a dance climax; the various characterizing phrases remain fragmentary, instead of developing into a coherent lively dance form. The young audience, however, does not realize what it is missing, and enjoys what it gets. The performance itself was a very pleasant one. Rex Cooper, who as the Wolf has the best part, dances it expressively, and he did, among other things, a very neat backward roll. Miss Alonso was a charming Bird.

The matinee also brought the second performance of Lichine's new ballet, *Fair at Sorochinsk.* A second view of it confirmed this reporter's impression that Lichine's gift as a choreographer is a highly notable one. It is shown clearest in the Russian folk-dance scene ("At the Fair"), which has a dance impetus that is straightforward and surefire. Its effect is derived from the sharp shifts of the movement back and forth from soloists to ensemble, and from the shift of attention between slower choral arm movement and rapid solo leg-and-foot steps. But these shifts, large though they are, are so well placed for the eye that the continuity is kept and the climactic effect is inevitable.

Lichine's gift as shown in *Fair at Sorochinsk* is a gift for broad and rousing dance effects. There is clearly no great seriousness in his treatment of diabolic forces—they are not frightening. Clearly, too, the choreography is without the complex overtones we are accustomed to in our best choreographers. There is no psychological strain, there is no poignant tension in the conception of dance form. Lichine is not a poet-choreographer as Balanchine so pre-eminently is.

But the firm control of frank vigor which Lichine has—and he alone, it seems—is a quality to be highly admired. His good scenes are straight and impulsive dancing, with no apologies to what is fashionable. And the quiet lyric section at the end of the fair scene strikes me as being sincere and from the heart. OCTOBER 17, 1943

REGRETS ABOUT "MADEMOISELLE ANGOT"

The indulgent public applauds Massine's new ballet, *Mademoiselle Angot*, and this reviewer, though he does not care for the piece, is glad that the production promises to be no financial loss to the company. It is a pity, however, that so much effort and expense ($35,000, according to rumor) should have given no more positive result than one more piece that gets by. The materials out of which it is made are good ones. The music of Lecocq, though dry, is animated, of excellent workmanship, and easy to listen to. The décor by Doboujinsky is perhaps clumsy, but it has nevertheless more presence than many sets in current ballet repertory. The dancers are first-class and do whatever they do with enthusiasm. The trouble with *Mademoiselle Angot* is simply that for all its constant commotion it seems endless and pointless; the successive dances seem to flounder around without either a steady subject or any consecutive form.

The dancing might have expressed the plot of the operetta the ballet is based on, *La Fille de Madame Angot*. The latter has a solid plot—solid because it shows the character development of its heroine, as she comes in contact with a foolish but loving workman, a fascinating but unreliable intellectual, a self-important plutocrat, and a brilliant, temperamental demimondaine. The heroine begins as a bright slum girl educated in a good convent; she falls in love with the intellectual, goes to jail for him, is released by her rival, the influential demimondaine, is disillusioned about her first love, and ends by good-humoredly making fun of everyone and staying friends with everybody.

During the rehearsals of the original operetta the people around the theater had no faith in the piece at all. A seasoned pit musician said to Lecocq, "It's a good job, but there's not a laugh in it." On the first night the manager (who had skimped on the sets) was dumbfounded by the tremendous success. No one had realized during the rehearsals that the serious logic of the libretto gave warmth and humor and pathos to the comedy situations.

Massine, however, in adapting the piece has passed over the human drama of the characterizations. He has turned the people of the story into dance marionettes, and the plot becomes merely a peg to hang dances on. No character is ever surprised at the action, and none of them cares at all about anyone else on the stage. His heroine is as knowing at the beginning as at the end, and so you feel that in the end nothing has happened to her at all.

When the choreographer fails to individualize his dancing characters he gives up his chance for narrative interest and humor of situation. But in place of a story ballet, he can still make an amusing dance suite. Massine has made successful suites of this kind in *Capriccio Espagnol* and *Gaîté Parisienne*. This time, in *Mademoiselle Angot*, too many of the dance jokes—particularly the gags in Massine's own role—are in the most foolish ballet-boy-acting-cute manner, and the dance sequences give no sense of plan or climax. The line of movement is so blurred and cluttered with conflicting simultaneous dance figures that you don't know which place to look and your eye can't follow anything longer than a few seconds. What you see is a jerking, leaping, twisting, arm-waving running in and out, and if it stops, it stops in a pose that is pointlessly difficult and that sums up nothing.

A layman might answer to what I have said: "So what? It's just a show. Who cares?"

Well, there is no sense in thinking comedy ballet is just a sop to morons. Ballet has always had light pieces as well as heavy ones, and the light ones have often been of high quality—pieces that the audience can remember with affection. The oldest ballet still running (it dates from 1786) is a comedy ballet, so is the 1870 *Coppélia*, and two excellent recent ones are Lichine's *Graduation Ball* and de Mille's *Rodeo*. These ballets are all of them serious comedy—that is, they present a real situation in a humorous light.

Beside comedy ballet proper, there is room in the repertory for a sort of super stage show, a lively dance suite, a ballet equivalent of an ice show or a festival dance program. Such pieces generally take for an excuse an evocation of exotic places and periods, and their fake exoticism can be amusing too; but their theatrical virtue lies in the clarity and logic of the dance arrangements. They are not so much humorous as athletically buoyant. When a great dancer appears in them they can be very thrilling; and with competent dancers they are as attractive to people who enjoy dancing as a horse show is to people who like to watch horses.

Massine's reputation does not rest on the success or failure of one more novelty. It is merely a matter of regret that this year he has given us neither a good comedy nor an effective dance suite, two styles he has often been highly successful with before and no doubt will often be equally successful with in the future. OCTOBER 17, 1943

TUDOR'S "LILAC GARDEN"; LICHINE'S "HELEN OF TROY"

Saturday night's Ballet Theatre performance at the Metropolitan was brilliantly executed throughout. First came the new *Fair at Sorochinsk*, the choreography of which has been previously reviewed. Dolin, as the Devil of the Ukraine, danced his part (which, if I saw right, includes even two gargouillades) at astonishing speed. His toe steps—Caucasian style—make him look as if he were dancing on a claw. Eglevsky, in the part of young Gritzko, did a pirouette followed by a triple tour in the air as if it were the most natural thing in the world. His simplicity in the part is admirable.

The men in the piece do all the hardest varieties of those Russian dance steps done in a crouching position, and they do them with bravura and enthusiasm.

Second on the bill came *Lilac Garden* in an especially fine performance. The choreography in this case is full of carefully adjusted detail, rushes cut short, impulses constrained, half gestures, lightning lifts and reversals. The detail suits perfectly the story, and also the music's constantly shifting emotional stress; but it requires of the dancers the most meticulous control in execution. The entire cast in *Lilac Garden* danced not only so that every detail was defined, but with an impetuosity that was theatrically convincing. Miss Kaye and Laing in particular were thrilling to watch.

Interesting, too, is how different the two dancers make the characters they portray in *Lilac Garden* from those they do, for instance, in *Pillar of Fire*. It is to their credit as actors and equally to Tudor's as choreographer; but I point it out to balletgoers as a striking example of characterization by dancers.

The evening closed with David Lichine's *Helen of Troy*. The newspaper deadline usually prevents this reviewer from seeing the last ballet on the bill, and I had not seen the piece this season. In fact it happened that I had not seen it since the first performances here last spring, and so had missed the many changes that had been made in the dances and the stage business. Though I am way behind the other ballet fans, I should like to say that I was quite surprised Saturday night and that I found the piece in its present form sunny, civilized, and very enjoyable. The story is well told, the characters are clear, the jokes are amusing. The solos are pretty, and the love duets even have a little tenderness, so that the sweetness of Offenbach's humor is not—for once—wasted on a ballet.

The cast for *Helen* couldn't be better. Everyone on the stage deserves praise for the happy charm the piece has, and the audience loves them all. Jerome Robbins, as Mercury, has of course the most original part, and he does it beautifully. It is a part in straight American—real Third Avenue, in fact. One of the interesting things about it is that, where everyone else dances with a particular vivacity, he moves with an American deliberateness. The difference is as striking as it used to be in peace time abroad, when a stray American youth appeared in a bustling French street, and the slow rhythm of his walk gave the effect of a sovereign unconcern. So Robbins on the stage, by being very natural, looks different enough to be a god; and that a god should be just like someone you see any day on the street is a nice joke. OCTOBER 18, 1943

ARGENTINITA'S "PICTURES OF GOYA"; TUDOR'S "JUDGMENT OF PARIS"

Last night's performance of Ballet Theatre at the Metropolitan was—like that of the night before—full of verve, and the crowded house applauded the dancers in the friendliest spirit.

The program brought the second performance of Argentinita's new suite called *Pictures of Goya*, danced by herself; her sister, Pilar Lopez; and their two partners, José Greco and Manolo Vargas. It was a distinct hit with the audience.

At the first performance of the piece, I had found it too unclear in its phrasing to be effective as dancing, and it did not seem one of the successful creations of Argentinita. Last night it was danced with more precision and more expression and its effects—which are small ones—carried. Argentinita's Fandango is an interesting number, and the Jotas at the end by all four dancers are charming. The piece is not a very original one; it has neither the lambent grace of the Goya tapestries nor the exacerbation of his *Caprichos*; it is a modest and agreeable number.

Tudor's satiric *Judgment of Paris* followed on the program. Miss Reed danced Juno; Miss Karnilova, Venus; Miss Chase, Minerva; Tudor himself was the Customer; and Laing, the Waiter. This little picture of three ladies of the oldest profession trying despite their varicose veins and their boredom to stimulate the interest of a seedy and sodden customer is as elegant in its horrid detail as it is virulent in its humor. The dancers put across each of its points with phenomenal accuracy; and I am surprised that the audience seems to take it all as good clean fun. It's a ghastly little piece. OCTOBER 18, 1943

TUDOR'S "DIM LUSTRE"

Ballet Theatre presented at the Metropolitan last night the world premiere of *Dim Lustre*, a ballet by Antony Tudor, the brilliantly original choreographer of six other ballets in the company's repertory. *Dim Lustre* is weaker than any of the others, both in the inventiveness of the dance detail and in the general overall dramatic effect. It seems to me that the one real distinction it has is Tudor's name on the program and the incidental presence of Tudor, Nora Kaye, Rosella Hightower, and Hugh Laing on the stage.

The story of the piece, a "psychological episode," is that of a gentleman and a lady at a ball. As they dance among the other couples, a chance gesture, a perfume, a kiss reminds one or the other of what once happened—a shadow of memory that dims the real present for a few moments. It is the stream of consciousness technique in storytelling. In *Dim Lustre* each time the memory sets in the lights go out; when they come on again the hero or heroine is brought back to reality.

It struck me that there was little difference in rhythm or dance style between the world of reality and that of imagination. There was a slight change in the mood, two of the memories were a trifle tender, two were a trifle frustrated; but I didn't see that the characters had much to choose between dreams and facts. And at the end, though they seemed disconcerted for a moment by their memories, hero and heroine ended by dancing like everyone else at the party. This slight touch of bitterness, of accepting an unsatisfactory reality since it is expected of you, is, I imagine, the real theme of the ballet. For *Dim Lustre* Tudor has chosen as dance style something closer to exhibition ballroom dancing than to ballet. The dancing does not keep stopping in a pose as it does in other ballets of his; it is a continuous movement, reminiscent of *Lilac Garden*. Arm movements are of little interest. The dancing has an agitated rather than a sweeping effect; it looks heavy too.

The agitation is heightened by the empty loquacity of the score (R. Strauss's *Burleske*, an early piano concerto written previous to his conversion to Wagnerism). It is heightened, too, by the flat cartoon quality of the overloaded backdrop.

The dancers, however, especially the principals, dance as handsomely as one expects of them; Miss Kaye looks particularly lovely, and both Laing and Tudor are highly interesting as usual.

OCTOBER 21, 1943

"DIM LUSTRE" AND "ROMEO AND JULIET"

Ballet Theatre's program last night at the Metropolitan brought back into the repertory Tudor's beautiful *Romeo and Juliet* and followed it with the second performance of his new *Dim Lustre*.

Dim Lustre was played and danced not at presto (as on the opening) but this time at allegro. With the change of tempo the agitation that had puzzled me last time in view of the slightness of the dramatic accents had subsided, and the ballet made on me also the effect intended, that of a light, intelligent anecdote. Tudor's point is: Do memories of other flirtations make it easier to fall in love? Almost, but not quite. Even in the flurry of a ball, people are often a little troubled.

As dancing, the piece is not as rich in variety or as exact in placement as the serious Tudor piece; but there is no special need in this case. What the ballet has instead is an interesting attempt on Tudor's part to keep the dance more continuously in motion than he has previously tried. There is a slight lack of freshness in the ensembles, but the momentum carries through to the last very pretty pantomimic finish.

Miss Kaye and Miss Hightower, Mr. Laing, Mr. Tudor, and Mr. Kidd were all excellent and distinct, and Kaye and Laing particularly give wonderfully the sense of an inner life. The ballet was this time cordially applauded.

Romeo and Juliet seen again turns out to stand up extremely well as drama, notwithstanding its generally slow tempo. It is a touching ballet and a very curious one. In a sense, the dance is all recitative, or like a highly figured prose. It is in pantomime style. But so exact is the invention of the gesture, so varied is the timing of motion from figure to figure, as you look, and from one narrative detail to the next, that you have very clearly a sense of rhythmic strength. The rhythm envelops you in a spell.

The scenery and costumes for this ballet by Eugene Berman again astonished me by their poetic power. When the ballet occasionally lapses, the scenery still sings. And how it takes lighting effects.

Miss Kaye took the part of Juliet, so strikingly done last year by Miss Markova. It may seem strange for a reviewer who called Miss Kaye Miss Markova to speak of the difference between them. Miss Markova's phenomenal balance, her quickness in those movements of the body which are generally heaviest (movements of the thigh and hips) give her a lightness that is all her own. Her lightness made Juliet a creature of another sphere, and gave the ballet an extra dimension. Miss Kaye does the part—a very difficult one—very handsomely indeed; but one is not so convinced of Juliet's innocence of heart or of her unique spirit. Miss Kaye is beautiful, of course, and I thought her particularly fine in the bedroom scene.

Mr. Laing was a magnificent Romeo, as he had been before. Mr. Robbins was Mercutio (combining the part with that of Benvolio) and performed it with an excellent attack. Tudor's and Laing's deaths were especially fine.

OCTOBER 23, 1943

A BALLET THEATRE MATINEE

At Ballet Theatre's matinee Saturday—the matinees have a charming family atmosphere—the program consisted of *Swan Lake*, *Petrouchka*, and *Mademoiselle Angot*. The company dances for the children as excellently as it does at every other performance, and the afternoon was a pleasure to everyone.

Swan Lake had Rosella Hightower and André Eglevsky again in the leading parts. Eglevsky gives the part the sustained sincerity, as well as the quiet elegance, that it deserves; he expresses the poetry of his part and of the piece. It is perhaps a carping criticism to refer once more to the one blemish in his general style: the way he often breaks the line of arm and hand at the wrist, and so loses the expression the palm might have. Notwithstanding this, he is the best, because he is the most wholehearted, classic dancer we have.

Miss Hightower began her part with what seemed to me too much vehemence and haste. But the adagio duet was even better than last time, and the solos that followed were this time highly plastic—she made perfectly clear the very interesting three-dimensional values in these classic variations. Younger soloists in general do not seem quite limpid in the use of shoulder, upper backbone, and breastbone—in the use of the upper torso. But the present popularity of *Swan Lake* and *Aurora* will no doubt clarify for them (and perhaps for men dancers, too) this wonderful resource in dancing.

In *Petrouchka* Massine was in his best form, with that clarity and tautness of silhouette that he has the secret of, and with all his intense and very intelligent stage presence. Ensign David Nillo (on leave from the Merchant Marine) danced the Moor convincingly, and that has become rare; his dead pauses were fine, and so was the absence of any of that cuteness which so often spoils the part. Miss Chase began a trifle too amiably but at the end was very good. Miss Hightower made the Street Dancer shine.

Mademoiselle Angot—like the other novelties this year—looks much clearer now it has settled into running order. Though in the choreography one can still object to the overabundance of detail—much of it a little commonplace, all of it equally stressed, and all in the same inelastic rhythm—one sees some of Massine's better qualities as well. I was delighted that much of the ballet is perfectly good entertainment after all, and it gets across as that. OCTOBER 24, 1943

THE DE MILLE "TOUCH"

Miss de Mille's dances for *One Touch of Venus* shine by their good sense. Among our choreographers she has always had in particular that touch of nature that the title of the piece suggests. It is a striking virtue in musical comedy, where nature is the last thing you expect. Miss de Mille has not this time the chance for human warmth she had in *Oklahoma!*, but she certainly makes the most of what opportunity she has; and in *Venus* she again succeeds in touching the heart of the average audience through the dance numbers in a way no other musical comedy dance director can. The specialized dance lover, on the other hand, who naturally has special standards in the originality and the emotional interest he expects from dancing, will readily recognize in the course of these dances the intelligence of a fine choreographer.

Most interesting of the four numbers is the "Venus in Ozone Heights" ballet in the second act, which depicts what goes on in Venus's mind when she faces the possibility of becoming a suburban housewife. It begins lightly with children playing, they gradually get to be a nuisance, they grow up and start leading their own lives. The goddess remembers more and more distinctly the nymphs and fauns who do not change with time; and finally, with a last salute to human romance, she reassumes her divine majesty. Here at the end, when Mary Martin enters upstage, tall and remote, when she tosses with a quick, high gesture a handful of spangles as a blessing to the Aviator and his Girl, and then paces unperturbed across the luminous stage with a retinue of flying immortals, the dance reaches a clear statement of why a goddess is simply undomesticable—a statement that is vital to the plain story of *Venus*, and which is Miss de Mille's (and Miss Martin's) contribution.

The effect is a true one, and the change of mood from comic and intimate to remote and grand is convincing. It is achieved not so much by novel dance detail as by a change in the rhythm and a change in the bearing of the dancers. It is made possible by the fact that the entire dance is serious in the sense that the dancers represent an action; they do not—as musical comedy dancers generally do—exhibit their personal charm. They have a clear story to tell, and they tell it. And this successful change of mood gives (in *Venus* as in *Oklahoma!*) a direct dramatic life to Miss de Mille's ballet.

Among the other dance numbers "Forty Minutes for Lunch" is a new version of the city traffic theme that modern-dance groups used to like. But the topical introduction of the French sailor, the simple intelligibility of the action, and the absence of an overearnest straining make it a pleasant number, if not a novelty.

The prodigious success of Sono Osato as the star of the dance company is good news to her many admirers who know her in her former ballet roles, but it doesn't come as a surprise to them. In the first act she dances with a precise sharpness in every limb and a rhythmic punch that startles; she is a galvanic comedienne. In the second act, she then transforms herself into a glamorously alluring comic Nymph, who at the end is quite serious and beautiful.

The jitterbug number in the first act, arranged, I believe, by Lou Wills, Jr., for Miss Bond and himself, is a particularly original and happy one. The way they dance it, it stops the show too.

There is no doubt that the public loves any show Miss de Mille touches. And, personally, I look forward to the humanization of musical comedy, which her successes are bringing about, with the greatest enthusiasm.

OCTOBER 24, 1943

TCHAIKOVSKY AT BALLET THEATRE

Ballet Theatre presented at the Metropolitan last night *Swan Lake*, *Aleko*, and *Princess Aurora* on an all-Tchaikovsky program. Private Yurek Lazowski, who last year danced *Petrouchka*, the hero in *Russian Soldier*, Peter in *Peter and the Wolf*, the Devil in *Three Virgins and a Devil*, and many other leads, was in town on a pass, and appeared as one of the Young Boys in the third scene of *Aleko* and as one of the Three Ivans in *Aurora*. He danced with wonderful exuberance and precision, and it was a great pleasure to see him on the stage again.

Aleko was danced by the entire company with the fine enthusiasm they always give it. Miss Kaye as Zemphira is not the impetuous gypsy princess Miss Markova was in the part; she is instead a sensually avid girl. Markova's Zemphira when she was in love with Aleko was annoyed by the look the Young Gypsy gave her; then she found herself in love with him instead of Aleko. Miss Kaye wants Number One and Number Two both at once, right away. When Number Two makes scenes about it, she is just bored with him. Well, last night at least, I couldn't blame her for being bored with him. I thought the great Massine (who was Aleko) played his deep grief over Miss Kaye's faithlessness rather too much in the Ochi Chornaya style of emoting. But the performance rushed along and was enthusiastically applauded. Hugh Laing (the Young Gypsy) was, as usual, superb.

The costumes and the backdrops by Chagall I am eager to praise as highly as possible every time I see them. What a mastery of color, of perspective, of clothing; the horse in the sky on the last drop is sadder than anything that occurs on the stage. OCTOBER 29, 1943

"BILLY THE KID" AND ITS DANCE FAULTS

The ballet *Billy the Kid* is a peculiar piece. Any sensible person can point out its absurdities, yet sensible people like it. It bobs up year after year in one company or another, always in inadequate performance, but it keeps on the boards. It is not satisfactory while you look at it, it is obscure and pieced out awkwardly; but something of it stays with you, something original that it alone has. I find its flavor very different from that of *Rodeo*, our other serious American ballet. *Rodeo* is about the West as it is lived in; *Billy* is about the West as it is dreamed of, as it is imagined by boys playing in empty lots in the suburbs of our cities. And for this reason *Billy* is unreal in its local description, but real in its tragic play. An anthropologist would recognize it as an urban puberty ritual; I like it because there is somewhere in its folderol of stylization the sense that tragedy is natural, and this is, after all, the most interesting emotion that the theater can present.

Because *Billy* as a theater piece has a sense of the tragic, because the music is of the finest quality, and because *Billy* was frankly conceived as a serious artistic collaboration, I admire it sincerely. All the more because it was made around the corner and talks about things I know. Of course, if our big ballet companies could afford it, we should have, after all these years, more than merely two American ballets that are meant as a serious and touching image of the spirit. But till we get more such pieces we should at least pay attention to the two we have, watch and criticize and generally participate in their existence. Both ballets have naive faults of choppy, gesture-by-gesture pantomime; just the same, both of them, in their main overall expression, appeal to the imagination and get across a suggestion of reality to the audience. They are truer, in this respect, than many more adroit and more celebrated ballets.

Looking at the pantomime movements that Loring invented for *Billy*, I find them more interesting when they tend to be literal than when they tend to be symbolic. The storytelling gestures—those of the cowboys riding or strolling, the gun play, the sneaking up on the victim, Billy's turning away from his sweetheart or lying down—all this has more life as dancing than the gestures meant as "modern dance." The latter pound a beat, but often they don't add up to a dance rhythm.

The eye gets snagged on them, one at a time, as by sign language. In the "March," for instance, the energetic horizontal arm thrusts with open palms look as if our ballet dancers were mimicking "pushing back the frontier." The "Come on out West" gestures back to the electricians offstage, the praying, digging, running, housekeeping, ever westward, ever westward are meant as a frieze of history; but it is history like that shown us in the slick-paper ads.

The technical fault is that the gesture does not lead out into space and relate to the full dimensions of the stage; it only leads back into the dancer's figure. It makes the stage close in on the dancer, instead of showing him boldly taking possession. Only the double turns in the air at the end of the "March" give an effect of real vigor.

On the other hand, the "Street Scene" that follows is most interesting. The wandering individual floor patterns by not emphasizing a fixed place on the stage and the gestures by not emphasizing a climax in rhythm give the sense of unfenced spaces and of all the time in the world. Nothing could be more characteristically American or more original as a dance conception.

But it is the lack of emphatic grouping, of a compact center of attention, which makes the "Macabre Dance" a foolish letdown—much later on in the ballet. The center-stage ladderlike floor pattern of the "Gun Battle" just before has been so insistent that it would refresh the eye (and indicate a new scene) if there were a sudden focus on a new, completely different grouping off center. Instead, there is just a wavering lineup. (I wish, too, that the scene were danced straight as a naive celebration; the "macabre" element is mere la-dee-da. The steps themselves are all right.)

The halfhearted placing at this point blurs also the wandering scenes that follow. Then, just in time, the climax is saved by the interpolated waltz adagio, which is especially effective if the girl seems to spin out the distances of her dance from Billy's fixed position downstage right. Billy's death itself is excellent as a scene and very much in character, particularly if there is no nervousness in his movements, only wariness.

The character of Billy derives its interest not from his murders but from his attempts at human contact, contact with his mother, with his friend Garrett, the sheriff, and with his sweetheart. His feeling for them is reciprocated. When this is clear then the story of his solitary fate becomes tragic—really tragic because he never appeals to us for sympathy or considers himself wronged. He accepts his isolation and lives the life he has. Billy's real enemy is the plain crowd of frontiersmen, who being a crowd can ignore him and whom he ignores by an act of pride. Billy's friend, Garrett, is at ease in the crowd, but different from it; Billy and he are both individualists, but of opposite social types. I regret that the crucial dispute between the two—over a card game at night on the prairie—no longer expresses either their natural interest in one another or their profound difference. And I regret that in the crowd scene (Billy's first murder) Garrett does not—now that Lew Christensen no longer dances the role—remain distinct enough from the crowd either in the sustained smoothness of his movement or in his stage presence.

Often Loring's contrasts between relaxed American movement and jerky, accentuated, Massine-style gesture are effective, often they seem accidental. But there is no doubt that Loring was the first to bring this different quality in movement into a ballet. It is this that gives *Billy* its core of dance sincerity, its fascination. And its further tragic implications, though obscure and hesitant, are perfectly real if you look closely, and they make the ballet a very remarkable American theater piece. I haven't mentioned in this the role the Copland score plays, but it is a masterpiece, at every point a decisive help to realizing the poetic meaning of *Billy*.

OCTOBER 31, 1943

"CONCERTO BAROCCO" AT NEEDLE TRADES HIGH SCHOOL

The American Concert Ballet, a small company, opened last night with a recital at the Central Needle Trades High School on Twenty-fourth Street, as the second concert in the series of the Students' Dance Recitals, managed by Joseph Mann. The subscribers who packed the hall saw what was the most interesting ballet evening of the season, because it brought four novelties, all of merit and one of them a masterpiece. That is certainly a record.

The masterpiece is George Balanchine's *Concerto Barocco,* made two years ago for the South American goodwill tour of Kirstein's Ballet Caravan, and shown here then only in a dress rehearsal at Hunter College. That performance was sufficient to give the piece celebrity among dance lovers, and many of us have waited impatiently to see it again. Performed last night in practice costume, it was once more a delight. It is straight dancing, animated, complex, and completely clear. Like the Bach Double

Violin Concerto to which it is set, it does not register emotion, it presents an infinite variety of energy and repose, a balance of force that expresses in itself a happy movement of the spirit.

Concerto Barocco is in the new Balanchine manner; there is no deformation of gesture, the dancer's body dances as a unit, fluent and at ease. The company of dancers look natural whatever they do; especially the arms are natural. Sometimes a nod of the head, to avoid another dancer passing above, astonishes you by its simple directness. But the variety of invention in the choreography is unparalleled. In the adagio the lifts are breathtaking as well as unheard of. And the syncopations of the first and third movements are wonderfully apt and American.

The ballet was beautifully danced, though the slippery floor gave it perhaps a slight timidity. Miss Shea and Miss Lanese are dancers of the highest quality, and Miss Lanese—who has a wonderful dance impetus—has also the most magnificent legs of the season. Mr. Moncion carried her superbly. The entire company is astonishingly well trained, and I particularly admired their simple and expressive arms all evening.

Todd Bolender's *Mother Goose Suite* (to the Ravel score) is a dream ballet, tender and just a little frightening, like a dream. There are many original happy details, and there is an interesting personal flavor. It has a real intimacy.

Mary Jane Shea's *Sailor Bar, 1943* (to a Honegger score) is realist ballet. You see a sailor bar, and you feel the atmosphere of frustration that underlies the brutality, the swagger, and the fancy steps that sailors dance. The gesture Miss Shea has invented is sharp and true, and the piece is all the more touching because the theater rather shies away from the real life of the contemporary sailor or soldier. There is also a symbolic couple that I did not care for so much; but the sailors and their girls, their dancing, and their fights are excellent, and are convincingly danced by the company.

I had to leave after the first scene of William Dollar's *Five Boons of Life*, after Mark Twain's story and set to variations on a nursery rhyme. But the opening is certainly a stunning tour de force, and thereafter the dance seems to keep continuously and exuberantly in motion. It is much more dance ballet than *Mother Goose* or *Sailor Bar;* and I left the audience applauding the successive variations of the soloists. I saw enough to be delighted with the fluency of Mr. Dollar's inventions, and with the remarkable execution.

Simon Sadoff and Angelo Caffarelli accompanied extremely well on two pianos. The evening was one of no pretension but of really remarkable distinction.

NOVEMBER 1, 1943

ALONSO'S GISELLE

Ballet Theatre at the Metropolitan Tuesday night presented the great 1841 ballet *Giselle*, with Alicia Alonso in the title part. The house was crowded and Miss Alonso received a great ovation at the end. It was brave of her to dance a role not only so exacting in itself, but also danced with incomparable brilliance by Miss Markova.

Miss Alonso is a dancer of merit; and, by good fortune, the shape of her head, neck, and shoulders is most attractive. In the first lifts of the second act, in the diagonal series of leaps on both toes in the solo that follows, she was lovely to look at. In the first act she had a very remarkable moment of miming just before her death. But neither the plastic clarity of the entire figure nor the dramatic variety of the role was really sufficient.

As the first trial in the part by a young dancer who is physically not quite strong enough for it, the performance was admirable; but as theater this great ballet looked Tuesday night merely charming and quaint. With Miss Markova dancing, *Giselle* is a tragic action with the most touching and the most mysterious implications; her genius brings its real nature to life. But no other dancer begins and ends a dance phrase as distinctly or gives such dynamic variety to dance phrases as she does.

The company gave *Giselle* a magnificent performance. The ensemble, and the quartet of Giselle's girlfriends in particular, was excellent. Mr. Dorati conducted magnificently. Mr. Dolin danced Albrecht with assurance, though in this part he has too much attack and not enough sustained flow.

NOVEMBER 3, 1943

SOME BALLET BOOKS

If you are one of those who have come to enjoy ballet and would now like to know some more about it—technically and practically—the best way, of course, is to attend lessons. If you go to any ballet school, introduce yourself to the secretary, and say you would like to watch a class at the school's convenience, you will, I am sure, be welcome. The pupils will give you a stare and then forget you are watching. The exercises will puzzle you, but it is likely that in the course of an hour you will see some beautiful moments and you will perhaps feel some of the special atmosphere, so serious and so innocent, that characterizes a good dance lesson. You may begin to see, by comparing the pupils, how the personal physique of a dancer changes the plastic value of a regulation step, and you may even see how the character of the dancer colors and vivifies the correctness of execution. Only, just as the dancer shouldn't strain for an effect, so the observer shouldn't try at any cost to see something significant or lovely. Take dancing as it comes, and when you see something you like, then remember the impression.

But books, too, can help you to exercise your eye. There is a new English one, *The Ballet Lover's Pocket Book: Technique Without Tears for the Ballet Lover*, which is exactly what its title describes. It is written and illustrated by Kay Ambrose, a lady whose action drawings of ballet dancers have appeared in previous books. This one contains clear (and quite charming) drawings of dancers, showing many basic exercises, steps, leaps, and poses, giving the French names and diagramming the sequence of motion. It also contains in its sixty small pages an amazing amount of sound information about ballet art and ballet life—for example, useful advice to fans, to beginners, and to "ballet mamas." It is a sensible, accurate, and cordial book.

There is an older (1939) American book I also recommend highly to ballet lovers who are looking for technical information, Lincoln Kirstein's *Ballet Alphabet*. It gives an immense amount of fundamental theory and history, cleverly compressed into seventy pages, and it has few but very vivid illustrations. *Ballet* (1938), by the London ballet critic Arnold Haskell, is another easy introduction. I read it with interest, but it is written in a rather careless style, and I am not sure that a layman who takes it up can distinguish between what are the facts and what are the author's private opinions.

A new book by Mr. Haskell—his fifteenth—has just arrived here, *The National Ballet: A History and a Manifesto*. Although it is meant for British consumption, as a boost for the London Sadler's Wells Ballet company, it also brings much information on productions and personnel, past and present.

It is a pleasure to read about the wartime Ashton and Helpmann choreographies; it is interesting to look at the photographs of dancers and speculate about them. And then one is curious whether that is all there is of value in English ballet, for five other English companies are now dancing over there.

There is, however, one aspect of Mr. Haskell's "national" idea that is peculiarly puzzling to us over here: his omission from it of the English dancers we have come to admire. Antony Tudor, for instance, is barely mentioned in passing; Hugh Laing and Frederic Franklin, not at all. Markova, the very paragon of English dancers, although treated with deference, is not invited to join a national British ballet. Well, we are only too glad to keep them all if they care to stay.

But I don't believe Mr. Haskell could have meant to slight the English dancers who so brilliantly exemplify for us the idea of English ballet. And there are things in the book better worth speaking of. Fundamentally, Mr. Haskell pleads for a ballet that will be a part of the normal cultural life of its own country, and this is exactly what we too are after. He points out that such a ballet needs a permanent home, where it can rehearse with concentration; it needs a permanent school to train its dancers; it needs all the local collaborators it can find; it needs serious artistic guidance. He also makes the excellent points that such a company should not restrict itself to self-conscious nationalism in theme or dance style, and that it should preserve the masterpieces of the past as points of comparison with the present.

Unfortunately, we are still far from a national ballet in this sense. But I believe we need such a stable organization if our ballet—so glamorous at the moment—is not to deteriorate sharply in the next five years. There is no substitute in the arts for artistic integrity. And integrity needs a home where it is valued. That is a plain fact that any sensible person knows from experience.

NOVEMBER 7, 1943

ROSELLA HIGHTOWER; JEROME ROBBINS

The Ballet Theatre's Saturday night program at the Metropolitan contained *Petrouchka*, *Dim Lustre*, the Grand Pas de Deux from *The Nutcracker*, and *Bluebeard*. The news event of the evening was Rosella Hightower's dancing in the pas de deux, which was of exceptional brilliance and classic finish.

This time her poses were completely plastic and her timing of the dance phrases was sure. She gave the sense of finishing one phrase before the next, of fulfilling one impulse and completing it before the next impulse alters the figure of the dance. It is astonishing how rarely dancers are able to have so clear a control—a control which Miss Markova, of course, possesses to a phenomenal degree.

Because of Miss Hightower's technical brilliance, her naturally forthright manner of dancing was more than ever attractive. And Eglevsky, her partner, was at his very best, too; not only technically superb and magnificently simple, but with that large openheartedness that he alone brings to classic dancing. His warm and loyal manner toward Miss Hightower added a great deal to the freshness the whole dance had; and in her spontaneous delight Miss Hightower looked really radiant. It was a great pleasure to see her in this final triumph at the close of a season in which she has been so remarkable.

In *Petrouchka* Jerome Robbins took the title part. In distinctness and energy of gesture he couldn't have been better; he is a highly intelligent dancer, and he can make the meaning he intends his dance to have completely clear. I liked, too, the slight comic quality he keeps in this often exaggeratedly pathetic part, and I liked his makeup. But Robbins sometimes seems to like to jump about for the sake of jumping; and he forgets then not the meaning of his gesture but the illusion of the stage—that is, the reality of a character and of a story. I thought he was too anxious to get across to the audience, too eager to please; he would be more effective with more reserve. Technically, the gesture looks as if it started in the limbs, not as if it arose in the trunk and had the full strength of that; Massine, whom Robbins imitates so extraordinarily well, keeps the main expressive force in the torso—even in this puppet role. Robbins is evidently a dancer of remarkable talent, and the style he is developing promises a great deal of originality. NOVEMBER 8, 1943

SOME FAULTS OF BALLET THEATRE

In the recent Ballet Theatre season the new choreographies were—except for the fair scene in Lichine's *Fair at Sorochinsk*—disappointing. I am not referring to the disappointing roughness of execution of the opening nights, but speaking of the ballets as they look at their best. At its best, a little of Massine's *Mademoiselle Angot* was amusing in a sort of overcute, opéra-bouffe style; and all of Tudor's *Dim Lustre* was a competent dance version of a modern English drawing-room play. They both had less conviction than manner, and both tried too anxiously to play safe; they were meant to look elegant, but the effect they made was only a trivial one. Luckily we know Massine and Tudor well enough as choreographers so that we needn't judge them merely by what disappoints us.

Lichine, however, has not yet established a choreographic reputation. He has shown several ballets, and beside four inconclusive ones, I remember with sincere pleasure the comedy *Graduation Ball*, done by the de Basil company. *Helen of Troy* in its present state is an excellent farce, and he is officially responsible; but after its many changes and after the persistent rumors of large-scale collaboration, one hesitates to judge him by it. The qualities in the fair scene of *Sorochinsk*, however, are distinctive and add a new style to our ballet repertory. In this scene Lichine too plays safe (as do Massine and Tudor), but he does it in more innocent a fashion. For there is obviously never anything oblique about it, in intellectual or choreographic manner. The sentiment is straight, the dancing vigorous or plain, and the sequence of it is determined by dance contrasts. The points it makes are simple, but they are not stupid: in the moonlight dance, the way the girls sail easily across the stage when the boys have bowed to them, the moment of hesitation (against the music) before the boys grab the girls, the moment of delay (also against the music) when they all face toward the moon and lift their arms—these plain effects ring true after the multiple exuberance of the folk dances before. It is no use looking for an intellectual intentness or refinement in these dances; but it is a pleasure to find that whatever there is is aboveboard: the dancing carries as dancing, the sentiment carries as sentiment.

I am not speaking here of the foolish (witches' sabbath) scene in Lichine's ballet, but only of the fair scene. The good scene is so long and complete that the bad one in the same ballet doesn't change my high opinion of Lichine's capability; but the bad one does, I am sorry to say, add to the other choreographic disappointments of this particular season. Incidentally, the Mussorgsky music for the fair scene is magnificent to dance to; the "Bald Mountain" music of the witches' scene isn't as good for dancing, and unless the dancers keep clear of the music's rhythm and beat they look dwarfed by its force.

The great disappointment of this ballet season's dancing was that Alicia Markova could appear only briefly. It was to be expected that we should miss her technical brilliance, but we missed even more her brilliance of characterization, as Giselle or Odette or Juliet or Zemphira, or in her two comic parts as Elora and as Taglioni. She alone can make each of these different characters convincing, she alone can keep them wholly within the dance illusion, where we believe in them. She has the art of never attracting attention to her private self, and the art of expressing in her role a kind of love that makes the character a rare being we watch with complete attention as long as it appears on the stage before us.

Instead of repeating once more the praise already given the various excellent dancers of the company, I should like to criticize what I think of as Ballet Theatre's general dance intention. Ballet Theatre has always stressed—so it has seemed to me watching the dancers—the obvious dramatic expression in dancing. The method has the advantage of emphasizing decision and energy in the dancer's movement, of making him try to get across a specific point to the audience, of bringing him out of the secluded studio and onto the public stage. But it has the drawback of encouraging his stage vanity, because it tempts him to be personally a focus of attention. It also makes him think his dance part unimportant unless it has a logical and special narrative function. Many dance parts have an illogical atmospheric function. In many ballets old and new it is the delicate finish of the ensemble dancer's simple movements that makes the audience appreciate the poetic intention of the piece. These parts have dance meaning rather than dramatic meaning. And most solo parts have more dance meaning than dramatic meaning, if one looks closely.

Ballet Theatre in recent seasons has developed a fine rush and verve in dancing; they disregarded, I thought, the sensitive articulation of movement which people call elegance. Ballet Theatre got across to the audience boldly; at times I have seen them overdo their parts, though, and try to top each other till the effect has been silly and vulgar. This season I feel that the company as a whole has a new interest in the ballet classics, and an interest in them is the best corrective for the faults I have mentioned. For though the classics need dance verve and stage presence in dancing to bring them to life, they also need dance elegance and personal reticence; a classic dancer doesn't spill his personal glamour all over the stage and orchestra, as a dancer in a character part is sometimes tempted to. I notice that the audience also is getting more and more interested in these old ballets. The more they are danced, the sharper the audience's eye and the clearer the dancers' execution become, so that a choreographer finds himself after a few years with a more sensitive instrument and a more sensitive public, too.

NOVEMBER 14, 1943

ARGENTINITA AT CARNEGIE HALL

In the sanctified vacuum of Carnegie Hall last Saturday night Argentinita appeared with her small Spanish company and danced with the delicate exactitude of effect for which she is celebrated, and which makes her seem as you watch so witty a Spanish lady, and so charmingly intimate a friend. It was a particularly fine recital; and the other familiar dancers, too—Pilar Lopez, José Greco, and Manolo Vargas—were all at their very best, each adding a different characteristic to the evening.

Argentinita's style is not the explosive gypsy kind, nor has it the thrilling force that some Spanish dancers have had. Her dynamic range as a dancer is not startling. But the limpidity of everything she does and the perfect placing of nuance in the dance form are as rare a virtue. Not that she emphasizes detail. You are hardly conscious of the originality of her arrangements or the subtlety of her execution. Her numbers seem intended as slight ones. But the line of the dance is so sure, the variety so accurately calculated, that she can hold her audience with no visible effort and no unladylike insistence.

The evening brought seven new numbers, some of them by her sister, Pilar Lopez, all of them presented in as polished a manner as the older ones.

Technically I was particularly fascinated by one detail of Argentinita's dancing, the delightful delicacy of the feet. Her small steps have an especial rapidity and brilliance. The distance between the feet when she puts them down, the poise of them in the air, the lightness of little running steps in high heels—these are special refinements rare in contemporary dancing. They are properly Spanish, but they also revive for us a detail of an otherwise vanished eighteenth-century technique—a technique before the legs became visible, which made the feet dancing out from under long and heavy dresses fascinating in their own liveliness.

Fascinating in quite another way are the "hot" movements in Argentinita's new habanera number. Here she suggests what a Cuban rhumba may have been in Colonial days, and reveals a wonderful subtlety in those characteristic loin movements that have since become plain bumps. The close of the number, when she slides into a rocking chair and begins to rock without breaking the line of movement, is in itself a feat of dancing.

Different again is the charming evocation of a 1900 zarzuela, or popular operetta, style in *Scenes from Old Madrid*, danced by the entire company.

But Argentinita's programs are always notable for her immense knowledge of the innumerable varieties—historical, geographical, or racial—of Spanish dancing. NOVEMBER 15, 1943

AMERICAN CONCERT BALLET: THREE NEW CHOREOGRAPHERS

Imagine that our two big ballet companies could—at almost no cost to the management—add considerably to the prestige and to the interest of their seasons, if they were able to produce now and then a special program entirely by new choreographers, danced, say, by their less-known dancers, in practice costume and to piano accompaniment. Unfortunately the heavy touring schedules of these companies make such a project impossible because the dancers haven't the free time to rehearse extra novelties. It is a pity; whether such studio matinees produced remarkable works or not, they would find an interested special public, they would vary the dancers' routine, and best of all they would give young choreographers—and big ballet needs them for the future—a chance to develop. How is a choreographer to learn except by trying?

In practice, however, it has always been the small, unglamorous companies, on a semi-student basis, who have tried out most of the new choreographers. Though the execution is often rough, the performances are very valuable to the ballet public and the ballet industry. Among our best-known choreographers, Agnes de Mille and Eugene Loring began with small groups; so did Tudor in England and Balanchine in Soviet Russia. There is every reason to suppose that such small ballet companies are a necessity to the sound development of ballet in this country.

The American Concert Ballet is just such a group, a new one that has begun by showing us the work of two new choreographers, Mary Jane Shea and Todd Bolender. It also brings a new piece by William Dollar, whose last New York ballet was the *Concerto in F* at the Metropolitan some years ago; and, in addition, it dances Balanchine's *Concerto Barocco*, which had not yet been produced here.

Miss Shea's *Sailor Bar, 1943* is to my mind the most interesting of them. It is a realistic scene in a sailor bar—a place something like the sailor bars of the East Fifties or West Sixties. Sailors come in, meet their girls, they dance, they fight, they leave again. One sailor and his girl are the chief characters, and on the other side of the stage you see a young man and a young woman represent their ideal selves. As the sailor and his girl come closer to having confidence in each other, the ideal selves, too, have more contact; for a moment the gesture is even the same for both pairs; then the boy and girl in both pairs draw apart again, unable to believe in one another.

The psychological action is credible and the realistic gestures look astonishingly familiar. What is interesting is that they have not been stylized to fit into a definite dance style, they keep their natural contour and impulse; what has been stylized is the weight, the flow and tempo of the motion.

In this way held poses (such as sitting), slow motion (as if dazed), normal dance steps, and representational gestures keep their familiar realistic value, but they also combine into dance sequences. The sequence of the girl climbing onto the table, the long climax of the sailor dancing with two girls, quarreling with the one he likes, knocking her down, and being beaten up by two other sailors—these are excellent as continuities of movement. (And for once a fight in dance form and realistic costume didn't look silly.)

Not so successful are the two ideal selves. They are carefully directed in an abstract dance style, and seriously thought out; but they manage to say no more than what the realistic figures tell us already in a more convincing way. As ideal dance figures I should have liked to see them move with greater force and freedom than the realistic ones; their movement might have emphasized (where it barely suggested) the quality of spreading into space that differentiates abstract from realistic dancing, and it might so have heightened the restrictedness of the other figures. But as a whole, Miss Shea's first piece shows a very original dance intelligence, and a notable absence of false dramatics. And she uses the music she chose with exceptional adroitness.

Mr. Bolender's *Mother Goose Suite* tells several Mother Goose stories to a little girl, and it has a feeling both solitary and intimate, like that of a child's daydream. I liked how the movement seems to wait a long time and then flare up all at once, and how sometimes the space is very empty and then peculiarly crowded. I liked the tree that once picked up a little girl and carried her to a garden seat, and the slow clouds. But I wished the chief character had danced more, and that the many slow arm movements had held my interest better. The piece seems almost to make a virtue of indecision; but it has a quality of timing that is not derivative and serious workmanship is evident throughout.

Mr. Dollar's *Five Boons of Life* was the most fluent of the choreographies, but to me the least convincing. It is the kind of ballet I like, it has lots of dancing; but though it begins very well indeed, after a while the dances do not seem very different one from another, the effect becomes one of repetitious agitation, and one loses interest. But like the other two ballets, it is a perfectly honest piece of choreography; it is planned for dancing, not for an exhibition of stage personality.

The dancers performed all these ballets satisfactorily. Some of them are, I imagine, students, others are appearing in current shows, and some have appeared in solo roles in ballet. They are unequal in talent but they all dance straight: their bearing is clear, their acting is, in the best sense, modest, and the effect is one of general good style, with excellent individual moments.

The performance of Balanchine's *Concerto Barocco* was much less exact and able than that of the other pieces. It is a wholly admirable ballet. Its coolness and its simplicity are not in the current fashion; its musicality—for instance in the lifts in the second movement or in the percussive effects of the toe steps—is very bold indeed. I hope the piece will be seen often enough so that its noble qualities can become familiar; for the moment its lack of affectation and the natural look the dancers have in it seem to puzzle the audience.

The American Concert Ballet has made an intelligent and very attractive debut.

NOVEMBER 21, 1943

DUDLEY-MASLOW-BALES

The local modern dance season opened a week ago yesterday with a recital by Jane Dudley, Sophie Maslow, William Bales, and their New Dance Group, who appeared at the Central Needle Trades High School as the third event in the Students' Dance series. The Dudley-Maslow-Bales trio has become the unit that represents best the younger generation of modern dancers, a generation that follows Martha Graham's, and that she has formed. These three dancers in particular are not, I think, the most interesting in this class, but together they establish on the stage a level of workmanship, of finish, that is obviously professional and worthy of respect. They are reliable.

The work they do is aboveboard: the dances are clear in subject, reasonable in form, unpretentious in presentation. In composing, they tend to avoid the modern effects of several years back—the harsh arm thrust followed by a wait, the gloomy straddle, the solemn cramp, the long writhing on the floor. They would like dancing to look friendly for a change. So they try for lightness, for fluency, for rapidity in the feet and mildness in the arms. They try for dance sequences rather than for gesture sequences, but the dance is made for the sake of the subject, not just to look pretty. And in all this the trio reflects a general tendency of modern dancing in recent years, which has changed a good deal since those unwieldy "Revolt" numbers many people still think of as typically "modern."

Watching them dance, I like the trio best when the dance forms are simple, as they often are, and when the dancers can present themselves as pleasant young people, which they do very convincingly. In such passages I find that their work carries. In character dance passages their characterization is not bold enough, not distinct enough from their usual stage personality.

I also did not think the trio at their best in complex quick dance passages that require a continuity in dance rhythm. The rhythm of modern dancing has been in the past a gesture rhythm rather than a dance rhythm, a rhythm in space rather than a rhythm in time. But the clearness of a dance passage is based on a rhythm in time (musical rhythm) far more than on a rhythm in space. In musical rhythm the modern dancer hasn't the chance to do all the interesting gestures that occur to him; so he crowds them too close and doesn't finish any one of them properly.

Or one can look at the modern dancer's difficulty from another point of view, that of the balance of the body in motion. The moderns have developed highly interesting movements by emphasizing action in the arms, by extreme torso displacements that violently shift the body's weight. They take their own time and their own way about changing from one such dangerous equilibrium to the next; the dancer, one might say, pulls herself together after one of them and then is ready to launch into the next. This discontinuity produces striking details and dramatic accents, but it is no preparation for unbroken continuity in a light and rapid dance sequence. Such a continuity is based on far slighter shifts of equilibrium and on subordinating the action in the extremities of the body to a steady support at its center. Either type of dancing can be expressive, but the two of them are very different indeed in method.

What I sincerely like in modern dancers is the thoughtful way they keep attacking such fundamental questions of dance form from all sorts of novel angles. They are willing to make it hard for themselves. They don't really take anything for granted; they leave all kinds of possibilities open. They intend, at least, to make every kind of experiment in person.

The program of the trio and their group brought two new numbers, *Sea Bourne* and *Llanto: We Shall Avenge Our Tears. Sea Bourne* shows us six persons of Yankee Clipper days—four women and two small girls—looking out to sea and thinking of an absent sailor they each love in a different way. He appears—returning in their thoughts, I imagine—and we see him dance first with his wife and two daughters, later with two women who are not so respectable ("Two Who Knew Him"), and last with a girl who is in love with him. He disappears and they all stand waiting once more, perhaps not quite so strange to each other as at first.

The piece is clear to follow, it is meticulously worked out in its detail, and several moments are very good. The theme is a fine one for a contrasted dance suite: I should think a man would seem very different indeed to various people who love him. But too many of its possibilities remained timid hints. The sailor's part in particular was too colorless, despite lifts and jig steps; he had no chance to show why he was desired by six longing women, and no chance to be a man of mystery either. The various episodes could have been more boldly different in dance quality. The passage with the girl in love (very well done by Ethel Winters) seemed to promise a different flow, but then it turned into pantomime. I think the fault all through the piece was that it kept too close to plain sense—to what the sailor might have done had he returned to these plain women in person. The dances were logical, they were reasonable, but uninteresting.

The other new number, *Llanto*, was a brief trio by Miss Maslow to a Spanish "traditional song record." It was antifascist in its intention, but it was hardly more than the beginning of a dance, and it had, I thought, too little relation to its brave subtitle, *We Shall Avenge Our Tears.* Mostly I saw Miss Dudley going around gloomily bent double, Miss Maslow sitting on the floor with an angry look in her fine eyes, and Mr. Bales trying to do Spanish heel-taps in slippers that had no heels. But he did give the number what force it had by the taut Spanish bearing of his body; in fact, he really was very good indeed.

The rest of the program was composed of pieces seen in previous recitals. Miss Dudley's comic *Harmonica Breakdown* was, as usual, a sure-fire success, and had to be repeated. Miss Maslow's celebrated *Folksay* was given a particularly fine performance. It is a charming number in an artfully naive manner, though at some performances it seemed to me a little on the Sunday-school side—it seemed to present the "folk" as a bunch of well-washed children. At this performance, however, its openness and friendliness and the easy variety it has were completely winning. And at every performance Woody Guthrie, the folk singer, who accompanies the piece with songs and jokes, is superb. The audience, I should add, is invariably delighted with *Folksay*. They take it perhaps as the reflection of a lovely summer day, and that is what it really is.

DECEMBER 5, 1943

A RECITAL OF DANCE STYLES

At the Barbizon Plaza Concert Hall Friday night, Miss Joze Duval with a company of eight dancers, a pianist, and a guitarist presented a program entitled "Dance Styles," beginning with seventeenth-century social dance forms, including evocations of eighteenth- and nineteenth-century ballet, and ending with modern interpretative ballet numbers. The numbers were of a mildly decorative nature.

Miss Duval herself is attractive; she has a good face and figure for the stage, a clean small style, and she is, I think, talented. But she dances and composes, as beginners generally do, with a clutter of detail and no sweep or impetus. She might well learn these by joining a ballet company and dancing the compositions of mature choreographers. The rest of the dancing was like that of a student performance.

Miss Duval is to be congratulated sincerely on her remarkably fine costumes, the designer and executor of which were not named. I had the impression, however, that she wore her eighteenth-century costumes over crinoline hoops instead of paniers. The latter are, I believe, flatter from front to back, and show the foot better.

As for the historical numbers, they indicated a good deal of erudition but not quite enough. Miss Duval's eighteenth-century number, for instance, followed too closely that remark by the great Camargo's necrologist, that she performed all her steps beneath her, and so could dispense with those precautionary drawers that other dancers needed to satisfy the demands of modesty. I wish Miss Duval had instead followed Noverre's remark that Camargo was so lively and leaping a dancer that one couldn't notice her dance faults. Good dancing has always been a lively show.

DECEMBER 11, 1943

ANNA SOKOLOW; "CARMEN JONES"; BARONOVA

Anna Sokolow's modern-dance recital brought back to mind the striking impression she had made a few years ago in intense numbers evoking proletarian adolescence. Her figure with the small head, the solid neck, the small sloping shoulders and elongated limbs was immediately touching. Her hands and wrists were lovely, her arms light. Her dancing had the directness of a child's motions. When she lifted her forearm, when she ran and leaped, you watched the action itself. It was the action in itself that moved you. In composing, the way she derived dance gestures easily from pantomime, her simple formal arrangements—these "naive" qualities suited her adolescent atmosphere. And when she danced her numbers with subjective intensity the confusion between herself and her dance heroine did not bother anyone.

Conscious of Miss Sokolow's originality, I was puzzled to find her recital unsatisfactory. Her figure is still the ideal one for a dancer, her way of moving as graceful and distinct as ever. She worked with intensity; in fact, she often forced out an angry little grunt that sounded like an impatient Spanish "Eh!"—as if she were whipping herself on. But the atmosphere of her presence had changed; this time her own presence was not that of an adolescent. It was that of a lady, of an adult.

Unfortunately, Miss Sokolow's present adult subjective fervor no longer suits the girlish simplicity of her former compositions; the more intense she becomes the more she hides their real character. And so the old numbers dealing with such themes as slum childhood, juvenile delinquency, or Loyalist Madrid—numbers that once seemed natural as adolescent reflections—now, seen in an adult atmosphere, look artificial and false to their terrible themes.

In addition to old numbers, Miss Sokolow also showed a new long work, *Songs of a Semite* (for four dancers, a musician, a singer, and a speaker). It presents a Jewess who feels homeless and lost; she remembers—in the form of dance episodes—the courage of several women in the Old Testament, and then she finally joins them in a brave march. The theme is a special one and the audience applauded the piece. But, though I thought it rounder in movement and maturer in tone than the earlier numbers, it seemed confused in its storytelling and repetitious in gesture, and it seemed inadequate as an evocation of legends so heroic, or an emotion so religious. To me Ruth's dance looked only a little tender, Miriam's only a little exultant, and Miss Sokolow, as the meditating figure, seemed to move more like a torch singer than a real person. The truest moments, I thought, were small and sweet ones.

What about the big moments? I believe the trouble is that Miss Sokolow has not developed enough variety of expression in dancing, a wide enough variety in its technical resources, to represent a complex theme from an adult point of view. Technically, the dancer's trunk is loaded with energy, but the energy remains latent. It is not used in muscular actions that would give the torso plastic variation, not in weight in the arms, not in lightness in the thighs, not in the play of the feet with music. You don't see the impetus increase or decrease, the body soften or harden, the movement float or break, the figure gain expression by its path on the stage. Such qualities are only hinted at. But they are the expressive material of dancing, and it is to make their contrasts clearer to the audience that modern dancers, from Isadora on, have preferred to abandon the tradition of ballet forms.

Whatever the dance form (ballet, modern, or as yet uninvented), the actual realization of such expressive effects is what constitutes the dance tradition. A tradition is not a police regulation, nor is it a device for repetition. It is a practical aid to an artist. It is useful for suggesting practical methods, for reminding him of expressive possibilities, for encouraging him by showing him that other persons have been faced with similar difficulties. A tradition is an artist's home base; or, to reapply Wordsworth's remark, it is the "tranquillity" in which the event that is the artist's subject is "recollected." And his tradition also is, as Auden has said, what he can judge himself by.

Miss Sokolow's own *Songs of a Semite* has, at least in intellectual intention, this same point in view, since it draws the moral that a tradition is a good thing for an adult individual.

. . .

The dances in *Carmen Jones* are a lot of fun because they have the liveliness and grace of an excellent Negro dance company. Eugene Loring has made a nice airplane dance in the first act, and, in general, his work fits in perfectly with the production. I agree with Virgil Thomson, however, that the parody number in the third act (with jokes from *Gala Performance*) strikes a wrong note, though the dancers do it with charming good humor. Incidentally, Muriel Smith as Carmen was very fine indeed in her poses in the murder scene.

Irina Baronova is appearing in the present stage show at the Roxy, and she is presented there with reasonable tact. She looks as sumptuous as ever, she has all her phenomenal balance and ease. I thought she hunched her shoulders coquettishly and that her dance itself was foolish, but a great dancer can be forgiven a good deal now and then.

DECEMBER 12, 1943

ASADATA DAFORA

The African Dance Festival, which Asadata Dafora, the dancer from Sierra Leone, presented at Carnegie Hall last week, gave us another of our rare glimpses of African Negro dancing. The main impression was once again that of a completely civilized art. It was the nonritual forms that were stressed. The theme of the festival was a young man's arrival in a village to court his beautiful bride, and the village celebration which ensues; it showed us village dances, expressing the social good spirits of such an occasion.

Drummers set the rhythm; the country girls danced formal dances, the matrons sang; the young groom exhibited in dancing his buoyancy of spirit and his graceful decorum—qualities which in New York too make for a happy married state. As a New Yorker, however, I was struck by the charming ceremoniousness of these villagers. The young man, for instance, did not rudely go straight to his fiancée; he first danced a few steps with each of the other girls in turn, circling about each as if to pay her a special compliment—an attention which each rewarded by a lovely smile and a graceful undulation in her steps.

And later, when he danced a duet "Of Acquaintance" with his bride—

a dance which began with a boops-a-daisy and continued with a figure where she swayed her bright-colored bustle a little on the left or a little on the right, and his arms drew long caressing curves in the air just out of reach behind her—the elegance of their play and the lightness of their rhythm reminded me in its spirit of an eighteenth-century pastoral. The emotion was natural, but the manners were perfect. The amenities were being observed for the pleasure they really give. And though I had not expected social graces in African village life, they seemed at once completely authentic characteristics—perhaps because among our own citizens Negroes in particular value the ceremonial of gentle manners, and perform it with the greatest grace.

The dances of the village girls looked at first quite simple, with an odd hieratic stiffness about them. As the chorus moved forward, generally in single file, the feet kept reiterating sharply a syncopated rhythm of steps and sole taps. The tap was made from the ankle, without moving the knee. Meanwhile the arms performed the dance variations, creating a secondary rhythm. The shoulders were as flexible as the ankles and they often moved in an independent rhythm. Occasionally there were accented motions (like "bumps") in the upper spine. And when the torso turned or bent it seemed to move from the hips. The head was generally kept horizontal, as if unconcerned.

Such a bearing looked stiff; a further sense of stiffness came from the simplicity of the floor patterns as well as from the trait of repeating a small detail of movement over and over, then taking up a new detail and repeating that. And after several dances the insistent foot rhythms tended to sound and to look all alike.

On the other hand, the lucidity of the style was remarkable—the way the body kept clear to one's eye, the feet distinct from the legs, the legs from the trunk, the shoulders, the arms, the head, each separately defined. The definiteness gave to slight variations their maximum effect. And in the end one noticed that the exactness of the posture, the firmness of the rhythm gave to the dance both dignity and force; that the peculiarities of the style could not be "savage" or accidental, but were the outcome of a consistent and highly cultivated dance tradition. The odd grace it had was distinctly elegant and certainly difficult to achieve.

The solo dancers, Miss Premice (the bride), Miss Sutton, and in particular Mr. Dafora (the groom), showed the further technical subtleties of the style. In his dancing Dafora only now and then called attention to his percussive foot beats. Though they were continuous, you watched the upper part of his body, the brilliantly rapid, darting, or sinuous arms, the strangely mobile shoulders, the slight shift of the torso as it leaned forward or straightened, the turn of the head, the animated face. The way he phrased the rhythmic patterns in these movements and so heightened the meaning of the dance resembled the way a blues singer phrases her song and heightens its meaning against the steady beat of the orchestra. Dafora's free dance rhythms seemed to soar over the strict drum rhythms of the accompaniment and over his own steady foot beats. His musical instinct was extremely subtle, his dance intelligence striking.

The displacements in space, the motions of legs or torso, the dramatic accents were not large. His numbers were modest ones, as suited their subject, and they looked effortless. He did not exaggerate to attract attention, or try to be impressive. But there was never an empty moment or a lax one.

I think the qualities I have mentioned show him to be a remarkable choreographer as well as a fine dancer. The proportions and the sequence of the dances were excellent. But beyond this, the dancers he has trained are, after all, American girls, to whom life in an African village would be as foreign as life in a Russian one would be to the Russian-dancing Americans in our Ballets Russes. Yet this village festival (like Dafora's previous *Kyunkor* and *Zunguru*) had in performance a definite local atmosphere. It was not mere decorative exoticism. It brought with it across the ocean the sense of a real landscape and a real way of life. I wish it were possible for so sincere and intelligent a choreographer as Mr. Dafora to bring over across the ocean a small company of real West African dancers to add to his well-trained American pupils, and then show us more of the extraordinary wonders West African dancing holds.

For it is apparently extremely wide in its range. I wish I had space here for some of the vivid descriptions in Geoffrey Gorer's brilliant *Africa Dances*. When you read the book you can see the towns and the countryside, the people, their government, their diverse customs, their beliefs, their extraordinary magic, and, as a part of all this daily life, their dancing. There are ritual dances and play dances, hair-raising acrobatic dances and communal frenzies. In many primitive communities there are professional dancers, but the community dances too, when it chooses. Gorer seems to have seen dances everywhere and almost daily—an infinite variety of costumes, of intention, of expression. West Africans "dance with a precision, a verve, an ingenuity that no other race can show, the smallest group has its own ballet, distinct in costume, in movement, in tempo from any other. . . . Africans have only one art [Gorer claims their sculpture is largely connected with dances] but to what a pitch they have brought it!" Gorer was watching them in 1934. Nearly six hundred years before, the Arabian traveler Ibn Batuta was watching African mask dances, so old is this dance tradition. DECEMBER 19, 1943

GRAHAM'S "DEATHS AND ENTRANCES" AND "SALEM SHORE"

Martha Graham, no doubt the greatest celebrity in the American dance world, appeared last night at the Forty-sixth Street Theater, giving her first Broadway recital in two seasons. The house was sold out the first day of the ticket sale, and the performance is to be repeated January 9.

Miss Graham presented two new works, *Salem Shore* and *Deaths and Entrances*. *Deaths and Entrances* is a piece for ten dancers—six women and four men—and is described in the program as "a legend of poetic experience rather than a story of incident. It concerns the restless pacings of the heart on some winter evening." In performance it is long, obscure, of intense interest and extraordinary richness of invention.

The action concerns three sisters. The memories and fantasies that pass through their ardent hearts are personified by other dancers, whom they move among and touch, so that reality and imagination are no longer two distinct experiences. The Brontë sisters, who used to pace in the firelight on winter evenings at Haworth, imagining the passions of their novels, are a kind of model. But the piece is in no sense biographical.

One might describe it instead as a poem in the associative or *symboliste* technique, a sequence of tightly packed and generally violent images following a subconscious logic.

But it is Miss Graham's own performance that is the extraordinary and fascinating focus in which one sees this irrational world as a real experience. The intensity with which she projects agitation, wonder, fury, or—at the end—a heroic acceptance of fate is a unique quality. Unique, too, is the extraordinary technique with which she makes every movement seem that of an actual person, not of a performer. The other dancers, accurate and excellent though they are, cannot give their movement this sharp immediacy. Miss Graham constantly controls not only the active driving portion of a gesture, but also its passive, unemphatic phase. She changes the speed of a gesture after its instant of fulfillment, and so gives the motion a living rhythm that is wonderfully dramatic. This is in all kinds of dancing a perfection of technical intelligence, and you hardly ever see it.

The other novelty, *Salem Shore*, is a solo for Miss Graham, describing the longing of a young wife for her husband's return from the sea. It is not at all the wildly dramatic number one might expect; it is a discreetly poignant piece. By presenting her heroine as a reticent young lady of Salem, a girl who remembers playing on the shore as a child but knows she is now an adult, Miss Graham makes the character an interesting and real one. The handling of stage properties is particularly "natural," and quite unusual in that sense. Miss Graham looks wonderfully young in this piece.

The orchestra, under Louis Horst, performed the specially composed scores by Paul Nordhoff, Hunter Johnson, and Robert McBride. They were useful accompaniments, and their quality was generally good.

The costuming of the novelties by Edythe Gilfond was excellent, and the stage sets by Arch Lauterer effective, modest, and useful. The lighting by Jean Rosenthal was superb.

Among the dancers in the company Merce Cunningham's long dance phrases, his lightness, and his constantly intelligent head are very fine. Erick Hawkins and Nina Fonaroff shone particularly in the last number, *Punch and the Judy*, a sardonic comedy of white-collar married life first seen two seasons ago. In this Miss Graham can make the house laugh by a flick of the wrist, so accurate is her timing and her emphasis. As a comedian too her distinction is extraordinary.

DECEMBER 27, 1943

PAUL DRAPER

Paul Draper, the tap dancer in the Paul Draper style, and Larry Adler, the harmonica player in the Larry Adler style, are, as everyone knows, specialists as well as excellent showmen; they always get their audience, and they do it with ease and a deceptive reticence. And in their self-made specialties they are unrivaled.

I have never seen an audience that didn't go for both of them in a big way; for myself, I find them charming performers, but not interesting all evening long. The harmonica, even with all the extraordinary sounds Adler makes on it, has for my ears a tinny sound that doesn't carry the musical content of the serious pieces—Mozart, Bach, or Debussy—that Adler plays. "Blues in the Night," however, and "Begin the Beguine" are great fun.

Paul Draper combines ballet steps and gestures, as well as suggestions of Spanish and "modern," with tap dancing; the result is of course a mixture, but there is no harm in that. I do not find, as many people do, the mixture interesting in itself. I only wish it worked better. I find the "art dance" arm movement not free enough—the arms look put into position, accurately but not naturally. Tap technique requires relaxed knees, and so it blunts many of the lines that ballet technique tries to keep taut. The movement in Draper's dances does not seem large, because the extensions are so often modified and broken. But the effect is a delicate and a very pleasing one. There is lightness and a touching sense of innocence in it. And these qualities—and they are qualities of refinement—are clear to the audience and they delight in it.

I wish Draper had more freedom in his neck and shoulders. And I wish he had more rhythmic freedom in his tap rhythms. To my ear he seems to be embroidering the musical rhythm rather than to be creating an independently interesting parallel rhythm. But as after a few numbers I find the sound itself of the tapping a little insistent, expertly modulated though it is—I am not the best judge of this matter. I admire it most in his dance without music.

JANUARY 1, 1944

THE METROPOLITAN OPERA BALLET

Christmas Day the Metropolitan gave the Polovtsian Dances from *Prince Igor* as a ballet in a new choreography by Laurent Novikoff. Many of the steps and gestures were like those in the old Fokine version of *Prince Igor* (some of this material has an ethnological basis), but the choreography did not produce the effect of savagely brilliant force that Fokine's ballet does; the new dances were neither clear nor bold. They suffered, too, because Fokine's masterpiece has so often been executed by first-rate companies. It was foolish of the management to exhibit its choreographer and its dancers at such a disadvantage or to risk such comparisons. Had we been shown four or five "concert" dances, presenting the best dancers in their best light, the result might well have been pleasing. As it was, a great deal of hard work went into an embarrassing performance.

Embarrassing too was the rest of the production. The score was played mechanically. The singing chorus was placed in a way that crowded and dwarfed the dancers. The hundred costumes were so ill assorted in color that the stage looked like a dollar-tie counter pawed through by Christmas shoppers.

It is a good deal pleasanter to speak of the fourth-act ballet in *Carmen.* Miss Svetlova's toe dance with fan and mantilla and in a brief ballet skirt—I imagine this is some 1870s kind of ballet Spanish—was an amusing novelty and didn't look out of place at all. It was also the best dancing I have seen at the Met. Amusing too was the mock bullfight that followed her number; and after that the ensemble flung itself into the finale with delight. A good deal of this vivacity was due to Beecham's conducting; at another performance, which he didn't conduct, the ballet was much less lively.

I also liked the incidental dance in *Lucia*; it was simple, but spirited and neat. Of the ballets for *Tannhäuser*, *Samson and Delilah*, and even *The Bartered Bride*, the best I can report is that they were routine opera-ballet numbers, orderly in execution, but with foolish figures and dowdy costumes.

One may regret that the choreography at the Metropolitan has no freshness in movement, and regret that the young dancers seem to have no one who can awaken their vitality, who can teach them style and a clean line. But one can understand why the management prefers a routine ballet to a lively and stylish one. A lively ballet company is as much trouble to an opera manager as an infatuation is to a middle-aged man. When opera managers go overboard for really good dancing, they are in for extravagances, misunderstandings, recriminations, and triumphant premieres. For a man who is running singers and musicians besides, it is a terrible strain. So one can accept our present "well-meaning but not very able" Metropolitan ballet (so Paul Bowles called it) as a modest substitute for a glorious inconvenience. JANUARY 2, 1944

SYBIL SHEARER; CARMEN AMAYA

Sybil Shearer—generally accepted as one of the leaders of the younger generation of modern dancers—appeared last Sunday in the dance series at the YMHA in a joint recital with Katherine Litz. Miss Shearer was applauded most in three tragicomic numbers. While watching these one felt not so much in the special world of dancing as in the general world of the theater; they appealed directly to the general intelligence of the audience, and one could easily have enjoyed their acid wit without being aware of their finesse as dancing.

One of them, called *Spanish Reversal*, would certainly be a hit in a bright revue or in a nightclub like the Blue Angel. It is a parody of Spanish dancing as a housewife might find herself doing it, quite astonished herself at this outbreak of the gypsy in her. While the feet rap out "Spanish" taps with violence, the body stays limp and noncommittal, shaken now and then by the kickback from the explosions below. Another number, a new duet called *The Pulse of Death*, was even wittier in invention and was laughed at loudest. It looks as casual as a charade. Two figures dressed in a shapeless version of Grecian robes putter about the stage reciting brightly to each other the rhymed platitudes of a poem on the Vanity of Life. The motions they illustrate the verses with are small, careful, and absurdly domestic, and the horrid, middle-aged stoop in Miss Shearer's back is the realistic foil to their inane and spinsterish fussing.

These entertainment numbers, and one other similar parody, were what the serious modern-dance audience at the YMHA liked best on Miss Shearer's and Miss Litz's varied program. They were in line with the tendency of the modern dance toward the objective and the explainable. But they were the best pieces too, because Miss Shearer's delicate personality came through most warmly when she was telling a story about someone not herself. And to my eye her dancing during the whole recital had a pantomimic and descriptive inspiration that suited character numbers best. Her error was not to end boldly; instead, she pressed their "tragic" aspect; such intelligent pathos should close on a laugh.

But all of Miss Shearer's dances were remarkable for the infallible accuracy of their gesture. She has, I imagine, the most complete control of movement of any modern dancer in her generation. She and Miss Litz are both of them fastidious in taste, original in invention—especially in gestures derived from the little nervous motions people make in real life. Their costumes too are most intelligent. At this recital I missed the lyric spurt or play of dancing, and I missed the free sweep with which dancing can animate, can take possession of the stage space with all the air above it. But these are qualities pantomimic motion doesn't have.

The famous Carmen Amaya, now appearing at La Conga, is the antithesis of Miss Shearer in method. Amaya's method has nothing to do with visual refinements or delicate relationships; it is the fire of dancing and that is its entire passion. At the midnight show, when I saw her, she did only two solos—not enough. But the spring of her movement, the power of it, the assurance with which she controls its rhythm I found more stunning than ever. For a moment now and then I caught a glimpse of her trying to be impressive, but then the dance took hold of her again and nothing existed for her but savage dancing. For dance lovers not used to nightclubs I'll add that you can watch her very well from the bar, where a drink costs 85 cents, and ladies must come with escorts. You'll probably see some good jive, too, by the younger customers.

JANUARY 9, 1944

"DEATHS AND ENTRANCES" REVISITED

It isn't often I've seen the lobby in the intermission so animated in its discussion of a ballet as it was after Martha Graham's new *Deaths and Entrances*. The piece is a harsh one: it has neither a touching story, nor a harmonious development, nor wit and charm to help it along. But at both its recent performances it has held the audience spellbound. What fascinates is the movement itself as it takes place on the stage—the rapid succession of curiously expressive and unforeseen bursts of gesture, the urgency they have, and above all the intense vividness of Miss Graham's own dancing.

Her dancing does not look stylized or calculated; it looks spontaneous as movements do in life or as Markova's motion does on the stage. Miss Graham's effect of spontaneity comes from attention to that part of the gesture which is like the following-through in athletics, the part which restores the body to balance after an effort, which relaxes the tension after an outward stress. Most dancers do this mechanically and their dance, though accurate, looks wooden. Miss Graham, by making the speed of the unemphatic and relaxing movements just a little different from what one would have expected, gives animation and a personal rhythm to the ebbing of energy, too. It makes all her dance look elastic, fresh, and ungloomy. Such an unexpectedness of rhythm is what delights us in the playful motions of children and animals; in the calculated clarity of dancing only the great stars can look as free as children.

A spontaneous look has little to do with novelty in the general shape of a gesture. In fact, the more novelty of gesture, the less freedom of movement is the common rule. Just the same, Miss Graham wants every movement to be a novel one. She finds new varieties of hobbling, kicking backward, sinking in one's steps, going with a bounce; she finds caressing undulations, flights looking downward, reactions to the touch of a hand, spidery dartings of the arms, possessed shoulder-shakes, or a group of deformed graces holding hands. One has the impression of not having seen any of the movements the ten dancers do before, of never having seen bodies take these odd shapes.

Such extreme originality is shocking, and it is suited to the shocking subject of the piece. *Deaths and Entrances* is a homage to Emily Brontë, the stoic young woman who conceived the terrors of *Wuthering Heights*. It is meant in one sense as an image of her heart, and in the dance we see reflected some of the strange wonders that absorbed her—incestuous family love-and-hate, the duplicit need in a woman for both a brutal and a tender contact, "perverted passion and passionate perversity" mounting to real madness and ending heroically sane. Like the actions in Emily Brontë's novel, the movements of the dance look frantic, but not at all indecent.

The current of *Deaths and Entrances* is frenzied, and one is never at one's ease in it. One is never prepared for the next moment. What holds the piece together is the lucid concentration of Miss Graham in the central role, a personage to whom all the actions on the stage are completely real. They are images she contemplates within herself and also sees independently active outside her; and her mobile face lights up at the objective impressions. She is adolescently tender dancing with her two Beloveds at once; she is terrifying and horrible in her mad scene; her final gesture is adult, like tragedy. Very strange, too, is the mysterious elegance which never leaves her.

I hope that Ballet Theatre (or the Monte Carlo) when it comes to town will invite Miss Graham and her company to perform *Deaths and Entrances* as a guest production on its programs. As it is the most extraordinary novelty of the season, the general public will be curious to see it and to form its own opinion of it. JANUARY 16, 1944

HENIE'S ICE REVUE

Sonja Henie, appearing in person, opened her 1944 Hollywood Ice Revue last night at Madison Square Garden, this one being the seventh of the series. The spectacle is perfectly refined in the Hollywood sense of that word. Miss Henie is, too; she is smooth and cute and gets her public. Though this isn't news to anyone, the house was crowded and clearly pleased.

Miss Henie skates five numbers: a "Liebestraum" (performed this time with a partner), a waltz, a hula, a tango (by popular request), and a new solo in the concluding "Parisian Mardi Gras" scene, which I was unable to stay for. Only the first of these numbers contains striking feats of fancy skating.

But one feels sure she could execute any sequence she cared to, no matter how difficult. Her control of speed and her balance are perfect at all times, and she has a clear sense of musical phrasing. She has a smooth hip action, a nice way of leaning against her partner, and occasionally a fine lift in her waist. And all these qualities are rare enough in skating.

She has, of course, a very pretty figure indeed, and she is always smiling. She seems to show you how easy it is to skate gracefully, and it is a pleasure to think so. But she doesn't make her numbers express any more interesting emotion than ease. Her skating seems all for the sake of charm, and so much charm is a little silly now and then. Well, that is the Hollywood convention of elegance, and Miss Henie is the complete mistress of this effect.

Her partners are perfect partners, but they hardly get a chance to show more. The Cales sisters, however, are neat and effective. To my mind, the most interesting number was Freddie Trenkler's comic one, and I regretted missing his second very much. His humor is real and his skating is full of surprise and real skating rhythm.

Real skating rhythm is not the basis of the ensemble numbers, however. They are adaptations of dancing without skates, and include a bit of a jig here and a bit of a Schuhplattler there; and they seem to resort to skating between such nonskating suggestions only because they cannot avoid it. A Viennese waltz ("Ball in Old Vienna"), for instance, never got into the sweep of skating at all.

The pretty chorus, however, is chosen for looks, it seems, rather than for skating ability. In the latter it is rather spotty, with awkward extensions and awkward stops.

The show is well paced and nicely costumed. Perhaps one should not judge it so sharply; it is a big Hollywood spectacle, in an accepted convention. And the audience, which probably had come for just that, was quite satisfied with what it got. JANUARY 19, 1944

SKATING AS BALLET

Watching Sonja Henie's new ice revue from the point of view of ballet, as I naturally did, I found Freddie Trenkler's superb comic skating far more interesting than Miss Henie's celebrated sweet kind. And I imagine if skating is to become a form of real ballet, ice ballet is more likely to develop from the comic style than from the graceful one. For it is the comics who use most inventively and most dramatically the peculiar resources of motion on the ice. In the middle of a mad rush they stand quiet. They caper, spin, stop, rush off, fall, and scoot headlong. They leap correctly and oddly, they skate clumsily and delicately, and you see the point of the difference. They set the smallest movements against the biggest ones; they change the accent of a step, they change their direction, their skating impetus, for the precise value the change has, and they don't let the change break the continuity of their number. It is out of the extremes of rhythm that skating alone can have that they build their dramatic effects.

And their dramatic intention, even more than their technical range, is what makes the comedians the real models for a serious ice dancer. Like serious dancers in the theater, the ice comedians don't show off their own person, or even their own proficiency; they show you a number, a dance. They focus your attention on a drama of character or on a drama of contrasted movement. In any form of theater dance it is the dramatic focus that makes the difference between "legitimate" and "cheesecake."

Among the noncomic skaters I have seen, there was one who seemed pre-eminently to have this dramatic approach to a part—Skippy Baxter, who is now in the Army. Technically, too, he could be compared to the best comedians. Watching him made me hope a bold choreographer would make a serious group number, utilizing the full technical resources of skating for a legitimate dramatic purpose. Such a piece would lift the audience out of their seats by the incredible rapidity, the sweep and shock of its movement.

Miss Henie's special style, as far as I can see, does not tend in this direction. Admirable is the bland surfacing she gives her routines; she blends her steps, she joins the longer phrases, and she delivers the routine as a coherent whole to perfection. But both from the point of view of contrasted movement and from the point of view of dramatic interest her skating does not suggest anything like real ballet. In movement she avoids wherever possible extremes of force and tautness, she stays in the middle of the dynamic range where everything is nice and charming. It is Hollywood's device of crooning-in-movement. Taken out of the tiny camera field and viewed on a large stage, you see it is just a salon style of motion.

Even if it isn't ballet, there is nothing wrong with a salon style if it has objective dramatic interest—as for example the impeccable dancing of Astaire has. When he dances, he is showing you a dance, he gives it a dramatic focus. But Miss Henie seems not to be showing a dance, she seems to be exhibiting her proficiency and her own cute person. Her amazingly powerful personality rivets one's attention firmly on her personal attractions. I looked at them attentively for four numbers. Very nice, but no drama.

JANUARY 23, 1944

PEARL PRIMUS AND VALERIE BETTIS

Pearl Primus and Valerie Bettis, two young modern-dance soloists, gave the most dramatic recital that any young dancers have given this season. Miss Primus, the young Negro star who has been appearing at Café Society Downtown since last April, is vigorous, clear, and direct; Miss Bettis is intense, delicate, and intellectual. Both are thrilling to watch in motion, and neither has any of the careful academicism that makes many young modern dancers less effective on the stage than in the classroom. They represent a new generation of modern dancers, full of theater vitality.

Miss Primus's subjects were African, Haitian, and North American, several of the last quite naturally concerned with race oppression. What she intends her gesture to mean is always completely clear. But her sense of movement is so powerful that besides telling a story, her dance has constantly the direct force of dancing. The spring in her legs, the sweeping undulations of the torso and arms are thrilling. Her bare feet are not just feet without shoes; they can grip, caress, and strike the floor as if feeling the ground were natural to them. At several sudden high leaps the audience audibly gasped. But it is not her technique that she intends to display or that you admire, it is the dramatic form and the dramatic point of her dance. In several numbers she attains a fine Negro grandeur, and in a Haitian play dance she has a West Indian charm that is spontaneous and sweet.

In style nothing could be more different from Miss Primus than Miss Bettis is. Her dancing is about civilized frustrations, intense virginal quiverings, hesitations, momentary illusions of rest. Her phenomenally rapid leaping, her drumming delicate feet, her strange pauses that turn into a rapid shaking motion are admirable in their elegance; but they too serve her particular dramatic purpose. One has not the sense of watching a dancer's dance inventions; she looks like a beautiful young woman who is agitated, like a character in a situation. And one number, a dance play, where a number of voices offstage developed a story in dialogue, and Miss Bettis answered them in dancing or else in speaking, showed that she is an actress of very great talent, not unlike Bette Davis in her effect. To my mind, Miss Bettis has difficulty concentrating on a simple climax and resolution; she hesitates between a lyric and a dramatic form. But she is a dancer of real power and originality.

The recital had musical interest as well: Miss Primus's fine Afro-Haitian drummers, Messrs Koker and Cimber, whose drumming is fascinating in rhythm and intonation, and two pieces for Miss Bettis by John Cage, which as dance music were sensitive and very civilized.

JANUARY 24, 1944

HANYA HOLM'S "ORESTES"

Hanya Holm, a leader among the older generation of modern dancers, appeared for the only time this season last Saturday. She presented a new long work, for herself, soloists, and group, called *Orestes and the Furies.* It looked to me like a graduation event put on by the girls' physical education department—posture work, intermediate and advanced, neatly and seriously performed.

The trouble was Miss Holm's desire to arrange her pedagogic material in the form of a story. It led, as stories will, to groupings on the floor that presented the young ladies from rather awkward angles. (They were being Furies and were in tights.) However, when all these girls galloped friskily across the stage the effect was jolly, and the audience laughed happily, Furies or no Furies. Another time they ran across and each in turn did a leap that looked as if they might land on their faces (none did), and that was an exciting passage.

The program spoke of these Furies as "pitiless" and "relentless." It stated that the piece was a dance drama in two scenes and explained: "*Orestes and the Furies* relates in dance form, as Aeschylus' *Eumenides* did for the Greeks in drama, the mental torment of a man who had killed his mother." Such claims struck me as pretentious and confusing; the real interest was Miss Holm's gymnastic method.

Her method balances the spine on an oscillating pelvis; it moves the limbs as if from the waist and it holds the back straight. This makes for a good carriage in normal life. One can say that as training for a professional dancer it is insufficient; the limbs are not used in clear opposition to the trunk, and so they have the same look a trunk has; they have no vigor and no firmness in articulation, and so no brilliance in rhythm. The method does not touch theatrical expressiveness either; there is no impersonation in it and there is no sex, either adolescent or adult. But for college girls who do not aim to become professional dancers it affords a modicum of body control. And for educators who have to find some way of teaching "the dance" without offending civic prudery, Miss Holm's method recommends itself too by its Nordic innocence and its smooth look.

Her technique is sufficient also for dances in a sort of out-of-doors barefoot vein, a hygienic pastoral like those evoked by the advertising copy of summer camps. Miss Holm's *Suite of Four Dances*, in this manner, built on mild variations of speed and rearrangements of small groups, was thoroughly attractive. It was easy, clean, and simple. A duet in it was charmingly danced by Joan Palmer and Paul Sweeney, two dancers with a native instinct for the theater; and after that the rest of the number went off very well indeed. It would please on any program.

This light piece was helped very much by the light music of John Cage, written after the dance was set, which contrived to move delicately in opposition to the dancers, and so did not swamp their mild rhythm. John Coleman's earnest score for *Orestes* was well written, though he had so absurd a task set him.

The evening opened with a long group composition, *Song*, by Mr. Sweeney, to Hindemith music with an epigraph from Whitman. In style it resembled Miss Holm's pastoral manner, though with more emphasis on detail. A solo danced by Mr. Sweeney was a good passage, well performed. His ballet experience gave him energy and definiteness.

JANUARY 30, 1944

WHY NOT A NEW YORK BALLET?

For several seasons now the city, and for that matter the whole country, have enjoyed an attack of balletomania from which, happily, neither shows any sign of recovering. The touring companies are packing in customers from Kansas to California. New York could treat itself to a winter season of ballet, too, if there were a proper theater free and an extra company free to dance in it.

Is it too much to ask that New York should have its own ballet with a permanent home here? For such an organization touring would be only a secondary activity. So far, first-class ballet in this country has been leading a hand-to-mouth existence, keeping on the go year in and year out. In constant travel it wears out its strength and brilliance and productivity. Dancers need a home like anyone else. As artists they need to share the natural life of a city, like the people who know they belong there.

As professionals they need quiet to practice, to develop, to rehearse. The choreographers need confidence in the schools that train their young dancers, and they need confidence in whatever intellectual life the country has. These are slow things that have to be able to grow unconsciously over a long term of years. They are the things that eventually give ballet a sound and strong character. A racing stable needs sensible attention all year round and needs to plan for it; much more an ensemble of ballet dancers.

Will the public keep on wanting to see ballet for years to come? We think there are signs enough of a real affection for the art. For one thing, it is no longer considered "foreign" or snobbish; it is no more foreign than a symphony orchestra playing the usual repertory. And for another thing, the present public is not acutely star-conscious; it doesn't go to admire a superstar, regardless of the piece or the ensemble. Stars there are and stars there certainly should be; ballet cannot do without them any more than plays or films can. But the audience seems to go nowadays for the lift it gets out of the entire show. It seems to enjoy the cordial gaiety, the civilized tone a first-rate ballet evening can be counted on to have. Perhaps such qualities are valued more in times like these, when the sustaining warmth of the world of poetry rises in contrast to the vicious ruin of war. But these are qualities which will cheer many of us at any time. So we ask for nothing less than a New York ballet, a first-rate company identified with our home town.

FEBRUARY 17, 1944

"SWAN LAKE" IN EAST INDIAN

At the Ethnologic Theater Saturday afternoon La Meri presented a press preview of her new *Swan Lake* in East Indian dance idiom, and scored a distinct success.

The idea of this version of the famous ballet classic is the following: What would an East Indian, familiar with Indian but not with Occidental dancing, imagine *Swan Lake* to be like, were he to hear the score on records and be told the general action? That is what La Meri and her company show you. The story is there, and the music, and the choreographic outline—action scene, dance by the swan chorus, grand pas de deux, ballabile, and finale scene; all of them are done, however, in Indian steps and pantomime gestures. La Meri has added a prologue showing how the heroine was first enchanted; an Oriental-style combat at the climax between the Enchanter and the Prince; and a last glimpse of the swans that is effective.

To balletgoers this version offers a running comparison between ballet and Hindu dancing that is very interesting and sometimes—as in the Cygnet quartet—very witty. La Meri with her usual fine tact does not press the parallel too solemnly; her little joke is a tender and a touching one. She looked lovely as Hamsa Rani (the Swan Queen) and Aldo Cadena was a convincing young Prince.

The program opened with La Meri's East Indian pantomime comedy *Gauba's Journey to Paradise* and with *Seven Classical Indian Dances*, which familiarizes the audience both with the meaning of the Hindu pantomime gestures and with the technical resources of Hindu dance steps. La Meri and her Natya dancers present this ancient heritage in a delightful and completely unaffected manner.

FEBRUARY 20, 1944

THE ROCKETTES AND RHYTHM

The Rockettes at the Music Hall are an American institution and a very charming one. Their cheerfulness is sweet as that of a church social. Their dancing is fresh and modest, their rhythm accurate and light, and everyone can see that they accomplish what they set out to do to perfection. At the end of their routine when the line of them comes forward in a precision climax, the house takes all thirty-six of them collectively to its family heart. It is a very pleasant moment of contentment all around.

The Music Hall has a charming chorus of classic-ballet girls too, who, like the tap-dancing Rockettes, are perfectly accurate in their timing and exact in their motions. They too dance without affectation in a graceful and modest manner. Just as the Rockettes avoid what is "hot" and disturbing in taps, so the toe dancers avoid what is intensely expressive in ballet; instead they are phenomenally neat, they never blur anything they do, and everyone can see they fully deserve their applause.

The ballet doesn't, to be sure, establish a family feeling in the house as the Rockettes do, but then you rarely see toe dancing in the living room and you often see tap dancing there. Ballet is meant to be seen at a distance, it isn't relaxed or familiar in its bearing. But there is a further reason why the ballet is less effective at the Music Hall than the tap routine. In both of them the dramatic punch of the number lies in the unique (and apparently effortless) synchronization of all the dancers and of the entire dance with the music. While this feat heightens very much the sense of rhythm you get from the Rockettes, it doesn't somehow heighten the sense of rhythm you get from the ballet; though it's just as difficult a feat for the latter, it doesn't carry so in ballet.

The fact is that tap and ballet rhythm are different to start with, in the way they connect with the music. The tap dancer plays with the beat, he plays around it and he never leaves it alone. Whatever else he does in the way of elegant ornament, it's the beat that interests him, and each beat does. You see his relation to it in his motion and you hear it in his taps, and his relation to it is the excitement in the dance. The "hotter" he is, the more intimate and dramatic his relation to it becomes; but he can hold your interest just by showing a cool and a sure relation. And a tap-dancing chorus can by complete synchronization fix with a kind of finality the relation of the dance to the music and so reach a satisfying expression. You know what to follow and at the end you know where you are.

But you don't follow a ballet beat by beat. Ballet dancing probably once had a good deal of this percussive quality—so eighteenth-century dance music suggests. In 1890s ballet you can see a percussive dance number in the Cygnet quartet in *Swan Lake*. Contemporary American ballet tends to use this device more sharply—you see it in parts of *Rodeo* and particularly in *Concerto Barocco*. Here the sound of the dancers' toe steps is part of the effect. But these passages are details. More generally the rhythmic interest in ballet dancing isn't fixed on the beat or on the dancers' relation to it; the interest is in their relation to the musical phrase, to the melody, to the musical period. At such times their rhythm is a "free" one, more like that of a singer in its variety of emphasis than like that of a tap dancer.

Like the blues singer, the ballet dancer takes a freer emphasis for the sake of more intense dramatic (or lyric) expression, so he can change his speed against the steady music, so he can make more kinds of effects with his body and travel more freely about the stage. The spring that is the life and rhythm of taps is not tied to the beat in ballet; it has been extended, so to speak, into a lift in the expression of the dance; you follow the rhythm not by separate steps but by the rise and fall of extended phrases.

In taps you see and hear two different rhythms, both of them in the same strict musical meter. In ballet you often look at a free meter and listen to a strict one. Complete synchronization of ballet and music is a special effect that works by contrast to other rhythmic possibilities and it satisfies only when used for such a contrast. People accustomed to strict acoustic rhythm often take a while to get used to ballet rhythm so they can follow it, but there are many too who can't follow a tap dancer, who lose track of any dance rhythm unless it pounds the downbeat. Well, that's why there are several kinds of dance rhythm to suit different types of the human receiving set.

FEBRUARY 20, 1944

HUMPHREY'S "INQUEST"

Doris Humphrey's new *Inquest* is a dance that leaves no doubt as to its story or its point. The story is clearly told by a speaker, who reads a newspaper report of an inquest held in 1865 in a London slum. We hear of a destitute family, father, mother, and son, who lived in a squalid room. The son began to go blind; finally the father died of starvation. As we listen to the words we also watch the scenes they tell us of, they are acted out in quiet pantomime upstage, in a small space like a room. When in between the pantomime scenes a number of persons pass in files across the darkened stage it is easy to think of them as neighbors passing along the streets. When the story has been told and the neighbors begin a rushing dance sequence to music, it is clear that this dance is their emotional reaction to the story.

But the story has made a further specific point. By quoting sentences spoken by the two survivors at the inquest, the news account has shown us the devotion of the three central characters to one another and to their home. In the pantomime scenes Miss Humphrey, Mr. Weidman, and Mr. Hamilton, who portray the three, give the sense of the dignity of a united family very strikingly. They make us realize that the theme of the piece is the destruction of a home. And so when the movement, which during the story portion was slow and repressed, then bursts into rushing violence in the dance sequences, with stamps and clenched fists, we are quite ready to accept it as expressing our own anger and grief. And at the end, when it grows calm and sustained, we take it as expressing a firm and valid reproach. The piece has pointed out that poverty destroys humane values we all believe in. We applaud it as a sincere and eloquent sermon on the theme of the freedom from want.

If a dancer feels like preaching he has as good a right to do it as any other citizen, and the theater has always liked a sermon now and then. *Inquest* is a piece that appeals to our moral sensibility; it aims to be clear and its aesthetic appeal is secondary. The audience approved of it very much indeed. For my part, I was also interested in something that has often struck me in dances with an excellent propaganda purpose: the difference in speed between getting the ideas and following the dances. One grasps the moral implications quickly and agrees with them. But the full rhetorical exposition of these ideas in dance form takes a good deal longer. The result is that one's response is complete before the dance is finished; and at *Inquest*, too, I was ready for a new idea while, for the sake of emphasis, the dancers were still dwelling on the old one. As the secondary, purely aesthetic appeal was slight, there was a gap in the interest.

Intellectually speaking, an interesting dance is a continuous discovery. The ideas it presents do not precede it, they are formed after one has perceived the movement. And because an interesting dance creates new ideas, it is often not at all easy to understand nor in accord with what one would reasonably expect. This, of course, does not do for propaganda.

Inquest is concerned with reminding us of an idea we all approve and urging us to act on it—and that it does rationally, with complete clarity. It begs the question of how a dance creates its own novel meaning as it goes along.

MARCH 12, 1944

A NOTE ON DANCE INTELLIGENCE

Expression in dancing is what really interests everybody, and everybody recognizes it as a sign of intelligence in the dancer. But dancing is physical motion, it doesn't involve words at all. And so it is an error to suppose that dance intelligence is the same as other sorts of intelligence which involve, on the contrary, words only and no physical movement whatever. What is expressive in a dance is not the dancer's opinions, psychological, political, or moral. It isn't even what she thinks about episodes in her private life. What is expressive in dancing is the way she moves about the stage, the way she exhibits her body in motion. A dancer's intelligence isn't shown by what intellectual allusions she can make in costume or pantomime, or, if she is a choreographer, in her subject matter. It is shown by how interesting to look at she can make her body the whole time she is on the stage.

In the coming ballet season you may be able to compare Alexandra Danilova, Nana Gollner, and Alicia Markova, each as the Swan Queen in *Swan Lake* and each one celebrated in that particular part. Each will be interesting to look at the whole time she will be on the stage, but the effect they make will be different. Watching the three in turn you may see what differences in their physical movement parallel their difference of expression and see how the dance intelligence of each leads her to a slightly different visual emphasis in identical steps and gymnastic feats.

Far apart from questions of choreography, it is variety of visual emphasis that we see when we feel variety of expression. And there are many resources for visual emphasis in dancing. There are the shifts in the pacing of a sequence, the points where the dancer hurries or delays. An identical step or arm gesture can be attacked sharply or mildly, it can subside or be stopped short. These differences draw the eye to one phase of motion rather than another, to one line of the body rather than another, or to the dancer's partner, or else to her momentary position on the stage, or even to a moment in the music which sharpens our sense of her movement.

But the most interesting resource for visual emphasis is the heightened perception of the dancer's body not in a line or silhouette, but in its mass, in its all-aroundness. A dancer can emphasize a passage in the dance by emphasizing the shape her body takes in the air. When she does this she does not call attention merely to the limb that moves, she defines her presence all around in every direction. At such moments she looks large, important, like a figure of imagination, like an ideal human being moving through the air at will. The great dancers seem to do this throughout a dance, but they vary it in intensity.

These are some of the physical characteristics of dance expression, and the brilliant use of them to arouse our interest, to thrill and to satisfy us, is proof of an artist's exceptional dance intelligence. She may have several other sorts of intelligence besides, but it is of no consequence to the public if she has not. It is the boldness and tenderness of her dance intelligence that the public loves her for. MARCH 26, 1944

A FORUM ON DANCE CRITICISM

Agnes de Mille, speaking on a forum on dance criticism recently, made a point I should like to pass on to other dancers as the wisest advice I know on the relation of the dancer to the critic. She spoke of the alternate confident and uncertain periods through which artists pass and how in his uncertainty the dancer longs for assistance and clarification. He is tempted then to turn to the critic to lead him out of his confusion by an authoritative estimate of his individual creative gifts. But Miss de Mille warned against relying on reviews in such moments of doubt. A good critic will tell the dancer which elements in a work get across and which do not. But that alone does not necessarily indicate the most productive, the most sincere direction for the dancer to take. An artist will find his own real strength not by listening to what is said about his work, but in the creative process itself. And it is safer for him to rely on himself to find his own identity; for it is unlikely that anyone else can find it for him.

The forum at which Miss de Mille spoke so brilliantly was held at the YMHA during the storm last Wednesday night in a large comfortable crowded room. The other speakers were Mary Jane Shea, the very gifted choreographer of *Sailor Bar*, B. H. Haggin of *The Nation*, George Beiswanger of *Theatre Arts*, *Dance Observer*, and *Dance News*, and Milton Robertson, a young radio writer; I acted as chairman. The audience took a lively part in the discussion, which turned on the function of the dance critic, what one can expect of him and what he is good for.

Mr. Robertson affirmed that a critic should be a propagandist, that it is his function to create a movement in the right direction, to popularize good art and teach as large an audience as possible what and how to enjoy. But this radio-minded view met with opposition. Not one of the other speakers, and few, it seemed, of the audience, could see the critic as a glorified teacher with all a teacher's classroom authority. Most of those present agreed with Mr. Haggin, who stated that the best critic is a man of exceptional perceptiveness who reports as clearly as possible to his reader. His merit does not lie in dictating what is to be right or wrong. It lies in animating the reader's own perceptions, so that he can see the work more distinctly for himself. This much one can expect of a good critic. But to direct new movements, to popularize the appreciation of masterpieces, to encourage artists, these are not the critic's function; he has no power and no authority to affect them.

On the subject of the critic's lack of authority, Mr. Chujoy, the ballet critic, remarked from the audience that for ten years each season every dance critic has condemned *Schéhérazade*, but *Schéhérazade* continues to be given and is as popular as ever.

For myself, I too quite agree with Mr. Haggin's realistic view of what the critic at best accomplishes. I find the critic looks ridiculous in the role of a dictator of taste and also in that role against which Miss de Mille warned, that of a fortune teller for artists. And yet in practice both roles are constantly being assigned him. With charming good humor, some members of the forum audience, after agreeing that the critic was not a teacher, asked if he couldn't, though, teach just a little. I guess a critic won't quite avoid being a bit of a pedagogue and a bit of a charlatan. But I'm all for everybody's recognizing that these are not his functions, that his function is as Mr. Haggin said: to notice, to order, to report; or as Virgil Thomson has said: to put down a sort of portrait of what went on.

APRIL 2, 1944

MERCE CUNNINGHAM

At the small Humphrey-Weidman Studio in the darkness of Sixteenth Street, Merce Cunningham and John Cage presented a program of solo dances and of percussionist music last night which was of the greatest aesthetic elegance. The audience, an intelligent one, enjoyed and applauded.

It was Mr. Cunningham's first solo recital, though he is well known to dance audiences as soloist in Martha Graham's company. His gifts as a lyric dancer are most remarkable. His build resembles that of the juvenile *saltimbanques* of the early Picasso canvases. As a dancer his instep and his knees are extraordinarily elastic and quick; his steps, runs, knee bends, and leaps are brilliant in lightness and speed. His torso can turn on its vertical axis with great sensitivity, his shoulders are held lightly free, and his head poises intelligently. The arms are light and long, they float, but do not often have an active look. These are all merits particularly suited to lyric expression.

As a dancer and as a choreographer of his own solos, Mr. Cunningham's sense of physical rhythm is subtle and clear. His dances are built on the rhythm of a body in movement, and on its irregular phrase lengths. And the perfection with which he can indicate the rise and fall of an impulse gives one an aesthetic pleasure of exceptional delicacy. His compositions too were in no way derivative in their formal aspect, or in their gesture; they looked free and definite at the same time.

The effect of them is one of an excessively elegant sensuality. On the other hand—partly because they are solo dances, partly because they lack the vigorous presence of the body's deportment characteristic of academic ballet style—their effect is one of remoteness and isolation. This tone may well be due to the fact that Mr. Cunningham is still a young dancer, who is only beginning to discover his own dramatic resources. But I have never seen a first recital that combined such taste, such technical finish, such originality of dance material, and so sure a manner of presentation.

Mr. Cage accompanied the six dances on "prepared" piano and his compositions for them were perfect as dance accompaniment. He also played six piano solos of his own, accompanied Juanita Hall in two songs (one to a text from *Finnegans Wake*), and directed his quartet *Amores*, performed at the Modern Museum last year. The new pieces were applauded—as had been those heard last year—for the delicate sensuality of their odd timbres, for their rhythmic subtlety, and their willfully remote tenuousness of construction. His music, like Mr. Cunningham's dancing, has an effect of extreme elegance in isolation. APRIL 6, 1944

ROSARIO AND ANTONIO

Rosario and Antonio, the very thrilling and handsome young flamenco team from *Sons o' Fun* and the nightclubs, known as "Los Chavalillos" or "The Kids from Seville," gave their first Carnegie Hall recital last night, assisted by a Spanish ensemble. The long program included magnificent moments and inept ones. The audience—largely Hispanic—generously applauded throughout.

"The Kids" deserve the immense success they have had in America. Rosario is a good dancer, a good showman, and she has a very attractive stage personality. Antonio is a first-class virtuoso and a very superb dancer indeed. His youthful fire and his force, his speed and his sharpness of attack sweep her too into a real enthusiasm. His Miller's Dance from *The Three-Cornered Hat* was magnificent in its dance impetus. So were their duets together, whenever they did not stray too far from the established folk or gypsy dance forms. But their Spanish "classic," Madrid lowbrow, or storytelling numbers—concert numbers that require a sharp, special flavor both in choreography and in the pantomimic invention—these did not come off so well. And *Song Among the Shadows*, a long straggling group number billed as a ballet, bogged down completely in pink and white garlands and silly costume changes, with the superb Antonio looking merely complaisantly vain at the end, like a picture-postcard lover.

These lapses in Antonio's style I should blame on his long absence from Spain and on the "concert" school of Spanish dancing, which, at least in America, refines the decorative aspect of Spanish dancing at the expense of far more interesting qualities: violence of rhythm and a kind of compressed fury. Antonio seems to have learned here variety, clarity, and poise; but for so great a Spanish dancer his leaps are too airy, his silhouette not sufficiently held in, his love scenes tend too often to be cute. In the final number, however, he danced once more with that vehement seriousness that Spaniards alone seem to have. I trust he will find his way back to a nobler and severer style, the more chance he has to try it out on the public; he certainly has it in him.

In the supporting company, Antonia Cobos was much applauded for a neat and bouncing solo bolero, and Miss Acuña also performed a solo with success. In the first number I was delighted to see the famous Soledad—once celebrated as a dancer and as a bullfighter—dancing for a moment with an admirable and purely Spanish grotesque flavor, and in another number to hear her singing offstage a *saeta* with no voice but with a marvelous purity of gypsy style. She showed where Rosario and Antonio's real home still is, and where their inspiration should come from. APRIL 10, 1944

NIJINSKA'S "ETUDE"

On the rival ballet programs last night the Ballet Russe de Monte Carlo, appearing at the City Center, presented two premieres: *Etude*, by Bronislava Nijinska, and *Cuckolds' Fair*, by Pilar Lopez. The first looks like evolutions by a recently demilitarized heavenly host, the second is Spanish character ballet dancing with a cheerfully acid Spanish folk story as its excuse. Both are works of interest, though the second is the more winning and harmless. Argentinita, Miss Lopez's sister, meanwhile was dancing with Miss Lopez and a company of Spanish dancers in a premiere at the Metropolitan Opera House, on the program of Ballet Theatre. Her piece was her own version of *El Amor Brujo*, a classic of theatricalized gypsy dancing, famous in the great Argentina's version. This novelty I thought missed fire, perhaps in large part through a poor décor; but it received a good deal of applause.

Etude is Mme Nijinska's interpretation of the religious spirit in Bach's music—in a selection from his concerti and suites. The movement is formalized in a sort of Byzantine manner, and has a solemn rapture in the expression. The palms facing forward, wrists crossed above the head, suggest wing tips of icon angels; and the legs extended in arabesque sometimes hint at the line of the wing below. Because the movement is willfully stylized, it is difficult to give it sweep and vitality. The orchestra in addition played faintly and timidly, so that the dancers had no assurance of the beat. The costumes, too, were too light in their materials, and so failed to be noble (décor by Bilinsky). As a result one did not have the impression that these angels were controlling an immense power in their reserve, as I think had been the choreographer's intention. They seemed mostly stiffly regimented where they might have been magnificently lawful. Nonetheless, the piece has many interesting evolutions and brilliant passages for soloists; and Miss Tallchief, in some steel-hard pirouettes, seemed to indicate better than anyone else what the whole ballet should have looked like.

Pilar Lopez's *Cuckolds' Fair* is essentially one of those decorative dance-games in Spanish style (like Massine's *Capriccio*) that are very agreeable to watch. It has a story, a young wife who wants a child, who goes on a pilgrimage with her husband for the purpose, who goes off into the woods with the sacristan of the village while the husband has a good time drinking, and who presently returns to the husband with her pious wish granted. But this story is only lightly sketched; the point is in the dancing, and that is very pretty. Miss Lopez makes nice shifts of interest, from ironic arm gestures to quick hard turns. And Frederic Franklin (the husband) has a fine solo, which he dances hard and clear, with great force. He keeps his dignity like a Spaniard, and so saves the story. Miss Danilova as the wife is serious and captivating and sure she is right in the true Spanish manner. The costumes are a bit fancy, but the set is airy, and so is the group choreography. The music by Pittaluga is softened de Fallaese in its idiom, all right for this harmless purpose.

Argentinita's *El Amor Brujo* at the Metropolitan doesn't try to tell the wonderfully wry story of that piece very clearly. This story, too, is used as an excuse for short numbers by herself and her partner, José Greco, by Pilar Lopez and Manolo Vargas, and by Argentinita and six young ladies. The plainness of the group dances might have made an authentic folk effect, but neither the group nor Argentinita herself seemed to try for anything but the "concert" folk style. Superb as she regularly is in this style, I had difficulty in the darkness onstage and under her unattractive costume to make out what it was she was doing. The last part of the Fire Dance seemed to me to be very interesting. I liked Miss Lopez's number and moments in the groups I liked too. The set (by Oscar Weidhaas) confused the eye and overloaded the stage completely.

APRIL 11, 1944

DE MILLE'S "TALLY-HO"

Agnes de Mille's new *Tally-Ho*, which had its local premiere last night on Ballet Theatre's program at the Metropolitan, was not quite a hit, but it was certainly not a flop. And it is not an imitation of her previous ballets. She has created a new and touching character—the loving, intelligent, temptable wife, the woman of thirty. She has also found a different dance material for her wit to play with—the refined social dances of the French eighteenth century. She makes them over into something as lively, as sexy, and as American as Broadway dancing. The farce-comedy numbers are brilliant. But there isn't enough serious dancing for contrast, and so the piece seems too much of one thing, and long.

The story of *Tally-Ho* is a charming one. In the Louis XVI part of a French chateau, on a long, lovely summer day, the lively young people of the court amuse themselves; they aren't prudish, they have a good time. Among the guests is a serious young man, "a genius" (Hugh Laing), and his wife (Miss de Mille). He loves his wife and he loves to read. The atmosphere doesn't trouble him, but it does trouble her. The Prince, a very grand young man indeed (Anton Dolin), sees her, follows her, finally meets her alone. She returns to her husband, and the charm goes out of the long afternoon. He slaps her, gently but clearly. Finally an innocent girl who just came to court that day (Lucia Chase) reconciles them, and the Prince grandly bows out.

The production by Ballet Theatre is excellent. The choreography gives the principals (Maria Karnilova is also one) and the minor figures each a chance, and they all dance with distinction and wit. The décor is summery and out-of-doors (by Motley), the lighting excellent. The score—an arrangement of Gluck pieces by Paul Nordoff—has no musical distinction, but it is all of a piece, and it makes the Gluck tunes sound a little like a hit parade of a few years back; it makes them serve for farce-comedy dancing.

Miss de Mille herself is wonderfully real on the stage; she is a great actress-dancer. Her own part is the quietest and the most graceful she has ever had. Her brilliant pantomime inventions, her shifts of rhythm and timing, her use of ballet for jokes at the expense of sex, and her group arrangements, these are full of variety. But the serious parts of the story that should support the jokes, these parts are too much in pantomime, so that they don't get a lift that they would have if they, too, were dances.

She is poetic, and so is Mr. Laing in her presence on the stage; if her passages with him had been more "abstractly" dance passages, her comedy would have been a marvel. As it is, it is pleasant, but it relies on shock value, and that doesn't last all through.

The cast of the piece is admirable. Miss Karnilova, Miss Bentley, and Miss Golden as the "bad" ladies are wonderfully witty and Lucia Chase as the dumpy little innocent succeeds completely in one of her most subtle roles.

APRIL 12, 1944

BEECHAM AT THE BALLET

Sir Thomas Beecham conducted *Romeo and Juliet* last night at the Metropolitan. He made the Delius selections of which the score consists shimmer and glow, swell out and sink to a whisper. Ballet Theatre's orchestra, unusually good this season, never played so well; the rather ponderous music never sounded more sumptuous. Just the same, the dancers onstage, even the great Alicia Markova and wonderful Hugh Laing, did not seem comfortable, and did not seem sure of support. They have danced *Romeo* better when the music was played less as a showpiece, more as a high-grade soundtrack, which serves to time their gestures and often to underline their expression and dynamics. *Romeo* is a fine ballet, and there was no harm seeing if anything can be done to make the musical aspect of it fine, too; the experiment failed.

Sir Thomas's pauses between the selections were an improvement, though. Last night's *Romeo* was a little longer than the version of last fall. A good deal of new business has been added—or rather new details of rich dance gesture; last night some of these seemed confused, probably due to the surprise of the dancers to find a very familiar score ringing with so different an emphasis. Sir Thomas's legato obliterated the landmarks they were used to.

While Ballet Theatre was giving the Grand Pas de Deux from *The Nutcracker*, with Rosella Hightower and André Eglevsky, for a second number, I dashed uptown and caught that very number at the City Center, danced by Alexandra Danilova and Igor Youskevitch. They were performing it up there as part of the third scene of the Monte Carlo's three-scene version of *The Nutcracker*, with which that company opened its program last night. Coming in its proper place as the climax of a long ballet, the number is much more affecting than when it is given as an isolated parade piece. The grandeur of its grace, the poetry of its bodily acrobatics were perfectly expressed by these two great stars; and the noble sweetness of their manner, the melody of their movement were extraordinary. They both soften the contours without in the least blurring them; they find the perfect emphasis for the phrase; the suavity of their head positions and arms is especially remarkable. APRIL 13, 1944

NIJINSKA'S "CHOPIN CONCERTO"; BALANCHINE'S "SERENADE"

At the City Center last night the Ballet Russe de Monte Carlo opened its program with the oddly beautiful *Chopin Concerto*, a familiar ballet by Mme Nijinska set to the E-Minor Concerto. It is an oddly beautiful one because it is clear and classic to the eye but tense and romantic in its emotion.

The structure of the piece—like that of much of Mme Nijinska's work—is based on a formal contrast: in the background, rigid impersonal groups or clusters of dancers, which seem to have the weight of statues; in the foreground, rapid arrowy flights performed by individual soloists. One appreciates their flashes of lightness and freedom because of the weight they seem to rise over, as if the constraint of the group were the springboard for the soloist's release.

Sometimes Mme Nijinska—not unlike our own modern-school choreographers—may seem obsessed by her own neatness, by her own horror of leaving any loose ends of anatomy trailing around. But at her best—and *Chopin Concerto* is one of her best ballets—her stylization is strangely poignant. The contrast she achieves between the rigid poses and the tense brief freedom of ballet virtuosity has a romantic emotion very true to the brilliance and poignancy of the Chopin music. APRIL 14, 1944

"SERENADE"

Balanchine's *Serenade* was beautifully danced last night by the Monte Carlo at the City Center, and it is a completely beautiful ballet.

George Balanchine is the greatest choreographer of our time. He is Petipa's heir. His style is classical: grand without being impressive, clear without being strict. It is humane because it is based on the patterns the human body makes when it dances; it is not—like romantic choreography—based on patterns the human body cannot quite force itself into. His dance evolutions and figures are luminous in their spacing, and of a miraculous musicality in their impetus. Sentiment, fancy, and wit give them warmth and immediacy. But as the audience actually watches, it all looks so playful and light, so unemphatic and delicate, it doesn't seem to call for noisy applause. Ten years later, when noisier successes have faded, one finds with surprise that his have kept intact their first freshness and their natural bloom.

Serenade is a kind of graduation exercise: the dancers seem to perform all the feats they have learned, both passages of dancing and passages of mime (or plastique). There is no story, though there seems to be a girl who meets a boy; he comes on with another girl and for a while all three are together; then, at the end, the first girl is left alone and given a sort of tragic little apotheosis.

I was delighted to hear some giggling in the audience at the parts where all three were together—it showed how well the point got across; the audience at plays giggles too when the sentiment becomes intimate, it is our national way of reacting to that emotion. After giggling last night they gasped a little at some particularly beautiful lifts and then began applauding them. APRIL 15, 1944

A MONTE CARLO MATINEE

At the City Center, at the Saturday matinee, the Monte Carlo gave their three-scene version of *The Nutcracker*, and the children in the audience were impressed when little Clara—no older than they—came on in the third scene and all the dancers bowed to her and she to them. But at the jumping Chinaman they crowed and burbled with pleasure all over the house. Later, they approved the rodeo scene in *Rodeo* as audibly, especially when the heroine fell off her imaginary horse and rolled over on the floor. A few of them, I imagine, will remember many years from now the gently wonderful radiance of Danilova and Youskevitch in the *Nutcracker* duets, and will be in doubt if dancing could really have been as beautiful as that. But it was.

In *Rodeo*, Vida Brown took Miss Etheridge's part as the Cowgirl heroine. Miss Brown's version of the part is more open, more assertive, more horsey. She looks healthy and attractive, she puts the pantomime points across clearly, and she has no trouble filling a star role. On the other hand she does not give—as Miss Etheridge so brilliantly does—the sense of a girl who only gradually discovers what it means to be a girl. It is this gradual, painful, and at the end happy discovery that is the dramatic heart of the piece. And you realize that Miss Etheridge's Cowgirl is really in love with the honest and openhearted Champion Roper whom she gets, while Miss Brown's seems to take him good-naturedly as a second choice in place of the dark and fascinating Chief Wrangler.

APRIL 16, 1944

THE MONTE CARLO AT CITY CENTER

Is the ballet at the City Center really any good? People who haven't been ask me that question in a confidential tone. They assume it would be quite proper for a journalist to write as kindly as possible of a popular-priced ballet appearing at so praiseworthy an institution as the City Center; but just the same, civic virtues aside, they want the lowdown on it. Well, so far as the dancing goes, the Monte Carlo is a company of first-rate dancers, who are handicapped by two disadvantages: in the first place, the stars are overworked; in the second place, the Center was not built for ballet.

The Metropolitan wasn't built for ballet either. From the orchestra seats you have a hard time seeing the dancers' feet downstage, and dance lovers know that standing room at the Met is really the best place to see from. But the Met stage itself is beautifully proportioned for dancing. Of course the greasy-looking masking border should be raised out of sight. But apart from this blot, the proscenium arch frames the stage space harmoniously. The height of the proscenium, the absence of overhanging balconies in the house allow the lines of force in the dance movement to extend freely up and out into the air—and ballet, like orchestra music, needs a clear space to "reverberate" in. It is not only the plush and gold at the Met which gives ballet there an extra glamour; it is also the sense of air on the stage and in the house, for air is the medium of dancing.

The City Center has not these architectural advantages. The stage is not ample enough for the dancing to spread out in. It is too shallow to let all the backdrops be lit right (though the lighting staff does perform miracles with their equipment). And in the orchestra seat at the Center you either sit under a deep balcony or you sit too low and too close to the stage. Sitting close by at ballet is bad, because you can't see the whole stage without bobbing your head from right to left and because details and defects take on an exaggerated prominence when they aren't merged into the overall effect.

Let me add quickly, however, that these structural faults at the Center are not overwhelming misfortunes. First-rate ballet has been given in far worse houses, and any dance lover will put up with these drawbacks and more, if the show itself is good. I list them only to make clear that the Monte Carlo dancers are not assisted by the glamour which a good dance theater lends to ballet, their virtues are not enhanced and their slips are not mitigated as much as they might be.

The second handicap of the Monte Carlo, that the stars are overworked—Miss Danilova and Mr. Franklin dance every night and often dance two major roles on the same program—this is an old practice of our touring ballet companies; even Ballet Theatre has only outgrown it since, after Markova's illness, Miss Gollner and Mr. Petroff were added to the troupe. It is humanly impossible for a star to be brilliant day in and day out without some rest. To impose such heavy schedules on them is a monstrous abuse which should be stopped. While it continues one cannot blame the performers if in some pieces they look strained and weary. As it is they rarely do.

These then are the handicaps, architectural and commercial, which the Monte Carlo has to contend with. In the selections from their repertory I have sampled so far, they have been admirable despite them and, I may add, regardless of the merits of the piece they were dancing. Individually and collectively—for they have a fine ensemble spirit—they are young, pretty, full of dance vitality, well trained, and in earnest. They often have danced like a company of soloists.

And, of course, no dance lover will want to miss seeing Danilova, Youskevitch, or Franklin. These great stars are not eclipsed by any of the great stars at Ballet Theatre. They are irreplaceable and unique and as much a glory of dancing in America as are, for instance, such unique stars as Markova, Eglevsky, or Laing. I don't mean to compare the two companies or to bring up the question of the artistic policy of either one. But I want to say that the Monte Carlo seems to me a fine ballet company at any price.

APRIL 16, 1944

NIJINSKA'S "ANCIENT RUSSIA" AND "SNOW MAIDEN"

Ancient Russia, a new ballet by Bronislava Nijinska for the Monte Carlo, had its second performance last night at the City Center. It is a slight piece, adroitly danced, and mounted very prettily in the bright sets Natalia Gontcharova made six years ago for Massine's uninventive *Bogatyri*.

Ancient Russia is better than *Bogatyri* because it is shorter and doesn't try so hard. But the Russian dark ages haven't had any adequate expression in ballet since Mme Nijinska's magnificent *Noces*, twenty years ago.

Ancient Russia tells a little legend in a sort of expensive Russian candy-box style. The story is of Russian women held prisoners by the bad Tartars, liberated by the good Russians, and it ends with a wedding for the stars. Action and dances have been squeezed to fit to Tchaikovsky's B-flat-Minor Piano Concerto. They have no expressive relation to the music, and they don't have much invention. As dances they are small and pseudo-naive. The ensembles, except for a short moment of buffoonery, are nothing; Alexandra Danilova and Frederic Franklin have nothing of interest to do, but they remain agreeable and serious; Igor Youskevitch as the hero does two remarkably elegant brief numbers, extremely rapidly and whirling barely above the ground. His instant return to this quiet role right after the dancing is a prodigy of change of pace.

Saturday night the Monte Carlo had given its "new version" of Fokine's famous Polovtsian Dances from *Prince Igor*. The reason for a new version seems to be that the company is too small to dance the old one. The changes, at any rate, are all bad ones. Once again a few of the dancers, exuberant Frederic Franklin and the Polovtsian girls headed by Anna Scarpova, saved the day for the general public at least. The amazing costumes, as far as they are new, would serve better for a barbaric number Miss de Mille might compose to this music under the title of *Prince Igor on Second Avenue*.

Mme Nijinska's *Snow Maiden*, which I also saw over the weekend at the City Center, flirts with greeting-card effects and sentiments. But the groupings and the dance phrases often develop very interestingly, and by preserving just enough independence of rhythm in relation to the sugary Glazounov score they keep a certain acid edge. The total result, if not a thrilling work, is yet a very elegant one. I find that only Igor Youskevitch has the right note of elegantly indicating the idyllic sentiments and of making the peasant dances take on a worldly halo of suavity.

APRIL 17, 1944

"FANCY FREE"

Jerome Robbins's *Fancy Free*, the world premiere given by Ballet Theatre last night at the Metropolitan, was so big a hit that the young participants all looked a little dazed as they took their bows. But beside being a smash hit, *Fancy Free* is a very remarkable comedy piece. Its sentiment of how people live in this country is completely intelligent and completely realistic. Its pantomime and its dances are witty, exuberant, and at every moment they feel natural. It is a direct, manly piece: there isn't any of that coy showing off of "folk" material that dancers are doing so much nowadays. The whole number is as sound as a superb vaudeville turn; in ballet terminology it is perfect American character ballet.

Straight character dancing has to do with lowlife characters. *Fancy Free* deals with three sailors on shore leave who come into a bar. They pick up one girl who happens by, then a second girl. That makes two girls for three sailors. The three sailors first show off, and then they fight: result, they lose both girls. Now, too late, a third girl shows up. They decide it isn't worth getting into another fight about her. And then comes a tag line, so to speak, and a blackout.

If you want to be technical you can find in the steps all sorts of references to our normal dance-hall steps, as they are done from Roseland to the Savoy: trucking, the boogie, knee drops, even a round-the-back done in slow motion. But the details aren't called to your attention. Or when each of the sailors to show off does a specialty number you may take John Kriza's turn (the second) as a Tudor parody and Jerome Robbins's rhumba as a dig at Massine mannerisms. But they are just as effective without an extra implication. Most effective of them was the first dance of the three, Harold Lang's brilliant acrobatic turn, with splits like those of the Berry Brothers. It was in this number that the house took fire, and from there on the ballet was a smash.

Leonard Bernstein, the young composer of *Jeremiah,* wrote the score for *Fancy Free* and conducted it brilliantly. It has complex nervous rhythms and violent contrasts of thin and thick orchestral texture. I thought it a little overcomplicated, and not quite charming enough; but it was a hit, too, and the musicians I spoke to commented on the brilliance of its orchestration. I liked best the rhumba for Robbins's solo. Oliver Smith's set is in the style of vaudeville sets, it is a perfect space for the seven characters of the piece to dance in, but it is less interesting to look at than his previous sets. It, too, was applauded. Kermit Love's costumes for the three girls were perfect. So were the girls. APRIL 19, 1944

BORIS AND MOYLAN IN "SERENADE"

There were no novelties on Wednesday night's program of the Monte Carlo at the City Center, but I was happy to see Balanchine's *Serenade* once more, and to enjoy again its clean dance style and its atmosphere of serenity, both in animation and in adagio. The ensemble danced *Serenade* beautifully once again and the audience often applauded during the piece.

Among the soloists, Ruthanna Boris, who had the longest part, was remarkable in her precision and in her elegance. Like many young dancers, she tends to force her straightforward leaps (grands jetés) so that the taut forward leg drops a little before the body reaches its highest point in the air, and the clean rise of the leap suffers. Toward the end I found she slightly forced an expression of pathos, as if she were miming a part; it doesn't suit this particular ballet. But it is possible she was disturbed by a slight error that occurred in the ensemble near the climax; and, indeed, I wasn't sure she hadn't hurt herself earlier in the piece. In any case, these are minor errors in so very gifted a young classic dancer.

Mary Ellen Moylan again astonished with a particularly fine long-held arabesque that rose in height at the end as an opera singer's high C increases in volume in the last bar. Leon Danielian came on a little too portentously, and he flourished his hands too much, turning them back at the wrist. He is a gifted dancer, and doesn't need to show off to make his real effect. Nicholas Magallanes is very handsome indeed, strong and discreet, and he has a manly style; he seems a little lazy on the stage, but since this is his first season, it is good to note he hasn't any foolish mannerisms. In a small part blond Nina Popova was remarkably quick, clear, and straight. Since this ballet is in pure academic style, it gives all the dancers a chance to show how well they can do what they have so arduously learned; the total effect is one that combines dance brilliance and personal modesty, a wonderful effect that the perfection class in a ballet school gives to the morning visitor.

The second ballet on the program was *Ancient Russia*, which I recently reviewed far too leniently. Seeing it a second time, I think it a very poor piece, with no dancing to speak of, and the arbitrary discrepancy between the music and the movement forces the dancers into a fake execution. The entire company took it easy during the piece, and I thought they were quite right.

The company took it easy in a different way during the last number, *Gaîté Parisienne*. In this ballet, which has been danced several thousand times in its six years of life, the dancers know exactly which moments in each part count, and which moments will carry sufficiently with a minimum of effort. Wherever it counted, they were fine that night. As a performance of the piece at high tension is rather hectic to watch, I enjoyed *Gaîté* more than I expected to. Alexandra Danilova and Frederic Franklin were superb, especially in their duet; the simplicity of their stage manner, the sweetness and vivacity of their stage personalities, and their perfect musicality are a very great pleasure indeed. Alexander Goudovitch had a fine moment at the end of the free-for-all. The entire piece was as usual a tremendous success.

APRIL 20, 1944

"FANCY FREE" A SECOND TIME

Fancy Free, the new Robbins-Bernstein-Smith triumph of Ballet Theatre at the Metropolitan, holds your interest as consistently the second time you see it as the first. The pacing of the ballet is very fine, and the sober moment at the close is real and appealing without being in the least pathetic. The game the sailors play with the first girl's purse, the recognition scene between the girls, and the pauses before each of the sailor's solos—the passages all have a wit that is sound because it is not so affable as you expect. The piece is not conceived as a charm number.

The dancers don't play it as a charm number either. They dance it with a direct vitality and a sense of real life that are even more remarkable than their dance brilliance. The three sailors (Robbins, Kriza, and Lang), of course, have the best roles. But Janet Reed's transition from the stiffness she first gives her hardboiled part to the later natural abandon is superb. Equally astonishing is how Muriel Bentley and Shirley Eckl instantly convey the particular character of their roles; you know all about these girls, and you remember even the one you only see for a moment distinctly.

I noticed the second time how forcefully the score seconds the dramatic effects and builds big climaxes where they are needed and where the small cast couldn't quite create them alone. The orchestra under Mr. Bernstein plays magnificently. As for the set, when the curtain went up the house broke into real applause, and a gentleman back of me said "Solid!" under his breath.

APRIL 24, 1944

PEARL PRIMUS

Pearl Primus, the young Negro modern dancer, who has attained celebrity via ten months at Café Society Downtown, gave a solo recital at the Ninety-second Street YMHA last Saturday and repeated the program on Sunday. Both dates were sold out long ahead. Since her last recital in January (jointly with Valerie Bettis) Miss Primus has made striking progress in the technical finish of her dancing, and the revisions she has made in her numbers are all of them interesting choreographic improvements. Now her magnificent natural dance impulse is seen even better than before.

Strange Fruit and *African Ceremonial* were on Saturday especially impressive. In these dances the detail was exactly defined, the continuity consistent throughout, and in *Strange Fruit* the pacing was brilliantly contrasted. There were three new numbers on the program, of which *Study in Blues*, a little joke, was the most finished.

In one serious piece, the reiterated leaps were so fine that the house broke in with applause. And in *Hard Time Blues* Miss Primus did another leap that by its drive and height made the audience gasp. It happened that the second and third similar leaps in this number did not succeed so well: the second one, because it was turned the wrong way; the third, because when she came to it she missed her breath and so the run up to the leap was not sharp. It is proof of Miss Primus's taste that she does these startling leaps only rarely, and only for the sake of their expression at that moment in the number.

Miss Primus has astonishing gifts of movement—for flow, for lightness, for power; and her powerful body is beautifully plastic on the stage. With constant stage experience, her stage personality grows sweeter and more direct. Though the dance effect of almost any young dancer's solo recital is repetitive and strained, Miss Primus's seemed varied and easy. She seemed, too, to rely less on the moral sanction of her themes to awaken sympathy and interest, and more on the buoyant drive of her dance; and in the theater, whatever the theme, it is not the theme, it is the actual dancing that really wins the audience's faith.

APRIL 24, 1944

"DARK ELEGIES"

Tudor's *Dark Elegies*, on yesterday's program at the Metropolitan, is Ballet Theatre's *Parsifal*. A sort of *Weihefestspiel* given only once or twice a season, it is said to be Tudor's favorite among his works, and Miss Kaye and Mr. Laing, the stars who interpret his work so brilliantly, are said to consider it his masterpiece. The reviewer feels respect for these opinions, but he does not share them.

Dark Elegies is set to Mahler's *Kindertotenlieder*, a luxurious, slightly overstuffed symphonic setting of the touchingly intimate poems by Rückert on the death of children. In the orchestra a man sings the words. On the stage seven young women and four young men, dressed in the Youth Movement fashions of Republican Germany, dance a stylized version of Nordic folk dances. The dance figures have the flavor of a vestigial ritual and the solemn expression of the dancers is ritualistic also. They look a little like modern dancers of some years back doing a symbolic number.

The actual dance detail of *Dark Elegies* is willfully spare, but it is also of a remarkable elegance in its arrangement. The timing of the accents, the placing of the dancers, the correspondences of dance phrases to musical ones, the variety of invention—all this is completely interesting. The look of helplessness in the men's arm movements, in the women's toe steps, and in the remarkable lifts has a distinct pathos. The running circles at the climax are very effective. But the fact that this helpless and impoverished tone is continued so long, and continued even during the consolatory last section, leaves me with the feeling that at the end there has been no dramatic progress, that the stage characters have exhibited their suffering and have gone off content with that. It gives the ballet a faintly stuffy, holier-than-thou expression. APRIL 26, 1944

A TRIBUTE TO YOUSKEVITCH

The Ballet Russe de Monte Carlo closed its spring season at the City Center Saturday night with a program consisting of *Etude*, *Cuckolds' Fair*, *Pas de Deux Classique* ["Black Swan"] (danced by Alexandra Danilova and Igor Youskevitch), and *Red Poppy*. It was the pas de deux that was the event of the evening, and it was Seaman Second-Class Youskevitch—dancing on the last night of his shore leave—who made it so.

At the moment Youskevitch is at the peak of his classic style. His style is calm, rich, and elastic. It is completely correct. You see easily what the action is, how the trunk takes the main direction of the dance, and how the limbs vary the force and the drive by calculated countermovements. The changing shape of the dancing body is vigorously defined.

The weight of the body and the abundant strength of it are equally clear; and the two aspects blend gracefully in the architectural play of classic sequences. The distribution of energy is intelligent and complex. In his leaps, for instance, the noble arm positions, the tilt of the head sideways or forward, make you watch with interest a whole man who leaps; you don't watch, as with most dancers, only the lively legs. And while most dancers leap for the sake of the bound upward only, Youskevitch (like Markova) leaps for the entire trajectory, and for a mysterious repose he keeps as he hangs in the air.

The completeness of his dance education is unique among our classic male dancers. His rhythm is free, his characterization economical, his lift gracious. His stage presence has none of that hard insistence on attention that breaks the illusion and the flow of a classic ballet. It is unanxious and gently confiding. True, he has neither blazing temperament nor dazzling edge; at times I find his romantic miming a trifle too politely eager; I prefer Franklin's Hussar in *Danube* to Youskevitch's. But if Igor hasn't every quality imaginable, I, at least, know of no dancer anywhere who is nearer than he to perfection.

And now he is returning to his base, it is hard to think how the Monte Carlo can long continue as a first-class company without him.

MAY 1, 1944

JANET REED: LEARNING TO STAR

At the Metropolitan last night, Ballet Theatre presented *Fair at Sorochinsk*, *Pas de Quatre*, *Fancy Free*, and *Tally-Ho*. Young Janet Reed danced Cerrito in the second ballet, one of the passers-by in the third, and the wife in the fourth—three star parts and three very different roles on one program. It was a tour de force and redheaded Miss Reed carried it off with determination.

As a dancer, she is a born soubrette: petite, active, bounding, sharp, malicious, and strong. She is in her element in character parts where the gesture counts and the speed makes a point. Her fault on the stage is that she often has a tendency to force both in her movement and in her projection; the first breaks the continuity, the second isolates her own part from the general atmosphere and meaning of a ballet. Forcing, except in farce, destroys the dancer's dignity.

Last night she was not quite in her best form, judging by her Cerrito and her passer-by. I had not yet seen her in the lead in *Tally-Ho*, which she was dancing in place of Miss de Mille for the second time last night. Miss Reed's dance technique is superior to Miss de Mille's—the steps are more distinct and rapid, she is more at ease in the lifts. One misses, however, the sense of legato phrasing that Miss de Mille showed.

Miss de Mille, by lifting her chest and tilting back her head easily, by understressing her arm gestures and steps, gave the sense of a woman in the relaxed full flower of her thirties; she was also happily aware of her husband's presence, and happily at home in it. She projected not only her own role but their joint role as a couple. (And Mr. Laing, as the husband, does the same thing very beautifully on his side.) A happy marriage and the dignity of a happy wife are the focus of the story, even though the point gets insufficient expression in actual dancing. This crucial overtone Miss Reed does not convey.

A quieter approach, and movements timed just a trifle behind the beat, might help Miss Reed. And a sense of repose might help her, too, to give the feeling of being in the open air in summer, which Miss de Mille so beautifully conveys.

A young dancer so obviously talented and intelligent as Miss Reed is can be forgiven for such misjudgments; stage assurance is not learned without mistakes.

MAY 2, 1944

MARKOVA'S GISELLE: BALLET THEATRE'S GLORY

Alicia Markova in *Giselle* is Ballet Theatre's greatest glory. Last night was the second of three performances of *Giselle* on this season's programs; and it was a gala evening at the Metropolitan. Miss Markova danced once again with incomparable beauty of style—dazzlingly limpid, mysteriously tender.

There is no other dancer whose movement is so perfectly centered, and who controls so exactly the full continuity of a motion from the center to the extremities. There is no other dancer whose waist and thighs are so quick to execute the first actions that lead to an arm gesture and to a step, or who diminishes the stress so precisely as it travels outward along the arms and legs. It is this that gives her dancing figure its incomparable clarity, its delicacy, and its repose. It is this, too, that makes her dance rhythm so clear to the eye and so full of variety.

This superlative dance intelligence makes her dance fascinating, both as pure motion and as motion to music. The fragility of her figure, the dramatic conviction of her characterization give her dance another and equally strong expressivity. Her physical and intellectual concentration confer on her a mysterious remoteness and isolation, and this tragic dignity makes her expressions of tenderness extraordinarily touching.

All her qualities, of dancing, of mime, of presence, find a perfect use in the part of Giselle; the extraordinary effect Miss Markova creates in this part is obvious to the thousands who watch her, whether they are familiar with ballet or not. Last night again she received a unanimous ovation.

The costumes and set of the first act—dating from the early days of Ballet Theatre, when *Giselle* was taken as a cute period piece—are still a blot; in time we may get a new décor, and let us hope it will be Berman's projected one for this piece. MAY 6, 1944

WHERE ARE THE NEW SERIOUS BALLETS?

The April "war" between Ballet Theatre and the Monte Carlo would have been more exciting to watch if it had been a competition between artistic directions instead of a competition for customers. There were plenty of customers everywhere, so both companies won. Ballet Theatre, of course, had the smash hit, *Fancy Free*, and it had all through the smarter public. But it didn't allow its great choreographer, Mr. Tudor, to produce a new serious work; nor had the Monte Carlo allowed its guiding artist, Mme Nijinska, also a great choreographer, to create a serious new piece. Though the dancing was often superb and the audience got its money's worth, neither company can boast of a new production an intelligent citizen can get excited over; with all their rich resources neither company produced anything as remarkable as Martha Graham's *Deaths and Entrances*.

Ballet Theatre has given native-born choreographers a chance as long as they would entertain. The Monte Carlo has tried to get the foreigners to be cute. No doubt the heavy touring schedules of both organizations make it impossible for them to rehearse with concentration. And no doubt the general public likes light pieces. But it is striking how the daily public here in town responds to the heavy ones, the abstract ones, the classic ones. Both companies underestimate the intelligence, the sensibility, and the curiosity of the public. And they have no faith in the special power of a disinterested creation. One can't win an artistic victory without taking an artistic chance. And without such a special kind of victory no amount of success can counterbalance the decline of prestige.

Artistic prestige is ballet's chief economic asset. In order to survive, ballet has to keep in competition with the classics—as contemporary serious painting, music, and poetry do. It can't compete with commercial entertainment. This is not a matter of snobbishness, it is strictly a money matter. Ballet is too extravagant an apparatus to exist without subvention, public or private; it is as extravagant as a museum, or a symphony orchestra. In their artistic policy all of these enterprises must sell themselves to the kind of money that can pay for them—in their case the solid fortunes of trusts, foundations, and states. Once our ballet succeeds in interesting such money, it can stop living from hand to mouth and present itself in its proper splendor.

And it is the solid world of the classics and of their serious contemporary competitors—representing as it does long-term artistic capital—that is most congenial to such long-term fortunes; while the world of commercial entertainment—strictly short-term artistic capital—normally appeals to short-term fortunes as a congenial field for their erratic spending.

But there is a simpler argument in favor of a disinterested artistic policy. It is that a ballet company is a company of artists, and artists lose their vitality when they cannot feel around them an atmosphere of artistic conviction.

For the moment success is enough to give our dancers vitality. And though I feel that the glamour of momentary success is no solid foundation on which to build an American ballet, I am full of admiration for their freshness, their earnestness, and their unremitting intensity. Their own artistic integrity is unimpeachable. MAY 7, 1944

GRAHAM'S INTELLECTUAL FURY

Martha Graham—undisputed star of our modern-dance world both as a dancer and as a choreographer—opened with her company yesterday a week's "season" of nightly performances at the National Theater. Last night's program centered on Miss Graham's latest work, *Deaths and Entrances*, which had so extraordinary a success when first shown a few months ago, and which, seen again, has the same fury-possessed and tragic fascination. The other two numbers on the program were *El Penitente* and *Punch and the Judy*. During the course of the week Miss Graham's repertory will show eleven of her celebrated works.

In *Deaths and Entrances* Miss Graham gave once more an unmatchable performance. The work expresses with a phenomenal brilliance of fluctuating, frantic images the increasing horror which surrounds the human awareness in adult life. Memories of comparative innocence in earlier years are so many insults to the later consciousness. But Miss Graham's heroine survives these intellectual living conditions, as every intellectual must, and stands sane and calm at the end.

Last night everyone in Miss Graham's company was quite exceptionally fine. Their clarity in each detail and their ability to hold the urgency of the atmosphere and the rhythm made the piece as a whole easier to follow than it had been originally. It is a long, difficult, and fitful work; but it is so uniquely imaginative and magnificent a one that one can easily forgive what seem its occasional weaker passages for the sake of the total effect. As a whole it is certainly a masterpiece of romantic distortion in choreography, and of romantic insurgence in emotion.

Punch and the Judy, on the other hand, is a sardonic, urban farce that, with wit and personal charm, explains how married life is mere folly, family ties and marital fidelity are so much nonsense. It is far from simple good humor; it is a stinging comment, performed with a nonchalant smile. Here, too, the company was perfect in every witty or cumbersome detail.

El Penitente, which opened the program, is a trio for Miss Graham, Erick Hawkins, and Merce Cunningham. It depicts, under a religious allegory, with images derived from New Mexican "primitive" art objects, the mystery play of man and woman and fate.

These three pieces show something of the range of Miss Graham, and of her unique inventiveness in dance gesture. Her extraordinary stage presence holds these innumerable details in focus. But her company, too, understand her complex dance figures perfectly.

The new staging of the pieces is occasionally overheavy, and the music occasionally too shrill and disjointed. But the impression of the evening is one of magnificent intellectual integrity and dance discipline.

MAY 8, 1944

THREE GRAHAM SOLOS

Three of Martha Graham's celebrated solos, *Frontier*, *Lamentation*, and *Deep Song*, were the feature of last night's program of Miss Graham and her company at the National Theater, and in all three Miss Graham held the audience completely in her spell.

In their choreographic workmanship all three show the extraordinary precision and the astonishing range of her plastic intelligence. Miss Graham does not dance now with the unremitting tautness that characterized her execution seven or eight years back, and it seems to me that though a few of the accents in *Frontier* are less brilliant than formerly, the overall effect of each number is more coherent, more sovereign.

Lamentation (1930) is the least complex of the three solos. Miss Graham, seated, wrapped in what look like cerements, thrusts out her wrapped arms, her torso, her legs, straining against the drapery, and creating for the eye extraordinary sequences of triangular volumes; in this violent limitation her movements seem to reach out preternaturally far.

Frontier (1935) has long been one of her most popular numbers. Here again it is in her stationary poses that she is able in the thrust of the neck to give an extraordinary sense of enormous space around her. *Frontier* is incidentally an answer to those critics of modern dancing who claim it is technically too easy; *Frontier* is certainly technically one of the most difficult dances anybody has ever attempted.

Deep Song (1937), a homage to Republican Spain, is the longest, and richest, of the three solos. It is technically an extremely interesting derivation from Spanish flamenco dancing, from the carriage and rhythm of it—but it is a completely original and personal dance form that Miss Graham has evolved. I found *Deep Song* last night very noble and very moving.

The evening began with a particularly fine performance of *El Penitente*, in which Miss Graham—apparently rested from the exertions preceding this repertory season—was much more interesting than on the opening night, last Sunday. The piece is a tender and subtle one; I only regret that its new décor and properties are less delicate than those of the original production. The music, by Louis Horst, is charming and was well played. In fact, the orchestra was excellent last night throughout. The lighting in general is still overcomplicated and too harsh; but that, too, will no doubt improve.

MAY 11, 1944

GRAHAM'S "AMERICAN DOCUMENT" AND "PRIMITIVE MYSTERIES"

Last night's program of Martha Graham and her company at the National consisted of *Primitive Mysteries*, *Punch and the Judy*, and *American Document*. *Primitive Mysteries* is a gentle work of ten years ago which many recall with pleasure. Suggested—like several other of Miss Graham's works—by the Spanish-Mexican art of the Southwest, it is consciously naive in its gesture. It contrasts the rigid, heavy, underslung stance of the group of girls with Miss Graham's delicate refinement; she is a Madonna-like figure who sheds her grace gently on her peasant worshippers. The sense of communion on the stage is touching, and unforced. Only the repeated processional entrances and exits exaggerate the pseudo-naive stylization; as a whole the work is distinctly a happy one. The music by Louis Horst is flowing, beautifully shaped, and reticently expressive. Of all Miss Graham's scores his are by far the most musical and apt.

American Document, on the other hand, is in its present form a complete failure. Originally it seemed at least to conceal some sting of protest and to present our history as much for its disgraces as for its strength. At present it seems intended merely as smug glorification. It is monotonous as dancing and in sentiment varies from hollow solemnity to mawkish sentimentalism. The opening of Miss Graham's Indian solo and one sentence quoted from Jonathan Edwards are the only thirty seconds of interest; the rest seems as insincere as those patriotic full-page advertisements in color in the slick-paper magazines.

One can see that Miss Graham's intentions were to make the movement open, plain, and buoyant. Perhaps it is her own natural subtlety that defeated her. The movement turns out to be inelastic, it strikes poses, and it pounds downward. The company performed the piece very handsomely, and one failure is not a disgrace to any choreographer.

MAY 12, 1944

MARKOVA IN "LES SYLPHIDES"

On last night's program of Ballet Theatre at the Metropolitan the great Alicia Markova—whom we are not to see in ballet next year—appeared in *Sylphides* and in *Pas de Quatre*. There was no trace of the indisposition that had made some of her earlier appearances this spring uneven. Though she is perhaps not yet as strong as she was before her illness last fall, her dancing yesterday was again immaculately beautiful.

In *Sylphides* one could admire again the limpidity of her phrasing—how delicately she seems to let the musical phrase impel and lift her, and then how gently the impulse in her subsides into repose. Without blurring a detail of her steps, she can subordinate them to a retard or an acceleration of impetus. No other dancer can make her runs on toe or half-toe as exact and yet transfer her weight as imperceptibly. In complex sequences, it is the complete elasticity of her ankle and instep that gives her so light a step; but it is her keen sense of rhythm, her dance imagination that make the most of her exceptional technique. And what is uniquely Miss Markova's own is the rare grace of spirit which her dancing figure communicates.

MAY 20, 1944

HIGHTOWER AS SWAN QUEEN

Rosella Hightower, blossoming into New York's favorite among the younger classical dancers, gave a quite exceptionally fine performance as the Swan Queen in *Swan Lake* at Ballet Theatre's Saturday matinee at the Metropolitan. Dimitri Romanoff too, as her Prince, was remarkable in the poetic quality of his miming and of his support, a quality which John Kriza, as the Prince's Friend, shared with him. The emotion of *Swan Lake* comes from the sense of a mysterious understanding that exists among these three characters—and between them and the enchanted swans. And it is only out of their simple acceptance of a moonlight transfiguration that the bravura "arias" of the ballerina can take on their real poignancy. Saturday's performance was a touchingly sincere one, and Miss Banks as one of the swans was lovely, too.

Miss Hightower was superb in the great adagio, better than she has ever been in it before. Her phrasing was sustained, classical, and lucid. All through the piece her slow gestures had a beautiful repose. The quicker ones, at which she usually excels, seemed too hasty by contrast. But in her second allegro solo she was again very brilliant indeed. It is a great pleasure to watch her growing into a complete ballerina.

Swan Lake was followed by *Fair at Sorochinsk*, in which Jerome Robbins substituted for Anton Dolin as the Devil. As the striking rapidity of the part is based on toe work, Mr. Robbins, who doesn't, like Mr. Dolin, use toe shoes, had a hard time making much of it. The exuberant climax of the fair scene as usual went over in a big way; the subsequent quiet dances of the boys and girls have lost a little of their charming bloom because the dancers no longer start their phrases a fraction behind the beat, and in addition end the phrase too hastily.

The third number on the program was *Barn Dance*. I think that the orchestra in this has become too brassy for the attractive parlor style of the score, though of course the dances on stage are brassy if they are anything. In *Barn Dance*, however, Nana Gollner and Paul Petroff give their best performances of the season. Miss Gollner is ravishing to look at, and both of them are amusing and vivacious; the absence of sustained phrasing, which has for me spoiled their classic work this season, is no drawback in this high-pressure romp.

MAY 21, 1944

A BALLET LOVER'S VIEW OF MARTHA GRAHAM

Any one of Martha Graham's highly intelligent pieces would gain in theatrical brilliancy if she and her company could present it singly, say, as an item on a Ballet Theatre program. Her particular genius would flash more strikingly right next to the genius of other choreographers and dancers who excel at other aspects of dancing. Some of my friends are shocked by this genius of hers and they tell me she has no style, that she fascinates merely as heretics do, by her contrariness. But I keep being struck in all her work by its intellectual seriousness, its inventiveness, and its exact workmanship; and these are qualities I can't think of as heretical or contrary. They offer a moral basis for style. I see no reason why one shouldn't try to place her work in relation to the ballet tradition and see what is special in her dance method.

The special thing about Miss Graham is not that she is a modernist. Almost no one nowadays is anything else. Modernism in dancing is really a conservative tendency. Its first victories through Isadora and Fokine, its boldest ones through Nijinsky and Mary Wigman, its general acceptance in the twenties—these are facts of history. Inside and outside of ballet, modernism has emphasized the interest in bit-by-bit gesture, gesture deformed, interrupted, or explosive. It has done everything possible to break up the easy-flowing sequence of a dance.

But through all these modernisms well-trained ballet dancers made any gesture, however odd, with reference to their traditional center of motion, and so still gave to a series of disjointed gestures a logical dance continuity. And through all these modernisms, too, ballet retained its traditional formula of the architecture of a piece, with the long dance aria (like the central adagio in *Swan Lake*) as the basic type of an expressive climax. Ballet dancers had sound models for dance coherence and for dance rhythm all around them.

The modern-school dancers, however, had no models for long, serious poetic forms: for them the fundamental questions of dance rhythm and dance continuity could not be referred to a traditional type. Miss Graham, for instance, began with the decorative attitudes and the connecting walks of Denishawn "exotica"; her formal point of departure was an actor's loose gesture sequence, not a dancer's logically sustained dance sequence.

But against this enormous handicap she did succeed in discovering for herself a sound basis on which any sequence of gesture can keep a strictly logical continuity.

She has done this, I think, by developing an acute sense of the downward pull of gravity and of balance, and an acute sense, too, of where the center of pressure of a gesture is. By concentrating motion on these two elements, she can exaggerate or deform a gesture as far as she chooses without blurring it, and she can retract or transform a gesture without breaking the continuity of movement. She is the only one of our modern dancers who has really solved this fundamental problem in all its aspects.

Ballet began, one might say, on the basis of lightness, elevation, and ease; it could add modernism (which was an increased heaviness and an oddity of gesture) for its value as contrast. Miss Graham, beginning with modernism, made of heaviness and oddity a complete system of her own. Brilliancy in heaviness and oddity became her expressive idiom. This is one way of explaining why much of her style looks like ballet intentionally done against the grain, or why she has used lightness and ease not as fundamental elements but for their value as contrast. But Miss Graham's system keeps expanding, and this season her entire company now and again seemed to be using nonmodernist dance qualities not merely for contrast but directly.

Judged by what I look for in ballet, Miss Graham's gesture lacks a way of opening up completely, and her use of dance rhythm seems to me fragmentary. It does not rise in a long, sustained line and come to a conclusion. I find she uses the stage space the way the realistic theater does, as an accidental segment of a place, not the way the poetic theater uses the stage, as a space complete in itself. And I do not feel the advantage to dancing in these qualities of her style. But I am intensely curious to see what her next works will look like, and where the next ten years will lead her. I find watching her not a balm for the spirit, but certainly a very great pleasure for the intelligence. MAY 28, 1944

BALLET CONDUCTING: BEECHAM AND BERNSTEIN

The great Sir Thomas Beecham and brilliant young Leonard Bernstein conducting as guests for Ballet Theatre this spring—the first, *Romeo and Juliet*; the second, his own *Fancy Free*—not only added to the season's glamour, they also proved how immensely valuable a conductor can be to the dancers. For the conductor, leading a ballet is very different from leading a symphony. As a performer, he has to yield the spotlight to the ballerina; and even as a musician, he can't let the music take the spotlight. He has to adjust the score to the rhetoric of the drama onstage—and when a ballet story has been set to music composed for another purpose, the points of emphasis are often quite different ones. The ballet conductor has to take the cue for his dynamic climaxes from the theatrical moment. When the audience has become absorbed by the action, when it has grasped the situation, an increase in loudness may clinch the big effect; but if the audience is not warmed up, if it has not yet caught on to the rhythm of the piece, a big noise will only puzzle, distress, or alienate it. Most important of all, the conductor has to adjust to a speed that the dancer can use, according to the sequence she executes, according to her physical temperament; and if that speed is tough on the musical sense, he has to find a way of making it sound slower or faster than it is. The fixed common term between the dancer and conductor, between the rhythm of music and the rhythm of dancing, is the beat or pulse of the music. The more steady and reliable the beat is, the more freedom for inspiration the dancer will have.

In *Fancy Free* Leonard Bernstein's beat was steady and, better still, it was buoyant. His downbeat, delivered against an upward thrust in the torso, has an instantaneous rebound, like that of a tennis ball. He can give the illusion of an increase in speed by increasing his buoyancy and adding a dynamic crescendo; so he doesn't have to quicken the tempo to pep up the show. Such a beat gives a lift to the dancers and it gives them confidence; they feel that he won't hurry them breathlessly in a lively spot, or die out on them in a nostalgic cadence. And you could see that the dancers, even when they came on tired, responded to Mr. Bernstein like hepcats to Harry James.

Dancers and conductor didn't have so easy a time getting together in

Romeo and Juliet, but in this ballet there isn't any groove for them to get into. The Delius selections which serve as score don't by nature follow the logic of the action; nor is their beat or even their rhythmic lilt clearly distinguishable in the web of luxurious sonorities. *Romeo* has always been a theater hit, a richly involved and sensitive spectacle in a deliberately luscious neo-Pre-Raphaelite style. But the dancers have been lucky if they heard most of their cues, and they have had a good deal of trouble getting their complicated sequences and shifts of balance to flow with the music. On account of musical trouble, *Romeo*, after a year's run, still hadn't settled when Sir Thomas was invited in to conduct it.

Even he didn't solve the matter at once. But the eighth (and last) time he conducted, the audience saw throughout the most brilliant and the most exact performance the ballet ever had. This time the orchestra was astonishingly transparent. One heard distinctly the variety of impetus the interwoven musical phrases have, their devious and delicate qualities of motion, as they rise to the surface and shift and overlap and get lost again in a sort of harmonic undertow. The dancers not only recognized their cues, they could find in the musical phrase they were cued to the exact impetus which suited their momentary phrase of dancing. Tudor had counted on these correspondences of impetus from the first. But only Sir Thomas understood completely on the stage and in the orchestra what aspect of the score it was that Tudor had counted on, and he made this aspect musically plausible and expressive. The result was a unique performance by the entire company; in fact, the delighted dancers, especially Miss Markova and Mr. Laing, probably inspired Sir Thomas quite as much as he did them; artists like to reciprocate inspiration.

I wish Sir Thomas or Mr. Bernstein could conduct *Swan Lake* several times next season; it would give the company a clue to how much more they might get out of the music and out of the piece. Meanwhile Ballet Theatre is to be thanked particularly for having both of these distinguished guests conduct often enough so that the dancers could really profit by their exceptional musicianship. JUNE 4, 1944

MARIANNE MOORE ON PAVLOVA

An album of Pavlova photographs with "accompanying notes" by Marianne Moore is the very astonishing contents of the latest issue of *Dance Index*—price, one quarter; admirers of Pavlova and admirers of Miss Moore will not want to miss so remarkable an item. There are thirty-one photographs of the great ballerina, who holds the rank of greatest in our century, despite Kchessinska and Egorova, Karsavina, Spessivtseva, and Doubrovska, who were her brilliant peers in the days of her glory. And there are six pages of comment by our great poetess—scholarly, subtle, and accurate, in an impeccable prose that has the floating balance, the light pauses, and the recurrent soaring instants of classic dancing. The style is a homage to the dancer, precisely delicate and delicately spontaneous.

Miss Moore's article is first of all a collage of quotations from the celebrated appreciators—Svetloff, Levinson, C. W. Beaumont, Oliveroff, Dandré, and Stier. They tell very little of Pavlova's craftsmanship, of that technique she worked at so devotedly and which must have been full of discoveries and procedures worth passing on to later dancers and dance lovers. Miss Moore includes what technical hints she has found, but the eyewitnesses describe Pavlova's dancing mostly by the device of spiritual rhapsodies. Miss Moore quotes the most vivid evocation, Levinson's description of *The Dying Swan*, and translates it beautifully. From the innumerable other tributes she selects a phrase here, a sentence there and reassembles them with so keen a sense of style that they give you a clearer picture of dancing than in their original context.

Still, the quotations keep their bias—a parlorlike spirituality that is unsatisfactory. Miss Moore does not shatter their decorousness; she vivifies it by adding to it herself physical and moral perceptions of real elegance. Like Gautier, she can manage a rapturous moment without losing her balance. "In the photograph of her . . . in the grass . . . the descending line of the propped forearm, of her dress and other hand, of ankle and foot, continues to the grass with the naturalness of a streamer of seaweed—an inevitable and stately serpentine which imparts to the seated figure the ease of a standing one." Or, "We see her in the gavotte advancing with the swirling grace of a flag and the decorum of an impala deer."

But it is by her private moral perceptions, appearing for an instant and at rare intervals, that Miss Moore gives us the sharpest equivalent for the actual fact of classic dancing. She notes on a picture of twelve-year-old Pavlova "the erectness of the head, the absolutely horizontal brows, indicating power of self-denial; the eyes, dense with imagination and sombered with solicitude; the hair, severely competent; the dress, dainty more than proud." And after describing a hand pose, "These truthful hands, the most sincere and the least greedy imaginable," she notes Pavlova's use of the passive voice when the dancer wrote: "I was permitted to style myself Première Danseuse . . . later I was granted the title of Ballerina." This classic modesty Miss Moore refers to: "She had power for a most unusual reason—she did not present as valuable the personality from which she could not escape." And later, suggesting the quality of Pavlova's expression, Miss Moore asks, "Why should one so innocent, so natural, so ardent be sad? If self-control is the essential condition of conveying emotion and giving is giving up, we still cannot feel that renunciation had made Pavlova sad; may it have been that for lives that one loves there are things even love cannot do?" And later Miss Moore herself answers, "That which is able to change the heart proves itself."

Morally speaking, this describes correct classic dancing; it is a poet's metaphor of its final grace. A journalist asked the sprightly Danilova what was the most important quality for a ballerina. "Modesty," she answered quickly.

JUNE 18, 1944

THE MONTE CARLO MINUS FRANKLIN

Due to Frederic Franklin's accident during Monday's ballet performance—an accident he successfully concealed from the audience that night—two star parts of his had to be taken on short notice by other dancers at last night's performance of the Monte Carlo at the City Center. Yurek Lazowski substituted for Franklin as the Hussar in *Beau Danube*, and James Starbuck, formerly of the Monte Carlo, dashed uptown from *Song of*

Norway to do the Champion Roper in *Rodeo*. That their performances lacked the authority, the edge, and the vitality of Franklin's was to be expected. They got through creditably, and Starbuck was pleasantly natural in a part that calls for this. It is to the company's credit that, under the circumstances, the evening as a whole was an enjoyable one.

The gem of the evening was Alexandra Danilova in her familiar part of the Street Dancer in *Beau Danube*. After doing it for twenty years she is still the most radiant and the freshest dancer in the piece. She has by nature and by artistry a wonderful legato that gives to all the sharp accents and spurts of can-can steps that the part calls for a musical grace none of the younger dancers have learned. In comparison with her they seem to trust to luck for their balance, and so their dancing loses flow and sweetness. Danilova makes her temperamental vivacity count because the movements are so well placed. Where others look hasty she scintillates. But it is her feminine presence, her air of dancing for the delight of it, that captures the audience's heart. Her twists of awkwardness, especially in the wrists, do not blur the open line of the movement; they add a touching and inimitable accent.

Nathalie Krassovska unfortunately has not Danilova's poise or assurance. She has temperament and physical gifts, but they hardly get their full value because of her mannerisms in the hands and her tendency to mime emotion in the neck. Last night she was at her best in the Bluebird, to which she gave a nervous charm. Leon Danielian, highly gifted for leaps but still unsure of his shoulders and arms, was her partner. They both looked young and fresh, and brought down the house. Mr. Danielian had been excellent earlier in the evening in the part of the Dandy in *Beau Danube*; he is a promising dancer who keeps improving.

SEPTEMBER 13, 1944

"SCHÉHÉRAZADE": A FOUNDERING WARHORSE

Seen on a current ballet program, *Schéhérazade*, which was on the Monte Carlo bill last night, is an illustrious warhorse foundering in dishonor. Not that there isn't some kind of life left in the old girl. The bundling and the clinches are still fine for laughs and whistles and cries of "Take it off"; the piece would still be a wow on the GI circuit. One sees a great many people register sex all over the stage with an earnestness that is disarming rather than embarrassing. But one wonders what *Schéhérazade* could have looked like when it scandalized our parents or when Parisians swooned at the lushness of it in 1910.

In the 1910 photographs the slave girls look soft and abandoned. Nijinsky bounded about them like a panther in thrilling spasms that grew to a paroxysm of death at the climax. Bakst, the great decorator—the Berman of his day—dazzled the public by the sensual shock of his brilliant décor. And the "Slavic harmonies" of Rimsky's score dunked the orgy on stage in a bath of gold.

Nowadays the small orchestra, the clumsily executed décor, the earnest but overworked dancers can't create any sense of abandon. The trouble is that there is no dance form, nothing for them to do as dancers. There is only miming and hubbub, and that doesn't keep for thirty years. A dance ballet can keep fresh because of its form, because arms and legs stay arms and legs; but when the dancers have to pretend to be something they aren't, a ballet gradually disintegrates into a charade.

A pleasant charade when, as last night, the exquisite Danilova sits and stalks with an imperious delicacy and dies with an Oriental sincerity. It is at the end that Fokine's timing still makes good theater.

SEPTEMBER 14, 1944

BALANCHINE'S "DANSES CONCERTANTES"

The Monte Carlo's new *Danses Concertantes* is a glittering little piece, brilliantly animated and brilliantly civilized. As a production it combines the talents of Stravinsky, Balanchine, and Berman—a ballet composer, a choreographer, and a ballet decorator so eminent that each in his field can be called the best in the world. A new piece involving any one of them is something to look forward to; a piece that involves all three at once and allows each to do his sincere best is that rare luxury, a ballet production in the grand style—in the grand style Diaghilev insisted upon and thanks to which ballet acquired its peculiar artistic prestige. *Danses Concertantes*, with fourteen dancers onstage for twenty minutes, is a ballet quite small in scale. But as a new ballet by three great artists it is a big event, an event of interest to London, Paris, and Moscow, an event the American ballet world can take pride in.

The first thrill of *Danses Concertantes* is that of Berman's costumes and drops. Before an inner curtain the dancers cross over quickly by twos and threes, bowing to the audience, looking as brilliant as scarabs, if scarabs came in several colors. Then the inner curtain rises. Now the dancers stand assembled, glittering sharply against a black drop, but it is a drop that is as atmospheric as the open sky of night. You peer into nocturnal distance. And in this lofty blackness every motion of the dancers coruscates. Berman has emphasized their limbs and molded their bodies with black ornaments and with rhinestones so that each motion is distinct in itself.

The dancing is a suite of brief numbers, classically correct in steps but in surprising sequences that contrast sharply and have a quick effervescent invention. The changes from staccato movements to continuous ones, from rapid leaps and displacements to standing still, from one dancer solo to several all at once follow hard on one another. The rhythm is unexpected. But the shift of the figures and the order of the steps is miraculously logical and light, and so even fitful changes have a grace and a spontaneous impetus. What had first seemed separate spurts, stops, and clipped stalkings turn out to be a single long phrase or impulse that has risen and subsided in a group of dancers simultaneously. The line of the large phrase is seen in their relations to one another, and each dancer independently remains open and free in bearing, the arms natural and elegant.

One notices how each dancer in all this coruscating complexity remains a charming and a natural person. They are like characters in a garden, individuals who communicate, respond, who modify and return without losing their distinctness. The dance is like a conversation in Henry James, as surprising, as sensitive, as forbearing, as full of slyness and fancy. The joyousness of it is the pleasure of being civilized, of being what we really are, born into a millennial urban civilization. This is where we are and this is what the mind makes beautiful. *Danses Concertantes* makes it beautiful by presenting a sumptuous little garden pastoral, a highly artificial, a very exact, and a delicately adjusted entertainment.

The dancers performed the piece to perfection. Even those of them just out of school danced like soloists, with a light and civilized deportment. And Danilova and Franklin, the stars whose happy flirtation is the central theme of the piece—and a birdlike duet it is—characterized their parts charmingly and lightly, he with the fatuousness of a happy male, she with the willfulness of a tender woman.

SEPTEMBER 17, 1944

THE MONTE CARLO'S "COPPÉLIA"

The young Monte Carlo company danced through two Saturday and two Sunday performances at the Center with altogether astonishing grace and freshness. Coming after an arduous opening week made the more difficult by Frederic Franklin's knee injury, with consequent substitutions and extra rehearsals, it was a taxing weekend for the dancers. But it was all through a very pleasant one for dance lovers. Its prize was two performances of *Coppélia*, despite the cuts that Franklin's absence made necessary. Miss Danilova, wonderfully radiant in the leading role, made of the lovely piece a triumph for her company and for herself.

Coppélia, an 1870 classic, has a gentle modesty and a tender humor. It does not try for grandeur; it is an intimate piece that charms and delights. But the graceful clarity of the dances and the Delibes score are both masterful. And the Monte Carlo décor and costumes (by Pierre Roy) have a lovely serenity. They belong to the best ballet decoration in existence, although hardly anyone notes them consciously.

The Monte Carlo has newly rehearsed the piece, and the dancing of it is fresh and light and clear; the first-act ensembles were in fact the best classic ensemble dancing in several seasons. Among the men, talented Mr. Danielian, more firm in the waist and with consequently more continuity of phrasing, had never danced so handsomely; and Mr. Goudovitch, in this piece as in others, danced with the lively elegance that he has been showing more and more. But Miss Danilova is, of course, in a very different class from anyone in the company—she is one of the world's greatest dancers. Her wonderfully feminine charms, her wit and dance brilliance make of the Monte Carlo *Coppélia* a real event.

SEPTEMBER 18, 1944

"COPPÉLIA" TELLS THE FACTS OF LIFE

The Monte Carlo *Coppélia* might well be more celebrated than it is. With radiant Miss Danilova and either Franklin or Youskevitch in the leads, and given in its entirety—as it wasn't this fall—it is a very happy version of a delightful classic. The score Delibes made for it so carefully has lost none of its charms. And in the Monte Carlo production the choreography and the decoration are—like the music—distinguished, gracious, and light. *Coppélia* is a modest little comedy, but it has a peculiar grace, an 1870 secret, a bouquet as fresh as a summer morning in the country. The Monte Carlo dancers dance it clearly, they do it gaily and they do it straight. And thanks to their lack of affectation, I noticed with some surprise that if you follow the action quite literally it isn't a silly story, as people claim it is. A part of *Coppélia*'s secret is the serious good sense with which it treats a serious subject—the basis for a good marriage.

This is the action you watch: Two very lively and very real young persons love each other and are about to marry. But the boy is struck by the sight of a mysterious stranger, the beautiful Coppélia, who sits on a balcony. Naturally, his first girl is vexed and hurt. That night the mysterious Coppélia turns out to be only a mechanical doll. The flesh-and-blood girl breaks the doll, she harries the old dollmaker, she even rescues the boy, whom the dollmaker has drugged with a sinister intent. The boy acknowledges his fault, and the next day there is a celebration at which the local duke pays for everything, the boys and girls all get married and get money, and everybody watches dancing and dances happily, too.

Critics have claimed that the celebration scene added nothing and could as well be omitted. It cannot, because you haven't until then seen the boy and girl dance together and exhibit all their virtuosity, their combined dance power at its highest pitch. When you see their motions and physical proportions beautifully balanced, when you see them harmoniously overcoming impossible difficulties, you have seen a convincing image of what would make two young lovers happy in marriage.

And the divertissement that clusters round this grand duet bears logically on the same subject. The dances are entitled "Dawn" (a solo), "Prayer," "Work," and "Follies" (several of them); and taken together the series represents rather well the nonsexual basis for a happy domestic life. On the other hand, the pitfalls that prevent marriage are told in the earlier action, when the boy is infatuated by a beautifully mechanical ideal: he wants a real girl and he wants an ideal one in addition. In this psychological dilemma, like a man, he goes to sleep. But the girl, like a Shavian heroine, solves the dilemma by her independent courage. And then the boy proves his real worth by his strength and his gentle control in the nuptial dance duet. All these ideas of marriage are reasonable ones, though the lightness, the wit and tenderness they have in dancing are lost in retelling.

As you watch the dance you notice how the more perturbing the emotion becomes, the purer becomes the movement of dancing and the more open and free the dancer's bearing. You see the magic of the heart's sincerity, its most urgent necessity, transform a village girl into a grand and gracious ballerina. And what a solace the transformation is! But *Coppélia* has only two such really serious episodes; it shifts easily to a pantomime scene, to a folk dance, to a sparkling parody. Its theme is domestic, and it ends with a modest circle of dancers enclosing the stars in a running ring. I only wish the young Monte Carlo would take some lessons in classic pantomime; it is a charming game when dancers play it right. And I wish I had space to tell you about Danilova, who is the most wonderful *Coppélia* heroine in the world.

SEPTEMBER 24, 1944

BALANCHINE'S "BOURGEOIS GENTILHOMME"

Le Bourgeois Gentilhomme, the new ballet the Monte Carlo presented at the City Center Saturday, could have been a delightfully elegant trifle. But despite the magnificence of its decoration, it opened lamentably. The piece failed because the management showed it half-baked. The public came for a premiere and was shown a disheveled dress rehearsal. The ballet was ruined, the public imposed upon. This has happened before at ballet premieres, and it is a malpractice.

Your reporter, however, does not want to throw out the baby with the bath. *Le Bourgeois Gentilhomme*, even in its present puling state, reveals too much originality to be blamed for the debacle. It is—or someday will be—a dance entertainment by George Balanchine, mounted by Eugene Berman and set to Richard Strauss's incidental music to the play of Molière. The action of the ballet covers the love interest and Turkish ceremony of the play and serves as a framework for a series of dances, for a ballet vaudeville of several joking pantomimes, two character pieces, a classic number, and one very touchingly playful love duet. What survived of these dances Saturday night was never commonplace in detail, and their originality of tone lies in their relaxed unseriousness; *Bourgeois* is much more relaxed than *Danses Concertantes*.

Le Bourgeois has no intention other than to be a feast for the eyes, a dance dessert, fantastic and light, of a splendor evoking the after-dinner ballet amusements of Louis XIV and of the munificent Fouquet. The pomp of *Le Bourgeois* is a triumph for Berman. To see such novel invention and dazzling taste in splendor is an intense delight; it was on Saturday even though the costumes were pinned on and sometimes tore, even though the stage was abominably lit.

In the dancing Miss Moylan and especially Miss Maria Tallchief sparkled, and brave Miss Krassovska looked very pretty. The company was valiant, inaccurate, and frightened. The Strauss score is so amorphous that it would take several orchestra rehearsals for the dancers to catch their cues and the instrumentalists to mark the rhythm. It is a cumbersomely Teutonic score, but having accepted it the management was bound to rehearse it.

But the management's most shocking error was to open *Le Bourgeois* without a real star to pull it together, to be a focus of attention. After Franklin's accident two weeks ago Magallanes took over his part. Magallanes is an honest but far from a sparkling young dancer. In addition, he had turned his ankle two nights before the opening. After doing leads all evening before *Le Bourgeois*—and, according to the program, at the Saturday matinee also—it was no wonder that by 11:30, when the crucial love duet got going, he could barely hobble through it.

SEPTEMBER 24, 1944

"LE BOURGEOIS" TRANSFORMED

Le Bourgeois Gentilhomme, the Monte Carlo novelty at the City Center, at its second performance last night turned nearly into a hit. It may soon be a complete one. The transformation from Saturday was astounding. But the only changes were that yesterday the dancers did very nearly what they were supposed to at very nearly the right moment. *Le Bourgeois* is now one of the prizes in the Monte Carlo's bag. And Berman's mounting is certainly a marvel.

Now that the ballet is clear, one sees clearly that the originality of the dances lies in the unaffected ease of their long sequences. The rich detail they have is as naturally subordinate to the continuity as if they had been danced for a long time, or as detail is placed in the choreography of Petipa. After thirty years of stress on detail at the expense of flow, *Le Bourgeois* marks a complete turnabout in dance style. It is the opposite of "modernism," of the deformed, the stylized, the bizarre. It looks harmless and easy, and it holds the attention effortlessly by an unfailing naturalness in invention. It shows off the dancer, not the choreographer.

Interesting, too, is the boisterousness of some of the pantomime, moments of high spirits and fooling that are in the tradition of Molière, and so of ballet, too. *Le Bourgeois* in type belongs with ballet farces like, say, *Beau Danube*. But its sweet grace and spontaneity bring it nearer to Mozart's kind of fooling than Massine's.

The company began to shine in this second performance. Miss Krassovska was wholly admirable. Miss Moylan showed she can make her part dewy and sparkling; Miss Tallchief, hers warm and gay; Miss Boris and Messrs Lazowski, Danielian, Talin, Katcharoff were excellent; and Mr. Magallanes as the hero began to be convincingly tender and natural in the charmingly playful love duet.

He had, in *Swan Lake*, which opened the bill, given a remarkably good performance of the Prince, supporting Miss Danilova in perfect style. Miss Danilova, though a trifle tired, danced with a more beautiful phrasing and warmth in her movements than ever. Her head gestures were especially lovely. I hope the management will not overtax her on tour; she is a lovely glory of the American dance world.

Indignant as this reporter was with the Monte Carlo management over the totally inadequate premiere of *Le Bourgeois*, he must after its second performance congratulate the same management for having given us two such brilliant novelties as *Le Bourgeois Gentilhomme* and *Danses Concertantes*. And now I look forward with great pleasure to seeing the dancers when they return in February, with that great dancer Franklin back in his star roles. SEPTEMBER 15, 1944

PEARL PRIMUS ON BROADWAY

Pearl Primus, the justly celebrated young Negro dancer, and her troupe opened a ten-day season last night at the Belasco with a show that came across completely only in a few numbers. She has proved herself a quite exceptionally gifted and thrilling dancer before, and it is likely that later performances will not have the self-consciousness that she and her somewhat disparate troupe showed again and again in their first contact with the Broadway theater public.

The program, elucidated by a speaker, begins with "primitives"—that is, dances derived from African or Haitian origins. A second part brings dances of protest from the point of view of the Negro in the United States. And a final portion, more or less on a jazz basis, begins with several playful dance inventions and ends with more protest.

It is the playful dances, *Afro-Haitian Playdance*, *Study in Nothing*, *Rock Daniel*, *Mischievous Interlude* (the last a very brilliant solo danced by Albert Popfull), which delight the audience. They are witty, warm, and well made. Of the serious numbers *African Ceremonial* and *Hard Time Blues* are thrilling dancing. But a number of the other serious ones fail of complete effect because the audience agrees beforehand with the protest they make. An artist can protest passionately to a hostile audience and win them over; but there is little drama where the audience is quite amenable. In that case the propaganda can't excite the public, but only the elegance of the execution, and the dignity of the protest is compromised by no longer being the dramatic center of attention.

But it is Miss Primus's privilege to attempt these very earnest themes. One regrets that she hammed them occasionally last night. As a dancer, she has a unique power and unction in her hips, knees, and instep. The leaps can be thrilling, the quickness of the feet a delight. Waist and torso are strong and often beautifully pliant. She has the gift of motion, which controls the body easily in flow. The arms are uninteresting in formal movements, but charming when they play a subordinate role. One wishes she would dance more with a partner, less in the correctly "modern" manner and more in her personal, playful way, where her invention is most brilliant and free, and her personality warm and charmingly dignified.

Miss Primus's troupe consists of four male dancers, two excellent drummers (Messrs Cimber and Koker), Frankie Newton and his four-piece band, two pianists, two singers, and a speaker. The jazz drummer was excellent also. OCTOBER 5, 1944

LICHINE'S "GRADUATION BALL"; TOUMANOVA

The enthusiasm of the house was the really gala aspect of Ballet Theatre's opening Sunday night at the Metropolitan. The company as a whole has given and no doubt will give more brilliant performances. Sunday night the ensemble was tired and many had not been able to find hotel rooms. But the fans were rapturous at having them back and applauded everything with welcoming abandon.

The novelties of the evening were Ballet Theatre's revival of *Graduation Ball*, last seen with the de Basil company in the season of 1940–41, and the reappearance of three great stars who have not danced here since that same season. Tatiana Riabouchinska and David Lichine returned in the leads of *Graduation Ball*, which they created, and Tamara Toumanova danced the lead in *Swan Lake*, which opened the bill.

Graduation Ball is a juvenile comedy set in a quiet Europe of fifty years back; it shows us a party at a proper girls' school to which a neighboring proper boys' school has been invited. Its charm is light and true. The young exuberance of the dances is infectious, the little moments of sentiment unforced. It is the uncomplicated dance vitality of most of *Graduation Ball* that is its peculiarly happy characteristic, and the notable characteristic of Lichine as a choreographer.

But the happiest thing about *Graduation Ball* is Tatiana Riabouchinska, the sweetest and the quickest of dance comediennes. Lichine, too, is a master comedian, who keeps every moment of his dancing in character and in the story. Miss Hightower was a very funny hoyden and Miss Alonso and Mr. Kriza won particular ovations.

Mr. Dorati conducted, and rather milked the applause after each number, which diminished the total atmosphere and effect of the piece. The garishly painted scenery also diminished the effect; the liveliness of young people was more touching in the cold grandeur they danced in three years ago. But the applause was enormous in any event.

Beautiful Miss Toumanova in *Swan Lake*, too, won great applause. Her performance, however, was not a superb one. Though her line in arabesques and in développés was often dazzling, these moments had little connection with the continuity of the dance she was dancing. And she marred her beautiful leg gestures by a mannerism of undulating her arms sometimes snakily, sometimes mimicking the rhythm of the music. She lacked the inner repose from which the Swan Queen's dance arises; she forced her presence on the audience.

It is true she was badly supported by Mr. Dolin, who as a dancer, too, was disappointing Sunday night, failing once again to beat his entrechats at the end of his variation. The Ballet Theatre version of *Swan Lake* has often been a mechanical and unflowing one, and Mr. Zlatin conducted it with a heavy hand indeed. But as Miss Markova used to triumph over all these handicaps, so no doubt Miss Toumanova will also find a way to triumph.

OCTOBER 9, 1944

BALLET THEATRE BACK IN STRIDE

Our Ballet Theatre hit its stride last night at the Metropolitan, dancing consistently well to an audience less boisterous than the one on opening night, but a thoroughly pleased one. Miss Toumanova, who did the Prelude and pas de deux in *Sylphides*, danced far better than the day before, and her poses were often admirable. She has not yet reached her thrilling best form, which her admirers recall so well; but it is natural that an absence of several seasons from a ballet company should prove a handicap at first. Ballet lovers expect great things of her, and from all over the house they watch her like hawks for every good point.

But last night the event of the evening was Alicia Alonso's dancing. Despite an unhappy fall halfway through the program, she triumphed by her purity of style in three different ballets.

In *Graduation Ball*, which came last on the bill, she and Richard Reed did their classic pas de deux with a youthful strength that was charming. Earlier she had danced the about-to-be-abandoned mistress in *Lilac Garden* with a remarkably convincing womanly presence and with no trace of melodramatics; her interpretation was in a different way as fine as the best ones of this role—Miss Kaye's and Miss Karnilova's.

But Miss Alonso's greatest moment was in the Mazurka of *Sylphides*, where her perfection in the quick accuracy of leaps, in the lovely bearing of chest, shoulders, and head, and in the rapid and exact tripping toe steps was very exceptional indeed. Miss Alonso has a classically modest and undramatic stage presence which is quite her own in the company and most attractive.

Miss Hightower, too, excelled in *Sylphides*, particularly in the two ensemble numbers. While Miss Alonso keeps the gestures of her limbs academically dependent on the torso, Miss Hightower has a fine flinging abandon; it is difficult for her to phrase so much energy with delicacy, but one loves the spontaneous warmth of it.

Robbins's exuberant *Fancy Free* returned with last night's bill, and though one missed Mr. Bernstein's phenomenal vitality as conductor, the piece and the performers were sound and straight. The company looked rested and accurate throughout the evening, and what I was able to see of *Graduation Ball* was far less bumptious than it had been Sunday night; the piece is not a *Barn Dance* and should not be danced as one.

OCTOBER 10, 1944

BALANCHINE'S "WALTZ ACADEMY"

For the third time this fall George Balanchine has given us a dance ballet of the best quality, and for the third time the opening performance has not been a good one. Last night Ballet Theatre gave the local premiere of his *Waltz Academy* at the Metropolitan. One had to watch the sweet and open little ballet closely to see its remarkable virtues. The lambent grace, the joyous lightness in invention, and the gently rising climax of keen delight in dancing—these happy qualities of structure did not shine as brightly as they might have. But they are the qualities of which Balanchine has built *Waltz Academy*.

Waltz Academy is a dance suite which takes its departure from morning ballet practice in the rehearsal room. Oliver Smith's set suggests a loft under a wonderful cupola, a hint of the rehearsal room at the Paris Opéra and somehow a hint of the old Aquarium too. It is airy, modest, and alive, and his most distinguished set to date. Into this room the dancers come, the girls in bright tarlatans, the boys in the practice uniform of the Maryinsky (costumes by Alvin Colt). They do a few of the traditional exercises, there is a little joke or two, and soon they are crowding into the center for the second part of practice. But, instead, they start to dance, and the rest of the ballet is a suite of pretty dances that show young dancers in all their airy brilliance and vivacity.

Last night it was Nora Kaye who was the truest and sweetest (and most brilliant) of the young dancers. But Janet Reed, Albia Kavan, John Kriza, and Harold Lang (who held himself particularly well) were all of them excellent. The misfortune of the performance seemed to be trouble in the first pas de six, and a misplaced miming of glamour in the climactic pas de deux of Miss Gollner and Mr. Petroff, which did not look humorous and spoiled a beautiful dance. The score was played too slowly and that may well have troubled the company.

The score, a new one by Vittorio Rieti, is a melodious and witty and elegantly written one. It is excellent for dancing and agreeable to hear.

Waltz Academy is a great addition to the Ballet Theatre repertory, which lacks contemporary dance ballets that are neither ironic nor topical. *Waltz Academy* is dancing for the pleasure of dancing, a ballet for dancers and dance lovers. It will be a pleasure to see repeatedly, and to see emerge into full brilliance.

OCTOBER 12, 1944

BALLERINA TROUBLE AT BALLET THEATRE?

The Ballet Theatre company, in the first five days of the season, has seemed to suffer from a drop in its morale, unknown before in this admirably steady ensemble. The trouble has been, I imagine, that Ballet

Theatre has had to change classic ballerinas in midstream and that this delicate operation was not at once successful. For a ballerina is not only a superacrobat with extra publicity. She is also an artist whose performance shows you the heart of a ballet. She sets the tone; the other dancers can add to it but cannot go counter to it, and so her quality is of crucial importance to them. Indeed, company, ballerina, and chief choreographer need to have a sort of affinity, an unconscious confidence in one another if they are to become completely effective. The mutual adjustment comes by working together and there is no way of forcing it.

In Ballet Theatre's case the adjustment is especially delicate because the repertory has two tendencies, classic and modern. It was a stroke of luck that Tudor, the modern choreographer, and Markova, the classic ballerina, were united not only by mutual admiration but also by a common nationality. Even so it took some time for each of them to get what they needed at Ballet Theatre, to feel at home and shine in a homogeneous and confident company.

There is no way of replacing this particular confidence now Markova has left. Miss Toumanova, if she is to take the place of permanent classic ballerina at Ballet Theatre, will have to grow used to a company with a special tradition. And to start with she has further difficulties. She is cast in Markova's classic roles, and these are all on the serene side. Toumanova has in the past been superb in the opposite manner, the dramatically intense (as in the Black Swan, a role that is the evil counterpart of the serene Swan Queen). In the lyric roles she has taken these first few days, coming after Markova's gentle radiance and Danilova's warm and lovely presence in the same parts, Toumanova's manner seems a little grim. Technically she has not yet shown the control of arms or the sure phrasing Markova has led us to expect; on the other hand, her grand leg extensions and sharp toe steps have been phenomenal to see—especially last Thursday in the first section of the *Nutcracker* duet, where she was well supported by Dolin. Whether Toumanova can suit her temperament to these particular roles or will be given others, she is certainly a dancer of exceptional style and interest. And it is to Ballet Theatre's credit to be bringing her back to ballet.

The two new pieces Ballet Theatre has added to its repertory so far have been very agreeable ones and that is also to its credit. Lichine's revived *Graduation Ball* is a pleasant ballet comedy set to Strauss waltzes. Balanchine's new *Waltz Academy* is classic dancing so unselfconscious and spontaneous in its elegance it is art without a capital A. These novelties, Miss Toumanova's return, and two roles for two other great dancers, Miss Riabouchinska and Mr. Lichine, were calculated to open Ballet

Theatre's season with brilliance. But the mistake has been to begin by presenting Miss Toumanova, as prospective ballerina, in parts in which she was not at her own best. That has put a jinx on these first few days, I think. But I feel sure that by the time this appears our leading ballet company will have recovered from this moment of uncertainty and will be dancing again with the verve it has consistently shown, in the three years since it has been appearing at the Metropolitan. That's the way it has always solved its troubles. OCTOBER 15, 1944

RIABOUCHINSKA AND TOUMANOVA

The general impression over the weekend is that Ballet Theatre is headed up again. Sunday night's performance at the Metropolitan was lively and accurate, the best evening so far. The new *Waltz Academy* looked as it should have on its opening night, gay, unpresuming, and beautiful. Miss Alonso was dancing with new animation in her perfect neatness, Miss Gollner with a new simplicity in her fine feats, a directness we have waited for for two years. And the audience enjoyed the charming piece and the company cordially.

The bill included the Grand Pas de Deux from *The Nutcracker*, danced by Toumanova and Dolin. Miss Toumanova, with a prettier coiffure, this time superimposed a different manner on her dazzlingly perfect leg action, smiling and giving ecstatic little tosses of the head before big effects. I imagine a great classic choreographer like Balanchine could best correct the miscalculations of manner that mar her superb capabilities.

Sunday afternoon's *Sylphides* and Saturday night's *Aurora* billed both Toumanova and Riabouchinska, the guest celebrities of Ballet Theatre. Miss Riabouchinska, though no great technician in movement, has so warm and true a presence, so clear a sense of the musical enchantment that surrounds her, and so keen an instinct for a natural characterization that one watches everything she does—even her faults—with pleasure. Her greatest fault is a tendency to raise her shoulders too much, which gives her torso a dumpy look. But when you see her dancing with the happy absorption of a little girl, you wish other dancers in classic pieces would learn from her to believe in their imagination.

In *Sylphides* she seems to be one of the chorus dancing by accident; in the Bluebird she is a sparkling princess with a wonderful bluebird of her own; in *Graduation Ball* she is a little girl, mischievous, sweet-natured, and well-mannered. She creates a magic world around her—a very rare dancer indeed.

Graduation Ball on Sunday afternoon brought Harold Lang in Lichine's part, and he danced it with a fine natural charm and clarity, perfectly in character. He is developing particularly well this season. This piece is, happily, losing the strident stress that spoiled it at first.

OCTOBER 16, 1944

TOUMANOVA IN "GISELLE"

Miss Toumanova with her large, handsome, and deadly face, her sword-like toe steps, her firm positions, her vigorous and record-high leg gestures—and with her bold and large style of dancing—by nature makes a very different figure from delicate Miss Markova, whose star role in *Giselle* she undertook for the first time last night. Dancing at the Metropolitan as guest of Ballet Theatre in the familiar Ballet Theatre version (including Mr. Dolin as the star's partner), Miss Toumanova was very striking and was properly cheered. But Miss Markova's Giselle is still incomparable.

In Toumanova's performance, this Markova fan missed the sustained otherworldly floating quality and the calm completion of each pose and phrase that were Markova's specialty, and that helped make this ballet in particular extraordinarily thrilling. But Miss Toumanova not only gave her best performance of the season, she showed some of her dramatic gifts as well as her technical ones. She sustained the first act and built up an atmosphere of threat that might well lead into the second. And in the second act she gave her supported adagio section a very interesting sensual overtone, which might, if developed in the role, add to this whole act an unusual (but perfectly possible) macabre intensity.

Later in the second act, at the allegro climax, in the famous series of little leaps on both toes, Miss Toumanova leaped too far to keep her lightness, and she did not reach a sort of desperate quality she may have intended. In the lifts that follow she was too large for Dolin quite to create an effect of lightness. Indeed, Dolin's overpowering assurance in the part is now becoming his most serious qualification; he has to substitute a theatrical pose for dance brilliance. But he supported Miss Toumanova very handsomely.

The company was excellent indeed in the second act; here Miss Hightower as the Queen was at her very finest, with magnificent leaps, beautiful arm gestures. OCTOBER 17, 1944

"PRINCESS AURORA" AND PETIPA

Watching Ballet Theatre's *Princess Aurora* last Tuesday in a routine performance—no superstars around—I was struck by how sincerely the piece itself has come to interest the audience. They take to it as a piece, for its animation as dancing, its choreographic atmosphere. A few years ago this 1890 Petipa number used to interest the public very little and the company even less. Everyone waited around for the leaps in the Bluebird and then for the Rose Adagio, as a kind of obstacle course. And when Ballet Theatre first did its *Aurora* back in '41, as lively an effect as any was the one made by the King, who entered with a grand fanfare and without his trousers on. But that was before the present response to classic dancing. Now the interest of the audience is, it seems to me, teaching the company, too, to take a livelier interest. On both sides of the footlights there is a growing realization that the Petipa style expects all the dancing by everyone on stage to contribute actively to a theater spell.

The public begins to recognize the classic spell and it wants all the dancers to help create it and to keep within it. They are expected to keep the same animated and spontaneous elegance in simple steps that the ballerina shows in her grand-prize feats. The fine hint of abandon or of heartbreak that her acrobatics can have in a Petipa ballet needs the foil of youthful spirits in the rest of the company. One enjoys her firm delicacy far more in a surrounding atmosphere of clear and buoyant grace, and only accurate classic ensemble dancing can create such an overall spell.

Now that the public appreciates accurate ensemble dancing, we might also have longer versions of classic ballets. The climactic dance thrills make more sense theatrically in their context; the proper approach, the proper tempo for a climax are created by introductory numbers and by contrasting kinds of dances, and the big duets, coming where they were intended, look more touchingly noble, more natural, even. We might have a renovated *Aurora* as long as our present *Giselle*—and what a ballet for Eugene Berman to mount that would be! And to renovate *Aurora* handsomely, Ballet Theatre might also ask the great dancer Pierre Vladimiroff to dance Prince Charming and show us for once what the Maryinsky grand manner in supporting a ballerina really looks like.

The present *Aurora* is merely a selection from the three-act *Sleeping Beauty* of Petipa. The lovely string of solos, for instance, that now comes in the middle was originally intended as a string of dances by good fairies who are bringing gifts of beauty to the infant princess—the grace of pine woods, or that of hummingbirds, or that of songbirds, or that of particular flowers. The light evocation of these graces of nature—in the dances and in the Tchaikovsky score—and the sense of blessing a child with them are a part of the full effect of these solos. Placed as they are in *Sleeping Beauty*, their story point does not change the steps and gestures but it colors the dancers' attack. And similarly the Rose Adagio, too, has a story context which gives its formal bravura an amiable overtone.

It is a proof of Petipa's great power as a choreographer that even without their context those of his dances we see can create a wonderful spell. They are not showoff numbers; they all have some basis in human relationships. But they are not meant to be mimed, they are meant to be danced. Even without knowing what their story function may be, an attention to their rhythmic and plastic detail, a response to their impetus and current as dancing are enough to delight the audience and to make the dancer on stage look her very best. And by his choreographic virtue, Marius Petipa, who was born in France in 1822 and died in Russia in 1910, is now here in the United States—like a living man—enlivening dancers and audience, and actively animating an art he loved.

OCTOBER 22, 1944

TOUMANOVA'S SHOW

Dazzlingly handsome to look at in *Black Swan*, effervescently and girlishly temperamental in *Three-Cornered Hat*, Tamara Toumanova sustained and put across last night's Ballet Theatre show at the Metropolitan as a star performer should. Ballet can be more gracefully poignant and the Spanish style more controlled; but last night one was happy in the vigorous theatrical impetus Miss Toumanova gave both pieces she appeared in.

Black Swan is the grand pas de deux from *Swan Lake*, Act Three. The most correct version of the duet was the Monte Carlo's of 1941, danced then by Toumanova and Eglevsky, and a performance unparalleled that was. Mr. Dolin's present version is a straight bravura exhibition number, and Miss Toumanova rose to the occasion. The grand abundance of force she had in all she did was stunning; and her accurate line, her half-turn recovery from a deep back bend, her ballonnés and circle of turns—each effect was driven home magnificently. The house rightly gave her an ovation.

The same duet in its context in *Swan Lake* has an overtone of vicious evil; it can be danced with more reference to the ballerina's partner and projected less hard at the audience. It is more moving that way. But done as Miss Toumanova did it—a brilliant feat of unique prowess—it affords an honest theatrical thrill; and no other dancer could have delivered it with such physical magnificence.

Mr. Dolin was Toumanova's partner, and what he did was neatly done. His showmanship put it over successfully.

Three-Cornered Hat, with Toumanova and Massine in the leads, and David Lichine as the Governor, had a star cast. Here Miss Toumanova was very touching in the brief hand-fluttering solo after the Miller's arrest; and if her Spanish is awkward in the arms and vague in the feet, if her silhouette is diffuse—as Massine's even now is not—still the way she plays her role with conviction and dances with impetuosity brings back a long-lost freshness to this excellent little ballet. The Picasso drop and costumes are each time a joy to see. One wishes Ballet Theatre would also restore the Picasso front curtain. Lichine was amusing and discreet, though he does the role as impish comedy without any Spanish dignity to give it an extra sharpness. OCTOBER 24, 1944

"DON QUIXOTE" PAS DE DEUX

The Grand Pas de Deux from *Don Quixote*, which Tamara Toumanova and Anton Dolin performed last night for the first time, is the best dancing of the three classic duets they have done during this Ballet Theatre season at the Metropolitan. It is the best because it is closest to true Petipa style. It shows you arms as well as legs, and it projects an atmosphere. Miss Toumanova's powerful impetus and assurance, for once strictly disciplined, was thoroughly impressive.

The duet, now staged by Mr. Oboukhoff, the great Petersburg dancer, is from a full-length 1869 ballet by Petipa, and it was last seen here in 1926 danced by Pavlova. It is striking how Petipa as choreographer does not repeat his big effects, how clear and grand the line of the dance is and the figures the two bodies form, and how the emotion rises in joyousness from the opening straight lifts to the final brilliant zigzag of leaps by the man and the dazzling whirling circle by the ballerina.

In the adagio Miss Toumanova's arms were clearly placed, and her feats, particularly a climactic arabesque, were bold and stunning; the following pizzicato variation was for its steely sharpness even more extraordinary. One regretted a trifle the unconvincing broad smile she had, and even more the trick of milking the applause whenever possible. This dance is a brief joyous number, and would have a much greater cumulative effect danced right into incidental applause.

OCTOBER 26, 1944

"CARNAVAL"

Ballet Theatre presented last night at the Metropolitan a revival of Fokine's *Carnaval*, said to have been taught the company by Fokine himself some years ago. They must have forgotten meanwhile what he taught them. The Monte Carlo *Carnaval*—dilapidated as that is—has more precision and more flavor than this one. Ballet Theatre's looked amateurish, empty, and pointless despite a cast of fine dancers.

Carnaval is a very famous piece and the enraptured reviews of thirty years ago are perfectly convincing reading. In my own experience Danilova and Youskevitch as Columbine and Harlequin have been wonderfully fascinating, but the piece as a whole has never made any sense at all. Its effervescence, subtle characterization, malicious wit, delicacy of sentiment I only know from history books.

Last night Miss Chase mimed Columbine prettily but she didn't dance the part. Mr. Tudor strangely enough conveyed nothing of interest as

Pierrot. Lovely Miss Karnilova gave her Chiarina a dim trace of warmth and lightness. Orloff's Pantaloon had some wit but was rowdy. Hugh Laing had trouble with his hat. Miss Hightower's impetuous Papillon and several very good passages of Harold Lang's Harlequin were the only dancing done. Mr. Lang has not yet the sharpness of beats, pirouettes, and turns in the air, nor the lithe malice the part calls for. But he could learn; he has strength, naturalness, and animation, he is by nature a fine dancer, and one always likes to see him.

Set and costumes for *Carnaval* were rudely executed after the Bakst sketches. Well—poor Fokine! OCTOBER 27, 1944

A FAULT IN BALLET THEATRE'S DANCING

Each Ballet Theatre season, the more often I go, the more I admire the company. As a group they are gifted, strong, conscientious, untiring dancers; as individuals they are lively, attractive young people. Each season, as the weeks pass and they recover from the strain of touring and from the interruption of ballet classes on tour, you see first this one and then that one begin to blossom in their dancing. Just now they are better than ever, and among the soloists warmhearted Miss Hightower, Miss Alonso, and Mr. Kriza are often even strikingly expressive. And yet, despite all this, the general tone of Ballet Theatre's dancing has long had a tendency to seem heavy-footed and wooden. Watching Miss Riabouchinska and the illusion of animation she gives, I wondered what the technical secret of it might be.

For in the technique of a step, a leap, or a lift most of Ballet Theatre's company is far more accurate than she is. She fakes and she has no tautness. But when she dances she has a miraculous instinct for the atmosphere of a piece, so that her number fits naturally into the poetic illusion of it. Her dance makes sense in terms of the piece and it also makes natural sense as a dance. Her naturalness in action comes from the fact that she shows you so clearly the sustaining impetus, the dance impulse which carries her lightly through from beginning to end. Because the impetus is exactly right she strikes you as dancing her whole number on an impulse, spontaneously for the joy of it.

Ballet Theatre, by comparison, looks as if it tried manfully to do its duty. It doesn't dance as if dancing were easy; it doesn't quite seem to believe that a dance is a joy in itself. Instead of letting the number take wing and deploy in the make-believe atmosphere of the piece, Ballet Theatre is afraid to let it go at that; it "theatricalizes" a dance by mugging or glamorizing. Often it acts as if a dance were an argument, a string of points to be put across by fair means or foul. It hits hard one step or gesture, goes dead, and then with an effort begins the next one. You don't feel that the waist and the thighs are ready for dancing ahead of the feet and arms; the slight knee and ankle bend which connects steps isn't agile; the muscles around the small of the back aren't quiet enough. And so the feet stick and the arms drag. I am of course drawing a caricature here, but though I exaggerate the failing it exists.

Ballet Theatre has, I think, trained itself too little in the physical basis for continuity in dancing and it has not trained, either, the instinctive gift for it that dancers have. They have not been trained to sense accurately the dance impetus which will best carry them through all the detail they are called on to perform, which will give it coherence and expression. But it is when he discovers the appropriate impetus for his part that the dancer begins to look light and natural and captivating.

Unfortunately Ballet Theatre's repertory doesn't suggest lightness and naturalness to a young dancer. In spirit, its nineteenth-century revivals are often too self-conscious; its light modern pieces are often too smart-alecky—they comment on comic characters selfconsciously from the outside. And in technique Tudor's complex serious ballets are obviously hard to dance with spontaneity. Spontaneity in dancing requires, among other things, personal changes of pace which animate the prevalent rhythm, but Tudor's main rhythm is hard to get hold of, it has no beat or lilt. So it is difficult for the dancers to sense where their instinctive changes of pace (their rubato) would be proper. Much rehearsed, *Romeo* and *Lilac Garden*, thanks to the brilliant example of rubato that Markova and Laing have given, have recently been danced with a striking increase in animation. And the company is dancing the new *Waltz Academy* with a new naturalness, too. It gives hope that Ballet Theatre will plan its future repertory (and its future ballet classes) with an eye to remedying its faulty tendencies in dancing.

Ballet Theatre is our strongest dance company. Its accuracy and its steady drive are quite exceptional. But it might look lighter and more spontaneous and more unselfconscious. As a company it still needs more of the physical sincerity, the warmheartedness that it admires readily and generously when it sees its own home-grown ballerina, Rosella Hightower, dancing. OCTOBER 29, 1944

BALLET INTERNATIONAL

Ballet International, the ballet intended primarily as a New York company, opened its handsome home, the International Theater on Columbus Circle, last night, to a distinguished audience eager to be friendly. The occasion didn't quite come off. One had expected a clear sense of artistic unity, a sense of style, and that didn't show at this first performance. A sense of style in ballet is what we badly need just now.

This first program brought two world premieres in *Brahms Variations* and *Colloque Sentimental*, a revival of Fokine's *Sylphides*, and one of Mme Nijinska's *Bolero*.

The *Brahms*, which Mme Nijinska has set to the Haydn and Paganini variations, is two ballets in one. It is endless, highly ingenious, and pointless. Perhaps the décor by Vertès is its worst feature; in any case, it kills the dance. It makes the stage look like a perfume counter in a department store. One did see André Eglevsky dancing magnificently, better than he has ever danced, and looking extraordinarily handsome. All the other dancers were leaping about and forming uninteresting plastic groups. A good deal of soulful throwing back of heads didn't help. A disappointment generally.

Colloque Sentimental is a muted duet set to a rich, elegantly gloomy, and mellifluous score by Paul Bowles.* It has a brilliantly novel gray backdrop by Dali that crowds the dancers forward. Everything is tangled up in long white streamers of veils, and an enormous stage turtle with more veils and autumn leaves goes into action, crawling. The whole has a strange morbid calm. It has style and it is supposed to be about memory.

* Though credited to André Eglevsky, this work was choreographed by George Balanchine. It was danced by Marie-Jeanne and Eglevsky. See *Choreography by George Balanchine: A Catalogue of Works* (New York: Eakins Press Foundation, 1983), p. 166.—Ed.

Marie-Jeanne and Eglevsky were the principals and lovely they looked.

Les Sylphides, rehearsed by Mme Fokina, opened the program. It was interesting in a certain greater animation in the choreography that distinguished it from the usual versions, a clearer sense of climax. The corps de ballet was not of course as good as that of Ballet Theatre, or even of the Monte Carlo. Marie-Jeanne was delicate in the valse and pas de deux. William Dollar, who had the male role and did some rushing leaps, is an interesting dancer; he looks unsure but he also looks very alive.

One of the fine features of International is its excellent orchestra; it is a pleasure to have an accurate and also a sensitive orchestra, as it was under Alexander Smallens's direction. I am not sure he always helps the choreographic effects, but he certainly gives musical distinction to ballet, a place where it is badly needed.

Ballet International has a number of elements of distinction. They do not get their full value, because they are not given clear preponderance. The dancers themselves as an ensemble are not brilliant, but they are well rehearsed. Still, ballet companies are not created in a few months' rehearsal. It takes a good deal of dancing together in performance for everyone, including the management, to see what they are really after. But a resident ballet company, and one with excellent intentions in artistic directions, is something New York dance lovers can well be a little patient with, at its beginning.

OCTOBER 31, 1944

CATON'S "SEBASTIAN"

Ballet International's second program last night at the International Theater was more modest in its pretensions than the opening program of the night before, and in it the inexperienced company left a fresher impression. Edward Caton's new ballet *Sebastian*, his first, was the evening's feature.

Sebastian is a story ballet of love, magic, and murder in seventeenth-century Venice. It is not a subtle problem piece, it is straight melodrama. The excellently theatrical score by Gian Carlo Menotti, the period setting by Oliver Smith, and the costumes by Milena are not subtly elegant either but they are instantly effective, they have imagination and adroitness. Caton's choreography is like Tudor's in the point of being a dance stylization of fragmentary pantomime suggestions; it has a great deal of invention at first but is repetitive later on. Its theatricalism is promising, however, and it is a pleasure to have a new choreographer of imagination among us. Notably able was a long scene composed on a stage hardly more than a foot wide.

Lovely Viola Essen, who danced the lead, seemed nervous, but the flowing beginning of her solo in the third scene began to show her fine qualities. Francisco Moncion, as Sebastian, was highly remarkable, both in beauty of motion and in intensity of characterization. Last night he carried the piece. The ensemble did well in a dance interlude where they leaped and whirled across the stage in roles described as "Passers-by, Prostitutes, Priests, Peasants, etc." A lively scene it was.

Dollar's *Constantia* is a revival (with changes) of his *Concerto in F*, given some years ago at the Metropolitan. It is strictly a dance ballet in the Balanchine style. Though it lacks the continuity and easy fullness of Balanchine, though its group passages look a little monotonous, it has fine moments, notably in the adagio duet and in the roles for the two principals in the finale. Mr. Dollar danced the male lead with a spontaneity and a delight in dancing that made his many virtuoso feats very expressive. Delicate Marie-Jeanne, his partner, danced her difficult part admirably and seemed to gain from Dollar's performance in warmth as she went on.

Swan Lake opened the program with Miss Essen and André Eglevsky in the leads. It was a slightly more dramatized and characterized version than the usual one, but it did not seem a better one, partly because of the weakness of the ensemble, partly because of Miss Essen's constricted manner in dancing. The new set by Dunkel is, unfortunately, an inept one, and the way it is hung makes the stage far too small. Miss Houston's costumes for *Constantia* are also foolish ones, and dead in color. Mistakes in décor are an unpleasant surprise at Ballet International; but seen as the company was last night, as a modest and earnest beginning, the general effect is a perfectly agreeable one. For the moment at least, Ballet International is not competing with our other two ballet companies.

NOVEMBER 1, 1944

SEMENOFF'S "MEMORIES"; NIJINSKA'S "BOLERO"

Ballet International, at the International Theater, presented another world premiere Wednesday night, Simon Semenoff's *Memories*. The reviewer also saw Mme Nijinska's *Bolero*, which at its original performance Monday night had come too late to be reported on. *Bolero* is Radio City corn of incredible lugubriousness. *Memories*, Mr. Semenoff's first ballet, would make a passable though unoriginal production number in a show if cut to five minutes; lasting half an hour, as it seems to, it too is an incredible mistake in ballet production.

Memories is set to an endless series of Brahms waltzes—one of them, at least, from the Lieder. Brahms, a master at clogging the motion of a melody, is not a happy choice for dancing, anyway.

Mr. Semenoff's ideas aren't dance ideas, however—ballroom waltzing, cotillion figures, a few supported poses, and a messy bit of flash technique don't make a dance.

The ideas that went into *Memories* are pantomimic by nature. *Memories* mimes a ballroom scene of a hundred years ago, with some fancy idealized flirting by the principals. It is a story remembered, it seems, by a gentleman in Brahms's whiskers, who appears at the beginning and the end. What he remembers is lost onstage in a welter of pathetic gestures. Miss Essen was pretty and intelligent in one of the leads. Mr. Jolas in another was silly and slow. I can't imagine even a good performance by everyone would make the piece of any interest.

The set by Raoul Pène du Bois is pretty in a timid way. There is no point whatever for a new company aiming at artistic prestige to commission feeble period decoration, no matter how innocuously genteel. Broadway is the place for that. I may add that the audience applauded everything about *Memories* loud and long.

But *Bolero* is considerably worse than *Memories* because Mme Nijinska has proved herself in the past a great choreographer. Her Paris version of *Bolero* (for the Rubinstein ballet) was bad, but I did not remember that one as nearly so bad as this. This one begins with a chorus doing the "Volga Boatmen" and then whips them into doing spirituals in the style of Mr. Mamoulian. Miss Essen squirms around on a big table in the center, with a smile of autoerotic delight that Hollywood might consider enticing. There is nothing remotely Spanish anywhere around, despite mantillas, knives, flounces, and so forth. Of course, the soporific blatancies of the music would discourage any ideas of Spain or of dancing; one may claim that this *Bolero* is the good old sucker-trap number that the *Bolero* was composed for. But why should Ballet International present it?

What a pleasure to see *Sentimental Colloquy* in contrast. Dali's backdrop is mild in a way, but it is masterful. Bowles's score is beautifully made and the orchestration is sound and just. This little ballet doesn't get anywhere, but first-class materials have gone into making it.

The program opened with *Sylphides* with Miss Essen, Miss Maslova, Miss Golovina, and Mr. Eglevsky in the solo roles. Eglevsky danced handsomely, but the soulful style of miming and the wig don't suit him. The sort of abandon that Dollar gives the part is not in his line. Miss Essen, one can see, is an able dancer, with an agreeable unaffected personality and a dramatic gift. She, too, is not very convincingly entranced by the Chopin spell, but she doesn't overdo it. The International's version of *Sylphides* remains, however, choreographically the best of those we see.

Ballet International is at a disadvantage in trying out its new repertory here in town. It is essentially a pleasant company and I hope it has the stamina to live through this initial ordeal. NOVEMBER 3, 1944

NIJINSKA'S "PICTURES AT AN EXHIBITION"

Bronislava Nijinska's *Pictures at an Exhibition*, the world premiere of which Ballet International offered last night at the International Theater, is an orderly group composition in stylized Soviet-Russian clothes, a sort of mechanized Russian farm celebration, without much dancing or very interesting ideas. The company as a whole gave a perfectly satisfactory performance.

The choreography is a stylization of Russian folk steps and village games. It has a good many chain-gang huddles and a number of rows standing face upward, looking fervently glad. Instead of looking like a monument, however, the piece looks like a poster. The community farmers look careful and clean but not—as the farmers in Nijinska's *Les Noces* did—anonymously passionate and powerful. The sports and jokes, the joys and sorrows that the piece is about have not in the dance a rhythm startling or jubilant enough to be emotionally convincing. *Pictures* is a serious, a remarkably ingenious work, but it is not a bright one.

Pictures is based, the program states, on "the essentially Russian spirit of Mussorgsky's music" and set to most of his *Pictures at an Exhibition* (orchestrated by Ivan Boutnikoff). The score's descriptive side is very often ignored; its melodic line is ignored, too, and the rhythmic counterpoint that the dance offers is overheavy. The finale, which mimics pulling on ropes to ring bells, doesn't work in the dance and it doesn't work in the score either. Unfortunately all through the ballet the spirit of the music is much more amusing, cordial, and nobly direct than what you see on stage, much more alive and easy.

Pictures gains immensely by a clean stage design by Boris Aronson. The production is supposed to resemble Soviet staging of the present; there is in the dance action a certain reminiscence of the "Blue Blouse" or Agitprop technique of twenty years ago, but the photographs of present Moscow ballet staging are much more like International's *Sylphides*. Aronson has imitated pine boards, monk's cloth, and such materials; they would have been prettier real than painted; nevertheless I very much enjoyed the clear space of the décor and the general coolness. Miss Geleznova danced the lead very charmingly. NOVEMBER 4, 1944

TOUMANOVA AND DOLIN AT BALLET THEATRE

What really thrills in Toumanova's dancing is its horizontal and downward drive—the velocity with which she travels perfectly stiff, the force with which she rams her squared-off toe shoe into the floor, the solid slowness with which her free leg deploys its mass from the leg she stands anchored on. These are thrills where her prowess and her dance instinct coincide. She can simulate the motions of airiness—she did it perfectly in her second *Giselle* performance and in *Sylphides*—but she does not sustain for any length of time the impulse upward, the lyric breathing on which these roles are based. On the contrary you see her natural genius in *Tricorne*, when she sits down grandly and massively like a Roman river deity on the floor and waits for the farucca to begin. The true expression of her dancing comes from her passion for the floor and its rhythm is one of pressure and explosion. The tone is an unexpected one in ballet, it even recalls Mary Wigman at her best. Toumanova has some of Frau Wigman's scorn for the amenities of the theater, her force of self-isolation on stage, her hectic smashing rhythm. A ballet in which Toumanova could oppose her record feats and her quasi-Wagnerian grandeur to the airiness of the rest of the company would be completely sensational; what she needs is a choreographer to show her as she is.

She has, I believe, been presented this season mostly as she is not. Unable to use her natural expressiveness, she has improvised a fake stage personality and with that, with her unfaked acrobatics, and with her face, she has been wowing the customers in the old vaudeville way.

Mr. Dolin as her partner in classic numbers, equally unable to prove his real theater virtue, has resorted to the same vaudeville attack. He is not technically a classic dancer anymore. He can get applause, to be sure, merely by looking lovingly at his own right hand or by doing a leap (entrechat) in which his feet paddle in the air like Donald Duck's; but this is no proof of his classic technique, it is a proof of his genius and experience as a showman. Dolin is a first-rate showman and comedian. His natural wit, enthusiasm, great charm, and sense of caricature give a parody point to everything he does; they assure him of an immense success on the speaking stage, and those of us who sincerely admire him would like to see him add a fresh legitimate glory there to his former great glory in ballet. It is distressing to see two artists as fine as Toumanova and Dolin, both miscast, competing in a ballet number as to which will be the more audience conscious and stagey.

High-class vaudeville is not ballet. Ballet Theatre is a company of very fine dancers. If the management encouraged their native sincerity as artists, if it encouraged sincerely poetic dancing above vaudeville auto-exhibitionism, the management would be astonished both how its neglected classic ballets would increase in value and how its intellectual prestige would soar.

NOVEMBER 5, 1944

BALLET INTERNATIONAL AT TWO WEEKS

Ballet International, our new company, has several strong points which should not be overlooked. In the first place, it is a resident company. The dancers will not be exhausted by touring and their regular training will be less interrupted. Ballet dancers are athletes and they respond to a reasonable hygiene as much as other athletes do; they are also artists, and artists need a quiet place where they can work and they need an unconscious participation in the daily life of a city as anybody there lives it. A resident company can eat and sleep at home; it can practice and rehearse with concentration; it can be happy and unhappy in the same familiar drug store or elevator. International already shows a trace of the easy family feeling sensible working conditions induce. There is a serious and cheerful tone on the stage that a ballet company should have; there is no desperate anxiousness for personal applause that stage people resort to, as to a drug, when their vitality and self-respect are low.

But good points at International have been obscured by bad mistakes in artistic judgment. Of the nine pieces shown so far even the four more or less interesting productions—*Constantia*, *Sentimental Colloquy*, *Sebastian*, and *Sylphides*—have not been satisfactorily produced all around. The general impression of the repertory to date is that the new choreographies begin well, but instead of developing further they turn repetitious; the choreographers needed more discerning encouragement to go on. The new orchestrations of old scores are not dry, but they tend to banalize (and rather sour) the music they set out to amplify. Hardly any of the new costuming is properly calculated for the small stage; it takes up too much room. The cut is awkward (*Swan Lake* bodices) or conceals the gesture (*Sebastian*) or suggests foolish associations (*Constantia*), or the colors break up the dance (*Brahms Variations, I*). The problems of orchestral balances, of how a lot of costumes will add up in dancing, of how drawing and color in a drop create or destroy space onstage—these technical problems are outside of the professional experience of Broadway because they are vital only in ballet production. And so instead of commissioning Broadway stylists, International might have appealed for new scores and sets to the composers and painters in town who are perfectly familiar with ballet production from experience with ballet here and abroad;

their boldness and accuracy would have started the new repertory right.

When International started, the town was looking for a bold venture and it found a timid one. What we expected and missed was a clear sign of artistic direction, of intellectual drama and decision, of the nerve that creates style. Style can be created only at a risk; it is a form of courage, it is an exposed and often indefensible position. Stylishness even in the serenest classicism has a now-or-never edge and thrill, and even at its most playful it doesn't ask for a second chance. International has not been bold in style. NOVEMBER 12, 1944

COBOS'S "MUTE WIFE"

The Mute Wife, last night's novelty at the International on Columbus Circle, is a bright piece in perfect taste, a little dance comedy with intelligent choreography (Antonia Cobos), elegant mounting (Rico Le Brun), and excellent orchestration (Vittorio Rieti orchestrating Paganini). It is a trifle that is fun to watch and a first-rate production that puts you in fine humor.

The action follows the plot of Anatole France's play—a husband who has his pretty wife cured of muteness only to find her chatter unbearable takes refuge in deafness himself. Miss Cobos has left out France's Rabelaisian overtones and transposed the action to a politer eighteenth-century Spain; and her dance idiom is largely "classic" Spanish—an amusing novelty, too.

She herself acts and dances the lead with restraint and with an intelligence not unlike that of her fellow Californian Miss de Mille. She is not a strong dancer, but she is an interesting one. She expresses her muteness rather as an elegant frustration. Her operation scene, with hints of bullfighting, is inventive. When, after that, Miss Cobos chatters with castanets and heel taps, she rather draws out the effect too long, but the confusion of household is well timed in detail. It is a pity there is no general dance at least at the climax, but the smaller dance numbers are clear. Miss Cobos is a promising choreographer.

Mr. Moncion as the husband was excellent, and his miming of deafness at the end last night pulled the piece together just in time. In the smaller parts all the dancers were shown to their best advantage. They were inventively costumed, too, and Miss Cobos's own eighteenth-century "precautionary drawers" were charming. As a stage designer, Mr. Le Brun takes Eugene Berman for his model and does very well that way.

Rieti's orchestration is sour and sweet in happy juxtaposition, and though it seems sometimes a little too soft for the dancers to hear, it generally makes the orchestra sound rich and varied, and always musically elegant. George Schick conducted excellently.

NOVEMBER 23, 1944

ABOUT BALLET DECORATION

Because ballet dancers keep moving all over the stage and because in looking at them you keep looking at all the scenery all the time, ballet decoration is observed in a livelier way than play or opera decoration. In fact as a ballet unfolds and your interest in watching it grows, you become more susceptible to visual impressions and so more sensitive, too, to the decoration. In plays or operas you forget the scenery for long stretches while the performers stay still and you listen, more and more captivated, to their voices. The real dramatic power of a play or opera is felt to such an extent by listening that you can be thrilled even when you sit at the radio with no stage to watch at all. But the dramatic power of a ballet is in its visual impact. You feel it by seeing just how the dancers move, seeing their impetus in relation to each other and also their force in relation to the entire stage—how far they choose to go in contrast to how far they might go.

The force with which dancers approach, touch or separate, come forward toward you or retire, take possession of stage center or pause isolated near the wings, these changing intensities are meant to have a cumulative effect. You appreciate this best if you sit far enough back to view the whole stage at a glance, so that its height and width can act as a fixed frame of reference. Ballet scenery and costumes are meant to make the action of the dance distinctly visible at a distance and also to give a clear coherence to its variety, a livelier common term to its action than the mere empty stage area.

For this purpose a décor so busy that it confuses or so stuffy that it clogs the animation of the dances is of no use. But it cannot be timid. It must have power enough to remain interesting and alive as the dancing gradually sharpens the visual susceptibility of the audience. One of our finest sets—Pierre Roy's *Coppélia*—does this without attracting any notice to itself at all. The effect of a décor is right when as the ballet gathers momentum the dancers seem to have enough air all around to dance easily; when you see their long dance phrases in clear relation to stage center; when the flats keep the force of the gesture from spilling aimlessly into the wings; then the dancers—no matter how odd they looked at first—can come to look natural in the fanciful things they do, the natural fauna of the bright make-believe world they move in.

The present standards for ballet decoration were set by Picasso, whose *Three-Cornered Hat* is still pictorially alive after twenty-five years. The reason easel painters are better designers for ballet than anyone else is that they are the only craftsmen professionally concerned with what keeps pictures alive for years on end. When they know their trade they make pictures that hold people's interest for hundreds of years, so making one that will be interesting to look at for twenty minutes is comparatively easy for them.

A ballet set has to stand up under steady scrutiny almost as an easel painting does. At first sight it tells a story, it has local color or period interest or shock value. But then it starts to change the way a picture in a museum does as you look at it attentively for five or ten minutes. The shapes and colors, lines and textures in the set and costumes will act as they would in a picture, they will seem to push and pull, rise and fall, advance and retreat with or against their representational weight. The backdrop may tie up with a costume so that the dancer's figure seems to belong in it like a native, or it may set him plainly forward, where he has a floor to dance on. A good ballet décor, like a good painting, does different and opposite things decisively; like a painting, it presents a bold equilibrium of pictorial forces. And when the bold equilibrium in the décor corresponds in vitality to that of the dancing and that of the score, then the ballet as a production is alive and satisfactory.

The decorations by Picasso, Roy, Berman, and Chagall in our current repertory (Bérard's and Tchelitchev's are at the moment in storage) set a satisfactory standard—the highest in the world. It is a standard worth keeping for the time when other native American easel painters join Oliver Smith in working for ballet, as, despite management and union, they obviously should. Painters as they are, they will enjoy furnishing the pictorial power and nobility of presence ballet thrives on; and to see their American invention so openly presented would be a great pleasure to them and to us.

NOVEMBER 26, 1944

MEANING IN "THE NUTCRACKER"

Thinking of Christmas, I remembered the Christmas tree conspicuously onstage and the Christmas party in the first scene of *The Nutcracker*, the venerable fairy-tale ballet that Petipa's collaborator Ivanov set long ago to Tchaikovsky's lovely score. Has the action anything to do with Christmas? What is its nonsense plot really about, and how does *The Nutcracker* create its mild and beneficent spell? This serene old vehicle, complete with all the 1890 ballet conventions—pantomime scene, ballroom dance, grand pas de deux, divertissement, and ballabile, all of them strung in a row on a story nobody pays attention to—still works as a theater piece. It does even in such a form as the Monte Carlo's three-scene version, which though cut, patched, and mauled by years of hard wear keeps the formal continuity of the original three acts. At the Monte Carlo most of the young dancers show no manners in the pantomime part and they may do their stint in the dance scenes as if they were reciting "Thanatopsis." But the great Danilova as the Sugar Plum Fairy (especially with Youskevitch as partner) has a radiant and tender presence that lets you see the heart of the ballet and convinces you of its expressive power. Through her performance the choreographic intentions of the work emerge once more. If you are curious about choreography, you find that the dance logic of *The Nutcracker* is solid and that the nonsense plot—its idea content—has a rational structure too. The intentions of *The Nutcracker*, when you do catch on, are humane and sensible, and its 1890 formal method is highly intelligent.

What is the method? This is what happens on the stage. The long first scene is a clear pantomime story. The dance is plain, realistic, without embellishments, it does not lead to leaps; it is all terre-à-terre. The second and third scenes, in contrast to the first, tell hardly any story; instead they are dancing that clearly looks like dancing, with steps in patterns, leaps and lifts, dancing with "elevation." The two dance scenes are made up of successive dance numbers, each with a beginning and an ending, each a set piece, all of them together arranged in a suite ending with an ensemble finale.

The suite method in ballet, as in opera, does not have the urgency of the continuous, symphonic method. The suite ballet does not try so hard to get somewhere. The emotional tone is stable, it changes en bloc from number to number. The series of emotions that constitute the whole work are grouped in clear rubrics, the imagination dwells on one at a time and then proceeds satisfied to the next. The momentary detail is seen in relation to the number it appears in; when the number is finished one has a complete image, and the detail loses its insistency. There is a sense of repose in action, a control of the emotion that is both modest and noble. In short, the set-piece structure is not at all a foolish device.

The Nutcracker is not foolish in form, nor is it foolish either in its literal content. It is a fairy-tale ballet and certainly looks like nonsense. But nowadays, with psychoanalysis practically a household remedy, grown-ups take the nonsense of fairy tales more seriously than children. We call them narratives in free association and solve them like crossword puzzles. *The Nutcracker* is an easy one—the title gives it away. The story begins on Christmas Eve in an upper-class home, the locus classicus of ambivalent anxiety. An elderly bachelor with one eye gives a preadolescent girl a male nutcracker (the symbols and inversion couldn't be more harrowing). Her young brother tears it away from her by force and breaks it. But she takes it up from the floor and nurses it; she loves it. She dreams that the nutcracker turns almost into a boy. Then she dreams of a deep forest in winter with restless girl-snowflakes and a handsome young man who keeps lifting up a young lady (and who is this lady but the little heroine's own dream image?). And after that she dreams she is watching a lot of dancing Chinamen and Russians and oddly dressed people—all of them somehow "sweets"—and at last the previous young man and the previous young lady turn up again, too. They furnish a brilliant climax, and that leads to a happy dazzle for everything and everybody everywhere at once.

You can see that the suite of dances presents an intelligible association series, operated with unconscious sexual symbols; that the piece makes sense enough as a subconscious reverie beginning with a cruel sexual symbol, the nutcracker, which is also its literal title; and in this sense the various subjects of its pantomime and dance scenes are intelligible, too. It is the kind of sense one expects of a fairy-tale plot, since it is how fairy tales are rationally understood. But what you see on the stage is a suite of well-mannered dances, graceful and clear. The clarity of the dance-suite form controls the pressure of the unconscious theme and by easy stages brings on a pleasing change of emotion. Using the methods of 1890, *The Nutcracker* reaches an unconsciously satisfying final goal by a series of choreographic effects; and even in what appear to be merely formal evolutions, this old-fashioned dance entertainment follows a sincere emotional logic.

At the start of the piece, the effect of the pantomime scene—sadistic in content for all its upper-class Christmas party manners—is gloomy and oppressed; the dancers don't really get off the floor. What a relief when the dancing begins with leaps and airy lifts in the next snow scene. But the choreography here preserves a coolness and a remoteness that don't quite satisfy. The third, last scene is friendlier, lighter, more open to the audience, more animated, more playful in detail, and in the end there is a happy sense that everyone on the stage has leaped about freely and sufficiently. So they can all stop and smile straight at you, looking pretty without the least embarrassment.

And there is another unconscious satisfaction in the sequence of the dances. For the strictness of bodily control inherent in dance virtuosity, a strictness that grows more exacting as the dance becomes more animated and complex, seems at the end a satisfactory sublimation for the savagely cruel impulses suggested in the disturbing pantomime opening of the piece. And so *The Nutcracker* is really a dream about Christmas, since it succeeds in turning envy and pain into lovely invention and social harmony.

Compare this conciliatory dream libretto with the dream libretto of the Dali-Massine *Bacchanale.* The latter proceeds from anxiety to disgust and hysteria and bogs down in a pile of umbrellas. If one took the *Bacchanale* seriously one would find it a very unsatisfactory story.

No doubt Ivanov, the choreographer of *The Nutcracker*, didn't look for symbols in a fairy tale; he was interested in dancing that one could see clearly and that would have a cumulative effect. He would find my account of his ballet absurd, and so would the many thousands who like it and don't ask for a reason. Thousands of people all over the world find *The Nutcracker* touching and comforting without knowing why. My point is simply that if you look for a reason, if you are interested in what ballet means rationally, you can find a great deal of meaning in *The Nutcracker* and excellent reasons for its peculiar effect.

It is not quite by chance either that they are to be found. *The Nutcracker* was derived in one way or another from a long fairy tale of E. T. A. Hoffmann's, *The Nutcracker and the King of Mice*. The ballet has a little of the story and much of the tone of Hoffmann, his special note of hurt and tender assent. Hoffmann was one of the brightest of men and master of the free-association device. The free-association device was as familiar to educated persons in 1820 as it is to us, and practiced by them with more sense of humor. Their joke was: as long as the association of images is free, why not make it come out pleasantly? Perhaps this is the secret connection between Hoffmann's conciliatory fairy tale and the emotional control of the set-piece ballet form; and the connection, too, between the quality of the score Tchaikovsky composed and that of the dancing and the story. At any rate, story, score, and choreographic style join very beautifully in this academic ballet.

DECEMBER 10 AND 17, 1944

DALI'S "MAD TRISTAN"

Dali's *Mad Tristan*, which Ballet International offered at the International Theater Friday night, is a masquerade that only a genius could invent. Dali takes Wagner's music and Massine's choreography and uses them as props for a spectacle, and what a show he puts on.

Fantastic backdrops, costumes, stage effects tumble out over the stage for half an hour in frenzied profusion. It is a theater thrill that Billy Rose might envy; a proliferation of decoration no one in the world but Dali can rival.

Mad Tristan is meant as a hallucination in the mind of Tristan, who "sees himself devoured by Isolde's Chimera," the program says. The piece has two scenes. The first opens with Isolde waving the fatal scarf and proceeds to a horridly confused acrobatic love duet with Spirits of Death like shivering maniacs and Spirits of Love like enormous dandelions in seed milling about. It ends with the revelation of two Isoldes, both equally fascinating and differently horrid; King Mark with two soldiers wondrously armed enters.

The second scene shows Tristan on a version of Böcklin's *Isle of the Dead*, plagued by a sardonic Shepherd, plagued by a beautiful bouncing ship, plagued by the Isoldes and the Spirits and other faceless figures. It ends with Tristan dying for love as upstage his own repulsive mummy is lowered into a vault caressed by white wormlike dismembered living arms.

There is, as you can see, a vague connection with Wagner's *Tristan*, with Freudian symbols, with symbols that recur in Dali's work. The ballet has not, on the other hand, any of the exalted hypnotic immobility onstage nor any of the long-drawn climactic surge of *Tristan*. In fact, though excerpts from *Tristan* are played as accompaniment, the visual hysteria of *Mad Tristan* must be revolting to an absorbed Wagnerite; and as the music sounds thin with the small orchestra that plays, it is just as well to take the score not as Wagner, but as an effigy of a masterpiece, a literary reference.

As the score isn't music, so the ballet isn't dancing. Its best effects are properly stage effects, disjointed ideas rather than organized dances—such are the first shivers of the insane Dead, the parallelism of the two Isoldes, the Shepherd sticking to Tristan like a leech. Indeed, there aren't quite enough such nondance effects; they belong to Dali's passion for the inappropriate. One would like to see people reading the newspaper, or brushing their teeth; one would like to see a straight fistfight among the ballet steps.

Mad Tristan is nothing like a classic ballet, it is not something to be seen over and over. It is fascinating as a contradiction of classicism. It is fascinating too for its imaginative abundance, for the largeness of its pictorial presence. And it is wonderful how Dali turns whatever pictorial reference he offers into an immediate insignia of the unconscious world within us. To put it more simply, as a show and the first time you see *Mad Tristan* there isn't a dull moment in it.

Besides Dali, there was one other hero Friday night, Francisco Moncion, who took the part of Tristan. He carried off the most acrobatically strenuous part ever seen without a flaw, and more than that he projected the character and the story convincingly. He is a very fine dancer indeed, and a quite exceptionally imaginative one. Toni Worth, the real Isolde, is beautiful in a rather Vargas-like way. She and Miss Maslova, her double, who did the dancing of the part, were perfectly acceptable executants. The Flute Player, Mr. Armstrong, was excellent.

Mad Tristan murders Wagner, but does it to the hilt; with this novelty International has given us a first-class mental carnival.

DECEMBER 16, 1944

INTERNATIONAL'S FAREWELL

Ballet International closed its season at the International last Saturday night. Both last Saturday's and Friday's performances showed that the company, for all its mistaken timidity in production, has acquired a following of friends and showed also how steadily the inexperienced ensemble has improved.

Saturday's biggest applause went to André Eglevsky, a great dancer and established star who that night was dancing his best, as he does not always seem to have the heart to do. *Brahms Variations*, which he appeared in, is an exacting, ungrateful, and crabbed ballet, and its decoration is so awkward that the dancers look like several flavors of ice cream melting messily over the stage. Just the same, the piece is the only one in International's repertory that makes use of Eglevsky's phenomenal ability.

In the first part he stars by being the calmest in motion of all the busy dancers; in the second, by having the most powerful drive. The absurdly twisted arm and head positions required of him, the protracted poses, the sudden dartings—none of these can break the grand continuity of his dancing. The piece is especially a leg-action ballet: Eglevsky's leaps and steps are models of every variety of resilience. Fine, too, are the small entrechats, in which his calves, beating against each other, rebound with the taut quiver of a plucked string.

Eglevsky is an established great star; a star in the making is young Francisco Moncion, who Saturday appeared as Tristan in Dali's *Mad Tristan*. Moncion is the first dancer in the four Dali ballets since 1939 to create a stage character who remains convincing in the frenzy of the impressive set; and plenty of ballet's best artists have been in the other three. Moncion as a character dancer is the happy discovery of the season.

Looking back over the season, I find the agreeable side to have been the general seriousness of the dance company. Of the novelties, only *Mad Tristan* was produced on the professional level of our other two ballet companies. But people who dropped in at the International much as they might drop in at a neighborhood cinema for a quiet evening have found the general tone pleasant, modest, and acceptable. That is more than one hoped for after the first performance. DECEMBER 25, 1944

BALLET INTERNATIONAL IN RETROSPECT

The luckiest stroke of International's recent season was the discovery of the very great gifts of young Francisco Moncion. He had been doing classic as well as dramatic parts for some time in successive Kirstein companies, and a year ago his Sailor in Miss Shea's very interesting *Sailor Bar* had been especially remarkable. At the beginning of this season with International his parts weren't grateful ones. But later on, in the male leads of *Sebastian*, *The Mute Wife*, and *Mad Tristan*—three wholly different styles of movement—he showed that he is the most gifted American character dancer (if one may use the term for dramatic characterization in ballet) to appear—"the best thing that has happened," as Mr. Van Vechten, our greatest ballet critic, said to me, "since Hugh Laing came along."

Moncion, well trained as a classic dancer, strong and manly, is like a modern dancer in the freedom with which he can use torso, arms, and neck. But his exceptional gift is his intense imaginative sincerity. He creates a character completely, and he has power, musicality, and humor. His leg gestures when the thighs separate are not as clear as the others, and his feet can get a more expressive support from the floor, but his instinctive dignity in expression will teach him best. A fine dancer who believes in dancing more than in himself is a wonderful thing, and we can look forward to many seasons of growing pleasure in Moncion.

Sebastian and *Mute Wife*, in which Moncion made his mark, also showed the other dancers at their best. In the first, Miss Essen, though she has not the powerful, open line or the rhythm needed for a Swan Queen, was perfect as the Courtesan with a perverse young softness, a girl sincerely kind in little ways. In *Mute Wife* one saw young Guelis leaping up and hoped he might soon learn to be elastic above the waist. Among corps dancers, Miss Blum and Miss Shea were bright and cute, and one noticed a girl of quite exceptional grace and individuality, Miss Garfield, of whom her fellow dancers, too, prophesy great things. Among featured dancers in other pieces I admired Marie-Jeanne very much, with her classic openness and rapidity in the thighs, her clear rhythm, and regretted her reticence in yielding motions and gestures above the head—and sometimes a little neglect of line in the instep. There was William Dollar, whom I like for his musical delight in dancing when he is in form, but whose mannerism of relaxing his loins in the air and his neck in poses has cost him the popularity he long since deserved; and forthright Miss Patterson, musical Miss Golovina, Maslova, Geleznova, and from the corps Miss Hill, Mr. Beard, Mr. Raher, Mr. Armstrong. International's company is still not homogeneous and it is a bit heavy, but it is talented.

But International's great dance attraction was of course the superbly easy, clean, classic virtuoso Eglevsky. Unfortunately, he was not well presented. One would have thought that International, faced with showing a green company in an untried repertory on a shallow, narrow stage under inadequate lighting facilities, would have built its first season around Eglevsky, and built it to some extent around its unusually fine orchestra. Instead, it wasted both these exceptional features by pretending to have as well all the other resources for ballet in the grand manner, which it too clearly didn't. International's personnel as well as its plant suggested a repertory of ballets in the concert style, small individualized ensembles, novel music, decoration planned to make the stage look freer. As gifted and experienced a choreographer as Nijinska might perhaps have given the company several striking concert-style ballets, had she been told to. The limitations of the form might have led to a freshness of conception and ideas, qualities that would have given vitality to the whole enterprise. And the small stage would have turned into an organic advantage.

DECEMBER 31, 1944

CUNNINGHAM SOLO

Merce Cunningham, a brilliant soloist in Martha Graham's company, and the most gifted of the young dancers who follow her, gave a solo recital last night at the Hunter College Playhouse. Though his first recital last year had been a distinct success with the audience, this second one was not. But Mr. Cunningham's quite exceptional merits as a dancer were as clear as ever and as interesting to a dance lover.

As a virtuoso in our modern-school technique he is second only to Miss Graham herself. His face is always expressive. The elasticity, strength, and quickness in the legs and feet, the variety of bearing in the torso and neck, the clarity of motion in arms and hand allow him very striking effects. Better still is the variety of drive and speed which phrases his dances; and best is the improvisatory naturalness of emphasis which keeps his gestures from ever looking stylized or formalistic.

With his physical elegance and originality of gesture Mr. Cunningham combines a rare good sense in what a man dancing alone on the stage may with some dignity be seen to be occupied in doing. A man alone can suggest he is looking for something invisible, that he is trying out a trick, that he is having a bad time, or that he is just fooling. Cunningham's dances express these lyric possibilities with real imagination and subtlety. The unhappy numbers have dignity and the joking ones have humor.

One funny one, *Mysterious Adventure*, with an absurd object on the stage (designed by David Hare), was long but alive all the time.

In short, Mr. Cunningham is an exceptionally gifted and exceptionally intelligent dancer. For dance enthusiasts whatever he does is a pleasure to watch. But the variations of solo lyric dancing he shows are not sharp enough themselves to attract the intelligent audience he is equipped to interest. He does not create onstage different objective characters, but rather lyric variations of his own character. His genre, which hovers between lyric and character, is one that expresses itself best in comic numbers, in which the divided personality is a virtue.

A virtuoso like Mr. Cunningham is a rarity, and his ability is of the greatest value to modern-school dancing. For the moment, he shines best, however, in group compositions, where his character contrasts with that of other dancers. His solo recitals, impeccable as they are in taste, are not yet bold enough in expression to communicate to a general audience. But he has all the possibilities of becoming a great dancer, and we need as many of those as we can get. JANUARY 10, 1945

INDIA-HAITI-AFRICA

Hadassah, an Oriental-style dancer with an excellent studio reputation, made her debut last night at the New York Times Hall with Pearl Primus and Josephine Premice, Haitian singer, as guest artists. But it looked like a debut with a hex on it. Hadassah was disappointing and so last night was Miss Primus in two of the three familiar numbers she appeared in. It was Miss Premice with her little folk songs, her charming Haitian timbre, her loose-jointed West Indian vivacity and elegance who saved the evening.

Hadassah was much the happiest in a parody-Hindu Jack Cole–style number at the end of the program; the joke isn't new, but it is still a good one. Her serious numbers, four East Indian and one Javanese, were her own arrangements of Oriental material, set to recorded Eastern music. If one were to judge her as an Oriental dancer, one would note that she missed the basis of the style, the pelvic concentration from which the movement of Indian dancers ripples upward through the torso and out into the fingertips with a lithe and sinuous strength. Similarly her thighs were not firmly turned out, and she had no assurance in them. In consequence her rhythm was choppy and often hasty, and her poses were not plastic. Her elegant wrists, her pretty head were very attractive, though, and perhaps for the rest this was not an evening by which to judge her.

Authentic neither Hadassah nor Miss Primus really intends to be; but authenticity is the basis of Miss Premice's Haitian songs. Her charming delivery, mixed with dance steps, may have been suggested by Belle Rosette, the Trinidad dancer with whom I believe Miss Premice appeared here, at Louise Crane's brilliant Coffee Concerts some seasons back. (Miss Primus and also Miss Ellis, now a star with Katherine Dunham, were, I think, on Miss Rosette's program, too.) Dance lovers will also recall Miss Premice as the charming leading dancer in Dafora's African program last year at Carnegie Hall. Her Haitian folk songs, however, are a novelty.

JANUARY 12, 1945

"ON THE TOWN"; "SING OUT, SWEET LAND"; "SONG OF NORWAY"

Jerome Robbins's dances for *On the Town* are fresh, neat, direct, and sincere, and that is how they are danced. The spirit they are danced with is where you see his originality much more than in the steps. You can tell what an exceptional gift he has as a director by how clearly the dancers know what to stress and by how spontaneously they do it. All of them, chorus as well as principals, give you the sense of a happy cooperation with the piece and with each other, a cordial glow that they share, newcomers and experienced dancers alike. Looking at them, one wishes some such vivifying warmth had brought together the dancers of Ballet International too and given them a freshness on the stage they might easily have had. International couldn't cooperate in this way because it often didn't get the point of what it was doing in terms of ensemble ballet rhythm. In *On the Town* the company knows how their movements work in terms of ensemble pacing; so they know what they are after, and they can all look intelligent when they dance, unselfconscious and lively.

There are lots and all sizes of dances; they generally tell a little pantomime story, but you don't think of them as distinct from the rest of the show. They generally emerge from the stage action and melt into it again so as to give value to a scene rather than a hand to the dance. Often they express a sentiment, too, much as Miss de Mille's musical-comedy dances do. In *On the Town*, the sentiments suit the farce plot especially well, and besides, Robbins's sentiments are naturally intelligent and attractive ones anyway—serious or funny without affectation.

Just now his dance ideas do not develop in space easily, but he doesn't try to cover up by complicated patterns or ornamental gestures; he concentrates instead on clarity of impulse and variety of pacing. In detail, though, I admired particularly the end of the "Lonely Town" number and the way the singer's one nod completes a dance; the equally simple ending of Miss Osato's "Turnstiles" number; the brief strange rush of the Times Square finale; and the monkeyshines of the principals in "You Got Me," which was for me the most striking moment of all. Less successful, I thought, was the dream number, but Oliver Smith's wonderful scenic effects here are more than enough to carry it.

Miss Osato danced in the dream and everywhere else with brilliant rhythm and a brilliant sense of shades of character (and of hardness and softness). She is an impish and a warmhearted comedienne, completely natural in the general New York hometown atmosphere. And the fun of the whole evening is the grace of feeling at home here where we are.

Sing Out, Sweet Land wants to make you feel at home, not here and now, but in our historic customs. Doris Humphrey and Charles Weidman have furnished historical steps (from "squares" to Charleston), and Peter Hamilton's Charleston is a brilliant dance moment. But as for the rest, if you begin to compare the heavy accents and strained postures of the dancing with the limpid, relaxed, and delicately elastic rhythm with which Burl Ives, the balladist, sings his songs, you notice how "unauthentic" the dance effects are. You will notice it, if you enjoy our country folklore straight and appreciate its inherent modesty and unassertive spaciousness. But it takes a unique artist like Ives to put across such mild and sweet effects.

Song of Norway, when it opened in August, had nothing less than the Monte Carlo, headed by Danilova and Franklin, as its dance company. The stars have since been replaced by Olga Suarez, a highly promising newcomer, and by Dorothie Littlefield, Messrs Guérard and Starbuck, artists familiar to balletgoers. Revisiting the show last week, I found the numbers fresh, cool, and clear as ever. In one sense they are the boldest on Broadway, for they rely on the most civilized of dance virtues—a striking simplicity of line and purity of classic style. Unobtrusive as these Balanchine numbers are, anyone can see that they are pretty and the final ballet offers you, without insistence, modestly, and touchingly, a sentiment not at all commonplace. *Song of Norway* does not falsify ballet as most musicals do, on the ground that adulteration is the first principle of showmanship. Balanchine's numbers are simplified ballet, but of the purest water.

JANUARY 21, 1945

DUDLEY-MASLOW-BALES AND CUNNINGHAM

Recent recitals have presented the Dudley-Maslow-Bales trio (with Frieda Flier taking the place of Miss Maslow) and Merce Cunningham. These are four of the leading soloists who have been trained in the modern-dance technique, and they show in different ways the direction the young modern dancers are taking. The modern dancers have been shifting their attention from social protest to lively dance action. They are taking ballet lessons, they are listening to the beat of dance music, learning a friendly stage manner and quick, neat footwork. They will leap up lightly whenever they get a chance. Probably they will soon dress as elegantly onstage as they already do off it. They go in more for professional finish and less for creative personality. And many are finding work in musicals. I think it will all help those among them who are really serious to find out just how serious they are.

The Dudley-Maslow-Bales trio has for some seasons represented a moderate point of view in this general tendency. Their recitals have looked capable, varied, unpretentious. They combined modern-school inventions of gesture with an easier audience appeal—a flavor of country dance, of jazz, a hint of de Mille and now of Robbins. Miss Flier, the substitute member, is a very well-trained dancer, with defter feet and a quicker balance than the other two, and she has a feminine delicacy that is attractive and that is still unusual in modern recitals.

But I was disappointed in the general effect of the evening. As intelligent moderns trying for a friendlier, more open style, the trio had raised expectations. They seemed to be looking for a lilt in dance rhythm and for an objective impersonation of character; and one forgave the clumsy side of their first attempts in this new direction. But now instead of working ahead on the line they took, they mostly go on repeating their old numbers and slick over the mistakes. Watching them once more, one cannot help noticing how lifelessly the gesture is clamped to the beat of the music, how wooden the characters are, how fussy and unmusical the setting is for such a folk song as "On Top of Old Smokey." Mr. Bales seemed self-conscious as soon as he defined his movements clearly or raised his head. Miss Dudley changed her silhouette at will to practically anything in Picasso, but she had no resilience of rhythm. They may well be tired of the numbers; in any event, I hope next winter they bring us a new program.

If the trio represent the eclectic popularizers in the modern school, Mr. Cunningham reminds you that there are pure dance values in pure modern technique. He is a virtuoso, relaxed, lyrical, elastic like a playing animal. He has an instinct for a form that makes its point by repetition, each repetition being a little different, and the phrasing of each difference exceptionally limpid. He has a variety of drive and speed which phrases his dances, and better still an improvisatory naturalness of emphasis which keeps his gesture from looking stylized or formalized.

The kind of elastic physical rhythm he has strikes me as something peculiarly American, and it is delicately supported by the elastic phrases of John Cage's music. But Cunningham's stage character is still too cautious to carry a solo program. He appears either as a lonesome youth or as a happy hooligan; you would like him to show a franker character, too, or see him in contact with different people. So strong a body should also harden and strike, force one phrase and throw away another; it could risk a firm beat, or an attack open and generous. A serious solo program calls for more risks in expression. Amiable popularizers like the trio don't lead you to expect much of a risk. Cunningham does, by his poetic style, by his brilliant gifts. There is no reason why he shouldn't develop into a great dancer.

JANUARY 29, 1945

"DEATH AND ENTRANCES"

Martha Graham and her company made their first metropolitan appearance of the season last night, presenting *Salem Shore*, *Deaths and Entrances*, and *Every Soul Is a Circus*. *Deaths and Entrances* was the most absorbing dance work that opened in New York last season, though it competed with plenty of ballet novelties. If its original shock value no longer operates, both the piece itself and Miss Graham's dancing in it have lost none of their first fascination.

Suggested originally by the life and works of the Brontës and by their atmosphere of passionate intellectual sensuality, heroic in despair, *Deaths and Entrances* in its dance gesture evokes the romantic stage tragedies of a hundred years ago—the ferocity, tenderness, and grandiloquence, the ancestral manor, the duel, the ball, the mad scene, the garland of wildflowers, the goblet, and the cushion with an embalmed heart in it.

Our forebears when they saw these tragedies started with horror and wept. They sensed their secret obscenity. Miss Graham brings back the true romantic impact and effect; it is as immediate now as then, and this is an achievement of genius. If we had expressive tragic actors they would go to *Deaths and Entrances* to learn their trade. For the general theatergoer, the ballet is an absorbing experience.

In recapturing romantic fervor Miss Graham has reinvented the gestures, the poses, the rhythms it needs, and made them startling afresh. Her tumultuous dance sequences are clear and firm. She herself never loses the ladylike elegance, the womanly look that makes formal tragedy communicative. And she does not force her private emotion into the passionate role she impersonates.

Her own role strikes me as the only completely rounded one in the wordless drama. The two men, though handsomely danced last night by Hawkins and Cunningham, are expressive only in their relation to the heroine; they have no independent existence as real characters would. The parts of the three little girls, though small, seem more autonomous than last year. The heroine's two sisters, danced so brilliantly last year by Miss Maslow and Miss Dudley, done now with care by Miss Lang and Miss O'Donnell, have become sketchier. FEBRUARY 6, 1945

MARIE MARCHOWSKY AND JEAN ERDMAN

At the Town Hall of the modern-dance world, the YMHA on East Ninety-second Street, Marie Marchowsky and Jean Erdman, well known for having been in Martha Graham's group, made their joint debut last Sunday afternoon as solo recitalists. Each dancer presented new solos and one long trio; and the whole program was meticulously produced in its dancing, music, costuming, and lighting. The audience, familiar with the effort and expense such an occasion requires, applauded warmly and eyed the performers professionally. Debut or no, I found the program far easier to take than the usual solo recital and of considerable interest to watch.

Marie Marchowsky, the more experienced of the two, demonstrated that she is a first-class professional as a dancer and choreographer of the modern school. She is up to the minute in modern-style technical problems and she has disciplined herself to evade none of them. She can be quick and sharp, she can be fluid and let her impetus subside like a breath; she executes a rhythm that vibrates evenly like a drumroll and she sustains the force of an out-thrust pose. She can dip close to the floor without losing her lightness, and she can stand massively erect. But by the standards she set otherwise, I thought that in lyric moments her shoulders were not easy enough, her ankles not quite deft. She moved her head from the base of the neck when she should have from the top and she held it chin-up too consistently—like a little commandant instead of like a graceful woman.

The first and the last one of her numbers were lyrical and, as dances, unforced, original in invention, skillful in flow. I liked them the best. Miss Marchowsky stressed more in three others that were dramatic in quality: a brief study in stiffened plastic relations called *Foreboding* (danced extremely well by Miss Wexler and Miss Chasnoff); a very long solo describing the frustration of a girl separated from her lover; and a long trio on maternal possessiveness. These all had striking inventions of gesture well set in the continuity. The sex-starved girl, for example, did peculiarly horrid crawlings on a table; and the viciously kind mother, arms outstretched, held hooked on them, hanging against her body, her grown daughter, cowered up and staring—as shocking an image as if one grown kangaroo were to sit in the pouch of another. It was a lift and an image Tudor might well envy.

A dance figure such as this one illustrates clearly the intellectual idea which the piece presents. For my part, however, I feel that an idea in a composition needs its own intellectual contradiction stated with equal emotion if it is to be convincing, just as a movement needs another movement in opposition to be convincing plastically or rhythmically.

Miss Marchowsky's formal model for her major numbers was a drama in pantomime and her continuity was narrative. In Miss Erdman's big number, a long trio, the continuity was rhythmic and the model was a dance (in this case a hula happily married to a "Gaelic theme"). Her dances in general suggested an anthropological fantasy and they had the tone of legendary games. Though Miss Marchowsky's psychological approach is that proper to a modern dancer, Miss Erdman's is a more original one and refreshing to encounter. But she had neither Miss Marchowsky's great discipline nor her variety of gesture. A piece about the Medusa looked almost collegiate in its timidity; and it wasn't till after two numbers that her body lost a sort of girdled decorum in the bustle, charming in a lady but not in a dancer. And yet her long trio, in which three young women swayed their hips and made wide snaky movements with their arms, waited in a straddle, joined in a ring facing outward, danced one here, one there, and then all three parallel—this long naive number to a marvelous score by John Cage fascinated and delighted me. Whatever the piece was meant to mean, there was a lightness in the rhythm, a quality of generosity and spaciousness in the movement that struck me as the content of a dance should, as a poetic presence. It did not seem long at all, it was charmingly danced. I was as happy watching it as when a friend took me to a bar on Ninth Avenue and showed me a poetic "primitive" landscape painted high up around the walls of lions and ships and wooded valleys and towns by the sea and people of various sizes walking or sitting by the water. FEBRUARY 11, 1945

MORE ARGENTINITA

The Spanish salon style—witty, well informed, lucid, and amiable—is Argentinita's great specialty both as a dancer and as a choreographer; and at last night's recital in Carnegie Hall her little company, which consists of Pilar Lopez, José Greco, and Manolo Vargas, was in perfect form to assist her. When the four of them are as lightly exact and as spontaneously responsive to each other as last night, Argentinita and her familiar style take on a new freshness.

It was the little ensemble's evening rather than the star's as it sometimes has been in the past, though Argentinita herself remained the subtlest and the most imaginative of the four. But Pilar Lopez, particularly in a new Bolero of her own, showed an unsuspected delicacy as a dancer and an agreeable originality as a choreographer. She stopped the show in her solo gypsy-style alegrías, and added a superb little coda as an encore.

José Greco, elegant and suave, has become a limpid virtuoso. To my mind he is still too consistently easy in the torso, and too consistently light on his feet; but the continuity of his dancing and the exactness of his gesture and his steps were very fine indeed. Manolo Vargas, harder, more sudden, and with gypsylike stops, is learning variety of nuance. He stopped the show, too, with a solo.

It is admirable how Argentinita has perfected and enlarged the dancing of these two gifted young men in a few years' time. She now can use their individualities together with her own and her sister's to give a little spontaneous drama and humor to her duets, trios, and foursomes without breaking the unity of the style. *In Old Madrid*, the 1900 Madrid zarzuela quartet, is delightful in its ingenuity at interplay. So is a new number, *On the Route to Seville*, where the city slicker (Greco) outwits and outsteals the three gypsies. Argentinita's tough arm gestures are very pretty in this; and Vargas incidentally did some remarkable pirouettes here, too.

If Argentinita's wit and storytelling gift are what immediately appeal to a foreign audience, her delicate differentiation between steps, her ingenious sequences, her excellent use of variety in the profile the dancer presents to the public, and the pretty rhythmic effects she achieves are what make them unique in their field. The ladylike tone she gives to them appeals more to some tastes than to others, which perhaps look for a greater forcefulness in Spanish dancing. But she knows what she wants and does it to perfection.

FEBRUARY 19, 1945

"BALLET IMPERIAL"

In *Ballet Imperial*, the novelty that the Monte Carlo presented at its opening last night at the City Center, the company looked miraculously renewed. It danced with an animation, a lightness and neatness that was far from the disheveled young valiance it showed only last September. The transformation that the dancing in Balanchine's *Danses Concertantes* then suggested is now in full view in his brilliant *Ballet Imperial*. And Mary Ellen Moylan, the leading ballerina of the piece, is a lovely jewel and a joy.

Ballet Imperial, which was first danced here by Private Kirstein's American Ballet a few years ago at the New Opera, is a vivacious, exacting, inexhaustibly inventive classic dance ballet, a ballet that evokes the imperial dazzle of the St. Petersburg style in all its freshness. It is no period parody. Everything is novel in its effect. But you recognize the abounding inner gaiety, the touch of tenderness, the visual clarity and elegance, the bold dance impulse that exist—often in only vestigial form—in the Petipa-school classics still in our repertory. Balanchine has re-created the spirit of the style which was its glory. And you look at *Ballet Imperial* with the same happy wonder that our grandparents may have felt in the nineties, when the present classics were novelties.

Ballet Imperial is a ballet without a plot, as luminously incomprehensible as the old classics were. It begins with a solemn, pompous, vaguely uneasy mood, groups and solos that turn into brilliant bravura; then comes a touching pantomime scene, with softer dances, a scene that suggests a meeting, a misunderstanding, a reconciliation, a loss; and then a third section succeeds, even more vertiginously brilliant than the first, in which everybody shines, individually, in clusters, the boys, the girls, the stars, and all in unison. The musicality of the choreography is as astonishing as its extraordinary ease in affording surprises and virtuoso passages.

Young Mary Ellen Moylan, dewy in diamonds, delicate, long, and with a lovely pose of the head and a beautiful freedom in her correctness, was the star. But Maria Tallchief, brilliant in speed and with a steely exactness, and Nicholas Magallanes, easy, sincere, and animated, were real stars as well.

The handsome backdrop, by Doboujinsky, suggests the architectural glories of Petersburg. The score, Tchaikovsky's Second Piano Concerto, was brilliantly conducted by Mr. Balaban. Rachel Chapman was ideal for dancers in the piano part, and the orchestra, too, was exact and strong, as it was all evening. FEBRUARY 21, 1945

"LE BOURGEOIS GENTILHOMME"

Balanchine's ballet *Le Bourgeois Gentilhomme*, which the Monte Carlo produced here in the fall in an unfinished state, returned at last night's performance of the company at the City Center, clear, light, and airy. The ensemble danced it as it should, cleanly and without forcing; but they seemed more subdued than they need have for so playful a piece.

Bourgeois Gentilhomme, which follows an episode in the Molière play and is set to the Richard Strauss music composed for the play, is gentle entertainment, a ballet divertissement with a few farcical and a few youthfully exuberant and youthfully tender moments; and it is a ballet that Eugene Berman has decorated with elegant splendor in a fantastic Louis XIV style that blends somber and delicately dry effects. The dances are full of diverting variety and effervescent ingenuity. There is a constant succession of happy choreographic novelties and they are thrown off without stressing. Unpretentiousness in abundance, ease in correctness are Balanchine's contributions to restoring ballet to its true cordial and civilized animation. Ballet isn't supposed to knock you flat like a vaudeville number.

The chief dancers in it, Miss Krassovska, Miss Moylan, Miss Tallchief, Mr. Magallanes, Mr. Katcharoff, Mr. Danielian, and Mr. Talin, are all easy and modest and it is admirable how they convey the nature of the characters they dance with no effort. A few changes in the choreography—notably the fencing scene—are excellent. And the audience likes the little jokes all through. The difficult music was reasonably well played, and sounded well from the balcony, at least.

Bourgeois was preceded by *Swan Lake* with Alexandra Danilova and Frederic Franklin in the leads. It was a quiet performance of the work, but handsomely in key all through. Miss Danilova, exquisite in the way she softly bends back between the shoulders, wonderful in the rhythm of her phrasing, was touching; and Mr. Franklin, a cleaner classicist than last fall, was as before warm and generous as a prince. Mr. Danielian danced the Prince's Friend's variation with vigor, a better posture, and a greater sense of continuity than in the fall, though his left wrist was awkward. He has evidently made great progress in style, without losing his natural verve.

FEBRUARY 22, 1945

"DANSES CONCERTANTES"; NIJINSKA'S "SNOW MAIDEN"

The Monte Carlo company presented last night an impeccable performance of Balanchine's *Danses Concertantes* and an agreeable one of Nijinska's *Snow Maiden. Danses Concertantes*, which has become a success with the audience, remains the boldest ballet of the season, the most original and singular.

Danses Concertantes is a triumph of succinctness. In fifteen minutes it offers as many contrasting dance images as if it took an hour. The more you look, the more you see. The clusters of dancers toss the current of motion up, down, they soften it for a moment, then whirl it, stop it, and flutter or stalk or run to a new departure. But though the single phrase looks very brief, it is bold and distinct; and the next phrase takes over its power, and in the end the force of the piece has been continuous and the effect is ample and grand.

But the magic of *Danses Concertantes* lies in its friendly and untragic atmosphere. It lies in the ease, the spontaneity and well-bred amusement which the individual gestures have, and in the young responsiveness to one another among the dancers which their composite dance figures so clearly show. The Monte Carlo company presents the piece with exact clarity and good manners, and further with a happy dancer's lightness and charm. And last night Danilova and Franklin danced the leads once more as the lightly natural comedians they can inimitably be.

The Snow Maiden, on the other hand, is as prolix as *Danses Concertantes* is succinct. It is rather like a fairy tale told by a poetical maiden aunt, who doesn't care to be hurried. But she is a well-educated and an intelligent lady, and she has a curious urban grace in her affectation of sweetness. In *Snow Maiden* the masculine assurance of the Shepherd, the timidity of the Snow Maiden, the open simplicity of the peasants all come through and strike a clear balance. And a number of dance passages, especially the hero's, play lightly over the cumbersome saccharine music in a highly intelligent manner.

Miss Krassovska danced the heroine with charm and exactitude. Mr. Danielian was a pleasant hero, and his leaps were superb; his main variation, however, still could gain in fluency. Mr. Lindgren, who danced the chief peasant, was lively in the steps, though he added little warmth to them; he is excellent, however, as the Fencer in *Bourgeois*. Miss Horvath was rather stiff as Spring, but in this part only Danilova has succeeded in spreading the radiance of spring on the stage. The peasants were very good indeed, and the tone of the whole performance was fresh and clear.

FEBRUARY 28, 1945

PAGE AND STONE'S "FRANKIE AND JOHNNY"

There were some laughs and applause for *Frankie and Johnny*, the little travesty which the Monte Carlo presented at the Center Wednesday night for the first time in New York, but as a novelty the piece is a disappointment. It would have been better to have left it honorably inhumed in our dance annals. The production is a revival of a Chicago 1938 WPA production of the Page-Stone Ballet, a company that with the Littlefield Ballet and the American Caravan pioneered in presenting native themes and sponsoring native dancers, composers, and scene designers. Brave as the experiments were, what we need now is more mature work by all then active.

The action of *Frankie and Johnny* follows the story of the ballad, and its dance style is an adaptation of barroom steps, grotesque pantomime, and acrobatics. The opening is serious, but after the murder the piece turns into conscious parody. It sacrifices the earnest tone which gives the song its stony eloquence; but it becomes rather apologetically amusing and harmlessly unpretentious.

The choreographers, Ruth Page and Sergeant Bentley Stone, have a great many pleasant improvisatory ideas, which hardly develop into dances. But the Frankie and Johnny duet suggests necking very nicely. Frankie's upside-down death is a clever joke, and so are the antics with the corpse. So is Nelly Bly's strut about the stage, excellently done by Vida Brown, and the many visits of gentlemen to her are neatly timed. But the chance the choreographers have missed is a straight sense of low-down life.

Miss Page, who, with Sergeant Stone, is a two-night guest at the Monte Carlo, is fragile but not very distinct or bold in movement. Mr. Stone has a very attractive open personality and considering he has been in the Army for a year he danced his part very well indeed.

The most interesting feature of the production is the score by Jerome Moross, which the composer conducted excellently. It is a youthful work eminently theatrical and with the integrity of simplicity; and Mr. Moross's recent *First Symphony* has, according to musicians, borne out the promise of it. The set, by Clive Rickabaugh, is satisfactory and unexaggerated and the costumes, by Private Paul Dupont, at least for the principals, are perfectly good for their purpose.

The evening, which ended with *Red Poppy*, began with a wonderful performance of *Swan Lake*, with Danilova, Franklin, and Danielian in the leads. The clear and honest classicism of the stars and the company—their power and simplicity—were admirable. Mr. Danielian stopped the show, and did it with no self-conscious overemphasis.

MARCH 1, 1945

"FRANKIE AND JOHNNY": AN INDECENT BALLET?

Frankie and Johnny, the 1938 Page-Stone charade which the Monte Carlo revived last week at the Center, is no bawdier than Nedick's orange drink. It tells the story of the ballad, but gives it the raciness of a daring sorority glee-club version. References to Frankie's and Nelly Bly's profession are strictly horsed, and when Frankie and Johnny get together what they do is a bit of high-school "necking." The lowlife characters milling about the stage are gloomily hunched up at first, and you think you are in for a social-consciousness number—German-expressionist style—but it all ends up as a nightclub joke, good clean fun, and nobody meant anything they did. They were just acting out the words like a charade.

A pretense of innocence, even in the most unlikely situations, is, if you will, an American custom, but it is not a characteristic of the ballad called "Frankie and Johnny." Its force and its humor in the best versions of the text—the Negro ones—come from its plainness. It describes the hero after being shot: "He fell down on his knees/Looked up at her and said/'Oh, Frankie, please/Don't shoot me no more, babe/Don't shoot me no more.' " Or when the sheriff approaches, " 'Well,' says Miss Frankie/ 'I don't care if I die/Take and hang me to a telegraph pole/Hang me good and high/ He was my man but he done me wrong.' " And after her arrest, "Passing through the jailhouse/Went by Frankie's cell/Asked her how she was feeling/She said, 'Go to hell.' " This is the Frankie that is poetic, and that is worth putting on the stage in a ballet or in any other form. The cute little Page-Stone Frankie isn't at all like her.

But besides missing the best point of its subject matter and the chance to present a plain American poem, *Frankie and Johnny* is muddled as a dance composition. The dancers step, jerk, and posture repeatedly, but no dances emerge, no effect of rhythm or of mounting vitality; they just seem to go on milling. Not that the piece shows no talent; far from it. It has a number of bright ideas, in stage business rather than in dancing, which call for laughs. And one cannot be angry with a piece that brings some original jokes, that aims to please in a harmless way, and that doesn't try for slickness; its talented amateurishness is perfectly aboveboard.

From this point of view, *Frankie and Johnny* has a perfect right to its good repute as a pioneer effort in amusing dance Americana, a repute it won in a 1938 Chicago WPA production. But *Rodeo* and *Fancy Free* have since then so far raised the standards—in dance construction, in humor of character and situation, and, best of all, in American savor—that *Frankie* can no longer compete.

The "unashamed" thing about this revival of *Frankie* is only that the management brought it to town. It should have been clear on the road, first, that it doesn't represent ballet Americana, and, second, that the piece makes the Monte Carlo dancers look foolish, since it doesn't give them a chance to dance. By keeping it in repertoire notwithstanding, the management harms the dancers, and it seems to bank on our gullibility—or, say, our natural leniency with native local color in ballet—to put over an inferior product. One sniffs the same smell of "sucker bait" that hangs about the Monte Carlo's equally inept but not so innocent *Red Poppy*. But I don't see there's a chance of its being closed for immorality even by Mr. Moss.

MARCH 4, 1945

BALANCHINE'S "MOZARTIANA"

Mozartiana, the new Balanchine ballet that the Monte Carlo presented last night at the Center, is in atmosphere light and subtle; it is as full of personal life as an ancient town on the Mediterranean on a holiday morning in the bright sun. In point of form, Balanchine recaptures the flavor of an old-style grand ballet like Petipa's *Don Quixote*, recaptures in novel terms its variety of playfulness, tenderness, and virtuosity, and he does it with only four principals and a chorus of eight girls. *Mozartiana* is another of his unassuming pocket masterpieces which restore to ballet its classic clarity and joyousness.

Mozartiana is a straight dance suite without a plot set to Tchaikovsky's Suite No. 4, an orchestral arrangement of Mozart piano pieces. Against an airy backdrop that suggests a crossroad at the edge of an Italian town, you see a young man in an eighteenth-century abbé's costume, dancing full of vivacity by himself. Enter a chorus of girls that are classic ballet's version of villagers, whom he joins in a little game.

They are followed by a girl who appears to be very sad and comes in carried by two veiled figures, a bit comic in their emphatic mysteriousness. She dances a touching Prayer. And after that comes a series of lively dances by the stars, by individuals from the chorus, by the first young man and the sad lady, now very gay in a tarantella costume. Then a poignant grand adagio by the stars, now crowned with gold leaves. And last comes a blithe little country-dance finale.

Full of novel sequences and novel bravura effects as all this is, it is striking how the variety of character in the principals becomes perfectly clear and how happily the chorus contrasts with them. Balanchine presents all the dancers at their best, and the Monte Carlo shines in *Mozartiana* once more. Danilova, both in her first pizzicato allegro and her second earnest and beautifully dramatic adagio, is a very great ballerina. But Franklin's joyous lightness, Lazowski's happy vivacity, and Miss Etheridge's serious grace and clear quickness are all wonderfully effective. And the little chorus is a chorus of soloists in achievement. *Mozartiana* was first produced by the Ballets 1933 in Paris; I thought I recognized some of the dances—they are all said to be the same—but the open, clear, and sunny tone of it now seems very different, very new.

MARCH 8, 1945

"COPPÉLIA": BALLET'S MASTERPIECE OF COMEDY

Fokine's *Prince Igor* dances, looking as pleasant as a newly weeded victory garden in August, reappeared nicely cleaned up in the Monte Carlo's repertory at the Center on Thursday. The event of that evening, and an event of local dance history, was the *Coppélia* performance which preceded *Igor*. It was all through in spirit and in style the finest presentation of an old-style classic that this reviewer has seen. Had it been shown in the flattering frame of the Metropolitan instead of the impossible one at the Center, it would have been not only the success it was, but the unique triumph it deserved to be.

If *Giselle* is ballet's *Hamlet*, *Coppélia* is its *Twelfth Night*—its masterpiece of comedy. Less effective dramaturgically than *Giselle*, it has more variety and vivacity. *Giselle* is grandiose and morbid. *Coppélia* is captivating and unneurotic. It treats of love and marriage, and beginning with adolescent joys and troubles, it suggests in its radiant last grand pas de deux an adult happiness. The range of its leading role is equal to *Giselle*'s, its incidental dances have far more fancy, and its score is far lovelier.

Last night's Monte Carlo performance was at nearly every point an extraordinary one. Alexandra Danilova, incomparably brilliant in coquetry, wit, warm feminine graces, and warm intelligence, was last night miraculous in classic clarity, in subtlety of rhythm, in darting and soaring elevation, in the biting edge of her toe steps and the wide, strong line of her wonderful extension. Her dancing of the "Ear of Wheat" and of the succeeding number with the village girls in the first act was both in its lightness and its nobility the most glorious dancing in the world; the elegance of her playfulness in this act and in the second were that of a peerless ballerina. The third act had here and there a trace of tiredness, but the grandeur and limpidity of the greatest ballet were there, and the last lift, for instance, to Franklin's shoulders, was entrancing.

But the unique merit of the Monte Carlo performance was the company's natural grace all through. Franklin, as the hero, shone happily with the incomparable vitality he has and in classic passages he was clean in style, manly, and imaginative. Quite extraordinary in their beauty of style were the eight girls who are the heroine's friends—the Misses Boris, Goddard, Chouteau, Lanese, Etheridge, Riekman, Svobodina, and Horvath, of whom I noticed the first four in particular. Never has such a chorus been seen here. But the rousing folk dances, the doll dances, the mimed passages, the divertissements all delighted by the sense of a happily inspired company. And on this occasion Miss Chouteau celebrated her sixteenth birthday by dancing alone a Prayer that was lovely in every way. MARCH 10, 1945

BALANCHINE'S "PAS DE DEUX"

Balanchine's new *Pas de Deux*, which Danilova and Franklin introduced last night at the Center, is a lovely incident in the grand manner but too brief a one. When you see these two stars dancing beautifully on the stage you want them to go on dancing; and though the piece isn't called a "grand" pas de deux, the audience nonetheless was hoping for solo variations and a coda to come when the curtain went down.

Not that the piece itself is fragmentary in feeling or in form. It is set to entr'acte music from Tchaikovsky's *Sleeping Beauty*, music composed to carry a mood of suspense through an interval required for a scenic transformation, but omitted in the original production at the suggestion of Alexander III, who thought it more amusing to speed up the machinists. Balanchine's duet too is a sort of transformation scene, an episode between conclusive actions. A prince appears with a lovely princess, he holds her gently, and as she flutters and turns and bends, he lets her free, and she returns to him, and they exit together. Their intimacy is that of young people in love and engaged, and their dance figures express the dewiness, the sense of trepidation in the girl and the generous strength of the man.

Technical feats are an integral part of the delicately nervous rhythm, of the romantic suspense that the music, too, has. And at every point the plastic clarity of the two figures in their many relations is as surprising as it is unemphatic. The style for the ballerina—the piece is hers—is not the bold but the gentle grand manner, the manner that requires delicate toe steps, lovely arms, a pliant back, and extensions that are not stressed. The marvelous Danilova, lovelier to look at than ever, is as perfect in this new field as if she had never danced in any other way. Franklin held and supported her perfectly, too, with his natural generosity of stage presence.

The bolder grand style they had both shown earlier that evening, in the completely different and equally beautiful second pas de deux they have in *Mozartiana*. MARCH 15, 1945

BALANCHINE: BALLET MAGICIAN

At the Center last night the Monte Carlo presented the first of two all-Balanchine programs, celebrating his twenty-fifth anniversary as a choreographer. (He was born in 1904.) At the conclusion of the second ballet of the evening the curtain rose again on the company, some of them in the costumes of *Danses Concertantes*, which they had just danced brilliantly, some of them already dressed for *Ballet Imperial*—a brilliant performance of which followed—the rest in street clothes, with Mr. Balanchine standing among them. Everyone applauded, the audience calling "Bravo!" Then Mr. Denham, the company director, made Mr. Balanchine an affectionate little speech and presented him with a package of Chesterfields and something to put them in. Enthusiastic applause, and a curtain call with Danilova and Franklin on either side.

The astonishing transmutation of the Monte Carlo this season is evidently the latest of Mr. Balanchine's amiable miracles. The five excellent new productions of his works added to its repertory this year have made the current season the most satisfying artistically in many years. But in the few months since the fall he has transformed the dancers as well. None of them has danced with such spontaneity, clarity, and modesty as now; and even Danilova, after twenty years of triumphs, has marvelously surpassed herself in these last weeks. The whole season has been properly a Balanchine festival.

And it is not only the delightful surprise of a single season that ballet lovers owe him. By showing us that the young Americans, who form most of the company, can dance straight classic ballet without self-consciousness—as naturally as people speak their native tongue—he has proved that ballet can become as native an art here as it did long ago in

Russia; and it can develop, as it did there, a native and spontaneous brilliance. Balanchine is indeed the founder of American ballet as an art, and ballet lovers in this country are happy to have an occasion to express their sincere admiration.

He has laid sound foundations for its development here by insisting on its integrity as an art, on its inheritance as a bicentennial tradition of expressive movement, and by working with Americans—in all our theater forms, for that matter—continuously for eleven years. He shows no nostalgia for Europe, either in his work or in his teaching. And his unique genius as ballet choreographer—he is the greatest and the most advanced of choreographers anywhere—has already made and will continue to make American ballet the envy and admiration of dance lovers all over the world. We hope they get a chance to see it soon and share with us one of our most civilized pleasures.

The second all-Balanchine evening, which the Monte Carlo presented last night at the Center, was once again a happy triumph of George Balanchine's magic. *Bourgeois Gentilhomme*, *Mozartiana*, the new *Pas de Deux*, and *Ballet Imperial* (all brilliantly danced), which composed the program, are in their striking variety of sentiment and form an indication of his inexhaustible classic invention; in their clarity and spontaneity, the dancing grace and wit, they prove his easy choreographic mastery. But the special secret of his magic is to make you forget the choreographer for the dancers you see before you, dancing in their lovely young freshness onstage.

Their freshness comes from the fact that they understand completely the classic dancing they are asked to do, understand it in dancers' terms. Classic dancing is what they chose as a vocation and carefully learned, what they are happy to do. For Balanchine they need not understand a dance by rationalizing psychologically, they need not put it over by emoting their role or glamorizing their personality. When they get the physical feel of a dance sequence, the bodily rhythm of the movement (and this is a profoundly personal and instinctively emotional recognition), they know they are right and that nothing will fail to carry. The audience will love them.

Nothing will fail to carry because Balanchine by accepting the classical system of body balance (foot positions) and the steps based on it has—for all his exciting invention—taken care of the flow of the dance phrase and the line of the deployed human figure. He has placed the gesture of the dancing figure in space so that you see it in positive relation to the visible stage center or the wings and to the figures of the other dancers.

And you see it too in happy relation to the music you hear, to its formal as well as its emotional stress or ease. So the dancer dances lightly, distinctly, rhythmically, and is constantly the natural focus of attention and the source of a happy excitement.

If clarity in excitement is one of the classic tenets, the other is human naturalness of expression. Balanchine, by asking his dancers to do what they best can, by allowing each to be independently interesting, by combining the figures easily and following the emotional overtones of the rhythm and line of a human body in action, leaves the dancer his naturalness, his freshness, his dignity. The secrets of emotion he reveals are like those of Mozart, tender, joyous, and true. He leaves the audience with a civilized happiness. His art is peaceful and exciting, as classic art has always been. MARCH 17 AND 23, 1945

THE MONTE CARLO NOW

The Monte Carlo in the season that closes tonight at the Center has shown us wonders: a buoyant and direct classic style, a string of Balanchine productions featured as they should be, and in Danilova an incomparable ballerina who is both the queen and the visible heart of the dancing company about her. No wonder that the spirit onstage has been high, with so much reason for a clear artistic conscience. The company's spirit has won out over obvious defects—the sad spots still in the repertory, the fewness of experienced dancers, the absence of Youskevitch, a wartime need of men, and the abominable visibility at the Center Theater. In respect to the theater, I find it scandalous that the Center administration has once more neglected to lower the fence of footlights that cuts off the dancers' feet for orchestra patrons as far back as row R, and absurd that the legs (side pieces) of the scenery are often hung in a way to make the small stage narrower than it need be. Just the same the dancing has been the happiest to watch in town for some years—unselfconscious in its manner, clear in its rhythm, fresh in its animation, light in its spring.

The new classicism which the Monte Carlo has accepted is the secret of its happy transformation. Classicism, in one sense, is a method of keeping clarity, continuity, and dignity in vigorous dance movement. Though it limits the dancers' movements, so complete a classic master as Balanchine finds within these limitations an inexhaustible variety of dance figures, of rhythm, and of human meaning. And the classic style as Balanchine understands it gives the dancer a means of personal expression without asking him to be an exhibitionist or to hypnotize the audience. There are no doubt other methods by which dancers can show their human dignity in their relation to an audience, but Balanchine's is a successful one. When they observe his classicism, dancers look clear and light, youthful and buoyant, and their personality that comes across is easy and fresh.

It has been astonishing to see how such thoroughly experienced dancers as the great Danilova, Franklin, Krassovska, and Lazowski have all revealed their best qualities under his influence. As for the younger soloists, they have seemed to be bursting into bloom like forsythia all over the stage. My favorite has been Mary Ellen Moylan, whose graceful intrepidity and air of candor make me think of those demure ballet heroines who a century ago leaped from the top of a twenty-foot scenic waterfall into the arms of a partner. With Moylan's arrowy exactitude, a special gift of hers is the young pliability of her straight back, and with it her instinctive grace in effacing or moving forward a shoulder or turning out an arm in its socket. Straightforward Maria Tallchief has not yet Moylan's grace of shoulder and she is now and then tempted to try for a solo effect when dancing with others, but her thrilling decisiveness and her brilliant legs are magnificent. Miss Boris, more experienced, has shown a scintillating clarity and a rich variety of dramatic temperament. All three do biting and beautiful toe steps. Imaginative Miss Etheridge, Miss Goddard, Miss Chouteau, Miss Razoumova, Miss Riekman have often been remarkable. Mr. Danielian, certainly the most brilliant American in leaps and beats, continues to gain admirably in classic rhythm and deportment. His weakness (like that of most young dancers) is a lack of expressive power in the connection between arms and torso. Far less brilliant than he, Magallanes has not this weakness and his handsome line as well as his miming is easy and natural. Bliss and Corvino are clearly gifted dancers, too, and Talin is remarkably so whenever he doesn't jut out his chin in an unfortunate way.

I rather think that the young dancers of the company have been dancing far better than they know how, and if in one sense that is the only way to dance, in another it means that to strengthen their gifts they need most to keep on dancing in the fortunate direction they have taken. I hope they will bring us as many new Balanchine productions next year as this. That would assure their style and their deportment in all the rest of the repertory (their manners are still rude in the first act of *Nutcracker*, in the ensembles of *Gaîté* and *Danube*, where good manners aren't solidly built into the choreography). And next year's repertory should by all means allow retiring *Frankie and Johnny*, *Schéhérazade*, *Igrouchki*, *Red Poppy*.

The Monte Carlo, as our first clearly classic dance company, has given us a happy season, it has regained its artistic prestige, it has won discerning friends, and it has awakened great hopes for the future. It can be proud of its wonderful achievement in the last five months.

MARCH 25, 1945

NIJINSKA'S "HARVEST TIME"

Harvest Time, presented by Ballet Theatre as a world premiere at the Metropolitan last night, is as foolish as the worst of the ballets Pavlova used to tour about in. Miss Toumanova, for whom it was constructed, is no Pavlova, however. Nor does Ballet Theatre look well when it is asked to super in vehicles for her. *Harvest Time* shows off Toumanova's record arabesque all right, but it is embarrassing as a world premiere by a great company.

Harvest Time—set by Mme Nijinska to a potpourri of Wieniawski pieces—is a series of showoff passages for a classic ballerina (with diamonds in her hair, of course) and for her partner. There are also evolutions and poses by six ballet girls (ballet peasants who carry a garland, of course) and by four peculiarly awkward men who crouch and stamp about in brown tights, indicating peasant "character." The piece might be explained as a pastoral scene—a Polish harvest—in the 1860 Petersburg style. But the trouble with *Harvest Time* is that it neither gets going as dancing nor offers a gracefully urban view of country sentiment. It is a perversity in corn that one wishes were at least intended as parody, though it isn't choreographically interesting enough even for that.

What can be said for it is that Nijinska at one point in a duet devised three or four poses in succession for Toumanova that are beautiful to see and that suit her peculiar personal style better than anything in the repertory. Their curiously static rhythm, their intensity of gymnastic prowess, their accent on powerful separation of the limbs rather than on a graceful deployment are strikingly effective. Three or four poses are very little really in a piece; but they serve to prove that what Toumanova needs is a choreographer to rescue her from her present too brutally acrobatic manner and restore to vivid expression her extraordinary capabilities.

APRIL 6, 1945

MASSINE'S "MOONLIGHT SONATA"

Poor Toumanova. Poor Ballet Theatre. With a kind of numb dismay, your reporter watched them submitting to a new choreographic indignity when Massine's *Moonlight Sonata* was shown Saturday night for the first time at the Metropolitan. Slick the performance was; but "Russian ballet" can hardly sink any lower than it does in offering us this clammy hallway chromo. And to have the great Massine and our fine Ballet Theatre responsible is ignominious for everyone.

Massine himself appeared as that stock chromo character "The Poet." Against a chromo backdrop representing a lake in the moonlight—it looked like an inexpensive Swiss lake in the off-season—he stuck out his chest, waved his arms importantly, and kept having to go somewhere offstage. Miss Toumanova was that other stock chromo character "The Young Girl." Unbecomingly dressed for her hip formation, she was still much the handsomest girl staying at the same deserted Swiss hotel as he. They seemed to realize stonily that there just wasn't anyone else to go around with—which is pretty much the expression of lovers on chromos.

Later, while Miss Toumanova was sitting in the moonlight alone upstage—and sitting very beautifully, really—two further characters came on, a Cupid and a Dark Lover. Cupid, in a ginger-ale-colored spotlight, turned out to be Miss Kavan, who hastily acted like the Cupid in Dolin's parody *Romantic Age*. The Dark Lover was less conventional. He turned out to be Mr. Petroff without a toupee, dressed in an old-fashioned black bathing suit several sizes too small so that he could get it up over one shoulder only. For propriety's sake, he also was wearing long black stockings. He looked as if he were employed at the local bathing establishment, though the program billed him as a figment of fancy. Fancy or no, he made persistent advances to Miss Toumanova and finally succeeded in lifting her so that she faced the audience in the air with—oddly enough—his backside on view just below her. Cupid came back and cleared up matters.

The orchestra all this while had been playing a fantastically brutal orchestration of Beethoven's so-called "Moonlight" Sonata, which, as everyone knows, has nothing to do with moonshine on Lake Lucerne or anywhere else. They had begun disemboweling it long before the curtain went up, clammy strings appropriating the left hand and loud brass the right. Beethoven expressed his views on orchestral transcription of his piano pieces the same year this sonata was published; you can imagine what they were. APRIL 9, 1945

MARKOVA AT BALLET THEATRE

There are only two real ballerinas in the country; the senior one is the great Alexandra Danilova and the junior one is the great Alicia Markova. Miss Markova, appearing last night with Ballet Theatre at the Metropolitan in two of her former ballets, *Romeo and Juliet* and *Pas de Quatre*, transformed this sadly disoriented company at a stroke into the splendid one it was during her marvelous final week with them last spring. She did it by showing them the quiet simplicity of a great style, by believing completely in the piece she was performing. They glowed, they danced, they were all wonderful.

Miss Markova's delicacy in lightness, in rapidity; the quickness in the thighs, the arrowy flexibility of the instep; her responsiveness in the torso, the poise of the arms, the sweetness of the wrists, the grace of neck and head—all this is extraordinary. But her dancing is based on a rarer virtue. It is the quiet which she moves in, an instinct for the melody of movement as it deploys and subsides in the silence of time, that is the most refined of rhythmic delights. The sense of serenity in animation she creates is as touching as that of a Mozart melody.

She is a completely objective artist. Who Markova is, nobody knows. What you see on the stage is the piece she performs, the character she acts. She shows you, as only the greatest of actresses do, a completely fascinating impersonation, completely fascinating because you recognize a heroine of the imagination who finds out all about vanity and love and authority and death. You watch her discover them.

Markova's Juliet is a miracle of acting. Every nuance of pantomime is poignantly clear and every moment is a different aspect of the cumulative tragedy. Her shy loveliness in the balcony scene, her moment watching Romeo die—but one would like to enumerate them all minute by minute. And the restraint of them all, the slow-motion continuum from which they each arise as dance gestures and which flows so steadily through the whole hour-long ballet are wonders to have seen.

The entire performance of *Romeo* was everywhere a glory. Laing, that beautifully poetic dancer, was an inspired Romeo. Mr. Orloff as Mercutio was distinguished indeed. And at the end, when Markova and Laing with the great Sir Thomas Beecham, who conducted the score with miraculous fluidity, and Tudor the choreographer (and Tybalt in the piece) took a joint bow, the enthusiastic audience applauded our quartet of British genius with the sincerest enthusiasm.

Later Miss Markova's Taglioni in *Pas de Quatre* was—as it used to be —a delight of sweet wit and stylistic brilliance. But I must add a word of sincere praise, too, for the semi-novelty of the evening, Argentinita with her enlarged company in *Café de Chinitas*. It is her best creation at the Metropolitan—in style, in sequence, in atmosphere—and it is fine to have it in the repertory. The Dali set and front curtain are grandiosely handsome, and the dancing (and Miss Miralles's fine singing) have true Spanish charm and distinction. APRIL 9, 1945

TUDOR'S "UNDERTOW"

Undertow, Tudor's new ballet which Ballet Theatre is giving at the Metropolitan, is well worth seeing. Though not so effective theatrically as *Pillar of Fire* or *Romeo*, it is a highly interesting, a very special piece, and a notable credit to the season. *Undertow* tells a story which appears to happen more in a young man's mind than in objective reality. The first scene presents quite realistically an image of his birth and his later interrupted breast-feeding. In the second, he stands, a shy and gentle adolescent in an imaginary city, and watches with increasing excitement the suggestive actions of passers-by. Other figures, innocent ones, which include a sort of innocent "brother" of his own self, try to divert his attention; and he, too, would like to ignore the horrid excitement he feels. He even persuades a girl, as excited as he, to join him in a kind of prayer meeting. But she breaks away, she invites his passion, and in an irresistible paroxysm of desire he strangles her. The next scene, set against a backdrop of clouds, shows him frenzied with terror and alone, while some of the previous characters, with a noncommittal air, stroll past. He realizes his guilt, he sees his innocence lost in the symbol of a balloon that escapes from a child's hand. And as he becomes conscious of the town once more, this very child, whom he had scarcely noticed before, points an accusing finger at him; the other characters, whether good or bad before, join her and point at him. An outcast, as if going to his execution, he walks slowly and resignedly off.

The theme of *Undertow* is that of an adolescent's neurosis, the terrifying dilemma which presents to him the act of manhood as equivalent to murder. The hero of the piece cannot find the normal solution of this, according to psychology, normal dilemma; the image of murder is so powerful in him it dominates and petrifies him, and in his impotence he kills. But despite Hugh Laing's completely sincere and sustained impersonation of the adolescent, the motivation does not convey itself to the audience, one doesn't identify oneself with him. The trouble is, I think, that the decisive initial scene, presenting a bloody birth, brilliantly shocking though it is, does not seem to be a part of the hero's inner life, it is not placed anywhere in particular. Later, at the climax, after the shockingly instantaneous murder (brilliantly duplicating the birth image), we see the hero trying to escape in vain an unseen force mightier than he; but we should have to see this antagonist of his moving in an active shape on the stage to know what the hero knows and feel as he feels. Because *Undertow* lacks such a physical release of opposing forces, it remains intellectual in its effect, like a case history, and does not quite become a drama of physical movement.

Indeed one keeps watching the movement all through for the intellectual meaning its pantomime conveys more than for its physical impetus as dancing. Its impetus is often tenuous. But its pantomime invention is frequently Tudor's most brilliant to date. The birth scene, an elderly man's advances to a prostitute, a hysterical wedding, drunken slum women, several provocative poses by the hero's victim, and quite particularly the suggested rape of a vicious little girl by four boys—these are all masterpieces of pantomime, and freer, more fluid, more plastic than Tudor's style has been. Brilliant too is his individualized use of the dancers and wonderful the way each one of them rises to the occasion. *Undertow* is worth seeing just for Miss Alonso's horrifying bit; and though not a successful drama, it suggests in many details that Tudor's style is more powerful at present than ever before. APRIL 15, 1945

THE TOUMANOVA PROBLEM

Ballet Theatre's current season closes next Sunday; judging by the improvement the company has shown this last week the final one may well be brilliant. Thanks to *Undertow* the company's spirits have recovered and so has attendance. During the first fortnight, however, Ballet Theatre looked generally demoralized. Poor its houses were, due to a general slump in theater business, but an experienced company is not bowled over by a week of poor houses. I shouldn't wonder if Ballet Theatre's jitters are serious and are due to an aggravated case of ballerina trouble. Ballet Theatre often seems like a tight little republic of soloists; though they once accepted Miss Markova as their queen ballerina, they have not accepted Miss Toumanova as her successor. And miscast as she has been—in absurd novelties, too—she has had the misfortune of not being fully accepted by the public either. Since she dominates the classic repertory, however, everybody is under an unhappy pressure, the general style of the company suffers, and the public is disappointed.

If this is so, it would seem that the solution would be to run Ballet Theatre without a queen ballerina until one emerges by public recognition of her merit. Miss Alonso, Miss Hightower, Miss Kaye have all been granted a joint first rank with Miss Toumanova and Miss Gollner by ensemble and public alike—in fact, despite the billing, this season has turned out to be more Miss Alonso's than Miss Toumanova's. It would be fine to see all five of them taking turns in starring.

Miss Toumanova is no doubt a more striking figure than the others. Her fascinating prowess is even more startling than in the fall; her aura of fanaticism, the impression she gives of devouring the stage suggest how thrilling she might be in a part suited to her. Even in the way she is now presented, as an athletic prodigy of incomparably powerful leg gestures, she supplies a special excitement welcome on special occasions. It is only in her current false position as the central dynamo of the company that she is lost.

For in classic ballet the queen ballerina of a company is its central dynamo; she sets the style, she exemplifies it at its most completely expressive. It is through watching her that the audience understands the style of a piece, and the style creates the poetic illusion in which the drama becomes real. She projects not only her own role, but the entire world of fancy in which that role becomes dramatic, in which everybody and everything onstage can play a part. Stage stars of all kinds project such imaginary worlds; Miss Holm and Miss Merman, for instance, do it in musical comedy, Miss Cornell and Miss Taylor in spoken drama. In ballet Miss Markova showed this quality pre-eminently two weeks ago in *Romeo.* Miss Kaye showed it last Monday in *Lilac Garden*, and Mr. Laing has it very strongly among male dancers. It is a quality that ballet language recognizes by saying that a real ballerina dances not a part but a ballet, not the Swan Queen but *Swan Lake.* I imagine that if Toumanova had shown this quality as steadily as Markova used to—as convincingly for the general ballet public—they would crowd to see her and give her similar ovations. And for myself, I notice she often gives me the impression of phenomenal sleepwalker moving isolated among dancers who are performing a different piece.

Her isolation comes, perhaps, from the special nature of her dance style, which has little in common with that of the other dancers, for all its apparent classicism. Her blocklike torso, limp arms, and predatory head position, her strangely static and magnificent leg control set her apart from the others. Her action looks not like what everyone does, done more subtly and naturally (which is a ballerina's function), but it looks like something radically different from her classic surroundings. It makes her seem less a classic heroine than an outcast.

And sometimes one wonders if Miss Toumanova doesn't play up her gift of chilly isolation onstage for an effect of exotic glamour, for a solemn impersonation of the foreign ballerina as Hollywood would type the part. It seems a foolish pose for her to take. Danilova, Krassovska, Riabouchinska, all as Russian as she, are all of them far too busy dancing to emphasize their Russianness among the Americans who surround them. But perhaps forcing her all at once into the position of top ballerina with Ballet Theatre—instead of letting them gradually become acclimated to one another—has been the real cause of a "Toumanova problem." Now, as I see it, the problem both threatens to disrupt the company and misemploys this great dancer's native genius.

APRIL 22, 1945

BALLET THEATRE'S SEASON

Though Ballet Theatre's season has proved disappointing on several counts, the individual performances of its soloists have frequently been very fine and a phenomenal performance among them has been Miss Alonso's as Ate in *Undertow*. In devising the part Tudor was at his most brilliantly horrid in the special angle of the head, the slightly lopsided ports de bras, the shoulder thrusts, the nasty accents of toes and knees, the fingering of the dress—all reminiscent, if you will, of the Youngest Sister in *Pillar*. Miss Alonso might have done all this as a series of striking gestures and given the impression of an acid caricature. Instead, by subordinating the separate detail to a continuous fluidity of movement, she gives you the sense of a real girl's instinctive rhythm of motion, she creates a real and living character. The coherence of her phrasing is as perfect as Markova's, and Alonso's classic precision and lightness give the part an air of distinction which makes it all the more frightening dramatically. Miss Alonso's gift for distinction is as evident for that matter in *Lilac Garden*, *Pillar of Fire*, *Peter and the Wolf*, *Sylphides*, or *Waltz Academy* (a moment of which is even a laughing little hint of her role in *Undertow*). Watching her, one wonders if a pointer or two from the older great Russian ballerinas on the large impetus of movement the famous classic sequences have in their finest phrasing would not be all Alonso now needs to triumph in them, too.

Rosella Hightower has shown, this season especially, a largeness of line Alonso still sometimes lacks, and Hightower's long-limbed Diana-of-the-chase figure is a handsome one to deploy. She still missed the edge that rapid translations give to slow extensions in classic phrases; her ankles do not respond sharply enough in these moments of an adagio. And in her readiness to meet the audience, she neglects, I think, the fairy-tale mystery which belongs to a classic role. But her sense of freedom, the beauty of her yielding movements, her cordiality, humor, and courage make her Ballet Theatre's best-loved dancer. Miss Kaye (if I may extend the term soloist for the moment), though finer than ever in *Pillar* and *Lilac Garden*, in other dramatic parts sometimes begins a gesture too hard and too fast, so that the rest of the movement has no carrying power, and because the moment of repose at the end of the phrase is blurred, she sometimes gets a rather busy look in action. She still lacks full confidence in her femininity. But her strength, her boldness, her accurate classicism, her growing sense of a large rhythm and of the stylistic unity of a piece have been increasingly remarkable. Miss Gollner has won a triumph in *Undertow* in the first part really suited to her natural looks and temperament, and in *Swan Lake* she performed a few calm développés in a lift that looked like real développés—nobody else at all seems able to do them just now. Miss Reed has been as successful a soubrette as ever.

In smaller parts Miss Adams, Miss Sabo, Miss Eckl, Miss Fallis, Miss Banks have struck me particularly this season for their clean style and graceful personality, and Miss Tallchief, as a comic mime. The little trio of bathers in *Aleko*—Hightower, Alonso, and Adams—is a moment when one sees clearly how fine an ensemble Ballet Theatre disposes of; or, for instance, the little trio in *Waltz Academy*—Miss Adams, Miss Eckl, and Mr. Kriza. Kriza has now a straight, free sweep and clarity of movement, a fine posture, and a friendly modesty of manner that are all first-rate; a little attention to ankles and feet is all he seems to need. In last Wednesday's *Fancy Free* he danced his solo with a sudden instinct for continuity in phrasing that showed very sharply his rich real gifts as a dancer, and Robbins, who followed him, quite as instinctively took his cue from Kriza, and phrased his own solo handsomely, too. This season Orloff's unfailing elegance has seemed to me very striking, as well as F. Alonso's clean style and charm. Kidd, though highly talented, has suffered, I think, from hasty timing. Young Lang is rumored to be leaving. He will be badly missed in all his parts, exceptionally fine dancer as he is.

Hugh Laing is, of course, among the men the special star of the company, and, in his style, in a class by himself. His exactness of gesture, his fine intellectual fervor, and his almost Sinatra-like suggestion have been as compelling as ever, and his balance has improved. Also in a class by himself, Eglevsky showed what great classic male dancing is like. He surpassed himself this spring in simplicity and power of style, and in his later appearances he has had a grandeur of rhythm that has made them great dance moments of the season.

Looking back on the two recent ballet seasons, I find that the Monte Carlo at the Center left an exhilarating impression despite its faults and Ballet Theatre at the Metropolitan, despite its merits, left a depressing one. Wondering why so strong an array of dancers and a number of fine performances should leave a ballet lover depressed, it struck me that Ballet Theatre's season had seemed like a number of disconnected efforts that had no guiding conviction to give them coherence and collective power. The performances of individual dancers had often been very fine, but too often they had had no dance contact with the rest of the ensemble onstage. Everybody did his job, but each worked for himself. Too often I missed the collective inspiration in dancing, the mutual dance response, that had been so exhilarating at the Monte Carlo. Ballet Theatre was slick, but not inspired. And most of its fine moments reminded me of the fine moments of a good jazz soloist playing with a high-class commercial band; slick the band is and it has a showy punch, but it can't pick up the animation of his rhythm.

The expressive virtue of any dancing is its rhythm, and its rhythm is felt only in continuity. Lightness and heaviness, the start and stop of a gesture or step, the thrust and return of a limb form the alternating rhythm of dancing, its stress and nonstress. But the two elements must not be so different in interest that they cannot combine into a continuity; and so to be able to combine them a dancer learns light-footedness, elasticity, and grace.

Classic dancing is our most expressive development of dance rhythm. It builds long continuities (or phrases) of movement that offer the audience variations of bodily impetus clearly set in relation to a fixed space. And these long phrases of movement convey the specific meaning of the ballet—its drama. As the impetus of successive phrases of music suggest to the hearer a particular quality of emotion and thought, so the successive phrases of a ballet suggest to the observer a particular quality of human action. When you watch a girl moving about a room you sometimes guess what the quality of movement "means." It is not that she expresses herself by making handies, she does it by the rhythm of her actions. We often understand animals that way and they us. And in love we all know how dramatic such a moment of understanding is. It seems to tell more than any words and say it more irrevocably. And this is the natural phenomenon on which the art of ballet is built as a convincing human expression.

I think it was this power of expression through rhythm that I missed at Ballet Theatre so often this spring, for, as a company, their dancing was convincing only now and then. It seemed somehow too heavy-footed, overstressed, discontinuous. I think it did because they defined the stress of the gesture emphatically but took no interest in the unstressed part. Perhaps they were thinking in dancing terms of key effects rather than in terms of a continuous melody. But they missed giving the exhilarating sense of dance rhythm that only the projection of a complete movement—stress and nonstress—can begin to create.

One can see that while it is possible for a dancer to smash the stress of a gesture at the public, he cannot do the same with the gesture's weaker phase. A complete movement (both parts of it as a rhythmic unit) gets its carrying power by a different attack—by being projected in relation to the stage space and the other dancers. This method has an air of modesty that doesn't catch the public as quickly, but it has the advantage of drawing the audience steadily into the illusion of situation and character which can exist only back of the proscenium. That is why the dramatic illusion and the dance illusion of ballet are broken by the punch of the hyperactive showman and are secured by the gentle-mannered and luminously calm ballerina.

If Ballet Theatre's fine company would aim for the continuity of movement of classic dancing and for the rhythmic power such dancing has, it wouldn't need to worry whether the ballet craze is over yet in America or not.

MAY 13 AND 29, 1945

VALERIE BETTIS

Valerie Bettis, who at the Adelphi last night presented a dance concert of solo and group compositions, is a modern-dance virtuoso with a devouring temperament and a hectic stage glamour. Unfortunately her chief subject matter (as choreographer) appears to be the very private discomfort of a hyperthyroid semivirgin—she tosses, quivers, whirls, kicks, darts, leaps, and falls all to no purpose, in almost every piece. The most distinct relief she found last night was a number in which she did some goofy clowning. And this reviewer suspects that her gifts would bring her general theater acclaim if instead of a serious recitalist she became a dance clown—like Mr. Victor—or else an actress starred in hysterically frustrated parts.

For as it is she seems to declaim one character's subjective troubles, but she does not present a character either in an objective conflict with another or in an objective variety of human emotions. And so her dance virtuosity instead of becoming dramatically thrilling remains merely a startling gift. Startling is her speed, her foot drumming, her shoulder thrusts, her twists, her sudden rests—only the hands seem clumsy, by contrast. Though not strictly musical, the rhythmic pulse of her phrasing is highly remarkable, as well as her gift for rhetorical emphasis. Her theater genius is unquestionable and her dance discipline is intelligent.

But though her gestures are most convincing in their pantomime aspect, and though the dances seem meant to tell a story, what that story is remains obscure. There was a number in which the group went through a routine of running, twisting, and snapping their fingers while an offstage voice read news items of the last five years; at the mention of Pearl Harbor the lights turned blue. But though Miss Bettis permitted herself a smile at her final exit, the point of the piece escaped me. Another group piece presented her in four "jokes" with pointless group dances before and after. A third group number seemed to show her distressed and fascinated by a man humiliated in public more than by another man who wasn't. Two solo numbers had offstage words but no visible dramatic progression. All in all I can only report her personal virtuosity as an event of interest.

The costuming was generally clumsy, but the assisting group performed admirably, especially Mr. Sweeney in *Dramatic Incident.* The music, apart from John Cage's *And the Earth Shall Bear Again* (which was also the best dance on the program), was undistinguished. The audience applauded a good deal. MAY 14, 1945

"APPALACHIAN SPRING"

Appalachian Spring is—as usual with Miss Graham's works—different from previous ones in style and like them in the convincing integrity of its differentness. It presents a pioneer celebration in spring around a newly built farmhouse in the Pennsylvania hills in the early part of the last century, when the country was still thinly settled. Miss Graham is the young Bride whose house it is to be; Erick Hawkins, the young farmer-husband. The ceremony presents the emotions, joyful and apprehensive, their new domestic partnership invites. An older pioneer neighbor (May O'Donnell) suggests now and then the rocky confidence of experience. And a Revivalist (Merce Cunningham) with a band of four ecstatic girl Followers reminds the new householders at this sacred moment of the strange and terrible aspects of human fate. At the end the couple are left quiet and strong in their new house.

All the characters are by turns playful and earnest and Miss Graham, who has suggested in the course of the piece the community aspects of girl-child, of wife and mother and neighbor, has near the end a wonderful passage as the individual human being each person in a community remains.

The dance style of the piece is abrupt and angular and it suggests in this way the rude pioneer artifacts of the place and time it describes. It suggests farmer vigor and clumsy farmer mirth. Dance episodes are joined to realistic passages which set the frame. But the more striking novelty in Miss Graham's choreographic style in *Appalachian Spring* is that each character dominates the stage equally, each is an individual dramatic antagonist to the others. So the piece is no passionate monodrama of subjective experience but an objective conflict united in its theme.

Appalachian Spring has a mysterious coolness and freshness, and it is no glorification by condescending city folk of our rude and simple past; it is, despite occasional awkwardness, a credible and astonishing evocation of that real time and place. To show us our country ancestors and our inherited mores as real is a feat of genius no one else who has touched the pioneer subject in ballet has been able to accomplish.

The company, and quite particularly Mr. Cunningham in a thrilling passage, were excellent. The stage design by Noguchi struck me as too sophisticated, but it served. Mr. Copland's score is a marvel of lyricism, of freshness and strength; and with thirteen instruments he seemed to have a full orchestra playing. The musicians under Louis Horst played admirably.

The opening number on the program was Miss Graham's solo *Salem Shore*, first presented last year and danced by her last night with a lovely youthfulness. Its picture of the waiting captain's wife, with its strange aqueous motions and seashore play, was once more a triumph of unforced impersonation. There is no American actress more sincere than Miss Graham, no dancer more strikingly, strangely inventive.

MAY 15, 1945

GRAHAM'S "HERODIADE"

Herodiade, a tragic dance scene for two characters which Martha Graham presented for the first time in New York last night, was first seen like her new *Appalachian Spring* at the Coolidge Festival last fall in Washington, for which both works—their score and choreography—had been commissioned. And here at the National, like *Appalachian Spring* on Monday night, yesterday's *Herodiade* was another complete audience success. But apart from that, the two pieces resemble each other not at all.

The scene of *Herodiade* as the program states is "an antechamber where a woman waits with her attendant. She does not know what she may be required to do or endure. Fragments of dreams rising to the surface of a mirror add to the woman's agony of consciousness. With self-knowledge comes acceptance; as she advances to meet the unknown, the curtain falls."

This is an accurate outline. *Herodiade* is an immolation scene and might take place in the antechamber to the Cretan labyrinth. It has the tone of a mythological rite and a classic sense of the grandeur of destiny. Miss Graham's motions are passionately and nobly contained, and marvelously natural as she makes them. A few large static gestures of tragic splendor and a few small desperate outbursts in complex hammered rhythms are enough to express the richness and dignity of the protagonist's fate. Her slow entrance; a later passage in "archaic" profile; a few crouching insane and blinded steps in which she approaches and touches the attendant; a twisting walk from the back with her feet parallel to the footlights; another with one hip thrust wildly sideways and held so; two grand poses heroically reminiscent of Isadora at the Parthenon: that is what gives to *Herodiade* its sustained wonder, its amazing human power and sense of human knowledge.

The second role, that of the Attendant, is far less interesting. It has a kind of coarseness that contrasts with the leading character's exquisite elegance. And the moment when Miss Graham, who is the victim of the action, turns to console the attendant is like a hint from the *Phaedo*. But one wishes this other woman had more character, either as a rude jailer or even as a comic foil. But this dramatic weakness in the piece is counterbalanced by the brilliant inventiveness of the chief role and the superbly restrained performance of Miss Graham in it.

The score of *Herodiade*, by Paul Hindemith, is a beautiful work, full, flowing, and somber, and the orchestra played it very well indeed. The title *Herodiade*, incidentally, is the title of the score—Mr. Hindemith chose Mallarmé's celebrated poem of that name for his subject. Though the ballet has very little relation to that poem, Miss Graham, who first had called her work *Mirror Before Me*, now uses Hindemith's title.

Miss Graham's second costume, an underdress, was beautiful too. The decor by Noguchi, however—in a sort of Bonwit Teller surrealism—added nothing. It looked to me like a doctor's office in a Hollywood fantasy.

MAY 16, 1945

GRAHAM'S "JOHN BROWN"

John Brown, the premiere on the program of Martha Graham and her company at the National last night, is a gesture-demonstration that enters a plea for the defense of the abolitionist hero—a plea part danced, part spoken. The first words suggest an identification of John Brown and Christ and the piece that follows hardly makes him a more earthly character. *John Brown* is a fine Sunday-school lesson, but it will hardly soften the hearts of unbelievers.

The text, mostly Brown's own words, with some questions put to him and answers he made after he was taken at Harper's Ferry, brings fragments of the noble Biblical forensics of the period. It is well spoken by Mr. Hawkins and by Mr. Will Hare, a nondancing interlocutor, who sometimes corroborates, sometimes mildly opposes. The movement is in gesture sequences—in biographical order—which Mr. Hawkins executes with superb exactitude, as a series of large assertions. They have a sharp outline and a sense of weight reminiscent of "primitive" American painting; they lack variety of flow or rhythmic lift.

Evidently Mr. Hawkins intended the effect to be a series of large assertions, and intended to present the figure as a hieratic martyr. Fine was the moment he rises from his litter to accuse his accuser; the hanging, too, was interesting in gesture, but it appeared to take place several times. The symbolic resuscitation was weaker. Though I was unconvinced by the piece, a friend of mine, who was thrilled, assured me it was a fine example of Japanese Noh drama.

The score was by Charles Mills. The decorative props by Noguchi were arranged with his knowing effects of perspective and included some charming little trees.

MAY 17, 1945

CUNNINGHAM'S "MYSTERIOUS ADVENTURE"

Thursday night's program of Martha Graham and her company at the National opened with *Mysterious Adventure*, a long solo composed and danced by Merce Cunningham with a score on prepared piano by John Cage and costume and stage prop by the sculptor David Hare. Cunningham, striking in each of his parts in Miss Graham's repertory, is a dancer of unique gifts, and *Mysterious Adventure* is a highly original number. It was, however, less effective last night than it had been when he first showed it at Hunter College.

Mysterious Adventure presents him as a sort of playful animal creature of fancy, with long quivering feelers on his black cap and colored quivering clusters attached to his black tights. This creature hops, walks, and bounds with a constant feathery elasticity. It sees an odd object, investigates, retires, returns to it, and then goes lightly hopping on its way. It would be a foolish number but for the fact that it has the curious rhythm—placidly agitated—of a robin visiting a strange bird bath and the unhurried sense of time which such a creature lives by. There is no mimicry of animal motion in the number, but there is dance illusion of a nonhuman world. It is a difficult and delicate effect to try but an original and a serious one.

The secret of the effect, however, lies in the unexpected but complete stillness that now and then for a moment the figure has. This was far more visible with the simpler (less quivering) costume and the simpler, heavier object Hare had made for Cunningham originally.

The Cage score is a very beautiful one in its delicate strength.

MAY 19, 1945

"APPALACHIAN SPRING" AND "HERODIADE" A SECOND TIME

On seeing Martha Graham's new *Appalachian Spring* a second time a quality which touched me particularly was the fresh feeling of hillside woods and fields the piece conveys. It does it partly in the way the still figures look off as if at a horizon of hills. The horizon is not the treetop garden horizon of *Letter to the World* nor the expanse of summer sky and sea of *Salem Shore*, but it is the real open air that is suggested in all three. *Herodiade* and *Deaths and Entrances*, on the other hand, happen in a room of some kind, and in these pieces, when Miss Graham suggests in her gesture a great space about her it is, so to speak, the intellectual horizon of the character she depicts. The precision of such differences in suggestion is one of the fascinations of watching her repertory.

Appalachian Spring describes the landscape not only in terms of its contour, but also in terms of living conditions. The separateness of the still figures, one from another, which their poses emphasize, suggests that people who live in these hills are accustomed to spending much of their time alone. Their outlines don't blend like those of townsmen. "In solitude shall I find entertainment" ("*Einsam und allein soll mein Vergnügen sein*") is painted on an early Pennsylvania Dutch bride chest, and the Bride in *Appalachian Spring* might well have read it. It is touching how gently the piece persuades you of the value of domestic and neighborly ties by giving you a sense of rural isolation.

The Appalachian isolation of the pioneer farmhouse in the piece is suggested even more imaginatively by a note of wildlife that keeps cropping up in the dances. A passage of Miss Graham's first solo looked to me as if she were a hillside girl darting after the little beasts her playing flushed from cover. And the Revivalist's four ecstatic girl Followers suggested in their fluttering and breathless darting the motions of chipmunks and birds on the ground, as if they were four small wild animals that were not frightened away by people; the Revivalist, too—part St. Francis, part Thoreau—seemed to treat them like tame wildlife rather than like girls. And the way his part merged evangelism with animism served in the ballet to join domestic ties to nature magic.

After seeing *Herodiade*, Miss Graham's other new piece, a second time I think Virgil Thomson's account of it in his article in today's music section more accurate than mine of last Wednesday. The secret of the piece lies much more in the complex and completely individualized elegance of the heroine than it does in the classic allusions of her gesture. Her elegance of motion is her private integrity. We watch it in conflict with her instincts, we watch her transform their force and gain in grandeur; and to watch so desperate a conflict being fought in middle age makes the drama the more poignant, the more heroic. But what makes it real in the first place is the real situation—a lady getting dressed by her maid. It is a pity the maid isn't some sort of real woman too; even her obscene gestures toward the floor look merely wooden.

MAY 20, 1945

"CONCERTO BAROCCO": BACH IN BATHING SUITS

Despite the weather last night, the Ballet Russe de Monte Carlo, opening its current season at the City Center, was welcomed with enthusiasm. In *Danses Concertantes*, the first ballet, there was applause at every entrance, with a culminating ovation when the great Danilova appeared. But the focal point of the evening was Balanchine's *Concerto Barocco*, the new production, which followed. Though presented without any grace of scenery or costumes, this extraordinary work triumphed by the limpid serenity of its choreography and its score. It was last night also a personal triumph for Marie-Jeanne, who had the major one of the solo parts.

Concerto Barocco is a dance ballet in classic steps set to the three movements of Bach's Concerto for Two Violins. It has no story. A group of eight girls dances first with two girl soloists, then with one of the soloists and a man who supports her, and finally with the two leading girls again. The excitement is that of a constant impetus of dance invention and figuration, now rapid and brilliant, now sustained, outspread, and slow. The emotion is now one of gradually gathered and released weight, now one of a free and even outpouring of energy. Its emotional changes are like those of the music, all contained in a wonderfully serene, limpid, and spontaneous flow. And indeed the musicality of *Concerto Barocco*, in phrasing rhythm and stress, is completely miraculous.

Particularly beautiful is the second movement with its climax of repeated lifts, in which Marie-Jeanne's extensions were grandly taut and Mr. Magallanes' lifting was extraordinarily expressive. But *Concerto Barocco* has innumerable beautiful details: the lively syncopation of the girls on toe, the sharp accents in the knee movements, the quick bows, the large, rapid changes of arm position. Patricia Wilde, the other soloist, and the chorus were accurate last night, though they seemed nervous. And the harshness of their little black bathing suits gave them all an unprepossessing, rather gym-teacherish air. It is certainly a great mistake to leave this ballet without decoration. SEPTEMBER 10, 1945

"DANILOVA AND RHYTHM"

Alexandra Danilova, dancing in Balanchine's *Mozartiana* on the Monte Carlo's program Monday night at the City Center, showed us once again how touchingly personal the grandeur of a true ballerina is, and how a ballerina's noble clarity of execution, her mastery over the many resources of dance rhythm, can make her formal steps and phrases seem poignantly unique and spontaneous, like a happy event in real life.

In all the severity of exact classicism Danilova's dancing rhythm fills the time quantities of the music to the full; it does not, like the rhythm of lesser dancers, jab at a stress and then drag for a moment till the music catches up. Stress and release in all their variety are all equally vivid, equally expressive to watch. And in watching her, you feel, in the sustained flow of Danilova's rhythm, the alert vivacity of her personal dance imagination, the bite and grace of her feminine temperament, and a human sincerity that makes an artist both unpretentious and great.

The performance of *Mozartiana* was in every way charming. Franklin, Danilova's partner, danced with his happy flow of dance vitality and his wonderful generosity as a partner. Miss Etheridge was very fine indeed in both her numbers—the beautiful Prayer and the gypsy dance. Mr. Zompakos and the virtuoso chorus of eight girls (Maria Tallchief particularly) were light, exact, and full of verve. The piece was, as usual, a complete success. SEPTEMBER 11, 1945

"CONCERTO BAROCCO"

Concerto Barocco, the Balanchine novelty of the current Monte Carlo season at the Center, is an unpretentious and good-tempered little ballet and it is also the masterpiece of a master choreographer. It has only eleven dancers; it is merely straight dancing to music—no sex story, no period angle, no violence. It does not seem to be trying to win your interest, but before you know it, it has absorbed your attention and doesn't let it go. It has power of rhythm and flow; in a wealth of figuration it is everywhere transparent, fresh, graceful, and noble; and its adagio section is peculiarly beautiful.

Concerto Barocco was recognized as a masterpiece at once when it was shown here in dress rehearsal four years ago by Lincoln Kirstein's American Ballet. It had just been created then for the Rockefeller-sponsored South American tour of that company. And though this ballet tour has recently been spoken of as one of Mr. Rockefeller's inter-American mistakes, as a ballet critic I can say that in showing *Concerto Barocco*, he was showing our neighbors choreography of the best quality in the world—showing a United States product that no country of Western Europe could have equaled. A mistake such as that does anyone honor.

It is a pleasure to report that the Monte Carlo production of *Barocco* is excellent both in the dancing onstage and in the playing in the orchestra pit. Unfortunately, though, the piece has in the present production been given a backdrop of meager, dirty blue and a set of harsh black bathing suits for the charming girls. Meagerness and harshness are not in its spirit; some of the wonderful clarity in its spacing is dimmed and in so poverty-struck a frame the rich title of the ballet strikes one as absurd.

But *Concerto Barocco* comes by its fancy title quite honestly. The name might lead you to expect an evocation of baroque dancing or baroque mannerisms; still, what the title actually promises is a baroque concerto, and that is just what you get. Balanchine has set his ballet so happily to Bach's Concerto for Two Violins that the score may be called his subject matter. The style of the dance is pure classic ballet of today, and the steps themselves follow the notes now strictly, now freely. But in its vigorous dance rhythm, its long-linked phrases, its consistent drive and sovereign articulation, *Concerto Barocco* corresponds brilliantly to this masterpiece of baroque music.

The correspondence of eye and ear is at its most surprising in the poignant adagio movement. At the climax, for instance, against a background of chorus that suggests the look of trees in the wind before a storm breaks, the ballerina, with limbs powerfully outspread, is lifted by her male partner, lifted repeatedly in narrowing arcs higher and higher. Then at the culminating phrase, from her greatest height he very slowly lowers her. You watch her body slowly descend, her foot and leg pointing stiffly downward, till her toe reaches the floor and she rests her full weight at last on this single sharp point and pauses. It is the effect at that moment of a deliberate and powerful plunge into a wound, and the emotion of it answers strangely to the musical stress. And (as another example) the final adagio figure before the coda, the ballerina being slid upstage in two or three swoops that dip down and rise a moment into an extension in second—like a receding cry—creates another image that corresponds vividly to the weight of the musical passage. But these "emotional" figures are strictly formal as dance inventions. They require no miming in execution to make them expressive, just as the violin parts call for no special schmaltz. And this modesty of stage presence combined with effects so strong and assured gives one a sense of lyric grandeur.

The adagio section is the only movement with a lyric expression. The introductory Vivace is rather like a dance of triumph, strong, quick, and square; while the concluding Allegro is livelier and friendlier, with touches of syncopated fun and sportive jigging. Both these sections have sharply cut rhythms, a powerful onward drive, and a diamondlike sparkle in their evolutions. There are, for instance, many lightning shifts in the arm positions and yet the pulse of the dance is so sure its complexity never looks elaborate. The eight girls who execute the little chorus and the two girl soloists are precise and quick and their grace is wonderfully natural. They are all so earnestly busy dancing, they seem more than ever charmingly young, and their youth gives an innocent animal sweetness to their handsome deportment.

SEPTEMBER 16, 1945

BOLENDER'S "COMEDIA BALLETICA"

Comedia Balletica, the new ballet the Monte Carlo presented last night at the City Center, was applauded by the audience with enthusiasm. But though it was danced with frequent brilliance, and though a promising work, I thought the piece as a whole an unsatisfactory ballet. It marks, however, the big-time debut of a young local choreographer, Todd Bolender, in whose gifts many young dancers have great confidence.

The title is a fancy one for a work that is so unpretentious in manner. *Comedia Balletica* is a dance ballet for five dancers, set to Stravinsky's *Pulcinella* Suite. Against a somber little cutout in false perspective, representing, one guesses, some sort of ballroom that is being used for rehearsal, the dancers—Miss Boris, Miss Marie-Jeanne, Miss Tompkins, Mr. Danielian, and Mr. Bolender himself—appear in conventional ballet costume. They present themselves to the audience, sit down on stools, take turns in solos, duets, and ensembles, changing seats at each conclusion. It is a sort of party, a party of professionals; each does his or her turn as an entertainer.

The style is straight ballet with an ironic sharpness and quickness in timing suited to the acerbity of the orchestra. The fun as you see it, though, is rather like that of a little clique of professionals indulging in acid gossip. There is no ill humor in it, it is clean and lively, but it is not as intelligible and charming to an outsider as to the performers and the jokes seem all pretty much alike.

Brilliant in this tight intramural manner are, for instance, the quick quivers of Marie-Jeanne's solo, or the Spanish spurt of Miss Boris in the minuet, and both were brilliantly executed. As well danced were Danielian's sharp-footed solo and Bolender's more easy-footed one. And Miss Tompkins had an adagio intentionally clipped in rhythm. But this variety in tightness is not boldly enough differentiated to make one enjoy the various flavors. And the sharpness needs the contrast of longer, more flowing phrases to make it carry. The connecting passages are wooden instead of being relaxed. Mr. Bolender is highly inventive in many details, but it strikes me he has missed the Neapolitan amiability, the naturalness of Pergolesi's flow which Stravinsky's score embroiders in such violent and witty color. The music is a pretty fancy joke, but it is a larger joke than the ballet. SEPTEMBER 18, 1945

TO ARGENTINITA

The death of Argentinita brings to many Americans who loved to see her dance a grief like that of a personal loss. Only the greatest dancers can awaken so personal a response by as restrained an art as hers was. Her spell as a star was that of a special Latin bearing, discreetly sensible and delightfully polite; she seemed a lady vivaciously entertaining her guests, and one could imagine that her expertness as host was only the reflection of the pleasure she felt in seeing her friends. Her dances had the effect of captivating anecdotes about Spanish style easy for us North Americans to appreciate and enjoy. By her amiable gaiety of spirit, her wit, her tact in sentiment, her perfect grace and perfect courtesy, she established a sure contact, so that in her case the classic reserve of Spanish dance forms seemed even to sentimentalists like ourselves neither remote nor haughty. Argentinita was in this sense a triumphant popularizer of the Spanish style among us; and through her easy and charming approach she opened the eyes of thousands of Americans to the nature of the Spanish tradition she worked in, to its vitality of rhythm, its subtlety of expression, and its high sense of personal dignity.

Argentinita's knowledge of the Spanish dance tradition was prodigious. An accurate scholar, she knew it in all its historical, regional, and racial diversity, folk forms and theater forms, the special techniques as well as the special deportments. She knew it from living with gypsies, from traveling in the mountains, from talking to poets. But she did not try to reproduce this material literally. Like the circle of poet-scholars and musicians she belonged to in Madrid, from Benavente and Martínez Sierra to Falla and, greatest of them all, García Lorca, her aim was to keep the full savor and amplitude of local traditions in freely invented and consciously shaped personal works of art. Argentinita's personal nature as a dancer was, by witty edge and lyric grace, essentially Andalusian, and she was too honest an artist to falsify it. And so if her Peruvian Indian dance, for instance, or her music-hall studies or even her flamenco became her own graceful versions of these dance forms, they were nonetheless each completely different from the others, each composed in its own specific dance idiom and danced with its characteristic rhythmic impulse and its own dance attitude. And you would scarcely have imagined, watching her in recital, on how strict a discipline in characterization her charming little numbers had been built.

Argentinita's dances as you saw them had a charmingly ladylike air, with no athletics and no heroics. Sometimes the steps and patterns seemed naively plain and the best ones were never very elaborate, but her group numbers were always completely transparent and their comedy points rarely failed to register. Argentinita chose a small range of force as a choreographer, but she was a master in economy of detail, in proportion of emphasis, in sustaining interest and flow. Her gift for continuity and coherence (of impulse and of silhouette) made of slight variations distinct contrasts. Her own manner of dancing was suited to such delicate devices, for it was completely graceful, completely defined, and her rhythm was infallible. Her special glory as a dancer were her little slippered feet, in their tiny, airy dartings and in their pretty positions on the floor. Argentinita's dancing naturally included more spectacular elements, but it was in the clarity of small details that one appreciated best the classic craft of her dance technique.

A classic cameo artist she was in technique, in choreography, in characterization. But she was a born star in the quick grace of her movement and a born star in the vivacity of her theater personality. Though she knew for years she needed rest and care, she could not bear to stop dancing. And though her tours overtaxed her, though she was handicapped by halls too vast for her special quality, and sometimes perhaps by the illness she heroically ignored, her hold on the public increased with each appearance. Last spring she seemed more scintillating and more amusing than ever, and her last production, *Café de Chinitas* at the Metropolitan, was her happiest work in a larger form. From the peak of her success she has now slipped away into silence.

At Argentinita's funeral were many who had known her only across the footlights but who loved her. And many more, all over this country, will keep their memories of how delightfully she danced, surrounded by her charming company, by her high-spirited and witty sister, Pilar Lopez, and by Greco and Vargas, the young men she had trained so brilliantly.

SEPTEMBER 30, 1945

"UNDERTOW" REVISITED

Undertow, Tudor's case history of a juvenile sex killer, which saved Ballet Theatre's spring season last year, loses a good deal of its first confusing fascination on reseeing. One becomes too sharply aware of its lack of sustained rhythmic drive, of the sentimental foolishness of its long-drawn-out last scene, of the all-too-frequent little twitchings, peckings, and mincings in the stylized pantomime gestures that are meant to serve as dance effects. The score covers some of these mistakes by its massive presence; and at one point, where the backdrop rolls up, the set creates a theater moment. But the piece looks mostly like an excuse for several boldly lurid fragments—the birth, the slaps of the prostitute, the wedding couple, the rape of the horrid girl-child, and the murder. Though they don't, in default of a dramatic or choreographic counterweight, add up to a piece, they are in themselves worth seeing.

OCTOBER 9, 1945

MICHAEL KIDD'S "ON STAGE"

On Stage, the new ballet which Ballet Theatre presented last night at the Metropolitan, put its audience in a good humor partly by the adolescent liveliness of its execution, partly by the clearness with which it played up a good old-fashioned trooper's fairytale. *On Stage* is Michael Kidd's first big-time work as a choreographer. It is lowbrow in sentiment, ambitious in size, and its dance invention as such is not very striking. But as theater the piece creates a friendly atmosphere and projects an obvious charm.

On Stage is a Chaplinade about a handyman in a theater (Mr. Kidd) and a little girl in pink (Janet Reed) who auditions for a ballet master (John Taras) and fails because she is nervous. The audition comes in the midst of a ballet rehearsal on stage, and its painful failure is covered over by the entrance of the company's tough grand ballerina (Nora Kaye) ready for action. The handyman and the little girl watch the rehearsal proceed, and soon, first one and then the other, both are daydreaming of how beautifully they could do the star parts. After the company has been dismissed and the stage is empty, the handyman tries to cheer up the little girl by pranks which gradually lead to dancing. At the moment she has lost all self-consciousness he manages to call back the ballet master, the company crowds back too, and all applaud her. She is accepted into the company, she waves goodbye gratefully to the handyman, and he is left alone, as Chaplin used to be, privately pleased with his adventure.

The big dance scenes, as you can see, have a realistic excuse; they are mostly the parody of a classic ballet, which moves from rather obvious jokes to vigorous evolutions, parodistic in their rudeness of style rather than in their invention. And this vulgarity of dance style which sets the tone of *On Stage* is in keeping with the sentimental hokum of the story. Far more subtle are Kidd's funny pranks and Miss Reed's downcast features.

But in the dancing itself, though the detail is unsubtle, there is a plain vigor in the arrangements that shows Mr. Kidd's latent strength; some of the static groupings too are attractive without emphasis. The gifts he shows are all for the present more suited to musical comedy than to ballet, but they are real ones. And as he took his final bow, he made a little gesture of "I'll be seeing you," which the audience clearly approved of.

The new score of *On Stage* by Norman Dello Joio is good plain theater without being distinguished. Its sentimental close was most effective. The set by Oliver Smith is discreet and attractive and gives the action clarity and freshness. Alvin Colt's costumes, too, are plain and clear.

OCTOBER 10, 1945

SEMENOFF'S "GIFT OF THE MAGI"

Semenoff's *Gift of the Magi*, Ballet Theatre's novelty last night at the Metropolitan, is foolish corn and a big dose of it. It is both inept as a ballet and absurdly blown up as a production. Lukas Foss's score (the most lively element of the show) is constantly ambitious and overheavy. Raoul Pène du Bois's décor is sentimentally coy and ponderous on stage.

In this clutter of disproportionate trimmings Semenoff's stage action dribbles along meagerly, jerkily, and slowly. Pantomime points and dance rhythms are equally weak and the sentiment saccharine. Nora Kaye and John Kriza danced the leads admirably, and watching them one regretted the waste of their brilliant talents. It was all a bad moment for ballet and a long-drawn-out one.

Gift of the Magi is a story ballet that follows and clumsily embroiders O. Henry's short story of the same title. On Christmas Eve, Della Young sells her hair and Jim Young (her husband) sells his watch, each wanting to surprise the other with a fine Christmas present; she buys him a chain for his watch, he buys her combs for her hair. It is the pathos of young white-collar life, of taste without money. But O. Henry ends not in pathetic frustration, but with a rising little apotheosis of young love; and that is the point of the title. Semenoff, however, drags out the frustration until it subsides, exhausted. Luckily for him, Kriza and Nora Kaye saved the ending—as they had the beginning—by their personal charm and their sweetness of characterization.

One might have expected an O. Henry ballet to be American in atmosphere and flavor. There was nothing in the action that recalled New York in particular or real life anywhere, for that matter.

Foss's score for *Gift of the Magi* is program music in the grand manner. It describes everything, though nothing very intimately, and it changes its subject every few seconds without the least hesitation or loss of breath. It makes lots of big noises, some of them sour.

OCTOBER 16, 1945

"APOLLO": THE POWER OF POETRY

Ballet Theatre covered itself with a real glory at the Metropolitan last night by bringing back to us Balanchine's *Apollo* and by dancing it completely beautifully. *Apollo—Apollon Musagète* is the title of the Stravinsky score—has been performed in New York now and then by various companies during the last ten years, and each time its serene and sensuous poetry has won it a spontaneous acclaim. It is an untarnished masterpiece.

Last night, too, there were bravos, and not bravos merely for the virtuosity but for the poetic beauty of the dancing. For myself, seeing *Apollo* last night has left me—for the first time in the current season, I'm afraid—happily and unreservedly enthusiastic.

Enthusiastic about the piece, which moves me and delights me each time I see it; enthusiastic about last night's performance, in which Alicia Alonso, Nora Kaye, and Barbara Fallis were brilliantly delicate, brilliantly strong, and André Eglevsky magnificently powerful. Virtuoso they were, all four of them—Alonso's extensions, Kaye's speed, and Eglevsky's sweep were in detail dazzling; but the sweet earnestness, the classic modesty, the poetic naturalness of all four throughout the piece made one forget the unhappy tendencies to a more foolish kind of solo showmanship that seems to be creeping more and more into Ballet Theatre's everyday performances. Last night Ballet Theatre was dancing seriously again, and beautiful was the result.

Apollo is about poetry, poetry in the sense of a brilliant, sensuous, daring, and powerful activity of our nature. It depicts the birth of Apollo in a prologue; then how Apollo was given a lyre, and tried to make it sing; how three Muses appeared and showed each her special ability to delight; how he then tried out his surging strength; how he danced with Terpsichore, and how her loveliness and his strength responded in touching harmony; and last, how all four together were inspired and felt the full power of the imagination, and then in calm and with assurance left for Parnassus, where they were to live.

Balanchine has told this metaphysical story in the concrete terms of classic dancing, in a series of episodes of rising power and brilliance. Extraordinary is the richness with which he can, with only four dancers, create a sustained and more and more satisfying impression of the grandness of man's creative genius, depicting it concretely in its grace, its sweet wit, its force and boldness, and with the constant warmth of its sensuous complicity with physical beauty. *Apollo* is a homage to the academic ballet tradition, and the first work in the contemporary classic style, but it is a homage to classicism's sensuous loveliness as well as to its brilliant exactitude and its science of dance effect.

What you see onstage is strangely simple and clear. It begins modestly with effects derived from pantomime, a hint of birth pangs, a crying baby, a man dancing with a lute, and it becomes progressively a more and more directly classic dance ballet, the melodious lines and lyric or forceful climaxes of which are effects of dance continuity, dance rhythm, and dance architecture. And it leaves at the end, despite its innumerable incidental inventions, a sense of bold, open, effortless, and limpid grandeur. Nothing has looked unnatural, any more than anything in Mozart sounds unnatural. But you feel happily the nobility that the human spirit is capable of by nature. OCTOBER 23, 1945

ALONSO AND EGLEVSKY IN "GISELLE"

Alicia Alonso danced Giselle Tuesday night with Ballet Theatre and both Havana and New York crowded into the Metropolitan to cheer, in enthusiastic ballet fashion, Markova's heiress apparent in the company. Young, unaffected, and often very brilliant the performance was, on Alonso's part and on André Eglevsky's, who danced the great partner role of Albrecht magnificently. Both of them broke through the familiar Markova-Dolin interpretation with a sincere youthful fervor of dancing and of love that even the mystery beyond the grave could not repress. You can imagine how the audience cheered.

Alonso is a delightfully young and a very Latin Giselle, quick, clear, direct in her relation to her lover. She is passionate rather than sensuous. She is brilliant in allegro, not so convincing in sustained grace. Her plié is not yet a soft and subtly modulated one and this weakens her soaring phrases. She has little patience for those slow-motion, vaporous effects that we Northerners find so touching. But there is no fake about her, no staginess. Her pointes, her young high extensions, her clean line, her lightness in speed, her quick balance are of star quality.

Her first act was the more distinguished of the two in its dramatic interpretation. She is no tubercular ballerina-peasant but a spirited girl who stabs herself. The dance solo was hidden from me by latecomers, but loudly applauded. The confrontation scene and the mad scene were convincing, simple and large in their miming. In the second act the first whirls were thrilling, and the famous passage of lifts with the following solo of échappés and spins stopped the show by its cumulative bold, clear speed. If there was little that was spectral in the second act, there was nothing that was not vividly young and straightforward.

But it was Eglevsky's dancing in the second act that was a superb revelation to those New Yorkers who have only seen Dolin in it of what this part is really like. Eglevsky's grandeur of rhythm, his magnificently easy elevation, his masterful, clean, and unstressed beats, and even more than that his modesty and young sincerity show how stagey, fidgety, and absurdly weak, technically, Dolin's Albrecht has recently become. Eglevsky's "fish leaps" (pas de poisson) near the end were beautiful indeed. And though he is clearly happier dancing than miming, and though the more difficult the passage the more beautifully he dances it, there is in his naive acting none of the empty showmanship of Dolin's. The way Eglevsky sustained an atmosphere of remoteness in his second-act solos showed that these passages can heighten the mystery of the second act and need not smash it in pieces as Dolin does each time he gets set for a solo. Eglevsky's Albrecht is something for ballet lovers to see.

The Ballet Theatre company danced *Giselle* Tuesday with a happy and spontaneous animation, particularly the first-act ensembles, and the second-act scene with Hilarion. Their interest in the mad scene, done so differently this time, was vivid, and the general support they gave Alonso made the company charming, too. I hope we shall have many more such bright Alonso-Eglevsky *Giselles*. OCTOBER 24, 1945

CHAGALL'S "FIREBIRD"

Marc Chagall's décor for the new version of *Firebird* is as wonderful a gift to the season as a big Christmas present to a child. It is heartwarming and scintillating, it is touching and beautiful, as the eye plays in its fairy-tale depths and fairy-tale coruscations. You can fly in the sky, you can peer into a magic wood and see people living in a dragon. One sits before it in childlike enchantment, watching the drops and costumes while the orchestra plays Stravinsky's elegantly enchanted score rather poorly and while, alas, Markova, Dolin, and the Ballet Theatre company wander about, hop, lift each other, or merely stand endlessly like an opera chorus waiting for a big effect. Dancing there is none to see.

I saw Markova once being lowered from a lift into Dolin's arms and she looked ravishing for the moment, in her loveliest style; and I saw Miss Adams bend and yield charmingly several times in the Berceuse. But the poverty of the choreography was amazing. Adolph Bolm, the choreographer of this new version, is a justly respected great figure of the ballet world—thirty years ago one of the greatest of character dancers, and since 1916 an indefatigable figure in American ballet. But his *Firebird* is mere nonsense, if you should go expecting a ballet.

The charms of Chagall's décor left me in so happy a frame of mind, I couldn't be angry at the silly sequences the poor dancers had to execute. But since the décor is so beautiful a work of art, one hopes Ballet Theatre will get a first-rate choreographer to reset it completely. It could be a glorious ballet.

OCTOBER 25, 1945

TARAS'S "GRAZIANA"

Graziana, the new piece at the Metropolitan last night, was Ballet Theatre's final novelty of the season, and turned out to be the one most cordially approved of by ballet first-nighters. What is striking in this success is that *Graziana* has none of the zippy Broadway showmanship Ballet Theatre has been trying to deliver to its public. *Graziana* is straight academic classicism, without apologies, without vulgarity, without straining for attention. It isn't very interesting; but the ballet audience seemed to be saying demonstratively that it prefers its ballet straight and not Broadwayized, and that it approves highly of a young man who seems likely to produce what it prefers.

The young man is John Taras, a soloist in the company whose first ballet *Graziana* is. It is an ambitious effort—no less than setting a Mozart violin concerto (K. 216) with four soloists and thirteen supporting dancers. They appear against a neutral blue drop in dance costume and dance ballet very well; and that is all that happens. The title is simply a word to identify the piece with.

Taras's approach to classic dancing is completely direct and aboveboard, with no nervousness or evasion. But though there is considerable variety in the steps, there is not much variety in dance expression. The figures are clear and they change without confusion. But one does not get a lift out of varieties of lightness, of speed, of rhythm, out of effects in spacing and timing. *Graziana* solemnly misses the expressive quality of its score, the Mozartian animation in grace and intimacy of sentiment, and hints boyishly at such qualities only in mild Balanchinisms. But young Taras is nowhere fussy or strained. He has happy moments of his own (in the transition to the adagio, and in the adagio foursome); and the public is clearly ready for more of his work. OCTOBER 26, 1945

"APOLLO"

Balanchine's *Apollo* is a ballet so simple in story, so rich in dance imagery, so exciting in invention, I should like to describe a little what happens. The piece calls for a string orchestra to play the Stravinsky score and for four superb dancers; it has beyond that only three small parts, no chorus, almost no scenery. It is quite unpretentious as theater. The scene is on Delos, Apollo's birthplace, and the action begins a moment before his birth, with Leto, his mother, high on a rock in a sharp ray of light, tossing grandly to and fro in the labor of a goddess. Then Apollo appears standing wrapped rigid in swaddling clothes. Two nymphs bring him forward and he bawls infantlike. The nymphs begin to unwrap him, but with a godlike vigor before they are done he makes a ballet preparation and whoosh! spins himself free. Free, he makes a grandly clumsy and babylike thrust and curvet or two, and the prologue is over.

When the lights come on again, he is grown to boyhood and alone. The nymphs have brought him a long-necked lute and he tries to make it sing. But his solitary attempts, first entangled, then lyrical, then determined, look inconclusive. Three young Muses appear and the four of them dance together. They dance charmingly and a little stiffly, reminding you of the inexpressive seriousness and shy, naive fancy of children. But as they end, the boy gives the three girls each a magic gift, a scroll of verse to one, a theater mask to the second, a lyre to the third. And holding these emblems of poetry, each seems to be inspired beyond her years. The first girl dances flowingly with an airy and lyric delight. The second bounds with dramatic speed, with sudden reversals of direction as if in mid-leap; just at the end one hand that has seemed all through to be holding a mask before her face seems to sweep the mask away, and she is herself again and frightened. The third Muse, Terpsichore, invents the most adventurously brilliant dance of all, boldly cutting her motions in startling divisions, as if isolating the elements of her art, without in these diamond-clear stops breaking the cumulative drive. She combines suspense with calm. And as she ends, Apollo gently touches her bright head. But, the dance over, she ducks away like a child and runs off.

Then Apollo, his strength awakened, dances by himself, leaping in complex virtuoso sequences, in a grandly sustained sweep of powerful motion. It is no showoff number, it is a masculine surge of full dance mastery. Terpsichore returns just as he ends and together they invent a series of adagio surprises, extremes of balance and extension, boldly large in line, boldly intimate in imagery, and ending with a tender and lovely "swimming lesson" that he gives her. And now all three Muses dance together in darting harmony and dance inspired by poetry's power, swinging from Apollo like birds, curving from his body like a cluster of flowers, driven by him like an ardent charioteer, and ending, when immortal Zeus has called through the air, in three grand accents of immolation. Then calmly and soberly, in Indian file, all four ascend the rock of the island and a chariot comes through the sky down toward them as the curtain falls. They will go to Parnassus where they will live ever after.

You see as *Apollo* proceeds how from a kind of pantomimic opening it becomes more and more a purely classic-dance ballet. More and more it offers the eye an interplay of lines and rhythms, of changing architectural balances, the edge of which becomes keener and keener. In this sense *Apollo* conveys an image of increasing discipline, of increasing clarity of definition. It grows more and more civilized. But the rhythmic vitality of the dance, the abundance of vigor, increase simultaneously, so that you feel as if the heightening of discipline led to a heightening of power, to a freer, bolder range of imagination. Since the piece is about the gods of poetry, and how they learned their art, it seems, too, to be describing concretely the development of the creative imagination.

And as the dance images grow more disciplined, more large, and more vigorous, they also grow grander in their sensuous connotations. As Apollo and the little Muses grow up, the intimate contact between them seems to develop from an innocent childlike play to the firm audacity and tender inventiveness of maturity.

Suggested in no sense mimically but purely by dance architecture, the range and richness of *Apollo*'s sensuous imagery is marvelous; and because of this consistent honest but unselfconscious sensuousness, the "abstract" classicism is at no point dehumanized or out of character with the dramatic situation. So for example the taut ballet extension of a girl's leg and toe—used in *Apollo* as an insignia of poetry itself—grows increasingly poignant to watch as the piece proceeds; and you experience everywhere the cool sensual luminosity of civilized art.

So *Apollo* can tell you how beautiful classic dancing is when it is correct and sincere; or how the power of poetry grows in our nature; or even that as man's genius becomes more civilized, it grows more expressive, more ardent, more responsive, more beautiful. Balanchine has conveyed these large ideas really as modestly as possible, by means of three girls and a boy dancing together for a while.

But the immediate excitement of watching does not depend on how you choose to rationalize it. *Apollo* is beautiful as dancing and gloriously danced.

OCTOBER 28, 1945

UPS AND DOWNS AT BALLET THEATRE

Ballet-hungry New Yorkers continue to crowd into the Metropolitan, and Ballet Theatre serves them performances that vary from rude or slipshod to superb, from nondescript to imaginative without warning. The valiant company struggles sometimes against overwork, sometimes against under-rehearsal, sometimes against feeble choreography, and almost constantly against the quite unexpected noises the conductor and orchestra are contriving for it in their pit. Just the same some performances come off with verve and brilliance. The public accepts everything that happens with the best of good nature and is grateful for ballet even with handicaps.

Thursday night the orchestra played the most extraordinary things during *Apollo*, and yet the dancers, particularly Eglevsky and Alicia Alonso, were often magnificent. Pity it was the sold-out house hadn't justified the management in paying for an hour's additional orchestra rehearsal.

The music seemed much better in *Firebird*, but in *Swan Lake* Mr. Horenstein started out with a record-breaking tempo that left no time for dancing at all. It was Nora Kaye's only *Swan Lake* of the season and it was a pleasure to see a careful, serious, and accurate interpretation. Consistently brilliant she was last night only in the last rapid solo; at other times she often could not in shoulders and head find the completion of the dance phrases that so often must subside in an arabesque.

The recent repertory has seen in the men's roles the changes enforced by Hugh Laing's departure. Michael Kidd has taken the most hectic ones—those in *Pillar* and *Undertow*. Both ballets are among the few that the company as a whole still does with real care, and Kidd, though he cannot be expected to grasp at once the constantly shifting rhythms of his long roles, does not mar them. The darting motions he does with amazing speed, but he still misses the consistent sensual legato and the imaginative grasp of evil that Laing had.

Harold Lang substitutes in *Aleko* but misses the sinuous independence the part requires. Romanoff in *Tally-Ho* is not as convincing a husband nor as real a sweet-natured intellectual as Laing, but he is agreeable. He is too eager in Tudor's part in *Lilac Garden*, but excellent indeed as the hero in *Pillar*.

But it is the lyricist John Kriza who in the character parts he now takes shows the finest new character talent in the company. True, in *Romeo* and *Lilac Garden* he has not the suppressed drive of Laing. But neither does he force the facial miming, or the speed; he takes each part large and easy. Easily and charmingly, too, he handles the lowbrow comedy of Hermes in *Helen*, and superbly the sensual high comedy of the Prince in *Tally-Ho*. Here in *Tally-Ho* is at last an American male dancer who is not self-conscious in acting an evil character; Kriza is elegant, unstrained, and adult in his characterization, and never works it for farce laughs as a less sincerely imaginative dancer would do. Kriza's development both as a first-class classicist and as a first-class character dancer is one of the really happy features of this Ballet Theatre season.

NOVEMBER 2, 1945

ROBBINS'S "INTERPLAY"

Robbins's *Interplay*, once in Billy Rose's *Concert Varieties* and now a success in Ballet Theatre's repertory, is of serious interest both for being young Robbins's second work and for being, of all the ballets by American-trained choreographers, the most expertly streamlined in dance design. *Interplay* looks like a brief entertainment, a little athletic fun, now and then cute, but consistently clear, simple, and lively. You see four boys come out and then four girls and all eight join in improvised games (such as follow-the-leader) done in dance terms; there is a boy's joking showoff solo, and a duet with a touch of blues sentiment in the air, and then all eight together play another game, competing in leaps and spins with the effect of a collective speed-up finale. It looks rather like an American outdoor party where everyone is full of pep and naively rough and where the general unfocused physical well-being is the fun of the occasion. Still, it isn't always clear from the way the dancers behave to each other if they represent twenty-year-olds being cute or ten-year-olds on their good behavior.

But leaving aside the subject matter (which the program doesn't clarify either) what immediately captures your attention is the pace of the piece, the clear drive of its dance impetus, and the athletic verve of the cast—a perfect cast, in which Harold Lang is especially brilliant. The physical spring of the athletic phrases obviously suits the dancers and the impetus of the movement obviously suits that of the score as well; and the whole continuity is perfectly clear to the eye as dance architecture. There is nothing subtle about the dance—nor about the score, Gould's *Concertette*, for that matter; the texture and the expressive accents are commonplace, but nowhere does the piece break down and become fragmentary, fussy, or thick. And this is a serious achievement. Robbins alone of our native choreographers has grasped at one stroke that the basis of ballet logic is a view of time and space as a closed entity. The time of a ballet is that specified by the musical architecture of its score and the space is that of the stage area as a static whole. These two architectural frames of reference, so to speak, give to the mazes of a ballet its coherent and cumulative distinctness. And the cumulative distinctness in spacing and timing *Interplay* has in action is of serious ballet quality.

Not of serious ballet quality is *Interplay*'s specific dance technique. Robbins does not show the resource of deploying the body unselfconsciously, of a sustained and natural soaring and sailing; the foot positions are only approximate and this spoils the buoyancy and sharpness of floor contact and of phrase construction; he tries for vivacity by again and again overspeeding pirouettes; his jokes are sometimes too coy; he does not distinguish between the timing of pantomime and of dance gesture; and the accents of the dance are likely to be energetic thrusts expressing a shot-in-the-arm vigor rather than an individual response to a dramatic moment.

But perhaps Robbins feels that both the score and the subject matter of *Interplay* call for a general vigor rather than for a modulated and individual grace. The characters of *Interplay* seem to be urban middle-class young people having a good time, who know each other well and like being together but have no particular personal emotions about each other and no special keenness of response. They know about sex as a jive joke or as a general blues sentiment; they don't know it as an individual focus of passion. From a hint of personal sincerity they turn untroubled and vague with a coltish playfulness, expert in strength but blunt in edge.

In this unpersonal aspect of *Interplay* there might be the poetic subject matter of an American flavor of sentiment. And Robbins has, I think, a poetic love for the air of rudeness and unresponsiveness in our national manners. But in *Interplay* he has glossed it over by a general mutual amiability that is humanly unconvincing and a bit goody-goody; he has for the moment confused love of America with flattery. Such criticism is nonsense if *Interplay* is taken as passing entertainment, but not if it is taken as some sort of serious ballet. And the intellectual vigor, the clear focus of its overall craftsmanship suggest—as *Fancy Free* suggested in another way—that Robbins means to be and can be more than a surefire Broadway entertainer, that he can be a serious American ballet choreographer.

NOVEMBER 4, 1945

MARKOVA'S FAILING

Ballet Theatre's season, which closes tonight, has been very successful commercially, but artistically it leaves a disappointing impression, and one of its unexpected disappointments has been the lessening of Markova's marvelous magic. Sunday night in *Romeo* and the night before in *Giselle* she was an exquisite figure to watch, clearly Ballet Theatre's loveliest dancer. But she who in her own miraculously fragile way used to illuminate the meaning of an entire ballet and spread a radiance over the rest of the cast and the entire stage seemed too often to be upstaging the company and to be dancing her own steps merely to look as deliciously graceful as possible, not for the sake of a larger dramatic expression. This has often been her failing this season.

Graceful she still is, and incomparably so, in the lovely bearing of the head, the beautifully effaced shoulders, the line of arms and wrists, the arrowy ankles and feet. Her variety in speed, her general exactness of positions, the limpidity with which she reveals the contrasting accents in direction of a dance sequence without breaking the smoothness of its flow are all of ballerina quality. Her leaps, her way of soaring and gliding, her wonderful lightness in downward motions are unique. But one notices that she tends this season to preserve these graces by lessening the vitality of her dancing, by understating the climaxes. It is as though a singer were to get the mannerism of taking fortissimos in half-voice, a kind of crooning in ballet.

One sees climaxes this season (in *Nutcracker* and *Aurora*) that are tricked out with flicks of the head in pirouettes, with flicks of the wrist in poses; one notices (in *Giselle*, too) the wrists beating time in sustained passages, and broad smiles held throughout a classic number. She seems, no doubt unconsciously, to indicate a discourteous aversion to dancing with Eglevsky and Kriza; and in dancing with Dolin she sometimes gives the effect of a private understanding between them—as is customary and proper in exhibition ballroom dancing but hardly in great classic roles.

These are no doubt inadvertencies which can be blamed on her year's absence from serious ballet. But they are unfortunate mannerisms in a great ballerina. They give an impression of sufficiency that is especially not in keeping with Markova's shy style. And though the audience still applauds her wonderful moments of grace, it does not now thrill to her performance as it used to and as it will again when she gives herself wholly to her parts. I don't doubt that so great an artist will soon tire of the effects she now toys with. NOVEMBER 5, 1945

THE AMERICAN BALLET SCHOOL AT CARNEGIE HALL

The very pleasantest kind of an evening for a civilized and curious audience was what the National Orchestral Association offered its members last night at Carnegie Hall, for its second Monday-series concert. The music was lovely and unusual—what with a Tchaikovsky never played here before and a Stravinsky (*Elégie*) played only once in a different version. The dancing was beautiful, unpretentious, and novel, having been arranged for the occasion by Balanchine and Todd Bolender for fifty or so pupils of the American Ballet School. And the many young musicians and dancers—some of the young dancers were of the kindergarten generation—all performed most handsomely with a real attention to the amenities of their profession and with as little nonsense as if they were playing and dancing in the family. The whole of it was like a delightful family party, where everyone does something interesting, and where the joint practice of art is a refreshing family habit.

The purely musical parts of the program were inspired in various ways by dancing, and the dance portions showed the sincerest respect for the music danced to. The dance material of them was naturally simple, since it was invented for pupils. But with the simplest of materials Balanchine and Bolender achieved a constantly interesting variety, effects of real dance expression and almost of dance brilliance. The pupils never had to strain beyond their assurance, and they never looked unnatural in anything they did. And the assured cleanness, lightness, and modesty of their execution gave the evening its sincerely youthful charm. A few of them, Miss Le Clercq, Miss White, Miss Hyatt, Miss Rechenmacher, and the young lady in Bolender's adagio duet, were often beautiful in line and bearing. But especially delightful was the impression of all the fifty or so of them dancing lightly and simply all together, in a cumulative rush of motion.

Choreographically the most striking was Balanchine's setting of the *Elégie*, which was done by two young girls with hands entwined, turning, rising, interlacing, spreading, crouching, and folding in a long, uninterrupted, beautiful adagio sequence. But Bolender's crisscrossing crowds of dancers in the *Valse*, though not so limpid as the crowds in Balanchine numbers, was very interesting too, in its romantic expression. The Mozart *Symphonie Concertante* was kept fresh by successive brief entrées, and there were lovely passages in the adagio. And the *Circus Polka* with tiny Miss Kursch as the central elephant was a happy little number, after which an enormous box appeared from which Mr. Balanchine and Mr. Barzin handed everyone a happy little bouquet. That the dances could all be invented in a month, and executed so cleanly, was well worthy of bouquets to all concerned.

Mr. Bolender and Frank Moncion, the excellent dancers who assisted as guests, performed as handsomely as one would expect. Karl Braunstein and Hugo Fiorato, who played the solos in the Mozart and the Stravinsky, were excellent, too. And it was also a pleasure to see for once the solo musicians who were playing for the dancers.

Mr. Barzin conducted with his customary positiveness and clarity. And this happy occasion also marked Lincoln Kirstein's first participation since his discharge from the Army in New York's artistic life: it was, I am sure, a happy augury of other interesting evenings to come that we shall be able to thank him for.

NOVEMBER 6, 1945

BALLET THEATRE IN DECLINE . . . AND A FAREWELL

Ballet Theatre is on the decline and its decline is due to mistakes in its management. That is the impression the recent season has left despite the crowds at the Metropolitan. Fine performances there were, bright moments of glory. But the defects which last spring grew less marked as the season progressed, this fall became more pronounced and new ones joined them. Many people noticed this time the increasing rudeness and heaviness of Ballet Theatre's general dancing; they noticed more than ever dancers in solo passages drawing attention to themselves at the cost of dance style and dramatic illusion, and a growing laxness in executing the older pieces in the repertory. People noticed too that the production routine was more careless—in hanging and lighting the sets, in replacing old costumes, in dragging out intermissions—and that the orchestra was more than usually unreliable. And even Markova, whose return to Ballet Theatre had been eagerly looked forward to, did not thrill the public as she used to.

Last spring Ballet Theatre had been saved only by *Undertow*. Last spring, too, the company was overtired and discouraged; but with *Undertow* they felt they had accomplished something worthwhile and had justified their existence as artists. So their morale soared and everybody—including those who had no roles in that piece—danced everything in the repertory with a new zest. But the management did not learn from that example. This time its novelties—though worthwhile as the first steps of new choreographers—were too timid as ballet to give the season a lift. There was no large risk in them. The management took only three other risks this fall, and though none was brave enough to lead to a decisive victory, in each case it spoiled even the small victory it could have won with them. They were the Chagall décor for *Firebird*, which had no choreography of interest to go with it; the Alonso-Eglevsky *Giselle*, which was done only once and in Alonso's hardest week; and the revival of Balanchine's 1928 *Apollo*—the high point of the season but marred at the two repeat performances by insufficient orchestra rehearsal. Poor management indeed.

And that was not all. When the recent season was planned last spring, the management saw it had no challenging novelty, and so it scheduled the best of its former repertory. It could so have presented a respectable season if it had also planned in advance for the best performances possible. Obstacles were the departures, some certain, some threatening, of Hightower, Gollner, Dorati, Tudor, Laing, and a number of others; the cost of rehearsals needed for many changes of cast in so large a repertory; and the strain such a season would put on Kaye and Alonso. But if money had been spent on understudy rehearsals last spring (with Tudor) and on several weeks of extra rehearsal for the company this summer, the dancers would not have been exhausted by trying to learn everything in a hurry. It was poor management to save the money and instead to show Kriza, Kidd, and Lang at short notice and manifest disadvantage in Laing's crucial and complex roles; to wear out Kaye in trivial parts that added nothing to her range or her value; and to lead tired Alonso to save herself in *Swan Lake* and *Waltz Academy*, which she could otherwise have done brilliantly. It was poor management to present the whole company overtired, often underrehearsed, with a conductor who had to keep his eyes on the score and with awkward stage management.

Under such handicaps any dancers spoil their style, and their best style is what a performance depends on for its vitality and thrill. When she is tired, even Alonso, that meticulous stylist, falls into the great Toumanova's error of exhibiting prowess or the great Markova's error of seeming to snub the company and the piece. Even ardent Kaye—who, like Alonso, far bettered her previous best this season when she was rested—when she is tired begins to turn in and to hitch up an arabesque after it has been extended. This has become a general failing with Ballet Theatre's girls, and when tired they dance—it's not their fault—with a violence that reminds one more of a tennis game than of limpid ballet. Perhaps, too, the insistent self-assertiveness of Marjorie Tallchief and the undisciplined roughness of Rall, besides spoiling these two very gifted dancers, give a bad example to the rest. The young dancers who came through this strenuous season most happily were, I thought, the Misses Fallis, Adams, Eckl, Lanese, and Herman, the Messrs Tobias, Beard, and Dovell. Eglevsky—who wasn't used so hard—was magnificent when possible, though his facial miming is overdone; Orloff was remarkable. But John Kriza, overworked as he was, was everywhere Ballet Theatre's brightest mainstay, and his verve in his final Romeo woke up Zlatin and the orchestra to a fine musical performance and even almost woke Miss Markova out of her season's trance.

Ballet lovers are distressed by the wasteful handling of so fine a company of dancers as Ballet Theatre during this last season. The rumor that a new international company is being formed by De Basil, De Cuevas, and De Hurok is no palliative to watching the demoralization of so much of our most valuable native talent. Mr. Kirstein tells me our ballet ensembles are stronger than any he saw abroad. The future of American ballet depends on them, and their growing powers should not be frittered away by poor management.

With this article I end my duties as dance reviewer for the *Herald Tribune* and turn the department over to Walter Terry, back from more than three years of service in the Army. NOVEMBER 11, 1945

Reviews and Appreciations

THE MONTE CARLO DISTRACTED

The Ballet Russe de Monte Carlo opened in New York September 4 in a distracted state with too little illusion of grace or style. During the course of its twelve-day season at the City Center the company had brighter moments (notably *Serenade*, *Concerto Barocco*, *Ballet Imperial* when Marie-Jeanne danced it) and the big news was the dancing of Ruthanna Boris, who showed she deserved further ballerina parts. But the disappointments of the season remained too great. The repertory had been exposed to view in a ragged state to ragged music; Danilova, owing to a knee injury, hadn't appeared at all; Tallchief, injured too, had had to stop dancing after a few days; and the only novelty had been Ruth Page's *The Bells*. Such a string of misfortunes, whether you blame it on the theater jinx that dogs all treatments of Poe (*The Bells* in this case) or blame it on errors of management, was disheartening to watch.

The management had gambled on opening with only two weeks of rehearsal. The company looked tired out without having had time to get into form. Some dancers hadn't recovered the spring they lost practicing on a concrete floor during the summer season in Hollywood. Others were insecure in new parts. The orchestra muddled and dawdled; Mr. Boutnikoff, the conductor, coated the scores with schmaltz, including Stravinsky's. And there was no time to correct the stage lighting. Two weeks more of rehearsals might well have saved the situation and saved the management's face.

A second gamble the management lost was one on its great ballerina. Just before opening, the overworked company gave an out-of-town preview of *The Bells*, and after a six-hour bus ride Danilova was asked to dance without time properly to rest and to warm up. On the management's part this was inviting bad luck; and it was at the preview that Danilova hurt herself.

But the company's misfortune in presenting *The Bells* wasn't even a gamble. Miss Page had produced the piece in Chicago last spring and it was open to inspection then. *The Bells*—choreography by Ruth Page, music by Milhaud, décor by Noguchi—claims in a pretentious program note that it "parallels the psychological development" of Poe's well-known poem. Incidentally, the program doesn't bother to quote the poem correctly.

The Bells is a piece that goes on for half an hour being puerile in public.

First there is a good deal of blithe maidenhood on toe. Then a young man in yellow comes in and the heroine and he have a nice long wedding. After a while, the corps waves some cloth between them and they look unhappy. In due time enter the King of the Ghouls, a young man with a headdress. Our hero abandons his bride to stamp around with the newcomer, and this offends her. She takes to an umbrella. Everybody suffers more and more and works hard at it. By now everybody is tangled up in black streamers and in each other and so eventually everybody gets down on the floor except the King of the Ghouls, who after breaking up one happy home still stands menacing the audience. The program book says this indicates "Beauty divorced from Truth and . . . the Moral Sense."

Not that *The Bells* is incompetent in its own manner. Cut down to ten minutes it would be an unusually good stage show at a movie palace and would have an immense success. It is a good stage show because it has lots of different steps, difficult lifts, pretty lineups, smooth transitions, an anodyne story, and even a dash of what in stage shows passes for modern dance. No doubt its stereotype dance ideas and its puerile expressive passages are never anything but girlishly cute; its characters gesticulate in clichés of love and despair, its dances beat time to the music and have no surge or freedom of dance rhythm. But that is what the audience in a movie house expects of the stage show. It is only the pretentious insistence with which *The Bells* keeps up its triviality for half an hour that isn't good form in a movie house, and that wouldn't be allowed in one, either.

In ballet neither pretentiousness nor triviality is good form and the management shouldn't allow them. Even a good stage show is not a good ballet. It is because the good dance execution of *The Bells* and the celebrity of its collaborators might mislead that it is necessary to point out the nature of the work. Otherwise, out of deference to Miss Page's many efforts for ballet in this country, one would have preferred to pass it off with a joke.

To Poe lovers in the dance public, not *The Bells* but the mysteriousness of Balanchine's *Night Shadow*—a novelty of last season—is recommended. Mysterious is the interaction of its elements: the vapid ballroom dances; the winsome exhibition numbers that have a perverse and cruel undertone; the elaborate, encircling artifices of the Coquette's pas de deux; the directness and space of the sleepwalking scene; the massed mime chorus in unison at the end. The progress of the piece is "romantic"—it is disconcerting, absurd, and disproportionate; but its effect when it is over is powerful and exact. It gives you a sense—as Poe does—of losing your bearings, the feeling of an elastic sort of time and a heaving floor. As a friend of mine remarked, "When it's over, you don't know what hit you." *Night Shadow* bears no resemblance to the recent Balanchine "classic" pieces—no resemblance to their firm dance lilt and their formal transparence; though it is not a mimed piece, its effects are related to mime effects.

At the opposite pole from *Night Shadow* in form and in sentiment is the reconstruction by Danilova and Balanchine of Petipa's *Raymonda*, which the Monte Carlo also introduced last spring. Not only its air of leisure but its candor and sunny clarity are qualities unusual nowadays. It is difficult at first to be so unnervous, so relaxed and unresentful as this long and peaceful ballet invites you to be. The surprise is that it can be so long and so peaceful without turning foolish or false in sentiment. *Raymonda* has an easy amplitude and graciousness in good spirits; there is a sweetness in the air like that of a large, happy, well-mannered, and gifted family living in a large, old-fashioned summer house. And you feel in it, too, the family note that distinguishes so pleasingly the Monte Carlo company itself.

There is, I am told, little of the original Petersburg *Raymonda* in this version, though the most fantastic dance invention, the ballerina's third-act czardas on toe, is authentic Petipa, and Petipa's, too, is the large, bold force of the male pas de quatre in that act. But all through this American *Raymonda*, the resourcefulness in simplicity, the vitality of dance rhythm, the clarity in plastic contrasts, the grand relief of the human figure are in the honest Petipa manner. The dances are by no means easy to do, for a blurred or unintelligent movement shows up at once. Everywhere they look as if it felt good to dance them, and it feels good to watch them. With all their profuse variety there is not a mean gesture to be seen for a whole hour. Some people find this escapism, but as a conception of society it strikes me as revolutionary.

Without Danilova to dance them, her great parts looked pale and some fine passages meaningless. Franklin too was not at his best without her. Magnanimous and buoyant lyricist as he is, and an excellent actor, he seemed a little tired and distressed and his style suffered; he looked as if he were counting for everybody else on stage and keeping a weather eye out for everyone's mistakes. In Danilova's parts, Krassovska, lovely and sweetly feminine when she can be yielding and modest, rather lacks the authority in development, the vitality and variety of dance rhythm that make grandeur lively. Marie-Jeanne, fantastically sharp in *Imperial*, excellent in *Night Shadow*, was on the other hand lost in *Baiser*, in which her intention to look soft and sweet made her slur the steps, vaguely wave her arms, and miss the drama. Tallchief was wonderfully fascinating at moments, but her bad ankle restricted her.

A dancer who was constantly a pleasure to watch was Boris. Her lovely figure, her bearing and balance, her line, her clean, swift steps and harmonious ease, her reliability in every part were very remarkable. So was the intensity of her acting in *Frankie*. Her variations in *Raymonda* and her duo with Lindgren in *Night Shadow* were a delight; but her best part was *Serenade*, where she showed a sense of what she seems still a little to lack—a wider scope in rhythm, a bolder timing of main accents, and a more elastic change of speed which will sustain and join the phrases of a dance in what in music is called a period. With her sure instinct for both drama and music and Danilova's example, she should be able to find the large sweep of classic continuity. Young Chouteau, as careful though not nearly so finished, but clear and intelligent in her dancing, has by nature a vivid sense of rhythm and without pretension or bad manners she can quite naturally be herself. If her development continues as happily, she seems to me to have very great possibilities. There isn't space for more, but one should at least mention Tyven's excellence this season, Goddard's Nelly, Magallanes's noble support, especially in *Barocco*, young Weamer's cleanness, Kokitch's Wrangler, Bliss's Roper, and above all Danielian's really superb dancing in *Raymonda*.

Watching the dancers in good and less good performances, and considering the handicaps the management imposed on them this fall, I have no doubt that with a little planning the company can get its repertory back in shape; that it can bring us next time a novelty as brilliant as those of last spring; and that with Balanchine to clarify the execution of *Night Shadow*, *Baiser*, and the classic pieces, with Danilova dancing and the rest back in their best form, the company as an ensemble can show again the light, clear, intelligent dance style they specialize in and that ballet lovers have justly admired them for.

Dance Magazine, NOVEMBER 1946

BALLET THEATRE VS. HUROK: A WAR OF ATTRITION

The current exceptionally full New York ballet season has not yet shown any exceptional luster. One might have hoped to see it as a lively competition between a prewar and a postwar style of dancing, the first as represented by the Original Ballet Russe of Col. de Basil, and the second by Ballet Theatre. Instead, it has taken on the gloomy appearance of a war of attrition between Ballet Theatre and S. Hurok, the impresario. Sadly enough, the return of the Original after five years' absence has proved an event of no interest at all.

When Mr. Hurok and Ballet Theatre split last spring over differences of artistic policy, he booked the Original in Ballet Theatre's place. For twenty-two weeks this fall and winter the Original replaces Ballet Theatre, first at the Metropolitan Opera House here and later at many of the large and profitable theaters in other cities. The Original, to be sure, following a previous split with Mr. Hurok, had lost its most celebrated dancers and had had to spend five years arduously touring Latin America. But for its return Mr. Hurok added to it dancers such as Markova, Dolin, Eglevsky, Rosella Hightower, Skibine, Frank Moncion, and excellent young Marjorie Tallchief. To the de Basil repertory of standard classics, early Fokine, and several prewar successes, he added three American choreographies—Dollar's *Constantia*, Cobos's *Mute Wife*, and Caton's *Sebastian* (all three from the Marquis de Cuevas's short-lived Ballet International), as well as *Giselle* and Dolin's *Pas de Quatre*. Even a good orchestra was engaged. And when the boat bringing the company from South America was delayed, local dancers were engaged to rehearse the American ballets as well as a New York premiere, *Camille*, and to dance in them till the Original had time to learn the new roles and take over. All in all, a very considerable and expensive effort; but the secret flaw in this plan was the five lean years the Original had been through since it was last seen here. They could not be patched over in a hurry.

The Original arrived September 27 and opened at the Metropolitan September 29 for a three-and-a-half-week season. Ballet Theatre arrived a few days earlier and opened September 30 for a five-week season at the Broadway Theatre. Both openings were crowded and demonstrative; the Original had the dressier, and Ballet Theatre the livelier crowd. But by the third night the weather prophets were foreseeing that by next fall Ballet Theatre would be back at the Metropolitan, and that faced with their respective deficits, Ballet Theatre and Mr. Hurok would soon find themselves in overwhelming artistic agreement.

People go to the Original out of curiosity and because it appears at the Metropolitan; but despite the extra attractions they find the troupe as a whole depressingly second-rate. Ballet Theatre, on the other hand, has not the money either for the bold new productions or for the enlargement of the company that it needs to keep its spirit and its vitality at their best. It is, of course, clearly much the better ballet.

The best part of the Original's season so far has been the individual work of the dancers newly added to it—notably Markova and Eglevsky. But such isolated moments of brilliance do not blend with the rest, and the American dancers already look uncomfortable. The general style of the Original is very different from the accurate, large, and buoyant American style. It is a survival, though only a faint one, of the prewar Franco-Russian style, with its dramatic sweep of phrase and its keen edge of temperament. In clarity, speed, line, and bearing, however, the dancers are now too weak to give their dramatic intentions brilliance. One admires their instinct for coloring their dancing according to their roles—an instinct Americans are weak in. But their dancing too often is rudely forced and approximate, their stage presence emptily emphatic. The principals, such as Stepanova, Moulin, Stroganova, or, among the men, Tupine, Dokoudovsky, are dancers of obvious talent one would like to see after six months of intensive class work. Only Jasinski in character mime roles shows a fine dignity and style, and watching the company as a whole one can well believe the story that they have not had a class for four years. One does not feel like criticizing them in their misfortune. That these young people, many of them Latin Americans, have kept on dancing any kind of ballet with the touring conditions they have been under so long is touching to every ballet lover.

As for prewar successes, so far, I have seen Fokine's *Paganini* and Lichine's *Francesca da Rimini*. The latter looked too foolish to be worth keeping; the former, for all its simple and large-scale amplitude of rhythmic continuity, was hard to take in its complacent mawkishness of sentiment.

The novelties of the Original's season are Taras's *Camille*, Lichine's *Cain and Abel*, and Psota's *Yara*. *Camille*, Taras's second ballet, is set to a Rieti arrangement of Schubert piano pieces, and is dressed and decorated by Cecil Beaton. It shows us Marguerite Gautier, in her last illness, haunted first by the memory of a ball at which Armand appears, later by the vision of a happy afternoon spent with him in the country, and recurrently by the figure of his father; recalling her promise to the father, she awakens and sinks back in despair. The dances are gently inventive, clear, and fluent; they are also too lightly tinted and too innocently reticent to seem suitable to so passionate a subject or make much of a ballet. In addition, the dancing was smothered under the opulent elegance of Beaton's crinolines and decorative graces. Markova danced Camille with enchanting delicacy and clarity; Dolin as Armand was wooden and his costume gave him a hump.

Lichine's *Cain and Abel* has a score of Wagner excerpts and a décor by the Mexican Prieto of big snaky boulders, from the top of one of which Cain pushed his brother—a six-foot headlong drop onto a concealed mattress. *Cain and Abel* is an athletic romp for two muscular boys in bathing trunks, sometimes together, sometimes intertwined with two slightly dressed girls representing Good and Evil. There is a good deal of rolling, squirming, and bumping on the floor and on rocks. It is a Hollywood conception of biblical tragedy, and a ballet wit described it accurately as "Tarzan in a Turkish Bath." Cain and Abel beat their chests, yodel for an echo, and when the characters dance they look as awkward and as simpleminded as devotees of the Body Beautiful improvising Creative Expression on a beach. *Cain and Abel* is too simpleminded to get angry at; as a ballet it must be one of the most fantastic absurdities ever offered.

The opening night of Ballet Theatre began with a brilliant performance of *Interplay* and ended with a tired one of *Fancy Free*. In between, Nora Kaye had danced *Pillar of Fire* as beautifully as ever, and Alonso and Youskevitch had danced the *Swan Lake* Act Three pas de deux. Youskevitch is currently replacing Eglevsky as Ballet Theatre's classic premier danseur, and this was his first appearance since his return from the Navy. That evening, as well as two nights later, in the *Nutcracker* pas de deux, his grace of bearing, the lightness, the elegance in effacé positions, the entire absence of mannerism were wonderful to see again. He has not yet regained the complete control of arm poses in leaps that he had before, and had alone—where Eglevsky's style is one of forthright power, Youskevitch's is one of insinuating strength; and both are superb.

Ballet Theatre's novelties this season are Ashton's *Les Patineurs*, Keith Lester's *Pas de Quatre*, a new Berman investiture for *Giselle*, and Robbins's first "serious" piece, a psychological drama for three characters called *Facsimile*, with a score by Bernstein and a set by Oliver Smith. The last, announced for October 17, is naturally awaited here with intense interest. Of the other novelties, only *Les Patineurs* has so far been given, and it was at once a popular hit.

Les Patineurs was charmingly danced by the company, with Kaye and Laing discreetly and convincingly romantic in the pas de deux, and Kriza very witty in the variations; and it looked in Cecil Beaton's decoration like the most graceful of correct Christmas cards. People agreed that the piece was fun, that it was easy and fresh in its plainness, and had a certain inconspicuous elegance of taste that keeps it from quite being musical comedy. Ballet lovers regretted that Ballet Theatre had not brought back a more ambitious work of Ashton's, the English choreographer many of us are particularly curious about. Ballet Theatre's season would certainly seem more brilliant had it done so. It was a great pity to have missed so fair an opportunity, and one hopes Ashton will soon come over and rehearse works of his with both Ballet Theatre and the Monte Carlo.

Ballet Today, NOVEMBER 1946

BALLET THEATRE WINS

New Yorkers never spent so much money on ballet as in October and it was a pity they didn't get a dazzling season. The novelties of interest were only two, both of them given by Ballet Theatre—Jerome Robbins's new piece, *Facsimile*, and a new staging of *Giselle* danced by Alonso and Youskevitch and decorated by Berman. Ballet Theatre's season was a very pleasant one as a whole, though distinctly uneven; but it set a superb standard compared to that of the Original Ballet Russe, which was cluttered with shabby performances and shoddy productions. The Original's was far the poorest Met season in ten years, even though it included Markova's beautiful Giselle.

The Original had not been here since '41. For five years it toured Latin America, repeating its prewar repertory, changing personnel, recasting roles. Such as it was, the company remained committed to the Franco-Russian Ballet Russe tradition. For its return to New York, however, a dozen or more dancers, raised in or acclimated to our own different standards, were quickly added; Markova and Dolin, Eglevsky, Hightower, Antonia Cobos, George Skibine, Francisco Moncion were put in as extra stars; four New York choreographies, plus *Giselle*, Dolin's *Pas de Quatre*, and standard pas de deux, were hastily stuffed in among the repertory. The ballet grab bag that resulted had no collective vitality or style. It was the added dancers and choreographies that gave the Original season what bright moments it had; but the Ballet Russe contingent far outnumbered them, and in their dilapidated state offered one dismal sight after another.

There were times when these prewar Ballet Russe productions evoked a ghost of the company's prewar grand manner—evoked as in a parody the former sweep of phrase, the former temperament, the former gift for color and impersonation. The old effects failed now because the technical basis for them had rotted away. The usual dancing of even the principals—such as Stepanova, Moulin, Morosova among the ladies, or Tupine (a dancer of great gifts), Dokoudovsky, MacKenzie among the men—was rudely forced or vague in rhythm, in line, in step; it was thick in the shoulder, heavy in carriage, lacking in courtesy, and emptily emphatic in stage presence. That there was talent buried under these ruins only made the spectacle more morbid. If the Ballet Russe section of the Original is to be revivified as a company, it will take a year of rigorous classwork and a new repertory to do it.

Danced without grace of any kind, the prewar repertory was no pleasure to see. Massine's *Fantastique*, for instance, looked merely hectic and brutal; Fokine's *Paganini*—despite its often large-scale rhythmic continuity—merely complacently mawkish in sentiment. The Original also displayed two lengthy 1946 novelties. One, Psota's *Yara*, had a pleasing Brazilian score and décor (Mignone and Portinari) but no dance interest. The other, Lichine's *Cain and Abel*, stressed manly Body Beautiful poses by two rugged boys in tiny trunks, and sexy entanglements with two girls called Good and Evil; Cain and Abel also bumped around together on the floor a good deal and perspired freely; and the orchestra played *Siegfried* to it.

Fresh and quite clear by contrast were the non–Ballet Russe productions added here under local direction, and with non–Ballet Russe dancers to set the style. The only new piece among them was John Taras's *Camille* (score, Schubert-Rieti; décor, Cecil Beaton), described as a dream of the dying Lady of the Camellias. The graceful and cool correctness of its dance invention and bits of mime made it an agreeable though an excessively slight ballet. Markova danced the title part delicately and the first dim glimpse of the set was remarkable. On the other hand, seen in any relation to its subject matter, *Camille* was preposterously virginal.

The Original's two superstars were guest artists, Markova and Eglevsky. Markova danced more carefully, elegantly, and imaginatively than last year. Like last year she diminished, wherever possible, high leaps, high développés, large displacements, all that required unusual physical strength. But within this diminished scale of dance values her control of momentum, the limpidity of rhythm and gesture were as miraculous as ever. That her dramatic genius has found no big part since Juliet—and is now restricted to Giselle—is a great loss, greater as the years hurry by.

It is a loss too that, since his triumph in *Apollo* last year, no new part has been found that suits Eglevsky's special large and deliberate soaring rhythm. The magnificence of his force at present is unequaled among dancers. He was unusually meticulous this season; but an entrechat with his back to the audience (in his Black Swan variation) was an impolite error.

Eglevsky's leaps and Markova's Giselle had long been Ballet Theatre attractions; to make up for losing them this year, Ballet Theatre offered two of its three finest new features—the new production of *Giselle* with Alonso, and Youskevitch as regular classic premier. Where Eglevsky's virtuosity is one of forthright power and breadth, Youskevitch's in the same great passages is one of elegant and even insinuating grace. Youskevitch's art of plastic harmony (of contrapposto) can give his strength a sort of mild luster; his miming is unmannered; his support is superb; his courtesy and his modesty charm; and his bows are in good taste. These were his first weeks of real ballet in more than three years, and his achievement in general was excellent.

Ballet Theatre's new *Giselle*, which he danced in, was, though unfinished, an event of importance. Formerly it was only Markova's piece, now it is on the way to becoming the whole company's. Alonso's Giselle is young, lovely, much more carefully worked out than last year. In the crucial second act she is stronger than Markova in many virtuoso feats; nonetheless Markova is still dramatically more thrilling. One watches Alonso imitate to perfection several of those touching "Victorianisms" of Markova's that are close to mincing; they are effects that suit Markova's figure but not always Alonso's. (Alonso's head, for example, when she holds it forward is not fragile enough to be innocently wagged.) Markova, too, attains expressive effects by a sovereign evenness of momentum, which makes her motion seem floating and her lift seem under a spell (as when, for instance, the unbroken impetus at the start of her lifts prepares for the vaporous descent). Alonso tends to a more sforzando-edged attack and it sometimes breaks the continuity of her characterization, too. (So, in *Giselle* as in *Swan Lake*, she can first look a bit too consciously familiar in the arms of her lover and then start away a bit too willfully, twice breaking the spell.) Alonso's Giselle is a brilliant effort still incomplete; when she gains full dramatic power, she will have found an overall dance impetus (or attack) for the part that suits more intimately her own genius as a dancer. (Incidentally, Alonso's bows "in character" are unfortunate.)

The new production aimed in many details for clarity of motivation. I was sorry it missed motivating, through Myrtha, Giselle's return to dancing stage center after her flight with Albrecht to the cross—and this, the beginning of the climax, was the point at which the dramatic continuity broke down. The "love death" climax of *Giselle* was best conveyed years ago in Serge Lifar's version, and his own rise in elevation toward the end, like an ecstatic possession, was magnificent.

Marvelously dream-loaded and miasmic in atmosphere, in subject matter, color, and perspective were Berman's backdrops; beautiful too were his two front curtains (all superbly executed) and several costumes. On the other hand, the Wilis looked interesting but too substantial and the chorus costumes in Act One were a mistake. As a whole, Ballet Theatre's production was a real theater event, full of imagination, amplitude, and devotion to a central tradition of ballet.

Robbins's new piece, *Facsimile* (score by Leonard Bernstein, set by Oliver Smith, costumes by Irene Sharaff), is an earnest satirical image of a flirtation between an idle woman and two idle men. You see how these people, by anxiously pretending they feel a mutual attraction, get themselves into an awkward *amour à trois* tangle, which turns viciously hateful as the frenzy rises. At a momentary stalemate that postpones the climax, the woman stops the action with a hysterical cry. Politely the men stop. Humiliated but polite, the three leave separately and the stage is empty.

To pretend to be sexy is a farce situation and Robbins hasn't missed the jokes. But he has given his characters a spasmodic grasping drive that indicates they are passionately pretentious. The devouring drive of vainglory is a tragic subject. But *Facsimile* doesn't go that far. Its characters stop prematurely; after the embarrassing cry there is no further development, no shock of terror, no fury, disintegration, or resolution. And so the disaster remains pathetically trivial.

Though timid in that more serious sense, the stage craftsmanship of *Facsimile* is immensely capable. There is no padding, no hesitancy, no drop, no blur. Though made up of fragmentary, often constricted gestures, the continuity is unbroken, the pacing sharp, the rhythm bold, the musical tact remarkable. So is the cartoonist wit; and remarkable as dance invention is the long main climax. *Facsimile* is a big step forward by an honest, exceptionally gifted craftsman. It was excellently performed by Robbins and John Kriza and with consummately rich brilliance by Nora Kaye. The set was intelligent, remarkable in the opening light, the score trivial and efficient.

Ballet Theatre's other novelties, Ashton's *Patineurs* and Lester's *Pas de*

Quatre, two ten-year-old charm numbers brought back from England, were pleasant and in good taste but too slight. Ashton should be invited over to rehearse some of his serious pieces with our companies.

The attractive general character of Ballet Theatre's season was due to the return of a happier, more homogeneous company atmosphere. Though smaller and not quite so strong as once, it is still as pretty a company and, despite overwork, it managed generally to look fresh and crisp.

The management has restored the company's collective harmony and morale; the dancers are fresh, bold, and strong; it looks like a good opportunity for some conscientious technical development.

Dance Magazine, DECEMBER 1946

WIGMAN AFTER THE WAR

Harald Kreutzberg danced here a week ago, and tried out some new, decoratively surrealist numbers that looked silly to me; but I'm not a Kreutzberg fan. The public here was divided much as at home—he's a success but not with dance lovers. At the recital I saw Mary Wigman, light-eyed, red-haired, with a wild, ruined face and a wonderful human warmth; she was in Locarno (the next town) for a few days' vacation after giving a two-week course in Zurich (with Kreutzberg) and before going back to her school in Leipzig (Russian Zone). She was having a wonderful time staring at all the luxury of the West: clean trains, meals on the lawn, whipped cream and coffee on the sidewalk, and the palms and flowers and mountain peaks of this place. She told me she has a school and a new dance group formed since the war, and it toured in a program she made for them called *Aus der Not der Zeit* (*Out of the Rubble* is a free translation). She also was director at the Leipzig Opera for *Orpheus* (two months of rehearsals), doing it with a dance group onstage continuously almost. It was considered the best production in Germany since the war. She stopped dancing in 1942; the Nazis were always hard on her, and finally forced her to sell her school.

She says that modern dance didn't evolve under the Nazis or produce a new crop of dancers, and it's still too early since the defeat. A class of young people of hers to whom she mentioned the word "Olympus" didn't know what it meant, not one in thirty. Of course there is hardly any money for lessons, also no food. She was wearing a gray dress sent from New York. She is not well. But she had been sent a book of photographs of Martha Graham and wanted to hear all about her. She thought Graham must be marvelous and also so intensely American, an embodiment of the country. And she spoke of Martha's having described the Grand Canyon to her—those subterranean mountain ranges—long ago in New York, and of the American landscape she remembered, and how her American pupils each one sooner or later danced a dance of spreading out into space.

A former pupil of hers, Pola Nierenska, was here too, said to be the best modern dancer in England. C. 1947 (UNPUBLISHED)

ASHTON'S "CINDERELLA"

The big hit of Ashton's *Cinderella* is its pair of Ugly Sisters, Helpmann and Ashton himself, and it is the one Ashton plays, the Second Ugly Sister, who becomes the charmer of the evening. She is the shyest, the happiest, most innocent of monsters. She adores the importance of scolding, the fluster of getting dressed up—in a rush of milliners, hairdressers, jewellers, violinists. To do a little dance transports her, though she keeps forgetting what comes next. At the Prince's she is terrified to be making an entrance; a few moments later, poor monster, in the intoxication of being at a party she loses her heart and imagines she can dance fascinatingly—in the way Chaplin at a fashionable tango-tea used to imagine he could slink like a glamorous Argentine. But after the slipper test she accepts the truth as it is, she makes a shy state curtsy to the princely couple, to the power of Romance and Beauty, and paddles sadly off. No wonder such a monster wins everybody's heart. Ashton does it reticently, with the perfect timing, the apparently tentative gesture, the absorption and the sweetness of nature of a great clown. He acts as if he never meant to be the star of the show and very likely he didn't. He cast Helpmann, England's greatest mime, as the First Stepsister and gave that part the initiative in their scenes; he himself was only to trail along vaguely, with one little solo in the second act. After all, he was busy at the time choreographing the three acts of the piece, his and England's first full-length classic ballet, and doing it in six weeks. Ashton's unexpected triumph onstage is the sort of accident that happens to geniuses.

The farce mime in the ballet is so amusing and so long in each act it is in danger of killing the dance scenes; as choreographer of it, Ashton keeps the clowning gentle and, what is more, all the pantomime completely comprehensible—a lovely feat. As dance choreographer his great moments are a set of classic variations for girls representing the Four Seasons (the Good Fairy calls each in turn to attend Cinderella), and a number of entrances for the Jester during the ball. What a Harlequin-Jester was up to in the piece and how he got so big a part I didn't find out till several days later, but I was so delighted with the vitality and style of all he did, I never thought of wondering about it while I watched. The part is Alexander Grant's, the company's most interesting male dancer. Like a jet of force he darts forward in deep plié, in renversé, bent sideways, bent double, leaping down a flight of stairs, springing into the meager dances of the guests with a smiling threat. In the Jester's leaps Ashton has timed the rhythm to the leap's arrival (instead of to its departure from the ground) and because your ear anticipates the rhythm, the crouching dancer's downward course through the air keeps the beautiful suspense of an animal pounce. More delicately Ashton uses the same device in the feminine Seasons variations and there too it gives the dancer an other-than-human presence. These four classic solos in their conciseness and grace of style, their freshness of fancy and purity of evocation are Ashton's masterpiece. They don't look like Petipa or Balanchine and are worthy of either. The Seasons' passage is also the best incident in the score and in the decoration, as if composer, choreographer, and decorator each drew a breath of relief at being free for once of the logic of the libretto.

Seasons, Jester, Second Stepsister are Ashton's most expressive figures but they aren't in a position to carry the central action. *Cinderella* is a three-act ballet in the grand manner—it consists of miming, of classic, demi-caractère, and character dancing, of processions, lineups, tableaus, and apotheosis, all of them (including farcical female impersonation) traditional elements of the form. Ashton has composed in each style easily, correctly, clearly, without oddity, camp, or other subterfuge, each kind true to its nature and function (so he keeps the farce to mime, never extends it to classic steps). Such a piece leads straightforwardly to the entrances of the ballerina, of the ballerina and her partner, as its moments of intensest poetic illumination around which the piece revolves and reechoes. The critic, delighted with Ashton's openness, is eager for the big climaxes ahead. He wants to love the ballerina not only for her dancing but even more for what the imagery of her dances can tell of her nature as a human heroine. And the libretto of *Cinderella* is so direct, her dances have to be logical parts of the story. An anxious critic is willing to excuse that in the first variation early in Act One (she is daydreaming of the ball at her housework) she looks mostly ornamental and not-quite-naively playful. She doesn't dance again till at the climax of Act Two, she enters, meets the Prince, and is in love. They have a pas de deux and each a variation. The two solos are bright and lovely—like youthful talk, the girl's more original, the boy's more amiable; but after this they could still fall in love with someone else. And when they dance together the rhythm is nervous, hasty, the figures crowded but not intimate—two people being obliging in a difficult situation. Aren't they in love? The eye doesn't catch any luminous movement-image of a dazzling encounter, a magic contact, and release of romance. Even the three-act form hasn't world enough or time for so many preliminaries. After that, when the third act opens and Cinderella in a morning-after variation remembers the ball, instead of retrieving the situation by a radiant kind of *Spectre de la Rose* recollection, she fiddles with her broom again and offers an adroit, ingenious anthology of bits from Acts One and Two. What a cold fish she is! Even here in private she won't give a hint of the marvel she has seen, of the kiss she has felt. Her shy Ugly Sister has more heart than that, and the smoldering, demonic, horsey First Stepsister has more vitality. Here they are—wonderful again—with the slipper, and what a lively family scene it becomes with its motley swirl of characters! Poor, silly Prince, of course the slipper fits only his ballerina! But they haven't danced yet in this act, by rights we'll get another pas de deux. Transformation, rapid procession of our old friends the Seasons and attendant Stars—the magic powers of time that create the bloom of beauty—and here we are in the bridal pas de deux. Noble style, calm rhythm. And here a lovely dance figure—the Prince kneels and she tenderly touching his bent shoulders extends away from him a lovely arabesque—a shy moment of forbearance in contact, a moment of clarity once more worthy of Petipa. Now the ice is broken, they can begin to really dance together—but no, the pas de deux is over, it's all over, they will never get any closer. Bitterly disappointed in them, I watched them get into a galleon the size of a telephone booth and sail off, while the Stars and Seasons and all Beautiful Powers sank back and subsided in a brief sweet pianissimo close like a gentle sigh. Curtain.

From the special standpoint of dramatic impact or drive, *Cinderella* would be more exciting if its central characters were more expressive, if it had a joyous ensemble dance in Act Three and a livelier one in Act

One. (I even wished the First Stepsister's grim limp at her last exit could be dramatized to a scene of hatred and eternal horror.) The piece's success in impact is the long ensemble dance climax at the ball and the claustrophobic crowd that ends it during the fatal strokes of midnight.

But *Cinderella* hasn't the disharmony of a piece that can't do what it wants to, and impact and drive are not its method of being interesting. The fun of the farce keeps relaxing the hold of the central story and in the story the dances don't try for intensity and fail, they don't look silly, they look agreeable. Ashton's sense of character is a true one as far as it finds expression but he doesn't strain for drama any more than he does for humor. Comfortable in the pace of its developments and transitions, always amusing or attractive to watch, never embarrassing or insistent, the piece succeeds very well in what it chooses to do. In that so-to-speak domestic key is its harmony, the harmony of an untroubled voice at home telling once more the same fairy tale.

The fact is *Cinderella* lasts two hours and a half and doesn't seem long. The current that carries it is easy and gentle. Its hold on one's attention is so mild that an American like myself is hardly aware of being in the theater. The spell it creates doesn't crystallize in a climax or a specific dance image but no mean gesture breaks the continuity of it. English in the lightness of its fragrance, the charm it holds is a grace of spirit, an English sweetness of temper. It doesn't excite, it ever so mildly refreshes. To keep in a three-act ballet such a tone, to sustain it without affectation or banality, shows Ashton's power, and he shows this in doing it as simply as possible, by keeping the dancing sweet.

The dance impetus of his piece, mild though it is, is open and confident. The variety of ballet styles blend without a blur, each springing as fresh as the other from the score, and the spell of being inside the imaginary world of music where dancing is natural doesn't break all evening. The processions and lineups, for instance, don't disturb the dance pulse of the action, nor does the action jump in and out of the music when the ballerina dances right after the mimes have been funny or when a flurry of character dancers dance in the farce scenes. The jokes come easy, and the miming looks free, it isn't stylized or Mickey Moused to fit the notes, but it derives its phrasing and the emphasis from the shape and the stress of the musical phrase as spontaneously as the dancing does. Ashton responds to whatever is buoyant in a musical phrase as a whole, he responds to a musical phrase with a dance phrase and he takes the spring and momentum from the precise form of the other. So the score flows easy and clear and the dancers in motion look fresh and airy. They don't exhaust the music, nor vice versa; they can be many or alone, they can stop or continue.

Ashton is sometimes too relaxed and then, though the impetus in the trunk still is right, the arm shapes and step shapes don't count for much; but if he is wary of dramatic tension it is that an expression which isn't in the phrasing clutters a dance and depresses it. The drama of his best ones is in their harmony and pulse. Even when his dances are slight they have in passing a spontaneous air of grace. They look on pitch, they make up a tune. He has disciplined his gift to sincerity, to an inability to fake or strain or impress or aggrandize, all of them uncivilized practices, that make successes but take the fun out of dancing. He could reach grandeur, but he is in no hurry to get there. The pleasure he offers is that of ballet classicism, which says what it does say in a tone at once civilized and innocent, a tone which is personal to him. In such a tone even a slight message makes an evening one is glad to have spent at a theater.

But the fact is, too, that for all the pleasure *Cinderella* gives, it is too slight to hold one's interest a second time. It has enough passages fascinating to see repeatedly, mime effects and dance effects, to make a brilliant one-act piece; but they don't make sense by themselves because they are those of secondary figures. In their own secondary range they express the idyllic human message or tone of the ballet; but the rest of it doesn't widen the range of feeling, doesn't make the idyllic feeling more poignant at the climaxes or more ample in the main ensembles. One may say that Ashton has been weak as a dramatist, weak in the contact between figures. But I think his fault has been an uncertainty of emphasis in the structure of many passages. It seems to me that a dance simultaneously with its impetus develops a quality of human motion contained in a phrase of classic movement, that a dance does this in the way a piece of music develops its "thought" by developing and refracting an expressive cadence contained in the harmony of music. The spontaneous emphasis of a dance falls at any rate on one phrase of movement more than another, an emphasis which makes a momentary look in motion of a thigh or flank or forearm or instep or neck more dramatic as it passes, with an effect like an unconscious characteristic gesture. These transiently emphatic images reverberated in the harmony of their context determine the particular expression of a dance, its poetic character, its human implications. When they appear large, free, and clear, a dance is fascinating, it is expressive. (I don't mean that expression is necessarily rationalizable—the Waltz of the Flowers in *The Nutcracker*, for instance, is completely expressive.) Though the dances of *Cinderella* are clear in many ways—but the emphasis of them is not always clear—the emphasis doesn't make luminous the special kind of motion that is the dance's subject matter. This is why the ballet seems slight. But because *Cinderella* shows that Ashton, in the many passages where he has expression, has it without oddity, without forcing his gift or his discipline, it shows his natural power and his achieved craftsmanship. I think the piece shows these qualities further developed than *Symphonic Variations* or than *Scènes de Ballet* (his best), though these two are better theater, more sustained in brilliance. Because of its slightness and its length the good qualities of *Cinderella* are likely to be overlooked when the sameness of its gentleness in everything it does, even in its clowning, begins to make itself felt more strongly than the harmony of its tone. And for people not susceptible to its charming transparency the piece must seem a weak one the first time they see it.

It may be Broadway hawks would find so transparent a piece invisible. For myself, I might have been less open to *Cinderella*'s shy spell had I been in an audience less forbearing than that of Covent Garden. Even at the premiere they looked at the ballet so to speak discreetly, almost as one watches family theatricals, as if the dancers weren't professionals. Afterwards in the lobby I was to find that they saw as clearly as any other audience, but while the performers were working they gave the impression of seeing only the good things. The rules of first-night sportsmanship are very different in New York and Paris. But at the *Cinderella* opening, the audience's county family serenity (wonderfully exotic, so it seemed to me as a foreigner) was also due to the influence of a local ritual I knew nothing of, of which I became aware only a few days later when I saw another *Cinderella*, this time at the Palladium. Watching my first Christmas pantomime, with piping children around me and elders beaming at everything, with slapstick-clowning Dames and Cinderella in the same costume as Moira Shearer, and a Good Fairy to wave her wand (the same model as at Covent Garden) and start transformation scenes, and with a Harlequin-descended Buttons—and what a good one!—who "placed" for me the Jester in Ashton's piece, I realized how many childhood echoes the ballet awakens in its public which a foreigner can't share. To the British public *Cinderella* is not in a revived ballet form; as soon as the curtain goes up, the travesty Ugly Sisters at their sewing make everyone feel safe at home in the living pantomime ritual the audience has known all its life.

Thanks to the ritual Ashton was able to use two of the company's three strongest theater personalities—Helpmann and himself—in long parts which made the ballet's success. Margot Fonteyn, the greatest of the three, was cast for Cinderella, and her presence when she dances again will of course change the value of the central figure. Shearer in Fonteyn's part is lovely to look at, graceful and true in movement, and her legs are fine; Violetta Elvin in the same part is more interesting and alive on stage, and while she isn't more proficient, she has a grander kind of schooling (a more forceful bearing and thigh action); but she creates at best her own role, she has not the imaginative radiance by which a ballerina creates a world of romance on the stage all around her. Somes is a clean dancer and is unusually vivid at his first entrance. Nerina's Spring is charming. No part is done poorly, the whole company is attractive, bright, and well trained (though in too small-stepping a style) and they did all Ashton asked. He could have given them more had they developed in themselves more boldness and vivacity, qualities which involve a love of acting as well as dancing. But their general outlook of honesty, their sense of good manners, and their reticent willingness to dance has a touching quality of its own. Helpmann in the piece is a model of generosity and intelligent good taste. He gives everyone, particularly Ashton, every chance, knowing very well he could upset the balance at any moment by a single gesture delivered full force.

The costumes by Malclès are pretty; his decoration, though less stiff than the décor of several British ballets I have seen, aims for a homey-timid charm that only partly comes off. The Prokofiev score is in a homey style too, but not in the least timid. It is much more vigorous theater than the ballet. It is completely adroit in continuity, always ready with tunes and lively rhythms, never dull or thick, and also with no noticeable counterpoint, completely danceable, brilliantly sustained for the ball. All this can't be praised too highly and it helps Ashton immensely. But a facile and casual irony in it, suited no doubt to the brilliant Moscow production, doesn't suit the quiet London one. The score doesn't ever gather in a nonnarrative, a contemplative climax, an expression of the faith in a marvel which a fairy tale has. It wasn't Prokofiev's intention to repeat what Tchaikovsky had said so well already, but for all the score's large-scale vitality its character seems guarded compared to the innocent sweetness of nature of Ashton. Ashton's spontaneity is nearer to Haydn.

So Ashton has made *Cinderella* well and made it fun; it isn't a great ballet but he is a great choreographer, and proves it in this piece; and that it is a complete popular hit is a pleasure too.

Ballet, FEBRUARY 1949

AN OPEN LETTER ABOUT THE PARIS OPÉRA BALLET

I wanted to write you an article about ballet at the Maggio Musicale as you suggested, but I couldn't, so I started a letter and then began to rewrite it to find out what I meant; here it is, it turned out to be just about the Paris Opéra.

What I most looked forward to at the Maggio was my first sight of Vyroubova. I agree with you about her entirely. After three steps I loved her—delicious figure, limpid style, sweet absorption. To be sure by the time she had done four ballets I didn't love her as much more as I had looked forward to when she first began; but there was no reason either to love her any less.

She has the sweetest Russian-style virtues. A long foot, quick thigh, delicate bust, small head far from the shoulder. The step has edge, the arms are a classicist's dream, the carriage of the head has distinction, the face makes sense. She is unusually accurate and musical. I thought her best number here was that in *Suite en Blanc* (Vaussard's part, I think), which she did with a kind of demi-caractère liveliness in grace that suited the steps perfectly. She did each of her four parts as if it were a different woman dancing, discovering the impersonation in the impetus of the steps, sustaining it without a break from the first move to the last, with no mannerisms of her own showing ever. (Her other ballets were *Mirages*, *Dramma per Musica*, and *Divertissement*, all Chauviré parts.) It was adorable to see how she—a dancer of little experience dancing new parts in a company new to her—by instinct at once accepted the complete responsibility for the piece; to see her go straight for the main thing, the reality of her role and of the imaginative world in which it can be real; to see her conceive of the importance of a character not in terms of rank but in terms of purity of motive, and impersonate beauty in the cleanest steps she could make. Her decision on all this was unhesitating. And it gave her that lovelier authority onstage which I am sure Margot has always had.

It's all there, but on the other hand not yet pronounced enough. Her technique is well rounded and sufficient but not virtuoso. Her waist is weak. And the last two nights here she tired. Nor did she show the variety of accentuation, the nuance in phrasing a finished dancer can; in this particular Chauviré was more interesting than she. And Vyroubova, at least here, did not make her parts magnificent with those movements of complete climax, of lovely stillness that a ballerina is born to express. She is a darling, but she should turn into a marvel, a complete marvel. I wish she could join Sadler's Wells and have the benefit of all you discreet idealists; and since she is the brightest hope in Europe for another great ballerina five years from now, in a sense it's your duty. I think, too, that in a couple of years Balanchine could make her long legs twice as long and give her a stunning elegance of attack.

Toumanova was here too, just the opposite of all V.'s virtues, and wonderful. She was at her worst: careless feet, limp and wormy arms, brutally deformed phrasings; in allegro she was a hoyden, in adagio it was a bore waiting for her to get off that stubby toe; she waddled complacently, she beat time, she put on a tragically wronged stare (Second Avenue style—lower Second Avenue), she took absurdly graceless and completely unconvincing bows. It upset me while I was in the theater; but the next day it seemed only ridiculous, I'd half forgotten it, and it had no connection with moments I couldn't help remembering the grandeur of: a few terrifying extensions, a few incisive strokes that counted phenomenally. At those moments she had so much vitality she made everyone else look as if they merely crept or scuttled about her while she danced. It wasn't ballet she did, it wasn't any kind of dancing anybody ever heard of, but it was dancing on some sort of grand scale, it was the real thing in that sense.

I liked Renault very much. His acting is naive, his waist wiggles and his wrist-flaps are silly, he has learned no distinction (Blasis ports de bras and head positions, effacés and harmonies of contrapposto—men look raw without them). But each time the steps grow difficult and strenuous, he forgets his foolishness, and I don't care about his faults. He whirls and leaps in the rush of action, he likes pouring out his strength, he dances on a big scale, and the joy of it then is contagious. And when he looks honest, simple, and sweet natured.

The season as a whole was received in a friendly way, not with the enthusiasm I had seen here last year for Sadler's Wells.

I enjoyed *Palais de Cristal*, though friends who know the New York version complained bitterly of the slow tempos which they told me disfigured it. Lifar's ugly edition of *Sleeping Beauty* (*Divertissement*) makes me cringe like a knife scraping on a plate. His own works at their best have a curious antimusical and desperate pound; apart from this personal quality—at its strongest in *Suite en Blanc*—I can see no interest in them that lasts. With poor choreography ballet loses for me its nerve; but usually I am happy anyway watching a good company dance.

As companies go, the Paris Opéra one seems to me very good, and here the credit is Lifar's; they looked fresher, better disciplined, and better rehearsed than when I last saw them a year and a half ago. I liked them all very much as professionals. They are attractive, well built, loyal, and gifted. They believe in doing what they do with attention and individual imagination. When they begin they suggest a kind of glitter of stylishness onstage that fills me with happy expectation. They show at once that they are going to have variety of expression, that they are not going to do the immature juvenile charm act far too many adult Anglo-Saxon dancers do. So I look forward to the dance action to come when their interesting expressions will become an interesting grace of movement, when it will bloom and shed a radiance over the stage as a dancer's expression does in dancing.

Instead, what I see is different. The dance action looks small and constricted and close, it makes the dancers become short-limbed. In the general effect of shrinkage, the dancers keep their pointed expressions, and the result is arch. Affectedly so, it often seems to me. When I see them stepping out gingerly, when I see a large bold step modestly diminished and a stabbing rapid one becomingly blurred, see the girls separate their thighs as if reluctant to do that in public, the world of decent domesticity it conjures up appals me. And when I catch fretful flappings and crookings of elbows, dissatisfied glances of the girls toward each other and irritated ones at the conductor, a fluster of waist wriggles, wrist flicks, and head tosses, the expression reminds me of a nervous woman who can't resist tidying up her furniture and her person after the guests have already sat down. The boys seem to take the feminine flurry with a slightly superior or interestingly sullen male detachment, though their own action is not free of what look like fatuous flourishes and they promenade about with a tight bouncy step that looks silly. All this is my first impression and at this point I realize I have misunderstood everything so far and missed the point completely. So I look more closely at what is happening.

The dancers are well built and strong; but I begin to see that the Opéra style transforms them according to its own ideas of grace. It makes their figures in action look thick and droopy in the middle, stumpy and brief at the ends. The figure doesn't hold its shape in the air as it moves. Necks shrink in, shoulders hunch, waists sag and bob, thighs seem to take on weight. The step becomes unresilient, timid, and short; the tempo spurts nervously and drags. The pulse of the rhythm is weak. The style makes the dancers look like sedentary persons dancing.

They are painstakingly trained to. They do the step correctly, but they do it only from the hip joint down. Similarly they do arm motions from the shoulder out. (The ports de bras are altered as a rule from a correct shape into a resemblance to expressive gesture.) The Paris Opéra style avoids using the tremendous strength of waist and back to move with, to move the thighs and upper arms freely and equally. The Ballet Russe or Russian-derived style uses the full strength of the back to initiate, to sustain, and to reabsorb a movement, as Negro dancing does too. It gives these styles a kind of follow-through effect, an ease in flow; it gives the dancers a straight but not stiff back, a long neck. In ballet, without the full strength of the back their figures bunch up awkwardly in motion, they lose the carriage in large steps, they don't deploy fully in the air. They lose their speed, their spring, their impetus, their vigor in resilience. They don't sustain the continuity, they don't reach the large-scale virtuosity or the large-scale vitality they otherwise would. The Paris Opéra dancers don't, not through weakness, but because the style avoids such effects.

The style's idea of musical grace in dancing is as peculiar as its idea of grace of movement, I mean equally puzzling to a balletgoer used to the Russian-derived style. The Opéra dancer likes to put the dance stress where the shape of the musical phrase gives it no support; so it gets a petulant look. She likes to begin a shade behind the beat as if prettily taken unaware, and end a little ahead as if in confusion; then she adds a vigorous flip of the wrist on the last note, which by being synchronized makes the wrist suddenly look disproportionately big, as big as a leg. I speak from the standpoint of the Russian style, which treats the score like a glorious partner on whose strength the dancers soar and dart and effortlessly end. By contrast the Opéra style has the music run along beside the dancer like a stray dog—it keeps shying away from her when she stops and getting underfoot when she goes on again. An accomplished Opéra dancer is one who makes one forget what a nuisance it is.

But such a view is based on the assumption that the Paris Opéra style is doing worse what the Russian style does better. Looking at it closer, the Opéra style indicates on the contrary that its intentions are different to begin with. Its conception of rhythm and of phrasing inclines away from that of the music and toward that of speech. The general effect is not unlike that of speech rhythm. The dancer shapes her phrases by giving them point, as one would in speaking. She selects a step in the sequence and points it up, giving it a slight retard and a slight insistence, and she lets the other steps drop around it so to speak casually and a shade hastily, much as a glittering conversationalist stresses the telling word, delivers his epigram and seems to throw the rest of the sentence away. Following the step rhythm as speech rhythm—and as speech rhythm set against music—one can find virtuoso subtleties and ingenuities in the phrasing of an Opéra soloist, odd little vivacities, implications, hesitancies, bursts of rhetoric, tiny gusts of inspiration that hurry her onward. We Anglo-Saxons think a dancer looks like a lady when she dances divinely; but that is our lack of realism. The Paris style doesn't mean to transport you so far from the appearances, from the awkward graces and characteristic reserves of normal sedentary city life. The point of unprofessional carriage and unmusical rhythm is to make the dancer look less like a marvelous vision and more like an opinionated Parisian with all her wits about her whom one might meet in a room full of conversation.

Other traits of the Opéra style seem to resemble characteristics of French conversation, too. Ranking dancers are expected to dance against each other as acute conversationalists are expected to talk each other down. Agreement is not considered interesting and when everybody dances it's like everybody talking at once. To pause awhile onstage is like keeping still; it's a sign of respect, not of listening. Listening doesn't count, it's nothing to make a point of; and a dancer doesn't make her stillness a part of the rhythm of the general dance—in the way a singer makes her silence as well as her voice a part of the music.

The Paris Opéra style has its own view of what a performance is about. The dancers do not present a ballet as though it were a stage drama. There is no collective attempt to create the illusion of a poetic event taking place before our eyes. They don't come on as imaginary characters whose fate is unknown but foreordained. They come on instead in their official character as Opéra dancers. The ballet is a ceremony which offers them an occasion for the exhibition and the applause suitable to their various ranks. The excitement of the official ceremony is in the suggestion they individually convey of being people it would be delightful to know at home. And that is perhaps why the dancers scatter in all directions a great many of those little shakes, peckings, and perks of the head that look so pretty around a Paris dinner table, though coupled to the foot activity of ballet they unfortunately give an effect of witlessness.

I am under the impression that Parisians of taste (who can remember Diaghilev) take the Opéra style far less seriously than I have. They are surprised anyone should. They know there is no one onstage who does it with the acuteness of wit, the stylishness of presence it calls for, or with imaginative scope; and that there are many whose airs and graces are more respectable than stylish. The best Opéra dancers try to Russianize their dancing, and even the Opéra fans encourage them to.

And as for me, I see that by instinct I can hardly be fair to the style. The weak rhythm it has by choice depresses me as I watch. The fun of ballet is in the feet—in the feet and the bearing and the mutual response of the bodies in motion. The spring and edge and lift of ballet is in its relation to the beat—and to the beat in the full variety and extension which the musical animation of a piece of music gives it through musical structure. Of course, dancers are actors too, and their acting gestures can be delightful, noble, even thrilling. But their most wonderful moments of all come when they are in the middle of dancing. Their expression then looks unintentional. The wit or the sentiment it communicates, the ravishing lyric flight or sweeping collective transport is in the impetus of the dancing bodies, in the sustained pulse of their motion in space. The force of the communication, its imaginative scope, is in a kind of reverberation with which the resilient pulse of a rhythmic stream enlarges the hint of natural behavior that appears in a momentary movement of dancing, transfiguring it in the exhilaration of sustained buoyancy into a poetic image as innocent as the action of fate. I love the thrill of such a grace in meaning. But large-scale vitality in ballet, even apart from any meaning, is also a pleasure, deeper than it seems. The Paris Opéra style has too weak a pulse, too weak a dance rhythm for these two kinds of exhilaration.

Poor Lifar. He looks older onstage than Dolin or Massine. He has had the misfortune to put on weight all over him except between knee and ankle. (And he insisted on leaving no doubt in the matter by appearing as a Greek statue.) Dolin and Massine at least have extraordinary stage presences and are able to conceal some of the weaknesses of their dancing. Here in Florence Lifar wasn't able to conceal any weakness of his; but what surprised even more, he had no stage presence at command with which to pull his performance together. He worked harder than anyone and completely in vain. I haven't the heart to blame him, remembering his beauty and his genius; but if one doesn't, one has to blame Hirsch.

And one has to blame Hirsch too for not suppressing the three recent short ballets of Lifar which were shown here, *Pavane*, *L'Inconnue*, and *Entre Deux Rondes*. The first might have been devised for an end-of-the-year party at a desperate dancing school. The other two looked just as batty. One was earnest about the Decay of Western Civilization and resembled an apache number; the other was gay about Our Enduring

Cultural Values and offered gambols by a Greek Statue and a Degas Ballet Girl. Tudor could have made wonderful little pieces out of both by making them loathsome intentionally.

There was a piece of business in Lifar's *Giselle*, Act Two, which was new to me. Mourning at her tomb, he seemed for some time unwilling to part with the flowers he had brought. He held them out, snatched them back, looked at them appreciatively. Mastering his emotion, he sacrificed them and fainted. But Giselle, dead as she was, rushed out from the wings with a much bigger bunch and pelted him with it headlong. So prompt, so sweet of her, so fitting. He lay drowned in flowers. If only the audience had given way to its impulse, had leapt to its feet in rapture and tossed hundreds of bouquets more, aiming them from all over the house, what a perfect moment of art it would have been for all of us to share with him!

Still, I believe Lifar inspires his company. Their devotion to him, their faith in virtues of his no longer visible onstage, is touching. A few company mannerisms seem imitations of mannerisms formerly his own as a dancer; that is foolish but not meretricious. Distasteful, however, is the way his choreography keeps making the dancers look pompous.

Ballet, JULY–AUGUST 1950

A LETTER ABOUT ULANOVA

About Ulanova. She is a very great dancer, no doubt of that, even seeing her as we did very awkwardly presented. What we all saw first was the magnificent schooling and the admirable personal discipline. You know how touching that is when you see a dancer not allowing herself to monkey with the rules. What we saw was a wonderful flow of movement sustained and sustained, a sort of cantilena style of dancing with beautiful legs (marvelously shaped arabesques of all kinds, and so clearly differentiated too), and beautiful elbows. The very beginning of a movement is fresh and quick and almost at once the motion so begun slows down to a strong full velvet flow; and before the flow has stopped, without any break (like a fresh current that appears from below in a wide even stream of water), the new next motion begins, clear and decisive, and that one too seems to·be already flowing calm and sustained. It isn't the bird or dragonfly style of dancing, it's a kind of aspiration upwards: lightness as a longing and a dream rather than as a possession. I can't think of any one dancer we know who has that particular quality; nor is it one that goes with being a model pure-classicist: it's romantic. Ulanova makes herself more heavy and more light, too, like a romantic. And another quality she shows is that of not presenting herself to the audience, of being like someone who is dancing for herself, a sort of half-in-shadow-in-the-deep-woods quality. There isn't much conscious response between her and her partner, I mean all those conscious little consciousnesses. In the same way that the pulse of the rhythm is broad and slow, so the characterization or flavor or key of the dance is barely noticeable; it's there but it's only appreciable after a while. There's something covered, a sort of inner life unconsciously revealed, that carries her more than it directs her. (I'm speaking not of her personally but of the kind of stage personality that comes across.) Of course one can fall in love with such a special creature; or else not. Some people were crabby—I mean a few ballet fans I spoke to.

Of course it's nonsense to pass judgment after seeing her dance half a dozen numbers with piano accompaniment in front of black curtains, awkwardly costumed, without a company or a ballet to set her off, and with a foreign audience, who probably expected a triumphant beauty and saw instead a modest little-girl-style creature. The general theater style that was indicated—I mean the kind of overall performance atmosphere or manner, which is different according to whether the dancers are Parisian, Danish, British, or from New York—that theater style was quite different from any of our various ones; which makes a confusion too. Just as what Parisians think pretty New Yorkers are likely to think affected, and just as Parisians think mechanical what we see as unaffected and friendly, so there was about the Soviet atmosphere a strange absence of chic or bite or risk or individualized projection. It struck us who were foreign to it as homey, and goody-goody. And sometimes this tone made Ulanova seem a bit puss-in-the-corner, which I imagine one wouldn't think in a big long piece where she can gradually make the character clear.

Her weaknesses as a dancer seemed at this performance to be a kind of thickness, a kind of lack of ease at the base of the neck and all round there in the region of the breast and shoulders. This makes her neck look short, and doesn't give her head that queenly port that is so lovely; but then queenliness isn't her style. Her feet aren't delicately placed when she steps, nor are the hands and wrists so good. But the arms don't suffer, and she has a marvellous lightness in the knees. Though her pas de bourrée weren't beautiful, her feet stretched in the air always were. And particularly beautiful were all her poses in lifts. Really beautiful lifts. I liked a few mime gestures she made very much too.

I liked her second number immensely—for the lifts, much more exact than we make them, and more varied. It's practically the *Sylphides* pas de deux. Next best I liked the *Casse-Noisette*. Number three, *Chopin*, to music from Schumann's *Carnaval*, was a Greek supported adagio with veil, by Chaboukiani, absurd in style to us. The final Rubinstein waltz was an allegro with bunches of flowers and a very pretty saut de poisson, I couldn't find out by whom; but this also looks to us very démodé in style. The style it resembles is a sort of super dinner-dance adagio couple style; of course it's done so very prettily. *The Dying Swan* I liked least, but she got an ovation for it. The choreography of the two other pieces, the Rubinstein and the *Red Poppy*, was uninteresting, but the style is too different to judge at a glance.

Perhaps what I missed in Ulanova's dancing was the want of those moments that affect me so, those moments of rest in a dance when a movement resolves for a hair's breadth of time into repose and finishes, and there is like a sense of eternity from which the dancing and the movement re-arise. I didn't see this completion of repose in her dancing.

Her partner, Kondratov, was a pleasant young man, with no intentions as to what we think of as style or grace, a trifle muscle-bound, completely unaffected. He was a marvelously sure partner, and one who could support her on one upstretched hand, and so forth. Her balance wasn't sure at this performance, and his support was both unnoticeable and pleasing. I don't approve of dancers who don't dance like dancers, but it was interesting to see one so well trained and so simpatico. The Parisians, however, were utterly dismayed by such an apparition.

The musical part of the program was bad. The dance accompanists were wonderful as such. (A good deal of rubato, but never noticeable.)

Oh yes, I forgot to mention Ulanova's wonderfully lyric entrances and exits, so soft, merging into an infinite continuation.

This is what I saw so far; I'm coming again to her second concert. (I came back from Greece for her, and was so excited the afternoon before she danced I had to go to bed with a fever.) Maybe next time I'll see more calmly. Beryl de Zoete exclaimed afterwards that she'd never seen dancing before, which was the reaction I hoped to have, but didn't. That she belongs with the half-dozen great geniuses we know is obvious too.

Ballet, AUGUST 1951

A LETTER ABOUT ULANOVA AND THE ROYAL DANISH BALLET

I went back to Florence for Ulanova's second recital. She danced, I think a critic would have said, even better: the same large clear strong movement, the same calm lightness of strength, and the wonderful velvet flow. The timing is perfection: each phrase of movement, of the step or arm gesture, materializes at the exact speed and with the right urgency to make it visible in itself and coherent in the sequence, as movement and as plastic image; a perfectly proportioned continuity or dance phrase. Great musicians play music with a similar absolute clarity of proportions in the continuity, so you follow it completely, and it makes sense. Whether that sense is interesting as sense is not what I am speaking of at the moment; the quality of making sense of a dance as dancing is in itself rare and beautiful in the extreme degree in which she has it.

In details of action I saw again the same beautifully distinct and sure arabesques and attitudes, the same beauty in lifts and complicated lift sequences, a beautiful small développé (her style is so much in the développé spirit that I wish she had had occasion to do lots of large slow ones). She did a very pretty quick five- or six-turn finger pirouette. She did very clear large renversés, but I liked some small ones even better. She did some nice bourrées this time, but they aren't apparently one of her great gifts; nor did balance seem to be. I didn't get an impression of her gifts in second position; I saw (at the first performance) a pretty leap, but not how much bounce she has in a series; that wouldn't seem her style, but then her Giselle is famous. The shape of the knee is perhaps not quite ideal by nature, but the leg extension and stretched foot in the air are always beautiful.

I was left in doubt on one major point of the schooling, that impression of opaqueness I mentioned in the chest and shoulders (the line of the body in motion doesn't seem to travel through the upper thorax up into the neck and head easily; the head doesn't seem to have enough—how shall I say?—harmonious dignity). I didn't see the effects of schooling in Blasis's head positions, which is another way of putting it, perhaps. And floor contact and hands (wrists) seemed to have been understressed in schooling. Here in Italy, where in daily life one sees so much elegance and ease of carriage, so many pretty hands and feet, one's eye notices these things more than elsewhere. Neither Ulanova nor her partner has a "sensuous" grace of movement, or any intention of having it.

The number I liked best on the second program was a dance from *Cinderella*; she was completely pervasively "in character." I don't mean that she was an English or an Italian Cinderella, but she was her own kind. She was first gently pleased to be waltzing with him, then gently sportive in a sort of period step; gently she refused a crown he offered and then was gently proud when after she'd put it on him he nicely put it on her; and she was happy, oh! so mildly blissful; then, resuming the waltz at a quicker tempo, she was gone. It was all completely clear and convincing, touching and sweet; her head was too sweet in its little gestures. And yet I wondered that the contact between the two of them seemed so generalized that it didn't seem an extraordinary, unique event, it seemed too blunted to me in its particularity, in its keenness.

Partly, I thought, from the lack of keenness of definition in the movements of the extremities; partly from the plainness in the plastic images of the choreography. As plainness, the choreography was excellent: every stage of the encounter entirely clear in statement, smooth in flow, and convincing in development. Their spiritual intimacy was expressed by supported arabesques and attitudes. (Her promenade en arabesque is marvelous, especially penchée.) But I thought of those encounters in Balanchine, those extraordinary images of unique moments of fate, Shakespearean in the startling brilliance they have, and with such delicacy in the power of their imagery as contacts.

She repeated *The Dying Swan*, and though she did it even more meticulously than the first time (and received an even louder ovation) I wondered that I saw neither the uniqueness of the swan creature nor the image of death. I saw a pang and then it was over; I was puzzled. The execution had been so careful. She also did a "Danse Russe" (mixed character and classic), which she began as a smiling village beauty and, gradually becoming mystical, ended as a sort of icon figure. It seemed neither suited to her (she isn't "earthy" or "abundant") nor a good dance. Even so, the timing of the execution couldn't have been better.

As for Kondratov, he had an opportunity of being more varied in style, and he was suiting the style to the number, characterizing (as she did) in a pervasive rather than a scintillating manner, but staying completely in the role. In *Cinderella* he had, in particular at the climax, a kind of free manly courage in the pose of the head for a moment that was very good. He also did a fine Russian dance (big leaps, a pirouette that slowed down, rousing rush and all), which was a great pleasure. He couldn't have been more straightforward, and the audience at his second time liked him very much; so did I. I don't care for the opaque look about the shoulder blades or the walk with not-quite-stretched hip joints (vaguely hurt style); but he is a very good dancer in a style intentionally athletic.

Curious, I thought, the effect the dancing as a whole gives of being built as a continuity rather than as a rhythm; it flows and flows with a slow pulse under its rubato and it never suggests an edge or an end. I missed in it the sharpness, the brilliance of edge and the daring, the risk and commitment. I didn't enjoy the blunted effect, the sense of a generalized blur in contact, in the mutual contact of the figures of the dance too. I missed seeing a human keenness of mutual response which makes a dramatic moment on stage unique and marvelous, that instinct for beauty in the face of the very present. I felt again that homeyness of the first time, like that of a party where everybody acts nice and sweet and "good," but no one thaws out or ventures to commit himself, so that the goodness becomes stuffy and thick-skinned. There was a Wordsworth quality about it. I've seen American dancers with a similar quality, but choreographers counterbalance it by a sharpness of edge in execution and in the plastic images themselves—what the literary critics call poetic irony. All I mean to say on this subject is that on these two programs I missed seeing it. (The Chaboukiani number, at second view, seemed to have a richness of plastic imagination, in the lifts rather than the steps; but Petipa is much bolder in imagery, more decisive and keen.)

The general impression as poetic theater was far more disappointing than I expected. Obviously one doesn't draw general conclusions from a few excerpts, from seeing only two dancers, poorly programmed, badly costumed, with very uninteresting musical numbers performed between the few dances. Her I liked best in the *Sylphides*-style number on the first program, where her "slow-motion" gift and art shone at its brightest and clearest. And the exit was ravishing. That at least was a moment which I shall always remember, and remember as beautifully her own. A marvelous dancer.

Trudy Goth saw Ulanova, and said she was definitely unhappy about performing excerpts. Also she loved the baskets one can buy in Florence; very sweet and mild.

I had such a good time reading about your Danish holiday, being back in Copenhagen and watching them again, and was so happy seeing those dancers have a big success. I would adore seeing all of *Napoli*, which I agree with you is a work of genius, of the happy kind. I saw the first act in rehearsal, and what a pleasure it was, and how very Neapolitan-inspired! I loved the ensemble dance saying "A storm is rising," which ended by all the men (or was it everyone?) holding up one finger the way one does to see which way the wind is coming. And I loved the hero's return from sea: exhaustion, then realization he was safe, gratitude, and only then—so Italian, so un-Anglo-Saxon—did he realize that his beloved was lost in the waves? And then he was furious. He didn't rush to save her; he first cursed his destiny. Adorable! I thought the Lander *Etudes* very effective, but heavy and with little grace of spirit. The Galeotti piece on the other hand I was all enchanted by; and admired how neatly placed, how agreeably varied and clearly timed it was. I don't agree about *Coppélia*, though; I think the U.S. Monte Carlo version the best by far I know, and one of the great ballets—especially when Balanchine cleaned it up in '45. (He said then that the pas de huit in Act One—the girls' number after the Ear of Wheat—was the inspiration for all his choreography.) But if you have my book you'll find something about this version, also explaining why the Hours, Prayer, etc. are important to the poetic story; just folk dances at the end don't make the transfiguration necessary to a real ballet story.

But I agree with you entirely about the mime marvels at Copenhagen. I liked Gerda Karstens very much, but didn't see *Sylphide*: I only saw her giving a class in mime to the eighteen-year-olds of the scene where James is rude to the Witch; and deliciously they did it. I remember an excellent boy and excellent girl, but not their names. I remember Larsen's Coppélius as *very* fine, also everything else he did. (Didn't see the Greenland number.) In fact he was my favorite of all. I thought the company didn't have much training in continuity of movement or in large-scale line; their small, that is parlor-size, line is very good; its timid hint of line has a charm with the general Copenhagen sweetness. That is, the girls'. Margot Lander had a bigger style and much more projection. I wasn't entranced; thought she was doing it a bit too hard, a bit too star "effectiveness"; a bit too tired and without that dear sincerity of the others, whose ineffectiveness obviously bored her. (Ineffectiveness in the sense of lack of projection and theater accent where it counts.) The *Giselle* version I saw her in was a poor one, too. She was best in the *Napoli* rehearsal. I thought the company didn't turn well, or balance or land from jumps well. They have extraordinary second positions, and probably, though I don't remember, fine passés; fine batterie, charming though small arm poses, a delicious parlor propriety, excellent stage manners (all except that dear hot Icelander of theirs), and, of course, above all, a perfectly serious and poetic mime tradition.

It's the real pre-Russian style: I have an idea everybody but the Taglioni-

Grisi-Elssler geniuses used to dance with small steps. However, the Blasis figures show big steps, so I'm wrong.

Ballet, OCTOBER 1951

IMPRESSIONS OF MARKOVA AT THE MET

Alicia Markova has become that legendary figure, the last of the old-style ballerinas. Her second *Giselle* with Ballet Theatre this fall season broke a box-office record at the Metropolitan Opera House. Five people fainted in standing room. She did the contrary of everything the new generation of ballerinas has accustomed us to. With almost no dazzle left, Markova held the house spellbound with a pianissimo, with a rest. A musician next to me was in tears, a critic smiled, a lady behind me exclaimed "Beautiful!" in an ecstatic, booming voice. Her dancing was queerer than anyone had remembered it. A few days later, meeting a balletomane usually far stricter than I on the street, I asked him what he thought of her this season. "More wonderful than ever," he cried aggressively. When I asked if he thought she had shown this defect or that, he admitted each in turn, but his admiration was as pure as before. This is the sort of wonder a real ballerina awakens, one our young dancers are too modest to conceive of, and that Markova's dancing used to do for me, too. Though I wasn't carried away this time, I found watching her so-different method intensely interesting.

Details were extraordinary—the beautiful slender feet in flight in the soubresauts of *Giselle* Act Two, how she softly and slowly stretches the long instep like the softest of talons as she sails through the air; or in the échappés just after, how they flash quick as knives; or in the "broken steps" of the mad scene of Act One, when, missing a beat, she extends one foot high up, rigidly forced, and seems to leave it there as if it were not hers. I was happy seeing again those wonderful light endings she makes, with the low drooping "keepsake" shoulders, a complete quiet, sometimes long only as an eighth note, but perfectly still. I recognized, too, the lovely free phrasing of the *Sylphides* Prelude, so large, though not so easy as once. Best of all, better than before, I thought her acting in *Giselle* Act One. Surer than I remembered is the dancelike continuity she gives her gestures and mime scenes—all the actions of the stage business embedded in phrases of movement, but each action so lightly started it seemed when it happened a perfectly spontaneous one. In this continuity, the slow rise of dramatic tension never broke or grew confused. It was the technique of mime in the large classic style.

In classic miming, a sense of grandeur is given by stillness that is "inside" a phrase of movement the way a musical rest is "inside" a musical phrase. Markova's strong continuity of phrasing, the clarity of shape that mime gestures have when they are made not like daily-life gestures but like dance movements from deep down the back, and her special virtuosity in "rests"—these give her miming grandeur. But for dancing, her strength is too small for the grand work of climaxes. She cannot keep a brilliant speed, sustain extensions, or lift them slow and high; leaps from one foot begin to blur in the air; her balance is unreliable. In ballet it is the grand power of the thighs that gives magnanimity to the action; there is no substitute and a ballet heroine cannot do without it. Once one accepts this disappointment, one can watch with interest how skillfully she disguises the absence: by cuts, by elisions, by brilliant accents, by brio, by long skirts, by scaling down a whole passage so that it will still rise to a relative climax.

A second disappointment for me was that her powerful stage presence (or projection) no longer calmly draws the audience to herself and into her story on the stage. Markova used particularly to practice that art of great legitimate-theater personalities of drawing the public to her into her own imaginary world; she used to be fascinatingly absorbed in that world. But now she often seems like a nervous hostess performing to amuse, eager to be liked; she pushes herself out on the public. It is a musical-comedy winsomeness and looks poor in classic ballet. It was, I thought, a serious mistake for a ballerina of such wide experience to make. Another error, a more trivial one, was the absurd way she danced the *Nutcracker* pas de deux—more like a provincial *Merry Widow* number than the *Nutcracker*—with a shrunken, slovenly action, bad knees, affectations of wrists and face; and for a Sugar Plum Fairy to be carelessly dressed was unfortunate.

But despite even bad mistakes, there remains her phenomenal old-fashioned style of delicate nuances in dancing. The methods she uses showed here and there and it was fun to look. For instance the divine lightness of attack: Merce Cunningham, with whom I was discussing her technique, spoke of the illusion she gives of moving without a preparation so you see her only already fully launched, as if she had no weight to get off the ground (the stretch from plié is so quick). He remarked very vividly that in a leap she seemed at once "on top of her jump, like an animal." He also pointed out how she uses this illusion to disguise the weakness of a développé—she throws the leg up in a flash with knee half extended, but all you become aware of is the adagio motion immediately after that—a slow dreamy extension of the beautiful instep.

Markova achieves her illusion of lightness not by strength—for strength she has only the instep, shoulder, and elbow left. But she draws on other virtuoso resources—the art of sharply changing the speed without breaking the flow of a movement; the art, too, of timing the lightninglike preparation so that the stress of the music will underline only the *following* motion, done at the speed of the music, which is meant to be displayed. As in her phrase beginnings and leaps up, so the same transformation of speed from presto to adagio is used for her weightless descents and her phrase endings—though for the latter, it takes her a beat or two more to subside into stillness than it used to. For the full effect of being stilled and immobile, she often brings forward her low shoulders into a droop, a gesture like a folding-in of petals, like a return into herself. This motion softens the precise stop of the feet, because it carries over for an unaccented count like a feminine ending, like the diminuendo effect of a port de bras which is finished a count later than the feet finish the step. Her softening forward droop in the shoulders also alters the look of the next new start, since the dancer takes an upbeat of straightening her shoulders, and so seems to lift and unfold into the new phrase. Such nuances of color or breathing or dynamics give to the old-fashioned style its fullness; but they easily become fulsome. One can watch Markova, however, use them to carve more clearly the contour of a phrase, to make it more visible and more poignant. Our current fashion in classicism is to avoid these nuances to make sure that they will not be used to conceal a cardinal weakness.

In contrast to the solid, sharp, professional, rather impatient brilliance of our grand and powerful young ballerinas, the kind of effect Markova makes seems more than ever airy and mild, transparent and still. The dancer seems to begin on a sudden impulse, and to end in an inner stillness. She seems less to execute a dance than to be spontaneously inventing. She seems to respond to the music not like a professional, but more surprisingly, more communicatively. It is an "expressive" style, as peculiar looking in New York as any Parisian one. It is one our dancers look quite clumsy at, and not only our own, who hardly ever try for it, but many Europeans too, who constantly do.

I have wanted to focus attention on the difference, but I don't mean to judge between these two styles. For my part, I enjoy our own new one because the neutral look of it, a sort of pleasant guardedness, seems to suit our dancers better. Someday they will find out how to open up, but in terms of a technique that suits them. Markova happened to learn a style that suited her physique, her temperament, her environment; and a born ballerina, she made the most of it. The public responds to her now, not because of her style, not because it is the right one, but because she is a wonderfully compelling theater artist. For me she was, this fall, exhibiting her highly elaborated style rather than dancing a dance or a role, and that limited my enjoyment. But for fans who love classic dancing, and because they love it are happy to see as much as they can of its possibilities, of its richness and scope, it is well worth seeing her perform effects no one in our generation is likely to make so lightly and so lucidly.

Dance Magazine, DECEMBER 1952

OBITUARY FOR "BALLET"

The London magazine *Ballet* closed suddenly after the October issue and went into voluntary bankruptcy. Founded just before the war, it had been resumed in '46 and in a short time became a publication unique in the dance world. "Ignorant," "irresponsible," "snobbish," "effete," "unpatriotic"—a string of adjectives by which one comes to recognize the presence of a critic of value—were hurled at its editor, Richard Buckle, more often and more vehemently than at any dance critic in English. A more honest word for his way of writing and of editing would have been "aristocratic."

Ballet had become the most attractive looking of dance magazines. Pleasing in its small size, handsome in its typefaces, appetizing in the transparent blacks of its reproductions, it presented itself with a specifically English elegance. It seemed to promise that inside the covers one would be addressed not as a harried fellow-professional, but—for once—as a guest at a pretty supper party. Pretty, but not entirely safe. As one looked inside, a line drawing or a photograph among the rest met one suddenly like a quick disconcerting glance.

Buckle let everyone else in his magazine talk more than he and louder.

But his own piece—commentary or a book review—was the first that one read in each new issue. His criticism was vivid, malicious, and well-bred; never niggardly. It had the mark of a born stylist. Written simply, it often took the dry tone of gentlemanly understatement that is a virtue more of the old England than of the new. To a New Yorker, it sounded unassertive. In London, as I found, it was the most feared, the most infuriating and valued. Despite its low-pitched voice and air of frivolous luxury, *Ballet* became the most powerful dance magazine in Europe.

Rereading them now, one finds in Buckle's opinions nothing freakish; they are reasonable and bright, they reveal a man of educated taste but also a man of character and constancy. He has faith enough in England to look at foreigners with interest. And he often reminds the British dance world of the stodginess that a complacent insularity leads to. Such a reminder is valuable in any ballet-producing city—New York as much as London. So, for instance, when the sweetly extravagant young Champs-Elysées company at its brightest first arrived from Paris in '46, though many Londoners loved it, the prevalent insular view condemned it as undignified. Buckle pointed to the value of such vivacity of imagination in dancing and such a grace of décor. It was only years later, when the Champs-Elysées itself had dimmed, that Sadler's Wells nodded its great head in assent to Buckle. Similarly when the authoritative opinion was that the Americans lacked French vivacity and English dignity, he noticed virtues; when the average London critic, educated on story ballets, complained that Balanchine's were undramatic and all alike, Buckle countered that whoever cares to look at the dancing in them will see how various, how noble, how powerfully dramatic they become. Last summer—so a local fan whose work makes him follow the English press told me—the reviews of the New York City company sounded, in general, even intentionally obtuse. (For my part, after sampling a few I had to stop; I felt an acute attack of chauvinism coming on.) Buckle took the situation as an English as well as an artistic impropriety. And besides pillorying the august London *Times*, he brought out a sheaf of really enlightening articles, the most original of which were his own and one by a young painter, Ronald Wilson.

Buckle influenced British taste by expressing his own more adventurous one. He kept looking. In a profusion of pictures, in special articles (many by Beaumont), and in the editor's commentary, *Ballet* offers the record of new ballets as they appeared in London and of English dancers. But it includes, richly illustrated as well, news from abroad; a special appreciation of the Royal Danish Ballet; accounts of all kinds of exotic dance styles seen by travelers or presented in London; vivid reminiscences by people of note; line drawings that the editor enjoyed looking at for a change; antiquarian iconography and texts in lively presentation. The energy of the editing is striking as one sees it expressed through the course of years. Buckle also took ballet lessons. He watched the development of young dancers. So, for instance, when David Blair was still a minor member of the Sadler's Wells junior company, it was he who took Dolin to see him dance; it turned out to be the decisive event in the career of this young man who at present is the only one of his generation who shows the gifts of a danseur noble of the very first quality. Buckle's guess then was wild, but it was lucky for England. And though so great and so unique an artist as Margot Fonteyn is showered on all sides with praise, Buckle's tributes, particularly the one when she was first to appear in New York, evoke her image with a delicacy of respect that is touching and poetic.

Naturally an English critic's chief concern is Sadler's Wells. In a sharp review of a new ballet, Buckle, touching on general questions it seemed to raise, spoke of the three directors, de Valois, Lambert, and Ashton, as the "three blind mice" of the nursery rhyme. It got him into real trouble. He found himself accused in the press of having caused the death of Lambert by his review. The accusation (by Sir Osbert Sitwell), though in vague words, seemed definite enough to people in the dance world, and Buckle would have been marked for life if he had left it unchallenged. To future gossip it would not matter that Constant Lambert, superbly gifted, proud, and combative, had died a month after the notice on his new ballet. He had died of diabetes. But bad as it could become for Buckle, the charge was also ignominious to the memory of Lambert. It is a pity that Ninette de Valois did not at once contradict it—for the sake of her dead friend and in view of Buckle's value to British ballet. Instead the accusation was repeated with emphasis. Buckle, abandoned by those who should most have defended him, was forced to clear up the shameful muddle in *Ballet*, and he did it in a brilliant polemical piece. He emerged from this sordid and dangerous episode with honor, and everyone shook hands all around.

Buckle is at his driest in danger. In his "Adventures of a Ballet Critic"—his own reminiscences occasionally printed in his magazine—there are passages as dangerous as snapshots of well-known persons caught in absurd situations; they are not unkind at all, but very lifelike and very funny. He does not diminish the good qualities of his subjects when he makes one laugh at them. But the fact that the humor lies in the literally reported actions and words of his victims leaves them no escape but to laugh at themselves. There are moments in an active life when this is difficult. Dame Ninette once exclaimed one was afraid to speak to him because one couldn't tell what he would print. "Aren't you afraid?" she asked me with indignation. "Of course," I answered timidly. "So you see!" she cried. But what I saw was that this dauntless woman was resenting his independence, resenting it volcanically like the empire builder she is. And I realized how much personal courage goes into Dickie Buckle's aristocratic sense of humor.

Ballet had behind it the personal courage necessary for elegance. A colleague, Miss Manchester, when she was told that the magazine had folded, exclaimed, "He had to have it beautiful." It is the highest of professional tributes. The magazine tried for the distinction of appearance and of character that ballet itself demands, and it maintained that effort under every conceivable difficulty. To do so was Buckle's personal responsibility toward the art he loves, his act of loyal homage. This aristocratic attitude was the unexplained source of the fascination *Ballet* exercised. Buckle is not the only educated and intelligent Englishman who writes about ballet, not at all. The other British dance magazines are sound and earnest, but I find I rarely read them. Their character lacks romance. Odd that in London, a city so proud of its culture, so proud of being the capital of Western ballet, the one monthly that reflected this pride gracefully for an international audience should have been allowed to close. Now it will no longer sting with momentary shame and it will no longer inspire with faith either.

Dance Magazine, JANUARY 1953

"STARS OF THE RUSSIAN BALLET": A FILM REVIEW

Stars of the Russian Ballet tries very nicely to give a front-row view of Soviet ballet. The dancers in it are members of Russia's two best companies, the stars are among the country's most brilliant. They dance *Swan Lake* (a revised version), *The Fountain of Bakhchisarai*, and *The Flames of Paris*; the latter two are Soviet productions of 1934 and 1932 and are based on character steps. At the Bolshoi each of the three would last a whole evening, but the film condenses them to eighty minutes all included.

On the screen flashes of dance and mime delighted me. It was fine to catch glimpses of many dancers, men as well as women, whose leg action was powerful and easy and whose mime was wholehearted. They created plenty of nervous excitement. But the effect as the film continued was disappointing. The dances kept disintegrating into banality, the mime into hubbub. Only in the *Swan Lake* adagio did a few film sequences suggest the grand theater power of a poetic image. The rest left me with an overdose of vitamins and virtue.

The men were thoroughly wholesome, the girls more earnest than gracious. The dancers enjoyed giving a big dynamic charge, being excited, strenuous; messiness and hamminess didn't bother them as long as there was a passionate conviction about whatever story content the piece afforded. Now and then, in a flash of mime, the storytelling was brilliant. But the dancers didn't leave it at that. They forced the emotion in blurred gestures, they tried to mime it at every step of a dance. The overall theater effect was repetitious, thick, and airless. They showed only one side of ballet, the side without wonder. They never created as a company the stillness in which wonder begins.

According to this film the Soviet choreographies are ineffectual and meager, the dancers are inelegant. That they are at their weakest in the court scenes of *Swan Lake* is only incidental. Elegance in ballet is not a mime effect or an imitation of court life. It is a sustained visual harmony of movement out of which ballet builds its theater effect of continuity and sweep. Without elegance the dancers can show no wit, no joyous freedom in absurdity; without it the choreographers cannot orchestrate a dance. Elegance is like the clean pitch in a musical instrument. Without it a choreographer cannot sustain a clean development; he cannot give his themes the larger powers of grace, of freshness, and of grandeur which sustained choreography can—nor the brilliant caress of a larger meaning, like that of poetry. In classic theatre, Western or Oriental, elegance is the medium for the communication of serious feeling. The film showed Soviet ballet attempting serious feeling without elegance, and wasting the power of its dancers. The theater excitement they created was what we call corny.

But film all over the world is poor at catching the beauty and very good at catching the silliness of any ballet. Film is like a scatterbrain with a beady swivel eye. Its field of vision is totally unlike that of a theater seat. This film showed the best intentions. But one could observe that the director had not stopped for retakes of a few dance errors, and that he had passed a few musical errors in synchronizing some *Swan Lake* sequences when the sound didn't fit the steps. Maybe he liked a bit of extra messiness as "more real," maybe he asked for an extra violence of attack in dance and mime (that a choreographer would not have permitted).

One cannot be certain how far this film falsifies the overall theater effect which the three ballets create on stage in Moscow or Leningrad. But it does photograph details of action that fans who are curious about Soviet ballet will enjoy being able to look at. A number are interesting. Beautiful are the two novel lifts in attitude (Ulanova carried by Sergeyev) in the *Swan Lake* adagio, which replace the Ivanov lifts with a développé and lead into the arabesque penchée promenade. The promenade itself did not eclipse the same passage as shown in the film *Russian Ballerina* (whenever the two films showed the same passage the older one made it look better). But the penchée of farewell in the last act was very fine. To see Ulanova's iron force clinch the leg at its extreme height, holding it against a backward arch in the spine tense as a bow, is like hearing a soprano hold a fortissimo high D without a tremor. The weightless look her body has in the air in lifts is extraordinary, and admirable the assurance with which her foot reaches the ground as she is lowered. And in the pas d'action, when she first meets the Prince, she descends beautifully from a piqué to full foot. Her shoes, and those of the chorus too, had no apparent blocking; though they gave her little support and spread easily, they gave an unusual delicacy to a number of toe steps. I admired less a mannerism she had of hopping up on toe, and another of bending back the hand emphatically from the wrist. In one renversé moment, when first one leg circled way back, then one arm with the wrist, then another arm with another wrist, she looked like a parody of herself, like an uneasy octopus.

In the girls of the swan chorus, too, one saw the handsome extreme sweep of a port de bras to a backward arm extension typical of the Maryinsky school, and which our good teachers also teach. The Soviet dancers add to such a movement a strong arch backward with both shoulders pulled back too; it gives the dancer the so-called "pouter pigeon" silhouette, and when the neck bends back as well, and one leg is stretched or lifted at the back, it makes a very grand deformation. But the Soviet dancers use it so much it turns into a mannerism. Sometimes they force the head forward despite the backbend; this gives the head a kind of clandestine look, as if it peeked out from behind a decapitated girl. Kind of creepy.

The swan chorus did the little it had to do perfectly. The Cygnets danced the steps ours do, but we should have judged their performance as average and a little slow.

Dudinskaya, who danced the Black Swan, often showed, like Ulanova, a poor neck. Her speed and sharpness were of virtuoso strength, but the violent way in which she danced her variation seemed to me very close to parody. It would be absurd to judge so celebrated an artist on the faults of one variation, especially as the passage seemed the worst-photographed spot in the film.

Sergeyev's classic action was large and harmonious. His leaps were fine in the air, but did not end cleanly. In his variation he presented the buoyancy of the dramatic moment very well, and neglected technical refinements we are used to seeing. Foot positions merely sketched, no turnout, no clear stretch in the ankles or groin, or at the base of the neck. He did not have the force of a hero or the polish of a prince, but he had a manly mildness, an uncompetitive projection, that were attractive.

In *The Fountain of Bakhchisarai*, Plisetskaya, a strikingly handsome woman, filled the part of Zarema, the harem queen. Her waist was a trifle square and the costume did not flatter her. But she had a big-scale dramatic temperament and proved to be a very strong dancer, somewhat acrobatic in style. It was noticeable that she spoiled several fine leaps by after-motions in the arms or by putting the accent of the leap not on the leg that reaches out, but on that which follows after. All through the film, in one way or another, one noticed similar deficiencies. Many striking dancers looked unevenly trained. Physically, men and women tended to look stocky in the waist. And the film sets and costumes were not at all imaginative.

In *The Flames of Paris* the great Chaboukiani appeared, whirling with a grandiosely volcanic temperament, an extraordinary whipping brilliance; but the miserable staging and direction of this ballet wasted the impact he made and blurred several other attractive moments.

The film showed as much mime as dancing. There was one interesting invention, that of Ulanova's death in the harem. She drooped against the wall on both pointes and slid, turning the feet so they sank with the arch against the floor. This moment of extinction and the brief last look of consciousness before it were wonderfully acted. As an actress she sustained the character of each of her two quite different major roles with an extraordinary wealth of nuance and no interruption. But her intensity of projection became in the film almost formidable. The shape of her gestures was often poorly invented and overcomplicated, and she delivered many of them in a half-crouch that made the feeling look ungenerous. None of these defects were apparent when she appeared onstage a few years ago in Florence in several concert numbers; her mime moments then were subtly and delicately poignant.

The mime of everyone in the film was completely sincere, and several of the male stars had flashes of grandeur. But as movement a great many of the gestures were foolish, confused, and poorly timed. Some of the chorus mime consisted of taking a very deep breath and coming up with a distorted face or a wildly flung arm. The general effect was what we call chewing the scenery. The part of acting that an actor feels seemed highly trained in these dancers; the part an audience sees, neglected.

In the last two ballets the choreography was based on national steps suitable to the story and often danced in heeled shoes. The folk steps appeared in simple forms, they were quoted and repeated. One did not see the elements of them return in more striking shapes, varied in accent and rhythm, building to a visual dramatic climax. Neither were the mime gestures clarified, ordered, and timed for a theatrical emphasis. Constantly throughout the film the absence of invention, the want of composing power were unmistakable and depressing. The new music too was hackneyed, uninventive; it was danceable, but commonplace.

Dance Magazine, OCTOBER 1954

"ROMEO AND JULIET": A FILM REVIEW

The Russian feature-length ballet film *Romeo and Juliet* is more fun to watch if you don't like classic dancing than if you do. The whole cast keeps behaving like the operatic boyars and muzhiks one is acquainted with from Russian historical films. They rush up and down stairways, they fence by hundreds, they stare, feast, dance, and mourn with an unquenchable agility and vehemence. Seen close up, they ham an emotion with a capital letter. They do a little classic dancing too, and tie it in by heavy character acting. They are completely convinced, if not completely convincing. You can't miss any point they make, but you do miss a delicacy of implication. The action hasn't that aura, or overtone, of grace and human sweetness that in Shakespeare or in classic ballet lets the wonderful side of a meaning appear as if of its own accord. Instead, the film has a great deal of energetic obviousness, the enthusiastic conventionality we are used to in the ballets of our screen musicals. On that level *Romeo* does very well.

But one expected another level. This *Romeo* is intended to show Russian ballet at its best. It has been adapted from one of the best postwar stage productions, the *Romeo and Juliet* of the Bolshoi of Moscow. It has been choreographed and co-directed by Leonid Lavrovsky, the choreographer of the theater version. The original ballet score by Prokofiev is the film score. It is danced by the Bolshoi Ballet, headed by the most celebrated of Soviet ballerinas, Galina Ulanova, who created the same Juliet in Moscow. Very likely the film keeps the style, the general plan, and many of the best moments of the stage version; certainly it shows every sign of care and devotion in its realization. And on this level one looks for a general effect much more interesting, and for a show with more sparkle.

But a local ballet fan is too curious about Soviet ballet to leave it at that. He comes to the film delighted with the chance to see the differences in style between these dancers and ours. He watches the detail for moments when what they do will show the kind of force the style has.

And he does see effects that communicate. Juliet, with the Friar's potion in her bodice, as she begins to dance with County Paris has a moment when she thinks she is dancing with Romeo; the insane flash of it is real, though the style is melodramatic. Romeo has a strange rushing entrance in the tomb scene, and he lifts high what he believes is Juliet's corpse with a gesture that brings back the grandeur of the verse. Mercutio in the midst of the sword fight in which he is to die has a rush of darting and twisting leaps that makes one see his spirit all quickness and no venom. Two acrobats leap through the carnival crowd with a vivid gusto. And when the whole population of Verona is dancing its stamped and Slavic step in the carnival square, in the general enthusiasm the remoter groups can't bear the beat and gradually shift to a later one of their own; this shift is so real it pulls you right into the crush of the crowd. These moments are not effects of classic dancing, they are effects of acting, of mime. And I was delighted as by a sort of virtuoso mime specialty, when Tybalt made his face look the absolute peak of fury, and then slowly altered it to look twice as furious.

But the local fan keeps thinking, what about showing us some choreography? There are groups strolling, crowds milling, pretty girls in tears, people running very fast or standing still, cutting capers, feasting, brawling, and constantly making faces and violent gestures. At the ball there is lots of genial ogling and drunken lurching, and with this motivation, slices of four or five dance numbers. But as far as their choreography goes, that turns out to be surprisingly commonplace, uninteresting in its material or in its development to the score. The big folk dance in the square, choreographically speaking, is nothing at all. But the unimaginative choreography of the two decisive pas de deux is what astonishes the fan most. The situations are the greatest—those of the balcony and of the bedroom scenes; the dancers are the best. And here at the poetic climax Juliet's dances have no brilliance of choreographic invention, no power of choreographic expression at all—they are elementary; while Romeo's part consists of giving his partner support with now and then the crumb of a leap thrown in. The dancers carry the situation by mime, like fine actors putting across a decisive scene in which they have only a banal text to work with.

The choreographic text is consistently elementary so as not to distract from the mime expression. Very likely the point of our best ballets would be lost on them if they saw them. They would take them for exercises in virtuosity. How could they know that they were meaningful when all the dancers looked so pleasant and so civil?

One comes to see that these Russians don't try for the same lucidity of dance action and of dance rhythm that we are used to, and that an interesting choreographic text calls for. They like to be off the measure. They prefer to fling out a whole step sequence to the general rush of a musical phrase or two, as if they heard in the music only its rhetoric or drive. They prefer to let the mime element—the acted emotion—blur the shape of the step and the classic carriage of the body. There is an exception in the classic-style group dance with mandolins, but the discipline here is meant to register as nice party manners. Only Ulanova shows a consistent powerful exactness of line in feet and legs, but even with her the mime emphasis makes the shoulders rise, the wrists tense, the floor contact thicken. And the habitually lifted rib cage breaks the line of her back and shortens her neck.

Once a local fan gives up looking for what we call choreography and classic style, he can see that the whole of this *Romeo*—dancing and mime—is keyed to a dominant mime image, a melodramatically violent one intended to characterize the environment of the brawling Capulets and Montagues. That the violence is a Slavic one, and not an Italian, is natural enough. But Shakespeare uses the brutal families as a foil for the marvelously civilized lovers—whose strength and delicacy suddenly become a wonderful and growing power that gives to the tragedy its joyous radiance. The kind of point Shakespeare makes can be and has been made by classic ballet when the piece (as in Petipa) takes its key from its lucidly dazzling grand pas de deux, just as the English play takes its key from its most dazzling sweet moments of verse.

But the Russian choreographer has turned the foil into the protagonist, and has taken his key from the rude and heavy mime motions that signify brutality. Everything in the ballet is oppressed by some reflection of the key. And the insistent intentionalness of the mime key has a depressing effect in another way. The effect is that the only human relations left in the piece are intentional ones.

Anyway the heavy mime style bores you. So when Lady Capulet, with an awesome gesture, rends her bodice in grief over Tybalt, you find yourself peeking at her underwear to see if that too is in period. When Juliet in the bedroom scene keeps falling agonized to her knees, you notice that it isn't in front of the Madonna that she drops but in front of a full-length mirror—and you see Ulanova-Juliet with a ballerina's practice mirror in her bedroom.

But after an irreverent breather, the fan can watch again. Not the acting, but the movement. And how beautifully Ulanova runs. How handsomely they all run. And the fan is struck by how the men sail through the air, all of them, with a fine sustained stretch that few of our boys achieve. They sustain the extension through the powerful middle of the body, they don't hold it as well in the ankles, knees, and nape, classic style. So they increase the effect of a weight that sails. The weight the dancers suggest in their action becomes the men better than it does the women. And the men's strong stance is a pleasure. And as the fan watches, he gets to see that the expressive vigor of their action comes from the dynamic sforzando attack they give to a stretching motion, a sforzando that comes from the midriff, and that has been trained in many gradations. Ulanova is a virtuoso of both the attack and the development that follows.

And one can well imagine—when a stage is full of heavy men and women dancing with this kind of powerful sforzando thrust and leaping up with a powerfully sustained extension in the air, so that a continuous pulse of ferocious energy pours out over the audience while the orchestra blares full strength—that the theater effect becomes so overwhelming one doesn't so much watch the dance as abandon one's self to the orgiastic discharge of it. One can well imagine the mass scenes of *Romeo* or any other piece creating such an effect, so that when Ulanova appears, so slight and small compared to the rest of the cast but so rapid and decisive and so occupied with a particular inner life, the shock of seeing an individual again is shattering. One doesn't ask for more, one sees her through tears of gratitude. One can well imagine it, but the film doesn't show anything like it.

Nor could it. A large stationary stage accumulates energy (or else lucidity) in a way that the swiveling narrow field of a camera can't. A camera can't keep its mind on dancing. In a mass scene its eye catches a hardness of strain in a movement and reminds you that the dancers have been repeating this take so often they are past their best form. The camera eye looks at a few steps of Ulanova's and observes that her waist is not a pretty one. It also observes her worn face, but after a few moments that turns out to be in its own way quite pretty. Of all her many dance qualities, it is her lovely airiness in lifts and supported leaps that best keeps a trace of its stage magic in this film.

It has been a long film but it is over now. The fan has caught the copious visceral vitality of these dancers, which would make them a stage success anywhere. Their style has less visual and musical continuity than it has visceral. Conventional ideas when they take this expression become what some of us call vital, human, and earthy. What a wow this company would make of *Schéhérazade*. The expression of their style is strongest just where that of our ballet is weakest, and vice versa. When they come to New York, what fun it will be to see the contrast. As for myself, as I went down into the subway on my way home, I began to wonder what Rubens would have done if he had been a Russian choreographer.

The Nation, MAY 12, 1956

THE BOLSHOI AT THE MET

In the spring of 1959, The Great Moscow Bolshoi Ballet disappointed some balletgoers. "We'd all expected so much, and they aren't superhuman after all," a bright young lady exclaimed as we met at the door after a performance of *Swan Lake*; she quickly added the warmest praise for Ulanova in *Romeo and Juliet*.

About Ulanova I quite agreed. At first sight her vividness of motion, unique among the dancers around her, reminded me of Martha Graham's. As for the company, the first half hour shows it is a great one—highly skilled, convinced, attentive, lively. In *Romeo* everybody did a great deal of pantomime. They didn't all prove striking actors—nor would that be possible. But the company doesn't make hasty or shrunk-up or "unpurposeful" gestures. The movement of a gesture has that amplitude of strength, that full support from the waist, traditional among Russians, but which the Bolshoi has excellently trained. The large-scale easy power of movement, whether of mime or dance, I found a remarkable pleasure.

But let me describe the Bolshoi *Romeo and Juliet.* The score is Prokofiev's; the story, Shakespeare's. Costumes and sets look like stock nineteenth-century stage properties—Renaissance style. The action shows you, one after another, the familiar "big" scenes of Italian grand opera—the morning market, the street affray with drawn swords, the ballroom festivity, the carnival, the duel with a slow death followed by another with a quick one, the clan oath of vengeance, the family row, the burial by night with torches and tapers. Regulation opera-house humor is offered; the regulation populace of Italian opera turns up, wenches, pedlars, down to the ragged urchins played by girls en travesti. Every bit of it done in earnest, with complete conviction, and, of course, total laryngitis. It goes on for nearly four hours. At first you wonder that despite the Italian opera model nobody onstage behaves with an Italian irony or elegance; then you realize that everybody is behaving like the brutal boyars and dimwitted serfs in a conventional movie about Ivan the Terrible.

The pantomime points of the crowd scenes are made obvious and then made obvious again. Succinctness, surprise, leaps in logic—the fun of pantomime—are avoided. The crowd slowly prepares a mass climax, then it slowly milks it, then comes a lull in interest, a cover scene, carefully protracted. The pace is that of an army's indoctrination lecture.

When the crowd dances, the dancing is more stage business. Briefly the love scenes—the balcony, bedroom, and tomb duets—hint at a kind of dance that isn't stage business: on the balcony, a few classic steps; in the bedroom, a few lifts; in the tomb, a single lift, a very fine one. But even alone together the lovers keep pantomiming: the ballet doesn't venture into the other world of metaphor a dance can develop. In Shakespeare the love scenes develop an expression wonderfully alien to the Verona scenes, and that radiant difference makes the drama. Pasternak says of the play, "And to the din of butchery and cooking, as to the brassy beat of a noisy band, the quiet tragedy of feeling develops, spoken for the most part in the soundless whispers of conspirators."

The company's opening bill in New York was *Romeo.* Balletgoers here had seen many a pantomime piece more brilliant and beautiful. But what they had looked forward to seeing was the Bolshoi's fabulous dance power, and *Romeo* kept that under cover all evening.

Ulanova's vividness saved the first night. When she bent her neck toward her partner in a lift of the bedroom scene, the gesture had the tragic quiet Pasternak speaks of. Or take the opposite kind of moment. Faced with marriage to County Paris, Juliet, her mantle flung round her, desperately rushes along the apron to Friar Lawrence; armed by him with the sleeping potion, she flings the mantle round her again, and rushes desperately along the apron back horne. The fling, the rush, the exact repeat are pure *Perils of Pauline*. But Ulanova's art at that moment is so brilliant the audience breaks into delighted applause.

You can find out something about Bolshoi style by trying the gymnastics of Ulanova's fling and rush yourself. Standing in the middle of the room, fling an arm across your chest, and at the same time raise the breastbone as high as it will go, bending it over at the top so it pushes the neck back. Don't let go, keep forcing the breastbone further, but in addition push the neck forward as hard as you can, and lift your head until you feel "desperately resolved." (It may make you cough.) And now, keeping the stance you are in unchanged, rush about the room with an incredible lightness and rapidity. If your family is watching, they will pick you off the floor, and urge you to try harder.

The special stance of fling and rush you just tried (it involves a backbend between the shoulder blades) is not classical. It has been called the pouter-pigeon silhouette by Walter Terry, and that is just how it looks. But when Ulanova does it, you feel it means "Here is my heart."

But if you notice that, you also notice her feet. In light runs on toe (bourrée steps) they seem to touch the floor sensitively. You see how keen the pointed foot looks in the air, during attitudes, arabesques, and passés, how clearly the leg defines and differentiates the different classic shapes. Below the waist Ulanova is a strict classicist; above the waist she alters the shape of classic motions, now slightly, now quite a lot, to specify a nuance of drama (for example, the pouter-pigeon silhouette). Neither element—the lightness below or the weight above—is weakened for the sake of the other; the combined motion keeps fluid. And often while one movement is ebbing to its end, another seems already welling up in the midriff.

The Bolshoi women share Ulanova's method, but not her vividness. The pacing—the pulse—of their movement is less varied, more predictable. Ulanova shows the unguarded timing of a spontaneous gesture. And she keeps that "motivation" throughout a role. You watch the rhythm of a specific character, the irremediable individuality. The imaginary creature onstage is much more unforeseeing than anyone around her. That holds your eye and your sympathy. Ulanova uses no other charm. She does not take the audience into her confidence; she attends to the literal mimic meaning at every moment. Her manner is that of a heroic postmistress. And yet in the pas de deux from *Sylphides*, where the meaning lies in a particular buoyancy of dancing to music, she was also at her most poignant.

At the age of nearly fifty, Ulanova does not have the luscious ease of a young ballerina. Other women of the company are stronger, more acrobatically striking, or fresh and sweet. None of them can give to a stage heroine a convincing heroism.

Though not as vivid actresses as I had expected, the principal women of the Bolshoi are dancers with authority, handsome feet, and charming figures. The impression of heaviness they give is due to effects of Bolshoi style. The pouter-pigeon stance, for instance. The first time you see the *Swan Lake* Swans hit it full strength, stepping in slow straddles and uncoiling their arms Hindu style, they look like women of great weight specially trained to move; they looked prepared for immolation. When several women go into the stance with men on stage, you wonder that the men pay little attention. Later you see why. The Bolshoi women go into pouter-pigeon in all kinds of situations, at several angles, with different steps and gestures, and out again. The stance is a regulation formula. For a formula, it is rather unattractive. It shortens the woman's neck, it makes the head look helpless, the figure dumpy. Other formulas are no less hard on the women. You keep seeing open mouths, hunched shoulders, jutted chins, arms turned inside out at the socket and avidly reaching; you keep seeing elbows bent stiff or stretched stiff, hands crooked at the wrist, impatient arms, agitated hands, bobbing heads. When the women go into this formula they look fidgety. Another formula has them look so preoccupied with an inner trouble they can't be gracious to each other or to the men. The general idea seems to be that when a woman feels deeply, she looks a bit countrified.

The men of the Bolshoi haven't the women's light feet, or their heavy emotion. They are pleasant to each other and to the women, and four-square in their bearing. They don't try for a classic distinctness in low shoulders, upright neck, and level head; they don't much turn out at the thigh, or clearly stretch their feet, or define their descent from a leap. They are self-effacing, and reliable lifters; but given the chance, several become striking dramatic dancers and mimes.

The difference between the style for men and the style for women throws the sexes into relief. On the other hand, relations between the sexes keep to a Victorian propriety. This isn't so easy in some of the big lifts, where the mutual holds and tosses are far from Victorian.

But in two folk-hero parts, Vasiliev, a very young man of nineteen, showed what the Bolshoi style for men is capable of. One or two other men leapt as high as he, but none as they leapt and danced had his power of sculptural contour in motion or his power of upbeat in rhythm. None as actors had his lion-hearted magnanimity toward the heroine, the entire company, and the whole world. In dance or mime Vasiliev's instinct for generosity and delight couldn't be bigger and truer. His style is plain; his poetic gift—no simple one—is as radiant as that of the fabulous Russian dancers of the past.

Three of the youngest women principals, Timofeyeva, Maximova, Kondratieva, are ravishingly pretty and only the least bit stuffy. A fourth, Bogomolova, according to the local experts, can meet both Bolshoi and Western standards of ballerina technique. Samokhvalova could too, very likely. Bolshoi technique stresses big jumps more than quick toes; it stresses mobility of shoulder and upper spine, and acrobatics like those of a vaudeville adagio team. Western ballerina technique requires a sharply versatile, high-speed exactitude of step and of ear and a high-tension stamina—which are not Bolshoi characteristics.

But as one grows used to Bolshoi style, the gifts of a score or more of principals, men and women, become evident. The "Highlights" programs showed their dance power best, and on those, in good-natured acrobatic audacity, the ballerina Plisetskaya outdid anybody in the world. I grew to like the individual dancers better and better.

The productions however did not gain by being seen twice. *Swan Lake*, a revised version, developed less momentum than the traditional one in London, and no poignancy. *Giselle* began well, but, becoming longer and longer, lost its drive in each act. *Stone Flower*, a Moscow novelty, tried for dance momentum and fun, but like the other Bolshoi choreography, it kept losing the upbeat of the rhythm.

The Bolshoi's dance rhythm—choreographically speaking—is neither big like Fokine's nor clear like Moiseyev's. The dances are apt to go on without gathering momentum, without getting anywhere. They come down heavy on the downbeat and slur the upbeat. At a climax they pound the downbeat. They haven't the lilt of lifting off it, or the fun of matching a counterrhythm to the musical rhythm. They miss the upbeat buoyancy of a musical momentum, the exhilaration of a rising sweep of impetus. The rhythm is weak on resilience.

The dancers are expected to perform it with rubato, ahead or behind the music. They "shape" each phrase, treating the time values of the rhythm more elastically than the orchestra does. Each phrase has urgency, each phrase lacks repose.

You see the dancers do with devotion what they are asked to. During climaxes of emotion they are not asked for the calm and completely erect carriage of the classic ballerina and of her partner. They are not asked for the climactic suspense, the extreme responsibility of the lightest finish, the lightest musical phrasing. Since Diaghilev's time great Russian dancers have been showing us these extreme traditional resources of their art. At tragic and at happy climaxes they have shown us the power of radiance ballet can achieve. The lovely young Bolshoi ballerinas do not spread that radiance. The young Soviet violinists and pianists who visit us are in command of all the traditional musical resources, not only of amplitude of strength but also of edge and elegance and quiet. No reason the dancers should not have them too.

The Bolshoi has formalized its style and it does what it does on principle. It covers up with care the brilliantly unreasonable resources of expression which are the glory of ballet dancing. It does so to stress instead an acted mime meaning. Four or five in the company can do this convincingly; the rest, though sincere and convinced, haven't a gift for vivid acting. Nor has the choreography a gift for narration. At a three-hour stretch the company's mime of deep feeling and psychological motivation isn't absorbing. Where the Bolshoi convinces all evening is in the ample strength of a movement, and in the weight of one. And for these dance qualities, too rare in the West, it will always be welcome.

The Bolshoi means to uncover its dance power in the next few years. When it does, it will add to the literal meaning of pantomime the metaphorical meaning of dancing. As of now, Western ballet—and even our own part of it—offers more fun, a fiercer luster, more grace of irony, and much more imaginative excitement and poetic courage, though it isn't stronger and is ever so much less secure.

Hudson Review, WINTER 1959–60

A NOTE ON KABUKI

In 1960 an ensemble from the Tokyo Kabuki, headed by three great actors, Kanzaburo XVII, Utaemon VI, and Shoroku II, came to the New York City Center, invited by Lincoln Kirstein. The company brought with it a new idea, the running translation of the dialogue via transistor. It opened with a famous play, *The Subscription List.*

After twenty minutes of attention to everything onstage, helped by the transistor—and by having read Professor Ernst's book—the Kabuki stylization did not seem mysterious. But the great actor who took the second lead was so uninsistent that I began watching him. He acted his part when the drama required it; when it didn't, he marked it—and that was most of the time. He was very old. The voice had lost the lower register, which the Kabuki falsetto "breaks" into and out of to stress a syllable. But his diction was exceptionally distinct and melodious. His stylized movements too were beautifully clear in shape. Though the old man tended to lag in the middle of a long phrase, as it finished he somehow delivered the final accent unhurried in the nick of time. He sat erect and motionless during the hero's interminable tirades; gradually his gaze would blur; but when his cue came, the freshness of his reply was instantaneous. I recognized these professional traits from having seen them in very old, very fine Western actors. At one point his young attendants preceded him single file in a quick march to the "hurry door," a narrow exit about three feet high. Approaching it, the young men took two rapid steps in a deep knee bend and on the third passed through. I was distressed for the aristocratic old actor, who must have been in his late seventies and who was wearing a tall hat besides. In fast tempo, thin and erect, he took the first knee-bend step, then the second, then, even deeper, the third, and was safely through.

The soldier hero of the play, disguised as a monk, at the climax pretends to have achieved illumination. The more he speaks of it, the more one realizes that the silent old man with his mysterious moments of freshness must really be an illuminated sage or a Rishi who knows all the truth; and the play's ambiguities beautifully deepen. It was not by the stylized forms that the actor had achieved this, but by his actual age, which had modified the forms very slightly at any moment, but over an hour's time unmistakably.

At the end of the same evening the same actor (Kanzaburo XVII) reappeared as the plump young husband in a farce, his black eyes snapping, his stylized speech and gestures vivid with physical charm, his foolishness delightfully comic.

On the next program the company performed several highly dramatic scenes from another famous play, *The Forty-seven Ronin*. The three stars were each extraordinary; so was the rest of the cast and the entire production. I will describe some of the climax. The hero, a spirited young nobleman (acted by Kanzaburo XVII), has been condemned to commit suicide by an unscrupulous provincial governor. Immediately after his death, his estates will be seized, his noble young wife and his many retainers will be destitute. In a room of his mansion, the ritual preparations have been completed. The hero sits Japanese fashion on the floor, forward of stage center, his eyes straight at the audience, the honed short disemboweling knife laid at his side. He is alone except for two government witnesses, expressionless on chairs against a side wall. The young man's eyes are half-closed, sharp, motionless. He is steeling himself. No one moves. A pause. His face unchanged, he flicks one shoulder and his kimono slips from it. A pause. He flicks the other shoulder, the silk kimono drops, a swift gesture of his hands tucks it back. His position has not changed, his eyes have not moved. A pause. He is wearing a second kimono. Again he flicks a shoulder, and pauses; flicks the other, tucks the fallen silk back, and pauses. You see he has tucked the garments away from the abdomen he will pierce. Now he is wearing a third, thinner snow-white kimono and you sense that he will not shed it; he will stab the broad knife through it. Horrifying though the heroism of the ritual was, I noticed by this time that the recurrent pauses had each been a trifle too long. I was sorry that so great an actor should overplay so great a scene, even with the uncertainty of playing to a foreign audience. In any case his gleaming half-closed eyes held us. Without moving them, he picked up the disemboweling knife, plunged it to the hilt, deep into the far left side of his belly; and screwing up his face pulled it slowly with both hands in a straight line toward the right. As he reached his middle, a commotion occurred at the back of the audience. Keeping his face screwed tight, he stopped, and held the knife firmly where it was. A retainer ran toward him across the hanamichi and prostrated himself, wailing and sucking in his breath. The hero in a thin clear voice asked him a commonplace question. The terrified retainer answered yes, and again prostrated himself whining. The hero was past hearing him. Both hands gripping the hilt, he steadily pulled the knife to the far right of his belly, eased it out, raised it to slit his jugular, and dropped awkwardly forward. As the knife clattered to the floor, away from the dead man, I was surprised to see no blood on it. So convincing had the scene been.

But the next day, recalling the actor's marvelous miming of the scene, the slightly overlong pauses came back to me, and with them the gleam of the steady half-closed eyes. They were not those of a man steeling himself. I had seen that specific expression somewhere else, under quite different circumstances. Then I remembered. I had seen it in the eyes of a composer friend, at the orchestra rehearsal of a manuscript work of his; he had been intently listening in the web of sound for wrong notes, due either to a copyist's mistake or to an instrumentalist's. The hero onstage had had exactly that look. Then I remembered the rest of the drama. He had in fact been listening for the approach of his chief retainer. He meant to pledge him to vengeance. It must have been to gain time that he prolonged the ritual pauses; but since the government witnesses were watching, he could prolong them only a trifle. He had fooled the witnesses and me too. And when the retainer had at last run in, the hero fooled us again. His commonplace remark (like a dying man's absurdity) had actually been his demand for vengeance. So the listening look in his eyes, and the slightly overlong pauses, which spoiled the perfection of form, were decisive to understanding the scene and the character of the hero. They were not stylized effects, they were realistic ones.

The Kabuki's great stylized effects are famous in the West; decisive realistic effects, such as those I have described, are also worth calling attention to. The Kabuki style plays in and out of its stressed stylized forms in a number of unstressed ways which a theater fan will enjoy discovering for himself. Its elasticity in this respect makes for surprises, it distributes the tense moments, and the evening as a whole gathers a genial warmth of playacting.

As dance the Kabuki stylization has less range than that of Chinese classic theater, or than that of the two Balinese aristocratic styles. Its logic is less boldly nonverbal or acrobatic; it stays closer to the text. Dance logic as such appears to be furthest developed by Western ballet; the stylized Far Eastern theaters appear to have developed the art of mime the furthest.

They have also developed furthest the pictorial intelligence of stage decoration. The Kabuki, which elects (like our own scenic tradition) a middlebrow or nineteenth-century pop style, exhibits within that style an acuteness of pictorial intelligence that puts an observant Westerner in the best of humor. For its New York visit, the Kabuki had brought with it sets built to the measurements of the City Center stage—less than half as wide as its own. A Japanese warship had brought them to New York.

1960

THE ROYAL BALLET IN NEW YORK

The Sleeping Beauty

The Royal Ballet's first night at the Metropolitan Opera House was, as usual, a success—a gala for those members of the New York public who feel at home with English manners.

They welcomed the company, Fonteyn in particular, with a solid warmth; they stayed on at the end to show their solid friendliness by many curtain calls; and finally they drifted out into the drizzle of an incipient hurricane with a thoughtful glow of approbation.

The Sleeping Beauty, as the company gives it, engenders a comforting glow one is grateful for. Fonteyn, sweetly reasonable, sweetly lucid in every motion, looked lovely; she danced better and better as the evening went on, and was in her full glory in the final fish dives. As at every point in her career she carried the whole company, the whole drama steadily to a climax.

The Bluebirds (Page and Shaw) thrilled; Powell's wicked fairy and Grant's dance timing were extraordinary; Farron's mime as the Countess, and Larsen's as the Queen, excellent; Bergsma's mime as the Lilac Fairy, and Somes's as the Prince, very attractive. The costumes were opulent in colors like good British food; the scenery was enormous, wishy-washy; the divine music, a bit tight and sour.

But the second night, the music opened and sweetened. The young Lilac Fairy, determined to do it right this time, danced beautifully. In the next act, after a slightly forced Rose Adagio, Fonteyn's dancing quickly recovered all the gleaming freshness of Aurora. It rose from there to the marmoreal suavity of the Vision, and rose again to the magnificence of the final pas de deux. The company rose with her. A beautiful evening.

Ondine

In Ashton's *Ondine* everybody loved the magically liquid sparkle of Fonteyn. She was bewitching endlessly and with ease. Every action seemed the spontaneous one of the character she was playing. Of her last-act swim, in itself a stage trick, she made a beautiful dramatic image; the fatal kiss-of-death pas de deux she filled with grandeur. All evening she was a supreme artist at her greatest, and simplest.

The ballet surrounds her with an expensive spectacle and, much more valuable, with a devoted company. Ashton keeps her onstage most of the evening; what he invents for her is never unbecoming or forced, and now and then it turns excellent.

A delight, too, is Grant's fantastic running, sometimes spinning upward in full career, or at top speed stopping magically. When this sea god in fury calls on naiads and tritons one is surprised that what happens is a sedate-style stage show. Then and later one is surprised that so marvelous a creature as Ondine should pick her friends from among shoddy people and trivial immortals. The ballet is foolish and everyone noticed it.

Antigone, Le Baiser de la Fée, Giselle

Cranko's tragedy *Antigone* has a dance style that combines American Modern and Greek Modern, both of them at their most pompous and both delivered with a BBC accent. To me it looked like first-rate material for a farce: all it needed was some tourists wandering about. A pity Cranko missed the chance.

In MacMillan's *Baiser de la Fée* the first half of the mill scene showed his striking gift for poetry. Seymour, the Bride, became adorable in an odd way, and the Bridegroom, MacLeary, very promising. But the Fairy (Beriosova), though no woman was ever busier, never became supernatural. Unless she is supernatural, there is no drama.

The Royal Ballet's *Giselle*, now restudied by Ashton, seems to me preferable to the Bolshoi's for style and often for sense. Fonteyn is extraordinarily good, both as a sensitive country girl and as a tender imponderable ghost.

Ashton's Peasant pas de deux, delightfully danced by Page and Usher, is a jewel of 1840 pastiche. And his changes have done wonders for the old harvest number. The serious characterizations of Albrecht, Bathilde, Hilarion (Somes, Farron, Edwards) are lively and very touching. Larsen as the Mother becomes thrilling in a passage credited to Karsavina. *Giselle* seems to me more direct when it is cut; that question apart, Ashton's version is the best, and the company does it handsomely.

La Fille Mal Gardée

La Fille Mal Gardée had a very big success on its first night, though the leisurely pace of the ballet seemed several times, particularly toward the end, in danger of losing the public. However, it responded happily to all other elements—the sunniness and summeriness, gentle as in England; the good nature, good health, good humor of a mild countryside; the pleasant country dances attractively reinvented, gracefully interwoven with classic and with music-hall numbers; the many amusing finds in steps, in ribbons, in props, in lifts—an adagio supported through a window, for instance, was quite miraculous.

Most of all the public responded to the sweet-temperedness of stars and ensemble (including a white pony)—a company in which no one ever insistently pushed a motion or a gag or a character projection. Neither an American nor a Russian company could have sustained for so long so airy, childlike, and unemphatic a good time.

The stars, Nerina and Blair, were perfect in step and gesture. Holden, the farcical Widow, excellent everywhere, in a clog dance gained a sweet radiance that was adorable.

Grant as Alain was even more extraordinary. In dance and mime he made the full foil for a whole evening of blandness, without the least hint of intending to. No other dancer in the world could have done it.

For all this that Ashton has so happily evoked, guided, and invented, he cannot be praised too highly. His idyll passes, for me, too blandly and too evenly. But now that I know the kind of piece it is and the kind it is not, I am curious to see it again.

The Times (London), SEPTEMBER–OCTOBER 1960

MARTHA AT SIXTY-EIGHT

Martha is sixty-eight. The moves she makes are sketched. At crucial moments the timing is extremely vivid. She holds her audience by imagination. She does it all evening long in *Clytemnestra*, several seasons old now, a masterpiece as weird as Melville. But her public wants to see her every year, and that keeps her troupe going. The news is what the troupe has done to itself. It has blossomed.

It hadn't found out how to until the end of last season; it had been a strong severe bud for about twenty years. It had been bold about being in earnest, but timid about being lively. (Remember the then Sadler's Wells on its first postwar night in Paris?—like that.) Now it dances with "go," taking headlong risks, a nervy, vivid, big-time performance style. This year's new pieces were on the daft side, but that didn't stop the ensemble performance style. The troupe caught its fever from the amazing dancer in it, Paul Taylor; but the point is, the Graham style doesn't blur when the troupe gives it a whirl—it gets clearer. That is Martha's latest victory.

Twenty years ago I used to watch her get herself into an amazing full-force move or stance that left her no way out; then she found an astonishing way to get out and go on. That was how I began watching her technique. When the drama got stuck tight, she would pick up a prop and find a way to go on. I watched her drive her role so far into tragedy, she was stuck with it; she shook it, got it loose, and went on with it.

What has got her ensemble style unstuck has been ballet—not the steps, but the balance and spring. On its own account and in its own terms ballet has reinvented several of her inventions—the starfish- or octopus-type mobility, the angular accents, hip or shoulder thrusts, asymmetrical stances and moves, the sudden changes of pace. There are more. To be sure somebody or other in daily life keeps inventing all these kinds of moving and stopping, if only a child.

Not that the Graham style and ballet are fusing. Music parts them. Ballet moves inside it, modern dance outside. A Graham piece makes a free-verse-type rhythm different from the musical rhythm of the score it is timed to. Its form is unlike the form of the score. That makes me "read" it as a kind of mime.

As I look back on twenty years of Graham choreography as on some ritualized kind of mime, the vivid decision of its action, the rapidity and range of its gesture meanings jumping by free association from close at hand to remote, the turbulence and vehemence of the dramatic powers invoked have been extraordinary. It has been unique. I know ballet fans who feel passionately that the work is wrong in principle. As for me, its principles make those of ballet the clearer. A life of such enormous energies that keeps pouring itself according to its fate into the imaginative world of dance is a godsend. SPRING 1961 (UNPUBLISHED)

PAUL TAYLOR

Taylor's choreography at his first recital ten years back was antidance and avant-garde. For example, in the opening number a man in street clothes took a great many instantaneous nondance poses that had no mime meaning, usually taking a few steps between; this action was set to a tape of the voice on the telephone, "When you hear the tone, the time will be . . ."—a tape that kept telling the actual time every ten seconds for twenty minutes. To another tape, fifteen minutes long—this one of rain noises—two girls stood or ran in curves, nothing else. And to a three-minute score by John Cage, a sitting girl and a boy standing beside her, both in street clothes, did not move.

Ten years later, Taylor is choreographing to Ives, Schuller, Handel, Haieff. The action, though different from classic ballet, is no more avant-garde than the music. Today's avant-garde is as engaged, now as in the past, with antimusic, antidance, antitheater, and everybody agrees it is a good thing to have around.

Taylor's first choreography was antidance with a beautiful clarity and ingenuousness. He admired more than anything the shoreless beauty of Cunningham's dancing antidance, and he still does. But the more he danced and choreographed, the more a powerful and complexly fluid dance momentum engaged him. His gift defined itself as one not for antidance but for prodance. What he has been doing since 1960 is new in the sense that such dance momentum had not existed before in the modern dance (i.e., in nonclassic technique). The technical as well as the creative discovery is his.

Taylor is one of the few choreographers who can sustain a large-scale dance with only from five to eight dancers. He is the first New York choreographer since Robbins who has taken the trouble to teach himself the continuous clarity of a well-made ballet. He has given the modern dance a new resource, one equivalent to (but not identical with) the classic dance-step phrase. PROGRAM NOTE, SPOLETO, 1964

MERCE CUNNINGHAM

At first he was quite extraordinary because of the sloping shoulders and long arms and long legs. What a spring—so sudden and soft. There was something that kept your attention, which was his own intensity and his intensity of imagination in the part which he was doing. It wasn't as though he had thought it out, but as though he was entirely in it at the moment he was doing it onstage—though of course it must have been choreographed. But the choreography didn't resemble Martha's even when he was dancing with her. She had a wonderful way of using him in dramatic opposition to her own part, without altering what was characteristic of Merce himself. And that sense of character in a dramatic part which he had was not an ordinary character or a rational, psychologically motivated character. It was something more extraordinary than that and in a sense more like spirit—not an ordinary person—different from the way people are, but a kind of person that you have sometime known in your life.

When he stopped dancing with Martha and gave recitals of his own, though, I remember Virgil Thomson saying to me that Merce was "Happy Hooligan," who was a famous old-time American comic-strip character. There was something that was just that. It was a very apt expression because Merce had that way of moving very happily over a situation and being perfectly aware of it without forcing it.

But in *Appalachian Spring*, where he was the Revivalist, when he made his sermon it got extraordinarily exciting, as though he were carried away in his own vision, as though he were or became—as a great revivalist can—an artist of the forces of nature. Everything about it was terrifying, but not hostile. A friend of mine who saw it was telling me recently he remembered Merce very well as that Revivalist with a long brown suit and a big hat and attended by the little girls who thought he was marvelous (they were the followers of the Revivalist in the piece). And he made marvelous leaps that were quite terrifying, and the little girls all seemed to be terrified at this and were as if beginning to scream. But I also remember that the little girls looked, to me, like chipmunks and like little birds in the way they ran around him. And he (in his part) understood that. I mean he in his part understood that possibility of the little girls like pet animals around him.

From the start Merce was an extraordinary dramatic dancer with a very special and a very large dramatic imagination, and there hasn't been anybody like him since in that particular field. And even though he later gave it up, it still is quite strong when he wants to use it, as he did, for instance, in *Sixteen Dances* in an abstract way, and as he does from time to time in the current repertory—in the soft-shoe dance, for instance, that everybody remembers. But also he can suddenly turn a strictly neutral lyric abstract sequence of movements into a dramatic situation by the force of his dramatic imagination. You see this appear and you see it disappear again in the piece, and the shift is very light and wonderful.

As far as his technique and his technical inventions are concerned, they are very interesting and I think that they are generally understood now though they weren't for a long time. I have felt that by avoiding the drama out of which Martha Graham made her pieces, he discovered lyric aspects of dance that were much lighter than any that were discovered by people who were closer to Martha. And as he was doing this—as he was inventing this kind of abstract, noncoherent, non–logically coherent, nonnarrative piece—he also invented the technical basic stance (out of which to dance) which gave him and his company freedom of movement that was very difficult in the early Martha Graham kind of movement at the time when he was in her company. Her company changed their kind of movement a great deal later. But at the time, although Martha herself was always in complete command of her freedom of movement and she stood as straight as a ballet dancer as her own basic stance, her other dancers didn't seem to have understood that basic stance of hers.

When Merce found a similar basic stance it wasn't, I think, through her as much as through his own sense of where the body feels able to move and finding the place in which the body can move in any direction at any speed, without hesitation, without stammering.

The strange thing about making pieces that have no logical narrative or logical formal structure is that it needs an exceedingly dramatic gift that Merce has, and so a strange sense of freedom and of space is created.

No doubt, Merce and John Cage work very closely and it is difficult to know where ideas come from. They probably didn't come from anywhere, they just evolved through a mutual interest in doing something different from the way it was done before. I rather think that the basic ingredient in Merce's chance choreography is a question of deciding beforehand what movements to use in a particular piece. The sequence, of course, is afterwards determined by the chance method or some other.

But to do this, certain kinds of movements are used and the piece is made up out of them. If these movements are different enough and harmonious enough among themselves, it makes an interesting piece to see them reappear in all kinds of different sequences and timings. But if you don't know enough about movement to begin with to select the set of movements that can combine with each other interestingly in many kinds of ways, then your piece isn't going to turn out interestingly even though you do it by the proper chance formula. The chance formula, I suspect, doesn't have to be followed literally with complete exactness each time, but then no compositional formulas or discompositional disformulas ever are.

Seeing Merce is always a very great pleasure.

Dance Perspectives, SUMMER 1968

Balanchine and the New York City Ballet

I remember that Doris Hering told me that you should thank your teachers on this occasion, that it was customary, and I'm only too glad to. But there are so many of them that I can't even name them all. Of course there's one man who has taught me to see and hear more than anyone else, and you can guess who I mean—Mr. Balanchine. And he goes right on teaching me. I am very much interested in not only all the variety in which he sets the music and the different kinds of events that happen to the musical events, but also the fact that all his great ballets are very different from each other in a way that has to do with subject matter—but that subject matter is never directly expressed. You go home and can feel the subject matter, and perhaps you can think it through, but he hasn't actually told you. And that keeps you interested because the subject matter is so much larger than if someone had just said "This is what happens." It's so much more like the real subject in life and the things that you feel which are always much too big to be put into words and to be classified because they go off in all directions.

DANCE MAGAZINE AWARD
ACCEPTANCE SPEECH, APRIL 1966

A NOTE ON BALANCHINE'S PRESENT STYLE

Since 1940, it seems to me, Balanchine's choreographic style has more and more clarified the dancer's momentum in motion. That is what you follow as you watch the dance. You follow the variable momentum of the dancer's phrase, and the dance impulse in it that animates her is clearly defined. The spring of the steps and the thrust of the gesture clarify and characterize the dancer's changing impetus. Easy and elusive, she moves positively in coherent and unforeseen sequences. Her energy suits their emphasis, the figures of the dance suit her dancing figure. Free in following her impetus, light in responding to its surprising variations, her own human figure keeps its plastic unity. The unity it keeps for your eye makes the dancer a consistent character in your mind. You see her as an active, intelligent character on the stage whose variable play fascinates by its natural coherence. Because she creates her own momentum unimpeded and because you see her so clearly doing it, you watch her with pleasure as if she were doing what she spontaneously liked to. And because the rise and fall of the dancer's momentum is so clear and so expressive and the extended phrases appear to be the free dance impulse of an interesting human character, the dancer herself remains the force onstage you watch, the force that moves you. And since in performance there are many dancers to watch, stars and chorus, young men as well as girls, and since the impetus of each remains free and clear whether they dance solo or in harmony with others, the ballet onstage is full of variety, exhilarating and touching in its lively mutual responsiveness.

The novelty in this is the fact that Balanchine's style, like the classic Petipa-Ivanov style of the nineties, moves you by the act of dancing and not, as the fashion was from 1910 to 1940, by opposing to that act obstacles of various kinds of mimicry—pictorial, psychological, musical, or social. Choreography from Fokine on had made the most of such obstacles to dancing and of the intermittences in rhythm, the oddity and distortion of the human figure (the stylization) which resulted. Fanciful, startling, intelligent, and stylish it often was, and Balanchine himself began by rather outdoing other choreographers in all these qualities. "Modernism" was the liveliest fashion of its day, and it made every new piece obviously very peculiar: but it tended to focus one's interest not on what the dancers were doing but on what they were supposed to do, what they had been told to do. Dancers solidly trained in classic continuity of rhythm and balance projected an eloquent pathos by overcoming the choreographer's willful obstacle course; but dancers with little experience in a straight dance attack couldn't be effective in the oblique two-things-at-once impetus of stylization. Balanchine's shift from "modernism" may be due to the fact that he has worked for the last eleven years wholly in America, and generally for American dancers, whose incompletely trained dance impetus had to be stressed to make it carry in performance. But this new style may also be due to a spontaneous change in his point of view, to a new interest in classic coherence, limpidity, and grace that contemporary poetry and music are also beginning to show. In any event his present style is not an oblique neoclassicism, it is a direct new classicism. It is the new choreographic style of the forties, which is in emotion unlike the preceding style, the style we know from *Les Sylphides*, the *Faun*, *Tricorne*, *Noces*, and *Apollo*—each one a masterpiece, as everyone knows. Tudor's work too has been "modernistic"; and I have no intention of suggesting that the style has no life left in it, I am merely trying to analyze the novelty of a newer one.

One can of course point out that back in Diaghilev's day Balanchine was already recognized by the discerning as a classicist, and classicist he was in comparison to the modernistic choreographers. But even *Cotillon*, which in its open flow gives a clear indication of his present manner, is in its theme a stylized representation of a nonballet form of dancing.

Serenade is directly classic in its style of dancing but it makes many of its points by gestures and arrangements that have a sort of pictorial symbolism. I have the impression that *Balustrade* in the first and last part of it, in which the movement was simple and open and made its effect directly by its dance rhythm, was more definitely in the present direction, although it was the wonderfully sensual acrobatics of the middle section that delighted one part of the audience and shocked another. Shocking Balanchine has not been since then, perhaps because shockingness, especially in America, injects a nondance excitement that interrupts and diminishes the straight dance emotion. At any rate, *Concerto Barocco*, *Ballet Imperial*, *Danses Concertantes*, *Waltz Academy*, and the new *Mozartiana* (and in a simpler form the big number in the second act of *The Merry Widow* and the one at the end of *Song of Norway*) are direct dancing, limpid and exhilarating. *Bourgeois Gentilhomme*, in its present form, has some brief low-comedy and pantomime scenes, but *Bourgeois* is a variegated divertissement and not a consistent ballet; the stylized movement is used as it is in a Petipa divertissement or pantomime scene for occasional relief, not to communicate lyric emotion.

Despite the popular success our two ballet companies have had with his new pieces this winter on tour, many people feel that so straight and ungloomy a style as this does not convey emotion. They are distressed by the absence of a literary subject by which to get at the ballet. They feel that Balanchine's *Baiser de la Fée* was because of its story and pathos a greater work than his new ones. More grandiose in scale it was, and I wish this grandly morbid piece were still in repertory. It is a loss certainly that Balanchine has not had an opportunity to set a long and ample work. I should be happy, for instance, to see a 1945 classic hour-long version of a Tchaikovsky ballet, right next to the familiar 1890 classic versions in our repertory. But a plot and its attendant emotional situations are after all a device for continuity, an aid to attention: it is not the situation that achieves emotion but the impetus of the dance that creates it.

Balanchine in these new animated, constantly shifting, plotless, and unneurotic pieces by stressing the dancer's impetus makes one follow a dance performance with consistent interest without drawing your attention to familiar unhappiness. You don't watch the dance to see if the dancers come up to an emotion you expect beforehand, you watch to see what they do, and their variety in animation exhilarates; you are interested without knowing how to label the emotion. And so you are not tempted to excuse your pleasure, or rationalize it, or appreciate it mentally. I think that this direct enjoyment of dancing as an activity is the central aspect of ballet style that Balanchine has rediscovered. As in the new style the dancer is no longer divided between divergent impulses of motion, and as there is no longer a conflict for precedence between dancer and choreographer, so there is as you watch no painful split of emotion between your social consciousness and your dance pleasure. These classic and free pleasures of peace are as great as those of a tortured romantic disorder. They offer us a new emotion one is eager to enjoy.

Dance Index, FEBRUARY–MARCH 1945

"THE FOUR TEMPERAMENTS"

The Ballet Society, New York's new subscription organization for producing ballet and opera, opened with startling brilliance on November 20, presenting to its subscribers Ravel's one-act opera *The Spellbound Child*, and a new Balanchine ballet, *The Four Temperaments.*

The audience, an experienced one, welcomed the executants and welcomed *The Four Temperaments* in particular as a novelty of extraordinary fascination and power.

In its flavor *The Four Temperaments* is unlike any other Balanchine work. In form it is a half-hour dance ballet, without plot or locale, set to Hindemith's score of the same title (originally commissioned for it). The score consists of a set of three long themes, first stated directly, then varied four times. These variations, called "Melancholic," "Sanguinic," "Phlegmatic," and "Choleric," follow in their plan the four temperaments (or humors) of Hippocratic and medieval physiology. And the plan of the choreography scrupulously observes the musical plan. But the ballet as one watches it can better be described as a suite of dances of amazing richness and variety that illuminate an exceptionally powerful thick-flowing score.

The ballet holds one spellbound by the constant surprise of its dance development, by the denseness and power of the dance images which the figures onstage create from moment to moment. One seems to be watching innumerable novel dance possibilities realized without the least hesitancy in the drive or the least awkwardness in the continuity. The continuity is like nothing one has seen and it looks completely self-evident.

Unpredictable and fantastic the sequences are in the way they crowd close the most extreme contrasts of motion possible—low lunges, sharp stabbing steps, arms flung wide, startling lifts at half height, turns in plié, dragged steps, révérences and strange renversés; then an abrupt dazzle of stabbing leaps or a sudden light and easy syncopated stepping.

Neither sequences nor figures look familiar. The grandiose force of these crowded large motions seems to correspond in its accents to the dense tensions of the score's counterpoint, and the unexpected continuity (as the phrases evolve) to the score's smooth melodic surfacing.

But it is the pressure and shift of the musical as well as of the dance images that is the heart of the piece; no choreography was ever more serious, more vigorous, more wide in scope or penetrating in imagination. And none could be more consistently elegant in its bearing.

Dance News, DECEMBER 1946

A LETTER ON NEW YORK CITY'S BALLET

I hadn't expected so intense a pleasure, looking at New York again,* in the high white February sunlight, the childishly euphoric climate; looking down Second Avenue, where herds of vehicles go charging one way all

* In February 1952, Denby returned to the United States after four years abroad.

day long disappearing into the sky at the end like on a prairie; looking up a side of a skyscraper, a flat and flat and a long and long, and the air drops down on your head like a solid. Like a solid too the air that slices down between two neighbor skyscrapers. Up in the winter sunlight the edge of such a building far up is miraculously intense, a feeling like looking at Egyptian sculpture. Down in the streets the color, the painted colors are like medieval color, like the green dress of the Van Eyck double portrait in the National Gallery, intently local and intently lurid. And New York clothes—not a trace of charm, dressing is ritualistic like in Africa (or the Middle Ages); the boys are the most costumed; dressed men and women look portentously maneuverable; one set looks more dry-cleaned than the other, and those count as rich. New York is all slum, a calm, an uncomfortable, a grand one. And the faces on the street by day: large, unhandsome, lumped with the residue of every possible human experience, and how neutral, left exposed, left out unprotected, uncommitted. I have never seen anything so marvelous. A detachment from character that reminds me of the Arhats in Chinese painting. Women as well as men in middle age look like that, not comforting but O.K. if you believe in marvels, "believe in" in the sense of live with. They have no conversation, but a slum movie put on its marquee: "Sordid"—*Times*; "Unsavoury Details"—*Herald Tribune*. I never saw so civilized an advertisement in Paris. Manners are calm, everybody is calm in New York except where maybe somebody is just having a fit. No one looks dominated. But one minority looks sometimes as though it suffered acutely, the adolescents. They throw themselves about the city, now supersonic, now limp as snails, marvelously unaware of adults or children. Suddenly across their blank faces runs a flash of anguish, of huntedness, of brutal vindictiveness, of connivance—the pangs of reformatory inmates; a caged animal misery. They are known as punks and jailbait and everybody defers to them, everybody spoils them as people do to what they recognize as poetic. They are not expected to make any return. A few years later they have put on weight, whether girls or boys, and the prevalent adult calm has commenced for and closed in on them too, and others are adolescent. Another magic thing about New York is that everything you look at by day, people, buildings, views, everything is the same distance away, like in Egyptian sculpture too. When I look about me in New York I feel as if I saw with an eagle's kind of eye; lovely Italy I looked at with a dear simpatico horse's eye. But you want me to tell you about the city's ballet company, which I adore.

The day after I arrived, friends took me to see a morning run-through of a new Balanchine that was to open a few days later. The dancers were in practice clothes under the poetic work-light with a piano onstage. You can imagine how eagerly we started to watch. And the pleasure at first was so keen and so peaceable it seemed to me we might easily have been Orientals watching our local court ballet any time during the last millennium or two. As the piece lengthened measure by measure I understood that nowhere in the world could I have seen a more beautiful new one nor anywhere else seen dancers able to perform its fantastic academic ritual with such an air of ease and virtuoso calm; such pretty dancers, almost Oriental in their impersonalness. Not that they behaved in any way but natural New York. That was my first impression of the New York City Ballet and of *Caracole*.

Later in the season I saw the piece several times, and though it had lost some of its delicacy in the glare of performance, the power of it had become more active and stranger. I saw a number of the company's programs and liked a great deal of what I saw. I was interested to find it a non-Diaghilev-style company. Star composers, star painters, star dancers, star poets—the NYC doesn't try to reproduce this famous formula as every other company still does. Stern as Puritan Fathers, Kirstein and Balanchine deny themselves (and us) all but two pleasures: dancers who within the limits they are kept become unique, and choreography which is the best anywhere. Not only the Balanchine pieces. But the best of his are of course for me unmatchable beauties.

The Balanchine ballets in the repertory are of every known variety: dance ballet, drama with plot, drama of atmosphere, comedy of situation, divertissement (musical show number) sentimental or farcical, exhibition grand pas de deux. (A pas de deux I like very much is the *Sylvia* one, with a very beautiful part for the man, canonically danced by Eglevsky.) Of the entire repertory the pieces that fascinate me the most are three dance ballets, *Caracole*, *Four Temperaments*, and *Concerto Barocco*. *Four Temperaments*, overloaded with brilliance like *Caracole*, is its opposite in material. It is full of Beckmesserish dance jokes, classic steps turned inside-out and upside-down, retimed, reproportioned, rerouted, girls dancing hard and boys soft, every kind of oddity of device or accent, but never losing the connective "logic" of classicism, never dropping its impetus, and developing a ferocity of drive that seems to image the subject matter of its title: internal secretions.

Classicism is extended in these three dance ballets (as generally in Balanchine's work of the last decade) without upsetting the principle of equilibrium, or shifting the terminal points of a step or port de bras—on the contrary; and still the diversity of movement they have, the range they show in setting steps to music, and the range in lyric expression are astonishing. It is easy to see they are models of style—easy to see how each step in time is undistorted, distinct, fleet, spontaneous; how phrases, periods, and sections flow on unexhausted with a deep powerful impulse. In the earlier of his dance ballets a few pantomime images like bodily *mudras* emerge from the rushing evolutions of steps; later these pointing hands become indistinguishable portions of the constellated configurations of the dancing.

One can take such dance ballets as just fooling of a fanciful kind or one can take them to be beautiful and serious; they look like both. What they show is young people dancing onstage and how lovely the bodies look. The choreography shows them graceful in the way they dance with one another, or look alone as they move, in the way they hear the music or take a climax or present themselves to the public. It makes an image of behavior, and many momentary ones; a sense of instinctive manners and cruel innocence; unconscious images suggested by devices of structure rather than by devices of gesture. So the individual keeps all her natural ambiguity as you see her decide, and see her swept on past the moment in the stream of dancing. And the force of the image comes not from her will but from the rhythm of the company's dancing and from the physical strength of the step. Often these images of unconscious action seem to me grand and intrepid; and what I love so is the undisturbed bloom like in real life that they have as they flash past. But whether Balanchine meant this I have no idea. I naturally think in terms of a story when I get excited; for people who prefer to avoid human interest, I imagine that the fantastic ingenuity of the arrangements, the costliest of hypertrophic pleasure-domes built up on nothing, the sweep and the lift of them, is fun enough.

The dance ballets invite you not to bother with a "meaning," but the drama ballets on the contrary have explicitly the meaning that their story has. The drama of them sometimes catches me like off guard. I have watched the beginning, noticing I wasn't much interested, that it was barely holding my attention; and then not noticed if I was interested till, a long time later, transported far from Fifty-fifth Street, onstage in front of me I saw Destiny striking down a child of mine—a real poet—and I realized suddenly that it was I who had been watching it done, realized it only as I saw the Fifty-fifth Street curtain come down. And I was too absorbed still in the solemnity of the vision to wonder then how Balanchine could have circumvented my tense mistrust at the beginning, and made me accept his magic; and grateful to him too, because though I knew what I had seen was real, he at least assured me it was just a trick. Balanchine's gift for seriousness in the theater is a rare one. While anything happens it looks like ballet, like a step or a joke or a grace; but when it is finished it suddenly can look serious and real. The victim has been struck square. By the time it is over, the immolation has been thorough. Look at it in *Orpheus*, *Prodigal Son* (where it is a conversion), or *Fairy's Kiss*.

Prodigal Son is told, since it is about good and evil, in two kinds of pantomime: the dry, insect-light, insect-quick elegance and filth of atheism, and the fleshy biblical vehemence—so Near Eastern and juicy—of sin and of forgiveness, the bitter sin and sweet forgiveness. Still bolder as an image seems to me the leisure in the pacing of the scenes, which transports the action into a spacious patriarchal world, like a lifetime of faith. Very different is the ancestral religious Greece of *Orpheus*. The overslow adagio motions at the beginning and again at the close evoke the magic passes and stalkings of ritual—Orphic and Orthodox both. The forest creatures who witness Orpheus's grief appear in this magic slowed-down time from so remote and so pristine a country, it feels like a pre-Homeric Parnassus. (And don't they form a kind of protopediment or roodscreen?) Eurydice writhes at her husband's feet like a mountain lioness in heat, like the Worm of Death, like an eternal image. A pity the Furies' dance in Hell is of no value. But on earth the Maenads shudder possessed, swallow the spurted blood. Different again is the brutal romantic Switzerland of *Fairy's Kiss*. It is a land of fairy tale, reduced from the country of myth by industrial encroachment. Here the poet is only unconsciously a poet; as long as he may he thinks of himself as an average mill-owner boy. Poignant as is the reduction of consciousness, it is in this particular "world" that the image of looking under the bridal veil in horror becomes so grandiose and takes on so many tragic dreams. And the world of the believed-in fairy story is evoked by the nineteenth-century style of *Fairy's Kiss*. It isn't straight classic, but "like a classic": you can see it in the pantomime and the timing of dance steps, though the company isn't likely to distinguish.

Images such as these familiar ones (I mean to suggest) build up an imaginary country in which the story becomes credible; we recognize it as the particular country of our imagination where people would act as they do in the story, would do the deed they do. And the largeness of the images makes it a country wide enough so that the victim could escape, if he chose—like Achilles. But it is the rhythmic power of the dancing, of the dance scenes, that turns the pantomime quality of a gesture into an emblem, into an image with all its own country all around it. Dance rhythm is a power that creates the validity of the grand style. It is not rhythm used as a wow effect; I think it begins instead by quietening the audience; but it collects the audience's magic mind, its imaginative attention; it puts one into another time sense than that of practical action. One can recognize the same use of rhythm in the nineteenth-century classics, and that is I think the reason for their enduring magic. I imagine that many ballet masters and dancers don't know what to try for in preparing the old ballets, and choreographers don't know what to try for in preparing new ones. The weakening of the rhythmic power of a ballet in respect to its story is the defect of West European ballet in general. And Balanchine's effort to restore it choreographically—and also in dance execution—is a matter of interest for balletomanes to consider and discuss. He seems to me the active choreographer who best can give in his story ballets the impact, the truth, and the scale of the grand style, the structural devices to be recognized. Or at least he gives critics an opportunity of calling attention to grand values in contemporary choreography.

As for the less-grand-style ballets of his in the repertory, I'll have to skip them this time. Except for one I want to mention because it's George doing a turn disguised as Dame Ninette: a carload of respectable ideas, props, pantomime, orchestra noises, all of it honest and none of it dancing. It's *Tyl Ulenspiegel* I mean, and I don't mean to praise it, but I enjoyed seeing within its eleven minutes how many kinds of ideas did get across to me—history, economics, sociology, psychology, morals; how changes of pace presented a gesture in its actual as well as in a symbolic meaning; how casually introduced, how cleanly concentrated, how free in untying each situation was in turn. *Tyl* is a hearty Flemish grab bag—dirt and folk and anarchism and Robin Hood-ness, Bosch and I suppose Rembrandt and a Flemish philosophical novel, and the final dénouement even offers the concept of the gifted man who from the solitude of intelligence slips gratefully into ordinary human happiness, the progress from "the hero" to "a man." *Tyl* is also charmingly acted by Robbins, and it has a decor by Esteban Francés, who is the company's one discovery as a big-scale ballet painter.

There is another piece too I want to call your attention to, not for its choreography, though, but for its score: it's *Bayou*. Balanchine has made it a sort of Dunham number, gently graceful, that needs only a stage surprise near the end to be a divertissement. But he missed the originality of the score, its subtlety in candor, the sense it gives of clear repose in a secret spot. The liquid continuity of the music, the easy breathing of the melody, the transparency of the harmony, the unelliptic, unabridged, so-to-speak circular or stanzalike forward motion it has—these are peculiarities of structure that might have looked beautiful reflected in dancing. Like the Furies of *Orpheus*, *Bayou* is a disappointment, because one can see that with better luck it could so well have become an event. Virgil

Thomson, the composer, is also the composer of the opera *Four Saints*, a heavenly opera—in score, libretto, and singing—that I hope you saw in Paris; such pretty dancers, too.

Watching Balanchine's choreographic genius pouring out its gifts in profusion in the NYC repertory is as great a pleasure as I can imagine in the theater. Many fans here enjoy watching his choreography as keenly as if it were dancing itself. They are used to the dancers and to the dance style and you know how much easier that makes seeing the choreography. But I don't think anybody really wants to separate the dancers from the dance; I like ballet best when all about it, décor and music too and the evening's special good or bad luck for that matter, are all mixed up and indistinguishably beautiful. But I am trying in this letter to isolate what I think are the two remarkable features of the NYC, the grand-style choreography and the company dance style. The company dance style is particularly different from what Europeans try for and want and so on this tour it is particularly open to question and remark.

When you see the NYC doing *Concerto Barocco* or *Symphony in C* and see the de Cuevas or the Paris Opéra doing them, you realize in how different a direction the dance style of Balanchine's company is headed. And then when you have seen a good deal of the repertory, you see too what the limits are in which the dancers are quite strictly kept at present. These limits no European company would care for or be able to keep, but they do make the Americans brilliant. American ballet is like a straight and narrow path compared to the pretty primrose fields the French tumble in so happily. The NYC style is the most particularized and the clearest defined of all the American ones; the most Puritan in its uprightness. For me an immediate attraction of the NYC's style is the handsomeness of the dancing, and another is the absence of glamour, of glamorization. To have left glamour out is only a negative virtue, but there is a freshness in it to start with.

Handsome the NYC way of dancing certainly is. Limpid, easy, large, open, bounding; calm in temper and steady in pulse; virtuoso in precision, in stamina, in rapidity. So honest, so fresh and modest the company looks in action. The company's stance, the bearing of the dancer's whole body in action is the most straightforward, the clearest I ever saw; it is the company's physical approach to the grand style—not to the noble carriage but to the grand one. Simple and clear the look of shoulder and hip, the head, the elbow, and the instep; unnervous the bodies deploy in the step, hold its shape in the air, return to balance with no strain, and redeploy without effort. Never was there so little mannerism in a company, or extravagance. None either of the becks and nods, the spurts and lags, the breathless stops and almost-didn't-make-it starts they cultivate in Paris, and cultivate so prettily. (On the analogy of painting the French go in for texture, the Americans for drawing.) As clear as the shape of the step in the NYC style is its timing, its synchronization to the score at the start, at any powerful thrust it has, at its close. So the dancers dance unhurried, assured and ample. They achieve a continuity of line and a steadiness of impetus that is unique, and can brilliantly increase the power of it and the exhilarating speed to the point where it glitters like cut glass. The rhythmic power of the company is its real style, and its novelty of fashion. Some people complain that such dancing is mechanical. It seems quite the opposite to me, like a voluntary, a purely human attentiveness.

It is an attention turned outside rather than inside. It is turned not to sentiment and charm, but to perspicuity and action. It suggests a reality that is not personal, that outlives the dancer and the public, like a kind of faith. The company is not trying for an emotional suggestion; it seems to be trying for that much harder thing, a simple statement. A painter who is a very bright critic told me that at the opening of *Symphony in C*, during the rush and surge of the finale, tears came to her eyes because it was all so entirely objective. There the company must have showed exactly what it meant to; and it is no trivial expression. They are tears such as Fonteyn can make one feel. But for a company effect I felt them only once while I was abroad, at the rehearsal of *Napoli* by the Royal Danish Ballet, for the company's objectivity of miming.

This, I think, is the general direction the NYC style has taken, and its achievement so far. I don't mean to suggest that it is the only right one in ballet; I like having different styles to look at. I think it is an interesting one, and suited to American physical traits and habits. The limits and limitations of the NYC style were not nearly as much fun to try to identify. I tried on the ground it might be amusing to hear what an American fan finds fault with.

So the NYC dancing its best looks beautiful in the dance ballets. In the story ballets when one looks for miming, for acting too, one sees with surprise the company isn't performing at all. For instance in *Prodigal Son*. By exception this was badly rehearsed and the boys danced it so soggily they looked like a YMCA gym class. But that wasn't the trouble. Robbins was attentive, simple, modest, a touching actor; but no one else acted at all. They were as neutral as in *Concerto Barocco*. The stinging butterfly hue and desert grandeur of the choreography turned into an airless Sunday-school monotone. How I wanted to see *Prodigal* done by the Danes. And *Tyl* too. Or *La Valse*: it looked like an orphanage. Fortunate young people at a ball have a hectic, mannered, almost frivolous way which is correct for stage ballroom dancing too (it's a character style, it's not classicism). In *Valse* the steps invite this edginess, this overquickness; it would have made the ballroom vault over us all, and evoked that more and more unbearable, more unfulfillable longing of juvenile self-consciousness and soft mortality in which the mime scene could strike like an exploding thunderclap. Le Clercq and Moncion acted the scene well, but without the company to prepare it, it looked like a timid beginning. (And such miracles of rising choreographic climaxes; what a wow this would be done by your Covent Garden dancers, after a year or two of getting accustomed.) *Serenade* is danced even more meticulously than *Valse*; but despite its constant success, I would prefer it danced, so to speak, demi-caractère, not straight academic. Done as it used to be before the war, with a slight "Russian" retard and dragging in the waltzing, that tiny overtone of acting gave the whole piece a stylistic unity and coherence in which the beautiful gesture images (from the one at the opening to the very last, the closing procession) appeared not extraneous but immanent in a single conception. *Lilac Garden* is more effective too danced here and there with a slight advance before or retard behind the beat.

In *Swan Lake* Tallchief's head positions were a sharp pleasure. The neat, on-the-note timing of several striking steps in the adagio seemed to me of theoretical interest, but not this time interesting onstage. The entire adagio was taken too fast and too soldierlike in cadence to have the beauty and power it can: a développé has no force at this speed. The quartet was bad. But after the two new beautiful Balanchine Swan dances—a delight in their musical spring, their bird-look, and perfect too in their anonymity of style—after the beautiful long finale they led into—hundreds of birds beginning to take off, swirling in the air all over the stage, a beating of wings as they rise up, these great birds at arm's length—after they had gone and the toy swans were swimming back along the drop and Eglevsky looked at them immobile, and I looked with him, then as the curtain began to drop and applause started, just then I realized with a miserable pang that she had been transformed back into a beast, and that she was lost, lost forever. Lost to me too. It was as real as Danilova and Petrov had been in the adagio. Acting or no acting, it was the drama of the story that Balanchine saved, and I was grateful to Eglevsky too for it.

Maybe the acting in the ballets I mentioned demands some familiarity with European manners. But the NYC has a chance at character dancing without European precedent in the high school jazz style of *Pied Piper*. The Negro dynamics of the jazz style (such as an overslow follow-through, a razor-sharp finesse in the rhythmic attack, an exaggerated variety of weight in playing with the beat) are special; but the NYC dancers all have shagged from way back. So I was mortified to see them dancing still in the style of *Swan Lake*, dancing the piece wrong and looking as square as a covey of mature suburbanites down in the rumpus room. All but one dancer, Le Clercq, who does the style right, and looks witty and graceful and adolescent as they all so easily might have by nature. The piece has a Robbins-built surefire finale, and the public doesn't even guess at the groovy grace it is missing.

After concentrating awhile on muffed effects like these I got so peeved with my favorite company that I started looking for mistakes in the part of the company style I like so much—the neutral, classic part; and I found a few. The boys for instance were girlish about the knee. They were pleasing in personality and partnering but what they had for plié was indecently small. Their silhouettes in the air were weak because they didn't lift the knee enough; on the ground they relied too much on their instep in place of the knee, and so were getting to mince, even when they came out to bow. They had no élancé at all. They imitated Magallanes's unobtrusive inactive way (without its singular beauty), rather than the big-scale action of Eglevsky.

In the dancing of both girls and boys, the fault that troubled me seriously was a bluntness in the rhythm, a monotonous singsong or marching-style meter; it looked like tiredness at first, but after a while it looked as if it might grow into a habit. The sameness of attack at all times (as the military say) is the danger that the company's beautiful steadiness and continuity create. And the classic, the school kinds of variety of attack, and the steps that train variety were what I next tried to watch for and saw little of. A long-sustained adagio flow where the pulse seems to vanish in the controlled développé movement; the various changes of speed possible in a passé-développé; the sudden change from slow to fast in ballonné; the unexpected pause in demi-fouetté; the change of speed in a plié with ritardando drop and accelerando rise, or a port de bras with ritardando finish in free meter—where steps with possible variations of speed and of meter occur the NYC does them in a regularized athletic one-two one-two meter. But when these steps cease being rhythmic "variables" they lose some of their interest and color; what is more, they no longer sharpen the dancer's sense of rhythmic delicacy, her sense of variety of accentuation, her sense of the difference between the artificially prolonged and retarded follow-through of adagio and the plain swing-back of allegro. The classic overrapid meeting and separating of thighs when they pass one another in an adagio movement is never seen at all, and that is a failure; and I am sure that the classic plié with a quick rise is much better in *Symphony in C*, in the syncopated preparation passages of Reed's section—because I used to see her do them correctly and now see only a mechanical plié in even meter, and the passage has lost transparency and zip in consequence.

No company I ever saw performed such subtleties of technique reliably. A great star might, but a company indicates them often rather roughly under the stress of acting, or of a collective atmosphere, or a surge of group rhetoric; similarly in other companies the boys dance with a slight difference from the girls not through technical differentiation but by getting the habit when they began to study dancing in the character of a boy or man. The NYC, however, not only does not care for such messy uncertainties but also does not encourage any character-dance approach. (To be sure, character dancing also involves rhythmic liberties.) So we have reached the limits of the company style—the present ones.

It would be absurd to suppose that so great a dramatist as Balanchine (and so great an actor) is delighted to see dramatic implications of such scope and power as his not realized by his own dancers. If they perform every piece alike in the style of virtuoso finger exercises, it is because he made the choice. But the negative advantages are clear. The company doesn't offer the fake glamour, the vulgar rhetorical delivery, the paltry characterization that often have become the defects of a company that tries to act, to characterize and make personal everything it dances. I have seen companies act in a serious ballet so that they looked the way dressing-room gossip sounds, the same kind of expression except it wasn't even occasionally fun. Better than that is dancing a few years without any "expression," just neutral. That leaves the choreography unsoiled, and also the public. It doesn't spoil the effect of the physical aspect of the grand style the dancers neutrally dance in. And it doesn't begin them in habits of silly acting. The limitation to a neutral company style made it possible to force the bloom, if one may say so, of qualities stronger in Americans than big-scale acting is, made possible the company's large and powerful impetus, its large and candid unspecific expression.

Perhaps one can guess something of the latent powers of the company style by looking at the qualities the principals and stars show that don't look out of harmony with the ensemble. There are unnervous and unfake acting performances for instance. In *The Cage* the way Kaye throws away most of her part (throws away the detail for the sake of the large shape she so can give it) is very fine and grand. (She looked exhausted when I saw her but I thought that was because of rehearsals for *La Gloire*.) She and Robbins long ago learned to do without the insistent projection that so often spoils American ballet acting, because it gives everything the same tough edge and so turns every move into a comic gesture. Moncion I saw act too little to speak of any change. Hayden and Laing, formerly very fine in a tense and even overwrought style of acting, now seemed feeling their way toward a calmer and larger kind, such as Kaye and Robbins use. Together with the acting that Tallchief and Le Clercq show, it looks as if the NYC would welcome a simple and steady kind of acting whenever it begins to show.

Tallchief, though weak in adagio, strikes me as the most audacious and the most correctly brilliant of allegro classicists. She can lift a ballet by an entrance, and she has flashes of a grand decision that are on ballerina scale. What I missed seeing was that expressive radiance which makes beautiful not only the ballerina herself, but the whole company with her, and the whole drab area of stage space and bright imaginary world of the ballet that visibly and invisibly surrounds her—a gently indomitable radiance that is a classical ballerina's job, and that several times in my life I have seen a dancer accomplish. Le Clercq has a heavenly radiance and a lovely adagio, but neither has been trained to spread indomitably. Her New York elegance of person, her intelligence in every movement, the delicacy of her rhythmic attack we all adore. Adams has a perfect action, the best adagio, a ravishing figure, and a sweet manner that is our equivalent of your "county." Wilde has a beautiful Veronese grandeur and plasticity of shape in her dancing, a glorious jump; and Hayden has a Lautrec edge and vehement stab and a strange softness in her she seems to hate: a great actress, I would guess, if she learns calm. They are all in *Caracole*, each with a line as pure as a great ballerina's, and as characteristic as a great horse's in a horse show. And intent little Reed with the heart of gold—but individuals isn't what this letter is about, as I said to begin with. I love them all. I went by the air station when the NYC was off for Spain and when your Juniors were off to London, and how ravishing they looked, the station full of dancers both times; such an elegant and rich habitual way of moving, the little faces green from the farewell parties the night before, but the bodies delicious to watch in their unconscious young feline assurance. So they flew up into the sky.

About some of the other choreographies. Ashton's two [*Picnic at Tintagel* and *Illuminations*] are sound workmanship and each has first-rate passages. I find the subject matter of each too magnificent to suit their official-style scores, to suit, either, Ashton's own wonderfully intimate and ironic poetic eye. The more trivial the subject, the deeper and more beautiful is Ashton's poetic view of it. *Picnic at Tintagel* has a fine mystery-story opening and very pretty indecent lifts in the pas de deux. To me it seemed that Ashton's Isolde behaved like a Potiphar's Wife with a willing young Joe. She appeared in the lobby of her Central Park apartment building in her slip, found a big schoolboy there, seduced him instantly, and then again. A couple of bellhops peeked. And King Mark and some flags murdered the poor punk. Whether young Tristan ever noticed what it was he was doing with the lady—that is left in doubt; and that is the little private poignancy of the piece. It has nothing to do with the legend and very little with love; but it is a fact of life, it is true to life in its way. Tudor's *La Gloire* I was disappointed in; it didn't look like a piece to me in any direction, and Beethoven kept trampling madly on the bits of it. I saw Tudor was interested in "aplomb." The people around me, however, applauded earnestly as if they had seen something interesting; so I leave it at that. The Dollar and Bolender pieces I missed, and Boris's I'm sorry I didn't enjoy.

The Robbins ones—altogether exceptional of course in their gift for form and their ambition for sincerity—are exceptional too in the way they are unrepetitive, disciplined, driving, sharp-sighted. The dramatic pressure of *The Cage* is extraordinary. It devours the notes, it die-casts the gesture; when the curtain comes down, as Thomson said to me, there isn't a scrap left over. I was fascinated by the gesture—so literally that of the important Broadway people at parties and in offices. Bothered to be caged in with them, I looked around unhappily. No exit. But the murderous power that led to the climax and beyond—I couldn't really sense it in the force, the propulsive force, of the gesture; I felt it outside the characters. In *Tintagel* a discrepancy between what the story forces the dancers to seem to do and what it is I see them really doing onstage strikes me as harmless and fun; faced by the much greater dramatic force of *Cage*, if what is gobbling up my attention seems to be a discrepancy somehow, I get confused. No one else was bothered, as far as I could see. But I liked *Ballade* better because it didn't get started in that fascinatingly literal gesture of his that is wonderfully contemporary but so resistant to development, to the spontaneous growth kind of development. I liked it better too because at the end one girl at least discovers a way out of the trap that Robbins evidently intended to catch all of them in; she wasn't sure she wanted to get out, but it was clear she could if she chose. I liked the musicality of *Ballade* very much. And the Aronson décor too, so Debussy and real peculiar.

Something in the development of the subject matter seems to put me on the defensive. I'll blow up the impression and analyze it in terms of criticism and see where I get. Robbins's method is that of pantomime. The composition draws attention to descriptive gesture, incidental gesture made by peripheral movements; it does not draw attention to the central impulses of the body that dances. The gesture sequence is accentuated in spastic counterrhythm (an insistent device common to modern or Central European dancing, but used too, though ever so gently, by the Paris ballet dancers in inventing mannerisms for themselves). Robbins's dramatic line, the dramatic power of a piece, is developed not from the central impulses to dance—in ballet characters normal as breathing—but it is developed by applying an obsessive rhythm to what for the characters is incidental gesture. It is like seeing somebody punished very heavily for a small fault, and the main drama never coming to light. It is as if the characters were not free agents—they act under a compulsion. The effect is that of a kind of prehypnotic vortex. It destroys the reality of facts—sex, war, the South, money—and some facts one doesn't want to see destroyed; that is its danger. American writers to be sure very often use this device, but the honest and beautiful one among them is Poe. He is very careful. I think that Robbins's present technique would perfectly suit a "Fall of the House of Usher."

Robbins makes delightful and perfect ballets for musical shows, but at the NYC he wants to do something more. *Cage* as drama is as good as the best Hollywood or Broadway successes. I would say that ballet when it is more is something quite different, something freer. What bothers Robbins is that vast size, that space all around offstage of an imaginary world. But I think he takes serious ballet so seriously he is willing to get lost trying to find it; and I like that, I feel that way myself. Balanchine, Kirstein told me, believes in him entirely. So does the public, and the company's first all-Robbins night brought out a crowd of bright people who wanted to express their confidence and appreciation. I liked that too.

I think there are perhaps a few "background" notions about our ballet that we accept unconsciously but that you wouldn't know about.

First, something yours and ours have in common, a pallor, a whiteness of spirit, a thinness and meagerness of temperament that the French say they are so bored by, in our ballet, and in yours too; I think we had better not stop to sigh over it. Henry James describes the same characteristic in American acting of fifty years ago; he calls it an Anglo-Saxon shiny white hardness, as the French still do. Fonteyn has now for four years been leading a revolution against it in your country, and you were lucky she undertook it; after her ten years of the correctest rule she was the only person with the authority to try a change. I love the decisiveness of her action, and perhaps her new lovely warmth will influence our "Anglo-Saxonism" too, our own much more pronounced athleticism and shamefacedness. But actually the NYC is hardly more than ten percent Anglo-Saxon, and it is as likely to be as Negro as white in another decade or so. Actually you English are West Europeans and can still enjoy your different classes and you can still have the pleasant characterization and glamour that come from noting the differences of manner—noting them without envy or moral disapproval. We haven't that tradition anymore. But what a ballet company needs first is an instinctively homogeneous style, an unconscious character. The NYC is less "theatrical" than Ballet Theatre was at its best; but it seems to me to be more natural in its dance behavior, to be better founded on unconscious local manners.

It may seem odd to you that we over here put up with an absence of glamour in our best ballet company in a way that Europeans never would. The normal American attitude (I recognize it in myself too) is the one expressed recently by a local anthropologist in a book about our character (*The Lonely Crowd*): "Wherever we see glamor in the object of our attention we must suspect a basic indifference on the part of the spectator." Can you imagine a European speaking so slightingly of his own local glamour? It's a Puritan point of view. But considering what a mess American dancers have so often made of glamour and of acting, it's quite as well not to force the issue of inventing them both. The balletomanes are tactfully quiet about that aspect of our ballet, and express instead their approval of the simplicity, the openness and honesty of the NYC style. They feel that the company is developing in classic action a larger scale than any other American company so far, and it is a scale they like. They remember the mistake of Ballet Theatre in glamorizing and characterizing our ballet dancing on the European plan.

Massine whipped up Ballet Theatre once and gave it (with Tudor's help) a brief glory. But he couldn't solve the two main troubles: he couldn't unite the ballerinas to the company and he couldn't get the American dancers to open their hearts instinctively to dancing as the Russian ones had done. Massine proposed success as the magic formula to solve these problems. That sounded American. He had success. He had a triumph. But not a thing was solved. Instead everybody just got nervous. So now Balanchine proposes a different magic. He begins with attention on everyone's part to carriage, to correctness, to the score. This makes a kind of objective, nonegotistic focus, and it gives a kind of disinterestedness of expression. Do you see how this might make a basis for collaboration between chorus and principal other than individual applause, and a basis too for pride in one's work and for giving one's best imagination to it? It makes one moral law for all. You may find this attention to the craft of dancing not enough to hold your interest, you luxurious Europeans; but it's not ugly.

Europeans keep forgetting what a poor country America is. We can't afford those enormous, secure, pensioned, resident, officially respected companies you all do. We have no such luxuries as your wonderful Elvin, Nerina, and Grant dancing a young life away under the ancestral Petipas, and growing more and more beautiful through the deep decades of peace that prepare their triumphant accessions. The NYC never knows if it will last another season. It is either underpaid or overworked or both. With so small a company and so large a repertory—about a dozen novelties a year—there is no time for more than a memorizing of parts. How could they work so hard and act too? You can see for yourself how impecunious the company is—so poor it can't even afford to dress all its repertory, and has to run out every now and then in little whatyoucall'ems. Under the circumstances Balanchine and Kirstein might as well give up trying for tiny advantages as the managements of big vested interest must; they can keep in mind the biggest prize of all, the true grand style. (Fortunately in art there are as many first prizes as contestants, even if so very few ever win one.)

Ballet, AUGUST 1952

A LETTER ON "CARACOLE"

I haven't yet managed to speak of *Caracole*, and that was what I most wanted to do when I began to write you—so very interesting. The plebeian costuming of it is a pity and an indignity to Bérard too. But I think the NYC décor is so bad and so monkish generally that except for all of us to make fun of it every chance we get, there is no use in discussing it. (I don't mean the extraordinary lighting.) And yet I saw few ballet sets in Europe either that I wanted particularly to see again. They often looked better dressed than the NYC's and they showed better if a dancer was forward or back; but they rarely stood up as architecture for twenty minutes on end, stood up architecturally imaginative while the music and the dancers swept across again and again; no prettiness of backbone. In Europe what I was happy over was the delicious execution of costumes possible in Paris, and a grace in it sometimes in Italy (and in Italy a sweet sensibility for lights). No use getting into all of that. Despite its hard clothes, *Caracole* is a heavenly piece to see, and everybody knows it immediately. At second sight, it has a so-to-speak Miltonic grip in its suavity; and it takes wild Miltonic risks with having enough air to breathe—it isn't airy like *Mozartiana.*

But fanciful and sudden, ingenious and beautiful the ballet is over and over. Densely so in the long variation's movement and again in the Andante; in the introductory movement amusing and sweet; in the last, quick with a *Figaro* kind of wit (a little thinness here doesn't hurt); everywhere with a Mozartian current in continuity and a Mozartian lightness in beginnings and endings. Only the Minuet movement seemed mistaken—it struck me as too tight; though the spikey hooflike steps of the girls seemed to be pricking patterns like those on baroque prints of horse ballets and carousels. The baroque Spanish Riding Academy of the Hapsburgs is meant to be suggested by the word "caracole," too; and often the girls' light dances evoke an animal power in grace and—even more beautiful—an animal innocence in display. I remembered Belmonte, a Lippizaner who performed *haute école* here on a variety stage ten years ago, how the massive horse enjoyed himself majestically dancing for us, how he glowed and beamed with princely pleasure. Perhaps you've seen him too. The variations have something of that; the Andante in turn has a lovely suggestion of great mares being led by the bridle, grandly displayed like in baroque paintings. When you start thinking this way, the quick nods as the curtain rises become horsey, and the flurry of the Finale like the flurry of a race. But you don't have to—nothing in the sequences is literal, or insists on allusion. Strange that graceful academic dancing can evoke the heavy animals; strange to feel these powerful performing beasts related in their play to Mozart's tender intimacy. Strange how they become other images if you look close at the overpoweringly metrical choreography.

If you watch the steps, in the variations for instance, a single step or brief combination will flash out oversharply visible, so astonishing is the contrast to the step before it. The shape of the step appears unexpected as lightning and, lightninglike, vanishes—or like the pulsating brilliance of a butterfly on the ground, as its wings open and shut. And through these disparate flashings the dancer's impetus never falters. The powerful muscular pelvic thrust that renews her impetus step by step intensifies the image's visual pulsation. The deep dance beat of these powerful flashes strikes the eye sometimes even twice to a bar (like on 1-3-1 or 1-4-1), and it is set to music light, light in its beat, easy and fluid. The meter is strictly identical; it nails the dance to the music; and feeling them nailed fast to one another, the deep divergence between them in the weight of the beat becomes monstrous and ritual-like. But neither voice falters in its onward movement, and how felicitous each is; as one watches these contours lengthen, their grace covers over the secret between them and seems to obliterate it.

But something as strange as the incommensurableness of the two synchronized beats recurs in the action of the Andante. In this succession of fragmentary pas de deux, a new duet sometimes takes over with the boy changing partner merely on an upbeat, and the shift cuts into the continuity of the melody; you feel the wound of the cut, and yet you see across it the same tender intimacy continue undisturbed as if dreamlike, continue through each shifted pair and across the flowing melodic periods poignantly unbroken as long as the movement lasts, as if there were tenderness enough forever, the beautiful couples dismembered and recoupled, three boys and five girls, with no jealous failure in their lovely awareness. But as if to give no pathos to this image, the dance does not touch any of the "moments of expression" of the music—the young people onstage seem not to by some delicacy of instinct. Apart from the fateful identity of meter, they have another phrasing, another rhetoric and fashion of behavior than the music—the dancers keep a Maryinsky-Byzantine grandeur of deportment, the music a Viennese spontaneity of sentiment; separate ways of enduring. And when the Andante is finished, it is as if you had seen on two separate faces the same brief look of angelic irony; though they seem strangers, you know how close they have been in a secret they will never tell. The closest description of *Caracole* was that of a poet friend who said, smiling, when the curtain had fallen, "Balanchine probably made it as fast as Mozart did, or only a little slower."

That is what the excitement of the piece seems like to me. Looking at it more objectively, more relaxed, it seems meant to be as sweet as possible. There is not one novel "expressive" gesture to tax your nervous sympathy; not one step is twisted or odd, each limpidly departs from and returns to a neutral equilibrium; everything is academic convention; nothing but the body in plastic motion in beauty—the dancer appearing effortlessly fantastic. And yet stroke by stroke, so much fantasy, so ceaseless a jet, there is too much to watch, it leaves no time to breathe, to assent. It is a dense choreography one can call impossible to dance and to see the way some pieces of music are called impossible to play and to hear—impossible except that everyone recognizes them right away as miraculous. It is overpowering, as to some people may be their first sight of the brilliantly peopled heaven of the circus—acrobats and beasts. For me it made me think of how a boy in love hears a man's voice telling what love is like—so much more of it everywhere than anyone cares for, so much more than too much and every bit lucky—the boy believes that what he is feeling for the man is anger; and it seemed to me that the heavy thrust of its pulse was like the sound almost regular year by year of a heart in a breast. I don't mean Balanchine intended any of these ideas—no, no, not at all—only that I found it so innocent and insoluble; and how wonderful to see such a grandiose work come into being onstage in all its glitter and beauty, danced with a sweetness and a clarity that are disarming. *Ballet*, SEPTEMBER 1952

SOME THOUGHTS ABOUT CLASSICISM AND GEORGE BALANCHINE

The beautiful way the New York City company has been dancing this season in the magnificent pieces of its repertory—in *Serenade*, *Four Temperaments*, *Symphonie Concertante*, *Swan Lake*, *Caracole*, *Concerto Barocco*, *Orpheus*, *Symphony in C*, and the new *Metamorphoses*—not to mention such delicious small ones as *Pas de Trois*, *Harlequinade*, or *Valse Fantaisie*—made me want to write about the effect Balanchine's work has had in developing a largeness of expression in his dancers, and in showing all of us the kind of beauty classic ballet is by nature about. Thinking it over, I saw questions arise on tradition, purity of style, the future of classicism, and Balanchine's intentions in choreography; and I wondered what his own answers to them would be, or what he would say on such an array of large subjects. So one evening after watching an excellent performance of *Four Temperaments*, I found him backstage and we went across Fifty-sixth Street together to the luncheonette for a cup of coffee.

He began by mentioning the strain on the dancers of the current three-month season, dancing eight times a week and rehearsing novelties and replacements all day. After it was over, he said, smiling, the real job of cleaning up their style could begin; for the present it was like a hospital, all they could do was to keep patching themselves up just to continue. I assured him they had just danced very well indeed, and then told him about my general questions. He paused a moment. Then, taking up the issue of style, he answered that there were of course several styles of classic dancing; that he was interested in one particular one, the one he had learned as a boy from his great teachers in Petersburg—classic mime and character as well as academic style. He spoke as a quiet man does of something he knows entirely and knows he loves. He sketched the history of the Petersburg style. Then he took up aspects of other styles he did not care for—a certain sanctimonious decentness in that of Sadler's Wells, a note of expensively meretricious tastiness in that of the Paris Opéra—these are not his words, but I thought it was his meaning. He was not denying the right of others to a different taste than his own; nor did he mean to minimize the achievements of these two great bodies, but only to specify points of divergence. He said he believed in an energetic style, even a soldierly one, if one chose to put it that way.

Passing from the subject of style to tradition, he mentioned as an example the dance we know as the Prince's variation in *Swan Lake*. He told me that it used to be done all in brisés and small leaps, but that one time when Vladimiroff was dancing it in Petersburg this great dancer changed it to big jetés; and now the big leaps are everywhere revered as tradition. I gathered he thought of tradition rather as a treasured experience of style than as a question of steps; it was a thought I only gradually came to understand.

At this point he noticed that Steve wanted to close his luncheonette, and so we went back to the theater and continued to speak standing in the backstage corridor. We got on the subject of notation. He emphasized the continuity of movement it could reproduce. I asked if *Four Temperaments* had been notated, adding that I felt sure the public in forty years time would enjoy seeing it as much as we do, and would want to see it danced in the form it has now. "Oh, in forty years," he said, "ballet will be all different." After a momentary pause, he said firmly, as if returning to facts, that he believed ballet was entertainment. I realized he meant the word in its large sense of both a social and an attractive public occasion. But he looked at me and added, in a more personal tone, that when one makes a ballet, there is of course something or other one wants to say—one says what one says. He looked away, as if shrugging his shoulders, as one does after mentioning something one can't help but that one doesn't make an issue of in public.

At the far end of the corridor the dancers were now assembling for *Symphony in C*, the final ballet, and he returned to the subject of style and spoke of two ways of rising on toe—one he didn't like, of jumping up on point from the floor, the other rising from half-toe, which he wanted. Similarly in coming down in a step, he wanted his dancers to touch the floor not with the tip of the foot, but a trifle to one side, as if with the third toe, because this gives a smoother flexion. He spoke too of different ways of stretching the knee in relation to flexing the ankle as the dancer lands from a leap, and of stiff or flexible wrist motions in a port de bras. Details like these, he said, were not consciously noticed by the audience, nor meant to be. But to him they were important, and a dancer who had lived all his life in ballet noticed them at once. They corresponded, he suggested, to what in speaking one's native tongue is purity of vocabulary and cleanness of accent, qualities that belong to good manners and handsome behavior in a language one is born to and which one recognizes in it with pleasure. At that point I felt that he had, in his own way, replied to the large questions I had put at the beginning, though he had avoided all the large words and rubbery formulas such themes are likely to lead to. So I thanked him and went back to my seat and to the first bars of *Symphony in C.*

Balanchine had offered no rhetorical message. He had made his points distinctly and without insistence. It was several days before I realized more fully the larger ideas on the subject of style that his points had implied. He had suggested, for one, that style demands a constant attention to detail which the public is not meant to notice, which only professionals spot, so unemphatic do they remain in performance. The idea, too, of style as something a man who has spent many years of his life working in an art loves with attentive pertinacity. A classic dancer or choreographer recognizes style as a bond of friendship with the great artists he remembers from his childhood and with others more remote he knows only by name. For in spirit classic artists of the past are present at a serious performance and watch it with attention. And as I see Tallchief dance now in *Concerto Barocco*, I feel that they invisibly smile at her, they encourage her, they blow her little Italian kisses. They danced steps that were different but they understand what she means to do; her courage night after night is like theirs. And I think that they find a similar pleasure in the work of the company as a whole. For dancers have two sets of judges: the public and its journalists, who can give them celebrity, and the great artists of their own calling, who can give them a feeling of dignity and of proud modesty.

The bond between classic dancers is that of good style. But Balanchine in his conversation did not say that style in itself made a ballet, or that the entertainment he believed in was an exhibition of style. On the contrary he said that when he made a piece there was something or other he wanted to say. He was affirming the inner force that is called self-expression. And no doubt he would recognize it as well as an inner force in dancing. But for him there was no contradiction between creative force and the impersonal objective limitations of classic style. He knew in his own life as an artist—and what a wide, rich, and extraordinary life it has already been—that his love of style and his force of expression could not be divided, as they could not have been for others before him, and I am sure will not be for classic dancers of the future either.

That Balanchine expresses a meaning in a ballet is clear enough in those that tell a story. And he has made several striking story ballets even in the last decade. Among them are his recent vivid version of *Swan Lake*; *Night Shadow*, a savage account of the artist among society people; *Orpheus*, a large ritualistic myth of poetic destiny; and *Tyl*, a realist and antifascist farce. It took our bright-eyed young matinee audience to discover how good the jokes are in *Tyl*; and now the children have made it clear, the grown-ups see how touching are its sentiments.

The subject matter, however, of the so-called abstract dance ballets is not so easy to specify. On the point of the most recent, *Metamorphoses*, it happened that while it was being rehearsed, I met him and asked if what I had heard was true, that he was making a ballet on the Kafka short story, "The Metamorphosis." He laughed in surprise, and said no. But he added that as a matter of fact, about a month before, going down from his apartment one night to buy a paper, there on the sidewalk in the glare of the stand and right in the middle of New York he saw a huge cockroach going earnestly on its way. As for me, Olympic athletes, Balinese dancers, Byzantine seraphs seem all to have contributed images for this ballet, besides that Upper East Side cockroach. But onstage these elements do not appear with the expression they have in life. In the athlete section the explosive force of stops and speed makes a dazzle like winter Broadway in its dress of lights; hints from Bali are wildly transformed into a whirring insect orgy; the joyous big-scale nonsense of it and then the evanescent intensity of an insect pas de deux are as simple and childlike in their vitality as a Silly Symphony cartoon; and the end is a big sky swept by powerful, tender, and jubilant wings. What Balanchine has expressed is something else than the material he began with, something subjective; and I so respond to it.

His dance ballets each express a subjective meaning. I feel it as the cumulative effect of the many momentary images they present, dramatic, lyric, or choral. And the pleasure of them is seeing these images as they happen; responding to the succession of their brilliant differences that gradually compose into a structure—an excitement rather like reading a logically disjointed but explosively magnificent ode of Pindar. One might say they are dance entertainments meant to be watched by the natives in New York rather the way the natives of other places than this watch a social village dance in West Africa or watch a Balinese kebyar or legong.

I am supposing at least that natives take their dance forms for granted and watch instead the rapid images and figures. I like that way of watching best myself; and the closer I so follow a dance ballet, the more exciting I find it, and the more different each becomes. I do not enjoy all of Balanchine's equally, or all entirely. Some, like *Firebird* or *Card Game*, have disintegrated in large sections. Others, despite brilliant dancing and passages I enjoy, do not appeal to me in their overall expression—*La Valse*, *Scotch Symphony*, *Bourrée Fantasque*. So capricious is a subjective taste. And it is unstable too.

There is a perhaps less capricious way of following a dance piece. It is that of watching its formal structure. And the excitement of doing it is a more intellectual one. I am not sure that it is a good way to watch, but I will mention some of the discoveries one so makes, since they are another approach to the meaning of a piece.

An aspect of structure, for instance, is the way Balanchine sets the score, how he meets the patterns in time, the patterns of energy from which a dancer takes his spring. When you listen closely and watch closely at the same time you discover how witty, how imaginative, how keen his response at every moment is to the fixed architecture of the music. *Pas de Trois* and *Symphony in C* are not hard to follow in this double way, and their limpid musical interest helps to give them their light and friendly objective expression. More complex are the staccato phrasings of *Card Game*; or the interweaving of melodic lines and rhythmic accents in *Concerto Barocco*; or the light play—as of counterpoint—in the airy multiplicity of *Symphonie Concertante*. In this piece the so-called imitations of the music by the dancers, far from being literal, have a grace at once sophisticated and ingenuous. The musical play and the play of dance figures, between them, create bit by bit a subtle strength—the delicate girlish flower-freshness of the piece as a whole. But in relation to the score, the structural quality his ballets all show is their power of sustained rhythm. This power may express itself climactically as in *Serenade* or keep a so-to-speak even level as in *Concertante* or *Card Game*. It makes a difference in applause but not in fascination. Taking as a springboard the force of the extended rhythms—rhythmic sentences or periods—music can construct, Balanchine invents for the dancing as long, as coherent, and as strongly pulsing rhythmic figures; whatever quality of the rhythm gives the score its particular sweep of force he responds to objectively in the sweep of the dancing. And this overall rhythm is different in each piece.

Not that one doesn't recognize rhythmic devices of accent or of climax that he repeats—such as the rhythmic turning of palms inside outside; the Balanchine "pretzels," which I particularly like; or "the gate," an opening in the whirling corps through which in dynamic crescendo other dancers leap forward. He likes bits of canonic imitation; he likes the dramatic path of a star toward a climax to be framed in a neutral countermovement by satellite dancers. And there are some devices I don't care for too, such as the star's solo supported attitude on a musical climax, which (despite its beauty in Petipa) sometimes affects me in the way a too obvious quotation does. But to notice devices in themselves apart from the flow of rhythm and of images they serve to clarify tends to keep one from seeing the meaning of a piece.

Quite another surprise in his ballets if you watch objectively is the variety of shapes of steps, the variety of kinds of movement, that he manages to make classic. "Classic" might be said, of course, to include all kinds of movement that go to make up a three-act classic ballet: academic dancing, mime, character, processions, dancers in repose. And as folk and ballroom steps have been classicized in the past in many ways, so Balanchine has been classicizing movements from our Negro and show steps, as well as from our modern recital dance. In his more recent pieces, the shapes of the steps go from the classroom academicism of *Symphony in C* and the academic virtuosity of *Caracole* through ballroom and more or less traditional character dancing to the untraditional shapes of *Four Temperaments* with its modern-style jokes and crushing impact, or of *Orpheus*, or of *Metamorphoses* and its innocent stage-show style. What an extraordinary absence of prejudice as to what is proper in classicism these odd works show.

But in what sense can all his variety of movement be classical? It is so because of the way he asks the dancer to move, because of the kind of continuity in motion he calls for. For the continuity in all these pieces is that of which the familiar classroom exercises are the key and remain a touchstone. Classic dancing centers movement in a way professionally called "placement"; it centers it for the advantage of assurance in spring, balance, and visibility. The dancer learns to move with a natural continuity in impetus, and a natural expression of his full physical strength in the thighs—thighs and waist, where the greatest strength to move outward into space naturally lies.

Balanchine's constant attention to this principle develops in his dancers a gift for coherent, vigorous, positive, unsimpering movement, and a gift too for a powerful, spontaneous rhythmic pulse in action. And a final product of it is the spaciousness which their dancing—Tallchief exemplifies it—comes to have. Clear, sure-footed dancing travels through space easy and large, either in its instantaneous collective surges or in its slow and solitary paths. So space spreads in calm power from the center of the stage and from the moving dancer and gives a sense of human grandeur and of destiny to her action. In his conversation with me he had of course only stressed the small details of motion from which the large effects eventually can grow.

The final consistency that classical style gives to a performance comes from its discipline of behavior. Handsome behavior onstage gives to an entertainment a radiance Broadway dancing knows little of. Balanchine often builds it into the dance—even when he works on Broadway—by so timing the action that if it is done cleanly and accurately the dramatic color becomes one of a spontaneous considerateness among the dancers for one another and of a graceful feeling between the girls and boys. Further subtleties of behavior, subtle alternations of contact and neutral presence, are a part of the expression his pieces have. They seem, as is natural to Americans, unemphatic and usually even like unconscious actions.

But where drama demands more conscious relationships, these require a more conscious kind of acting. What Balanchine tries for as classic acting is not an emphatic emotional stress placed on a particular gesture for expression's sake. He tries instead to have expression present as a color throughout a dance or a role, sometimes growing a trifle stronger, sometimes less. It is as if a gesture were made in its simplest form by the whole body as it dances. This is a grand style of acting not at all like the usual Broadway naturalism. In ballet a realistic gesture if it is overstressed, or if the timing of it makes the dancer dwell on it "meaningfully," gets clammy; the grand style remains acceptable at any speed or intensity; and Tallchief often exemplifies it at a high intensity—in the writhings of Eurydice, for instance, or in the quiet lightness of her last entrance in *Firebird.*

What I have tried to say is that the meaning of a Balanchine piece is to be found in its brilliance and exhilarating variety of classical style. There is nothing hidden or esoteric or even frustrated about the expression of one of his dance ballets. The meaning of it, as of classical dancing generally, is whatever one loves as one watches it without thinking why. It is no use wasting time puzzling over what one doesn't love; one had better keep looking, and sharply, to see if there isn't something one does, because it goes so fast there is always a lot one misses. Pretty people, pretty clothes, pretty lights, music, pictures, all of it in motion with surprises and feats and all those unbelievable changes of speed and place and figure and weight and a grand continuous rhythm and a tumultuous sweep of imaginary space opening up further and forever, glorious and grand. And because they are all boys and girls doing it, you see these attractive people in all kinds of moments, their unconscious grace of movement, and unconscious grace in their awareness of each other, of themselves, of the music, of the audience, all happening instantaneously and transformed again without a second's reflection. That is what one can find to love. That is the entertainment, different in each piece. All these beauties may be gathered in a sort of story, or you may see them held together only by the music. It is up to you to look and seize them as they flash by in all their brilliant poetry. And many people in the audience do.

Classic ballet is a definite kind of entertainment, based on an ideal conception of expression professionally called "style." It does not try to be the same sort of fun as some other kind of entertainment. It tries to be as wonderful as possible in its own beautiful and voluntarily limited way, just as does any other art. What correct style exists for, what it hopes for, is a singular, unforeseen, an out-of-this-world beauty of expression. In our own local and spontaneous terms this is what Balanchine intends. I wish I had found a less heavy way of treating so joyous and unoppressive a form of entertainment; for a tender irony is close to the heart of it. But I hope I have made clear at least that neither classicism nor "Balanchine style" is, as one sometimes hears people say, merely a mechanical exactness in dancing or in choreography, no personality, no warmth, no human feeling. As for his dancers, this season in particular has shown us that the more correct their style, the more their individual personality becomes distinct and attractive onstage.

The strictest fans realize that his work in creating a company is still only half done. But though still unfinished, the result is already extraordinary. London, Paris, and Copenhagen have striking stars, have companies excellent in many ways, larger, wealthier, more secure than we know how to make them. This winter the hard-worked little New York City company has shown itself, both in style and repertory, more sound, more original, more beautiful than any you can see anywhere in the Western world.

In the last five years George Balanchine has come to be recognized as the greatest choreographer of our time abroad as well as here. Such a position has its drawbacks. But for my part, though his prestige may add nothing to my pleasure in his work, I have no quarrel with it.

Dance Magazine, FEBRUARY 1953

"OPUS 34"

Opus 34, despite its press, is powerful theater, brilliantly produced and performed. Once more Balanchine has made a striking ballet different from any in the repertory, different from any anywhere. It is a powerful and it is a paradoxical ballet. It looks like modern dance, but it is entirely classical; it shows no sweeping discharge of physical energy, but it generates as much force as if it did; it is frightening in its pantomime, but the effects seem ludicrous. The fact is it combines the ludicrous and the tragic in a magnificent tragic glee. It is the same glee that is so intolerably enormous in *King Lear*. Children like it, but adults shudder. They wish *Opus* were meaningless, or even a joke at their expense; it isn't, its theater power is exact at every point.

Opus 34 is a piece in two parts not at all similar at first sight, but both set to the same darkly glistening and oppressive Schoenberg score. The first part is straight dancing in a peculiar range; the second is a fairy tale told in pantomime. The audience watches the first part absorbed and impressed; it watches the second fascinated, frightened, and giggling. Then the curtain comes down and there is a curious vacuum, the blank state of not knowing what hit you. One tries to get one's bearings; one can't seem to bring all one has seen in focus.

What has happened onstage has been peculiar. When the curtain goes up, thirteen dancers face you, dressed alike in plaster white, each standing alone. They quiver a knee and stop; they lunge forward and stop; they dangle their hands; crouching, they throw a hand wide, slip it between the legs, grab a knee and stop; they turn up their faces to you and stop; they stand erect again. They are not tense, but very alert. The gestures are swift and clear, done without any sentiment; they look a little comical—yet somehow like those of terror. Stops and movements build into phrases, complex classic figurations, sections. The dance develops a powerful rhythm. The dancers touch themselves, each other, sharply and without feeling and go on; groups start and stop in a narrow compass, they scarcely leave the ground, they stretch their strength oddly downward. By flashes the stops give a sudden supervisibility like a film close-up. It looks funny and dreadful, yet the movements are so elegantly done, the rhythm so strong, the variety so surprising, one has a sense of great dynamism. It is as if people were under an oppressive force, meeting it keenly and swiftly, using to the utmost the space left them. But the dancers come to a repeat, as if there were no issue from the trap. Then, very slow, they mysteriously merge into a close clump of people, and together they meet extinction candidly and without complaint. It is an image of strange tenderness.

At once the pantomime begins. A brother and sister stand with their backs to us at the footlights, facing the darkness upstage. They go forward into it, a witch beckons them aside. As they turn toward her, swooping creatures tear them apart, kidnap them, they disappear. Out of the dark comes a fat squad of nurses, two operating tables, a surgeon. An operation is performed. Bandages, bandages, bandages. Dumped off the tables are the brother and sister, horribly altered, dreadfully fascinating to see. They quiver fantastically, grovel in anguish, they reach for and find each other blindly, ludicrously. A slithery heap of something viscous appears, like a wave. The girl steps into it for relief, it slowly mounts, swallows her. A second wave absorbs the boy. In the heaving waves, the victims wriggle, they try to reach each other, they meet wallowing topsy-turvy, are separated. The brother is scooped wondrously upward, gone forever. The girl is stranded ashore and rises. She finds a frightening memento of him, she hoods herself in it; hooded, she paces forward to the footlights. She turns, finds herself where the two of them were once together, facing the enormous dark that bears down on her from everywhere. Alone she slowly paces into it. Blinding lights hit her head-on, set fire to her, and, erect, she paces on into them. Curtain.

The pantomime is clearly a fairy tale—the dark wood, the witches, the cruel wizard, the bewitched waves and lights. The grisly events are vivid but not naturalistic. They appear and disappear in an unnatural black void. And like a fairy tale, as we accept the truth of the story, we find ourselves back safe in a familiar domestic lamplit room, back in the familiar theater.

What I have described is what anyone sees who watches the stage. The action is lucidly shown and straightforward. The piece has no surrealist ambiguity; there is no mystification, no siding with the monster, no confusion or violation of personality. Still less is it a hoax, a "period" spoof. Both parts move steadily to a heroic ending, a moment of quiet for an image of final courage. Both show people meeting an overwhelming inhuman force with courage, without complaint. The destiny, savage and ludicrous, that they meet seems to be, as a friend said, "the end of everything"; but that is merely what none of us escapes.

The tragic horror of *Opus* is not a gloomy fancy the choreographer wants to make a personal point about. It is given by the score. You hear it insistently evoked by the music. And the program notes tell you the story Schoenberg had in mind. It is contained in the titles of the sections of his score: "Threat. Danger. Fear. Catastrophe." The choreographer has dramatized this four-word libretto as convincingly as he could and in two parallel ways. He has projected the rising horror it calls for through striking images of savage irony and human heroism. The glee and the tenderness of these make the unescapable catastrophe not a pessimistic defeat; no, they make it lift tragically in the midst of horror. And the dramatic impact it achieves is terrifyingly real.

As for the dramatic device of mingling the ludicrous and the tragic, that has long been legitimate, and even a glory of theater. Balanchine has used it before: in *Prodigal Son*, for instance, and in *Night Shadow*; used it without a story reference in *Four Temperaments*. And he has long hoped to make a *Don Quixote*. He has certainly used a great many other and gentler devices when they were called for. The particular effect of this one is double: first it shocks one's stuffiness, then it delights one's sense of truth.

People shocked and puzzled by *Opus 34* have taken to the comfortable cliché that its devices and ideas are "the old-fashioned ones of the German twenties." This is nonsense for anyone who knows those twenties. Their characteristic was the protest, the resentful whine, the morbid self-dramatization. The ideas of *Opus* are consistently and clearly the opposite ones. It looks destiny in the face; it accepts catastrophe as a test of courage.

But what makes the ideas in the ballet appear with such expressive power is the way the stage action at every moment seems to fulfill the intense dramatic potency of the music. When the ballet is over you are convinced that you "understood" the score, you have felt its grandeur and theater. The music is Schoenberg's Opus 34, "Accompaniment-Music for a Motion Picture." Balanchine has set it twice: the first time he makes you see the forces of its tight logical form, the second the wide stream of its expressive rhetoric. In the first part of the ballet you watch the compressed phrases, the reversals, the intricate developments; wonderful how the dance reveals the hidden majesty of rhythm, reveals the intense spring of action left in the interlocking structure. In the second part, the music floods out like a soundtrack, weird as a spell of science fiction, inexorable in the timing of its dreadful stream. The sounds of it, the whirrs, squeals, reverberations, hums, and thuds, have frozen the first time on strictly limited dance movements, as if crystal by crystal their logic immured the dancers; then, the second time, the same sounds have liquidly lifted up a few solid gobs of nightmare, like the whisper of ghosts in a river that foretell what has happened already. Even if you don't look for the consistent narrative meaning *Opus* has, but follow it merely moment by moment as movements set to a particular score, the ballet makes its grand effect. That it offers two stage versions of the same very difficult music, each musically right and dramatically right, is a fantastic feat of choreographic virtuosity; but the expressive power, not the virtuosity, is what you feel as you watch.

In the pantomime the episodes become frightening because their exact timing projects them so forcefully. Note for instance the scary effect of the waits between when nothing at all happens. The gestures themselves are not those of psychological pantomime, nor are they stylized; they are the large simple factual actions that classic ballet has preserved from earlier theater. Note how real the effect is when the surgeon backs away from the tables, turns once, and then backs further away into the wings; or when legs wiggle without bodies out of the clasp of the waves; or the scare you feel when the sister picks up the piece of silk, though there is nothing special about the prop, and only a change of pace in her movement. The simple costumes and props by Esteban Francés, the complex lighting by Jean Rosenthal are to be sure marvels of theatrical imagination, so beautifully they suit every shade of the action.

The tense consistency of the pantomime's dramatic atmosphere might have been shattered at the point where the two dancers make a few startling dance movements; it isn't broken because these steps are in key with pantomime, they have the specific pantomime quality of movement. Similarly in the dance part of *Opus* the gestures derived from pantomime or modern dance do not jar with classic steps because they have been purposely given the specific quality of classic movement. They are made from a classic center, in classic balance, and in the classic rhythm of musical meter. They do not have a narrative continuity, but become—like classic steps—momentary shapes whose only urgency is that of musical rhythm and dance action. Such a shape will look oppressive not because the dancer dances it oppressedly, but because of its own visual and rhythmic nature. Whatever the look of the shape, a classic dancer can dance it clearly and securely; she keeps her swiftness, her elegance, her ease of bearing. And so the ballet allows for a steady confident brilliance in performance, and whatever it says is said nobly.

Brilliant the company looks as it performs, both girls and boys. No other company could duplicate the quickness of ear of these dancers; that they learned the piece in two weeks is an achievement unique in ballet history. Happily, the score is also played very handsomely and it is because the management provided for enough orchestra rehearsal—another admirable feat.

Opus 34 is a great ballet, and fans—even if they get angry—shouldn't miss it. It is in every way an exception among ballets, but it is legitimately classic wherever you test it. Such an exception is an honor to the company. It is worth a fight. It affirms the company's stand as the most adventurous anywhere, and it offers an adventure to the public.

My one objection is to the light that (if you sit in the orchestra center) shines in your eyes at the very end of the piece. It shines for nine seconds; the effect of the first four I like very much and wouldn't miss; during the last five seconds nothing more happens onstage, and I close my eyes and listen to the last grandiose whirrs of the music. If the light hurts your eyes too, you can try this solution. But just now a fan who has come into the room tells me he likes the whole nine seconds very much.

Dance Magazine, MARCH 1954

"THE NUTCRACKER"

The New York City Ballet's *Nutcracker* is a smash hit at the Center. It is Balanchine's *Oklahoma!*—a family spectacle, large and leisurely, that lasts two hours and sends people home refreshed and happy. A troubled New York poet sighed, "I could see it every day, it's so deliciously boring." The sentiments are those of family life, Christmas Eve, children growing up among adults, a little girl's odd and beautiful imagination. And the miracle is that these familiar sentiments appear onstage without vulgarization or coyness, with brilliant dancing, light fun, and with the amplitude of a child's wonderful premonitions.

The Nutcracker begins its large-scale entertainment pianissimo. Two children are sleeping in an armchair, left alone. Clara, the little girl, wakes up and goes to the door, peers through the keyhole. She wakens her brother, Fritz, who pushes her aside and takes the keyhole for himself. In the next room Father and Mother and the maid are trimming the Christmas tree. Guests arrive, children and parents. For the children there are games and gifts, a box of sugarplums; for the grown-ups, tea and conversation. Little girls behave, boys grow rowdy. An odd guest comes in late, bringing huge packages. He is an inventor, fascinating and a bit frightening, an artist who makes singular clocks and mechanical toys. He brings three that can actually dance; he also brings a wooden nutcracker for Clara. And he brings his Nephew, a boy of Clara's age, but with the glamour of being a stranger and of having almost grown-up manners. Clara and he get along very well, too well for Fritz. He grabs his sister's nutcracker and stamps on it. But it isn't badly hurt and Clara puts it to sleep in a new doll bed. There is a traditional party dance for everyone and Clara dances with the clock-maker's Nephew. Then the party is over, the guests say goodbye. And the room is empty.

Clara steals back in her nightgown to see her wounded nutcracker. But strange things happen. Huge unlikely mice rustle in and frighten her. The Christmas tree grows and grows enormous. The toy soldiers have become as big as she; so has the Nutcracker, with his sad wooden head. To protect her he leads the soldiers to battle against the mice. But the mice are taller and they win. The monstrous Mouse King appears; the Nutcracker himself rolls on the ground. A brave rabbit pulls the royal tail. The King flings around; Clara throws her shoe and hits the Mouse King on the back. As he whirls again to attack her, the Nutcracker leaps up and runs him through. The fight is finished. The victorious Nutcracker walks through the wall into the moonlit snow. And Clara sleeps on his bed as it glides after him outdoors. The bed wanders about the snow-laden forest, gliding to the music, with Clara asleep on it all alone.

Among the moon-bright firs the Nutcracker turns into a Prince. He wakes Clara and gives her a crown. They go deeper into the woods. Snowflakes begin to drift—like snowflakes you watch through a windowpane. First one or two dart past, then more come, they skim and scatter, they spin and thicken and vanish, they gather and rush, and they rest. Clara and the Prince walk through them to start their nighttime journey as the voices of the boys' choir rise once. The first act is over.

The second act is in the Sugar Plum Fairy's gold palace on a pink underground lake. Sailing up in a walnut shell, the Prince and Clara dock at the pier. The Fairy asks the Prince where they are from. "We come from way over there. This is what happened. I was sleeping. The mice attacked. I fought them. I fought the Mouse King. And Clara threw her shoe and saved me. I killed the Mouse King. That is what happened." The Fairy answers, "You have a brave heart." She tells some angels who are there to bring a throne and something to eat. As they eat, wonderful sweets run out and dance for them. Hot Chocolate, bold and pleasant, from Spain; Coffee from Arabia, a strong, peculiar, funny flavor; Tea, spry and Chinese. There is Marzipan, very sweet, crisp to nibble; candy canes with a sharp peppermint bite; a kind of tea-cosy giantess who keeps under her skirts small precise candies. And there is a big Christmas cake of many layers, with roses on the icing and a transparent silvery sugar

Dewdrop—so much cake it might be a garden with tunnels. The Fairy then dances with her Cavalier—so light, gliding, and quick, so respectful to each other, so easy in their whispering surprises, soft jumps, and airy twists. They are like adults at their very best, and wonderfully well behaved. Everybody dances for a moment more, and then Clara and her Prince say goodbye; we see them a last time in their walnut-shell ship, alone on a wide rippling blue sea, sailing to still other adventures. And that is the end.

The Nutcracker tells the story of a party at home and then of a party at the Fairy's house. The agitations of Christmas Eve lead to a small nightmare, a nostalgic journey, a glorious arrival. At the Fairy's there is everything that is best at home, radiantly clear. But then one leaves; ahead is another journey, still further.

These are the meanings I see as I watch, but the ballet doesn't press them. Nothing is insisted upon. The dances of sweets are straight dances, if you don't want to think of so much candy. But a small boy near me said, "Isn't there any more food or things to drink?" The pantomime too makes its narrative points straight and clear; but it doesn't force them on you. As little Clara was walking grandly with her Prince in the snow, a mother ahead of me whispered to another, "Poor thing, look, she's lost a shoe." Her seven-year-old daughter spoke up: "She lost it because she threw it at the Mouse King." It was a dramatic point, and she had seen it, and understood it.

The Nutcracker is a fantasy ballet for children, like a toy that a grown-up makes with thoughtful care. Grown-ups watching can slip back into a world they have left. The buried longings of it are there glittering still, but so charmingly, so lightly offered one doesn't have to notice. It is enough to notice the amusing family bits in the party scene, the fun of the transformations, the jokes in the dream, the sweet brilliance of the dancing, the pervasive grace of the music. And there is the pleasure of seeing children onstage who are not made to look saccharine or hysterical, who do what they do naturally and straight.

Of course, there are many more special pleasures. One of them is the novelty of watching so much pantomime; the more you watch, the odder becomes the difference it makes in a classic ballet, and the more interesting. *The Nutcracker* has several kinds of pantomime. There is that of classic gesticulation—the sequence of gestures by which the Nutcracker Prince tells his story to the Fairy. Each has a specific meaning so old nobody invented it. The gesture of revolving the hands one about the other chest-high (as in a muff) means: "This is what happened." It comes from antiquity, and is related to the silent gesture of "Keep on talking, give out with some more" used in radio booths. "Far from here," "sleep," "mouse," "king," "brave heart" are all gestures you can guess.

Stylized pantomime is quite another thing. It invents a dancey movement that intentionally half-resembles or suggests something else. Light touches of it are in the amusing mouse-and-soldier sequences set by Jerome Robbins. Still a third kind of pantomime is in the movement of the people at the family party. Their actions are not stylized at all, not part dancing, part mimicry; they are the plain normal movements everybody employs in daily life. But the pacing of them, the musical stress of the movement, and their relation to other actions add up to a little drama that is individual; they seem to tell it unintentionally.

Such an action is the deadpan shove—deliberately walked up to and away from—that Fritz gives the clock-maker's Nephew; also the Nephew's watching him walk away, watching steadily. Later, when the party breaks up, you can see two pairs of children who want to stay together, who are parted by their parents in two quite different tempos. The party scene has many details less prominent, which you discover only gradually. But they are all relevant to the story, they tell you the kind of family, the kind of social pressure in which Clara is growing up. The leisurely oppressive pacing of the party is in one sense the token of a responsible ruling class; but in another it creates the large time in which childhood events occur, the amplitude out of which fantasy takes shape. The party unfolds a story of mutual behavior, good manners and bad, those of children, of parents, of grandparents, guests and hosts, of a family servant, an eccentric artist. All these manners sharpen one's eye for the so-to-speak heavenly manners of the Fairy's palace, the graceful behavior of classic dancing. And *The Nutcracker* is also the story of a child's presentiment of handsome conduct, of civilized society; it is no foolish subject, and it gives the ballet its secret radiance.

So the pantomime becomes the dramatic reason why the grand pas de deux appears as a climax of fulfillment. It tops the shining sweep and rush of the Waltz of the Flowers that precedes it by the unexpected intimacy of its grandeur and glitter. The phrases are brief and intertwining; the star is free, but lightly she stays near her partner and swiftly turns as if diving each time in a different way into his supporting hands; leaps and lifts hover at half height; the adagio extensions move between or across the supporting figuration. The Cavalier's movements are clear, grand, and supple. And in the Fairy's variation (her solo) the brilliancy in intimate effects is delicious. The steps play across the pianissimo music in counterrhythms, counterphrases inventing feats of instant top-speed and instant rest, miraculously easy, so lightly do they dart from the spring of the music, ending (one of the times I saw it) in the featheriest of dazzles. The variation suits Maria Tallchief's soft powerful speed to perfection, and she dances it ravishingly. It is the triumph of her career. In the middle of the pas de deux, my four-year-old friend slipped an arm around his father's neck and whispered, "Are the people real?"

George Balanchine is the choreographer of this *Nutcracker.* The libretto is the old one, the steps and pantomime are new, without looking specifically like Balanchine. That much any balletgoer can see; but fans who like to watch more closely will find the original Balanchine contribution which does not strike one at first sight. For the music's sake, he accepted the old spectacle-ballet action—an action that the score wonderfully plans for and paces. He opened a few dance cuts in the score. In the pantomime, he wove several new theatrical details, all of them derived from the E. T. A. Hoffmann story that the libretto is based on (e.g., the keyhole episode, the role of a nephew, the wandering bed). For the apotheosis, originally "A Hive of Bees" (representing civilization), he substituted a simpler image, but one also derived from the German story.

In setting the pantomime, Balanchine did not force the German 1820 flavor. He made an old-fashioned Christmas, but kept to actions and manners that his company, including the children, could do naturally. In the group dances he tended to steps and figures of Ivanov's time, one might say to steps that Tchaikovsky had seen. Balanchine's dancers like to use their fine speed and sharpness, their rhythmic flexibility and musical ear; so he gave them the old steps with swifter displacements, in rhythms that are fresh, or in new virtuoso combinations. The dancers everywhere in the piece have an easy spontaneity in an old-fashioned look, a spontaneity which—if you stop to think of it—is astonishing in a long show whose theater concept is unfamiliar to us all.

The spontaneity of the new *Nutcracker* is the mark of its originality. It is central to it. Fanciful ornaments, curious details, the usual signs of originality disappear; their absence gives the piece a kind of classic impersonality. Balanchine liked two numbers from Ivanov's second act, knew them accurately, and quoted them unchanged. But there is so little Balanchinism in his own numbers that these quotations pass without a break in style; I took them for his inventions. They are the Prince's mime scene and the hoop dance. (Balanchine danced the steps of it thirty years after Ivanov made them; now thirty years later Robert Barnett dances them, and brilliantly too.)

Balanchine uses the modern effect of strikingly contrasted movements in constant succession only in the Marzipan dance and the pas de deux (where, however, they are separated by flashes of rest, and give a sense of closeup). The long Snowflakes waltz looks as if it used only a dozen elementary steps, but it is one of Balanchine's most magical inventions. The second-act dances make a sustained burst or a repeated surge; the power of each grows from only two or three movement motifs. The drama of each is in its striking rhythmic identity. The dances reflect gaiety or joyousness intimately or at a little distance, light and mild or bright and bold. The other sentiments of the score are expressed by the story situation, the timing of scenic effects, by the contrast of child and adult, of pantomime and dancing. In a nostalgic setting the dances are positive and sanguine.

But there is a powerful dramatic expressiveness in the large opposition between the so-to-speak forest-thick pantomime that fills the first act and leads only to a small clearing where snowflakes dance, and the spaciousness of the second act, with its clear dances that appear and disappear as free as shapes in the sky. The choreographic originality of the second act is not (where I had expected to find it) in decorative fancy. It is in the suddenness with which a dance shape, the shape of a dance, appears and vanishes. Each dance is instantly specific, it keeps its solidity as it rushes through the air, and is instantly gone. It has the grandeur of being complete, of asking nothing, of creating around its brief form a sense of airy stillness, of spacious calm. It seems impossible that so complete an image can be produced so suddenly, prolonged at will, and be so suddenly withdrawn. The effect is magical and powerful. And as I was watching it, wondering, my four-year-old friend seemed to feel a similar wonder. Looking at the same dancers I was, he asked his father very seriously, "How do they get out?" *Center*, MARCH 1954

"WESTERN SYMPHONY" AND "IVESIANA"

The two new pieces presented by the New York City Ballet during its fall season—*Western Symphony* and *Ivesiana*, both by George Balanchine—are as far apart as possible from one another in the kind of theater appeal they offer. *Western* is likable and lively, with good-natured jokes and fireworks, and it develops a dance momentum that for stamina, speed, and climax is irresistible. *Ivesiana* develops no speed of momentum at all, no beat; it is carried onward as if way below the surface by a force more like that of a tide, and the sharp and quickly shifting rhythms that appear have no firm ground to hold against an uncanny, supernatural drift. *Ivesiana* is a somber suite, not of dances, but of dense and curious theater images. Its expression is as subjective as that of *Western* is objective. But both ballets take as their subject matter familiar aspects of American life. And both are set to scores by native composers.

Ivesiana is set to six orchestral pieces by Charles Ives. They represent themselves as impressionist music, and the six titles specify what each is about. The material is noises of nature and scraps of everyday music treated as of equal musical value. The stream and pulse of the sonority, the extraordinary harmony, the eddies of conflicting rhythms sound unlike European music and fantastically apt to their local subject matter. The dimensions are compressed rather than intimate. The wonder of the score lies in the nobility of expression in relation to its subject matter that it achieves. It does so with the utmost succinctness but with no meagerness—quite on the contrary, with a kind of eerie grandeur as true and sure as that of an Emily Dickinson lyric.

This queerly magnificent music is not in our regular concert repertory, and it is worth going to the ballet just to hear it. Watching the ballet, however, one hears it as if with a heightened distinctness, hears its characteristic nuances and its grand expressive coherence as the theater images on stage shockingly confront one.

Such a theater image is the action onstage to the music entitled "The Unanswered Question." Out of the darkness a beautiful young girl in white appears aloft, carried by a team of four men, and a shadowy fifth precedes the cluster, turning, crawling, reaching toward her. Carefully, as in a ritual or a circus act, the girl is lowered and lifted, revolved in fantastic and horrifying fashions. In all the shapes her body takes, she is never any less beautiful or less placid. At moments her hair brushes the questioner's face. There is no awareness of his question or of his humiliation on anyone's part but his own. And the cortege moves forward again and disappears—like a great ponderous knot floating about in a shoreless obscurity. This scene, with its casual ghastly incident when the girl falls backward head-first into space, is the central one of the ballet.

The ballet begins with "Central Park in the Dark." A close wedge of girls appears way upstage in the dark and oozes forward spreading, covering the stage, kneeling, swaying. A girl runs in searching among them, a boy enters, they meet, and the stage looks like an agitated wood that surges around them—oddly bushy like the park itself—as they struggle together, lose, and catch one another in the monstrous dark. She drops; instantly with a frantic gesture he rushes off. Slowly the wood shrinks to the faraway clump it first was; much more slowly the girl feels her way with her hands across the deserted forestage. Next comes "Hallowe'en." It is a rushing whirl and whirr, a flurry as brittle and spooky as that of leaves at the end of New England October; and leaves too, or with the leaves, a boy and girl whirl and leap forward and away together and are struck down.

After the hymnlike "Unanswered Question" comes a noisy city scene, "Over the Pavements." Five boys and a girl jump, crawl, intertwine, innocently brutal, while several bands blare at once—a sightless massive energy like that of city streets—then the girl drops her head on a boy's shoulder, he runs off after the others, she skips unpreoccupied in another direction. Next, to a jazz that is small, sour, meticulously insane, comes "At the Inn." It is the elegant summer "inn" of New England, and a young couple side by side—with an intoxicated abandon and a miraculous rhythmic edge—invent a dizzy fluctuation of tango, maxixe, Charleston, and mambo steps, wander into a horrid combination and out of it, and approach a rough climax, but stop, shake hands, leave each other. After that comes a brief concluding section called "In the Night," in which, in a phosphorescent dark light never seen before, a great number of erect figures move on their knees very slowly onward in unconnected directions; and over the nocturnal murmur of the orchestra, as if across invisible meadows, float the smallest and purest notes of bells. As one listens for them, it is as if the stage, as if the whole company, had sunk half out of sight into another and slower world.

It all happens in twenty minutes, and it makes a great deal to see as it piles up. Painful situations, strokes of wit, local allusions, kinds of movement, shifts of impulse, intertwined rhythms, hallucinating contradictions—there is nothing comfortable to rest on. Details are as cozy as gravel. Events happen unexpectedly quick or distressingly slow, very odd or very obvious. The point of view contracts and expands: at one moment a part of a body grows overvisible, at another the sides of the stage overempty. The scale telescopes and so does the rhetoric: suddenness of expositions, brevity of climaxes, conclusions that open instead of shutting down. One can find it very irritating.

But the piece in its appalling shifts is steadily expressive. The theatricality is sanguine and decisive. It doesn't waste a note or a motion. There is no vagueness for ear or for eye. *Ivesiana* juxtaposes anguish with innocent fact. It compresses a conflict and drops it into a reach of eternity.

The tone is keen and positive. The ballet as one listens and watches moves very rapidly through an enormous range of fancy without a disproportion or a discontinuity. The speed kind of turns your stomach, but no harm.

There are many jokes at lightning speed. For instance, the innocence with which the boy and girl separate at the end of "Pavements" comes as a quick joke. But it makes the characters much more actual. The unexpected handshake in "At the Inn" looks like a gag. But the way it fits the musical conclusion that immediately follows gives it a second expression, a scary realness. At the climax of "Central Park," when the boy tosses and grabs the drooping girl in an awkward position, the flash is comic; but the shock of the humor is that it suits the tragic situation so realistically. In "The Unanswered Question" the views of the revolving girl which are ludicrous only make her body the more personal and the poignancy of heartbreak the weirder, the more intimate. Jokes such as these show you a concise flash of fact at the moment you expect a flow of sentiment. They take the place of a tragic pathos, which would need a great deal more time and repetition to develop. Such queer fun is typical of New England. Both Ives and Balanchine theatricalize in it a large-scale tragic glee.

And so for the general audience, the meaning of the piece is not elusive. The meaning is the same in the music and onstage. It offers a view of our local life, not from the point of view whether it is good or bad, whether it is pleasant or unpleasant, but seen as a vivid fact wide open to tragedy. The view is Ives's. Balanchine has inserted no different meaning of his own. He has taken that of the score, its condensed amplitude, the characteristic structural devices, the particular evocations of feeling, and has found steps, qualities of movement, situations, theater effects that correspond.

For the more special dance fan, Balanchine has found fresh developments, fresh values in familiar steps and in figurations he himself has already used. The startling weights, reversals, sequences in multiple rhythm flow with a miraculous easy vigor. To experienced classicists "Hallowe'en" and "Over the Pavements" will be a delight; a pity they were blurred on opening night by an unsteadiness in the pit. Classicists will find that the surprises (of action as of sound) are created by an imaginative tension of classic syntax. Onstage the surprises develop by a tightening of the gesture value of classic elements. The tenseness of continuity gives to such a surprise the appearance of a normal event—the look not of a stop but of a flowering. I want to see it all again. "It's a dictionary of movement," a painter exclaimed after the opening; and a teenager kept repeating, "It's fantastic movement, that's what he does, it's fantastic movement." Intermission talk had a look of concentration I remember seeing last at the premiere of *Deaths and Entrances*. The gallery had booed and cheered the ballet loudly. And one young man up there, just as the boy onstage rushed off at the climax of the first section, had cried out as if at pistol point, "Svengali!"

Ivesiana for a critic is as remarkable a novelty as *Four Temperaments* was. At first sight it is more phenomenal, less appealing. The older piece fuses weighty dance contrasts in the driving sweep of a strong beat; the newer one, with nearly no beat, condenses contrasting elements of gesture into solid theater images and floats their weight fantastically on a sustained acuity of harmony. In ballet theory this cannot be done successfully. But neither could the other. Ballets such as both of these are an active part of intellectual life in the United States; they are, it seems to me, among its triumphs. In any case, they are a fight. That is why the spirit, the vitality of the New York City company depend on dancing them. The way the company undertakes the incredible difficulties of *Ivesiana*—no other company in the world would be equal to them—shows it enjoys the battle. It danced *Four Temperaments* several years before it won that one. *Ivesiana* is still a draw.

The ballet is wonderfully lit by Jean Rosenthal. It is performed in practice clothes as an economy: the score was so difficult to play that extra orchestra rehearsals were expensive. I wish there were costumes, but the money could not have been spent better. And the New York City Ballet orchestra won a musical distinction our symphony orchestras can envy.

The other new ballet of the season, *Western Symphony*, was also danced in practice clothes. Costumes had been designed and are promised next season. I heard by chance what they were like: cowboy clothes for the boys, and for the girls dance-hall dresses of the Golden Eighties. There is a subtle and pervasive something in the dances of *Western*, a situation between the girls and boys, that these costumes would make charming and clear. Without them, one may unconsciously question what sort of American girls these dancing partners are, and why the score by Hershy Kay so insistently evokes a honky-tonk or dance-hall glamour.

Actually no one questions anything, the piece is so much fun to watch. Clear in any case is the healthy, normal Western American quality of movement it has. And Walter Terry in a brilliant first-night review in the *Herald Tribune* stated at once the historic aspect of the ballet: that the Americanness of the boys and girls is expressed in terms of strictly classic steps. He pointed out that the expression they have does not come from "Westernizing" a familiar step. The step is left intact but the sequence gives it a novel speed, metric accent, and visual emphasis which create an overall Western look—a Western strength in physical impulse and rhythm, in playfulness or sentiment. He showed how different this procedure is from that used in other Western ballets—*Rodeo* or *Billy the Kid*—and other Americana. It is like the difference between writing in dialect and in straight English, one might say. Mr. Terry's point will become more and more interesting and will be long remembered.

In *Western*—the action is like a big dance party, nothing but dancing—the dancers do everything possible with a four-bar and an eight-bar phrase. In the first section they fill it neatly full; in the second, they brush away a bar or two as if with a sigh; in the third, they leap over the bar marks in a long rolling motion like an easy canter; in the fourth—I get so excited by the syncopation I can't tell you what they did, but it was wonderful. The fourth section is all climax and goes on and on getting more so—at least it does if the orchestra keeps to tempo. I liked especially the manly mixture of false dreams and true in the sentimental second part—a part that is like a cowboy's vision of a pure ballerina. At a rehearsal I saw Balanchine miming this cowboy; it was so real, one would have thought he had never been anything else.

Something about the dancing gives an illusion of the clear desert air. "It clears your eyes," a young poet remarked to me as we came out after the performance. The company never looked so easy and fresh, though the piece isn't easy at all to dance. Tanaquil Le Clercq and Jacques d'Amboise were the special heroes of the first night. But Patricia Wilde and Herbert Bliss had danced beautifully, and Janet Reed and Nicholas Magallanes couldn't have been more touching and true in their delicate comedy. Miss Le Clercq and Miss Reed were brilliant too—quite differently brilliant—at the opening of *Ivesiana*, together that time with Allegra Kent, Todd Bolender, and Francisco Moncion.

The two ballets, one sociable, the other singular, are Balanchine's first direct treatment of American subject matter. He seems to know all about it, and have a great deal more to show us.

Center, OCTOBER 1954

"ROMA"

Roma, Balanchine's new ballet, is delightfully buoyant and firmly formal. The feeling of buoyancy it has is like a sense of many fountains splashing and purling deep in the quiet of a baroque garden. The formality of it is that of classic ballet—of the strictest French Petipa tradition. As one watches it, hearing the clear music, what one feels in the lightness is the graceful intimate impulse of the dancing. The grace of it seems modest as it takes place; but the sense of happiness it gives remains fresh in one's memory in a quite magical way.

Balanchine has set *Roma* to three movements of Bizet's *Roma Suite*—an extended pas de deux to the adagio, and lively dances for a large cast to the two faster movements that frame the slow one. The classicism is as correct as that of *Symphony in C*, but the spaces of *Roma* are more enclosed, more sheltered, more unspectacular. Within its closer world, the dancing of the new ballet skims and sparkles, it eddies and rushes. The fun, light-footed and happy natured, is a crisscross of accent between the boys and girls, a mutual grace of behavior. And even the "folk dance" romp at the end, with its elegant fireworks of leaps, flutter of steps, and rustle of tarantella tambourines, creates the unpresuming dazzle of a sophisticated friendliness.

One can see *Roma*, too, as Italian in character. The dancers do not pretend to be Italians, and very likely they would look foolish if they did. They dance as American dancers do, with a clear accuracy. But the figurations give them a particular lightness and quickness. It has in the very dance impulse of it a voluble vivacity, an easy politeness, a physical delicacy of contact. Not mimically, but in the quality of its impulse, it recalls the quick and sophisticated sociability of Italians.

From this point of view the three movements of *Roma* recall Italian qualities of gesture: the manners of young people promenading; a graceful sincerity in courtship; the candor, the crowded happy suddenness of a Neapolitan holiday. From this point of view *Roma* is a traveler's valentine to Italy, a happy and tender recollection of her daily life.

Her daily life as a foreigner knows it passing through the streets. It was the same domestic charm of Italian streets that young Bizet wrote about in his *Roma Suite* a century ago. His score is intimate and lucid, sprightly in rhythm, and charmingly orchestrated. Very much the formal young Frenchman amused by Roman sensuousness, he loves the sweet weather, the light bubblings of speech, the rapid guitar tunes; he loves the cordiality around him. As for pomp and grandeurs, he isn't so interested—he enjoys the personal grace of everyday people. That is what his valentine is about, and very handsome it is.

The painter Berman, with Bizet and Balanchine the third of the travelers who have made *Roma*, has designed the set and costumes. The girls wear bright and soft-cut bodices, full-billowing skirts, and underskirts from which the knee peeps demurely or boldly advances. The young men—a trifle military—have sleeves and short trousers of crushed-fruit colors with white tights up to mid-thigh (like boots). The white massive legs look particularly quick-footed. During the tarantella the caps everyone wears give the figures an extra succinctness. The costumes—period of Bizet in their allusions—are in the formal tradition of classic-ballet dress. Within that tradition—in which Berman is a master—they recall how flavorsome a feeling for the figure Italian clothes naturally have.

The set—like a lofty ruin and like a slum square—evokes a Roman massiveness, russet golden and many-storied against a heavy green sky. An iron railing, the railing one finds on a height in ruins and slums, opens at the back on a vastness of air. One feels the unseen view lying beyond and is drawn to it. Particularly during the pas de deux, which is magically lit, the scene is noble in its sentiment. For the concluding tarantella, a wreath of bulbs lights up story over story, like at nocturnal illuminations of local southern saints. Laundry appears, too, strung up high from wall to wall—very natural looking—and gives the neighborhood a Neapolitan friendliness. The scene is one of Berman's finest. It has an intense Italian presence of the open air that accords with the sociable dances, and an ancient melancholy that contrasts with their liveliness.

Roma was not much of a success at its opening. Its modesty turned out to be an extremely avant-garde effect. People went to see what new twist Balanchine had dreamed up and when they were shown the innocent art of dancing they were too bewildered to recognize it. But a bright-eyed lady beside me for her part was delighted. "So wonderfully buoyant," she said. "That's just what I wanted to see. No, I don't want to look at any more ballets, I want to go home and remember this one." She remarked too that though she had always enjoyed the manliness of Eglevsky's dancing, this time she enjoyed it much more—a more gentle considerateness for his partner gave it a grace of expression it often had lacked. She was delighted with Tanaquil Le Clercq and spoke of the beautiful turns of her head—"like those of long-necked Italian Madonnas"—as improbable as the painted ones and as delicious. "She has become a classic ballerina," she said, and spoke of her beautiful feet. I was delighted that my friend, who had not been to the ballet for some time, had so readily seen the new fantastic beauty of motion Le Clercq has shown a number of times this winter, and which has struck me as a major dance event of it. She has become a marvel.

The long adagio pas de deux for Le Clercq and Eglevsky is a most unusual one. It has an equable current and a stillness that do not allow the dancers the relief of a big climax. One can feel the attention of the audience, but also how new the quiet is to them. Onstage one notices an astonishing invention—a supported arabesque that slides over the two dancers' linked hands, and as it rests there and the ballerina is turned on point, it changes to a renversé extended in first, and the girl looks miraculously cradled as she is slowly spun. In the classic formality of the dancing one may sense the current of a more and more absorbed conversation—from a gentle pleasure in acquaintance, in tentative contact, to a playful ease in intimacy, and then to a sweetly earnest profession of faith. After that there is a mysterious courtesy between the two young people that spins to rest in a still pose swooping like a swallow's flight at dusk. Then the girl withdraws a little, smiling, and returns instinctively to a final pose of trust. It seemed to me a touchingly honorable and a very Italian and happy courtship. The lovers were interrupted by the explosive rush downstage—with their heads down—of two threesomes of tarantella dancers, a wild dash like that of Naples's children.

The charm of the pas de deux is a spontaneous delicacy of feeling between two young people alone. The novelty of it is a modesty in the accentuation of heroic dance feats. The quiet climaxes of the music give the dance its intimate stress. Beautiful for instance is that on a moment when the dancers pause separated upstage, each against the sky. Or that on a pose twice repeated—an arabesque grandly supported from the front (as if grandly sheltered), an arabesque felt rather than seen. The two dancers dissolve the pose before the musical climax is quite over, and the particular emphasis of it is like a poignant cadence of verse. To paraphrase such images in story terms does not convey the spontaneous pleasure of them or the transparency.

The way the pas de deux is set to the score gives the drama its sincerity of character. One responds to the inner impulse of the music as one sees that of the dance spring from a particular note or more amply lift from a phrase or a crescendo. Before and after the adagio, the faster dancing suits its steps to the measure, the phrase to the phrase. The dancers dance on the beat, as people naturally do; but being dancers they hardly touch the floor, or play with the beat several ways at once in counteraccents and syncopations.

The strictness of classicism in *Roma* and the strictness of the musical setting of the steps show the nuance of dance impulse more clearly. Dancers classically trained find in classicism a theatrical spontaneity and transparency. The expression of their dance can look sincere. And their personal quality in classicism—unconsciously transparent—can become a view of what the stage character represented is like "really." So for instance Le Clercq's delicacy of timing can give her characters a grace in courtesy, a quick awareness, that makes them exceptionally interesting. Fonteyn—a quite different dancer—has a similar courtesy.

It gives a wrong view of *Roma* to saddle its lightness with ideas. Interesting ones are present in it if one chooses to recognize them. One can enjoy so happy a grace and not notice the sophistication it also shows, or the theater modesty. *Roma* is brilliantly danced by the company, which deserves every praise, or very nearly—particularly by Eglevsky, who at the last performance reached a new peak in his career. I hope the piece stays with us awhile. *Center*, APRIL 1955

THREE SIDES OF "AGON"

One

Agon, a ballet composed by Igor Stravinsky in his personal twelve-tone style, choreographed by George Balanchine, and danced by the New York City Ballet, was given an enormous ovation last winter by the opening-night audience. The balcony stood up shouting and whistling when the choreographer took his bow. Downstairs, people came out into the lobby, their eyes bright as if the piece had been champagne. Marcel Duchamp, the painter, said he felt the way he had after the opening of *Le Sacre*. At later performances, *Agon* continued to be vehemently applauded. Some people found the ballet set their teeth on edge. The dancers show nothing but coolness and brilliantly high spirits.

Agon is a suite of dances. The score lasts twenty minutes, and never becomes louder than chamber music. Onstage the dancers are twelve at most, generally fewer. The ballet has the form of a small entertainment, and its subject—first, an assembling of contestants, then the contest itself, then a dispersal—corresponds to the three parts into which the score is divided.

The subject is shown in terms of a series of dances, not in terms of a mimed drama. It is shown by an amusing identity in the action, which is classic dancing shifted into a "character" style by a shift of accentuation. The shift appears, for example, in the timing of transitions between steps or within steps, the sweep of arm position, in the walk, in the funniness of feats of prowess. The general effect is an amusing deformation of classic shapes due to an unclassic drive or attack; and the drive itself looks like a basic way of moving one recognizes. The "basic gesture" of *Agon* has a frank, fast thrust like the action of Olympic athletes, and it also has a loose-fingered goofy reach like the grace of our local teenagers.

The first part of the ballet shows the young champions warming up. The long middle part—a series of virtuoso numbers—shows them rivalizing in feats of wit and courage. There is nothing about winning or losing. The little athletic meet is festive—you watch young people competing for fun at the brief height of their power and form. And the flavor of time and place is tenderly here and now.

Two

Agon shows that. Nobody notices because it shows so much else. While the ballet happens, the continuity one is delighted by is the free-association kind. The audience sees the sequence of action as screwball or abstract, and so do I.

The curtain rises on a stage bare and silent. Upstage four boys are seen with their backs to the public and motionless. They wear the company's dance uniform. Lightly they stand in an intent stillness. They whirl, four at once, to face you. The soundless whirl is a downbeat that starts the action.

On the upbeat, a fanfare begins, like cars honking a block away; the sound drops lower, changed into a pulse. Against it, and against a squiggle like a bit of wallpaper, you hear—as if by free association—a snatch of "Chinatown, My Chinatown" misremembered on an electric mandolin. The music sounds confident. Meanwhile the boys' steps have been exploding like pistol shots. The steps seem to come in tough, brief bursts. Dancing in canon, in unison, in and out of symmetry, the boys might be trying out their speed of waist, their strength of ankle; no lack of aggressiveness. But already two—no, eight—girls have replaced them. Rapidly they test toe power, stops on oblique lines, jetlike extensions. They hang in the air like a swarm of girl-size bees, while the music darts and eddies beneath them. It has become complex and abstract. But already the boys have re-entered, and the first crowding thrust of marching boys and leaping girls has a secret of scale that is frightening. The energy of it is like that of fifty dancers.

By now you have caught the pressure of the action. The phrases are compact and contrasted; they are lucid and short. Each phrase, as if with a burst, finds its new shape in a few steps, stops, and at once a different phrase explodes unexpectedly at a tangent. They fit like the stones of a mosaic, the many-colored stones of a mosaic seen close-by. Each is distinct, you see the cut between; and you see that the cut between them does not interrupt the dance impetus. The novel shapes before you change as buoyantly as the images of a dream. They tease. But like that of a brilliant dream, the power of scale is in earnest. No appeal from it.

While you have been dreaming, the same dance of the twelve dancers has been going on and on, very fast and very boring, like travel in outer space. Suddenly the music makes a two-beat cadence and stops. The dispersed dancers have unexpectedly turned toward you, stopped as in a posed photograph of athletes; they face you in silence, vanish, and instantly three of them stand in position to start a "number" like dancers in a ballet divertissement.

The music starts with a small circusy fanfare, as if it were tossing them a purple and red bouquet. They present themselves to the public as a dance team (Barbara Milberg, Barbara Walczak, Todd Bolender). Then the boy, left alone, begins to walk a Sarabande, elaborately coiled and circumspect. It recalls court dance as much as a cubist still life recalls a pipe or guitar. The boy's timing looks like that of a New York Latin in a leather jacket. And the cool lift of his wrong-way-round steps and rhythms gives the nonsense so apt a turn people begin to giggle. A moment later one is watching a girls' duet in the air, like flying twins *(haute danse)*. A trio begins. In triple canon the dancers do idiotic slenderizing exercises, theoretically derived from court gesture, while the music foghorns in the fashion of musique concrète. Zanily pedantic, the dance has the bounce and exuberant solemnity of a clown act. The audience laughs, applauds, and a different threesome appears (Melissa Hayden, Roy Tobias, Jonathan Watts).

For the new team the orchestra begins as it did for the previous one—first, the pushy, go-ahead fanfare, then the other phrase of harmonies that keep sliding without advancing, like seaweed underwater. (The two motifs keep returning in the score.)

The new team begins a little differently and develops an obvious difference. The boys present the girl in feats of balance, on the ground and in the air, dangerous feats of lucid nonsense. Their courage is perfect. Miss Hayden's deadpan humor and her distinctness are perfect too. At one point a quite unexpected flounce of little-girl primness as in silence she walks away from the boys endears her to the house. But her solo is a marvel of dancing at its most transparent. She seems merely to walk forward, to step back and skip, with now and then one arm held high, Spanish style, a gesture that draws attention to the sound of a castanet in the score. As she dances, she keeps calmly "on top of" two conflicting rhythms (or beats) that coincide once or twice and join on the last note. She stops and the house breaks into a roar of applause. In her calm, the audience has caught the acute edge of risk, the graceful freshness, the brilliance of buoyancy.

The New York audience may have been prepared for *Agon*'s special brilliance of rhythm by that of *Opus 34* and *Ivesiana*, two ballets never shown on tour. All three have shown an acuteness of rhythmic risk never seen and never imagined outside the city limits. The dangerousness of *Agon* is as tense as the danger of a tightrope act on the high wire. That is why the dancers look as possessed as acrobats. Not a split second leeway. The thrill is, they move with an innocent dignity.

At this point of *Agon* about thirteen minutes of dancing have passed. A third specialty team is standing onstage ready to begin (Diana Adams, Arthur Mitchell). The orchestra begins a third time with the two phrases one recognizes, and once again the dancers find in the same music a quite different rhythm and expression. As the introduction ends, the girl drops her head with an irrational gesture more caressing than anything one has seen so far.

They begin an acrobatic adagio. The sweetness is athletic. The absurdity of what they do startles by a grandeur of scale and of sensuousness. Turning pas de deux conventions upside down, the boy with a bold grace supports the girl and pivots her on point, lying on his back on the floor. At one moment classic movements turned inside out become intimate gestures. At another a pose forced way beyond its classic ending reveals a novel harmony. At still another, the mutual first tremor of an uncertain supported balance is so isolated musically it becomes a dance movement. So does the dangerous scoop out of balance and back into balance of the girl supported on point. The dance flows through stops, through scooping changes of pace, through differences of pace between the partners while they hold each other by the hand. They dance magnificently. From the start, both have shown a crescendo and decrescendo within the thrust of a move, an illusion of "breath"—though at the scary speed they move such a lovely modulation is inconceivable. The fact that Miss Adams is white and Mr. Mitchell Negro is neither stressed nor hidden; it adds to the interest.

The music for the pas de deux is in an expressive Viennese twelve-tone manner, much of it for strings. Earlier in the ballet, the sparse orchestration has made one aware of a faint echo, as if silence were pressing in at the edge of music and dancing. Now the silence interpenetrates the sound itself, as in a Beethoven quartet. During the climactic pas de deux of other ballets, you have watched the dancer stop still in the air, while the music surges ahead underneath; now, the other way around, you hear the music gasp and fail, while the two dancers move ahead confidently across the open void. After so many complex images, when the boy makes a simple joke, the effect is happy. Delighted by the dancers, the audience realizes it "understands" everything, and it is more and more eager to give them an ovation.

There isn't time. The two dancers have become one of four couples who make fast, close variations on a figure from the pas de deux. The action has reverted to the anonymous energy you saw in the first part. Now all twelve dancers are onstage and everything is very condensed and goes very fast. Now only the four boys are left, you begin to recognize a return to the start of the ballet, you begin to be anxious, and on the same wrestler's gesture of "on guard" that closed their initial dance—a gesture now differently directed—the music stops, the boys freeze, and the silence of the beginning returns. Nothing moves.

During the stillness, the accumulated momentum of the piece leaps forward in one's imagination, suddenly enormous. The drive of it now seems not to have let up for a moment since the curtain rose. To the realization of its power, as the curtain drops, people respond with vehement applause in a large emotion that includes the brilliant dancers and the goofiness of the fun.

The dancers have been "cool" in the jazz sense—no buildup, inventions that did not try to get anywhere, right after a climax an inconsequence like the archness of high comedy. But the dramatic power has not been that of jokes; it has been that of unforeseeable momentum. The action has had no end in view—it did not look for security, nor did it make any pitiful appeal for that. At the end, the imaginary contestants froze, toughly confident. The company seems to have figured jointly as the offbeat hero, and the risk as the menacing antagonist. The subject of *Agon*, as the poet Frank O'Hara said, is pride. The graceful image it offers is a buoyancy that mystifies and attracts.

Three

A program note says that "the only subject" of the ballet is an interpretation of some French seventeenth-century society dances. The note tells you to disregard the classic Greek title (*Agon*) in favor of the French subtitles. It is a pity to. The title and the subtitles are words that refer to civilized rituals, the former to athletics, the latter to dancing. Athletic dancing is what *Agon* does. On the other hand, you won't catch anyone onstage looking either French or Greek. Or hear musically any reason they should. French baroque manners and sentiments are not being interpreted; elements or energies of forms are.

The sleight-of-hand kind of wit in the dancing is a part of that "interpretation." You see a dancer, rushing at top speed, stop sharp in a pose. The pose continues the sense of her rush. But the equilibrium of it is a trap, a dead end. To move ahead, she will have to retract and scrounge out. She doesn't, she holds the pose. And out of it, effortlessly, with a grace like Houdini's, she darts away. The trap has opened in an unforeseen direction, as music might by a surprising modulation. At times in *Agon* you see the dancer buoyantly spring such traps at almost every step. Or take the canonic imitations. At times a dancer begins a complex phrase bristling with accents and a second dancer leaping up and twisting back an eighth note later repeats it, then suddenly passes a quarter note ahead. The dissonance between them doesn't blur; if you follow it, you feel the contradictory lift of the double image put in doubt where the floor is. Or else you see a phrase of dance rhythm include a brief representational gesture, and the gesture's alien impetus and weight—the "false note" of it—make the momentum of the rhythm more vividly exact. These classic dissonances (and others you see) *Agon* fantastically extends. The wit isn't the device, it is the surprise of the quick lift you feel at that point. It relates to the atonal harmonies of the score—atonal harmonies that make the rhythmic momentum of the music more vividly exact.

At times you catch a kind of dissonant harmony in the image of a step. The explosive thrust of a big classic step has been deepened, speeded up, forced out farther, but the mollifying motions of the same step have been pared down. In a big step in which the aggressive leg action is normally cushioned by mildly rounded elbows, the cushioning has been pared down to mildly rounded palms. The conciliatory transitions have been dropped. So have the transitional small steps. Small steps do not lead up to and down from big ones. They act in opposition to big ones, and often stress their opposition by a contrariness.

The patterns appear and vanish with an unpredictable suddenness. Like the steps, their forms would be traditional except for the odd shift of stress and compactness of energy. The steps and the patterns recall those of baroque dancing much as the music recalls its baroque antecedents—

that is, as absurdly as a current Harvard student recalls a baroque one. Of course, one recognizes the relation.

Agon shifts traditional actions to an off-balance balance on which they swiftly veer. But each move, large or small, is extended at top pitch. Nothing is retracted. The ardent exposure is that of a grace way out on a limb.

The first move the dancers make is a counteraccent to the score. Phrase by phrase, the dancers make a counterrhythm to the rhythm of the music. Each rhythm is equally decisive and surprising, equally spontaneous. The unusualness of their resources is sumptuous, like a magnificent imaginative weight. One follows the sweep of both by a fantastic lift one feels. The Balanchinian buoyancy of impetus keeps one open to the vividly changeable Stravinskyan pressure of pulse and to its momentum. The emotion is that of scale. Against an enormous background one sees detached for an instant the hidden grace of the dancer's individual move, a chance event that passes with a small smile and a musical sound forever into nowhere. *Evergreen Review*, WINTER 1959

IN THE ABSTRACT

Take the aspect of rhythm which is familiar to everybody when they first learn ballroom dances, the matter of stepping to the measure or beat of music. When you watch couples dancing on the dance floor, most of them step to the measure, but they seem to first hear and then step with a sort of tiny lag. That is the respectable or "square" way of dancing. Other couples, particularly to soft music, don't hold to the beat, they also step across it—now a bit too soon, now a bit too late—with a swooping flow that corresponds over several measures to a phrase of the music. They look gracefully sentimental, or, as the children say, like creeps. These are two kinds of dance rhythm, the first with an even beat, the second with an uneven one, and neither of them builds up pressure in the long run.

The high school couples cultivate a third kind, a kind that builds up pressure. They dance with a rhythmic thrust that is quick and exact, but percussive, not staccato. Watching the beat both as a pulse and as a time unit, they can take the exact lift of the upbeat to dance on. So they dance on top of the beat. They seem to me to keep on the edge of the upbeat awhile, getting their double balance on it, and they explode in a counterrhythmic break, like wire walkers turning a somersault in the air and landing on the wire again. It isn't only the gift and the nerve I notice, it is also the strict discipline of ear nobody has imposed on them but they themselves. They are absorbed and dance all-out.

Quite a lot of Americans have danced "on top of the beat" in high school, or have recognized the thrill of it then, watching classmates; and some recognize it in the second generation watching their children and their children's friends. Locally, that type of rhythm has those associations.

If you take the three ways of ballroom dancing I described—behind the beat, across the beat, and on top of the beat—as three types of rhythm, you can more or less recognize them in other kinds of dancing too. "On top of the beat" is a jazz expression. But with quite different music, with quite different steps, gestures, and accents, what you recognize isn't any derivation from jazz, not at all. What you recognize is an on-top-of-the-beat type of dancing, the percussive kind of continuity and its special pressure of pulse. You see individual great dancers who have that rhythm, dancers black, yellow, red, white, and greenish pink. The Balinese little girls and grown men dancing in "noble styles" have that type of rhythm to perfection. And a strong tendency toward it distinguishes the New York City Ballet from the great classic companies abroad. You see it here and there in European troupes, but their main tendency goes in another direction.

Of the great European companies, the Paris Opéra and the Moscow Bolshoi specialize in phrasing. You keep seeing the dancers not hit the beat; they prefer to hit it just now and then, and in between step a trifle ahead or a trifle behind, accelerating or retarding within the length of the phrase more obviously than the orchestra. Within the length of the phrase, they keep gaining and losing impetus. The art of this across-the-beat rhythm is that of a dramatic recitation. And when the dance phrase occurs at a dramatic story crisis, the across-the-beat rhythm can be very striking, like, "Is-this-a . . . DAGGER . . . that-I-see-before-me." But everybody who dances onstage isn't in a state of story crisis all evening long. Many of the dances add no more to a story than "tralala, tralalee, tralaloo." The company phrases these too. It gives to the rhythm a suggestion of local speech rhythm—the Parisians make it staccato, chattery, and charming, the Muscovites make it legato, singsongy, and soulful. To appreciate their artistry, you need only watch it in the right language. So too in the old-fashioned Bournonville style of the Danes, when a dancer "swallows" part of a classic step now and then, she isn't being careless; she is echoing an adorable "glug-glug" of the local polite speech rhythm.

If the Royal British danced with an Oxford accent, what glorious swallowings we should see. But it doesn't do that. It phrases across the beat only where the story justifies it, and then discreetly. And the Royal Danish in contemporary choreographies does the same thing. Both of the Royals generally follow the beat, follow it with a tiny lag. Nothing reprehensible about that type of rhythm. It gives these excellent companies—as it does to dancers in a ballroom—a touching look of civic virtue. As companies, they dance with an air that is discreetly majestic.

Many people notice that the New York City dances more strictly to the measure than the Europeans. It holds as strict a beat, whether in rhythm or counterrhythm, as the orchestra does. That gives to the dancers the lift of a steady upbeat pulse. To hold that pulse, that impetus, they do the step with a distinct and steady action—soberly. And the steady impetus allows—like in on-top-of-the-beat dancing, or driving a car—a quicker timing and a higher speed. Many people have noticed that the New York City is unique in the lucidity it keeps at high speed; none of the other companies is able to remain as distinct in complexities of beat and step continued so long at top speed. None has the high-tension stamina necessary. The strictness of the New York City has been called its Swiss-watch technique.

If the company is a watch, I never but once saw as pretty a one; that was the one I was given when I was nine, and that lasted three days.

Balanchine's Swiss-miracle watch, when he sets it to music and winds it, knows what it is doing. The dancers keep not only on top of the beat, but also on top of the mounting momentum. What does that mean? Well, the musical momentum of a score has a force of traction which begins to pull when it gets ahead of the dancers. That is a dance effect of 1910 which nobody goes all-out for today. So one doesn't see the New York City company dragged by a score's momentum, with opulent, swooning eyes and arms like a raped Europa. Instead, one sees the company's active impetus and hears that of the score. At moments one sees the dancers on the edge or brink of the surging momentum stepping out beyond it with their lovely impetus. And the music reaches out its edge of sound into the void ahead just as they need a place to land. Sometimes the dancers and the music compete till the curtain falls and the momentum catches up and hits full force with its accumulated images.

The impetus of the New York City seems to me more fierce and more fun than that of the companies abroad. The impetus makes some scores unexpectedly "listenable"—scores whose momentum is unforeseen by the public—the Schoenberg of *Opus 34*, the Ives of *Ivesiana*, the Stravinsky of *Agon*, the Webern of *Episodes*. They become listenable because Balanchine's choreographic rhythm and the company's dance rhythm focus moment by moment on the concrete impetus of the music. Quite as extraordinary is to listen moment by moment to Mozart's *Divertimento No. 15* or the *Gounod Symphony* as if they were music with an unforeseen momentum. You come to appreciate the orchestra, the most intelligent ballet orchestra in the world.

While dance ballets like these are going on, you can recognize the pattern game that music and dance are playing. In the music you recognize the classic conventions—or at least the classic type of noise. In the dance—at least for the most part—you recognize steps and figurations, the classic harmony of motion and grace of behavior, the drama of solo, pas de deux, and ensemble. Like in a familiar game, you catch the surprise of a fast play. You catch the sudden image the play leaves. And as you follow the nervy, personal impetus by which each of the dancers is individually creating the composite dance, you begin to sense between dance and music—as if it were a slower and larger image that took time to communicate—the image of a real quality of motion the vitality of which is a secret of art.

What does "a quality of motion" mean? A girl walking down the street looks wonderfully pretty at one moment and average pretty at another. It is your luck if you can see her at the right moment. At the right moment she has for you her real life and all of that real life from beginning to end is wonderfully pretty. In art that luck is an image, but in art to really have that luck, a flash isn't enough, it takes some time.

In California Khrushchev asked, "Which is better, your ballet or ours?" The fact is, the Bolshoi choreographers couldn't have imagined dances like *Agon*, *Episodes*, or *Divertimento No. 15*. Bolshoi dancers couldn't have danced them, or the conductors played the scores so straight. It may be that the New York ballet public is the only one quick enough of eye and ear to enjoy these pleasures. Does that prove our ballet is better? It only proves it's different. No matter. I am willing to prophesy that forty years hence, a decrepit New York City fan, huddled one night around a launching pad far far from home with a bunch of youthful Uzbeks, will suddenly be asked in awed tones, "And did you really see the New York City in 1959? Did you see *Square Dance*?" And a spark will flash in the aged eyes. "And *did* I? Pat's gargouillades—absolute heaven! You know, the music goes . . ." and so forth in the Uzbek tongue through all the legendary names till dawn.

New York City Ballet Souvenir Program, 1959-1960

"LIEBESLIEDER WALZER"

Liebeslieder Walzer, a ballet by Balanchine, was the peculiar glory of the New York City Ballet's recent season. Peculiar, to put it mildly, is the setup of this piece. Duration an hour; no orchestra, no story; the music, two Brahms song cycles all in waltz time with German text; eight dancers. Evidently the master had gone mad.

The curtain rises on a lamp-lit garden room; a summer night at a *Schloss*. The women are in pale, long, voluminous gowns, the men in tails. A group has gathered at the piano, intent on the score, ready to sing in four voices and accompany four-handed. The other guests, four couples, stand in the room about to dance. And in a moment they all begin.

At first one listens more than one looks; the dances begin with graceful Victorian ballroom forms. Then deeper in the music these waltz forms begin to tell what they know. The sensuousness isn't adolescent, the dancing has a boldness of romantic fervor and intimacy one recognizes with astonishment the range of, as much as the grace. There has been no impropriety: nothing, so to speak, has occurred. The dancers open doors into the moonlight and go out.

The curtain falls; when it rises again the company at the piano remains. But the room, moonlit and starlit, has turned mysteriously transparent; the dancers stand poised in it, but the women, now in dresses of transparent gauze, have become ballerinas.

At the first phrase of the music they soar weightlessly high into the air, lifted by their cavaliers. The dances, set angelically to the richness of the music, have an unearthly brilliance, a buoyancy in which images, gay or seductive or tragic, float or flash at play. Not that it is possible, but one believes it is happening.

The dancers have vanished. At their corner of the empty moonlit stage the musicians begin a last song. And the full force of one's feeling listens. In the shadows the dancers return, the ladies in their voluminous evening gowns now sit listening, the beautiful song ceases, the curtain falls.

Liebeslieder Walzer is Balanchine at his most glorious. Adams, Hayden, Jillana, Verdy, Carter, Ludlow, Magallanes, Watts all outdid themselves.

Balanchine made four more pieces, each quite different. *Monumentum*, to the recent Stravinsky-Gesualdo score; *Ragtime*, to Stravinsky too; *Don*

Sebastian, to Donizetti; and *Variants*, to Gunther Schuller. The last was jazz at its most longhair, and I never saw jazz-derived dancing develop so much concentrated power. We also had new works by Bolender, Moncion, Taras. A busy season, and the company flourished on it. As usual, nobody knows what will happen next.

The Sunday Times (London) (JANUARY 22, 1961)

"ELECTRONICS"

Electronics, Balanchine's latest, is Radio City–type art. It takes place in a cellophane cavern of ice to an electronic score. There are some people in long white underwear with cute horns who are a bit squirmy. Creatures in black underwear, almost invisible, come in; they want to do something to the white ones, but can't think of much, and it's too dark to see anyway; so everybody leaves. Some cellophane columns jerk around, semi-tumescent. At the end, the chief white-underwear couple make a very odd ball of themselves and roll around awhile.

This may suggest science fiction, spookily funny and horrid. But what *Electronics* looks like is Sundayfied abstract ballet. It looks like an undertaker. It achieves an impeccably fatuous banality. Balanchine's workmanship is there, his imagination isn't. Not worth making an exception for some details.

The come-on of the piece is the score (Gassmann-Sala). It is a tape of electronically produced noises, but it has nothing to do imaginatively with electronic music. It sounds like gems from Sinding played on a Hammond organ by a flustered maiden aunt. Because it sounds like sentimental parlor music, it would be perfect for slapstick onstage. Instead of having fun with the score's maiden-auntiness, Balanchine solemnly mirrors it.

Electronics is not a ballet to be proud of. It puts on a highbrow act, but what it delivers is middlebrow Radio City corn. And it has the success of that kind of a fake—it is a big hit with press and public. I hope it moves to Radio City.

Nothing fake about the dancing of the piece, or about the dancing of the company generally. An old curmudgeon who sits in the last row because from there you can see the feet, I notice that the New York City dancers are extraordinary.

The Sunday Times (London) (MARCH 9, 1961)

BALANCHINE CHOREOGRAPHING

When George Balanchine was about to choreograph *Variants*, to a new score by Gunther Schuller, I was asked to report the process as clearly as I should be able to; Rudolph Burckhardt was to take photographs. Mr. Balanchine very generously gave us permission to attend rehearsals.

The wall-clock in a large classroom at the School of American Ballet marked five minutes before the hour. Two dancers, Melissa Hayden and Arthur Mitchell, were doing a few final stretches at the barre; they paused and began to wipe their faces and necks. Balanchine stood beside the piano intently reading his copy of the score. He turned to the pianist and asked a question; the pianist played several dissonances and they discussed the point for a moment. Balanchine went back to reading. The dancers had come to the center of the room, where they stood gossiping in subdued voices, glancing toward the piano and then into the mirror which faced them the whole length of the wall. Still absorbed, the choreographer put down his score, looked pleasantly at the dancers, and went over to join them. He signaled to the pianist. The music began with a single note, then a pause, then a chromatic tinkle of rapid notes; the tinkle stopped, started off willfully in another direction; dissonant chords accompanied unpredictably. Balanchine clapped his hands and the pianist broke off. The pianist then repeated from the beginning and broke off at the same point.

Balanchine took his dancers to a far corner of the room—equivalent to the upstage wings, stage left. He placed the boy in front of the girl. At the single first note, they were to run to the center of the room and stop at the beginning of the tinkle. They did this to music. Then without music he showed the boy how to step aside, turn toward the girl, take a step sideways upstage, and offer her his right hand. Taking the girl's part, he showed her how to take the boy's right hand in her left, at the same time turning to face him and stepping boldly back, so that she ended clasping his hand at arm's length, standing with bent knee on one foot, leaning toward him, her other leg extended horizontally behind her in a ballet pose called arabesque. The moves for both dancers were very fast, the final pose was held for a moment. All this the dancers did at once with no difficulty, and repeated it to music. Then Balanchine, substituting for the boy, showed him how to step back, raising the hand by which he held the girl; the action pulled her forward; she caught her balance on both feet, her knees bent a bit like the boy's. Still clasping each other's hand, but with rounded backs pulling away from one another, the two bodies seen in profile made a kind of O figure, which held them poised. The dancers did this at once and repeated everything from the beginning, to music. "Tha-at's right," said Balanchine in an absorbed way, looking at the final pose. "Then maybe we do this."

Taking the girl's part, he showed her how to raise the hand which joined her to the boy, bending her arm at the elbow, and at the same time turning away, so she pulled him after her in profile for a few rapid steps on toe toward the side of the room. That they did easily. Next, as she stood, one foot before the other on toe (in fourth position), the boy, pulling back from the waist, and bracing himself one foot against the other, stopped her. At this stop their bodies made a second and different O figure. But the dancers could barely manage it. The boy couldn't, in this fast move, brace himself very firmly. Balanchine, who had first done it, now did it again. He showed the boy the foot position—the left on the ground, the right turned out, pressed on the instep of the left and pointed down. The dancer tried again, the choreographer showed once more. When Balanchine did it, the pull back from the waist looked quicker and sharper; when he braced his feet, the toe of the raised one seemed to cling to the floor. But when at the third try the dancers did this figure no differently from at first, he said, "Tha-at's right," and went on. Taking the girl's part, he showed her how to turn the wrist of the hand by which she held the boy, then turn that arm at the shoulder, and extend it, so without letting go she now had room to step ahead. She took two steps, swung out in a deep lunge, and ended poised on one foot, with bent knee; her free arm had swung ahead, the free leg back in arabesque again. She had pulled the boy a step or two after her. With this move the dancers had no trouble.

Now Balanchine asked them to go back to the beginning and set the whole sequence to counts. They went back to the far corner; but as they stood ready, he stopped them. He now put the boy behind the girl instead of in front of her. This required a change at the end of the first run to center, because now when they stopped, the boy had to step aside and downstage to give her his hand, instead of aside and upstage. No difficulty. They were about to start when he stopped them again. He told them not to run in on the first note as before, but to wait a moment and run in on the silence; he explained that the single first note would be played on the vibraphone, and would reverberate; there wouldn't be a silence onstage as there was now with the piano. They now began again.

The run looked different. Before, the boy running ahead seemed to be blocking the girl's escape. Now she stopped of her own free will and gave him the opportunity to invite her to dance. It was less tense; but with less time, the run became faster and fresher.

At the first note of the tinkle they started to count. They counted aloud by eighth notes to a bar or half-bar, doing the motions and rests at the same speed, or within a hair's breadth, as they had been doing them before, but with more edge. They were delighted to find when they reached the last lunge that everything fitted. "Tha-at's right," the choreographer said. The second O figure, the bothersome one, had lost a half count's rest in the process, but he went ahead. Taking the girl's final lunging pose, he found after a few tries that she could easily step back erect, and then whirl toward the boy, still holding his hand. Whirling around twice, she wrapped herself first in her arm and then in his. As she whirled, her unattached arm was wrapped in with her. She now stood facing front, close to the boy, imprisoned so to speak, and he could step closer yet, and put his free arm lightly around her waist. But no further initiative was left her. Balanchine took the imprisoned girl's part; then he took the boy's part; he seemed to consider various directions but he found none he liked. The dance had run itself into a blind alley. He asked the dancers to repeat the last moves, and watched them twice. They looked as if their hearts were bravely sinking. Then as they stood in the final pose, he went up to the girl, took her by the shoulders, and started pushing her toward the floor. After a moment, she understood and tried sinking out of the arms wrapped around her. Balanchine took her place and did it easily. She tried again, and struggled hard, but something or other was in her way. It couldn't be done. Watching her closely as she struggled, he went up to her and started pulling on the unattached arm that was wrapped in front of her, her right arm. With a happy smile, she caught on; she went back to the previous lunge, and the whirl that followed; wrapping herself up, then extricating the extra arm, she found room easily to sink down out of her imprisonment, duck under the arm she held the boy's hand by, and come up outside, free to move anywhere, but still holding his hand. For the dancers this move was a Houdini-style joke, and they were delighted. Setting the move to counts was easy.

The girl now stood facing center stage, and in a few steps she led the boy there; now they both stood center, facing front; they let go of each other's hand and began to a $\frac{5}{8}$ count a stylized lindy kick figure, in counterrhythm to each other, just as the music burst into a $\frac{5}{4}$ bar of jitterbug derivation.

By that time three quarters of an hour had passed since the rehearsal began; everybody had worked cheerfully and fast. But beginning with the $\frac{5}{8}$ lindy-type figure everybody's concentration seemed to double. Balanchine invented one novel figure after another. They began and ended within what seemed to be a bar or two. The figures kept the dancers within hand's reach of each other, and now more, now less, kept the flavor of a lindy-type couple dance. Very rapid, unexpectedly complex, quite confined, the figures, sharply contrasted, kept changing direction. But in sequence the momentum carried through. When the entire ballet was finished, this turned out to be a general characteristic it had.

At that first rehearsal, the choreographer did not mention that he intended it, or what he intended. Nor did the dancers ask. They concentrated on the moves he was making. They hurried to learn each figure as it was invented, to repeat it by counts, and to memorize the sequence by counts to the score. At the end of two and a half hours about one minute of the ballet had been made. Onstage this turned out to be the first half of the fourth of the ballet's seven sections—a section for solo vibraphone and a chamber-sized orchestral group.

As for the part described in detail—the ten-second introduction—onstage it turned out that the composer wanted for it a tempo radically different from the one it had been choreographed at; the steps were changed, and passed unnoticed.

Making a ballet takes an unbounded patience from everybody concerned. An outsider is fascinated to be let in on the minuteness of the workmanship. But then he finds no way out of that minuteness. Listening to the same few bars pounded again and again on the piano, watching the same movements started at top speed and broken off, again and again, the fascinated outsider after two hours and a half of that finds himself going stir crazy. Seeing a ballet in the theater one is carried into a world of zest and grandeur by the momentum of action and music. In performance the dancers look ravishing. In rehearsal they look like exhausted champions attempting Mount Everest, knowing how limited the time is, step by step, hold by hold, roped together by the music, with the peak nowhere in sight.

In the second half of the Hayden-Mitchell pas de deux, Balanchine invented a figure in which the girl, facing front, poised with bent knee on one toe, performed a little "turned-in" adagio exercise, as she reached back for support to her partner, who was doing a sideways shuffle behind her in $\frac{5}{8}$. The dancers caught on after a few tries. Even after they had, the choreographer, calling the counts sharply, made them repeat it—quite unlike his usual procedure. He did it again at a much later rehearsal after—though he wasn't aware of it—Miss Hayden had pulled a calf muscle the night before onstage. As she repeated the figure again and again—so she told me—the injury became painful. But as she kept repeating it, angry though she was, and trying to give the rhythm a keener edge, she found the key she had been looking for—the key to the character of her role.

At the third rehearsal, Balanchine began a pas de deux for Diana Adams and John Jones. From the start it was a violently explosive dance. Within a few minutes, Miss Adams stopped with a slightly pained look and turned away, but a moment later she was back at work. She didn't mention that her right arm had been badly wrenched. For the rest of the rehearsal, many of the very fast moves she memorized required her partner to give her sudden pulls to her arm, now to one, now to the other, often while the arm was suddenly being turned inside out. Rehearsal the next day was even more strenuous. After two hours of it, at a move the unsteady execution of which puzzled the choreographer, she apologized, saying she was sure she could do it right at a later rehearsal when her arm was better. He at once changed the next move to her good arm, saying, "We need that arm tonight." And work went on. That evening she was to dance the ballerina part in the full-length *Nutcracker*, the season's first performance, and all the reviewers would be watching her. She danced it beautifully.

Variants was rehearsed during the ballet season, when the dancers in addition to performance and class have repertory rehearsals as well; union rules specified the hours available. Besides inventing his ballet at such hours, Balanchine also had every morning and evening decisive responsibilities in running the company and planning its future.

Between September and November, he had made four new pieces. The first, to the most recent Stravinsky score, was followed by a ballet to Donizetti music; then he presented an hour-long ballet set to two song cycles by Brahms and called *Liebeslieder Walzer*. *Liebeslieder Walzer*—with a cast of eight—turned out to be a masterpiece, glorious and magical. No other choreographer, no other company could have done it; but one isn't aware of that, the poetry of it—the secret image—is so absorbing. Two weeks after *Liebeslieder* he presented *Ragtime*, a duet witty and deceptively elementary in the way the Stravinsky score is. Six days after *Ragtime*, he began *Variants*.

Balanchine usually prepares a ballet far in advance. He has said that he prepares for a long time by playing and studying the score—"I listen, listen, listen, listen." On the other hand, he does not look for steps until the actual performers are with him in the rehearsal studio.

Variants had been commissioned at his request. Like some of Schuller's previous music, it was to be in third-stream style, scored for the Modern Jazz Quartet and symphonic orchestra. The choice implied a third-stream-type ballet, a nonexistent species. Balanchine prepared for it by listening to jazz albums. He didn't study the score during the summer layoff while he was growing roses, because until September Schuller was too busy to begin writing it. The last installment of the piano version was delivered in November.

The composer's plan—a suite—featured the Jazz Quartet artists singly and jointly accompanied by small orchestral groups; the introduction was for full orchestra, the conclusion for full orchestra plus the Quartet. The choreographer's plan was a dance suite. He wanted half the cast—two solo boys and eight ensemble girls—to be Negroes; but the girls weren't found. He picked his dancers, cast each of the dance numbers, decided which numbers to make first. At that point the first rehearsal sheet was posted, the date for opening night confirmed.

At the start of the first rehearsal he chose a way of working which he kept until the whole piece had been created. At every point he took each role. The process looked like this. Standing near the dancer, he signaled the pianist to play ahead, and clapped his hands when he wanted him to break off. The pianist repeated the fragment once or twice while Balanchine listened intently. Then without music he took the position in which the dancer would have to start, and stood absorbed, sometimes turning his head very slightly in this direction or that, sometimes slightly moving on his feet. He was inventing the next figure. He seemed to test the feel of it, and decide. That done, he glanced at the dancer, stressed the starting position, and without music showed the move. The first time he showed it, he did it from start to finish at full performance force and speed.

The dancers reproduced it, adding to it at once—in ballet style—the full extension of the body, the turnout of legs and feet, the toe step or leap he had merely implied. A nondancer might have wondered how they could guess so much; but they seemed to guess right almost always. As expert dancers they were following out the logical balletic consequences of the main move he had shown. Sometimes they asked about a detail left in doubt, and he specified the answer in ballet terminology.

Moving at the speed and force he had shown, the fully extended bodies of the dancers sometimes developed a sudden momentum that was scary.

But the jet of it took the dancer to the right spot at the right instant. The impetus came from eccentric swings from the shoulder or waist, the support from handholds. When the choreographer first showed such a move, he literally threw himself into it, and let his feet take care of themselves. When the dancers couldn't manage the move, he repeated it. Between them they tracked down the trouble to a change of hand, a specific angle or stance, or an extra step which he had taken instinctively and which the dancers had overlooked.

Soon, when he made such a move the first time, he repeated it at once, stressing how the feet stepped and the hands reached for support. At the second rehearsal, he spent more than a half hour on a fantastic sequence lasting a few bars that wouldn't work to counts; after that whatever took too long to learn he discarded before it was set by counts to the music. (Had he been making a piece in regulation ballet steps to music easy to remember by ear, the process would have been far less cumbersome.)

Balanchine's care was for the mechanics of momentum. He did not mention expression. Watching him do a move full force, an outsider might often have been struck by his expression in it—a quality of gesture which was directly to the point. It was beautiful. The dancers did not imitate that. Their expression when it appeared was their own, and he did not criticize it. Expression seemed to be treated as a Jeffersonian inalienable right. And perhaps it is.

Later rehearsals were moved to the theater building, to a gloomy echoing room upstairs modeled on a chapter room in a castle of the Knights Templar. Here Balanchine took the dancers by shifts and choreographed from ten-thirty to six. "I work like a dentist," he remarked. He sometimes looked exhausted, but a joke revived him. When dancers lost the count, he did not nag or look depressed. The phrases he made for the chorus were easy motions, but their peculiar timing required exact counts. He kept checking the counts in the score. During ten-minute or half-hour breaks, he stayed alone in the rehearsal room, rereading the score, playing it, checking on the metronome speed. The composer, who was to conduct the ballet, watched a rehearsal, and Balanchine brought up the metronome speed; he referred to the metronome speed given in the score; Schuller, experienced with orchestras but not with Balanchine choreography, evaded his insistence. Solo rehearsals, chorus rehearsals, stage rehearsals, orchestra rehearsals, dress rehearsals, lighting rehearsals.

The first orchestra rehearsal for the dancers came the day before opening. The dancers had become used to recognizing landmarks or cues in the piano score. The colorful orchestration obliterated these. But they had expected as much. Since they had memorized the score by counts, they could perform to the measure whatever unforeseen noises the orchestra made. Disaster threatened nevertheless. Finding the music difficult, the instrumentalists slowed down; but the dancers, rushing headlong, couldn't slow down without toppling. The momentum of their off-balance rushes worked at a specific speed that had been agreed on between composer and choreographer and fixed by metronome. The dancers had to rely on it and now it turned unreliable. The choreographer's well-known coolness adjusted what was possible. And suddenly the first night's performance was over. There was polite applause.

Having seen as I had how the ballet grew and the adorably unselfish work that went into it, my view of the first night was not that of a theatergoer or of a critic. But the first night flop did not deter later audiences. They came at least to hear the Modern Jazz Quartet and the new Schuller score. The concentration of the dancers, the virtuosity of the ballerinas were watched by these music fans with close attention; they appreciated the range of resource by which the dancing matched the twelve-tone logic of the score.

The dance fans agreed about all the virtuosity, but they found the twelve-tone "third-stream" angle more strain than fun. In addition, the piece had been announced as "new jazz," and it wasn't contemporary jazz in its dancing. They objected to the thirties-type jive steps, to the show biz–type gesture, to the sour night-club look of the staging. As for the dancing, the partners couldn't let each other alone for a moment, the dances couldn't leave out a beat, nobody could dance except on top of the beat. Current jazz dancing separates partners, omits beats, lets the beat pull away, anticipates it; and that elasticity of attack characterizes the gesture, and varies it. The source of style isn't professional, but year by year emerges in the private dancing of a few high school students; the measure of style is its "go." The dance fans had seen the athletic overtones of *Agon*, which in some unliteral way came closer to the image of jazz than any jazz ballet yet has. They hoped that *Variants* would do for jazz what *Liebeslieder* does for the waltz.

In performance onstage, *Variants* keeps reminding one of conventional Broadway—that sort of jazz plus modern plus ballet. The numbers suggest corny types of stage jazz—the hot number, the ritual-magic one, the snake-hips, the arty, the pert one; the long finale quotes from the show, and ends with a decorative modernistic collapse for the entire cast, capped by a Brigitte Bardot "beat" pose for the two leading ladies. The dancers suggest that hard-shell type of dance very handsomely. But the rhythm they dance to isn't show-dance rhythm; it isn't quite jazz either. One recognizes jazzlike steps but one doesn't feel at home. The action of a step keeps being pointed up differently, retimed, rerouted, tightened, enlarged by ballet logic. At a retard several short numbers end with, one seems to watch a powerful momentum sink quickly from the dancers into the floor (like water into sand), leaving their last moves massive. The emotion is one of grandeur, the gesture is showbiz. Becoming interested, one sees a massive dance momentum started, developed, ended within two minutes, a drive different from one number to the next. By the time one has found out how to "see" the piece, the finale comes and ruins it. The finale, four times as long as the previous numbers, and crowded, has no momentum; nor has it any in the score.

Schuller's score features the shy, extremely musical sonorities of Lewis's Modern Jazz Quartet surrounded by orchestral sonorities, original in color or jazz implication. Such a texture takes more rehearsal than a ballet company can afford. The Quartet, progressive style, implies a jazz beat while playing a variable nuance behind. Not the orchestra. It plays by measure.

The progressive-style "delayed" beat, when featured, troubled the dancers who were dancing to the measure. But the jazz beat does not take over the score. The structural drive of the score is twelve-tone, not by beat but by phrase. To the specific twelve-tone phrase, to its momentum and shape, Balanchine had set the dance—first by ear, then checking and rechecking the count of the measure by the written notes.

Unlike Balanchine's twelve-tone part of *Episodes*—particularly the section danced by Paul Taylor, in which the shape of a "step" became equivalent to the shape of a musical phrase—*Variants* did not keep surprising the onlooker by the dramatic fantasy of its gesture. But it did have extraordinary moments—during the Adams-Jones duet, for instance, when, at the speed of fury, the complexity and the force of momentum disassociate the gesture from its Broadway connotations, and burst open its hard shell. At such moments *Variants* became a jazz ballet more powerful and grandly integrated than any yet.

Between two rehearsals Balanchine, after answering a question of mine about jazz, added, "In any case, we don't do jazz here, we do ballet; we try to make it as interesting as possible." Before rehearsals began, Schuller brought up the matter of jazz nuances of rhythm; the choreographer listened and then said that the way he made dances, the dancers were "inside the nuance."

Watching Balanchine at work, one could see he was thinking in terms of ballet action flavored by jazz action. One did not see him worry where the flavor might take him, or worry about the overall shape of a dance before he had made it. He seemed to be eating his way through the score, finding his way move by move. After he had found a move, one could see that it took its point from the pressure of drama and, if one may say so, the pressure of visibility which at that moment of the dance were at stake. (The previous move might be topped by a contradiction or an unexpected evasion, as in dramatic dialogue.) But looking for a new move, he seemed to find it by following an instinctive dance impulse of his body. Nearly always he trusted to his body's first response, while he was concentrating on the exact force of momentum the music offered for the next move.

The force of dance momentum derived from the score is a resource of ballet that he has developed further than anyone anywhere. He keeps enlarging its powers of speed, agility, intelligence, and fun. With twelve dancers he finds a momentum that feels like forty dancers; with forty, it feels like a hundred. His company dances three times as much per minute as any other.

Momentum and gesture are the dramatic resources of dancing, which ballet combines in several ways. One way is that of the nineteenth-century prolonged dance climax, a grand pas de deux with related choral and soloist numbers. The climax may be a tragic or a festive event but—like in opera—the scale of it is expressed by lyric meditations on it. In principle the shining virtuoso dance feat is also a gesture-metaphor derived from the dramatic situation, and an echo of the feat reverberates in the other numbers before and after, which prolongs the momentum.

Balanchine's so-called abstract ballets extend this traditional merging of gesture and dance momentum. The specific gesture is implicit in the actions of the step. It appears in the formal momentum in shape and rhythm so organically fused that one responds to both of these poles of dramatic meaning jointly, and follows the highly active meditation with delighted astonishment. The individual's absorbed gesture, carried by a powerfully developed momentum which reverberates its secret, reveals a grander and more innocent meaning than one expects to see. Remembered, it grows on the scale of the momentum. This power of poetry has long been the glory of ballet, and Balanchine's is that he succeeds in it so often. But the question of how he does it is not answered by watching him at work.

Kulchur, 1962

"A MIDSUMMER NIGHT'S DREAM"

Balanchine's *A Midsummer Night's Dream*, with a flock of children onstage and a well-known story, is family entertainment. It opens, as the Mendelssohn music does, deep in the magic forest. The children onstage are charming—their steps clean, their music cues prompt, they glisten with responsibility. Against their light rhythm—like an insect hum—the adult elves brilliantly dart and soar. As for the story, when you see the tiny Indian Changeling over whom Oberon and Titania are quarreling, a parent remembers the earnestness of a quarrel at home about whom the new kitten was to go to sleep with. And as the fairy royalties speak in Shakespeare—regal, delicate, with a child's heart—so they each dance beautifully among their separate elves in different clearings of the enchanted forest. It is a visible retelling of the story, close to its poetry. You see Oberon show Puck the magic flower, and send him circling round the globe. The lovers' misadventures are told in rapid dances, too fast to put pressure on them; Titania and Bottom-turned-donkey too—the gentlest of donkeys and delightfully convincing. In the forest the pace of events slows down or speeds up unpredictably. The first act reaches its climax with a long, unreassuring mixup of funny reality and scary dream, and at the last minute ends happily.

The second act brings Duke Theseus' wedding ball, where everybody dances extremely well. The first act has been remarkably interesting; the second somehow isn't, except during a brief virtuoso pas de deux and an epilogue back in the magic forest, a sudden sweetness and silence.

At home, after putting the family to bed, a parent reflects that the ballet gave both the children and the adults roles in which they could shine. Lithe, wonderfully live in unexpected pauses, sunny in action, the lead character, the Puck of Arthur Mitchell, is the truest Puck one is likely to see anywhere. Since Balanchine understood the play so well, the parent wonders why he avoided the Pyramus and Thisbe side of it, and its wide-open buffoonery. But though he did, what a pleasure to find in the ballet's many inventions the Shakespearean sweetness and lovely irony unfalsified. The aftertaste of the long evening is a very pleasant one.

This view by an imaginary parent seems to me reasonable, and I imagine that a choreography fan would agree. But while the parent drops innocently to sleep, the choreography fan wants first to identify the weakness of the second-act wedding ball. Most of it had been taken up by a divertissement, a pas de quatorze, that packed so many steps so amazingly close, it changed at every moment, and as drama didn't budge. But where did he get that impression? No clear picture comes back to him.

The picture that comes back to him instead is the wedding march with which the ball had opened—the music's interminable repeats, the chorus walking their designs looking as stuffy as in church, the orchestra blaring the tight two-bar phrase pattern. Obligatory boredom. The fan began to count on the next number for relief, the divertissement, the evening's climax. But the music for it, a Mendelssohn symphony, right away set the same tight phrase pattern, and the dance did too. The prospect of a grand climax confined to a two-bar seesaw—no travel—exasperated him. He watched the confined phrase pattern continue through the long divertissement, including the pas de deux. It continued through a court dance that briefly concluded the ball. Wedding march, divertissement, court dance, each had run to a modest ending, march and court dance keeping to the phrase pattern conventionally, the divertissement keeping to it, but not at all conventionally.

Not at all conventionally, though the steps of it were regulation school steps. Remarkably interesting to the fan, a brief men's pas de six. That moment of grandeur reminds him of more fugitive impressions. In the choral sections, delicate small steps, majestic open ones had flashed and vanished, finding room as if by magic. Oddly counted to the bar, a step found its buoyancy and time enough to open its classic shape and close it. The thicket of choral steps in a phrase seemed to turn on a dime, and hover an inch above the floor as they turned. Their momentum seemed to come from the melody—that was the music's energy, and none of it was lost to the ear. It sounded young, ingenuous, at moments heavenly.

It looked dense as a tapestry forest. Deep in the forest, a clearing—the brief pas de deux. (The variations for the stars had not been performed.) But brief as it was, the change from many dancers to just two gave a focus; suddenly the final dangerous supported falls made contact with the audience; a retard, an absorbing image.

The moment or image, ingenuously tender and noble, serious, had been for the fan the only absorbing one of the divertissement. The sweet Mendelssohn symphony develops very little drama, and so does its pas de quatorze. The number is more ornament than drama. The word "drama" taken in its pure-dance sense—the kind of drama of which Balanchine's *Valses et Variations* with its happy summer-morning dazzle is so full of. Had the pas de quatorze been so outgoing a climax as that, the fan and the public too would have been better satisfied. And yet, speaking for myself, I miss a regulation climax less than I miss before the number begins ten minutes of Pyramus and Thisbe buffoonery—that far-out timing and wildly off-balance gesture. It would make me ready for the divertissement's extremely far-in style, the vigor which keeps forming one unusual wholly positive classic phrase after another with the exact few steps there is room for inside the fatally predictable phrase length.

A fan, however, would point out that a contrast has already been made. The phrases of dance and mime in Act One are of constantly changing lengths. The whole first act has a pace livelier and more flexible than any full-length ballet had before. Dance and mime events move or pause with what seems a spontaneous variety of musical momentum. The beauty of the pauses strikes a fan's eye. Time enough to see what happens and not a moment more. But "time enough" changes in ballet: mime communicates instantly; dramatic dance tells its meaning fairly fast; lyric dance, which tells its meaning by many unfoldings and foldings, echoes and disappearances and returns, takes a good deal of time to happen. Act One of *A Midsummer Night's Dream* keeps sharp these differences of pace and even stresses them.

The dancers make their mime points so clear at high speed, they look like accomplished actors. More unusual yet, the ease with which they shift between mime, dramatic dance, and lyric dance. Such an ease is normally the secret of a few great classic stars. In *A Midsummer Night's Dream* mime and dramatic gesture do not try for a period style—Elizabethan or Greek—nor do they try for naturalistic theater. In principle they keep to classic-dance carriage and gesture, modified by situation and character; in practice, the vividness of action is that each gesture goes straight to its dramatic point, and that the "psychology" is perfectly clear by its timing. Timing is set to counts in the score.

The dramatic dances, based on familiar pas de deux figurations, can with as little as an unexpectedly averted head or a hastily extended hand make a story point without interrupting the dance. For instance, Titania dancing with Bottom in a supported figure when her back is turned to him makes clear by a slightly accentuated développé that she is imagining him a handsome partner; as the same figure an instant later turns her to face him and she sees he is actually a donkey, her next action is sweetly to find him some grass. The dance continuity gives its mime nuances lightness.

This kind of mime and dramatic dance has a pre-Fokinean precedent. Balanchine has long used it. A practical action—handling a prop dagger, or picking an invisible flower—is done literally; a gesture of emotion is done in the range of classic movement. A fan can compare the classic ballet mime of *A Midsummer Night's Dream* with the stylized ballet mime usually seen; the classic kind looks more direct and natural. It does when Balanchine invents it—no other choreographer has observed the gestural secrets of classic movement so lovingly.

Watching the cinematic cross-cutting between dance and mime at the climax of Act One, the rolling ground fog, the duels quick as Chinese theater, the dogs turned horses, the people turned sacks, Hippolyta vertiginously spinning with no floor beneath her, Puck watchful at the last moment not to repeat his former mistake, the fan recognizes that the scary omen of this prenuptial dream is one Hippocrates would have been delighted by. But the ominous tone of it is in the text—Oberon's "fog as black as Acheron" speech, and Puck's grisly answer.

But two other dreams, earlier in the act and deeper in the magic forest, delight a choreography fan even more: the weatherlike shifts of pressure between serenity and menace at Titania's court when Puck tries to kidnap the Changeling; and the unmotivated serenity of Oberon's court, like nature's unmotivated beauty, dancing her Platonic ideas among her moths and dragonflies.

Some balletgoers tell me they would like Balanchine to make a full-length ballet as extraordinary as *Agon*, *Liebeslieder Walzer*, or *Divertimento No. 15*. Such a ballet has never existed. Balanchine has mentioned a hope of setting the Ninth. One can imagine for some world festival of peace two hundred of the world's best dancers putting themselves at his disposal for it. How I should like to see it and hear Beethoven shouting, "We enter, drunk with fire, heavenly joy, your sanctuary." An equivalent quote from *A Midsummer Night's Dream* is "Shall we their fond pageant see? Lord, what fools these mortals be." The voice in one's heart that says it is a lighter one.

Dance 62, 1963

"DON QUIXOTE"

Balanchine's three-act *Don Quixote* tells the famous history of the Don's madness related to its social background—the Spain of Philip II. It is also a sumptuous spectacle, the handsomest in international repertory. It offers an enormous amount to look at—sets, indoors and outdoors, hundreds of costumes, props, beards, small children, a thirty-foot giant, animals, a penitential procession, a traveling marionette show, a village festival, a court ball, a divertissement, a masque, a long classic pas d'action, lots of pantomime—the way to watch shifts unpredictably. Rich and strange, bitter, delicate, and tragic, the piece gathers in one's imagination. When it is finished, it seems to have become a somber story of alienation. Its dramatic force has been an increasing pathos.

As the curtain falls, pathos has become the dramatic force, but the spectacle element has never been so unrepetitive in any large-scale ballet. As usual with full-length ballets nowadays, the scenic style is old-fashioned opera house. Unprecedented in that style is the subtlety with which the scale of the set to the dancers is varied, both in respect to size and to weight, and the variations of weight in the costumes. Effects of drawing and color in the set, which in a representational style on so large a stage often tend to harden and to dwarf the dancers, are not emphasized. The imagination and the sincerity with which Esteban Francés, the painter, has put himself at the service of the complex drama cannot be valued highly enough. Nor can the same qualities be valued highly enough in Karinska's execution of the costumes, or in that of the artists who made the props.

Imagination and sincerity are everywhere present among the performers, ranging from stars to children. Dulcinea, the heroine—pensive young Suzanne Farrell—is ravishing in the lucid grace of her mime and of her miraculous dancing. Joining her in the pas d'action climax, Mimi Paul and Marnee Morris dance too beyond belief. Before that, Gloria Govrin, Patricia McBride, and particularly Suki Schorer (in a duet with John Prinz) have been extraordinary. All the dancing is remarkable in strict dance numbers, and acceptable in the character-dance ensembles. But since the ballet tells a realistic story, it depends on the distinctness of its mime gesture and the conviction of its timing.

Don Quixote, a quiet part with a very large range, is acted by Richard Rapp with a beautiful honesty—even after Balanchine's marvelous performance, Rapp's was admirable. Lamont's Sancho too is a beautiful achievement. At Don Quixote's deathbed, the housekeeper (von Aroldingen) and the curate (Arshansky), together with Dulcinea and Sancho, doing almost nothing, shocked the audience out of its wits. Arshansky is very funny in another part. Nobody overplays. Each detail of mime in the ballet, if you look for it, counts.

The ballet starts with mime. It starts as the novel does with Don Quixote among his books of chivalry. He falls asleep. A great monster swoops down. A tiny blond girl perched on a book implores his help; tiny knights in armor and tiny armed monsters attack. He rescues her, she escapes. He is sound asleep in his chair when a young servant girl enters, quietly goes across the room to raise a curtain and let in the sunrise light. Her quietness tells she has often done this before. He wakes and sees her waiting by his chair. Now she washes his feet and with a quick gesture loosens her hair to dry them. She gives him his shoes and he kisses her forehead. He walks forward, thinking about chivalry. She runs after him, drops on her knees, and with a swift movement offers him his sword, pretending to be the page of an imaginary knight. Then she rises and goes out to her work without looking back. With the sword held high he is watching her. The room disappears and he is standing sword in hand facing an immense arid plain. On a cart the image of the Virgin appears. It is the same dancer who a moment before was the servant. To the Virgin Don Quixote, as if entranced, dedicates his sword. Sancho runs in, the armor and spear in his hand clattering, and takes a pratfall.

So one discovers at the start who Dulcinea is—the Virgin, a shy country girl growing up in his house, and a tiny blond princess in a nightmare. The gesture of drying his feet with her hair suggests the Magdalene; more than that it is an ancient gesture that belongs to washing a child. These clear pictures, one right after the other, add up to a complex emotion. Dulcinea is both very close and very far off. From then on, one is ready to see her through his eyes. In the novel, Dulcinea, heroine and motive of the story, is never seen, though she is a real country girl as well as an ideal empress of beauty. The Cervantes fan sees that these mime pictures recombine widely scattered details of the book, as well as adding visual metaphors of their own.

To follow the action of the ballet does not require more than a hearsay acquaintance with the novel. Here is an outline of the action.

After Don Quixote has made Sancho knight him they don't find adventures right away. Then grisly projections appear in the sky; onstage two incidents from the novel, briefly mimed, leave the knight and Sancho badly beaten up but beginning to recover as they so often are in the book. The scene changes to the ancient plaza of a remote small town with loungers and three village girls dancing. More girls and boys join in. Neither the scene nor the dance quite patterns. The dancing has something random in its shifts of activity. One friend of mine found no focus; another said it was the best village festival he had ever seen in ballet. I too had seen in a remote Spanish town, a couple of hours before High Mass, just such impromptu dancing as this suggested. (The steps onstage were ballet steps with a few Spanish arm positions.)

Sancho runs in hugging a stolen fish and dodging the fishwives. Two Guardia Civil grab him and turn him over to the loungers, who enjoy manhandling him. Arriving on horseback, Don Quixote rescues him. A further comic scene is interrupted by a man who drags in a shepherdess—Marcela. He points to a dead man on a bier; the villagers threaten to kill her. She is the same dancer who takes the part of Dulcinea, now in pastoral ballet costume. The knight rescues her, and she dances a classic variation. The program book quotes her beautiful speech to him from the novel; her dance is amazing, so transparent, so distinct, so unforeseeable in its invention. It is about virginal freedom. A painter friend exclaimed, "It's marvelous. There she is on toe, and everybody else is on their flat feet. What a theater idea."

A curtained cart appears. Its small curtain rises on a puppet show, adorable in action and in décor—a perfect pleasure. The tiny blond heroine of it is captured by the Moors. With drawn sword Don Quixote madly rushes to her rescue; the puppet theater collapses on his head and knocks him out. The local Duke and Duchess with some friends come onto the plaza, find the Don, and invite him to their palace at once. (They know him from the novel.) Barely conscious, he is lifted on Rozinante, Sancho follows on Dapple, the villagers are delighted, and the first act is over.

The curtain rises on a vast black and gold throne room in the Duke's palace. The noble guests in black and gold court dress appear followed by the Don, festive in scrubbed armor, and humble Sancho. The Duke and Duchess seat our friends near the throne; the aristocratic guests welcome the knight with exaggerated deference. He and Sancho watch a court dance which the Duke and Duchess soon join. Unexpected spurts of speed and individual timings make it look "real," as they did the unaristocratic village dance before. The Spanish arm gestures are amusingly elaborate. A divertissement of five numbers follows, performed by hired entertainers. Their garish bits of costume are as alien to Spanish hauteur as those of gypsies. (I remembered in Madrid at three a.m. deliciously haughty debutantes wearing family diamonds with young escorts in dinner jackets watching a gypsy entertainment such as I had never dreamt of.) Some demi-caractère steps of the divertissement, extremely virtuoso, are based on the frug in the sense that the Fairy variations of Petipa are based on the can-can. Several brilliant girls make the wit sharper by playing it to their partner or to a world of their own rather than to the public.

Suddenly one, then more masked aristocrats point to Don Quixote; and the Duchess invites him to dance. In a swirl of ironic masked figures she whispers to the Duke, and then returns to the courteous Don. It is a prearranged hazing. Sancho tries to lead his master away, but the Duchess prevents him. Master and man are blindfolded, are made sport of, Sancho escapes, thoroughly scared, brave Don Quixote is crowned Emperor and whipped and left exhausted.

A vision of Dulcinea appears, he stumbles after her, he recovers, he is about to follow her. A masked lady taps him on the shoulder, he turns to her, another taps him, you hear a soft thud and see his face blinded by whipped cream. He pauses, then turns blindly toward the disappearing vision of Dulcinea. The curtain falls.

The curtain rises on the third act. An immensely high gate fences in a moonlit forest in the foreground—the most mysteriously beautiful setting of the evening. Sancho is leading his exhausted master, and leaves him asleep by the trunk of a tree. Masked courtiers sneak up at once and cover him with a net. A moment later filmy girls appear—a dream, waving Elysian arms. Never has a moonlit dream begun more consolingly—this is the classic pas d'action. Dulcinea and her two friends are supported by three bold knights. Though Dulcinea's dazzling pas de deux ends on a hint of threat, miraculous variations follow, one girl boldly striding and turning, another at top speed resting utterly still for an eighth note, then dancing at top speed again. Like a dream, these dances remind you of something recent. Is it perhaps the divertissement, perhaps the shepherdess? The man's powerful variation (Anthony Blum) has arm gestures from the court dance. Dulcinea's variation—marvelous in the feet, in the novel and unorthodox épaulements—carries the hidden secret to its climax. Dancing faster and faster, more and more desperate, opposed by a woman in black like the Duchess, tortured by the enchanter Merlin, Dulcinea at last appeals to the sleeping knight—he starts up—the horror has vanished, faithful Sancho takes off the encumbering net. But the garden has turned into a landscape of windmills. He is challenged by a giant who grows as big as a windmill. Unappalled, the Don charges him; his lance caught in the windmill fan, he rises high in the air, drops, crawls still alive toward Sancho. Sancho binds his bleeding head. A charging herd of swine stampede him. Masked courtiers of the Duke carry on a cage and open the cage door. The knight on all fours feebly crawls away. They move the cage to catch him. Sadly Sancho heads him into it, and they shut it. Like a beast, he is carried to his own home. There Sancho helps him out, the old housekeeper, the old curate undress him and put him to bed in a fever. They leave. In a fever he sees the Inquisition approach. He sees the burning of his books. He is humble but does not recant. A vision of the Virgin on a cart appears—the image with which the ballet began—after a long pause she raises her head and looks at him. He is lifted in ecstasy, as mystics are by levitation. She vanishes, he collapses sobbing (at this point the machinery creaks) to his bed. His friends return with the shy servant girl. He dies and they mourn him. The servant girl picks up two small sticks, she goes very slowly to the corpse and lays them on his chest to form a cross. The curtain falls.

At the first performance the Don recognized his friends and died sane as he does in the novel. At a later one he was dead when they returned, a simpler effect.

The tragic pathos of the ballet is simpler than the enormous comic buoyancy of the novel. But the novel no less than *Romeo* or *The Tempest* has long been material for imaginative reinterpretation. Auden's brilliant reinterpretation of the novel, from which the program quotes, is quite as "free" as Balanchine's very different and equally brilliant one.

Balanchine has reinterpreted comic details of the book in a wider tragic sense—the hooded penitents transporting a statue of the Virgin become the Inquisition; the burning of books by his best friends becomes an auto-da-fé; ordinary pigs become half-human, their gleeful stampede morally swinish; the Don's cage, a kindly stratagem leading to broad jokes, becomes an image of horror; a buxom country girl becomes a delicate ballerina. Similarly the masked hazing of Don Quixote at the Duke's, gracefully as it moves, by the shock of its pauses—particularly the last pause, the face blinded by whipped cream, turned immobile to the public—becomes a bitter denunciation of society's meanness. The ballet is not only gloomily lit, but also somber in the ideas it suggests. Even if the Inquisition is shown as a hallucination, one recognizes the social fact it represents in a contemporary sense, and remembers the Inquisitor in Dostoevsky.

Man's inhumanity to man is one of the two forces at conflict in the ballet. The other is man's goodwill to man. It is shown by the touching pictures of Don Quixote's domestic friends, particularly humble cheerful Sancho, a stout man light on his feet. It is shown by the Don's cool and lovely Dulcinea; by the marvelous vision of his third-act dream—though even that ends in menace; by his innocent courage and his deeper idea of grace. Even in its strongest form this force does not triumph. At the end, after looking at him, it vanishes and leaves him sobbing.

The Establishment at all its levels pressuring the imaginative individual into alienation, into failure—that is what you watch. The ballet's images, like those of poetry, are fluid and contradictory. But they are not conciliatory. They are aggressive. The cruel ones get worse. On the other hand, though his ballet is about failure, Balanchine has never made dances more glorious in their novel beauty than that of Marcela and all those of the long pas d'action, or sweeter than the Mauresque duet; nor has he ever invented so many striking mime images, often extravagantly speeded up or slowed down without recourse to stylization.

A few times scenes are protracted beyond their active effect—the projection scene of Act One, the masked scene of Act Two, the vision of the Virgin in Act Three. I do not press the point. A full-length ballet so rich in imagination and with so complex a theater form, presented without dress rehearsal, can be allowed several uncertainties, even if they prove, like some of Shakespeare's, incurable.

Seeing Balanchine act Don Quixote, a number of fans got the idea that the ballet portrayed the choreographer. This ballet contradicts many others of his; but if this portrays him, all the others do equally.

As for the score by Nicolas Nabokov, it is descriptive, a bit of everything, well educated, rhythmically weak, with a tendency to fall back from a two-bar climax. A great composer remarked in conversation, "It's Louis Philippe. *Pièces de genre. Pièces de style*, everybody is bored with that, nowadays one can't keep that up more than five minutes. *Pièces de genre*, one can go on with that longer." As for me, I am grateful to the score for serving so interesting a ballet. I have heard many fans say the ballet isn't interesting. I find it is, and have said why, both from the point of view of a fan and a theatergoer. *Dance Magazine*, JULY 1965

BALANCHINE'S POETICS

Recently I was watching a revival by American Ballet Theatre of Balanchine's *Symphonie Concertante*. The stage seemed to be filled with dancers, and this surprised me because it is not characteristic of Balanchine. I don't remember that feeling of fullness in the original. The relationship between the dancers and the stage space seemed to have been altered. Things looked crowded and busy.

That relationship is very delicate, and it is difficult to define. But it is something which you sense being right in Balanchine, something you can see and feel. Balanchine's use of stage space is characteristically right for the movements he is using.

In *The Divine Comedy* Dante creates an image in only a few clear sharp lines and then changes the subject before you lose the image. The ability to do that in dance is just as extraordinary as achieving the same effect in poetry—to change the whole look of the stage in a moment or two without making the viewer painfully aware of what is happening. Balanchine does this constantly, and seeing his skill at work is a source of considerable pleasure. This is a rare gift today because so many choreographers intentionally—or so it seems—make their dancing as monotonous as possible, claiming that the impression of accumulated physical energy will be stronger. What strikes me so frequently about Balanchine's choreography is that it contains this desirable accumulation of energy, but it also has a delightful sense of variety. You are always curious about what's going to happen next.

Balanchine makes you feel the connection between the dance steps and the stage space. Instead of "space," we should say "air," because "space" seems to be such a dead word. Most choreographers rely on the subject matter of their dances to do this for them. But Balanchine thought of dance as having a *musical* subject matter, which is quite different from a plot. The sequences of steps, the variety, are all related to the music. The musical subject matter of Balanchine dances is difficult to describe, but it can be deeply felt. There is a completeness about Balanchine's dances within that context. It is not really so very difficult to understand if, in Balanchine's words, you are willing to "see" the music and "hear" the steps.

People respond to the unexpected variety that turns up and makes continuous sense in Balanchine's ballets. Again, to borrow an image from poetry—which is not unlike dancing, after all—certain words will sound different depending on their use. They sound one way on the written page when you first encounter them, then sound another way when used in a sentence. You can change their weight completely by putting words together with other words. You can say, "*Don't* do that," or say, "Don't do *that*," or "Don't *do* that." These possibilities—these shifts of emphasis—give life to conversation. Good plays are written that way. Shakespeare can be read in different ways, and, although his lines may not lose their music, the meaning will change depending on the actor who says them. Balanchine did the same thing when he created for certain dancers, who then came to embody the life of that dance.

Recently I was reading a collection of poems and felt a sudden shift, which at first I couldn't identify. In a very modest, unemphatic way a simple "it" had been slipped in which had the effect of changing the whole sense of the four lines before and the three or four lines which followed. In just one sentence everything had been changed as a result of the placement of one two-letter word. You enjoyed the feel of that, sensed the correctness. The same is true of the shifts in Balanchine's dances. As subtle as they may be, they are essential to the life and meaning of his work. Few choreographers have known how to do that.

And then consider that ballet steps are even more limited than our written language. The kinds of accents and thrusts selected by the choreographer are essential. I have admired one of Balanchine's late pieces, *Robert Schumann's "Davidsbündlertänze,"* because there was a great deal of drama in it without Balanchine's using a single dramatic gesture. The relation of the music to the dance made it dramatic, made you interested in the "story." You never know what these people are saying, the words they are using. But through those elements of which Balanchine is master, you sense that a lively and dramatic relationship exists.

The first time I saw Balanchine's choreography was in Vienna, when Spessivtseva and Lifar performed *La Chatte.* It was new at the time and didn't leave a lasting impression on me. A few years later in Paris I saw *Mozartiana,* which Balanchine created for Les Ballets 1933. It was a marvel of theater magic, everywhere unpredictable. Balanchine changed the way I looked at ballet, as he has done since that time for generations of balletgoers. I knew immediately that this was somebody whose work I wanted to see more of. I was totally fascinated, completely drawn into it. No other choreographer's work has had quite the same effect on me since. I was delighted with what I saw. I was astonished every moment with what was happening onstage. It was pure dancing.

Dancing is such a momentary impression. Balanchine always said that his ballets are like butterflies: they live for a season. He didn't much like reviving works because he didn't seem to remember them, being much more interested in new things. I have no idea what will become of Balanchine's butterflies now. I wish there were people who cared enough to preserve them as they should be preserved. Villella understood the Balanchine works so well, and of course Tanaquil Le Clercq. Tastes change, styles change, techniques change. Look at what has happened to Petipa in only seventy years since his death. But we know one very important thing about Balanchine: he changed the way we look at dance. Very few people in the history of any art have that kind of impact.

INTERVIEW WITH RICHARD PHILP,
Dance Magazine, JULY 1983

Essays

NOTES ON NIJINSKY PHOTOGRAPHS

Looking at the photographs of Nijinsky, one is struck by his expressive neck. It is an unusually thick and long neck. But its expressivity lies in its clear lift from the trunk, like a powerful thrust. The shoulders are not square, but slope downward; and so they leave the neck easily free, and the eye follows their silhouette down the arms with the sense of a line extraordinarily extended into space, as in a picture by Cézanne or Raphael. The head therefore, at the other end of this unusual extension, poised up in the air, gains an astonishing distinctness, and the tilt of it, even with no muscular accentuation, becomes of unusual interest. Nijinsky tilts his head lightly from the topmost joint, keeping this joint mobile against the upright thrust of the other vertebrae. He does not bend the neck back as some contemporary ballet dancers do. Seen from the side or the rear, the upward line of his back continues straight into the uprightness of the neck, like the neck of a Maillol statue. But Nijinsky alters his neck to suit a character role. The change is striking in the *Schéhérazade* pictures—and Mr. Van Vechten, who saw him dance the part, describes him as a "head-wagging, simian creature." Another variation is that for *Petrouchka*, where the shoulders are raised square to break the continuity of the silhouette; to make the arms dangle as a separate entity, and make the head independently wobbly as a puppet's is, on no neck to speak of. The head here does not sum up or direct the action of the body; it seems to have only a minor, a pathetic function. But it bobs too nonsensically to be humanly pitiful. In the role of the Faun the shoulders are slightly lifted when the Faun becomes dimly aware of his own emotion; but the neck is held up firmly and candidly against the shoulder movement (which would normally press the neck to a forward slant); and so the silhouette is kept self-contained and the figure keeps its dignity. Notice, too, the neck in the reclining position of the Faun. Another poignant duplicity of emotion is expressed by the head, neck, and shoulder line of the *Jeux* photographs—the neck rising against lifted shoulders and also bent sideways against a countertilt of the head. The hero in *Jeux* seems to meet pathos with human nobility—not as the Faun does, with animal dignity.

Looking in these photographs farther along the figure, at the arms in particular, one is struck by their lightness, by the way in which they seem to be suspended in space. Especially in the pictures from *Pavillon* and from *Spectre*, they are not so much placed correctly, or advantageously, or illustratively; rather they seem to flow out unconsciously from the moving trunk, a part of the fullness of its intention. They are pivoted, not lifted, from the shoulder or shoulder blade; their force—like the neck's—comes from the full strength of the back. And so they lead the eye more strongly back to the trunk than out beyond their reach into space. Even when they point, one is conscious of the force pointing quite as much as the object pointed at. To make a grammatical metaphor, the relation of subject to object is kept clear. This is not so simple in movement as a layman might think. A similar clarification of subject and object struck me in the bullfighting of Belmonte. His own body was constantly the subject of his motions, the bull the object. With other fighters, one often had the impression that not they personally but their cloth was the subject that determined a fight. As a cloth is a dead thing, it can only be decorative, and the bull edged into the position of the subject; and the distinctness of the torero's drama was blurred. Nijinsky gives an effect in his arm gesture of himself remaining at the center of space, a strength of voluntary limitation related, in a way, to that of Spanish dance gesture. (This is what makes a dancer's arms look like a man's instead of a boy's.)

An actual "object" to a dancer's "subject" is his partner. In dancing with a partner there is a difference between self-effacement and courtesy. Nijinsky in his pictures is a model of courtesy. The firmness of support he gives his partner is complete. He stands straight enough for two. His expression toward her is intense—in *Giselle* it expresses a supernatural relation, in *Pavillon* one of admiration, in *Faun* one of desire, in *Spectre* one of tenderness—and what a supporting arm that is in *Spectre*, as long and as strong as two. But he observes as well an exact personal remoteness, he shows clearly the fact they are separate bodies. He makes a drama of their nearness in space. And in his own choreography—in *Faun*—the space between the figures becomes a firm body of air, a lucid statement of relationship, in the way intervening space does in the modern academy of Cézanne, Seurat, and Picasso.

One is struck by the massiveness of his arms. This quality also leads the eye back to the trunk, as in a Michelangelo figure. But it further gives to their graceful poses an amplitude of strength that keeps them from looking innocuous or decorative. In particular in the Narcissus pose the savage force of the arms and legs makes credible that the hero's narcism was not vanity, but an instinct that killed him, like an act of God. In the case of *Spectre*, the power of the arms makes their tendril-like bendings as natural as curvings are in a powerful world of young desire, while weaker and more charming arms might suggest an effeminate or saccharine coyness. There is indeed nothing effeminate in these gestures; there is far too much force in them.

It is interesting to try oneself to assume the poses on the pictures, beginning with arms, shoulders, neck, and head. The flowing line they have is deceptive. It is an unbelievable strain to hold them. The plastic relationships turn out to be extremely complex. As the painter de Kooning, who knows the photographs well and many of whose ideas I am using in these notes, remarked: Nijinsky does just the opposite of what the body would naturally do. The plastic sense is similar to that of Michelangelo and Raphael. One might say that the grace of them is not derived from avoiding strain, as a layman might think, but from the heightened intelligibility of the plastic relationships. It is an instinct for countermovement so rich and so fully expressed, it is unique, though the plastic theory of countermovement is inherent in ballet technique.

Nijinsky's plastic vitality animates the poses derived from dances by Petipa or Fokine. It shines out, too, if one compares his pictures with those of other dancers in the same parts. This aspect of his genius appears to me one basis for his choreographic style, which specifies sharply plastic effects in dancing—and which in this sense is related both to Isadora and to the moderns. Unfortunately the dancers who now take the role of the Faun do not have sufficient plastic discipline to make clear the intentions of the dance.

From the photographs one can see that the present dancers of *Faun* have not even learned Nijinsky's stance. Nijinsky not only squares his shoulders far less, but also frequently not at all. He does not pull in his stomach and lift his thorax. Neither in shoulders nor chest does he exhibit his figure. His stomach has more expression than his chest. In fact, looking at his trunk, one notices a similar tendency to flat-chestedness (I mean in the stance, not in the anatomy) in all the pictures. It is, I believe, a Petersburg trait, and shared independently by Isadora and Martha Graham. In these photographs, at any rate, the expression does not come from the chest; it comes from below the chest, and flows up through it from below. The thorax, so to speak passively, is not only pulled at the top up and back; at the bottom and from the side it is also pulled down and back. Its physical function is that of completing the circuit of muscles that holds the pelvis in relation to the spine. And it is this relation that gives the dancer his balance. Balance (or aplomb, in ballet) is the crux of technique. If you want to see how good a dancer is, look at his stomach. If he is sure of himself there, if he is so strong there that he can present himself frankly, he (or she) can begin to dance expressively. (I say stomach because the stomach usually faces the audience; one might say waist, groin, or pelvis region.)

In looking at Nijinsky pictures, one is struck by the upright tautness about the hips. His waist is broad and powerful. You can see it clearly in the Harlequin pictures. If he is posing on one leg, there is no sense of shifted weight, and as little if he seems to be bending to the side or forward. The effort this means may be compared to lifting a table by one leg and keeping the top horizontal. The center of gravity in the table, and similarly that of his body, has not been shifted. The delicacy with which he cantilevers the weight actually displaced keeps the firmness from being rigidity. I think it is in looking at his waist that one can see best the technical aspect of his instinct for concentrating the origin of movement so that all of it relates to a clear center which is not altered. He keeps the multiplicity, the diffusion which movement has, intelligible by not allowing any doubt as to where the center is. When he moves he does not blur the center of weight in his body; one feels it as clearly as if he were still standing at rest, one can follow its course clearly as it floats about the stage through the dance. And so the motion he makes looks controlled and voluntary and reliable. I imagine it is this constant sense of balance that gave his dancing the unbroken continuity and flow through all the steps and leaps and rests from beginning to end that critics marveled at.

Incidentally, their remarks of this kind also point to an extraordinary accuracy in his musical timing. For to make the continuity rhythmic as he did, he must have had an unerring instinct at which moment to attack a movement, so that the entire sequence of it would flow as continuously and transform itself into the next motion as securely as did the accompanying sound. To speak of him as unmusical, with no sense of rhythm, as Stravinsky has, is therefore an impropriety that is due to a confusion of meaning in the word "rhythm." The choreography of *Faun* proves that Nijinsky's natural musical intelligence was of the highest order. For this was the first ballet choreography set clearly not to the measures and periods, but to the expressive flow of the music, to its musical sense. You need only compare *Faun*'s assurance in this respect to the awkwardness musically of Fokine's second scene in *Petrouchka*, the score of which invites the same sort of understanding. But this is not in the photographs.

Nijinsky does not dance from his feet; he dances from his pelvis. The legs do not show off. They have no ornamental pose. Even in his own choreography, though the leg gestures are "composed," they are not treated as pictorial possibilities. They retain their weight. They tell where the body goes and how. But they don't lead it. They are, however, completely expressive in this role; and the thighs in the *Spectre* picture with Karsavina are as full of tenderness as another dancer's face. It is noticeable, too, that Nijinsky's legs are not especially turned out, and a similar moderate en dehors seems to be the rule in the Petersburg male dancers of Nijinsky's generation. But the parallel feet in *Narcisse* and *Faun*, and the pigeon toes in *Tyl* are not a willful contradiction of the academic principle for the sake of something new. They can, it seems to me, be properly understood only by a turned-out dancer, as Nijinsky himself clearly was. For the strain of keeping the pelvis in the position the ballet dancer holds it in for balance is much greater with parallel or turned-in feet (which contradicts the outward twist of the thigh); and this strain gives a new plastic dimension to the legs and feet, if it is carried through as forcefully as Nijinsky does. I am interested, too, to notice that in standing Nijinsky does not press his weight mostly on the ball of the big toe, but grips the floor with the entire surface of the foot.

I have neglected to mention the hands, which are alive and simple, with more expression placed in the wrist than in the fingers. They are not at all "Italian," and are full of variety without an emphasis on sensitivity. The hands in *Spectre* are celebrated, and remind one of the hands in Picassos ten years later. I am also very moved by the uplifted, half-unclenched hands in the *Jeux* picture, as mysterious as breathing in sleep. One can see, too, that in *Petrouchka* the hands are black-mittened, not white-mittened as now; the new costume makes the dance against the black wall in the second scene a foolish hand dance, instead of a dance of a whole figure, as intended.

The manner in which Nijinsky's face changes from role to role is immediately striking. It is enhanced by makeup, but not created by it. In fact, a friend pointed out that the only role in which one recognizes Nijinsky's civilian face is that of Petrouchka, where he is most heavily made up. There is no mystery about such transformability. People don't usually realize how much any face changes in the course of a day, and how often it is unrecognizable for an instant or two. Nijinsky seems to have controlled the variability a face has. The same metamorphosis is obvious in his body. The Specter, for instance, has no age or sex, the Faun is adolescent, the hero of *Jeux* has a body full-grown and experienced. Tyl can either be boy or man. The Slave in *Schéhérazade* is fat, the Specter is thin. It does not look like the same body. One can say that in this sense there is no exhibitionism in Nijinsky's photographs. He is never showing you himself, or an interpretation of himself. He is never vain of what he is showing you. The audience does not see him as a professional dancer, or as a professional charmer. He disappears completely, and instead there is an imaginary being in his place. Like a classic artist, he remains detached, unseen, unmoved, uninterested. Looking at him, one is in an imaginary world, entire and very clear; and one's emotions are not directed at their material objects, but at their imaginary satisfactions. As he said himself, he danced with love.

To sum up, Nijinsky in his photographs shows us the style of a classic artist. The emotion he projects, the character he projects, is not communicated as his own, but as one that exists independently of himself, in the objective world. Similarly his plastic sense suggests neither a private yearning into an infinity of space nor a private shutting out of surrounding relationships, both of them legitimate romantic attitudes. The weight he gives his own body, the center which he gives his plastic motions, strikes a balance with the urge and rapidity of leaps and displacements. It strikes a balance between the role he dances and the roles of his partners. The distinction of place makes the space look real, the distinction of persons makes the drama real. And for the sake of this clarification he characterizes (or mimes, one might say) even such a conventional ornamental show-off, or "pure dance," part as that in *Pavillon*. On the other hand, the awkward heaviness that *Faun*, *Sacre*, and *Jeux* exhibited, and that was emphasized by their angular precision, was not, I believe, an anticlassic innovation. It was an effort to make the dance more positive, to make clearer still the center of gravity of a movement, so that its extent, its force, its direction, its elevation can be appreciated not incidentally merely, but integrally as drama. He not only extended the plastic range in dancing, but clarified it. And this is the way to give meaning to dancing—not secondhand literary meaning, but direct meaning. Nijinsky's latest intentions of "circular movement" and the improvisational quality *Tyl* seems to have had are probably a normal development of his sense of motion in relation to a point of repose—a motion that grew more animated and diverse as his instinct became more exercised. (An evolution not wholly dissimilar can be followed in Miss Graham's work, for instance.) And I consider the following remark he made to be indicative of the direction of his instinct: "La grâce, le charme, le joli sont rangés tout autour du point central qu'est le beau. C'est pour le beau que je travaille." I do not see anything in these pictures that would lead one to suppose that Nijinsky's subsequent insanity cast any premonitory shadow on his phenomenally luminous dance intelligence.

In their stillness Nijinsky's pictures have more vitality than the dances they remind us of as we now see them on the stage. They remain to show us what dancing can be, and what the spectator and the dancer each aspire to, and hold to be a fair standard of art. I think they give the discouraged dance lover faith in dancing as a serious human activity. As Mr. Van Vechten wrote after seeing him in 1916: "His dancing has the unbroken quality of music, the balance of great painting, the meaning of fine literature, and the emotion inherent in all these arts."

Dance Index, MARCH 1943

FLIGHT OF THE DANCER

If you travel all over the world and see every brilliant and flying dance that human beings do, you will maybe be surprised that it is only in our traditional classic ballet dancing that the dancer can leap through the air slowly. In other kinds of dancing there are leaps that thrill you by their impetuousness or accuracy; there are brilliant little ones, savage long ones, and powerful bouncing ones. But among all dance techniques only classic ballet has perfected leaps with that special slow-motion grace, that soaring rise and floating descent which looks weightless. It isn't that every ballet leap looks that way. Some are a tough thrust off the ground, some travel like a cat's, some quiver like a fish's, some scintillate like jig steps; but these ways of jumping you can find in other dancing too. The particular expression ballet technique has added to leaping is that of the dancer poised in mid-flight, as easy in the air as if she were suspended on wires. Describing the effect, people say one dancer took flight like a bird, another was not subject to the laws of gravity, and a third paused quietly in midair. And that is how it does look, when it happens.

To be honest, it doesn't happen very often. It is a way of leaping only a few rare dancers ever quite achieve. But it can be achieved. You can see it in the dancing of Alicia Markova, the English-born star of our present Ballet Theatre company; though no one else in this country—perhaps no one else in the world—can "fly" quite as perfectly as she does. No one else is so serenely calm with nothing underneath her. In *Pas de Quatre* she sits collectedly in the air, as if she were at a genteel tea party, a tea party where everyone naturally sat down in the air. There is something comic about it. That is because Miss Markova, who in the part of Giselle is a delicate tragic dancer, also has a keen sense of parody. *Pas de Quatre*, a parody ballet, represents the competition in virtuosity of four very great ballerinas at a command performance before Her Majesty Queen Victoria. (It actually happened in 1845.) In the ballet, Miss Markova takes the part of the greatest of the four, Marie Taglioni—Marie *pleine de grâce*, as she was called—who was a sallow little lady full of wrinkles, celebrated not only for her serene flight through the empty air, but also for the "decent voluptuousness" of her expression. Watching Miss Markova's performance, one feels that not even the eminently respectable British queen could have found any fault with the female modesty of such a look as hers. And that "refined" look is Miss Markova's joke on Victorian propriety, and a little too on the vanity of exhibiting technique just for its own sake.

Her expression is parody, but the leap itself is no parody of a leap. It is the real, incredibly difficult thing. Taglioni's leap couldn't have been any better. A leap is a whole story, with a beginning, a middle, and an end. If you want to try it, here are some of the simplest directions for this kind of soaring flight. It begins with a knee bend, knees turned out, feet turned out and heels pressed down, to get a surer grip and a smoother flow in the leg action. The bend goes down softly ("as if the body were being sucked to the floor") with a slight accelerando. The thrust upward, the stretch of the legs, is faster than the bend was.

The speed of the action must accelerate in a continuous gradation from the beginning of the bend into the final spring upward, so there will be no break in motion when the body leaves the ground. The leap may be jumped from two feet, hopped from one, or hopped from one with an extra swing in the other leg. But in any case the propulsive strain of the leap must be taken up by the muscles around the waist; the back must be straight and perpendicular, as if it had no part in the effort. Actually, the back muscles have to be kept under the strictest tension to keep the spine erect—the difficulty is to move the pelvis against the spine, instead of the other way around; and as the spine has no material support in the air, you can see that it's like pulling yourself up by your own bootstraps.

But that isn't all. The shoulders have to be held rigidly down by main force, so they won't bob upward in the jump. The arms and neck, the hands and the head have to look as comfortable and relaxed as if nothing were happening down below. Really there's as much going on down there as though the arms and head were picnicking on a volcano. Once in the air the legs may do all sorts of things, embellishments sometimes quite unconnected with what they did to spring up, or what they will have to do to land. And if there are such extra embellishments during the leap, there should be a definite pause in the air before they begin and after they are finished. No matter how little time there is for them, the ornaments must never be done precipitately.

But the most obvious test for the dancer comes in the descent from the air, in the recovery from the leap. She has to catch herself in a knee bend that begins with the speed she falls at, and progressively diminishes so evenly that you don't notice the transition from the air to the ground. This knee bend slows down as it deepens to what feels like a final rest, though it is only a fraction of a second long, so short a movie camera will miss it. This is the "divine moment" that makes her look as if she alighted like a feather. It doesn't happen when she lands, you see; it happens later. After that, straightening up from the bend must have the feeling of a new start; it is no part of the jump, it is a new breath, a preparation for the next thing she means to do.

In other words, the action of a leap increases in speed till the dancer leaves the ground. Then it diminishes till it reaches the leap's highest point up in the air. From then on it increases again till the feet hit the ground, when it must be slowed down by the knee bend to a rest; and all these changes must be continuously flowing. But most important of all is the highest point reached in the air. Here, if the dancer is to give the feeling of soaring, she must be completely still. She must express the calm of that still moment. Some dancers hold their breath. Nijinsky used to say he just stopped at that point. But however he does it, the dancer must project that hair's-breadth moment as a climax of repose. The dancer must not be thinking of either how she got up or how she is going to get down. She must find time just then to meditate.

When Nijinsky exited through the window in the *Spectre de la Rose* thirty years ago it was the greatest leap of the century. He seemed to the audience to float slowly up like a happy spirit. He seemed to radiate a power of mysterious assurance as calmly as the bloom of a summer rose does. Such enthusiastic comments sound like complete nonsense nowadays, when you go to the ballet and see a young man thumping about the stage self-consciously. But the comments were made by sensible people, and they are still convinced they were right. You begin to see what they mean when you realize that for Nijinsky in this ballet the leaps and the dance were all one single flowing line of movement, faster or slower, heavier or lighter, a way of moving that could rise up off the ground as easily as not, with no break and no effort. It isn't a question of how high he jumped one jump, but how smoothly he danced the whole ballet. You can see the same quality of technique today in Miss Markova's dancing.

In one respect, though, Nijinsky's way of leaping differed from hers: in his style the knee bend that starts the leap up and the other one that catches it coming down were often almost unnoticeable. This is a difference of appearance, of expression, but not really of technique. Nijinsky could make the transitions in speed I spoke of above with an exceptionally slight bending of the knees—a very unusual accomplishment indeed. When a dancer can do this it gives an expression of greater spontaneity to the leap; but several modern ballet dancers who try to do it aren't able really to land "light as a sylph or a snowflake," as Nijinsky could. The slight jolt when they land breaks the smooth flow and attracts more attention than the stillness of the climax in the air. And so the leap fails to concentrate on a soaring expression. The correct soaring leap is a technical trick any ballet dancer can learn in ten or fifteen years if he or she happens to be a genius. The point of learning it is that it enables the dancer to make a particular emotional effect, which enlarges the range of expression in dancing. The effect as we watch Markova's pure flight can only be described as supernatural, as a strangely beneficent magic. It is an approach to those mysterious hints of gentleness that occasionally absorb the human mind. It is a spiritual emotion; so Nijinsky's contemporaries described it, when he danced that way, and so did the Parisian poet Théophile Gautier when he saw first Taglioni and then Grisi take flight a hundred years ago.

It was a hundred years ago, most likely, that the trick was first perfected, together with that other trick so related to it in expression, the moment of airy repose on one toe. (Toe dancing, like leaping, has many kinds of expression, but the suggestion of weightless, poised near-flight is one of its most striking.) Toe dancing, like the technique of aerial flight, took a long series of dance geniuses to develop. The great Mlle Camargo two centuries ago, in Paris and in London, was already "dancing like a bird." But it seems likely that she fluttered enchantingly, rather than soared calm and slow. Certainly Camargo's costumes didn't allow some technical resources that are related to our technique of flight; they allowed no horizontal lift of the leg, no deep knee bends, no spring and stretch of foot in a heelless slipper.

In the next century, soaring of a different kind was being perfected. They literally hung the dancer on wires, and hoisted him or her through the air. Theaters had machinery called "flight paths," one of them fifty-nine feet long—quite a fine swoop it must have made. Maybe these mechanical effects gradually gave dancers the idea of trying to do the same thing without machinery. In an 1830 ballet, girls dressed as woodland spirits bent down the lower boughs of trees and let themselves be carried upward into the air on the rebound, which sounds like some wire effect. And in 1841 the great dancer Carlotta Grisi—Taglioni's young rival—opened in the ballet *Giselle*, in the second act of which there was one passage at least where her leaps were "amplified" by wiring. (She was supposed to be a ghost in it, and it was meant to look spooky.) In the little engraving of her in this part she certainly floats over her grave in a way no ballet star ever could; but probably the pose is only an imaginary invention by the artist. The same *Giselle* is still being danced today both in America and Europe, and, according to report, in Paris, in London, and in Leningrad, at least, this particular hundred-year-old wire trick is still being pulled. *Mademoiselle*, OCTOBER 1943

A TECHNICAL WEAKNESS OF OUR MALE DANCERS

In conversation with Roger Pryor Dodge—a man who is an authority both on jazz music and on ballet dancing—the subject of ballet rhythm naturally came up. He told me how some years ago when he was watching a ballet class here in town conducted by the great dancer Pierre Vladimiroff (who succeeded to Nijinsky's roles in St. Petersburg in 1913), Mr. Vladimiroff was giving combinations of leaps—jetés, entrechats, and sissonnes—to his pupils, among whom were some of the best young male dancers in the country. Mr. Dodge noticed that the young dancers executed the steps and leaps in a sort of one-two-one-two military rhythm, closing the sequence a moment after the end of the music. Their action was rapid, vigorous, and fairly neat, but the effect was colorless and undistinguished. But when Vladimiroff himself performed the same sequence, Mr. Dodge could see very clearly a variety of emphasis in the movement.

At one moment, for instance, the action of separating the legs was stressed, and though it was just a fraction of a second, the eye could distinguish it sharply. At another point in the sequence there was a passing stress on the action of holding the legs joined in the air, or else on the start upward of a leap; and the feet had closed the phrase and were firm in repose when the music stopped. In short, Mr. Vladimiroff had a free rhythm in his leg action, which gave color and form to the succession of steps, varying the stress of them and relating them to one another, much as the small differences in speed and in stress join together the words that form a well-spoken sentence (an art of phrasing one can admire, for instance, in President Roosevelt's or in Miss Hayes's elocution).

The young dancers in the class, however, by giving each leap an equal stress and an even metronomic regularity of time length gave the effect of a singsong recitation of "Hiawatha," or the effect of a pianist who pounds the beat under the illusion that he can thereby make the music move forward in lively fashion.

Mr. Dodge and I agreed that Miss Danilova and Miss Markova are both brilliant examples of dancers who can vary the time values of steps—or, more exactly, of the component phases of a step—so as to create in a sequence the sense of a homogeneous dance phrase with a rise, a climax, and a finish. Their sense of the time values in a sequence of motions is also a sense of the visual values that every sequence contains. The quickening or retarding of motion allows some moments in the movement to be seen more sharply than others, and these stressed moments become the central images around which the observer's mind groups the rest of the motion. And the sort of movement these central images stress—whether it is a spreading or joining, a movement toward the partner or away, a strong countermovement of one part of the body against another, or a pose in relation to the stage space—these central images by their momentary plastic and architectural tension afford the eye a point of reference in virtue of which a lengthy passage makes emotional sense, a little as a stressed musical motive gives the ear a point of reference in a lengthy passage of music.

The dance phrase is formed by variation in speed and variation in stress. Its total length is determined by the length of the musical phrase; its total dynamic range, by the nature of the steps and leaps that are used, by the amplitude that is given them in this particular musical setting. And from these different elements the visual reality of a dance phrase emerges; and in the course of a piece, the special dramatic characterization of a dance role.

But these variations of speed and stress which make the dance interesting or dramatic to look at are possible only with a highly developed leg and thigh and waist and back technique. It is possible our young male dancers who do not give us the sense of a live rhythm in dancing either lack a sense of rhythm in time or lack a sense of rhythm in three-dimensional stressing of movement. But it is just as likely that their thigh and waist training is insufficient. They cannot give variety enough to their steps and leaps because their technique has been directed to going through the motions of these steps and leaps as if they could be done only one way, in one sort of timing and with one kind of stress to the component parts of them. Their technique has not been directed to variety—human variety—within these traditional muscular sequences known as ballet steps and ballet leaps. That is what makes their dancing look monotonous. They should be able to make correct and similar jetés that if photographed by Mr. Mili with his stroboscopic camera would produce radically different patterns on the print.

Our young dancers, for all their admirable feats of athletics, are all too often engaged in repeating their poems in ballet by rote; they do not give them rhythm. They aren't able to give them rhythm in the sense that Harlem ballroom dancers, for instance, give rhythm to the traditional steps of the lindy. Of course the lindy isn't nearly as hard as the Bluebird; but it's not the difficulty of a dance that makes the audience happy, it's rhythm. *Mademoiselle*, DECEMBER 1943

BALLET: THE AMERICAN POSITION

Ballet is the one form of theater where nobody speaks a foolish word all evening—nobody on the stage at least. That's why it becomes so popular in any civilized country during a war. Its success here during the recent one surprised many people who didn't realize how civilized the country is. I have been asked to guess what will happen to it in the next few years. Anyone's guess is as good as mine. My guess is that its civilized qualities will continue to be remarkably attractive for some time; the difficulty will be for ballet to keep them, rather than for the public to appreciate them.

Ballet is absurd by nature. But its absurdities are civilized ones. It is as absurd as a symphony concert. A symphony is seventy-five men on a stage who make noises together very earnestly for a couple of hours; and music lovers beam at some of the noises and lose their tempers over others. Ballet is a lot of young people hopping about to music in a peculiarly exhilarating way. Sometimes they're being sad and sometimes funny, but they're always in the pink of condition, charmingly built, graceful, well mannered, and serious. Like an orchestra of musicians or a cast of actors they are busy building up the illusion of some sort of event; but they don't waste so much time about it as actors and they are pleasanter to watch at work than musicians. Dancers appear briefly in all the glamour of orchestral sonorities and surprising fancy dress, and you find intelligent people who long afterward remember with affection some brief illusion that dancers created. Ballet is in the habit of using the fantasy gifts of serious composers and painters without depreciating them. It is by nature a form of poetic theater and it is the form that is liveliest at the moment in this country. Theater lovers sometimes hope its popularity may even lead to a more imaginative spoken drama.

The fine moments of ballet frighten but they do it gently; and for that it needs accurate dancers. They have to be trained from early youth to precision in rhythm, to a clear, bold, large articulation (even in light or soft passages), to variety and virtuosity and personal modesty and ensemble work. Their way of building up a dramatic effect is to project its rhythmic beat or pulse and its individual rhythmic continuity. The quality of motion they show—now heavy, now light, rapid or still, gliding and stabbing, soaring or darting, successively solo, duet, or in chorus—gives the situation onstage its special imaginative meaning. You sense it in the clear shapes their bodies make, in their contact with each other in dance figures and in the cumulative transformations of choreographic architecture.

A ballet usually tells a story too and so it uses pantomime; but people don't go for the pantomime, they go for the dancing. Ballet dancing is not an imitation of anything else. It is an invention to convey imaginative meaning—an invention something like that of Occidental concert music, which isn't a very much older one historically but is one that has been far more widely practiced and elaborately developed. Concert music and ballet are each ways of communicating an interesting fantasy without the use of words or verbal logic. They each invented a nonverbal semantic system which audiences for the last few centuries have found agreeable and even internationally intelligible. Ballet now and then almost makes literal sense as pantomime; but a moment later it obviously doesn't, and then it is often more absorbing than ever as fantasy because then the beat and sweep of the dance become more powerful and its shapes seem to enlarge.

As everyone knows, ballet's international semantic system is based on a standard dance technique. The problem of theater dancing is how to keep a number of performers going with a steady liveliness that can weave a spontaneous spell. Ballet technique simplifies the problem for the choreographer in the way, say, a piano simplifies the problem of the composer who wants to arrange noises so they will be interesting to listen to in sequence. It limits but it is more workable. It is workable under theater conditions because that's how it was invented; and that's why its conventions are inseparable from the hard facts of theater music and stage architecture. Ballet technique was evolved by generations of theater dancers who were proud of their best effects and tried to pass them on to youngsters. It is a time-saving device for dancers as well as for choreographers. After only six or eight years of practicing it, dancers achieve a high standard of liveliness, clarity, and coherence in a wide range of effects. They can readily be used in companies, they can learn new dances quickly, they can do brilliant things reliably and easily. To achieve this, ballet technique limited itself to certain kinds of movement. But it discovered so sound and so flexible a language that new dance rhythms or dance images and new expressive qualities in dancing are constantly appearing in new ballets. It provides only one of the possible techniques of theater dancing; Javanese dancing has, for instance, a different and a very lovely one. The modern dance aims to provide a third, but so far its simplest units of posture, of movement, and of rhythm have been either too complex to be handy in the theater or else, with Jooss, too wooden. Modern-dance technique missed the simple bounce of growing up onstage with dance tunes around and children howling, the way ballet first did. For the present, ballet's technique is the most manageable, the most sociable and good-natured.

This is why ballet is a civilized kind of theater entertainment. It is by nature an exact and flexible language to communicate formal fantasy; and it is a medium of communication wonderfully fresh and sensuous, since it exists only while young people are dancing it conscientiously and happily to serious music and in imaginative fancy dress.

All this has been what ballet dancing is like by nature and what it intends as theater entertainment. Though difficult and expensive to produce, its graceful and civilized sense in nonsense makes it for many people a particularly exhilarating show, and in recent years audiences all over the country who were unfamiliar with it before have taken to its peculiarities without trouble. Ballet has now become acclimated because nobody thinks of it as foreign anymore. And it has become homegrown because almost everyone onstage nowadays was born and trained in America, and it is for their kind of dance gift and their American look that the new productions are intended. Their collective innocently American flavor in action is a novelty in big-time ballet but it looks natural to the audience that sees it here, and pleasing.

The charming figures, the long legs of American girls are a part of that new American flavor. In any kind of dancing a bunch of young Americans do together, they are likely to show a steadier and keener sense of beat and a clearer carriage of the body than Europeans would, and they are apt to wear a more sober and noncommittal look than European Latins or Slavs. In our ballet these national traits show up too and often turn out very handsomely. Large, clear, accurate, and unaffected our ballet style looks—and particularly among the slender young girls remarkable for speed, toes, and prowess; its phrasing is not very personal; and George Balanchine has mentioned a kind of angelic unconcern toward emotion as being perhaps a special charm of American dancers.

We would see our traits more sharply if we could see for contrast the current foreign companies. Till they come over, the only style we can compare ours with is the prewar Ballets Russes one of the thirties. Compared to ours its atmosphere was more hot-and-bothered, its rhythm in dance scenes made more sweeping climaxes, its techniques looked more casual and undefined, and its temperament was more exotically fiery. None of our companies since then has been as striking as that at its best. But if Ballet Theatre, the Monte Carlo, and Ballet Society were to pool their stars, soloists, and repertory and add the ex–Ballet Theatre contingent now with the Original (and two first-rate conductors) they would form a company of about the same size as the best prewar Ballet Russe and one of even finer dance quality.

How the present European dancers compare to ours I only know from deceptive photographs and conflicting reports by travelers. The general impression seems to be that our ballet is better in straight dancing and in dance invention than any of Western Europe. It is apparently less good in effects of imaginative impersonation, of imaginative atmosphere or stage presence—qualities which the Paris Champs-Elysées Ballet seems to project with especial brilliance and wit. As for the Soviet ballet, the magnificent abundance of energy and force of Moscow's enormous company would no doubt thrill anybody; but that innocent and unintentional subtlety of human response between fantasy characters which is the heart of our idea of style—how that looks over there, no one has clearly told us. All I have seen of it was an action shot of a supported leap in the *Sleeping Beauty* pas de deux, in which both stars showed a radiant glow of good nature all over, wonderfully simple in its amazing largeness of scale.

Till the contrast of foreign ensembles gives us a sharper view of our style, one senses its nature best in the clearness of our young ballerinas—Alonso, Boris, Hightower, Kaye, Moylan, and Tallchief, to list them alphabetically—but it shows too in thirty or forty good soloists. Ballet Theatre crystallized its version of our style with *Pillar of Fire*, and the Monte Carlo with *Danses Concertantes*. Our dancing would of course never have become so strong without a great deal of stimulus from abroad and from ex–Ballets Russes artists in particular. It is obvious that without Balanchine and Tudor as choreographers, without as stars Danilova, Markova, Toumanova or Eglevsky, Franklin, Laing, and Youskevitch, our stage would lose its current luster. And it would be silly to underestimate their decisive importance to our ballet in the years ahead. But one notices too that foreign-trained artists who stay in our companies acclimate themselves to the local dance atmosphere or else get fidgety and lose their power. When they stay they enrich our style by the example they give; but working here leads them to an unconscious shift of emphasis in their own manner. Eglevsky's present style—much more exact than five years ago—is an example. Danilova's new tautness in rhythm that a few years back gave a fresh power to her wonderful grace is another. A third is the change in emphasis Tudor has given the 1946 production of *Lilac Garden* compared to the one we saw five years earlier—the dancing now is far lighter and more flowing in arm motions, has far more impetus and three-dimensional clarity in phrasing. The stimulus that Tudor's work here has given our native choreographers and dancers is obvious; perhaps the increasing ease in his phrasing (which *Undertow* sometimes suggested too) is due to a reciprocal influence.

But the artist from abroad who has responded most to our special dance gifts and climate has been Balanchine. And he is also the man who more than any other individual created and founded our American ballet. The fact that we have not wasted time trying to imitate the Ballets Russes style, the local freshness and the high standards of technique in dancing and in choreography we take for granted—these are due above all to his quiet persistence and his pervasive influence since he came here fourteen years ago. He has developed the physical qualities and the zest of our dancers as elements of style. He has made our dancers look natural in classicism. His pieces carry onstage when they dance them classically clear and large, without nervousness or self-conscious glamour; he has shown how fascinating their buoyant rhythm can be in all sorts of variations of forthright impetus. That way they learn to dance correct ballet as straightforwardly and simply as one speaks the language one is born to, and learn from their experience in his contemporary classicism to dance the nineteenth-century classics as unaffectedly. Finding out how to dance these as real dancing is a big step in a young dancer's deprovincialization. They are dances created as far away from us in time and space as ballet reaches, and an American who finds herself bringing them to life feels her power as a dancer. Their undistorted gesture, their clear rhythm invite no faking, they are void of malice or acedia; but the theater effect of their good manners and large poetry is often more obvious to the audience than to our performers.

Balanchine too has shown us in his own choreography the kind of theater effect classic ballet can have. His pieces are not assertive smash numbers; they are pleasant the first time, and the more you see them the more you can find in them. They present themselves politely as ballet entertainment in which the dancers can look brilliant. Not the story, but the dance rhythm, the surprising dance figures, the witty solutions, the clarity, and above all the musicality of the action seem to carry the piece. It all looks like brilliant dance fun. And something else happens too. In your excitement as you watch the quick dancing, it will often evoke in passing an intensely poignant fantasy image of human relations. Such moments are not self-consciously underlined; they seem to happen of their own accord in the dancing and so they remain suspended in the world of fantasy. Their dramatic meaning or emotional relevance is no burden on anyone's conscience, least of all on the dancers'. Some people respond to these dramatic meanings sharply, some dimly, and some not at all; but it is fantasy of the highest imaginative honesty. The American ballet audience responds to his pieces with pleasure just as they do to *Giselle* or *Swan Lake*, and they like the peaceful excitement of them better and better the more they see it.

I have stressed Balanchine's classicism of dance "meaning" and the American flavor he develops in classic dancing because these are novel and unique qualities which just now we are contributing to international ballet and because they are based on qualities natural to ballet and to our dancers. They are important because they are novel dance qualities; but because they are dance qualities (not literary ones) they are hard to talk about. It is easier to talk about the novelty of our gay local-color Americanism in ballet or about the gloom-steeped psychological aspects of Tudor's gripping large-scale dramas of frustration. These pieces make a good deal of their appeal through their literary content, and from a literary point of view the value of them in nationalizing our ballet or in modernizing it has been properly stressed by many reporters. I myself do not think the literary ideas I see in Tudor or in the American folk ballet are very novel ideas as ideas go in contemporary literature—the local color generally strikes me as too cute and the sex psychology too weepy. But the action of these pieces onstage has many very brilliant passages. The qualities of novel dance invention and of dramatic confrontation, of observation and timing and punch shown in Tudor's work as well as in Agnes de Mille's and Jerome Robbins's are qualities of which American ballet—and the American theater in general—can well be proud. And it is. Of Robbins's choreographic genius, after his new *Facsimile* there can be no doubt. Our public loves the zest, the jokes, the local steps and vitality of the American-scene pieces and admires the intensity of Tudor's. Our intelligent public recognizes too that Martha Graham's modern-school choreography is an even more extraordinary achievement and that her personal stage presence as a dancer is a theater event of the highest class.

Ballet in America has developed a standard of technique internationally valid and a style founded on characteristics by nature our own. Though it is too early to be dogmatic about what is or is not American in ballet, people are aware that our ballet is not an imitation of the prewar Ballet Russe manner but a new manner entirely. It compares favorably in enough respects with the postwar ballet style abroad to make one hope it will continue a development so soundly started.

It strikes me that theoretically speaking what our ballet needs more and more to continue its development is lessons in serious impersonation, in transforming the dancer on the stage into a character of fantasy. Even a Petipa Prince Charming is a real fantasy character, not a glamour boy. Very few of our dancers dare transform themselves—they are afraid of losing that audience contact through charm which they are used to. They indicate a character but they want to keep in every case a simple juvenile sex appeal. When our dancers act a character they are likely to show what they mean; but they seem to be explaining him to you instead of turning into someone else. Impersonation in dancing comes less from explaining the "psychology" of the character than from sensing who he is from the dance rhythm of the part. For only the effects of dance rhythm can touch the heart in ballet. They are the only ones that look unselfconscious and innocent and therefore really serious. In that sense good models for a ballerina are our great vaudeville comedians, with their innocent air of not caring whether they are noticed or not.

The theatrical effect of the prewar Paris-Russian style lay in a gift for impersonation through dance rhythm. Even before the war, however, the gift was already disintegrating into a mania for rhythmic and gymnastic distortion. Our own musical instinct allows only a very slight latitude of phrasing against a firm beat, and when our dancers learn impersonation through rhythm it will be the simpler and the larger in its effect. Our current story ballets are good for giving them practice in dance impersonation but they stress oddity of pantomime rather than expression through undistorted rhythm. So far there are not more than four or five Americans who achieve the necessary air of complete unselfconsciousness in critical situations. Most of the others seem to confuse the issue by indicating a moral approval or disapproval of the character they are acting.

"Storyless" ballets on the other hand can treat almost any situation without impropriety or moralizing, and people can enjoy the excitement of watching as innocently as they can listening to music. For the audience to take in an exciting action without quite knowing what is going on can be an advantage over following a story self-consciously step by step. A story so easily becomes censorable at its most interesting moments; one watches it nervously. Nervousness isn't fun, it's excitement that is.

My point so far has been that choreographers, dancers, and dance public have established a new kind of ballet in this country which is inherently American and internationally valid. Our wartime eagerness for ballet, wartime isolation, and easy money brought it into flower. It sounds like a Horatio Alger success story. Unfortunately the weather prophets don't see the immediate future as rosy. But the difficulties ahead are organizational rather than artistic. Ballet normally runs at a loss, just as a symphony orchestra does, and the loss under current general conditions has already jumped. Our two American-style companies, Ballet Theatre and the Monte Carlo, strike the weathermen as growing timid artistically in proportion. Lack of artistic enterprise by the management quickly demoralizes the company's dancers.

Economy has also reduced the size of both companies to half-strength. Both companies are now so small that the dancers must be perpetually overworked. It is a miracle our dancers survive the strain added to the brutal beating that the months of touring bring. They have no time for technique classes; in performance they can't trust the orchestra; since they are overworked they dance negligently for half the evening and grow used to rundown productions. They dance wrong in parts they have to fill in a hurry, and aren't corrected. Tired as they are, it isn't doing a part right but getting as much notice as possible that they must aim for. They come to count how often they appear in good parts, not how well, and they come to wow a part, an effect of their individual "stage glamour." All these dishonesties in dancing are hard to resist in exhaustion. It is enormously to the credit of our dancers when despite such conditions they succeed in developing as artists. But the survival of a few individuals does not make such conditions rational. No baseball manager would expect his team to shine worked as our dancers are worked.

The only remedy is to double the size of a company and halve the burden on the dancers. If our two companies could combine to one of double strength the dancers could take classes, rehearse, and prepare their parts. They would appear less but appear in brilliant form—and it is only in their best form that dancers really develop. With a combined repertory, the rundown pieces could be dropped and the rest kept well rehearsed. With a stronger repertory and more rehearsal time a bolder and more long-range risk could be taken with novelties. A good ballet often takes a while to grow in performance and an original one may well take a year or more for the general audience or even the critics to come around to.

The necessary step of organizing an American company twice the present size would cost probably two or three hundred thousand a year in deficit. It would require above all a director of rare artistic integrity and courage. But by the end of last fall's New York season many people were troubled about the future of our companies. Ballet is no fun when it looks routine.

But the low point of last fall, its most discouraging and dismal experience, was not due to our local companies but to an imported one, the Original Ballet Russe. In prewar days the company of this name had been a brilliant one. Last fall, obviously a rundown company, shoddy in dance technique and in atmosphere, it presented in New York a decayed version of the prewar style. It was saved from collapse only by its astute impresario, S. Hurok, who added a contingent of local stars and local productions that had nothing in common with the atmosphere of the importation.

But in this sad picture the weather prophets agree that a new subscription organization in New York, Ballet Society, is a cheerful spot. Ballet Society is a deficit venture. It offers four programs a year of ballet and ballet opera besides an evening or two of lectures or dance films. (Ballet opera means an opera sung in the pit and danced onstage by dancers.) By January two programs had been presented, which included three novelties; two ballet operas never staged in New York; some lovely Javanese dancing by Ratna Mohini and the two young Javanese gentlemen Soekaro and Pamoedjo; some modern-dance solos; a new orchestra piece by Colin McPhee. Together these two evenings had more novelties of interest than the whole fall season of three big ballet companies. There had been décor by interesting easel painters too. One of the operas, Stravinsky's *Renard*, had brilliant animal costumes and a fine drop by Esteban Francés. Another painter presented was Kurt Seligmann, who did the décor for a ballet, *The Four Temperaments.*

A tenet of Ballet Society is to present novelties by local choreographers, the first of which was *Pastorela,* which Lew Christensen had set to a score by Paul Bowles. But the dance events of the winter were Balanchine's two new ballets, *The Four Temperaments* and *Divertimento,* the latter to a score by Alexei Haieff, the former to one by Paul Hindemith. *Divertimento* is quick and sharp. It has a hint of juvenile romance, a curiously tender, very novel pas de deux, a virtuoso girl's solo that looks all simple and dewy, and a wonderful ending. *The Four Temperaments* on the other hand is a large long piece packed close with intricate but boldly powerful dance invention. It appears to have the dispassionate ferocity of a vital process; its subject is the "four temperaments" (or humors) of medieval endocrinology and it suggests the grandiose impersonal drama of organic energies. It is an impersonal drama that appears to be witty, cruel, desperate, and unconsoling, like that of our time. Yet all that actually happens onstage is rapid exact ballet dancing in classic sequences that are like none you could ever imagine. In fact the technical procedure of both ballets is that novel aspects of classic ballet technique—aspects apparently contrary to those one is accustomed to—are emphasized without ever breaking the classic look of the dance continuity.

The originator and manager of Ballet Society is Lincoln Kirstein, who in '33 invited Balanchine to this country and who has worked with him ever since, running a ballet school, managing successive local ballet companies, producing repertories, commissioning untried choreographers, composers, and painters, inventing scenarios, writing books, and editing a magazine. The dance company of Ballet Society is composed of dancers connected with Kirstein's American Ballet School and is an excellent one; Mary Ellen Moylan is its bold young ballerina. I have here reported the Society's lucky beginning at quite disproportionate length partly because it is a new, much-talked-of enterprise, partly because it may well, after several years of trial and error, turn out to have been the origin and foundation of the sensibly organized, exciting American ballet company we need now so badly.

Sensibly organized to produce dancing as an art, which is a ballet company's proper function. Kirstein and Balanchine together have—as *Time* pointed out in reviewing Ballet Society—worked since 1933 to de-Russianize our ballet as art. Now they have begun the necessary organizational work to decommercialize it as a branch of our theater. At the moment it is the most effective way of keeping it civilized, though the method is obviously a lot of trouble. But unless it stays civilized, ballet is no fun. Staying civilized is always everybody's trouble, so why not ballet's?

Town & Country, APRIL 1947

A BRIEFING IN AMERICAN BALLET

Toward the end of the war, during several seasons, ballet in the United States had a bright moment of eagerness and glory. A number of strikingly original choreographies appeared, and with them a burst of dance talent, new stars, a new atmosphere onstage, and a lovely freshness in classic dancing. The choreographic innovations were ballets by George Balanchine in a dazzling new classicism; absorbing dance-pantomime-dramas of protracted anguish by Antony Tudor; and lively American local-color comedies by Agnes de Mille and Jerome Robbins. The two touring companies of the period, Ballet Theatre and the Ballet Russe de Monte Carlo, were largely composed of Americans, young, exact, strong, and charming. It was their new dance impetus that triumphed. They won their first decisive victory in 1942 in Tudor's *Pillar of Fire* at Ballet Theatre. Two years later, the Monte Carlo, its style suddenly transformed by Balanchine, presented his *Danses Concertantes*. From then on all over the country the vitality of both companies delighted a great new ballet audience night after night.

The difference between the two companies added to the pleasure. Ballet Theatre's aesthetics, under its English choreographer Tudor, tended to dramatic pantomime; the Monte Carlo's under Balanchine, toward a classic dance grace. They had different repertories, though both included nineteenth-century classics, Diaghilev, and prewar pieces. Ballet Theatre was the larger, stronger but somewhat heavier and harder company. Both companies had a few remarkable foreign-born principals. And each had a very great artist as its star ballerina. The Monte Carlo's was the witty warmhearted Alexandra Danilova. Delighted by the fresh stimulus around her, she reached in 1944–45 a new magnificence in strict classicism. Ballet Theatre's ballerina, on the other hand, was the frail English classicist

Alicia Markova; but Ballet Theatre's tendency toward pantomime developed her latent genius as an actress. For several seasons she showed us a shyly dazzling spirituality of expression, the secret force of which captivated alike war workers, housewives, and intellectuals. Her *Giselle* became New York's big ballet night.

Wartime, here as abroad, made everyone more eager for the civilized and peaceful excitement of ballet. More people could also afford tickets. And in wartime the fact that no word was spoken on the stage was in itself a relief. Suddenly the theaters all over the country were packed whenever the two companies appeared. They sold 1,500,000 tickets a year. The new public fell in love with the stars, with the dancers, and with ballet in general. It liked everything. It applauded a glaring variety effect and twenty minutes later applauded as eagerly a quiet poetic one. When the critics praised a piece, the public rushed to the theater and loved it; when they damned a piece, it rushed to the theater and loved it too. It was not so much a failure of taste as an abundance of stimulation. Thanks to the unconsciously American air the ensembles had in everything they danced, the new public found an unexpected contact with the brilliant strangeness of what they saw. As they watched any ballet, an indefinable something in the atmosphere, in the quality of movement and youthful manners, was unconsciously familiar and immediately touching.

The older balletgoers, familiar with prewar performances, had expected nothing like what they now saw. What they expected of ballet was the prewar Ballet Russe. When the war began in Europe, both of the prewar Ballet Russe companies, the de Basil Original and the Massine Monte Carlo, managed to reach New York intact. With the composers and painters of the School of Paris who were here, these extraordinary ensembles intended to continue a brilliant Ballet-Russe-in-exile in peace and comfort. But nothing of the sort happened. Within a few years hardly a trace of Paris-Russian atmosphere or dance style or choreographic fashions remained. Instead ballet had adapted itself to the American dance climate, as it had a few years before in England to the English, and more than a century earlier to the Russian.

The acclimatization of ballet in the United States had begun a decade earlier. It began with local semistudent companies in New York, Chicago, Philadelphia, San Francisco. (Europeans saw Miss Littlefield's Philadelphians tour in '37.) All these groups commissioned local choreographers, composers, and painters. The most interesting of them was Lincoln Kirstein's American Ballet in New York, of which George Balanchine was artistic director. About half of our current best talent seems once to have been in this group. On its first program in '34 it produced Balanchine's

Serenade, which when he presented it in '47 at the Paris Opéra astonished the audience by the abundance of its invention and the novelty of its style. But none of these groups was strong enough to compete with the Ballet Russe in scale, stars, or repertory. Finally in 1940 Lucia Chase's Ballet Theatre opened in New York, with the intention of becoming an American repertory company of as high a quality as the Paris-Russian ones.

Ballet Theatre, however, compromised on its chauvinism. It sought assistance from Fokine; Baronova joined it; it soon came under the guidance of its British artists Tudor, Dolin, and Markova. For a season it enlisted Nijinska, and it achieved the celebrity it aimed for as Massine and other Ballet Russe stars joined it. And it was Massine who awakened in Ballet Theatre's Americans the dance verve and drive that characterized the company ever after. During these same years, however, the Monte Carlo, as anxious to remain Paris-Russian as Ballet Theatre was to remain American, found itself forced to compromise too. Its ensemble atmosphere became more and more diluted. Its American contingent had grown too large to be assimilated. In '42 it even presented the first well-made ballet that had a real American tone and flavor, Agnes de Mille's *Rodeo*, and the "Russians" danced it convincingly. This double direction of ballet in the United States made the situation confusing as late as '42.

But until '42 for the public the prestige of the prewar Ballet Russe still concealed the changes that were taking place. What first-nighters still expected was the prewar fashion, its odd elegance and its nervous glamour. There was to be sure a sort of malaise in the air. One group—the Original—had disappeared. Some prewar stars had vanished, others grown lax; the ensemble style was no longer so vivid and the novelties had less and less point. No doubt the glorious Ballet Russe was a little out of order, but the spell of its prewar prestige covered everything.

The spell was broken by the overwhelming triumph of Ballet Theatre at the premiere of Tudor's *Pillar of Fire*. Neither in its style nor in its cast of dancers did it show any traces of Paris-Russianism. And by contrast it suddenly made apparent to everyone how devitalized the prewar formula had become. Now Tudor's earlier works already in the repertory became popular. Even the most effective of the prewar-style ballets created here during the war, Massine's *Aleko*, done by Ballet Theatre a few months later, could not change the current; though it had far more dance verve than Tudor, its melodrama could not compete with his real anguish. Now that the prestige of prewar ballet had collapsed, the old Monte Carlo was doomed; poor and desperate, it lost its prewar stars, all but Danilova and Franklin. Youskevitch joined the Navy. But when in the fall of '44

Balanchine took over the crumbling company and at a stroke rejuvenated it, the triumph of the American-style company, the new Monte Carlo, proved to have ended any interest in the resurrection of a Paris-Russian atmosphere. Indeed no one danced that way convincingly anymore; the old stars who remained had now assimilated themselves to the new style. Twice, however, an exhumation of the past was attempted—by Ballet International in '44 (its single season is said to have cost the Marquis de Cuevas $600,000), and by the de Basil Original brought back from South America in '46; both attempts failed.

The decay of the Paris-Russian ballet style in the United States was due to the isolation of the Ballet Russe from its natural sources of vitality in Paris. It affected the prewar Ballet Russe choreographers disastrously. Massine, for instance, created a dozen or so pieces in this country (including three with grandiose décor by Dali). But of Massine's work only *Aleko*—magnificently decorated by Marc Chagall—was at all comparable to his European work. Large in scale, hollow in sentiment, it had an ingenuity, a sweep, and a hectic activity reminiscent of his "symphonic" style. None of his other pieces were remarkable and some were appallingly shoddy. Fokine produced two ballets of no interest. Lichine created three or four, some pretending to great spiritual conflicts, but only one fine scene among them—one of exuberant South Russian folk dances. His 1940 *Graduation Ball*, a harmless comedy to Johann Strauss music, remained his best work. Nijinska created several ballets but none as attractive as her prewar *Chopin Concerto*. The new ones of the forties were highly ingenious, false in sentiment, willfully odd in musicality, and crabbed in their arbitrary construction of the dancer's actions; she retained, however, a greater force of style than any of the other choreographers of this group. It was sad to see how inexpressive they all became in the dance climate in which they found themselves.

These celebrities did not respond to the human medium which the more and more American ensembles offered to choreographers. A few of the stars sometimes developed interestingly in the choreographies in exile, but the effect failed because even then there was no resonance between star and ensemble, no coherent dance atmosphere to create a coherent poetic illusion. The fact was that several fine qualities the Paris-Russians had had by temperament and tradition, qualities their choreographers presupposed in a company, were foreign to the American dancers. Correct and clear the new dancers were, stricter in these matters than the Europeans; but the Americans, most of them too young ever to have lived abroad, did not understand those overtones of European local color, both geographical and historical, which the prewar Ballet Russe often suggested so imaginatively. Ballets presupposing such overtones (from *Petrouchka* to *Gaîté Parisienne*) lost in consequence most of their savor and point. The Americans were unimaginative too in suggesting nuances of social differentiation, or of sexual experience. The foreign choreographers for their part, even after living here, found no inspiration in local manners. But the American dancers had neither an instinct for imaginative characterization through liberties of rhythm and accent in classic variations, nor an ensemble instinct for the kind of rhythmic liberty the Ballet Russe had used for a sweeping collective climax. A European who sees ballet only in such terms may wonder if anything is left without these effects—if all that is left is not merely a machine, hard and monotonous.

The excitement and freshness of our ballet toward the end of the war, after the Ballet Russe impetus had disintegrated, proves the contrary. The American steadiness and exactitude of rhythm, its reticence of phrasing, have not the same but a different clarity and sweep. They do not underline the pathos of a scene by taking sides, but its tragedy by not taking any. They can show largeness of scope and power and they avoid greasiness of detail. The bold decision, the easy calm, and the large openness which Americans derive from the tradition of sports that permeates the country can give their dancing in complex dance figurations a noble clarity. Their sober friendliness of manner can have, as Balanchine once wrote, an expression such as one imagines angels would have, who can take part in tragic events without becoming themselves miserable. When one watches attractive young Americans in a ballroom or in a dance hall, one notes instinctive traits of dance style not unlike those I have mentioned; their dancing looks different from that of Europeans—it has a different style and expression—but style and expression it clearly has.

Of all the foreign-born choreographers who have worked in the United States, Balanchine has responded most to the stimulus of this country's natural dance gifts. Since he came here in 1933 he has worked successfully in all our forms of ballet, in musical comedy, in opera, in the films (where he was the first to compose dance phrases directly to suit the camera field and camera angle), in student performances (down to the age of six), and with both ballet companies. He can use Americanisms of rhythm or nuance in classic ballets without a trace of self-consciousness. Long before the war he lost interest in the Ballet Russe style of the period; and ever since he has been here he has worked by preference with American dancers. He is more than anyone else the real founder of the American classic style. He has shown our dancers how to be natural in classicism, and he has shown them how to become unaffectedly brilliant in their own natural terms. He has shown the public how effective they are with their charming long-limbed figures, their simple carriage, strong legs, their dazzling speed and their clean grace of line; how animated in the variety of their impetus, in their technical exactness and the exactness of their musicality; how touching in their unselfconscious delight in dancing, their cooperativeness, in the sobriety of their appeal, in the strength of their grace. And when he has come across a dramatic gift, he has placed it where it made its full effect without straining for emotional miming or for a verbal meaning.

Balanchine's choreography, whether during the Diaghilev period or the present one, has always suited the unconscious atmosphere of his ensembles and the innate gifts of grace of his principals. They have always looked both free and brilliant. His recent style differs from his European one in that it no longer shows his former lovely erotic interruptions. Since 1940 it has become strictly classical; the dancer's figure is a clear unit, the dance impetus is unbroken, sustained, and clear. Balanchine has inherited the empire of Petipa and Ivanov. You recognize their purity of idiom, their harmony of motion, and their power of rhythm. But the effervescence of invention, the exquisite musicality, the variety of momentum, the complexity of structure are new. The startling details are often, technically speaking, novelties in the timing, the size, the transposition, or the reversal of classic dance elements or of the phases of a step. Since they remain logical according to the classic technique of balance and impulse, the dancer in them keeps her free impetus. The expression she gives these inventions is merely her graceful freedom, her sovereign assurance; the drama of their happy surprise, of their startling development, of the poignant relations between dancing figures they suggest is resolved by the dazzle and sweep of the ballet's dance rhythm. Balanchine's classicism and his musicality give the dancers the spring in dancing that modern ballets don't have when they try for "meaning." And yet each piece of his touches the imagination with a mysterious expressive message.

The animating subject matter of these new classic ballets is no more explicit than that of *Swan Lake.* Their announced subject is occasionally a plot as unreal as that; more often it is merely the musical structure of the score. But each of Balanchine's ballets has a quality of motion in its development of impetus that is different and specific. One senses that at the core of this dazzling, joyous grace there is, as its source of energy, a specific human gesture, a real image, a slip of fate. Isolated in the imaginary rise and fall of musical time, it offers its transfigured drama in silence. It has become a game for dancers. And as one watches their rapid figures, happy in their animation, caught in their buoyant rhythm, the plastic emphasis of a dance gesture, defining for an instant the impetus, looks poignantly beautiful. Beautiful in its proportion, in its freshness. Beautiful in the innocent dignity of the dancer as she darts past. The echoes the instant awakens are worthy of her. The secret of the movement, its human characteristic, reverberates in memory as it does fantastically in the brilliant surprises of the dancing one is watching and of the music one hears. Neither the dancers nor the audience is required to justify the apparition of these evanescent dance images. They strike as lightly as the sound of a heartbreaking word. And the frightful truth of them remains suspended in an innocent and harmonious world of fantasy.

Of Balanchine's eight creations here since 1940 the most astonishing are three dance ballets of the purest classicism whose subjects are their scores: *Concerto Barocco* (1941) to Bach's Concerto for Two Violins; *Danses Concertantes* (1944) to Stravinsky's score of that name—a ballet brilliantly decorated by Eugene Berman; and *The Four Temperaments* (1946) to Hindemith's composition, danced in a décor by Kurt Seligmann. *The Four Temperaments*, formally a set of themes and elegant variations, is a long fantasy of incredible violence and amplitude, savage speed, and packed weight. *Danses Concertantes*, formally a comedy-style pas de deux with playful entrées by the chorus, is glittering in sharpness, in jets of power and tenuous resilient articulations, in witty grace, in the mystery of a menace withheld all one's life. *Concerto Barocco*, a long supported adagio framed by allegro chorus entrées, has the effect of an ample grace and a cheerful freshness accompanying like a landscape the savage wound of an individual, its untouched force persisting before and after the private event. At times the sweetness of its plastic harmonies is heavenly. It is a pity it is given in the most meager of décors. The Monte Carlo has had seven ballets of Balanchine in recent repertory, Ballet Theatre two, and Ballet Society, a new organization that presents four evenings a year in New York, also has two. For Ballet Society, Balanchine is now preparing Stravinsky's as yet unplayed *Orpheus*, a Rieti ballet, one to a Haieff score, and one to Mozart; for Ballet Theatre, Tchaikovsky's *Theme and Variations*.

In a completely different aesthetic as well as choreographic style is the work of Antony Tudor, artistic director and a principal mime of Ballet Theatre, who is the other ballet choreographer of genius working in the United States. Tudor's three major creations have all been very long pieces. *Pillar of Fire* (set to Schoenberg's *Verklärte Nacht*), half dream, half reality, tells the story of a love-starved English girl tortured by the fear that the young man who frequently comes to call loves not her but her younger sister; it turns out that she has no reason to, and at the end she becomes engaged. Full of self-humiliation, of gnawing envy, sex-frenzied orgiastic images, striking shifts of dance style, fragments of middle-class gesture, full of dance impulses suddenly released and suddenly frozen, it overwhelmed the audience at its first performance. It also established the young American Nora Kaye as a real dramatic ballerina, and the young English dancer Hugh Laing as an intensely imaginative dramatic star. Kaye has since won herself recognition as a classic ballerina as well and had a real success in London a summer ago, when Ballet Theatre danced there. A second major work of Tudor's was *Romeo and Juliet* (to several Delius pieces). Its effect is that of a reverie on Shakespeare's text that transmutes his fire into a Tennysonian pathos. It is a reverie luxuriously embroidered with quattrocento pictorial devices, as carefully cut as an Eisenstein film, and its rhythmic weight steeps the story deeper and deeper in a protracted and absorbing High Church gloom. *Romeo and Juliet* opened with a décor by Eugene Berman, which in its opulence, its wealth of invention and complex grace is itself an event in ballet annals. And Alicia Markova, slight, intensely still, intensely musical, was the most luminous of Juliets. Unfortunately the present state of the production is abominable. The third (1945) and least successful of Tudor's major long works was *Undertow* (to a score by William Schuman). It tells the case history of a sex murder, beginning with the hero's birth (breach presentation) and his infantile frustrations; later, grown into a repressed and gentle adolescent in the slums—which are full of sex—he strangles the girl who seduces him, and suffers remorse. There are dull stretches and a long evasively symbolic ending; but there are also brilliant passages, notably the rape of a horrid little girl by four little boys.

Tudor's ballets have obvious weaknesses. Their shock value, thrilling at first, does not last; their shaping force is discontinuous; they have a weak and fragmentary dance impetus; they peter out at the end. They can find no repose and no spring because balance is no element of structure in them. Their sentiment, acutely envious, acutely humiliated, weakens into self-pity. But they also have exceptional virtues. They are perfectly serious. Their sentiment is real till toward the end; they are full of passion, of originality, of dramatic strokes, of observation, of brilliant pantomime ideas and fastidiously polished detail. Tudor discovers dramatic gifts in his dancers and shows them off to striking advantage. There is no vulgarity in his obscene images. His ballets are not primarily dance conceptions, but their sustained expressive intensity is clearly large-scale.

On a much smaller scale than Tudor, derived from pantomime and novel character-dance elements, is the American local-color ballet. Its first great success was Miss de Mille's *Rodeo*, in which she dance-mimed the star role. It has an excellent scene suggesting cowboys rodeo riding and another of Saturday-night ranch-house dances. The dance steps are lively and the rhythmic sequences well contrasted. Its emotion is humorous-sentimental. It has a lively score by Aaron Copland, who had already written another "Western" ballet score, a beautiful and tragic one, for an interesting but now vanished prewar American piece, *Billy the Kid* (choreography by Eugene Loring). *Fancy Free*, by Jerome Robbins (score by Leonard Bernstein, décor by Oliver Smith), is about three sailors in town for an evening, and by far the best of the Americana to date. Its local color is sharply observed, its wry pathos is honest, and its jokes sound. The flow of movement, the rhythmic tautness, the concise storytelling are admirable, and it proved as successful in London as in New York. It is still a fresh piece to see after many repetitions. Robbins, a remarkable dramatic dancer himself, has since made two small ballets that show a great advance in construction but a sentiment more confused. Though his experience in classicism is not large, formally his choreographic genius is of the highest order. He understands by instinct the formal unity of a ballet in stage space and musical time, a unity created and filled by a coherent dance impetus. He also conceives every dance action in terms of a drama of real characters. In point of expression he has difficulty as yet in the complete transformation of specific pantomime images into the larger and sweeping rhythm and images of direct dancing. But there is no doubt that he is the most gifted of American-born ballet choreographers. At the moment unfortunately he is about to direct plays and films.

A remarkable choreographic talent appeared in the spring of '47 when Ballet Society presented *The Seasons*, the first ballet by Merce Cunningham (score by John Cage, décor by Isamu Noguchi). Cunningham, a pupil of Martha Graham and a prodigiously gifted dancer, is not a ballet dancer but a modern-dance or expressionist one. His piece, though not in classic idiom, was danced cleanly by dancers classically trained. Its subject was phases of weather and subjective states induced thereby, a subject in the tradition of Thoreau. The phrases were brief but clear, the plastic instinct forceful and imaginative. Though the emotion was tremulous and delicate, the piece showed strength as a dance structure. Cunningham may prove to be a choreographer as soundly gifted as Robbins, though in a style as hermetic as Robbins's is plain-spoken.

Though my subject is ballet and not modern dancing, I cannot omit mentioning Martha Graham, the greatest dance celebrity in the United States. Now past fifty, she is an actress of magnificent power, a dancer of astonishing skill; her choreographies abound in extraordinary plastic images of great originality. They are expressionist in rhetoric, violent, distorted, oppressive, and obscure; there is rarely a perceptible rhythmic unit or any dance architecture. But the ardor of her imagination, the scope of her conceptions, the intensity of her presence make her a dance artist of the first rank.

I have tried to give an impression of the character and of the resources of our new ballet. Among its greatest resources are the young American ballerinas now developing. The most interesting now are Alicia Alonso, Nora Kaye, Mary Ellen Moylan, Maria Tallchief; and Ruthanna Boris, Rosella Hightower, and Nana Gollner are in the same category. Kaye I have already mentioned; Alonso, Ballet Theatre's Cuban-born classic ballerina, with greater natural gifts than Kaye for a rapid and delicate grace, lacks Kaye's large-scale dramatic force. Moylan, with all the facility of a lovely virtuoso and its greatest gift of plasticity in motion, has a verve that suggests a genius for lively characterization; Tallchief has a tragic beauty and a distinction that set her apart. Among the students, Tanaquil Le Clercq looks like a ballerina to come and a great one. (Brilliant Tamara Toumanova, Ballet Russe ballerina, appears less and less.) Men of similar quality are rarer—John Kriza and, as a dramatic dancer, Francisco Moncion are the most remarkable; Leon Danielian has great gifts too; the most promising among developing dancers is Dick Beard. Our best male stars during the period have been Eglevsky, Franklin, Laing, and Youskevitch—all European trained.

Though the resources exist, though the public is still eager for ballet, since the war the two companies have not kept the high standards they had reached. Managerial disputes and rising costs have reduced both of them to less than forty dancers apiece; and a number of their best dancers have left them. Ballet Theatre's greatest loss was that of Markova some seasons back; unfortunately Markova herself, now touring with Dolin and their small group, has weakened noticeably as an artist. The Monte Carlo's greatest loss was that of Balanchine. It now has no master choreographer to inspire it and it is doubtful if it can long survive without one. Last season, however, the artistic energy which the big companies lacked was shown by Ballet Society, organized by Kirstein and Balanchine. In its first experimental season, together with its eight new ballets, it presented four one-act operas, and also gave us a glimpse of the lovely Javanese dancing of Ratna Mohini. After a remarkable second season—notable for the Stravinsky-Balanchine-Noguchi *Orpheus*—Ballet Society has now become the resident ballet company of New York's City Center.

I have suggested the elements of strength in American ballet style. Its chief weakness seems to be in the art of imaginative characterization. The Tudor ballets, with their many personages, give our dancers experience in the field. But his stylized gesture does not pose the question quite distinctly either. A dance character cannot be explained or justified; and he must remain himself in repose, where there is no distortion of mimicry possible. This is a problem of amplitude in style. Another problem of our style is that of differentiation from musical comedy. Our choreographers and many ballet dancers work in musical comedy and this tends to confuse and banalize their approach to ballet. These are not problems to be solved by verbal argument. They are questions the imagination of our dancers can answer only by dancing in ballets of imaginative force. American ballet is well paid, but its working conditions are the most exhausting in the world. The only thing that can refresh its spirit and enrich its style is the sense of artistic integrity, of imaginative abundance that the managements must supply by encouraging our best choreographers to create for them. This is the main problem ahead of our ballet. Contact with the work of artists from other countries with different resources of style will be stimulating too.

Kenyon Review, AUTUMN 1948

AGAINST MEANING IN BALLET

Some of my friends who go to ballet and like the entertainment it gives are sorry to have it classed among the fine arts and discussed, as the other fine arts are, intellectually. Though I do not agree with them I have a great deal of sympathy for their anti-intellectual point of view. The dazzle of a ballet performance is quite reason enough to go; you see handsome young people—girls and boys with a bounding or delicate animal grace—dancing among the sensual luxuries of orchestral music and shining stage decoration and in the glamour of an audience's delight. To watch their lightness and harmonious ease, their clarity and boldness of motion, is a pleasure. And ballet dancers' specialties are their elastic tautness, their openness of gesture, their gaiety of leaping, beating, and whirling, their slow soaring flights. Your senses enjoy directly how they come forward and closer to you, or recede upstage, turning smaller and more fragile; how the boys and girls approach one another or draw apart, how they pass close without touching or entwine their bodies in stars of legs and arms—all the many ways they have of dancing together. You see a single dancer alone showing her figure from all sides deployed in many positions, or you see a troop of them dancing in happy unison. They are graceful, well mannered, and they preserve at best a personal dignity, a civilized modesty of deportment that keeps the sensual stimulus from being foolishly cute or commercially sexy. The beauty of young women's and young men's bodies, in motion or in momentary repose, is exhibited in an extraordinarily friendly manner.

When you enjoy ballet this way—and it is one of the ways everybody does enjoy it who likes to go—you don't find any prodigious difference between one piece and another, except that one will have enough dancing to satisfy and another not enough, one will show the dancers to their best advantage and another will tend to make them look a little more awkward and unfree. Such a happy ballet lover is puzzled by the severities of critics. He wonders why they seem to find immense differences between one piece and another, or between one short number and another, or between the proficiency of two striking dancers. The reasons the critics give, the relation of the steps to the music, the sequence of the effects, the sharply differentiated intellectual meaning they ascribe to dances, all this he will find either fanciful or plainly absurd.

Has ballet an intellectual content? The ballet lover with the point of view I am describing will concede that occasionally a soloist gives the sense of characterizing a part, that a few ballets even suggest a story with a psychological interest, a dramatic suspense, or a reference to real life. In such a case, he grants, ballet may be said to have an intellectual content. But these ballets generally turn out to be less satisfying to watch because the dancers do less ballet dancing in them; so, he concludes, one may as well affirm broadly that ballet does not properly offer a "serious" comment on life and that it is foolish to look for one.

I do not share these conclusions, and I find that my interest in the kind of meaning a ballet has leads me to an interest in choreography and dance technique. But I have a great deal of sympathy for the general attitude I have described. It is the general attitude that underlies the brilliant reviews of Théophile Gautier, the French poet of a hundred years ago, who is by common consent the greatest of ballet critics. He said of himself that he was a man who believed in the visible world. And his reviews are the image of what an intelligent man of the world saw happening on the stage. They are perfectly open; there is no private malignity in them; he is neither pontifical nor "popular"; there is no jargon and no ulterior motive. He watches not as a specialist in ballet, but as a responsive Parisian. The easy flow of his sentences is as much a tribute to the social occasion as it is to the accurate and elegant ease of ballet dancers in action.

His warmth of response to personal varieties of grace and to the charming limits of a gift, his amusement at the pretensions of a libretto or the pretensions of a star, his sensual interest in the line of a shoulder and bosom, in the elasticity of an ankle, in the cut of a dress place the ballet he watches in a perspective of civilized good sense.

Ballet for him is an entertainment—a particularly agreeable way of spending an evening in town; and ballet is an art, it is a sensual refinement that delights the spirit. Art for him is not a temple of humanity one enters with a reverent exaltation. Art is a familiar pleasure and Gautier assumes that one strolls through the world of art as familiarly as one strolls through Paris, looking about in good weather or bad, meeting congenial friends or remarkable strangers, and one's enemies, too. Whether in art or in Paris, a civilized person appreciates seeing a gift and is refreshed by a graceful impulse; there is a general agreement about what constitutes good workmanship; and one takes one's neighbors' opinions less seriously than their behavior. Gautier differentiates keenly between good and bad ballet; but he differentiates as a matter of personal taste. He illustrates the advantages the sensual approach to ballet can have for an intelligence of exceptional sensual susceptibility and for a man of large sensual complacency.

Gautier assumes that all that people need do to enjoy art is to look and listen with ready attention and trust their own sensual impressions. He is right. But when they hear that ballet is an elaborate art with a complicated technique and tradition, many modest people are intimidated and are afraid to trust their own spontaneous impressions. They may have been to a few performances, they may have liked it when they saw it, but now they wonder if maybe they liked the wrong things and missed the right ones. Before going again, they want it explained, they want to know what to watch for and exactly what to feel. If it is really real art and fine great art, it must be studied before it is enjoyed; that is what they remember from school. In school the art of poetry is approached by a strictly rational method, which teaches you what to enjoy and how to discriminate. You are taught to analyze the technique and the relation of form to content; you are taught to identify and "evaluate" stylistic, biographical, economic, and anthropological influences, and told what is great and what is minor so you can prepare yourself for a great reaction or for a minor one. The effect of these conscientious labors on the pupils is distressing. For the rest of their lives they can't face a page of verse without experiencing a complete mental blackout. They don't enjoy, they don't discriminate, they don't even take the printed words at face value. For the rest of their lives they go prying for hidden motives back of literature, for psychological, economic, or stylistic explanations, and it never occurs to them to read the words and respond to them as they do to the nonsense of current songs or the nonsense of billboards by the roadside. Poetry is the same thing—it's words, only more interesting, more directly and richly sensual.

The first taste of art is spontaneously sensual, it is the discovery of an absorbing entertainment, an absorbing pleasure. If you ask anyone who enjoys ballet or any other art how he started, he will tell you that he enjoyed it long before he knew what it meant or how it worked. I remember the intense pleasure reading Shelley's *Adonais* gave me as a boy—long before I followed accurately the sense of the words; and once, twenty years later, I had two kittens who would purr in unison and watch me bright-eyed when I read them Shakespeare's *Sonnets*, clearly pleased by the compliment and by the sounds they heard. Would they have enjoyed them better if they had understood them? The answer is, they enjoyed them very much. Many a college graduate might have envied them.

I don't mean that so orderly and respectable an entertainment as that of art is made for the susceptibilities of kittens or children. But consider how the enormous orderly and respectable symphonic public enjoys its listening, enjoys it without recognizing themes, harmonies, or timbres, without evaluating the style historically or even knowing if the piece is being played as the composer intended. What do they hear when they hear a symphony? Why, they hear the music, the interesting noises it makes. They follow the form and the character of it by following their direct acoustic impressions.

Susceptibility to ballet is a way of being susceptible to animal grace of movement. Many people are highly susceptible to the pleasure of seeing grace of movement who have never thought of going to ballet to look for it. They find it instead in watching graceful animals, animals of many species at play, flying, swimming, racing, and leaping and making gestures of affection toward one another, or watchful in harmonious repose. And they find it too in seeing graceful young people on the street or in a game or at the beach or in a dance hall, boys and girls in exuberant health who are doing pretty much what the charming animals do, and are as unconscious of their grace as they. Unconscious grace of movement is a natural and impermanent gift, like grace of features or of voice or of character, a lucky accident you keep meeting with all your life wherever you are. To be watching grace puts people into a particularly amiable frame of mind. It is an especially attractive form of feeling social consciousness.

But if ballet is a way of entertaining the audience by showing them animal grace, why is its way of moving so very unanimal-like and artificial? For the same reason that music has evolved so very artificial a way of organizing its pleasing noises. Art takes what in life is an accidental pleasure and tries to repeat and prolong it. It organizes, diversifies, characterizes, through an artifice that men evolve by trial and error. Ballet nowadays is as different from an accidental product as a symphony at Carnegie Hall is different from the noises Junior makes on his trumpet upstairs or Mary Ann with comb and tissue paper, sitting on the roof, the little monkey.

You don't have to know about ballet to enjoy it; all you have to do is look at it. If you are susceptible to it, and a good many people evidently are, you will like spontaneously some things you see and dislike others, and quite violently too. You may be so dazzled at first by a star or by the general atmosphere, you don't really know what happened; you may on the other hand find the performance absurdly stiff and affected except for a few unreasonable moments of intense pleasure; but if you are susceptible you will find you want to go again. When you go repeatedly, you begin to recognize what it is you like, and watch for it the next time. That way you get to know about ballet, you know a device of ballet because you have responded to it, you know that much at least about it. Even if nobody agrees with you, you still know it for yourself.

That the composite effect of ballet is a complex one is clear enough. Its devices make a long list, wherever you start. These devices are useful to give a particular moment of a dance a particular expression. The dancers in action give it at that moment a direct sensual reality. But if you watch often and watch attentively, the expressive power of some ballets and dancers will fascinate, perturb, and delight far more than that of others, and will keep alive in your imagination much more intensely long after you have left the theater. It is this aftereffect that dancers and ballets are judged by, by their audience.

To some of my friends the images ballet leaves in the imagination suggest, as poetry does, an aspect of the drama of human behavior. For others such ballet images keep their sensual mysteriousness, "abstract," unrationalized, and magical. Anyone who cannot bear to contemplate human behavior except from a rationalistic point of view had better not try to "understand" the exhilarating excitement of ballet; its finest images of our fate are no easier to face than those of poetry itself, though they are no less beautiful.

Ballet, MARCH 1949

DANCE CRITICISM

People interested in dancing as a form of art complain that our dance criticism is poor. Poor it is but not poor in relation to its pay. Anyone who writes intelligently about dancing does so at his own expense. As a matter of fact the sort of semi-illiterate hackwork that oozes out shamelessly and pays off modestly in books and articles about music—educators recommend it—is hardly profitable when it deals with the dance. Almost all our dance criticism appears in the form of newspaper reviewing. But almost all papers would rather misinform the public than keep a specialized dance reporter. Even rich ones delight in skimping on costs by sending out a staff music critic who covers ballet as an extra unpaid chore.

In the whole country only three exceptionally well-edited papers have made a practice of employing specialized dance critics—the *New York Times*, the *New York Herald Tribune*, and the *Christian Science Monitor*—and a fourth, the *Chicago Times*, joined them in 1947. These four jobs, the best that specialists can hope for, carry an average salary below that of a trombonist in the pit and hardly comparable to that of a minor, not very reliable soloist onstage. If the profit motive is a sacred American right, it is easier to account for miserable performances by our writers than for acceptable ones. Nevertheless, among the mass of nonsense printed each year about dancing a few specialists and gifted amateurs do produce on their own initiative a trickle of vivid reporting, of informed technical discussion, of valuable historical research and striking critical insight. The conditions and the average quality of dance criticism seem to be similar the world over. Ours is no worse than that elsewhere, except that there is more of it packaged for breakfast.

Most of our criticism is poor but many readers hardly mind how foolish it is; they read it too inattentively to notice. Some of them glance at a review only to see if the verdict on a show is for or against their going. Others, who have opinions of their own, are eager to quote what the paper said either with rage or with pride. In their eagerness they often misquote what they read and catch the meaning of written words as vaguely as a playful dog does that of speech. Anyone who writes for a paper is expected to satisfy the canine eagerness of many readers. They love to be bullied and wheedled; to be floored by a wisecrack, excited by gossip, inflamed by appeals to bigotry or popular prejudice; they love a female critic to gasp or fret and a male critic to be as opinionated as a comedian. At this level the difference between good and bad criticism is slight; and if you have to read foolish criticism this is as much fun as you can get out of it.

There are, however, many people too who like to find sense even in a dance column. They expect a critic writing as an educated American to give them a clear picture of the event and to place it in its relation to the art of theater dancing. When good criticism appears in a large newspaper many people welcome and appreciate it. Many all over the country know very well what ballet is about and follow intelligent reviewing, not necessarily with agreement but with spontaneous interest. They realize that a good editor can give it to them and that one who doesn't is in this respect slovenly.

To judge a ballet performance as attentively as a work of imagination is judged and by similar standards is nowadays normal enough. To be sure, everyone doesn't respond to a high degree of imagination in dancing, and not every intelligent person is convinced that dancing can create the peculiar spell, intimate, sustained, and grand, a work of art does. But in the course of the last two centuries enough intelligent people have been convinced it can, so that now the possibility is normally accepted. Our stage dancing is less abundant an art than our music, painting, or literature; but its claim to serious attention is that it belongs like them to the formal world of civilized fantasy. In recent years ballet has been the liveliest form of poetic theater we have had.

Dancing that is pleasing and neat, that shows ingenuity and a touch of fancy, is no news in a luxurious city. But dancing that by its sequence of movements and rhythm creates an absorbing imaginative spell is a special attraction a journalist must be able to recognize and describe. The prestige position of a ballet company depends entirely on how well its performances maintain, for people who know what art or poetry is about, a spell as art and a power as poetry. It is these imaginative people who can watch with attention—there are many thousands of them in New York—whose satisfaction stimulates general curiosity and influences wealthy art patrons to pay the deficits. They go for pleasure, just as they might go to a concert by Gold and Fizdale at Town Hall or else read Stendhal or Jane Bowles at home. Dancing delights them where they see it become an art and it is to see this happen that they like to go. What they want to find out from a review is, Did an event of artistic interest take place, and if it did, what particular flavor did it have? And because they are the readers really interested in what only a dance reporter can tell them, it is his business to answer their questions distinctly.

If his report interests them, they will go and see for themselves, and incidentally they will notice the sort of news they can rely on him for. If his remarks often turn out to be illuminating, he is judged a good critic; too many foolish or evasive reports on the other hand make him lose his status as a valuable observer. They expect him to recognize and formulate the point at issue in a performance more quickly and sharply than they would themselves. But without considerable experience in several arts, and of dancing and its technical basis too, the observer has no standards by which to measure and no practice in disentangling the pretensions of a ballet from its achievements. That is why a newspaper that wants to inform its readers on interesting dance events has to keep a reporter with the particular gift and training needed for the job.

A dance journalist's business is to sketch a lively portrait of the event he is dealing with. His most interesting task is to describe the nature of the dancing—what imaginative spell it aims for, what method it proceeds by, and what it achieves. In relation to the performance, he describes the gifts or the development of artists, the technical basis of aesthetic effects, even the organizational problems that affect artistic production. The more distinctly he expresses himself, the more he exposes himself to refutation and the better he does his job. But beyond this the dance public wants him to be influential in raising the level of dance production in their community; to be enlightening on general questions of theater dancing, its heritage, and its current innovations; and to awaken an interest for dancing in intelligent readers who are not dance fans already.

What awakens the interest of an intelligent reader in a dance column is to find it written in good English. Even if he is not used to thinking about dancing he can follow a discussion that makes its point through a vivid picture of what actually happens onstage. On the other hand he loses interest if a dance column offers him only the same vague clichés he has already read elsewhere in the paper. After reading a movie review or a political commentator he is not thrilled to find that a ballet too is challenging, vital, significant (significant of what? challenging or vital to whom?). When a ballet is called earthy he recognizes the term as a current synonym for commercial-minded. Inappropriate visual images are suggested to him when he reads that a dance is meaty; or that dancers onstage were rooted in the soil and clung bravely to their roots; or that young choreographers are to be admired for their groping. No sensible person can want to watch a dancer brooding over a culture, or filling her old form with a new content, or even being stunningly fertile; or if he wants to watch, it isn't because of the dancing.

Our unspecialized dance reporters can't in sensible terms tell the public what is interesting and original in current dancing. Since 1942, for instance, strict classic ballet has become widely appreciated and acclimated in this country. It has changed so far from the prewar Ballet Russe manner that it has now a new and American flavor. But the nation's dance journalists have been notably unenlightening on the subject of classicism, its meaning, and its new development (some journalists even confuse classicism with stylized movement). To take another example, in the same period the modern dance has been trying for a new style, a new rhythm, and a different sort of theater appeal than before. Various aspects of the change have been due to Martha Graham's example, to her own shift in technique, to a new supply of male dancers, to the Party Line, and to contact with ballet; a new modern style shows particularly in the work of Shearer and of Cunningham. The nation's press knows that something has happened to our dancing in the last five or six years, but it doesn't yet know what.

During the same period the nation's press has not demonstrated its influence for raising production standards, either. All the New York critics together, for instance, have been unable to reform the miserable ballet company of the Metropolitan Opera. Neither they nor their colleagues elsewhere have been able to get the big ballet companies to keep fresh and clean the good productions (like *Romeo*) or purge the hopeless ones (like *Schéhérazade*). They have been unable to arrest the recent (1946–47) deterioration of dance standards, to protect dancers from being exhausted by overwork or demoralized by slipshod artistic policies. They have not ridiculed the illiterate English on ballet programs. They have even been unable to keep unmannerly latecomers in the audience from clambering over the rest of the public in the dark or to shush the bobby-soxers and showoffs who brutally interrupt a dance scene by applauding in a frenzy at any passable leap or twirl. If dance critics are meant to function as watchdogs of the profession they review, they will have to have sharper teeth and keener noses, too.

If only another half-dozen specialized and intelligent dance critics were writing on metropolitan papers, the public all over the country would profit considerably. Not that well-informed critics would agree on all details—far from it—but they could with a sharper authority insist on an improved general level of current production.

A special question of dance journalism is its usefulness to the choreographers and dancers who are reviewed. The point concerns few newspaper readers, but those it agitates bitterly. Ignorant criticism is naturally resented by professionals; but intelligent criticism when adverse often is, too. All critics would like very much to be helpful to a good artist. They love the art they review and everyone who contributes to it; they know the many risks of the profession. They are constantly trying to help, but the occasions when they are actually helpful seem to be happy accidents.

The professionals of the dance world are of course the most eager readers of dance reviewing, but they do not read their own reviews very rationally. For one thing a poor notice upsets them the way an insult does other people. For another, they argue that it endangers their future jobs. But in the touring repertory system of ballet the critics do not "make or break" a ballet or a dancer; managers do. To a dancer's career a bad notice is a much less serious occupational hazard than a poor figure, laziness, poor hygiene, tactlessness toward fellow professionals, or solipsistic megalomania—none of which a dancer who suffers from them complains of nearly so loudly.

A choreographer or a dancer, as he reads his notices, often forgets that they are not addressed to him personally but are a report to the general public. They are a sort of conversation between members of the audience on which the artist eavesdrops at his own emotional risk. What he overhears may make no sense to him; it may shock or intoxicate him; but it is astonishing how rarely, how very rarely it is of any use to him in his actual creative activity. It will sometimes corroborate a guess of his own, but it is generally silent on points he feels vital. Reviews cannot replace his own conscience, much less his driving instinct. A great dancer after twenty years of celebrity spoke of two reviews that had been valuable.

In my opinion reading reviews about oneself is a waste of time, like smoking cigarettes. To read reviews of rivals is more likely to be of use. Hardworking artists are refreshed by a rave for their "art," whether it makes sense or not, but blame is exhausting to deal with. Serious professionals often limit the value of reviews to the recognition of good craftsmanship and of technical innovations; and according to Virgil Thomson—great artist and great critic too—opinions beyond the recognition of these facts are pure fantasy. But for the audience—to whom the critic reports—the fantasy spell of art is that of conscious device multiplied by unconscious meaning. As long as the critic's fantasy remains intelligible to read, its forces and its scope are what give the reader a sense of the power and value of the work reviewed.

An intelligent reader learns from a critic not what to think about a piece of art but how to think about it; he finds a way he hadn't thought of using. The existence of an "authoritative critic" or of a "definitive evaluation" is a fiction like that of a sea serpent. Everybody knows the wild errors of judgment even the best critics of the past have made; it is easier to agree with contemporary judgments but no more likely they are right. It seems to me that it is not the critic's historic function to have the right opinions but to have interesting ones. He talks but he has nothing to sell. His social value is that of a man standing on a street corner talking so intently about his subject that he doesn't realize how peculiar he looks doing it. The intentness of his interest makes people who don't know what he's talking about believe that whatever it is, it must be real somehow—that the art of dancing must be a real thing to some people some of the time. That educates citizens who didn't know it and cheers up those who do.

When people who like dancing say a critic is right they mean he is right enough and that his imaginative descriptions are generally illuminating. He can hardly be illuminating or right enough unless he has a fund of knowledge about his subject. In theory he needs to know the techniques and the historical achievements of dancing, the various ways people have looked at it and written about it, and finally he needs a workable hypothesis of what makes a dance hang together and communicate its images so they are remembered. In practice he has to piece together what he needs to know; experience as a dancer and choreographer is an invaluable help to him.

The best organized and by far the most useful chunk of knowledge a critic has access to is that about the technique and history of classic ballet, in particular as ballet dancers learn it. Its gymnastic and rhythmic technique is coherent enough to suggest principles of dance logic—as expressive human movement in musical time and architectural space. But so far the best informed of specialized ballet critics have not formulated these clearly. And French ballet criticism as a whole, though it has had for several centuries nearly all the best dancing in the world to look at, though it has had since as far back as 1760 (since Noverre's *Letters*) a brilliant lesson in how to write about dancing, hasn't yet been able to bring order and clarity to the subject. Though they have been writing steadily for two centuries and more—and often writing pleasantly—the Paris critics have left us as reporters no accurate ballet history, as critics no workable theory of dance emphasis, of dance form, or of dance meaning.

The handicap to method in dance criticism has always been that its subject matter—dancing that can fascinate as an art does—is so elusive. Other arts have accumulated numerous wonderfully fascinating examples in many successive styles. Dancing produces few masterpieces and those it does are ephemeral. They can't be stored away; they depend on virtuoso execution, sometimes even on unique interpreters. They exist only in conjunction with music, stage architecture, and decoration in transitory, highly expensive performances. It is difficult to see the great dance effects as they happen, to see them accurately, catch them so to speak in flight, and hold them fast in memory. It is even more difficult to verbalize them for critical discussion. The particular essence of a performance, its human sweep of articulate rhythm in space and in time, has no specific terminology to describe it by. Unlike criticism of other arts, that of dancing cannot casually refer the student to a rich variety of well-known great effects and it cannot quote passages as illustrations.

This lack of precision, of data, and of method is not without advantages. It saves everyone a lot of pedantry and academicism, and it invites the lively critic to invent most of the language and logic of his subject. Its disadvantages, however, are that it makes the standards of quality vague, the range of achieved effects uncertain, and the classification of their component parts clumsy. Dance aesthetics, in English especially, is in a pioneering stage; a pioneer may manage to plant a rosebush in his wilderness next to the rhubarb, but he's not going to win any prizes in the flower show back in Boston.

The aesthetics of dancing—that is, a sort of algebra by which the impression a performance makes can be readily itemized, estimated, and communicated to a reader—is vague and clumsy. The dance critic's wits have to be all the sharper; he has to use aesthetic household wrinkles and aesthetic common sense to help out. And he has to pull his objectivity out of his hat. The poverty of his dance-critical heritage makes it hard for him to get a good view of his personal blind spots. A critic in the other arts learns to recognize his blind spots and develop his special gifts by finding out how he personally reacts to a wide range of much-discussed masterpieces. If he is annoyed by Mozart or Vermeer or even by Picasso and Stravinsky, he can read intelligent opinions different from his own. That way he learns who he is, what he knows and doesn't know. Gaps and crudities of critical technique are of concern to a professional critic; they are questions of his craft.

The earnest craftsman must hope that once a dance notation has become established, once the various hints toward a critical method (including those by modern-dance theoreticians and of exotic traditions) have been collected, sifted, and codified, dance critics will seem brighter than they do now.

At present a critic has to risk hypothesis. He can try, for instance, to distinguish in the complex total effect of a performance the relationships between dance effect and story effect, between expressive individualized rhythm and neutral structural rhythm, dance impetus and pantomime shock, dance illusion and dance fun, sex appeal and impersonation, gesture which relates to the whole architectural space of the stage and has an effect like singing and gesture which relates to the dancer's own body and so has the effect of a spoken tone. And there are of course many possible relationships of the dancing to the structure or momentum of the music which, by creating in the visual rhythm illusions of lightness and weight, impediment or support (for instance), affect the meaning of a passage. Dance criticism would be clearer if it found a way to describe these and other relationships in theater effect, and to describe just what the dancers' bodies do, the trunk, legs, arms, head, hands, and feet in relation to one another. The expression of a reviewer's personal reaction, no matter how violent or singular, becomes no immodesty when he manages to make distinct to the reader the visible objective action onstage he is reacting to.

Nowadays, however, a critic doesn't screen a dance performance according to such distinctions. What he actually does is to work backwards, so to speak, from the dance image that after the event is over strikes him as a peculiarly fascinating one. He tries to deduce from it a common denominator in what he saw—a coherent principle, that is, among uncertainly remembered, partly intense, partly vague, partly contradictory images. It takes boldness to simplify his impressions so they add up clearly to a forthright opinion; and it sometimes takes a malicious sense of fun too, to trust to his instinct where he knows he is risking his neck. But the intelligent reader need not be at all sorry that dance criticism is in a rudimentary or pioneering stage. It makes it more inviting to poets than to schoolteachers; and though its problems and possible discoveries are not colossal ones, still—if it succeeds in attracting poets—it should be for a century or so to come fun to write and to read.

An intelligent reader expects the critic—in his role of schoolteacher—to distinguish between good and bad dance technique, to distinguish between good and bad choreographic craftsmanship, to specify technical inventions and specify also the gifts that make a choreographer or a dancer remarkable despite defects in craftsmanship. Here the writer shows his fairness. But what one enjoys most in reading is the illusion of being present at a performance, of watching it with an unusually active interest and seeing unexpected possibilities take place. Reading a good critic's descriptions of qualities I have seen, I seem to see them more clearly. If I don't know them, I try looking for them in performances I remember or try to find them next time I go to the theater. And when you look for qualities a reviewer has mentioned, you may find something else equally surprising. For your sharpened eye and limberer imagination is still a part of your own identity—not of his—and leads you to discoveries of your own. The fun in reading dance criticism is the discovery of an unexpected aspect of one's own sensibility.

In reading the great ballet critics of the past one is impressed not by their fairness but by their liveliness. In reading Noverre or Gautier or Levinson, I find accounts that strike me as so unlikely I interpret them—by analogy to contemporaries—as blind spots, or propaganda and rhetoric; even if some of these accounts are accepted as facts of dance history. But it is not the partisan spirit with which they can blindly propagandize their own aesthetic views that differentiates them from lesser critics; it is the vividness of their descriptions that is unique. Gautier, who of the three gives a reader the most immediate sense of the sensuous fluidity and physical presence of ballet, expresses theory in terms of chitchat and ignores choreographic structure and technical talk. He seems to report wholly from the point of view of a civilized entertainment seeker; the other two, from the backstage point of view of the craftsman as well.

Noverre and Levinson advance theories of dance expression which are diametrically opposite. The force with which they are formulated gives their writing an elevation Gautier avoids, but makes them both far easier than he to misunderstand. Here in a nutshell is the dance critic's problem: the sharper he formulates a theory of the technique of expression, of how dance communicates what it does, the further he gets from the human vivacity of dancing without which it communicates nothing at all. And yet it is difficult to consider the central question of dancing—I mean, the transport and sweep that dance continuity can achieve, the imaginative radiance some moments of dancing are able to keep for years in people's memory, the central question Balanchine in his illuminating "Notes on Choreography" brings up in speaking of "basic movements"—unless the critic finds some way to generalize and to speak vividly of general as well as of particular dance experience.

I trust a future critic will be well informed enough to discuss such generalized principles of dance expression clearly. He could begin by clarifying our specific ballet tradition—the tradition called classic because its expressive intentions and technical precisions were long ago in some sort modeled on the achievements of ancient classic literature. It seems to me the elements of this theater-dance tradition, if they were vividly appreciated, are various enough to include in one set of critical values both what we call the modern dance and our present classic ballet—though at the moment the two are far apart in their gymnastic, rhythmic, and expressive structure and in their theater practicability as well. It seems to me that a vivid sense of such an inclusive tradition would set the merits of a choreographer or of a dancer in a larger perspective and would offer a way of describing his scope as craftsman and as artist in the light of all the achievements of past theater dancing.

So I should like to read a critic who could make me appreciate in dancing the magic communal beat of rhythm and the civilized tradition of a personal and measured communication. I expect him to sharpen my perception sometimes to an overall effect, sometimes to a specific detail. I should not be surprised to find in some of his descriptions general ideas stimulating in themselves, even apart from his immediate subject, nor to find in other descriptions technical terms of dancing, of music, of painting or theater craft. I should like him to place a choreography or a dancer with his individual derivations and innovations in the perspective of the tradition of theater dancing. I am far more interested, though, if a writer is able, in describing dancing in its own terms, to suggest how the flavor or the spell of it is related to aspects of the fantasy world we live in, to our daily experience of culture and of custom; if he can give my imagination a steer about the scope of the meaning it communicates. But as I read I want to see too the sensual brilliance of young girls and boys, of young men and women dancing together and in alternation onstage, the quickness and suavity of their particular bodies, their grace of response, their fervor of imagination, the boldness and innocence of their flying limbs.

A writer is interesting if he can tell what the dancers did, what they communicated, and how remarkable that was. But to give in words the illusion of watching dancers as they create a ballet in action requires a literary gift. An abstruse sentence by Mallarmé, the rhythmic subtlety of a paragraph by Marianne Moore, a witty page-long collage of technical terms by Goncourt can give the reader a sharper sense of what dancing is about than a book by an untalented writer, no matter how much better acquainted with his subject he is. Such examples lead to fallacious conclusions, but I am drawing no conclusions, I am stating a fact. A dance critic's education includes dance experience, musical and pictorial experience, a sense of what art in general is about and what people are really like. But all these advantages are not enough unless they meet with an unusual literary gift and discipline.

Now and then in reading dance criticism one comes across a phrase or a sentence that suggests such an ideal possibility. It is to emphasize these passages to people who wonder what good dance criticism is that I am writing. The fact that no criticism is perfect doesn't invalidate its good moments. Granted it is brilliant far less often than the dancing it commemorates; the fact that it is after all occasionally brilliant is what makes it as a form of intellectual activity in a modest way worthwhile.

The Dance Encyclopedia, 1949

SUPERFICIAL THOUGHTS ON FOREIGN CLASSICISM

Everybody knows that the principles of classicism are identical the world over. A ballet audience on any continent recognizes the same steps and the same elaborate theater apparatus, and knows what to expect in *Giselle* or *Swan Lake*. Everybody wants it that way and is proud of it, and with reason. And yet from experience everybody knows too that an American classic company as it dances a ballet has a general look that is not at all the same as that of a British company, and a Paris company is quite different from either. Different again is a Danish company, or an Italian, and further differences appear, no doubt, the farther you travel. It bothers the fans, this paradox.

It doesn't bother the general public. When a foreign company comes to a city accustomed to its own local one, the general public loves the exotic note, the picturesque stars, the novel repertory. Not so a fan. You can see him in any ballet capital, just such a real hard-shelled passionate fan hunched up morosely as a visiting troupe performs a piece he knows and loves. He can see that the company has gifts and works hard—but call that classicism! A few seats farther down is the other type of fan, the sociable kind, darting her sharp look brightly all over the stage at the funny foreigners, nudging her girlfriend and giggling, "Did you see his face when he offered that rose?"

When I first heard fans abroad bitterly resent our classicism, bitterly and inexplicably, I supposed they were being something like defensive or imperialist or chauvinist about their own; but later when I heard Americans complain as bitterly about European ballet, I realized it couldn't be the reason. The feelings of a fan about ballet anywhere in the world are deeper and sweeter than politics or economics. They are direct, more like the feelings of a passionate coffee drinker newly arrived in a strange country and for the first time tasting the brew that there is called coffee.

Just as the cut of a pair of pants which is sheer heaven to an ardent sharpie in one country is merely risible to the sharpie in another, so the sociable fan can't help giggling at unexpected behavior in a familiar spot.

Unexpected for me was some of the behavior onstage when I saw a piece called *Suite de Danses* at the Paris Opéra. The orchestra was playing a familiar Chopin piano piece, and when the curtain went up I expected some sort of *Sylphides.* Sure enough there was the moonlight and there was a man dressed for *Sylphides.* But instead of his standing in a grove with the demented bevy of girls in white, there were a fountain basin, and steps rising, and platforms, and more steps—and high upstage center on a raised podium in a vivid white spotlight was this man by himself. He executed a few beautiful Fokinesque ports de bras, rose on half-toe, and then, perfectly satisfied with himself, walked offstage on the third floor. Below in the dry fountain basin a huddle of partly grown kids knelt in an undisciplined lineup with one gangling leg extended. A quarter of an hour later when they got up, their little knees had gone stiff. And as they began to dance they kept glancing down at their knees and then out at us with slumlike grimaces of disdain and shrugged up their little shoulders. Finally came a polonaise for all the big girls in white. But they weren't at all Fokine's moony young ladies. These self-respecting Parisian dancers each brought with her her own cavalier to keep her company. To supply so many hadn't been easy, and some of the partners looked neither youthful nor attractive in their walk; one tubby one, to give himself a more romantic look, had shadowed his cheeks so heavily that he seemed to have a three-day beard. Each man, regardless of shape, was dressed in a short *Sylphides* suit and wore a long pageboy wig of the loveliest hair. The older ones looked at the audience rakishly. And the audience applauded and cheered.

Evidently the audience had seen something quite different from what I had. And as I went home I imagined that to a Paris fan our own *Sylphides* might seem quite as ridiculous. He might point out that without changing a single sacrosanct step of Fokine's, our Anglo-American versions have become—God knows how—as respectably dreamy as a bath-soap advertisement. No, they aren't always, but now and then they are, aren't they? And I went on imagining a Paris fan's dismay at the sight of our clean-washed girls, looking each one as like all the others as possible, instead of (as in Paris) as *un*like. How can you tell them apart, he might say—it was exactly what I had heard in Paris at the first visit of Sadler's Wells—what fun can it be to be a fan that way? I have heard the British answer: "*We* are perfectly well pleased, thank you—so self-indulgent the French, such a pity too, great institution, the Opéra." As for the Americans, when they see a huge gifted company on the vast stage in Paris, they wonder that the Opéra public likes its dance pleasure of so small a kind, inspected as though through an opera glass, a limb or a waist at a time. At home we like the way a company looks dancing as a company, a bold, large, and sweeping pleasure.

When I told a lady abroad that I thought it strange that classic dancing should look so different from one country to another she said: "But everything else looks different too; it would be very strange if ballet didn't." And when I returned, I heard Balanchine say: "When I first came to Paris from Russia, Diaghilev took me to the best restaurants, famous for their fine food. The waiter put before me a little dish with something particular on it. I complained: 'You call this fine food? I want a big plate. And bring me potatoes and beef and pork and turnips and cabbage and more potatoes.' And then I mixed them all up on the plate, and it was what I was used to. And I ate it and said to Diaghilev, 'Yes, they have very fine food here.' Ballet is like that. People like what they are used to."

And people are used to changes, too. It is changing all the time. Americans used to be used to the Ballet Russe style, now they are used to the American style—though a few fans still object to the change. Champs-Elysées style has modified the Sadler's Wells. I have heard French dancers sigh for the "great teachers" of New York, and Americans enthusiastic about schools in Paris. The Danes are delighted to have Vera Volkova teach them a style opposite to their own, the Italians and Turks have imported English teachers, and the English swear by the Cecchetti method.

But an American fan who travels in Europe from one ballet city to another sees, too, that the general look of the different companies in performance, different though it is, is more alike from capital to capital than the general look of a crowd moving in the street in the morning; the movement of the crowd, I mean, differs even more from one country to another. In Copenhagen the crowd has an easy stride, strong in the waist, light on the feet, with a hint of a sailor's roll. As they pass they look at one another briefly and trustingly without moving the face. They enjoy walking. In Paris they hate to walk. Each individual is going in an individual direction, at a different speed. And they hate it, but they refuse to bump. They carry their bodies with respect like a large parcel of dishes: sort of low. They jab their heels at the pavement, in short steps, each person differently; they trip, and strut, and jiggle, and waddle, and trudge, and limp; and every now and then a beauty passes among them sailing like a swan or stalking like a fine flamingo, completely isolated from the others. They notice her at once, but they refuse to look, and as she passes, every individual in the crowd from fifteen years old to sixty-five becomes more intensely himself or herself. That is their form of homage.

All over Italy half the population is constantly walking up and down hills carrying babies or parcels of food, a steady movement like breathing. The other half is in the street, the men leaning or relaxed in harmonious assurance, or lounging; the girls pass by just a little quickly, with an easy delicacy. Everybody enjoys everybody else's beauty—it belongs to everyone who sees it; they enjoy it all their life over and over with the same pleasure. One could guess that they had invented ballet. They know how to lift the waist imperceptibly as they turn half in profile, how to show a back, hold the head, raise an arm, point a foot, or extend a hand; they love doing it and seeing it. And they mistrust a person who won't make a scene; they all make them without getting confused or losing their sweetness; they do by couples, by threes, or by crowds at ticket booths, and breathe more easily for it. The only thing they will not tolerate is hurry and being hurried. They have no love for losing their habits of behavior; it makes them savage.

In London the crowd in the morning walks well, orderly, and the ears look delicious. Looking at the face isn't done. But then the beauties one would want to enjoy are in taxis, down from the country for the day. Truck drivers and dock workers have a curious autochthonous color sense—in subtle off-shade combinations—in their work clothes. After midnight, however, gentle monstrous creatures appear from underground, hideously primped and perfectly pleased with themselves, tell each other their secrets, and vanish, as natural to the soil as the creatures of Alice's dream.

As for the New York crowd, we all know it, and it doesn't resemble any of these at all.

How different the more consciously social movements are—coming into a room at a party, shaking hands, behaving at table, or sitting in a chair—everybody knows from foreign movies anyway. Dancers who grow up in a city naturally move in the way people around them have moved all their life. And that makes a difference in the overall or general look of a whole company, even if it doesn't show in one dancer doing a particular step. But classicism is so naked and enlarged a way of moving that any tiny unconscious residue in it of something else than the step—the residue of habit or of character—shows. And sometimes is beautiful. A dancer cannot intend such an unconscious overtone, for it is beautiful only if it is deeper than any intention. But a ballet fan can sense it and be moved. A faint reminiscence of a gesture seen with wonder as a child and long forgotten, an overtone characteristic of a city in the motion of someone one has loved and forgotten, returns sometimes in a dancer's innocent motion and makes its poignancy the more irresistible. Natural enough that an audience feels closest to the dancing of girls and boys of its own country. But the point of classicism is that local color is by an insistent discipline driven deeper and deeper into the unconscious imagination. There it becomes innocent, out of this world, unnationalist, and unsentimental.

I don't believe in an intentional local overtone in classicism. I believe that a good classicist should have less than as little as possible. But I never saw a homogeneous company that—besides tending to show a single style of teaching—didn't also in its general look show a common regional overtone. In a home company a fan becomes used to it and aware only of classicism; but when a foreign company first arrives the same fan is overpowered by its strangeness, its exoticism, and this keeps him from seeing the real classic dancing. It is very annoying. It takes time for this first confusion to wear off. That is why European fans respond more freely to our ballets with a local-color subject than to our classic ones: the general American look is plausible to them in an American number; in a classic number they want the unconscious regional overtone they are used to, as well as the conscious school style they are used to, too; that is the note which for them makes classicism plausible. Even Diaghilev, when he first came to Paris, had no success with *Giselle*; everybody adored the Russians when they were "barbaric" and "primitive," but in classicism these qualities seemed disturbing.

But I believe that fans here in New York are more and more ready to accept the initial shock of foreignness in classicism, curious to find out what a peregrine style may contain either of stimulus to our own or else of interest merely to widen a balletgoer's sense of the scope of international classicism. It was a similar curiosity that took me to Europe a few years ago to look around. Stay-at-home New Yorkers, however, have been able to see about as much as I. The only important Western company that has not been here is the Royal Danish Ballet, the importance of which I thought was its freshness and straightforwardness in presenting the touching (and soundly built) romantic ballets of Bournonville, of which no ballet fan can see too many. The choreography is simple, but original; the pace is easy, but sure; the dances are seen with a beautiful clarity; and the sentiment is both real and modest. It is a pleasure to see how simple, how chaste ballet can be and still go to your heart. A Galeotti ballet of 1786 (*The Caprices of Cupid and the Maître de Ballet*), in which a few steps have been, presumably at a later date, raised to real toe steps, but no other change has been made, is still alive and amusing as a piece, and even simpler in choreography. Their *Giselle* and *Coppélia* are the best one can see in their mime passages, but I don't care so much for the dance versions. I saw only two pieces of the modern repertory, and one of them, *Etudes*, seemed to me effective and clean, but not very distinguished. I imagine, however, that the full-length Bournonville ballets would have in New York the sort of gentle innocence we never see onstage, and that many of us would be happy not to resist.

But this extraordinary voyage back into the world of romantic ballet on which the Danish company can take one, refreshing though it is, is not an aspect of contemporary classicism. I wish one of their great mimes, Karstens or Larsen, could teach in New York. But the traditional atmosphere, the quiet ballet studios they work in, are very different from ours. What I wished very much, too, was that we could import the secure financial organization of those great European ensembles, which is founded on the practical experience of ballet as a long-term investment, analogous to the conception of our own cultural foundations. But the more an American looks at ballet abroad, where it is rooted in a city's life, the more he realizes that the most important way to improve our ballet is to keep it steadily and continuously living among us according to our local conditions, our own manners and behavior. In point of contemporary artistic interest our New York City Ballet is now in its own repertoire incomparably more exciting for me than any Western European company, larger and richer though they are, and brilliant though are some of their stars. And to my mind it is also in the dance style that it is close to achieving.

But I see no reason why one should dispute so unnecessary a question—which country's company is better; there is so much in all of them that is a pleasure, and particularly when one gets to know a company in its own home theater. The home audience responds so differently on points of manners, points that are unintelligible abroad, and that in fact have nothing to do with classic principles, but that become a part of the company's style. I was astonished and delighted watching a Parisian dancer save an awkward passage in performance. She seemed to be saying to the audience, "I'll tell you a secret: this is a passage of no consequence at all, and it doesn't suit my style either, such a stupid choreographer—oops, that elastic—again!—where was I? Oh yes, I'll just sketch in a few steps, I'm delicious at sketching in, you know—and then, just in a moment more, there's a bit—oh really so clever, you'll adore seeing how divine I am in it—ah, here goes now!" "How adorably alive," the audience whispered to its neighbor. A British dancer in a similar situation seems to say more decorously, "I should be happy if this weren't quite so undignified, but we must dance correctly, mustn't we, and it's such fun really, don't you think?" And her audience, staidly touched, breathes back: "Good old girl." I guess an American when the audience is losing interest goes on with her steps as if she muttered: "Don't bother me, I'm busy." She would seem rude to a foreigner, but, being an American, I know what she means, and I respect her for it. Better of course to go on dancing sweetly and not say anything at all; and I've seen dancers all over the world do that too, great dancers.

When you get to be familiar with any foreign style it becomes as misleading and absurd, as touching and delightful as daily life is abroad too. But I was curious abroad to find out if there was some particular regional style that was accepted as the best, and asking everywhere I found a general unanimity of opinion. The wisest fans were all agreed that, despite a few obvious defects, the one classic style that they felt in their hearts to be the most exciting, the most lovable and beautiful, was the style of their own country. I could not disagree with any of them, for I felt, so to speak, the same way, and so without going into particulars we parted with mutual expressions of sincere regard.

Dance News Annual, 1953

DANCERS, BUILDINGS, AND PEOPLE IN THE STREETS*

On the subject of dance criticism, I should like to make clear a distinction that I believe is very valuable, to keep the question from getting confused. And that is that there are two quite different aspects to it. One part of dance criticism is seeing what is happening onstage. The other is describing clearly what it is you saw. Seeing something happen is always fun for everybody, until they get exhausted. It is very exhausting to keep looking, of course, just as it is to keep doing anything else; and from an instinct of self-preservation many people look only a little. One can get

---

* This essay was prepared as a lecture to dance students at the Juilliard School but was never delivered. Denby was notoriously shy about public speaking.

along in life perfectly well without looking much. You all know how very little one is likely to see happening on the street—a familiar street at a familiar time of day while one is using the street to get somewhere. So much is happening inside one, one's private excitements and responsibilities, one can't find the energy to watch the strangers passing by, or the architecture, or the weather around; one feels there is a use in getting to the place one is headed for and doing something or other there, getting a book or succeeding in a job or discussing a situation with a friend, all that has a use, but what use is there in looking at the momentary look of the street, of One-hundred-and-sixth and Broadway. No use at all. Looking at a dance performance has some use, presumably. And certainly it is a great deal less exhausting than looking at the disjointed fragments of impression that one can see in traffic. Not only that the performance is arranged so that it is convenient to look at, easy to pay continuous attention to, and attractive, but also that the excitement in it seems to have points of contact with the excitement of one's own personal life, with the curiosity that makes one want to go get a special book, or the exciting self-importance that makes one want to succeed, or even the absorbing drama of talking and listening to someone of one's own age with whom one is on the verge of being in love. When you feel that the emotion that is coming toward you from the performance is like a part of your own at some moment when you were very excited, it is easy to be interested. And of course if you feel the audience thrilled all around you just when you are thrilled too, that is very peculiar and agreeable. Instead of those people and houses on the street that are only vaguely related to you in the sense that they are Americans and contemporary, here in the theater you are almost like in some imaginary family, where everybody is talking about something that concerns you intimately and everybody is interested and to a certain extent understands your own viewpoint and the irrational convictions you have that are even more urgent than your viewpoint. The amplitude that you feel you see with at your most intelligent moments, this amplitude seems in the theater to be naturally understood onstage and in the audience, in a way it isn't often appreciated while you are with the people you know outside the theater. At a show you can tell perfectly well when it is happening to you, this experience of an enlarged view of what is really so and true, or when it isn't happening to you. When you talk to your friends about it after the curtain goes down, they sometimes agree, and sometimes they don't. And it is strange how whether they do or don't, it is very hard usually to specify what the excitement was about, or the precise point at which it gave you the feeling of being really beautiful. Brilliant, magnificent, stupendous, no doubt all these things are true of the performance, but even if you and your friends agree that it was all those things, it is likely that there was some particular moment that made a special impression which you are not talking about. Maybe you are afraid that that particular moment wasn't really the most important, that it didn't express the idea or that it didn't get special applause or wasn't the climax. You were really excited by the performance and now you are afraid you can't show you understand it. Meanwhile, while you hesitate to talk about it, a friend in the crowd who talks more readily is delivering a brilliant criticism specifying technical dance details, moral implications, musicological or iconographic finesses; or else maybe he is sailing off into a wild nonsensical camp that has nothing to do with the piece but which is fun to listen to, even though it's a familiar trick of his. So the evening slips out of your awareness like many others. Did you really see anything? Did you see any more than you saw in the morning on the street? Was it a real excitement you felt? What is left over of the wonderful moment you had, or didn't you really have any wonderful moment at all, where you actually saw onstage a real person moving and you felt the relation to your real private life with a sudden poignancy as if for that second you were drunk? Dance criticism has two different aspects: one is being made drunk for a second by seeing something happen; the the other is expressing lucidly what you saw when you were drunk. I suppose I should add quite stuffily that it is the performance you should get drunk on, not anything else. But I am sure you have understood me anyway.

Now the second part of criticism, that of expressing lucidly what happened, is of course what makes criticism criticism. If you are going in for criticism you must have the gift in the first place, and in the second place you must cultivate it, you must practice and try. Writing criticism is a subject of interest to those who do it, but it is a separate process from that of seeing what happens. And seeing what happens is of course of much more general interest. This is what you presumably have a gift for, since you have chosen dancing as a subject of special study, and no doubt you have already cultivated this gift. I am sure you would all of you have something interesting and personal to say about what one can see and perhaps too about what one can't see.

Seeing is at any rate the subject I would like to talk about today. I can well imagine that for some of you this is not a subject of prime interest. Some of you are much more occupied with creating or inventing dances than with seeing them; when you look at them you look at them from the point of view of an artist who is concerned with his own, with her own, creating. Creating, of course, is very exciting, and it is very exciting whether you are good at it or not; you must have noticed that already in watching other people create, whose work looks silly to you, but whose excitement, even if you think it ought not to be, is just as serious to them as that of a creator whose creating isn't silly. But creating dancing and seeing dancing are not the same excitement. And it is not about creating that I mean to speak; I am telling you this so you won't sit here unless you can spare the time for considering in a disinterested way what seeing is like; please don't feel embarrassed about leaving now, though I agree it would be rude of you to leave later. And it is not very likely either that I shall tell you any facts that you had better write down. I rather think you know all the same facts I do about dancing, and certainly you know some I don't; I have forgotten some I used to know. About facts, too, what interests me just now is how differently they can look, one sees them one way and one sees them another way another time, and yet one is still seeing the same fact. Facts have a way of dancing about, now performing a solo, then reappearing in the chorus, linking themselves now with facts of one kind, now with facts of another, and quite changing their style as they do. Of course you have to know the facts so you can recognize them, or you can't appreciate how they move, how they keep dancing. We are supposed to discuss dance history sometime in this seminar and I hope we will. But not today.

At the beginning of what I said today I talked about one sort of seeing, namely a kind that leads to recognizing onstage and inside yourself an echo of some personal, original excitement you already know. I call it an echo because I am supposing that the event which originally caused the excitement in oneself is not literally the same as the event you see happen onstage. I myself, for instance, have never been a Prince or fallen in love with a creature that was half girl and half swan, nor have I myself been an enchanted Swan Princess, but I have been really moved and transported by some performances of *Swan Lake*, and by both sides of that story. In fact, it is much more exciting if I can feel both sides happening to me, and not just one. But I am sure you have already jumped ahead of me to the next step of the argument, and you can see not only that I have never been such people or been in their situation, but besides that I don't look like either of them; nor could I, even if I were inspired, dance the steps the way they do. Nor even the steps of the other dancers, the soloists, or the chorus.

You don't seem to have taken these remarks of mine as a joke. But I hope you realized that I was pointing out that the kind of identification one feels at a dance performance with the performers is not a literal kind. On the other hand, it is very probable that you yourselves watch a dance performance with a certain professional awareness of what is going on.

A professional sees quite clearly "I could do that better; I couldn't do that nearly so well." A professional sees the finesse or the awkwardness of a performer very distinctly, at least in a field of dance execution he or she is accustomed to working in; and a choreographer sees similarly how a piece is put together, or, as the phrase is, how the material has been handled. But this is evidently a very special way of looking at a performance. One may go further and say that a theater performance is not intended to be seen from this special viewpoint. Craftsmanship is a matter of professional ethics; a surgeon is not bound to explain to you what he is doing while he is operating on you, and similarly no art form, no theater form is meant to succeed in creating its magic with the professionals scattered in the audience. Other doctors seeing a cure may say, "Your doctor was a quack but he was lucky"; and similarly professionals may say after a performance, "Yes, the ballerina was stupendous, she didn't fake a thing"—or else say, "She may not have thrilled you, but there aren't four girls in the world who can do a something or other the way she did"—and this is all to the good, it is honorable and it is real seeing. But I am interested just now to bring to your attention or recall to your experience not that professional way of seeing, but a more general way. I am interested at the moment in recalling to you how it looks when one sees dancing as nonprofessionals do, in the way you yourselves I suppose look at pictures, at buildings, at political history or at landscapes or at strangers you pass on the street. Or as you read poetry.

In other words the way you look at daily life or at art for the mere pleasure of seeing, without trying to put yourself actively in it, without meaning to do anything about it. I am talking about seeing what happens when people are dancing, seeing how they look. Watching them and appreciating the beauty they show. Appreciating the ugliness they show if that's what you see. Saying this is beautiful, this ugly, this is nothing as far as I can see. As long as you pay attention there is always something going on, either attractive or unattractive, but nobody can always pay attention, so sometimes there is nothing as far as you can see, because you have really had enough of seeing; and quite often there is very little, but anyway you are looking at people dancing, and you are seeing them while they dance.

Speaking personally, I think there is quite a difference between seeing people dance as part of daily life, and seeing them dance in a theater performance. Seeing them dance as part of daily life is seeing people dance in a living room or a ballroom or a nightclub, or seeing them dance folk dances either naturally or artificially in a folk dance group. For that matter classroom dancing and even rehearsal dancing seem to me a part of daily life, though they are as special as seeing a surgeon operate, or hearing the boss blow up in his office. Dancing in daily life is also seeing the pretty movements and gestures people make. In the Caribbean, for instance, the walk of Negroes is often, well, miraculous—both the feminine stroll and the masculine one, each entirely different. In Italy you see another beautiful way of strolling, that of shorter muscles, more complex in their plasticity, with girls deliciously turning their breast very slightly, deliciously pointing their feet. You should see how harmoniously the young men can loll. American young men loll quite differently, resting on a peripheral point; Italians loll resting on a more central one. Italians on the street, boys and girls, both have an extraordinary sense of the space they really occupy, and of filling that space harmoniously as they rest or move. Americans occupy a much larger space than their actual bodies do; I mean, to follow the harmony of their movement or of their lolling you have to include a much larger area in space than they are actually occupying. This annoys many Europeans; it annoys their instinct of modesty. But it has a beauty of its own, which a few of them appreciate. It has so to speak an intellectual appeal; it has because it refers to an imaginary space, an imaginary volume, not to a real and visible one. Europeans sense the intellectual volume but they fail to see how it is filled by intellectual concepts—so they suppose that the American they see lolling and assuming to himself too much space, more space than he actually needs, is a kind of a conqueror, is a kind of nonintellectual or merely material occupying power. In Italy I have watched American sailors, soldiers, and tourists, all with the same expansive instinct in their movements and their repose, looking like people from another planet among Italians, with their self-contained and traditionally centered movements. To me these Americans looked quite uncomfortable, and embarrassed, quite willing to look smaller if they only knew how. Here in New York, where everybody expects them to look the way they do, Americans look unselfconscious and modest despite their traditional expansivity of movement. There is room enough. Not because there is actually more—there isn't in New York—but because people expect it, they like it if people move that way. Europeans who arrive here look peculiarly circumspect and tight to us. Foreign sailors in Times Square look completely swamped in the big imaginary masses surging around and over them.

Well, this is what I mean by dancing in daily life. For myself I think the walk of New Yorkers is amazingly beautiful, so large and clear. But when I go inland, or out West, it is much sweeter. On the other hand, it has very little either of Caribbean lusciousness or of Italian contrapposto. It hasn't much to savor, to roll on your tongue; that it hasn't. Or at least you have to be quite subtle, or very much in love, to distinguish so delicate a perfume.

That, of course, is supposed to be another joke, but naturally you would rather travel yourself than hear about it. I can't expect you to see my point without having been to countries where the way of walking is quite different from what ours is here. However, if you were observant, and you ought to be as dance majors, you would have long ago enjoyed the many kinds of walking you can see right in this city, boys and girls, Negro and white, Puerto Rican and Western American and Eastern, foreigners, professors, and dancers, mechanics and businessmen, ladies entering a theater with half a drink too much, and shoppers at Macy's. You can see everything in the world here in isolated examples at least, peculiar characters or people who are for the moment you see them peculiar. And everybody is quite peculiar now and then. Not to mention how peculiar anybody can be at home.

Daily life is wonderfully full of things to see. Not only people's movements, but the objects around them, the shape of the rooms they live in, the ornaments architects make around windows and doors, the peculiar ways buildings end in the air, the water tanks, the fantastic differences in their street façades on the first floor. A French composer who was here said to me, "I had expected the streets of New York to be monotonous, after looking at a map of all those rectangles; but now that I see the differences in height between buildings, I find I have never seen streets so diverse one from another." But if you start looking at New York architecture, you will notice not only the sometimes extraordinary delicacy of the window framings, but also the standpipes, the grandiose plaques of granite and marble on ground floors of office buildings, the windowless side walls, the careful, though senseless, marble ornaments. And then the masses, the way the office and factory buildings pile up together in perspective. And under them the drive of traffic, those brilliantly colored trucks with their fanciful lettering, the violent paint on cars, signs, houses as well as lips. Sunsets turn the red-painted houses in the cross streets to the flush of live rose petals. And the summer sky of New York for that matter is as magnificent as the sky of Venice. Do you see all this? Do you see what a forty- or sixty-story building looks like from straight below? And do you see how it comes up from the sidewalk as if it intended to go up no more than five stories? Do you see the bluish haze on the city as if you were in a forest? As for myself, I wouldn't have seen such things if I hadn't seen them first in the photographs of Rudolph Burckhardt. But after seeing them in his photographs, I went out to look if it were true. And it was. There is no excuse for you as dance majors not to discover them for yourselves. Go and see them. There is no point in living here if you don't see the city you are living in. And after you have seen Manhattan, you can discover other grandeurs out in Queens, in Brooklyn, and in those stinking marshes of Jersey.

All that is here. And it is worth seeing. When you get to Rome, or to Fez in Morocco, or to Paris, or to Constantinople, or to Peking—I hope you will get there, I have always wanted to—you will see other things beautiful in another way; but meanwhile, since you are dance majors and are interested and gifted in seeing, look around here. If you cut my talks and bring me instead a report of what you saw in the city, I will certainly mark you present, and if you can report something interesting I will give you a good mark. It is absurd to sit here in four walls while all that extraordinary interest is going on around us. But then education is a lazy, a dull way of learning, and you seem to have chosen it; forget it.

However, if you will insist on listening to me instead of going out and looking for yourselves, I will have to go on with this nonsense. Since you are here I have to go on talking and you listening, instead of you and me walking around and seeing things. And I have to go on logically, which we both realize is nonsense. Logically having talked about what you can see in daily life, I have to go on to that very different way of seeing, which you use in seeing art.

For myself, I make a distinction between seeing daily life and seeing art. Not that seeing is different. Seeing is the same. But seeing art is seeing an ordered and imaginary world, subjective and concentrated. Seeing in the theater is seeing what you don't see quite that way in life. In fact, it's nothing like that way. You sit all evening in one place and look at an illuminated stage, and music is going on, and people are performing who have been trained in some peculiar way for years, and since we are talking about a dance performance, nobody is expected to say a word, either onstage or in the house. It is all very peculiar. But there are quite a lot of people, ordinary enough citizens watching the stage along with you. All these people in the audience are used to having information conveyed to them by words spoken or written, but here they are just looking at young people dancing to music. And they expect to have something interesting conveyed to them. It is certainly peculiar.

But then, art is peculiar. I won't speak of concert music, which is obviously peculiar, and which thousands every evening listen to, and evidently get satisfaction out of. But even painting is a strange thing. That people will look at some dirt on a canvas, just a little rectangle on a wall, and get all sorts of exalted feelings and ideas from it is not at all natural, it is not at all obvious. Why do they prefer one picture so much to another one? They will tell you and get very eloquent, but it does seem unreasonable. It seems unreasonable if you don't see it. And for all the other arts it's the same. The difference between the "Ode on a Grecian Urn" and a letter on the editorial page of the *Daily News* isn't so great if you look at both of them without reading them. Art is certainly even more mysterious and nonsensical than daily life. But what a pleasure it can be. A pleasure much more extraordinary than a hydrogen bomb is extraordinary.

There is nothing everyday about art. There is nothing everyday about dancing as an art. And that is the extraordinary pleasure of seeing it. I think that is enough for today. *Center*, DECEMBER 1954

FORMS IN MOTION AND IN THOUGHT*

In dancing one keeps taking a step and recovering one's balance. The risk is a part of the rhythm. One steps out of and into balance; one keeps on doing it, and step by step the mass of the body moves about. But the action is more fun and the risk increases when the dancers step to a rhythmic beat of music. Then the pulse of the downbeat can lift the dancer as he takes a step, it can carry him through the air for a moment; and the next downbeat can do it again. Such a steady beat to dance on is what a dancer dreams of and lives for. The lightness that music gives is an imaginary or an imaginative lightness. You know it is an illusion, but you see it happen; you feel it happen, you enjoy believing it. There is a bit of insanity in dancing that does everybody a great deal of good.

It has been doing people good for a long time. Looking at Paleolithic cave paintings, one can recognize the powerfully developed dance sense our ancestors had fifteen thousand years ago. What are all those bison of theirs floating on, if not on a steady beat? A Brooklyn teenager would

* This essay had its genesis in a lecture, prepared in 1954, for dance students at the Juilliard School. Denby revised it extensively for book publication a decade later.

feel at home among the Magdalenian cave painters once the dancing started and he heard that beat. And a late-Paleolithic youth who dropped in on a gym or a ballroom going wild at two in the morning to the blasts of a name band would see right away that it was a bison ritual. And if he broke into a bison step, the kids near enough to see him would only say, "Wow," or "Dig that rustic shag."

And an educated late-Paleolithic magician, if he dropped in on a performance of classic ballet in an air-conditioned theater, would find a good deal he was familiar with—the immense, awesome, drafty cavern, the watching tribe huddled in the dark, and in a special enclosure the powerful rhythmic spectacle which it is taboo to join in. As a magic man he would find it proper that the dancers are not allowed to speak, not allowed to make any everyday movements, to show any signs of effort, or even of natural breathing; and equally correct that the musicians are kept hidden in a ritual pit. The orchestra conductor would strike him as a first-class wizard. This singular character stands up in the pit waving a wand and is respectfully treated by the audience as invisible. Though it is hard for him, he does his best not to look at the dancers; when his eyes stray to the stage, he pulls them down at once, visibly upset. He keeps in constant agitation, without ever doing a dance step or touching an instrument, and his costume consists of a pair of long black tails. The Magdalenian visitor, familiar with demented clowns who represent pre-male types of fertilization, would recognize the ironic function of this indispensable figure. And as the curtain fell, he would clap with the rest, delighted by a ceremony so clever in its nonsense and so sweeping in its faith.

If a New Yorker were to tell him, "But you're missing the point, ballet is an art, it isn't a ritual," he might answer, "You no like that word 'ritual'? You say it about our ballet, so I think maybe a nice word." And his Paleolithic girlfriend might add, "Please, are you a critic? We hear critics will roast fat dancer tonight, just like we do at home. Yum, yum."

Students of culture have suggested that an art of dance preceded that of Paleolithic painting. One can see it might well be so. One can see hints of dance at stages of living one thinks of as extremely remote. The stage of culture at which our species showed the first hints of dancing need not have been beyond that of several species of contemporary wild animals. Some of them that can be greedy and fierce have sexual maneuvers that are harmless and take time. On the one hand such a ceremony can be interrupted, it doesn't necessarily lead into the sexual act; on the other hand the act may occur with a minimum of ceremony. The animals seem to be aware of a ritual that is imaginative and that is fairly impractical. Their ceremonies aren't all sexual ones either. Wolves and fishes have special fighting ones. And the birds that swoop low and soar up sharply at dusk over a town square or in a clearing of the woods are very likely catching an insect in their open bills, but they seem to be ritualizing the action in a way they don't ritualize their feeding during the day. It is a special bedtime one. Standing among the ruins of the Palatine toward sunset late in October, I saw a flock of migrant birds keeping close like a swarm, beating their small wings almost in unison, forming—the swarm of them—a single revolving vibrating shape which kept changing in the air—a shape that distended, that divided like an hourglass, that streamed out like a spiral nebula and then condensed again into a close sphere, a series of choreographic figures which rose and fell above the city as the flock drifted upstream and out of sight. A social celebration and a prehistoric pleasure.

Birds seem to have made a number of dance inventions that strikingly resemble our own. They have sociable group numbers, intimate duets and perhaps trios, and private solos. You see the performers assume a submissively graceful or a show-off air. They seem to be enjoying a formal limitation as they move in relation to a center, and even as they move in relation to a lapse of time. Much as we do, they compose their piece out of contrasted energetic and gliding motions, out of reiterated gestures, out of circular paths and straight lines. Bees even use path patterns for a sign language. A returned honeybee performs for her hive-mates a varying number of circles which she keeps cutting with a straight line always in one direction, and her audience understands from her choreography in what direction and how far off are the flowers she has newly discovered. After that she passes around samples of the honey, as if she were giving her dance a title. Such an action does not seem like a ritual to us, but the bees find it very practical.

A formal path involves electing a base from which to move, it involves giving a spot an arbitrary imaginative value. It is a feat of imagination essential to dancing. Birds understand the feat. Cats are very good at it when they play games. One can see their cat eyes brightening with an imaginative light as they establish their base. Kittens begin to play with no sense of a base and gradually learn to imagine. It would be fun to see lions playing from a base the same way, pretending to hunt a bright rag on the end of a rope, pouncing, prancing, darting, tumbling head over heels. I imagine they do it in a wild state and would enjoy doing it in the circus if a lion tamer could be found to play with them.

Animals tame or wild do not seem to mimic anybody but themselves. One notices that their dancelike inventions are formal in principle. One may infer from it how far back in our history or how deep in our nature the formal aspect of dancing is.

But one notices too that the wild animals don't enjoy watching our performances as much as we do theirs. Rattlesnakes are glad to escape from a bunch of fertility-celebrating Indians. Hungry wolves and lions have never been known to venture on a group of enthusiastically stepping Russians or Africans. Our primitive social celebrations intimidate them. It may be they find the energy of them overpowering, or else that they are appalled by the excessive regularity of them, which is foreign to their habits. None of them time their movements to a regular beat of artificial noise as we do. Dancing to a beat is as peculiarly human a habit as is the habit of artificially making a fire.

Stepping to a manmade beat is a dance invention of a formal nature that we alone have made. Presumably we first danced without a beat, the way animals and small children do. Even trained animals don't catch the formality of a beat. Seals and monkeys like to clap, they can learn to play tunes, but they can't keep time either way. Riders can direct horses to keep time, and I remember a circus orchestra taking its beat from an old she-elephant who danced the conga, but it was her rhythm, not the orchestra's. How could our species ever have been bright enough to invent the beat? Nowadays we aren't even bright enough to explain it.

There used to be an opinion that the beat was invented by externalizing or objectifying our heartbeat, that it was first beaten and then stepped to. The prevalent opinion now seems to be that both the regular acoustic beat and the regularly timed step were invented simultaneously, as a single invention. One tries to imagine unknown races of men—tens of thousands of years before the elegant Magdalenians—as they hopped in the glacial snow for fun, laughing and yelling, and first heard a kind of count, an oscillating one-two in their ritual action. They may have heard it in the grunt of their own shout, broken as they landed full weight from a leap, over and over. Or else heard it when an older woman, out of pleasure at the tumultuous stepping of the young men, clapped sedately, and one of the boys found himself keeping time with her, and both she and he got more and more excited by the mutual communication. Or else they might have heard a beat when a word shouted over and over as they were stepping turned into a unison metric chant that they stepped to. Perhaps as they stepped and exaggerated a hoarse panting noise of breathing, they heard each other's breath and their own coming simultaneously and were thrilled by the simultaneous step action.

However people began to keep time, one imagines the eerie thrill they felt as they found themselves aware of hearing a beat from the outside and of taking a step from the inside, both of them at once. One can still feel a far echo of that thrill as one first finds oneself hitting the beat; or later in life, as one finds oneself stepping securely to a complex rhythm one isn't able to follow consciously. It is a glorious sensation inside and outside of one. For our ancestors the experience, subjective and objective at the same instant, must have been a wonderful intensification of identity. So peculiar a thrill could have been discovered and then forgotten and rediscovered by exceptional geniuses among successive races and successive climatic epochs. The invention ended by becoming an immensely popular one. But we cannot say that it has been entirely successful. Even now, after fifty or a hundred thousand years of practice, a number of us still can't keep time, and shuffle about a ballroom floor missing the measure.

Keeping time isn't the same thing as grace of movement. Animals, small children, and even adults moving without a beat but with the grace of dancing enjoy what they do and look beautiful to people who like to watch them. But doing it in strict rhythm as much for those who watch as for those who do it has a cumulative excitement and an extra power. The extra power is like a sense of transport. People are so to speak their better selves. They fly by magic.

People who dance till dawn in a ballroom or who are performers onstage can cheerfully pour out as much extra energy as they otherwise would be able to do only grimly in a matter of life or death. The wild animals cannot waste so much energy on fun. To our species the invention of stepping to a regular beat of manmade noise offers an occasion for the extravagant expense of powers which is the special achievement of our human civilization. And when there is grace in the extravagance and beauty in the excess, we are delighted with ourselves.

Looking back, then, one can see that animals invented for their ceremonies a formal limitation of movement. They do not move in every possible way, they move in a few particular ways. For us the added formal invention of the beat increased the artificiality much further. What had once been only instinctive animal patterns became human objective rhythms as well. They gained an objective measure. The subjective-objective or double awareness of stepping which the beat awakened gave an extra exuberance of power to the dancers. It also sharpened a sense of representation, the sense that a step action can also be a magic emblem. So dancing became exhilarating not only to do, but also to watch, to remember, and to think about. From being an instinctively formal pleasure, it became the kind of beautiful communication we call an art. In this way our ancestors invented an art—and perhaps all of art—when they regularized their dancing to a timed beat and a timed step.

The rhythmic stress of stepping is a habit of communication or expression which reaches into the present from unrecognizable races, from epochs and festivals when individuals of genius first made fires, first spoke in sentences. They grin and glare at us, and sit down beside us, these astonishing geniuses, and we feel their powerful wonder as they watch our young people dance, as they watch the bright ballet danced onstage at the same time as we do. They wonder at it, but they know how to watch it, they can see that it is some special kind of dancing.

I seem to be prowling about the subject like a nature photographer prowling about the countryside. The subject is expression in ballet. And I think you see what I am concerned with. I am bringing up some very general features of expression, and am trying to catch the expression of ballet from various points of view. Unless you can catch it in motion, you don't catch it at all. What I have caught of it seems to be as unspecific as a blur on the edge of the camera field. But you will notice something or other about it, I believe, and recognize something about the expression, and see it independently of what I say, as a fact of nature—I mean as a fact of human nature. That is what I am concerned with.

We were discussing the beat of the step in general terms. As you step to a beat, you feel the rhythmic pressure of your foot against the floor. You have the rhythm in your feet, so people say, and your feet start to dance. The rhythm of steps is beaten by the floor contact. It is stamped, or tapped or heel-struck, or shuffled. The onlookers catch the rhythm and they instinctively participate in the dancing as long as they stay with the step rhythm.

As the dancer steps he can hear the beat elsewhere than in the feet. And he often makes gestures that are visible rhythmic accents. In the Sahara there is a beautiful solo dance in which the girl moves only on her knees and beats the rhythm with sharp elbow, wrist, and finger positions. But in any dance the shape of the body is just as evident when it isn't hitting the beat as when it is. Between beats it keeps moving rhythmically, it keeps making contrasting motions. And as it does, it makes visual shapes the rhythm of which is a sculptural one. Watching the dancers, one sees this other rhythm of shape that their bodies make. Sometimes the dancers and onlookers are so obsessed with the acoustic beat of the step rhythm that they take very little interest in the visual shape rhythm; on the other hand, they sometimes take a great deal of interest in the action of the shapes.

Watching the shape of a movement is something we all do a great deal of in everyday life. You may recognize your friends at a distance by the shape of their walk, even unconsciously. One can often recognize foreigners in America or Americans abroad by a characteristic national shape of walking that one has never particularly thought about. As for average citizens passing down a city street, plenty of them have oddities in the shape of walking one notices right away—a turned-out forearm that dangles across the back, or a head that pecks, a torso that jiggles up and down, a chest that heaves from side to side. Men and women walking on the street keep making personal shapes with their legs—they snap their heels at the sidewalk, they drawl one thigh past the other, they bounce at each step or trip or stalk or lope, or they waddle, they shuffle or bombinate. Sometimes an oddity looks adorable, but one recognizes it perfectly well as an oddity.

Battalions of parading soldiers manage to avoid the oddities of civilian walking. They show very clearly the basic shape of a walking step—the swinging arm following the opposite leg, the twist at the waist, the dip in the figure's height and the roll. Marching West Pointers can give it a massive containment, and marching parachutists can give it an undulant grace. Young women marching don't seem to give it anything pleasantly collective. They don't seem to take an innocent pride in the achievement of a step the way young men do—a pride as innocent as that of a trained dog. A collective step becomes depersonalized or homogenized only after considerable training. And then it is a monotonous shape, of interest only in multiplication.

In a parade the body looks more two-footed than usual. Two feet traveling from place to place haven't mathematically much choice in the order they can go in. Soldiers at Forward March go from two feet to one foot, then they keep going from one foot to the other foot, and they go from one foot to both feet at Halt. That makes three kinds of step, and two more exist: a hop on the same foot, and a broad jump from both feet to both feet. These five kinds are all there are. Soldiers could be trained to do all five instead of only three, and you can see right away that once they were trained, the five would look hardly less monotonous than the three.

Dancers have no more feet than other people, and so they live with the same limitation. One could try to watch a ballet from the point of view of the five kinds of step, and see how it keeps scurrying about from one kind to another inside the narrow limits of a two-footed fate. One could try, but one doesn't. As you watch a ballet, the dancers do plenty of different steps and often some new ones you hadn't seen before. One doesn't keep watching the feet to see the sequence in which they are contacting the floor. You keep watching the whole shape of the body before and after the floor contact.

Between a ballet and a parade, take watching a ballroom dance, especially one where the partners break, like a lindy or a mambo or a Virginia reel. You see the steps exhibiting the dancer's figure, the boy's or the girl's, in a series of contrasting shapes. You see it advancing toward a partner, or turning on itself; it lightly bends and stretches; the thighs close and separate, the knees open and shut, the arms swing guardedly in counteraction to the legs, or they lift both at once. The feet, the hands, the head may refuse a direction the body inclines to or they may accept it. When the waist undulates Cuban-style, the extremities delay following it with an air of detachment. As you watch a good dancer, it all looks very cute, the figure and its movable parts, and you get to know them very pleasantly.

The contrasting shapes you see the figure making are as depersonalized as those of a military step—they are sometimes close to a marching step, and the difference is no more than a slight containment, a slight glide of the foot. But the next moment they are quite unmilitary. The dancers move backwards and sideways as much as forward, they kick and spin, they interweave and sway and clap, and the boys and girls keep making mutual shapes. One can see that the dance shapes add particular motions to the basic kind of step they relate to. But one also sees that if you take basic steps to be walking steps, then dance steps don't originate in them. Dance steps belong to a different species, so to speak. They don't give the body that useful patient look that walking does. They were invented for mutual fun and for the lively display of sculptural shapes. In Basque folk dancing and in ballet it is normal for a dancer to leap up and make a rapid quivering back-and-forth shape with his feet that is as far from common sense as a bird's brief trill. An entrechat suits the kind of common sense dancing has, but not any other kind.

The action of ballet exhibits the dancer's figure much further and more distinctly than that of a ballroom dance. The shapes are more exact and more extreme. The large reach of all the limbs, the easy erectness of the body regardless, the sharpness of pointed feet, the length of neck, the mildness of wrists, the keen angle of knee bends, the swiftness of sweeping arms, the full visibility of stretched legs turned out from thigh to toe, spreading and shutting; the figure in leaps, spins, stops in balance, slow-motion deployments, the feet fluttering and rushing and completely still. As it passes through such a dazzling series of transformations, you see the powerfully erect figure, effortless and friendly. It appears larger than life, like in an illusion of intimacy. And you are astonished when a performer who onstage looked so big, at a party turns out to be a wisp of a girl or a quite slender-looking boy.

A ballet dancer has been carefully trained to make the shapes of classic dancing, and one can readily see that they have specific limits. Classic steps limit the action of the joints to a few readily visible differences, so the trajectory of the body as it makes the shape is defined. A classic dancer has a habit of many years' standing of rotating, bending, and stretching the several joints of legs and arms, of the neck and spine in movements of which the start, the trajectory, and the finish have become second nature. How such a movement draws after it the rest of the body, or how it joins a movement before it or one after it, have become for him instinctive. The whole of the shape is second nature to him, and so are its component parts. He can alter a specific detail without becoming confused in the main shape. He is familiar with the impetus he must give that will mold it very clearly in each of its dimensions. And in all these shapes, whether large or small, the dancer has come to judge his momentum and his balance at varying speeds by instinct. So they appear effortless and unconfused and in harmony.

A classic dancer's legs seem to move not from the hip joint but from further up, from the waist and the small of the back; and the arms not from the shoulder, but from lower down, from the same part of the back as the legs; it lengthens both extremities and harmonizes them. The head moves at the end of a neck like a giraffe's that seems to begin below the shoulder blades. The head can also move without the neck, just from the joint where head and spine meet, tilting against a motionless neck. Then you see its small motion enlarged by the unexpected contrast to so very long and separate a neck. In the same way a flick of ankle or of wrist can be magnified by the long-looking immobile leg or arm it is at the far end of. So aspects of scale appear.

Classic action exhibits the dancer's body very clearly, but it steadily exhibits aspects of it that everyday life shows only at rare moments. Classic arms, for instance, keep to a few large trajectories and positions, they keep distinct from the torso, and the quality they exhibit in arms is the long lightness of them. They minimize the activity of elbow and wrists. In everyday life arms and hands do all the chattering, and the legs growl now and then. On the contrary in classic dancing the legs seem to carry the tune, and the arms add to it a milder second voice.

Classic legs, turned out from the hip joint down, look unusually exposed. One sees the inside surface of them, though the dancer is facing you. One sees the modeling of their parts, the differentiated action of the joints flexing or rotating—the lively bend of the knee especially. One watches the torque and powerful spread of the thighs at their base. The ballerina holds the bone turned in its socket rigid, and the leg extends itself to its complete stretch in the air, sideways, to the back, or to the front. The visually exposed action of the legs, fully turned out, fully bending and stretching, can look wonderfully generous.

No matter how large the action of legs and of arms, the classic back does not have to yield, and its stretched erectness is extremely long. It bends in or out when it chooses. The low-held shoulders open the breast or chest. But classicism doesn't feature the chest as a separate attraction the way advertising does; a slight, momentary, and beautiful lift of the rib cage is a movement of the upper back. At the back of the torso or at the front, it is the waist that one keeps looking at. Looking at it you see the figure's changing silhouette at a glance. The waist is the center of the dance shape, or the implied center. You seem to sense in its quickness a lightning anticipation of the next motion. The power of the waist is that of an athlete's, but the quickness of it is a child's.

Among the ways classicism exhibits the body that are different from those of everyday life, the most different is that of toe steps, which look like tiny stilts the girl is treading on. She can step onto them, or she can rise onto them, rising with a soft flick of both feet. She can step about on them with a fanatic delicacy and a penetrating precision. She can spin on them like a bat out of hell. When she jumps or runs on them one hears a muffled tapping that sometimes sounds fleshy. From the side you see the sole curving like a bending knife blade with at the back the queer handle of the heel. From the front they over-elongate the leg and alter the body's proportions; and the extreme erectness of the foot seems in keeping with the extremely pulled-up waist and the stretched lightness of the slender ballerina. Sometimes a figure on a single toe point, as its shape deploys from so narrow a balance, looks intently alone by itself, and, even if a partner supports it, intently individual. At other times one feels the contrast between the large pliancy of the knees, the lesser one of the ankles, and the scarcely perceptible give of the bones of the arch.

Toe steps sharpen one's eye to the figure's contact with the floor. The action of rhythm and the action of shape meet and keep meeting at the moment of floor contact. Classic dancing can make that moment keen to the eye so the rhythm it sees has an edge. Take for instance the moment on the ground between two leaps. You see the feet arriving stretched through the air, the ankles flex in a flash, you see the feet on the floor, motionless in their small position, catch the flying body's momentum, and instantly the ankles flash again as the legs stretch off into the air in the new leap. The feet have tossed the dancer's momentum forward, without a wobble or a blur. The eye has caught their moment of stillness the more sharply because the position they held is a familiar one that keeps returning. And that almost imperceptible stillness of theirs cuts the first shape from the second, and makes the rhythm of motion carry.

In these peculiar appearances and the recurrent complete stillness of the classic body, the eye recognizes or the imagination recognizes the sensual meaning of the exhibited parts, and the dramatic implication of their motions. It sees these implications and meanings appear and disappear. They are exhibited without the continuity or the stress that could present them as if in states of greed or of anxiety. Their moment-by-moment sensual innocence allows the imagination the more unembarrassed play.

The steps keep unfolding the body in large or small ways, and reassembling it in vertical balance like a butterfly. The peculiarity of its grace in motion is consistent and is shared by all the figures onstage. The expressive meaning is divided between recognizable details and the visual grace, the very light alternation of weight of an overall unrecognizable consistency. The consistency is as if the most usual and easy of ballet steps set a pitch for the eye—a pitch of carriage and balance in action—to which everything that is done onstage keeps a clear relation by its quality of impulse and of carriage. The overall effect is that of a spontaneous harmony of action. But its common sense remains that of a dance.

The peculiar values of classic style we have been considering are an invention extending from nowadays back into a collective past. They are in that sense traditional values. Ballet began as the kind of dancing current at village festivals around the Mediterranean from the times of King Minos and Daedalus to those of da Vinci. Young Boccaccio and young Dante before him danced these local steps; and Homer had danced them locally as a boy. The village dances changed so slowly that they were always traditional. At the edge of the holiday crowd, when the piper played, the tots tried to do the steps before they could keep time. Everyone had grown up knowing the sequences and the tunes that went with them, and knowing from having watched it the harmony that the dance could show. People always liked to watch the boys and girls do it, and liked giving a prize to the sweetest dancer. The steps were a part of the brightness of the recurrent holiday, and they brought back other bright faces and festivals that the little region had known in the past. The sense of such holidays was strong at the center of civilization for a long time, and one finds echoes of it reaching back from verses of *The Divine Comedy* to a carved Minoan cylinder three thousand years earlier depicting harvesters marching home with a band, singing and joking. In classic Greek representations of a dance step the harmony is sometimes so rich it implies contrary steps and extended phrases. Scholars have traced a number of ballet movements to classic Greek prototypes. No reason to suppose that the ancient dances were simple.

When, around the middle of the millennium before Christ, urban prosperity spread to Europe from the East, the country steps were theatricalized, first for Greek theaters, and later for the elaborate and ornate theaters of the Roman Empire. Then prosperity retreated eastward again, and for another thousand years dancing was again that of lively young people doing their local steps at balls or church festivals, with here and there some hired mimes or an anxious acrobat passing the hat. These hard-bitten comics were tramps and outsiders.

When prosperity and a pleasure in grace of behavior spread again—this time from Renaissance Italy—the country dances were theatricalized once more. Like the earlier Greek professionals, the new Italian ones rearranged the steps to new tunes, they turned them out a bit to face the public, and gave them a thread of story. They saw that the pleasure of the dances was their harmony. The pantomime they took over was that of the original holiday occasion, that of pleasant social behavior. Professionals developed indoors a sense of lyric expression in dancing. But the outdoor mimes, thanks to the same prosperity, had developed their capers and their insistent explosive pantomime into a rowdy Italian buffoonery. These two opposite kinds of expression had existed in the ancient theaters as well, and existed time out of mind, sometimes blending, sometimes not. By the seventeenth century, when theater dancing became organized, the ballet dancers were likely to sustain the sentiment, but the comics were likely to steal the show.

And here we are watching ballet in the prosperous mid-twentieth century. In a number of professional terms and steps dancers can recognize three hundred years of continuity behind them. Balletgoers can recognize two hundred years in a number of documents that evoke an artistic excitement related to their own. Though the comics still steal the show, the element which holds a ballet together and which creates the big climaxes is the one we call classic dancing. Classicism has stretched the ancient country steps and all the others it has added to them—it has stretched them vertically and horizontally to heighten the drama of dance momentum. But in its extended range of large-scale theater steps and their spectacular momentum, ballet has kept the gift of harmony it began with. Today's professionals of ballet are artists, they are virtuosos, craftsmen specialized for life. But as one watches them, just when they are at their best, history seems to vanish. The quality of character that makes a dancer seems the same as three or four thousand years ago. The nature of the pleasure they give by their genius as dancers does not seem to have changed much since Minoan times.

One July noon, in an Aegean village on the Greek island of Mykonos, two friends and I, after visiting a monastery, were waiting in the sun for the single daily bus. The torrent of heat and light was so intense that we went into a café for shelter. Inside the radio was playing folk tunes and a young farmer was dancing solo to it, while two stood around watching him and waiting for their turn. But when the second young man began, the miracle happened. The traditional steps produced an effect entirely different. The rapidity of decision, the brilliance of impetus, the grace were unforeseeable, as if on another scale. He was a dancer in the class of the classic stars one sees onstage. It was an extraordinary delight to watch him. He finished his turn. But while the next young farmer was dancing the bus honked outside, and we foreigners ran out to catch it.

An extraordinary delight such as this is the standard of theater performance. It is the standard that nature sets. A genius for dancing keeps turning up in a particular boy or girl who is doing the regulation steps he or she grew up with. Outside the theater or inside it, the gift creates an immediate communication. For some people watching such great moments at a ballet performance, the steps themselves disappear in a blaze of glory. For others the steps remain distinctly visible, but they make as much sense as if one could do them oneself. One understands them. It is like the sensation of understanding a foreign language because a girl has looked so ravishing speaking it.

But for professionals as they watched ballet dancers of genius at such great moments, and knew each step they were doing from long experience, it was the revelation of the large-scale effect possible in the familiar steps that fascinated them. Being professionals, they tried to catch the technical method. And what they caught of it during several hundred years has become classic style.

Style in its professional aspect is a question of good habits in the way steps are done. And so ballet has gradually settled on several habits it prefers. It has decided on the turned-out thighs, on the pulled-up waist that joins them to the erect spine, on the low-held shoulder line. It has decided on a few main movements of the head, of the arms, of the torso, of the several leg joints. And on fifty or so main steps. These main steps and the main movements that can modify them are the habitual exercises with which good habits of balance and carriage, with which habits of harmony and rhythm can be trained in apprentices to reach a large-scale theater effect. They form a common basis of action for professionals. And the history of them is that they have always been specifically dance steps or elements of dance steps, enlarged in scale by constant use in the theater.

In ancient Italian towns the narrow main street at dusk becomes a kind of theater. The community strolls affably and looks itself over. The girls and the young men, from fifteen to twenty-two, display their charm to one another with a lively sociability. The more grace they show, the better the community likes them. In Florence or in Naples, in the ancient city slums the young people are virtuoso performers, and they do a bit of promenading any time they are not busy. A foreigner in Rome who loses his way among the fifteenth- and sixteenth-century alleys and squares, hunting in those neighborhoods for the sibyls of Raphael or the birthplace of Metastasio, discovers how bright about their grace the local young Romans can be. They appreciate it in themselves and in each other equally. Their stroll is as responsive as if it were a physical conversation. Chunkily built though they are, they place their feet; they articulate the arms and legs; the boys stress the opening, and the girls the closing, of the limbs. Their necks and waists have an insinuating harmony. They move from the waist turning to look, or stepping back in effacé to let a girl pass, or advancing a sheltering arm (like in croisé). They present their person and they put an arm around each other's waist or shoulder with a graceful intimacy. Their liveliness makes these courteous formalities—which recall ballet—a mutual game of skill. The foreign ballet fan as he goes home through the purple Roman dusk, charmed by the physical caress of it, confuses the shapes of Raphael with those of the performance. But he realizes what it means that ballet was originally an Italian dance, and he becomes aware of the lively sociability of its spirit and of its forms.

The general question I have been considering is harmony in classic dancing. But I hope the reference to Italy has not been misleading. Classic dancing doesn't look Italian when Americans do it, or when English dancers do it, or Russian, or French, or Danish dancers; it doesn't, and can't, and needn't. But it has harmony when any of them do it. It has a visual harmony of shapes due to the specific action of the body that we were considering earlier. Let us go back to the single step, and make sure where we are, close enough to the Atlantic seaboard.

As one lies with closed eyes in bed or on a beach far from town trying to recall what a single step looks like, one sees several steps and dancers combined in a phrase, and sees the shape of a phrase as if it were an extended step, many-legged and many-armed, with a particular departure, trajectory, and arrival. And as phrases succeed one another, one sees them take direction onstage, and one sees the visual momentum their paths can have with relation to a center of action, or to several centers, coming downstage, retiring back, escaping to the sides, appearing from the wings. The momentum of phrases accentuates the angle at which a figure is presented, or at which it acts, the directions it takes or only aspires to take. The momentum disengages a leading quality of motion, hopping, fluttering, soaring, stopping dead. It carries along a single figure, or several mutually, or a group. It draws the figures deeper into dramatic situations, serious or comic ones.

But the action of a step determines the ramifications, the rise and fall of the continuous momentum. You begin to see the active impetus of the dancers creating the impetus moment by moment. They step out of one shape and into another, they change direction or speed, they erect and dissolve a configuration, and their secure and steady impetus keeps coming. The situations that dissolve as one watches are created and swept along by the ease and the fun and the positive lightness of it. They dance and, as they do, create in their wake an architectural momentum of imaginary weights and transported presences. Their activity does not leave behind any material object, only an imaginary one.

The stage by its stationary center and its fixed proportions accumulates the imaginative reality. Stage area and stage height appear to be permanent actualities. Within them the brief shape that a dancer's body makes can look small and lost, or it can spread securely and for an instant appear on their scale. One can respond to the visual significance—the visual spaciousness—of such a moment of dance motion without being able to explain it reasonably in other terms.

The shape the dancer makes at such a moment has no specific representational aspect. You have seen the same shape before with different feelings. And yet often the whole house responds to such a moment of classic climax. It seems not to insist on being understood rationally. It presents no problem, it presents a climax of dancing. One can leave the ambiguity of it at that and enjoy at once both the climactic beauty of it and the nonsense.

Or else as one responds in the moment to the effortless sense of completion and of freedom that its spaciousness gives one, one may feel that the expression of the motion one is watching has been seen throughout the piece without being fulfilled until now. It is the expression the piece is about. One feels the cumulative drama it rises on. Then its visual spaciousness offers to one's imagination a large or a tragic image to recognize. It is not frightening; the lucidity of the moment is as sweet as happiness. Like a word you have often heard that spoken without pressure at a certain moment is a final one, as large as your life, so the classic shape is an effortless motion that replies. To the symbolist poet Mallarmé, it appeared as an emblematic reply—as of blossom or dagger or cup—a climactic perception of mutual identity. As in a lucidity of perception there is in the motion no sense of intention or pressure. The significance of it appears in the present moment, as the climactic significance of a savage ritual appeared at the moment it occurred in our racial past.

As you lie on the hot deserted beach far from town and with closed eyes recall the visual moment of climax, and scarcely hear the hoarse breathing of the small surf, a memory of the music it rose on returns, and you remember the prolonged melodious momentum of the score as if the musical phrase the step rose on had arrived from so far, so deep in the piece it appears to have been.

The power of projection that music has strikes me as mysterious but it is a fact of nature. I have heard people who considered themselves unmusical modestly make acute remarks on the music of a ballet; and I once sat next to a deaf mute who followed the performance with delight and enrolled in a ballet school afterwards. However one is conscious of it, without music classic dancing is no more real than swimming is real without water around it. The more ballet turns to pantomime, the less intimate its relation to the music becomes; but the more it turns to dancing, the more it enjoys the music's presence, bar by bar. Even when the steps stand aside and let the music alone, they are intimately aware of it.

We spoke of the beat at the beginning and here we are back to it. Take a specific ballet step. An assemblé looks different if it lands on one of the measure or if it lands on four; an entrechat looks different if the push from the floor comes on the downbeat, or if on the downbeat the legs beat in the air. A promenade en arabesque done at the same speed looks different if it is done in three-four time or in four-four. The stress of the measure supports a different phase of the step; it gives the motion a different lift and visual accent and expression. And as the stress of the beat can give a different look to the step, so can the stresses of the other kinds of musical emphasis—the stresses of dynamics, of melody, of harmony, of timbre, of pathos.

All these stresses offer their various support to the steps. They are like a floor with various degrees of resilience to dance on. The steps step in some places and not in others. They make a choice of stresses.

But as you hear the piece the stresses merge into a musical momentum that varies and into a musical expression that changes; and they build into large coherent sections and finally into a completed structure of musical sound with a coherent identity. We are used to sensing the coherence of music sometimes in one way, sometimes in another. And while we sense a coherence it has, we can believe in the coherence of long sequences of dancing we are watching. We see their coherence from the point of reference of the musical meaning. A long dance gathers power by coherence.

But the relation of eye and ear is a mutual one. The visual action also makes particular stresses in the music more perceptible, and continuities more clearly coherent. Watching the sweep of the dance momentum, you feel more keenly the musical one, and the visual drama can give you an insight into the force of character of the score. A dance happily married to its score likes to make jokes without raising its small voice, and the thundering score likes it too.

But the steps of classic dancing have always enjoyed being timed to the notes of music, and their rhythm has always responded to musical rhythm. Inside the labyrinth of complex musical structures, you see ballet following the clue of the rhythm, you see it hearing the other musical forces as they affect the current of the rhythm, as they leave or don't leave the rhythm a danceable one. You see the dance listening and choosing its own rhythmic response. A dance ballet gets its power of projection by the choice of its response to the larger structures of musical rhythm. So its power of character reveals itself in a more complexly happy marriage. Timed as classic dancing is to strict measures of time, confined to a limited range of motion, lighter in the stress it communicates than everyday motion, the power of character, the power of insight it develops and sustains in reference to its chosen score, is a power of its own creation. Mutually to the music, you watch the dance take shape and make sense and show the dazzling grace of an imaginative freedom. It is worth watching for.

What we have been considering is what is usually called the form of classic dancing. I am not suggesting that a ballet has no content, and I am not suggesting either that its form is its content. I have heard these statements but they make no sense to me. I think the meaning of the two words is approximately clear, and that they describe different ways of approaching an event, or of discussing it. I have been avoiding the distinction because I have been discussing what classic dancing looks like regardless of the subject matter of the ballet, what one is aware of at the moment one sees the dancer move, what one is aware of before one makes the distinction between content and form. It is a fairly confused awareness, but it is real enough. One doesn't, as far as I can see, make any sharp distinction between content and form in the case of pleasant events while one is enjoying them, or of people one is in love with; one instinctively doesn't.

The forms of classic dancing are one may say no less instinctive for being formal. The way a cat comes up to you at night in a deserted city street to be patted, and when you crouch to pat her, the way she will enjoy a stroke or two and then pass out of reach, stop there facing away into the night, and return for another stroke or two, and then pass behind you and return on your other side—all this has a form that you meet again onstage when the ballerina is doing a Petipa adagio. And while cats one meets on different nights all like to follow the same adagio form, one cat will vary it by hunching her back or rolling seductively just out of reach, another, another night, by standing high on her toes as you pat her, and making little sous-sous on her front paws; a third by grand Petersburg-style tail wavings; a fourth, if you are down close enough, by rising on her hind paws, resting her front ones weightlessly on you, raising her wide ballerina eyes to yours, and then—delicate as a single finger pirouette—giving the tip of your nose a tender nip. When a cat has had enough adagio, she sits down apart; or else, changing to mime, she scampers artificially away, pretending to be scared by the passing of a solitary nocturnal truck. Dogs—dogs that you take on daytime country walks are virtuosos of allegro. They invent heroic dashes, sharp zigzags running low ending in grand jetés that slow down; or else in the midst of a demi-manège at cannonball speed they stop dead. They mean you to get the joke, and they make it deadpan like troupers. Then they come up to you at an untheatrical dog-trot, smiling, breathing hard, with shining eyes; they enjoy your applause, but they distinguish between the performance when they were pretending and the bow they take after it is finished when they are honest dogs again.

One watches ballet just as one would the animals, but since there is more to be seen, there is more to watch. More to be seen and also more to recognize: not only the formal shapes but also the pantomime shapes with their specific allusions. And everybody likes to see pantomime in the course of a ballet evening. It gives the feeling of being back in a more familiar rational world, back safe from the flight through the intuitive rhythmic world of irrational symbols and of the charming animals.

We have been considering ballet from its aspect as dancing. Its aspect as pantomime is equally interesting; so is its aspect as an art of the choreographer and as an art of the dancer. They are all part of ballet just as much as what I have been discussing—and I love them just as much, and they don't lose any of their beauty merely by being unmentioned.

Dancers, Buildings and People in the Streets, 1965

Appendix

From the Postscript to *Dancers, Buildings and People in the Streets* (1965)

I have not reworked these articles. I am astonished that I ever thought *Serenade* would be better danced in a demi-caractère way. Astonished, too, that the thrill I remember so distinctly of Le Clercq's climax in *La Valse*—throwing her head back as she plunges her hand into the black glove—is not mentioned here. Her solitary pacing that made the last minute of *Opus 34* so marvelous is mentioned but without naming her. Not mentioned is her leading part in developing the company's current dance style.

Introduction to *Dancers, Buildings and People in the Streets* by Frank O'Hara (1965)

In *Some Thoughts About Classicism and George Balanchine*, Edwin Denby writes that Balanchine's remarks had suggested to him "the idea, too, of style as something a man who has spent many years of his life working in an art loves with attentive pertinacity." This idea, I think, is the basis of Denby's prose and poetry, a style which "demands a constant attention to details which the public is not meant to notice, which only professionals spot, so unemphatic do they remain in performance." They were speaking of ballet performance, but the idea is equally true of Denby's writing performance, and one of the important secrets of its pleasures.

Since Edwin Denby is a good friend of mine, there are other secrets I should reveal. He sees and hears more clearly than anyone else I have ever known. No expressive or faulty quiver in a battement, no ingenious or clumsy transition in a musical score (whether by Drigo or Gunther Schuller), no squiggle in a painting and no adverb seems ever to escape his attention as to its relevance in the work as a whole. Having a basically generous nature, he is not at all guilty about pointing out mistakes and, unlike many poets who are also critics, he feels the moral necessity to point them out lest his praise be diminished by an atmosphere of professional "kindness." Most fortunately, his lyrical poetic gifts are tempered by the journalist's concern for facts and information. He works very hard at the above-mentioned "style" so as to give us a whole spectrum of possibilities: what he saw and heard, what he felt, what he thinks the intention was, what the event seemed to be, what the facts surrounding it were, what the audience responded to, leaving open with a graciousness worthy of Théophile Gautier the ultimate decision of the reader pro or contra his own opinion as critic. Thus, he restores criticism to writing, to belles lettres if you wish, to the open dialogue of opinion and discussion between writer and reader which is nonaggressive and has faith in a common interest as the basis of intellectual endeavor. Few critics are so happy as he to receive your re-interpretation or correction of what he has already seen or heard and already written about. He is truly and deeply interested, in a civilized, open-minded way.

On the other hand, he will not just put up with anything. Recently, at the premiere of Balanchine's *Don Quixote*, he was asked what he thought of the new work. Denby said, "Marvelous! I was very moved."

"I was moved right out of the theatre," his interrogator replied.

"That's where you belong, then," Denby said in the gentlest of tones.

He is always there, telling you what he sees and hears and feels and esteems, not caring whether you agree or not, because it is a friendly parlance about matters which are mutually important. The ballet, the theater, painting and poetry, our life accidentally in co-existence, is a rather large provenance which he tactfully negotiates and notates. As a theater man he is interested in The Public, and this gives his criticism a broad, general applicability, moral as much as aesthetic, for all its special knowledge and expertise. He is interested in his society, and those societies not his, without sentimentality. For our own society, how we act and what we mean, I cannot think that the two lectures ("Forms in Motion" and "Dancers, Buildings") have less than a major pertinence. For other societies Denby's essays have illuminations about us which are not available elsewhere and are admirably understated.

Denby is as attentive to people walking in the streets or leaning against a corner, in any country he happens to be in, as he is to the more formal and exacting occasions of art and the theatre. He brings a wide range of experience to the expression of these insights: his acting and adaptations for the theater here and in Germany; his work as ballet critic on the *New York Herald Tribune*; his acting in the films of Rudolph Burckhardt and other "underground" film-makers; his more personal and more hermetic involvement with his poems; his constant traveling and inquisitive scholarship; all these activities contribute a wide range of reference for comparison and understanding of intricate occasions, as well as of complicated implications in occasions seemingly obvious and general.

Like Lamb and Hazlitt, he has lightness and deftness of tone, and a sharp, amused intelligence, as evident in the method of perceiving as in the subject matter itself. Much of his prose is involved with the delineation of sensibility in its experience of time: What happens, and how often, if at all? What does each second mean, and how is the span of attention used to make it a longer or shorter experience? Is Time in itself beautiful, or is its quality merely decorable or decorous? Somehow, he gives an equation in which attention equals Life, or is its only evidence, and this in turn gives each essay, whatever the occasional nature of its subject, a larger applicability we seldom find elsewhere in contemporary criticism.

A Note on Sources

The information in the biographical essay was gathered mainly from primary sources and a decade of conversations with Edwin. No book-length biography or autobiography exists. The only comprehensive life of Denby is Ron Padgett's introduction to *The Complete Poems* (Random House, 1986).

Edwin helped a few writers with facts about his past. In the early fifties, he assisted his friend Lillian Moore when she was writing an entry about him for the *Encyclopedia della spettacolo*. A copy of her typescript is on file in the Dance Collection of the New York Public Library at Lincoln Center. He also aided the editors of *Dance Magazine* in their compilation of a one-page capsule for an awards issue (April 1966). The *Complete Poems* in which Edwin's "authorized" biographical paragraph appears was published by Full Court in 1975.

Transcripts of taped interviews have been useful. I have repeatedly quoted Edwin's words from John Gruen's *The Party's Over Now* (Viking, 1972), the 1979 interview conducted by John Howell (*Performing Arts/II Journal*, vol. 4, nos. 1–2, n.d.), and a Denby conversation with Mark Hillringhouse (*Mag City*, 1983). Other interviews and excerpts from interviews have been consulted.

Recordings of conversations have also been valuable. Among these number a delightfully coy 1974 non-interview with Padgett and Burckhardt, a 1981 phone conversation with Padgett, and the 1983 preparations for the Denby *Mag City* (which includes the Hillringhouse interview and other conversations with Edwin).

Edwin's interviews were useful, but not infallible sources. He remembered sequences well but time-markers badly. Perhaps recalling several friends' traumatic HUAC experiences, he chose not to tell most formal interviewers of his important Russian trip. Moreover, Edwin disliked the "hurry" of taped interviews. In a 1969 *Ballet Review* meeting of the minds with Don McDonagh, Arlene Croce, and George Dorris, Edwin insisted on a footnote protesting the flattening of conversation into print.

In my own intermittent transcriptions of Edwin's comments and memories, I used no tape recorder. (He once winced away a suggestion in that direction.) I tried to copy his words as exactly as I could as quickly as possible. Sometimes at dinner, Edwin's naps between the main course and dessert allowed me to consolidate phrases scrawled on paper napkins and torn envelopes.

Charles Denby Sr.'s two-volume *China and Her People* (L. C. Page, 1905) provides background information about its subject and biographical details about its author. (Edwin believed that most of the book posthumously attributed to his grandfather had been written by his father. Both Denbys wrote many articles about international topics.)

Standard reference books offer ample information about Edwin's statesmen forebears. Various editions of *Appleton's Cyclopedia of American Biography*, the *Dictionary of American Biography*, and the *National Cyclopaedia of American Biography* were utilized, the last yielding the long quotation about Charles, Jr.'s proficiency in Chinese.

Some of the graphic details about Martha Orr Denby were gathered from letters collected in John W. Foster's *Diplomatic Memoirs* (Houghton Mifflin, 1909). Edwin's papal aspirations were first noted in print by Doris Hering (*Dance Magazine*, February 1966).

Edwin's early schooling is documented in correspondence on file at the Hotchkiss

School and in copies of the *Hotchkiss Literary Monthly* and *Mischianza*, the school yearbook.

The years at Cambridge are illuminated by Edwin's Harvard transcripts. Other academic records include letters and telegrams about his overseas disappearance, other correspondence, and test results, all from various Harvard files.

An unpublished diary in the Denby Archives furnished the quotations and details for the period after his unwilling return to Harvard.

A copy of Edwin's diploma from Helleran is in the Denby Archives.

Early translations of articles and stories by Denby, including the fragmentary "mirror" story, are in the Denby Archives. The allusion to Moscow as "the cubical city" is from an unpublished poem. I relied on newspaper accounts for details about the two Denby brothers' wedding.

The Denby Archives contain a photocopy of the Lunacharsky note. They also contain Edwin's Russian journal, from which I quote extensively.

My account of Edwin's stay in Austria benefits from the reminiscences of Day Tuttle and the reconstructions of George Jackson (*Ballet Review*, Spring 1984). (Tuttle also knew Edwin at Hotchkiss.) With J. Michael Whitman, Jackson also translated Edwin's "Gymnastics" article (*Ballet Review*, Spring 1985).

Hermann Kaiser's *Modernes Theater in Darmstadt 1910–1933* (Eduard Roether, 1955) offers an exhaustive stage-history of the period relevant to Edwin. Wilhelm Reinking's *Spiel und Form* (Hans Christians, 1979) and Arthur Maria Rabenalt's *Das Provokative Musiktheater der Zwanziger Jahre* (Kiefhaber, Kiefhaber & Elbl, [c. 1980]) are important memoirs that place Edwin in context at Darmstadt. Sir Rudolf Bing's Darmstadt recollections form a chapter in his *5000 Nights at the Opera* (Doubleday, 1972). Bernhard Minetti, in his *Erinnerungen eines Schauspielers* (Deutsche Verlags-Anstalt, 1985) compares Eckstein with Bausch.

Citations from Virgil Thomson are culled from three sources: his autobiographical *Virgil Thomson* (Knopf, 1966), *A Virgil Thomson Reader* (Houghton Mifflin, 1981), and a memorial to Edwin (*Ballet Review*, Spring 1984). His autobiography provides a longer quotation from the Denby letter cited.

The history of the Denby-Eckstein partnership was pieced together with the aid of clippings saved by both principals.

Edwin added a reference to the Ballets 1933 *Mozartiana* when preparing his March 8, 1945, article for *Looking at the Dance*. He mentioned it in several interviews, including the one with Richard Philp (*Dance Magazine*, July 1983), on the newsstands when Edwin died.

Rudy Burckhardt described his early friendship with Edwin in his own *Mobile Homes* (Z Press [Calais, Vt.], 1979) and a memorial piece (*Ballet Review*, Spring 1984). The Denby Archives have a Meyenburg program.

Edwin's recollections about "unknown, uncozy, and not small-scale" New York are from his essay "The Thirties" (Poindexter Gallery, 1957). This article appears in *Dancers, Buildings and People in the Streets*, as does the "Willem de Kooning" piece (*Art News Annual*, 1964), the source of the citation about de Kooning's black kitten.

Minna Lederman Daniel writes about her long association with Edwin in *The Life and Death of a Small Magazine: Modern Music, 1924–1946* (Institute for Studies in American Music, 1983) and an untitled article in *Ballet Review* (Spring 1984). *Modern Music* files have also been consulted.

Paul Bowles's *Without Stopping* (Putnam, 1972) provides the quotation about his solo orchestra and some other details. The passage about Denby's eyes in de Kooning paintings is from Elaine de Kooning's memorial tribute (*Ballet Review*, Spring 1984).

John Houseman writes about *Horse Eats Hat* in *Run-Through* (Simon & Schuster, 1972). Hallie Flanagan's *Arena: The Story of the Federal Theatre* (Limelight, 1985) offers another first-person account. *Free, Adult, and Uncensored: The Living History of the Federal Theatre Project* (New Republic Books, 1978), edited by John O'Connor and Lorraine Brown, features an illustrated section on *Horse Eats Hat* which includes excerpts from an interview with Edwin. Barbara Leaming's reliable *Orson Welles: A Biography* (Viking, 1985) provides facts about the *Horse Eats Hat* and *The Second Hurricane* productions. A script of *Horse Eats Hat* is in the Billy Rose Theatre Collection, New York Public Library at Lincoln Center. At the same location are Federal Theatre scrapbooks and other clippings of reviews.

Burns Mantle's *The Best Plays of 1936–1937* (Dodd, Mead, 1938) records Edwin's contribution to *The Pepper Mill*. *Copland: 1900 through 1942* (St. Martin, 1984) by Aaron Copland and Vivian Perlis recounts the making of *The Second Hurricane* and *145 West 21* with interviews with Denby and other principals. *The Second Hurricane* was published (Boosey and Hawkes, 1957) and twice recorded before its 1985 revival at the Henry Street Settlement. Burckhardt's *145 West 21* can be screened at the Dance Collection, New York Public Library at Lincoln Center.

The Denby-Matthias translation of *The Criminals* is in typescript at the Billy Rose Theatre Collection, New York Public Library at Lincoln Center. The revisions from the German original are summarized in news clippings and reviews. Though still unproduced, the texts *The Sonntag Gang* (*Mag City*, 1983) and *Miltie Is a Hackie* (Z Press [Calais, Vt.], 1973) are available.

The Tennessee Williams comment is from *Tennessee Williams' Letters to Donald Windham, 1940–1965* (Holt, Rinehart, & Winston, 1977), edited by Windham. Millicent Dillon's *A Little Original Sin: The Life and Works of Jane Bowles* (Holt, Rinehart, & Winston, 1981) outlines Edwin's North African visit and other Denby-Bowles encounters. Dillon's edition of *Out in the World: Selected Letters of Jane Bowles, 1935–1970* (Black Sparrow, 1985) provides supplementary material. Richard Buckle's accolade of Edwin is from *In the Wake of Diaghilev* (Holt, Rinehart, & Winston, 1983). Buckle's *The Adventures of a Ballet Critic* (Cresset [London], 1953) describes Denby during his *Ballet* years.

Edwin's exclamation about seeing New York again is the opening of his August 1952 article in *Ballet*, pointedly titled "New York City's Ballet." His memory about meeting "these four boys" in the Cedar Bar was fixed in print by Anne Waldman's "Paraphrase of Edwin Denby Talking on 'The New York School' " (*The World* [St. Mark's Poetry Project], April 1974). Alex Katz recalls Edwin in a *Ballet Review* tribute (Summer 1984).

The gift of lilies was acknowledged by Alice Toklas in a letter in the Denby Archives. Mimi Gross's memories of Edwin at Provincetown are printed in *Ballet Review* (Fall 1984).

Arlene Croce writes of her friendship with Edwin in *Ballet Review* (Summer 1984).

A copy of the letter mentioning Frank O'Hara is in the Denby Archives. The proposed Brecht collaboration is mentioned in manuscripts of an unpublished poem in the Archives.

Jennifer Dunning's quotation was first published in *Ballet Review* (Winter 1985), as was Jerome Robbins's (Spring 1984). Frank O'Hara's tribute to the acuity of Edwin's perceptions is part of his introduction to *Dancers, Buildings and People in the Streets* (reprinted in full in the Appendix to this volume). The quotations by Marcia B. Siegel are taken from *Ballet News* (October 1983).

Some phrases ("a white old man, approved," "lucid Maine," "since freshman spring intimate") are from Edwin's poems.

—W. M.

Index

Acknowledgments

The editors wish to dedicate their efforts to Rudy Burckhardt and Katie Schneeman.

Our particular thanks go to Ron Padgett, Jacob Burckhardt, Kenneth King, Elaine de Kooning, Dale Harris, Claire Eckstein, Arthur Marin Rabenalt, Helen De Mott, Gret Masters, Jack Anderson, and Alice Notley.

The Dance Collection of the New York Public Library at Lincoln Center was our first resource, and its staff was helpful throughout. Other scholarly assistance was provided by the Billy Rose Theatre Collection of the Performing Arts Research Center, Walter E. De Melle, Jr., of the Hotchkiss School, Amy Fague of the Hotchkiss Alumni Society, and Lucy Wu of Harvard.

We are appreciative of the acumen and pertinacity of Eva Resnikova at Knopf. Beulah Cox expertly deciphered handwriting and yellowed newspaper clippings and made of them a cleanly typed manuscript. Patrick Dillon provided informed correction.

Mr. MacKay offers gratitude to the following people for their help with his biographical essay and more: Kenneth Ayers, Manus Canning, Jacqueline Deeter, George Jackson, William Dunas, Susan McCarthy, Mark Sullivan, Maureen Slattery, Joanie Anderson, Eugenia Pakalik, and Helena Hughes. He owes thanks also to Jack Cooper, Rick Campbell, Kaarin Lemstrom-Sheedy, Ellen Marin, Amy Galowitz, and Laura Jacobs.

Related-interest titles from University Press of Florida

The Art of Teaching Ballet: Ten Twentieth-Century Masters
Gretchen Ward Warren

By With To and From: A Lincoln Kirstein Reader
Edited by Nicholas Jenkins

Caribbean Dance from Abakuá to Zouk: How Movement Shapes Identity
Edited by Susanna Sloat

Classical Ballet Technique
Gretchen Ward Warren

Holding On to the Air: An Autobiography
Suzanne Farrell with Toni Bentley

Irina: Ballet, Life and Love
Irina Baronova

Maria Tallchief: America's Prima Ballerina
Maria Tallchief

Martha Graham: The Evolution of Her Dance Theory and Training, Revised Edition
Marian Horosko

May O'Donnell: Modern Dance Pioneer
Marian Horosko

Suki Schorer on Balanchine Technique
Suki Schorer

Vaganova: A Dance Journey from Petersburg to Leningrad
Vera Krasovskaya, translated by Vera Siegel

Winter Season: A Dancer's Journal
Toni Bentley

Writing in the Dark, Dancing in The New Yorker
Arlene Croce

For more information on these and other books,
visit our website at www.upf.com.